D1086452

Slavery, Fatherhood, and Paternal Duty
in African American Communities
over the Long Nineteenth Century

THE JOHN HOPE FRANKLIN SERIES IN
AFRICAN AMERICAN HISTORY AND CULTURE

Waldo E. Martin Jr. and Patricia Sullivan, editors

Slavery, Fatherhood, and Paternal Duty in African American Communities over the Long Nineteenth Century

Libra R. Hilde

The University of North Carolina Press CHAPEL HILL

Publication of this book was supported by a grant from San José State University.

© 2020 The University of North Carolina Press
All rights reserved
Set in Merope Basic by Westchester Publishing Services
Manufactured in the United States of America

The University of North Carolina Press has been a member
of the Green Press Initiative since 2003.

Library of Congress Cataloging-in-Publication Data
Names: Hilde, Libra Rose, author.
Title: Slavery, fatherhood, and paternal duty in African American
    communities over the long nineteenth century / Libra R. Hilde.
Other titles: John Hope Franklin series in African American history and culture.
Description: Chapel Hill : University of North Carolina Press, 2020. |
    Series: The John Hope Franklin series in African American history
    and culture | Includes bibliographical references and index.
Identifiers: LCCN 2020015444 | ISBN 9781469660660 (cloth : alk. paper) |
    ISBN 9781469660677 (paperback : alk. paper) | ISBN 9781469660684 (ebook)
Subjects: LCSH: African Americans—Family relationships—United States—
    History—19th century. | Fatherhood. | Masculinity. | Slaves—
    United States—Social conditions—19th century.
Classification: LCC E185.86 .H654 2020 | DDC 973.7092/2 [B]—dc23
LC record available at https://lccn.loc.gov/2020015444

Cover illustration: Henry O. Tanner, *The Banjo Lesson* (1893). Collection of the Hampton University Museum, Hampton, Virginia.

Contents

Acknowledgments

This project had its genesis in the classroom. In History 100W, a required writing course for majors, I often assign a comparative paper on Harriet Jacobs's *Incidents in the Life of a Slave Girl* and *Narrative of the Life of Frederick Douglass*. In semester after semester of discussions and guiding students as they crafted arguments based on these narratives, I kept coming back to the juxtaposition of Douglass's and Jacobs's commentary on fatherhood. There is a stark contrast between an enslaved man who desperately wanted to parent and free his children and died unable to accomplish these goals (unaware of the ways in which he shaped the lives and motivations of his daughter) and an unknown slaveholder who took no responsibility for his mixed-race son. I owe a debt to the countless students who have come through this class, as well as the masters' students who took my graduate course on slavery, as they all unwittingly contributed to the development of this book.

As the book moved from the conceptual stage to a reality, I made a common mistake and produced an unwieldy and unfocused draft. I then had the good fortune to spend the 2017–18 academic year on a fellowship at the Center for the Advanced Study in the Behavioral Sciences (CASBS) at Stanford University. In this beautiful setting, spurred by thought-provoking seminars and lunchtime conversations, I had ample time to completely rewrite the manuscript and rethink my arguments. I want to thank CASBS Director Margaret Levi and Executive Director Sally Schroeder for taking a chance on me amidst a field of applicants from research-one universities. I cannot name all forty-five fellows here, but know that spending a year up on the hill with each and every one of you shaped this book. A special shout-out is in order for Hector Postigo, Ariela Gross, and Francille Rusan Wilson for their invaluable suggestions.

I want to express my immense gratitude to Rose McDermott, a former CASBS fellow who was instrumental in convincing me to apply for and secure the fellowship, who read and commented on early iterations of two chapters, and who has been a cheerleader throughout. I'd also like to thank my former student Nicole Viglini for her contributions to the evolution of two chapters, and Alana Conner and Luci Herman for their last-minute editing. Finally, this book has benefited immeasurably from the comments of the anonymous reviewers who read the manuscript more than once.

This is a book about family. Enslaved people faced tremendous burdens in forming and maintaining the family ties that were of paramount importance in their lives and informed their sense of self. Writing this book has made me hyperaware of how lucky I have been to grow up surrounded by a loving family and to have been a part of creating my own. Thank you to my four grandparents who are now gone but not forgotten, to my expansive extended family, to my extraordinary parents and sister, and to my mother-in-law. To my children, Calder and Milan, who are now both in college, you are my inspiration. And then there is the man with whom I share everything, my husband Jamie, whose imprint is all over this book. Thank you for talking me through the rough patches, for reading and commenting when I felt stuck, and most of all, for being a consummate caretaker.

Slavery, Fatherhood, and Paternal Duty
in African American Communities
over the Long Nineteenth Century

Introduction

"My father, by his nature, as well as by the habit of transacting business as a skilful mechanic, had more of the feelings of a freeman than is common among slaves," Harriet Jacobs recalled in the opening pages of her narrative. "My brother was a spirited boy; and being brought up under such influences, he early detested the name of master and mistress. One day, when his father and his mistress both happened to call him at the same time, he hesitated between the two; being perplexed to know which had the strongest claim upon his obedience. He finally concluded to go to his mistress." Jacobs described the forceful reaction of their father, Elijah Knox. "You are my child . . . and when I call you, you should come immediately, if you have to pass through fire and water." In a system engineered to deny his patriarchal rights, Elijah attempted to assert his authority. He also attempted to provide for his children materially and emotionally. As a skilled carpenter, for a time he had permission to hire his own labor and he saved his money in a futile attempt to purchase the freedom of his children. Although unable to realize this goal, he did give his two oldest children the habits of mind and force of will that led them to seek and attain liberty.[1]

Slavery denied the enslaved control of their bodies and lives. Because slaves could be separated from their children at any time, parenting was a tenuous process. Masters appointed themselves paternalists and suppressed the rights of enslaved fathers. "The denial of black manhood was central to white manhood, American nationalism, and class relations," Edward Baptist argues. African Americans were not considered men because they lacked the essential attributes of American masculinity—control over their own labor, property, marriages, and children.[2] Enslaved fathers could not overtly protect their families without risking their own safety. They frequently lived on different plantations and apart from their wives and children. Despite a system designed to disempower them, however, enslaved fathers were often an influential presence in the lives of their children. Not all enslaved men could or wanted to be active fathers, but many endeavored to nurture their children in an atmosphere that was hostile to black men's open expressions of authority.

1

Slaveholders, on the other hand, were supposed to provision their dependents, including their slaves, as part of their paternalistic role as men and masters. On the slave market, white men purchased not only labor, but also a sense of masculine prerogative, buying slaves to provide for their white family members and then taking credit for the work those slaves performed.[3] To varying degrees, slaveholders materially "provided" for their dependents by usurping that patriarchal privilege from black men.[4] Some adequately maintained their human property while others did not. A fraction of slaveholders also regularly forced sexual attentions on enslaved women. The resulting offspring legally took on the slave status of their mothers. Few white men acknowledged their mixed race children or assumed the emotional responsibilities of a father. The slave system rewarded the white paternalist with the privileges of manhood and fatherhood, and denied those same rights to enslaved men. And yet, in the narratives of escaped and former slaves, African American fathers often provided physical and emotional sustenance to their children. In contrast, white fathers of slaves more commonly avoided their paternal obligations, though a handful acknowledged and even freed their illegitimate children.

This book is about fatherhood and slavery in the American South. What did it mean to be an enslaved man and a father? How did enslaved men handle the limitations of fatherhood within the institution of slavery? How did these men feel about their children, and how did their children feel about their enslaved fathers? How did slaves conceive of the paternal role? In what ways were men able to provide for their children, even if their time with their children was limited? How did these men shape their children's lives in a system that denied them authority, and, in many cases, coresidence with and physical proximity to their kin? Did children remember fathers they lost to sale, death, and escape? And, if so, what did they remember? Given the sexual dynamics of slavery, what did it mean to have a white father? How did former slaves feel about these men? How did enslaved women feel about the white fathers of their children?

A study of fatherhood, or of parenting more broadly, is fraught with difficulties. In any population, people exhibit a range of reactions to being a parent.[5] Some adapt quickly and take to the role of mother or father with ease, while others struggle and learn as they go. A few fail completely. Even under ideal conditions, some parents never adjust to the role, and some lack the basic motivation to succeed as a caregiver. This study encompasses a wide range of human experience, but that is not the main point. The critical issue is that slavery imposed tremendous constraints on and created painful dilemmas for enslaved parents. In a contemporary setting, many factors can complicate parenting, including lack of resources (human and financial), poor medical care, dangerous neighborhoods, unsafe homes, distance from extended family, tense adult relationships, domestic abuse, and more. Slaves faced not only these hurdles, but also the fact that they had little to no control over their own bodies and family integrity. Enslaved parents lived under a cloud of anxiety, knowing that no family unit was safe. Fortunate families lived together on the same plantation and were owned by masters who claimed to eschew forced separation. But a death or a debt in the white family could sever these fragile bonds, as professed slaveholder principles quickly broke down under financial pressure and the allure of monetary gain.[6] Under these decidedly adverse conditions, enslaved parents attempted to provide for and nurture their children.

In 1965, Assistant Secretary of Labor Daniel Patrick Moynihan published a report that discussed "deep-seated structural distortions in the life of the Negro American," which he traced to the legacy of slavery and the "tangle of pathology" created by the "fatherless matrifocal" family. Over the past half century, numerous scholars have refuted Moynihan's thesis about slavery's impact on succeeding generations, his characterization of the black family as a matriarchy, and his argument that failed patriarchy, rather than systemic factors, is the root cause of political dislocation and economic struggle within black communities. Despite many challenges to Moynihan's conclusions, his caricatures of black men, women, and children have persisted and had detrimental effects, including contributing to the contemporary mass incarceration crisis.

A main goal of this book is to counter the enduring stereotypes of black men's irresponsibility within the family. Too often, enslaved peoples' adaptations are used against them, with their adjustments to imposed and unchosen conditions being seen as signs of depravity rather than resilience. The distorted images of the missing father and the female matriarch fail to account for the flexibility of the enslaved family. These images also fail to account for the range of African Americans' lived experience in slavery and the post–Civil War period. Enslaved and then free African American fathers in the late nineteenth and early twentieth centuries regularly took care of their families and their communities in ways that were hidden from the dominant society.[7]

The legacy of slavery lies not in the pathology of black families or communities, but in the ongoing conditions of poverty, oppression, and structural racism that black Americans still face. Slavery also established black masculinity as subordinate to white masculinity, a hierarchy that persists. Enslaved men were privately allowed to exhibit the traits of manhood, particularly when such actions benefited the slaveholder. As long as black masculinity could be subsumed by white masculinity, black men could be men within the slave quarters. But when enslaved men threatened white power, they were quickly and often violently emasculated, a pattern that continues to define the contemporary experience of black men. The dominant society defines white males as men when it comes to authority and power and as boys when such a portrayal absolves their misbehavior. In contrast, the dominant society portrays black males as boys in relation to authority and power, and as men when such a description incriminates black men individually and African Americans collectively. White society carefully monitors and attempts to control black manhood.

Throughout the 2016 NFL season, San Francisco 49ers quarterback Colin Kaepernick knelt for the national anthem to protest police killings of African Americans and racial injustice. His silent protest provoked hostility from many white Americans, including candidate and then president Donald Trump. As during slavery, contemporary African American men are allowed to show attributes of masculinity in regulated environments and when it benefits those in power. Kaepernick's attempt to use his visibility to better conditions for black Americans—to provide for his people—threatens those in power. Many white Americans castigate Kaepernick as disrespectful to the troops and flag, but there is a deeper issue at play. Kaepernick opted out of his contract at the end of the 2016 season and, as of June 2020, has remained unsigned despite being considered an excellent football player. This extended blacklisting is a testament to how frightening the dominant society finds the public and unscripted performance of black masculinity, particularly when it moves into the realm of ideas and beyond white control.[8] A black man kneeling in silence due to the dictates of his own conscience threatens to upend the power structure and the masculine hierarchy. Kaepernick's actions fit into a long history of ideological caretaking by African American men and within black communities. He made visible and public what has long been invisible.

Family, Form, and Function

Scholarly assessments of enslaved fathers have generally been rooted in the study of the family. Early work argued that the legal, social, and economic forces of slavery destroyed the family and led to absent, emasculated fathers. Kenneth Stampp described the slave family as "matriarchal in form, for the mother's role was far more important than the father's." Because he could neither control nor safeguard his family, the bondman "easily sank to the position of a male guest . . . without respect or responsibility," W. E. B. Du Bois stated. Moynihan drew on this literature of dysfunction.[9] These scholars looked at the structure of households rather than the experiences of people within those households. While the enslaved father lacked externally recognized power, this did not necessarily mean that his family failed to invest him with respect and internal authority. Slavery undoubtedly weakened the enslaved husband and father, but he could still be and often was an influential presence in the life of his children. His loved ones often admired him despite his compromised position, and he could find ways to protect his children's sense of self even if he could not protect them directly. In the eyes of slaves, status differed substantially from sanctioned authority.[10]

In the 1970s, largely in reaction to the Moynihan Report, another generation of historians argued that a combination of slave agency and masters' economic incentives led to the widespread existence of the nuclear family. This second phase, the era of John Blassingame and "community studies," elevated black fathers. According to Eugene Genovese, the nuclear family was "the social norm," and the enslaved father acted as a provider and head of household.[11] Scholars reinforcing this vision of the two-parent family again focused on household structure. Although this camp overstates the insularity, uniformity, and stability of the slave family, it makes important points about how enslaved people adapted to an oppressive environment.[12] The third period, one of revision, is exemplified by the work of Peter Kolchin and Brenda Stevenson. While coming from different positions, these scholars raise the possibility that enslaved men failed to build stable relationships. Without investing in the Moynihan Report's rhetoric about matriarchy, which blamed black women for familial crises in the 1960s and accused them of emasculating black men, this scholarship still provides a prehistory of the absent father.[13] More recently, in a fourth phase, scholars such as Emily West and Daina Berry have reinterpreted relationships between enslaved men and women, arguing that fathers went to great lengths to build and maintain relationships with their children.[14]

Work on the enslaved family has increasingly emphasized regional variation and multiple forms. In the early 2000s, Wilma Dunaway challenged the paradigm of the stable, nuclear slave family. She argues that scholars based their analyses on the Lower South and large holdings and failed to adequately consider small farms and the Mountain South. In these areas, sale, hiring, and owner and labor migration led to higher numbers of one-parent households.[15] In his comparative study of three non-cotton-producing regions, Damian Pargas convincingly shows that the slave family varied "across time and space," as a result of both external pressures and internal agency. Different forms of regional agriculture shaped economic conditions, plantation and slaveholding size, and work patterns, which in turn affected family life, establishing a "basic framework of *boundaries and opportunities*," within which enslaved people could and did act.[16] A number of local and regional studies reinforce these findings.[17] The external pressures on enslaved people varied considerably by region, and also by locality, based on plantation demographics and slaveholder management style.[18] Outside forces affected household and family structure, but enslaved people everywhere prioritized family and took advantage of available opportunities. Most aspired to create two-parent households and did so when able, but in the face of obstacles and imposed and changing conditions, they adjusted their family life.[19]

Anthropologists and sociologists have pointed out the limitations of focusing on the household as a unit of analysis when studying the family. Based on fieldwork in an urban African American neighborhood in the 1970s, Carol Stack concluded that "an arbitrary imposition of widely accepted definitions of the family, the nuclear family, or the matrifocal family," failed to capture her participants' understanding of their own lives. Stack refuted the Moynihan Report, observing that "statistical patterns do not divulge underlying cultural patterns."[20] Nicholas Townsend's study of a Botswana village from the 1970s through the 1990s further reveals the insufficiencies of a narrow focus on residential household. According to government surveys, Botswana has a high percentage of female-headed households, leading to accusations of male irresponsibility. However, fieldwork shows that "domestic groups are not necessarily co-resident, and domestic arrangements are characterised by fluidity and adaptability. In particular, limiting investigation to the residential household conceals a great deal of men's connections with and contributions to children." Townsend urges scholars to move away from "cross-sectional definitions of the household as a group of co-residents at a particular time."[21]

In her analysis of white families in Walton County, Florida, after the Civil War, Barbara Agresti uses census data to counter the tendency among historians and sociologists to equate extended family structures with the preindustrial world. Agresti finds a high proportion of extended family households, particularly in later life cycle stages and during periods of economic stress. She counsels against making "broad generalizations about 'the' family of the past from cross-sectional studies. The findings suggest that the early American family was neither as stable nor as simple as we have often assumed."[22] Contemporary migrant agricultural workers, who face low wages, poor working conditions, and lack of opportunity, also respond to adversity with creative family arrangements. In order to find work and support their children, many Latino men have to live apart from their families.[23] Their remittances form the lifeblood of their communities, yet American culture adopts a normative, Eurocentric, middle-class view of paternity, equating responsible fatherhood with coresidence and direct economic and social support. Through this narrow lens, nonresident fathers are seen as irresponsible.[24] To fully understand the experiences of enslaved people, researchers must avoid normative, presentist definitions of household, family, and fatherhood. They must avoid the assumption that the form of the household determined the lived experience of its members.[25] Indeed, as enslaved people faced even greater economic and life stage challenges than many other groups, past and present, we may expect their family structures to be even more diverse and complex.

The domestic slave trade fueled the prevalence of female-headed households, especially in the Upper South. In addition to local sales, in the wake of the cotton boom, the interstate trade moved two-thirds of a million slaves from the Upper to Lower South between 1790 and 1860, breaking up families and communities. Michael Tadman shows that the trade moved "10 percent or more of slaves from the Upper to the Lower South" each decade, and half of these sales involved family disruption.[26] The Loudoun County, Virginia, slave households studied by Brenda Stevenson were often female headed as a result of the slave trade and local labor patterns. For Stevenson, "matrifocality was a fundamental characteristic of most slave families, even when fathers lived locally." Stevenson dismisses the influence of the slave husband and father as "much diminished," and conflates household structure and residence patterns with family structure. "Many slave families were not only matrifocal, but also matrilocal," she writes.[27]

Anthropologists developed terms for the residence patterns and family structures of free peoples, which makes applying such concepts to the enslaved family problematic. Matrilocality refers to residence patterns in which married couples live with or near the wife's family. Slaves were forced into matrilocal residence patterns because children followed the legal status of the mother and her owner's dictates determined household structure.

However, this term is not entirely accurate because unless a sale occurred, an enslaved husband could not move to his wife's plantation, nor was she free to move in with him to form a patrilocal residence. Slave households were matrilocal in that the children resided with their mother unless a family was broken up by sale or death, but where the husband lived varied. If an enslaved couple married on site, they were technically duolocal, though neither spouse might have extended family on the plantation, making both terms imprecise. "Matrilocality" fails to fully account for the complexities of enslavement and the fact that many physically divided families were still emotionally intact. Emotionally cohesive families with a husband living on one plantation and wife and children on another, or with older children hired out, were actually multilocal kinship networks scattered across multiple households.[28]

In a matrifocal family structure, the woman heads the family and the man has a less prominent role in childrearing. Enslaved households were frequently matrifocal in form, but this was due to imposed conditions rather than choice, making this concept even more problematic than matrilocal residence. Scholars must be careful when labeling either the enslaved household or family as matrifocal. A household could be matrifocal in form, but form did not always determine function. An abroad marriage with an engaged, visiting father created a technically matrifocal *household*, but many of these men did not want to be separated from their families and were highly involved in family life. A man and his children might see his wife's cabin as his home even if he could not reside there full time. In these cases, although the household was matrifocal, the *family* was not. While a household and family could be both matrifocal in form and function, at other times a household could be one parent and female headed in structure, and yet the kinship unit functioned as a two-parent or even patrifocal family. It is critical to consider and sometimes differentiate between the form of the household and the composition and function of the family. I thus refer to matrifocal households and do not assume that household structure dictated family experience or always led to a matrifocal family.

Matrifocal households resulted from children following the legal status of their mothers. This practice served the economic needs of slaveholders, who profited from the creation of more slaves. Many masters further centralized their human property by requiring that their male slaves marry, and thus reproduce, on site. However, local demographic constraints and enslaved peoples' preferences for choosing their own partners made this requirement hard to enforce. The combination of enforced matrilocality and slaves' tendency toward exogamy contributed to the practice of "abroad" marriage, in which partners lived on separate plantations, children lived with their mothers, and the husband visited his family on a biweekly, weekly, or monthly basis.[29] At times, abroad, or cross-plantation, marriages were a compromise between the demands of masters and the desires of enslaved people. However, because slaves generally preferred coresidential marriages and formed such unions when able, the matrifocal household and multilocal family with a visiting, nonresident father was most often a response to structural constraints.[30]

Regardless of how and why such unions formed, abroad marriages increased family instability by subjecting enslaved people to the whims and decisions of two slaveholders.[31] In addition, an enslaved man faced the disadvantages of not living with his family full time, including lack of oversight over his children and mate. On the other hand, he avoided some of the pain of seeing his family abused and had the opportunity to travel beyond his plantation. This form of regulated mobility enabled a man to gain valuable knowledge that could help in a potential escape attempt.[32] In an abroad marriage, moreover, enslaved women had more control over their family life, but had less help with household labor and childcare.[33] Abroad marriages were more common in regions with smaller farms, when masters owned only a few slaves, or where the sex ratio and ages of slaves on larger plantations made finding a suitable partner on site difficult or impossible. A man or woman might unintentionally fall in love with someone on another plantation, a spouse might be sold locally, or an individual might purposely seek a partner further afield. Abroad marriages could reflect unchosen circumstances, calculated decision making, or a combination of factors. Emily West calls abroad marriages in South Carolina "far from weak and nominal." Men's willingness to travel and take risks to visit their families points to their self-conception as "initiators, protectors, and providers."[34]

The slave household was often, but not always, matrifocal, and enslaved people contributed to this arrangement. However, a matrifocal *household* did not always mean a matrifocal *family*. To use the structure of the household as a measure of the quality of the relationships within and across households is shortsighted. How enslaved children felt about their fathers, and how they conceived of a father's role, even with men denied the authority to fully exercise that role, contributed to children's identity and development. In an abroad marriage, an enslaved woman could manage the household on a daily basis and yet the father could be highly involved and perceived by his children as the head of the family. If and when a father visited consistently, this was not a one-parent family. Where a man resided according to his owner and the place he saw as home often diverged.[35] In other cases, households were two parent in form, but not in function. Household structure cannot fully account for level of paternal or maternal involvement, which was also mediated by local contingencies. The early literature on the black family, including the Moynihan Report, mislabeled household matrifocality as matriarchy, thereby ignoring variation and lived experience, and defined this arrangement as pathological. Matrifocal households were, rather, adaptations to a pathological environment.[36]

This book highlights the precarious, varied, and adaptive nature of the enslaved family.[37] Slaves responded to local conditions and constraints and formed a diverse array of family structures within and across households.[38] In his work on the informal economy, Dylan Penningroth stresses the importance of family as well as the "flexible and negotiable" nature of kinship among slaves. Calvin Schermerhorn, examining networking as a way to protect family ties, writes, "Enslaved families tended not to form according to a regular structure."[39] As men and women started new families after market dislocation, kinship units regularly suffered partial or complete separation, and then reformed in a new configuration.[40] A focus on function rather than form, and on the interactions and relationships of family members, provides a sense of how individuals and family structures survived and adapted.[41] An examination of fatherhood shows that the enslaved family defied easy categorization because it shifted based on internal and external pressures.

Even in a hostile environment that denied them authority, many enslaved fathers managed to provide for their children in tangible and intangible ways. Elijah Knox, for example, could not keep his family together, but he did have a profound impact on his two children, Harriet and John Jacobs, in the limited time he spent with them. Harriet Jacobs exemplifies the many forms the enslaved family might take in the lifetime of a single individual. Until the age of six, when her mother died, she lived in a two-parent household that was part of a larger, extended family. Death and inheritance within the slaveholder family broke this nuclear slave family apart. When Harriet was twelve, she and her brother were acquired by a new owner and removed from their home. Their father's mistress married, and this new master rescinded Elijah's permission to hire out, requiring him to return to the plantation and further distancing him from his family.[42] He died roughly a year later, discouraged by his inability to purchase his children. For a time, Jacobs and her own children benefited from an extended family presided over by her grandmother, Molly Horniblow, who managed to achieve freedom. This fluctuating kin group increasingly lost members to sale, escape, and death.

Elijah's family was broken by slavery, and the institution broke him as a father and individual, and yet he had an outsized influence on his children. John and Harriet Jacobs escaped slavery and became abolitionist authors. Harriet's escape "evolves primarily out of her identification and association with the men in her family," writes Jennifer Fleischner, especially "her outraged and enraged father, who lives on in her mind after his death as a powerful internal imago." Furthermore, during Harriet's years in hiding, the men of the family nursed her when she fell ill. The "prominent symbols of caretaking, even in the womblike garret, are two men." Fleischner argues that Harriet's memoir functions as "a remembrance of her father, and an almost ceremonial enactment of Jacobs's father's command to reach freedom or the grave."[43]

In saying that some enslaved fathers had a meaningful impact on their children, I am neither negating the importance of mothers nor calling the slave family patriarchal. The slave family could be more egalitarian, matriarchal, or patriarchal, depending on local conditions, the constituent members, and the personalities involved.[44] Mothers, as scholars have shown, were crucial within the institution of slavery.[45] Moreover, I am not arguing that fathers were more important than mothers—I am saying that men, and their children, invested fathers and fatherhood with consequence. In her study of enslaved childhood, Marie Schwartz writes, "Women did not dominate the family, nor did family life center on women's activities. Rather, men and women cooperated as best they could to ensure the survival of children."[46]

Fatherhood

Scholars of the antebellum South have described the institution of slavery as abounding with contradictions.[47] When slaves had children, they affirmed their humanity and their ability to survive. Yet producing more slaves perpetuated the oppression of self, family, and future generations. Deborah Gray White calls giving birth "an act of defiance" on the part of enslaved women and "a signal to the slave owner that no matter how cruel and inhumane his actions, African Americans would not be utterly subjugated or destroyed."[48] At the same time, procreation and childrearing, for both men and women, created another emotional tie that could be used to compel and control. "Families were the greatest factors that slaves had to mitigate their conditions," Wilma King argues. "The manipulation of families was also the slaveholders' greatest source of control over bond servants." To nurture a child, to instill a sense of self-worth, and to teach them to survive in an arbitrary world was a form of resistance.[49] That resistance, however, augmented the master's stock. Slaves realized that nurturing their children brought bittersweet satisfaction and simultaneously contributed to the slaveholder's property. Parenting was thus an act of resistance that made slaves complicit in their own oppression. Slave labor also profited the master, but enslaved people did not love their labor as they loved their children.

Enslaved fathers faced additional agonizing contradictions. To act as caretaker deepened a man's social connections and provided one form of human meaning, but it also further tied him to a system that eroded his humanity. To be an involved, nurturing father was a form of resistance that was simultaneously humanizing and dehumanizing. Fatherhood imbued men with some authority, severely limited by slavery, and yet fatherhood also gave slaveholders increased leverage over a man. Fathers faced intractable dilemmas. To stand up for oneself or loved ones was to risk removal from and hardship for one's family. To be a man could mean compromising one's sense of duty as a man, and this remained true of the African American experience in the postwar period. African Americans articulated an abiding conception of paternal duty from the antebellum period through the 1930s because they faced consistent and ongoing challenges that did not end with emancipation. Slavery and Jim Crow placed two of the central imperatives of masculinity, duty to self and duty to family, in opposition. As a result, enslaved and then free fathers found alternate, indirect, and concealed ways to support their kin, often channeling their leadership and authority through ideas and religion.

This study considers the ways that the slave system undermined fathers and the considerable, and at times insurmountable, obstacles men faced in their attempt to parent. To be present and engaged in the lives of one's children meant negotiating behavioral constraints. A father might try to instill in his children a sense of self-worth, and yet a man who openly resisted the institution of slavery risked separation from his family. Masters manipulated men's love for their families to impose greater control and achieve financial gain. Proslavery ideology posited that slaves had weak familial connections, but the reality of slaveholder treatment of enslaved fathers contradicted those assertions. In addition, slaveholders used enslaved men's sense of familial obligation to economize, reducing material support to women and children and expecting husbands to make up the difference. Slaveholders destabilized enslaved men's authority more globally and yet often upheld men's position as the head of the family when it served them financially.[50] Just as plantation registers listing women as head of household can obscure internal family dynamics and fathers' contributions, especially in the case of abroad marriages, those designating men as head of household or cabin must be used carefully, as that role often had a dual function that bolstered slaveholders' managerial interests.

Paternalism included assumptions of male control of households, which offered enslaved men a way to navigate through the slave system. When permitted limited authority, including feeding and clothing their kin, however, fulfilling paternal duty left men further enmeshed in bondage. Slaveholders wanted men to produce children, and were at times eager to let them materially provide for their kin, but they feared emotional bonds and attempted to undermine these at any opportunity. Enslaved men were allowed to exercise some attributes of masculinity and paternity if, in doing so, they provided benefits to the slaveholder. When black fatherhood and provisioning threatened the power structure, enslaved men were denied access to masculinity in definition and in practice, a trend that continues to describe the experience of black men today. Craig Friend argues that antebellum Southern masculinity "required regular public performance. For enslaved men, of course, any attempts to demonstrate public masculinity had been met with physical and psychic violence meant to emasculate them."[51] Enslaved men could exercise paternal duty privately and within the bounds of the plantation and slave community, but they could not display their masculinity publicly.[52] Paternalism was an essential part of slaveholders' public performance of masculinity. Masculinity and paternalism were publicly available only to white men and informed white male identity. Both qualities reflected masters' self-conception more than the reality of slaveholder and slave behavior within the institution.

Historians have argued that slavery placed particular burdens on women, pointing to the double oppression of race and gender, and the "triple exploitation" of female slaves.[53] In terms of parenting, however, it was harder to be an enslaved father and maintain sustained contact with one's children. Fathers were more likely than mothers to live at a distance or be permanently separated from children. Slaveholders might congratulate themselves on keeping slave families intact and yet apply that practice only to mothers and their children.[54] Slavery placed heavy burdens on all parents, but motherhood meshed with white patriarchy and slaveholder control (to the disadvantage of enslaved families), whereas enslaved fatherhood mixed uneasily with masters' paternalistic self-image. Slaveholders further marginalized enslaved fathers by prioritizing the status of mothers in both law and custom. The antebellum ideology of mothers as nurturers and fathers as providers also worked against slaves. Enslaved men conceived of themselves as providers, but the institution of slavery effectively deprived them of full access to that patriarchal privilege.

Although the fear of losing kin to the interregional slave trade overshadowed the lives of all slaves, children were more likely to lose contact with their father.[55] An enslaved man knew he or his wife and children could be separated and sold away at any time and this anxiety shaped his role as a father. For children, losing a father to sale cut off physical contact, but many formerly enslaved people retained distinct memories of these men that informed their identity.[56] Slaves and former slaves considered having two parents ideal. To have one parent or the other was preferable to being separated from both, and those who had little memory of one or either parent understood something was missing from their lives. Former slaves blamed limited or lost contact with their fathers on the conditions of slavery, assuming that these men would have been involved in their lives had that been an option. The absence of fathers stemmed from the emasculation of slavery rather than choice or irresponsibility on the part of enslaved men.

To be utterly fatherless was to have no father in practice and no information about his identity, making it impossible to have any memory of him, real or constructed. Sexual abuse and white paternity most often led to utterly fatherless families. At least 13 percent, and probably more, of antebellum slaves had white parentage.[57] Scholars have highlighted the ubiquity of sexual exploitation within slavery. Deborah Gray White calls most sexual relationships between white men and enslaved women "exploitative," noting that while some women submitted to concubinage, their choice was "between miscegenation and the worst experiences slavery had to offer."[58]

Race mixing varied by slaveholding size and region, with the highest levels in the Upper South.[59] Labor conditions also contributed; areas where more men and women worked in domestic settings had more mixed-race individuals.[60] Some knew the identity of their white fathers, and a few had white fathers who acknowledged them. In twentieth-century interviews, a number of former slaves had no idea about the identity of their biological father because their mother withheld that information as a survival strategy. Still other informants withheld sensitive information about their parentage from fieldworkers. White paternity accounts for a significant but indefinable percentage of these fatherless families. The sexual dynamics of slavery thus led to an indistinct and unevenly distributed number of fatherless families, households, and individuals. Because white parentage affected family formation, variation in slaveholder sexual behavior and response to fathering slaves further exacerbated the uneven distribution of fatherless families.

White paternity of slaves also contributed to two diametrically opposed outcomes: it strengthened matrifocality while also erasing black mothers. When enslaved mothers resented the white fathers of their children and those men refused to acknowledge their children, mixed-race individuals tended to identify solely with their mother. This created *emotionally matrifocal families*, a phrase I use throughout the book. These were families in which the mother headed the household and she and her children felt little emotional connection to the father of her children. White paternity and forced pairing and breeding added another layer of complexity to the definition of the enslaved household and family and regularly led to fatherless and emotionally matrifocal families. At times, an enslaved concubine headed a family embedded within a white household, creating a kin group that was matrifocal but not matrilocal. However, when white fathers bequeathed freedom and/or property to their mixed-race offspring, those children had an incentive to identify with their father, sometimes at the expense of the mother. White parentage occupies two chapters of this book because it shows a different side of fatherlessness within slavery as well as illuminates the identity formation of former slaves. Attitudes toward fathers, black and white, known and unknown, reflected and shaped self-conception, and may actually tell us most about how people saw themselves. In addition, former slaves' criticisms of white fathers reveal their conceptions of paternal duty.

Imperfect information about one's origins or the putative white parentage of parents and grandparents makes accurately quantifying the degree of race mixing in the South impossible, but percentages matter less than the impact of such sexual practices on individuals, families, and communities.[61] What mattered was the exploitation itself and white men's reactions to their illegitimate children, particularly the hypocrisy of slaveholders abusing their power and then selling their own offspring. To own and sell one's blood relatives violated slaves' understanding of fatherhood. The presence of one or two biracial slaves, even on a neighboring plantation, was a reminder that enslaved people lacked control over their own bodies and of the fundamental instability of family life. "The children born of these assaults were potent symbols of the immense power that whites held over the most intimate spheres of black life," Brenda Stevenson writes.[62] A fraction of masters sexually abused their slaves, but enough did so to make paternalism and actual paternity hard to disentangle.

In the aftermath of the Moynihan Report, critics inside and outside the African American community accused enslaved women who had sexual relations with white men of colluding in their own subjugation. Black feminists refuted the charges of "castration" the report unleashed, addressing misogyny external to and within African American communities. Hortense Spillers argues that the African American family has "no Father to speak of," a condition that according to the Moynihan Report is "the Fault of the Daughter, or the female line." Captivity erased gender, slavery erased family, and the "matriarchist" misnaming of black women's power placed them "out of the traditional symbolics of female gender," and impinged on black men "in ways he cannot escape."[63] Yet the myths of the matriarch and indifferent father are not representative of the enslaved family or the lived experience of many African Americans. Although the slave quarters were far from harmonious, caretaking men who engaged in family life were supported by and supportive of their kin and recognized within their community.[64] Enslaved men felt most emasculated by slavery and slaveholders, not by enslaved women who headed households or were sexually victimized by white men.

Masculinity

In the wake of the market revolution, the Heroic Artisan model of manhood increasingly gave way to the idea of the Self-Made Man in the antebellum North. Meanwhile, Southern upper-class masculinity continued to enshrine the model of the gentleman patriarch, imbued with the characteristics of honor and mastery, whose dependents included women, children, and slaves. But, as Craig Friend and Lorri Glover point out, nonslaveholding white men could not fully access these traits, complicating the honor and mastery paradigm. They argue for a "diversity of Southern masculinities" based on age, class, and race. Although definitions of masculinity varied within Southern society, white men shared the belief that "domination of blacks bought manhood for whites." To be enslaved was to be emasculated and so "black men were the antithesis of honor and mastery—dependent, acquiescent, externally controlled." Friend and Glover highlight the importance of a public and private distinction in Southern masculine values: "Honor was externally presented for public consumption; mastery was internally realized for personal fulfillment." Regardless of regional and class variation, the central traits of American manhood were the same. A man was supposed to provide for and protect his dependents.[65] Enslaved people shared this vision of masculinity and adapted it to their own constrained circumstances. This enabled them to turn those characteristics around to critique white Southern manhood.

The most obvious model of manhood available to enslaved men and the one touted by fugitive authors was heroic resistance, which equated masculinity with dramatic action even to the point of death.[66] Scholars have tended to adopt this view of masculinity, seeing open resistance as an assertion of manhood.[67] Edward Baptist, Rebecca Fraser, and more recently, Jeff Forret, Sergio Lussana, and David Doddington have examined masculine identities within slavery and added greater nuance to this overly simplistic model.[68] In an article on enslaved men on the frontier, Baptist adds the "caretaker role" and "individualized manhood," as alternatives to heroic masculinity. Caretakers used religion to "emphasize ordinary virtue rather than heroic resistance and self-destruction." For many men, religious conversion was not only an acceptance of faith, but also a means of criticizing slavery and slaveholders. Individualized manhood entailed repudiating family and community ties and looking out for oneself, which sometimes placed these men at odds with the needs of the community.[69]

In a book-length study of masculinity, Sergio Lussana argues that enslaved men "created an all-male subculture" that emphasized public performance of masculine "exploits" and fostered "homosocial group solidarity." Although Lussana overstates group cohesion, he makes an important point about male sociability and friendships as a force for survival. I also emphasize sociability, but look at men's emotional investment in their kin. In his own exploration of "multiple masculinities," David Doddington counters the idea of masculinity as a force of solidarity and collective resistance, showing that varied expectations of and approaches to manhood could foster disagreement and conflict. "Enslaved men made different and difficult choices as to how to endure oppression while maintaining a sense of masculinity: These identities were intimately bound up within broader tensions over accommodation, resistance, and survival within slavery," he writes. While celebrated by fugitives and many enslaved people as the "apex of masculinity," heroic resistance was not the only route to manhood. Some assumed the role of provider and protector, achieving success through "industrious, energetic, and responsible manhood," and defining a masculine identity through work, a form of "limited accommodation." Men in "trustee positions," such as drivers and headmen, constructed a masculine identity based on "authority, responsibility, and power," which often undermined solidarity. Doddington stresses the competitive, comparative, and often hierarchical nature of enslaved masculinity.[70] Lussana, Doddington, and Forret rightly accentuate the importance of public performance of masculinity in the quarters. I agree, and when I discuss public versus private masculinity, I am differentiating between the slave community and broader society. Enslaved men displayed their masculinity within the bounds of plantation and cross-plantation slave communities. Beyond those confines, their masculinity remained subordinated to that of white men.

Doddington also discusses masculine identity tied to sexual virility, competition, and violence in leisure activities. "Some enslaved men accommodated themselves to the sexually exploitative framework of Southern slavery and validated their manhood through expressions of sexual dominance," he writes, an approach to sexuality that "crossed racial boundaries." Violence, sexual and otherwise, served as "a strategy to assert power."[71] Violence infused Southern life for both blacks and whites. Forret utilizes this social milieu to examine the perverse impact of slavery as well as how slaves appropriated aspects of Southern culture and made them their own. Exploring the "relationship between violence, honor, and masculinity within the quarters," he draws comparisons between enslaved and lower-class white men's conceptions of honor. Although violence certainly had a dark side, it enabled slaves to "impose a moral and ethical code of their own creation."[72] Where whites conceived of honor as a "vertical" construct that omitted slaves, enslaved people "understood honor's horizontal component," and forged an honor culture internal to the quarters. "The degradation slaves suffered in white society served only to enhance the sense of honor among themselves," Forret states.[73] Despite the emasculation that slavery inflicted, slaves achieved manhood and saw themselves as men, with violence offering one of several means of upholding and defending honor and performing masculinity in the quarters.[74]

A number of scholars have challenged the historiographical trend in the 1970s that presents unified resistance and community solidarity among the enslaved. Studies of family and internal economies have revealed stratification, tensions, and conflict within the quarters, adding human depth and multiplicity to a previously one-dimensional image.[75] In the most encompassing of these works, Jeff Forret's examination of violence offers insight into enslaved peoples' economic activity, family life, values, and gender and group identities. Likewise, Dylan Penningroth uses property accumulation to examine kinship and culture. Both authors employ the concept of neighborhood, arguing that social ties between enslaved people were not a given, but intentionally built. "The resulting portrait is not a single, static 'slave community' but a vibrant collection of multiple slave communities continually in flux and inhabited by complex, real people," Forret concludes. African Americans defined belonging through a "language of kinship, not race," Penningroth states. While fluid, kinship was not boundless. "The slave quarters was not inhabited by one big family."[76] Rethinking solidarity means rethinking and complicating slave agency, and decoupling it from communal action, resistance, and success.[77]

Calvin Schermerhorn draws similar conclusions about family and neighborhood solidarity using case studies of how enslaved people in the antebellum Chesapeake employed networking and new market opportunities to try to prevent market separation of families. "Enslaved people's relative lack of social, civic, and economic resources left them intensely reliant on one another," he notes, "which in the context of multigenerational families gave rise to an intense family-anchored spirit of solidarity and mutual support." This sometimes resulted in kin groups placing the survival of the family unit above community, a tactic I explore in chapters 4, 5, and 6. In particular, free black slaveholders and enslaved mixed-race people who identified with their white heritage at times valued family over community. Likewise, some concubines, through circumstance and choice, tended to see themselves and their children as set apart, an atomistic family unto themselves. These women placed their own needs and those of their closest kin above community.[78]

According to David Doddington, enslaved men who demonstrated "little allegiance to a wider slave community" were those who derived a sense of self and manhood from physical domination of fellow slaves.[79] There were also enslaved family men who were not caretakers. These men were individualists within family and adhered to a hegemonic conception of masculinity based on dominating others, a concept associated with slaveholders. Few men could escape slaveholder demands for reproduction, though these men could focus on self and remain emotionally aloof or unmoored from family. Commentary on enslaved fathers shows that men who used gratuitous violence within their family circles were criticized and likened to slaveholders. Violence might be a widely recognized sign of manliness, but depending on how it was dispensed, did not necessarily make for a good father.

A model of masculinity adopted by many enslaved men and their African American descendants was that of a caretaker.[80] This was not the only available mode of manhood or an identity pursued by all enslaved men, and individuals could be men without being fathers, but it was a fundamental model of masculinity in slave communities. Fatherhood obviously changes over time and means different things to people in different contexts. While conditions imposed on the enslaved family shifted regionally and locally, a range of sources written or dictated decades apart reveal continuity in what was expected of fathers. A good father emotionally invested in his family and assumed the role of provider and protector. Enslaved men provided material goods when able to do so, but their provisioning also took other forms, in the shape of cultural and ideological goods the slaveholder could not fully regulate, such as advice and religious guidance. What fathers gave their children varied regionally, locally, and individually, but across slave communities the attempt to provide was a hallmark of responsible fatherhood.

Although enslaved children followed the legal status of their mothers, enslaved men, their families, and slave communities acknowledged fatherhood and imbued it with significance. The system might negate a father's importance and efface his presence, but he, his children, and his community did not. Former slaves admired an array of traits in their fathers, traits that all came back to an ability to maintain their dignity in the face of oppression and a willingness to support others, whether that be the immediate family, neighborhood, or community. When former slaves evaluated their fathers, they praised caretakers and caretaking in various forms, and they criticized men who behaved like slaveholders, dominating others and abusing what little power they had within slavery.

The structural constraints of slavery placed two of the main attributes of American manhood at odds with one another. To be a man was to be a protector of self and kin, provider, husband and father. However, an enslaved man could not protect loved ones and hope to remain present in the life of his family. A man who defended self or others risked ending up dead or sold, and thus parted from family.[81] Faced with this dilemma and unable to uphold rigid gender roles, enslaved people adapted. Men found alternate ways to shield loved ones that were invisible to slaveholders, such as nurturing their children's sense of self-worth and humanity and offering protection in the form of spiritual counsel, but this hardly compensated for their circumscribed realm of action. Although enslaved men worked around slavery's erasure of manhood, this did not erase the psychic trauma of men's inability to defend self and kin. Former slaves did describe their fathers, and sometimes themselves, as emasculated. In their critique of slavery, abolitionist authors were more likely to explicitly make such arguments, whereas twentieth-century interviewees addressed the issue obliquely. Enslaved men understood how debilitating the institution of slavery was to their paternal role. However, while they realized their own limited power, they saw emasculation as external to and imposed upon them. Slavery weakened them, but they were not inherently weak.

When evaluating fatherhood, former slaves differentiated between those who had power and those who had honor. Depending on how African American men wielded the power available to them, their kin and communities judged them as honorable or dishonorable, moral or immoral. Slaveholders and slaves also diverged in their conceptions of manhood. As the slave trade intensified, white men increasingly defined manhood as the ability to commodify and dominate others, with status as a commodity signifying the absence of manhood. In contrast, enslaved people developed a strong definition of paternal honor—a willingness to take care of others, which is something they believed their oppressors lacked.

Caretaking was an adaptation to the constraints of the slave system. Men could be caretakers with or without being patriarchs or heads of household, roles often denied to them. Caretaking was thus a form of resistance. By taking care of kin, men upheld their own dignity and nurtured that of others. Caretaking has been overlooked as a fundamental aspect of the slave experience for several reasons. Slavery and paternalistic ideology obscured caretaking because enslaved men, who did not own themselves, were not seen as patriarchs. Scholars have overlooked caretaking because they focused on household structure and dismissed nonresident fathers. African Americans in the late nineteenth century also hid caretaking because postwar racial violence targeted men who were able to amass property. Caretaking has been most deeply obscured by the distorted image of black men stretching from slavery, through the Moynihan Report, to modern media images that misrepresent the complexity and multiplicity of the African American experience.

This study employs a broad approach, which has both advantages and disadvantages. Examining fatherhood across the antebellum and postbellum South blurs regional distinctions. However, in the decades before the Civil War, as the market moved large numbers of slaves around, looking at how men chose to be fathers, how they handled dislocation and constraints, and how children evaluated their fathers gets at the omnipresent challenges and contradictions of slavery.[82] A broad approach also allows for an exploration of adaptation. The main questions I consider are how individuals experienced family and how they assessed their fathers, including how they remembered fathers they lost. Even if children had only a memory of their father, he could still influence his children's identity. Fathering extended beyond physical presence, which means it extended beyond a specific time and place. I posit a fairly uniform sense of fatherhood shared by former slaves in the antebellum period, through the postwar, and into the twentieth century. This uniformity is underscored by fugitives' and former slaves' denunciations of white fathers of slaves. A range of sources from the early nineteenth century to the 1930s voiced consistent criticisms of white men who failed to provide for and protect their own offspring.

This does not mean I am dismissing regional or temporal nuances in the definition of fatherhood.[83] What I am arguing is that a basic set of values attached to fatherhood was a matter of survival. Defining paternal duty broadly enabled men to find their own ways to provide for and support kin. Family values shift over time and space, but again, what endured was the value placed on family regardless of its form. Another adaptation to the constraints of slavery was that gender roles were more malleable in slave communities.[84] The contingencies of slavery that gave enslaved women what Angela Davis calls "the deformed equality of equal oppression" also created space for men to approach their paternal duty adaptively and creatively. This more flexible approach to manhood and fatherhood did not mean that enslaved people lacked ideals or preferences. They did not have the luxury, or the limitations, of a rigid gender system. This approach was not liberating, because it was forced rather than chosen and slaves remained ensnared in a matrix of oppression and powerlessness. Because the enslaved and then free family faced similar and ongoing challenges, African Americans could not fully access the gender conventions of the dominant society. Discrimination, poverty, kidnapping, and abusive apprenticeships made it difficult for free black families in the antebellum North to uphold white, middle-class gender standards, as did discrimination and violence following the Civil War.[85]

Chapter 1 considers the considerable, often insurmountable, constraints slavery placed on family and fatherhood. Despite their adaptations, including multilocal kinship units, enslaved people faced encumbered parenting regardless of their household arrangements. Although emasculation imposed perverse dilemmas, enslaved men retained a sense of self, humanity, and manhood through love of family, religious faith, and their own definition of honor.[86] Chapter 2 examines how men managed to influence their children despite the structural constraints of slavery, with a focus on former slaves' commentaries on their fathers and the traits they appreciated and criticized. Because masters failed to uphold slave communities' vision of honorable manhood, slaves and ex-slaves compared negligent and abusive black fathers to slaveholders (a topic discussed in greater detail in chapter 8). Chapter 3 discusses enslaved men's attempts to provision their families materially, emotionally, and spiritually. Chapter 4 explores provisioning in more depth, focusing on men who purchased or endeavored to purchase freedom for themselves and their family members. The second half of the chapter looks at men who became fugitives, the painful decision some made to run away and leave loved ones behind, and commentary on family once free. In failure and in the infrequent cases of success, former slaves' words, choices, and actions as they sought to free self and family underscored the centrality of kinship and slave communities' definition of paternal duty.

Chapter 5 examines sexual exploitation and violence in the antebellum South and what it meant to have a white father. Feelings about white fathers varied considerably depending on how that father treated his illegitimate offspring, how the slave community treated mixed-race children (which also varied), and an individual's sense of identity, which was intimately tied to these other factors. Biracial children at times expressed admiration for the few white fathers who openly acknowledged their children and provided freedom and education. They tended to be more ambivalent about white fathers who offered a privileged status on the plantation but not freedom. A significant number of mixed-race children despised their white fathers, especially those who sold or physically abused their own offspring. Reactions to white fathers highlight slaves and former slaves' consistent notions of paternal duty. Chapter 6 focuses greater attention on enslaved women, exploring their feelings toward children born of rape and concubinage and the white fathers of their children. A white man who sold his own offspring likely sold his daughters into the sex trade, underscoring how deeply imbedded rape was in the market economy and in the role of white planters as *fathers*. The act of rape connected the private realm of the Southern home to the market.

Chapters 7 and 8 consider the lives of fathers and children in freedom prior to, during, and after the Civil War and into the early twentieth century. Ongoing challenges undermined patriarchal status and underscore the ways in which normative definitions of fatherhood and family limit a full understanding of the African American experience. Chapter 8 focuses on provisioning and ex-slaves' assessments, positive and negative, of their free fathers. A number of autobiographies written by and about church leaders skew the sample in favor of the caretakers, though the Federal Writers' Project narratives offer some corrective balance.[87] Despite such bias, the records speak to the importance of caretaking in the memory of former slaves.

Sources

While a range of sources speaks to paternity in slavery, I made a conscious decision to focus on sources that allow for an examination of the emotional aspects of father/child relationships.[88] Because I am concerned with former slaves' commentary on their fathers, fathers' commentary on their children, and the quality of these relationships, the main sources used are slave narratives, including the oral history interviews gathered in the late 1920s and 1930s. African American fieldworkers conducted the first interviews with former slaves. Between 1927 and 1929, A. P. Watson, a Fisk University graduate student in anthropology, collected religious conversion narratives of former slaves, published in the volume, *God Struck Me Dead*. Fisk researcher Ophelia Settle Egypt conducted an additional 100 interviews with ex-slaves, living mainly in Kentucky and Tennessee, from 1929 to 1930, thirty-seven of which were published as the *Unwritten History of Slavery*.[89] In 1929, while teaching at Southern University, John Cade sent African American fieldworkers out to interview former slaves. Excerpts of the eighty-two interviews were published in an article entitled, "Out of the Mouths of Ex-Slaves."[90] Between 1937 and 1938, white and black employees of the Federal Writers' Project, under the auspices of the Works Progress Administration (hereafter referred to as FWP narratives), interviewed over 2,300 former slaves in seventeen states.[91] This book draws on the volumes originally published as The Slave Narrative Collection, as well as the supplementary volumes of material later found in state archives and published by George Rawick.[92]

The problems of the FWP narratives, including the youth of the subjects during slavery, distant memory, interviewer bias, leading questions, and the racial climate in which the interviews took place, have been thoroughly explored by past scholars. Answers varied considerably based on the race of those asking the questions, with African American interviewers eliciting greater honesty.[93] The interviewer and subject sometimes knew one another, potentially biasing the responses.[94] Martin Jackson captured the difficulty fieldworkers faced in obtaining candid answers and establishing trust: "Lots of old slaves close the door before they tell the truth about their days of slavery. When the door is open, they tell how kind their masters were and how rosy it all was. You can't blame them for this, because they had plenty of early discipline, making them cautious about saying anything uncomplimentary about their masters." And yet, as Paul Escott notes, a remarkable number of informants were surprisingly frank, making these vital sources.[95]

C. Vann Woodward cautioned that the overrepresentation of house slaves in the FWP narratives, and the fact that nearly one-fifth of those interviewed were age five or younger in 1865, may have led to excessively rosy memories of slaveholders and means many respondents had little direct memory of slavery.[96] Karen Sánchez-Eppler counters "historiographic resistance" based on the age of the majority of the informants during slavery. Noting that 56 percent of the enslaved population in 1860 were younger than twenty, she argues that "once we recognize childhood as a crucial and devastating characteristic of the antebellum U.S. slave regime, those very traits and conditions that have seemed to undermine the reliability and relevance of the WPA Slave Narratives become instead a source of insight."[97] Because I focus on commentary on enslaved fathers and family, secondhand information and childhood memories are quite useful. Furthermore, when an informant praised their former owners to appease a white audience, this generally did not affect commentary on kin.[98] Informants felt obliged, particularly with white fieldworkers, to express respect for their masters, but they chose what to include about their family, making these comments far more candid.[99] If a family remained intact after freedom, moreover, many informants had decades of memories of their father even if they had little direct experience with slavery. Men are also overrepresented, as are those who had been enslaved on large holdings.[100] The second point biases the FWP narratives in favor of two-parent households, but still allows for an assessment of family relationships under a range of conditions.

John Blassingame considered the FWP narratives compromised sources due to problems of age and memory, the interview setting, the interviewers' lack of methodological rigor, revision and editorializing, and historians' unfamiliarity with proper use of oral history.[101] George Rawick found few cases of revision, with the exception of Texas, where heavy editing brought the material into line with contemporary race relations. More commonly, states such as Mississippi submitted only a fraction of the collected interviews, hence the now-published supplemental volumes of material Rawick found languishing in archives. Sharon Ann Musher has shown that fieldworkers sometimes changed meaning when editing narratives.[102] Editors at times deleted or reworded responses that did not fit into their vision of slavery.

Fieldworkers asked questions that prioritized information about the master–slave relationship over slaves' relationships with one another, making the main problem with commentary on fathers one of omission. Many former slaves with memories of their fathers likely never discussed those recollections, or did so in a cursory manner, providing a name but little further detail.[103] Because interviewers failed to ask follow-up questions about African American family relations, the information volunteered depended on what informants chose to add. A detailed picture of a family member emerges when the respondent wanted to discuss that individual. The absence of targeted questions about how subjects felt about their family members translates into a lack of substantive information and terse responses, yet it is still possible to glean a sense of family interactions and the emotional quality of those relationships.

Only fifteen FWP interviews from Virginia, at times in altered form, were sent to the national office. The *Weevils in the Wheat* collection consists of the extant material later recovered from archives, meaning that many remaining narratives are fragments of the original interviews. The collection consists of 159 interviews with 157 informants. African American fieldworkers conducted 100 of the interviews, with another nine collected by white fieldworkers. For the remaining fifty, the race of the fieldworker is unknown, though the interviewers were likely black.[104] Because the Virginia Writers' Project had an all-black unit, and Virginia was an area with a high preponderance of abroad marriages and dislocation due to sale and hiring, this is an ideal collection to evaluate family. However, the collection also presents problems due to the considerable number of brief and fragmented narratives and the fact that the list of questions used by black fieldworkers under the direction of Roscoe Lewis did not include specific queries about family history. Any analysis of family structure will therefore be compromised. In my analysis, which undercounts contact with fathers, 75 percent of respondents had contact with their mother, while 53 percent had contact with their enslaved father. The sexual dynamics of slavery account for some fraction of this discrepancy and 8 percent of the narratives discussed white fathers, while a total of 15 percent clearly identified or hinted at having a white father.[105]

Scholars have addressed some of the long-running concerns of the FWP archive, offering new ways of approaching the material. In her detailed study of the Federal Writers' Project, Catherine Stewart applies "vernacular criticism" to the Georgia and Florida narratives, recognizing ex-slaves as "strategic storytellers." Stewart uncovers the "veiled commentaries" of former slaves concerning "segregation in the 1930s, as well as alternate histories of slavery and emancipation." Her analysis explains how and why the FWP narratives contain "contradictory views on slavery and emancipation, at times even within a single interview." As ex-slaves appeared to accede to the Lost Cause nostalgia of white interviewers, "they also created their own counternarratives of black identity and experience by drawing on African American oral traditions to exert control over their interviews as well as the performance of their life histories." Informants used black vernacular, particularly signifying in its various forms, including figurative language, indirection, humor, evasiveness, equivocation, and disingenuous compliance, to "covertly contradict" the Lost Cause ideology of white interviewers.[106]

While the majority of FWP writers were white Southerners, the FWP led New Deal organizations in its employment of African Americans. Black fieldworkers elicited greater honesty, especially when informants discussed slavery. White FWP writers tended to use "minstrel-like, phonetic dialect," whereas African American interviewers more often eschewed dialect and recorded "graphic stories of abuse and slave resistance as well as the joy expressed by slaves when they learned of their freedom."[107] Interview subjects also employed signifying with black fieldworkers, but they "expected to be understood by their questioners," and black writers "actively collaborated" with their informants to ensure translation of the subtext. Although the "goals of black self-representation" were hampered, Stewart defines the FWP as a significant achievement. African Americans made a mark as informants and employees and the FWP amassed a "unique and unprecedented archive," comprising the "largest collection of ex-slave testimony, with arguably a far more extensive and diverse sampling of the experiences of the enslaved than the published autobiographies by former slaves from the nineteenth century."[108]

Though fewer in number, autobiographies written by former slaves offer richer detail. Men authored a far greater number of full-length narratives, and this body of sources is not representative of the average slave, with the

Upper South and fugitives overrepresented.[109] These are, nonetheless, invaluable sources. This book draws from the full range of slave narratives—narratives produced in divergent contexts and intentional in different ways. Antebellum authors carefully crafted their life stories, choosing their topics and language to appeal to a Northern audience. Twentieth-century informants, responding to questions selected and posed by others, offered calculated answers to placate a Jim Crow audience. All of these narratives were written or dictated from the vantage point of freedom. Abolitionist authors lived and wrote in a society steeped in domesticity, and postwar narrators wrote and dictated narratives from a Victorian perspective. The FWP narratives may say more about expectations of fatherhood in the 1930s than during slavery. Slave narratives produced across regions and over a century nevertheless articulate and share a consistent vision of paternal duty and denunciation of white morality and masculinity.

CHAPTER ONE

The God Part of Him

Slavery and Constraints on Fatherhood

Leonard Black associated the abuse he suffered as a slave with being removed from parental protection. "Here I was, a poor slave boy, without father or mother to take my part," he wrote.[1] Former slaves described the ways that slaveholders undermined and ruptured the slave family. Despite the constraints the institution placed on the formation of stable and enduring households, many enslaved people isolated from relatives realized what they lacked. They knew they had parents even if they had little personal contact with or distinct memory of their kin. Black also assumed that had his parents been near, they would have attempted to shelter him. Slaves and former slaves demonstrated an abiding understanding of the meaning of family even as they detailed impediments they faced and lamented their fragmented family ties.

Enslaved children frequently, but not always, had more sustained and longer contact with their mothers than their fathers. In an abroad marriage, children nearly always lived with their mothers and saw their fathers weekly or more infrequently. When separated by hiring or sale, children usually lost fathers earlier than and at higher rates than mothers, and because men absconded permanently more often than women, some lost their fathers to escape. When discussing family, former slaves viewed having two parents as ideal. To have one parent or the other was better than losing both. Having no memory of either parent due to early separation could lead to a sense of disconnection from one's roots. Like Leonard Black, former slaves blamed the institution of slavery for limited contact with or permanent separation from their fathers, believing that these men would have been involved in their lives had they been able.

Enslaved parents endeavored to nurture their children in an atmosphere that enforced neglect and denied parental authority across a range of household structures. In this emasculating atmosphere, enslaved men struggled to fulfill their perceived duties as fathers, as paternity and any attempt to act as a caretaker forced men to confront the painful contradictions and intractable dilemmas of the slave condition. These men retained a sense of self, humanity, and manhood through love of family, religious faith, and a definition of honor that stood in stark contrast to their criticism of white paternity and paternalism.[2]

Broken Families and Constraints on Fatherhood

When ex-slaves remembered only one parent, they more often knew their mothers. Having little knowledge of, memory of, or contact with a father resulted from several factors, including sale, disrupted abroad marriages, sexual exploitation in various forms, escape, and death. Regional labor patterns and economic conditions meant that children in the Upper and Mountain South had a higher likelihood of growing up in a one-parent household and being permanently separated from family, especially fathers. White paternity of slaves and intentional breeding also increased the likelihood that a child would have limited or no contact with their father and increased the prevalence of fatherless households. Paul Escott found that 4.86 percent of twentieth-century slave narratives commented on forced breeding and 12.26 percent mentioned interracial sex, almost certainly an undercount.[3] While the number of mixed-race people in the antebellum population varied regionally, and was higher in urban areas, these practices stemmed from slaveholder predilection and practices, leading to an uneven distribution across the landscape.

FWP interviews from across the South offered vague, incomplete information about unknown fathers that underscore the difficulty of accurately categorizing household composition and the reasons for family structure and disruption. At times, an enslaved mother purposely imparted no information about a child's father, most often because he was white, but also because a small number of masters coerced unwanted relationships between slaves. "I never seen a father to know. I never heard mother say a thing about my father if I had one. He never was no use to me nor her neither," John Patterson declared, shutting down this line of questioning. John Coggin had a similarly defensive response to a query about his family history: "I ain't neber had no paw an' I ain't wanted none." If a mother remained silent, her children grew up with no father, no idea of his identity, and no idea why he was missing. "Dar wasn't no niggers much in slabery times whut knowed nothin' 'bout dey pappys," Henry Green insisted. "Us neber hab no pappy, jes er mammy." Green contradicted his own statement about missing fathers when he discussed his maternal grandparents coming to collect his mother and her children after freedom and moving the entire family from southern Alabama to Arkansas. Green also related a story of having been born so light skinned that the mistress punished his mother, later apologizing when she felt she had been mistaken, indicating probable white parentage, one of the most common reasons for having little to no knowledge of a father.[4] It is impossible to know if Patterson and Coggin had white fathers, but it is clear that a large number of missing fathers were white. When former slaves made blanket statements about slaves not knowing their fathers, they left records that could be used to assign blame to black men for problems created, in part, by white sexual exploitation. Furthermore, all three of these men suggested, but never specified, that their mothers presided over female-headed households. These were emotionally matrifocal families, but without further information, it is impossible to fully assess the composition of the households and to what degree that structure reflected choice or external pressure.

Children who received vague or calculated responses when they asked about their paternity grew up with and passed on incomplete family information. "I ain't had no daddy case queens doan marry an' my mammy, Junny, wuz a queen in Africa," Ann Parker announced. "Dey would not talk to me 'bout who my father wus nor where he wus at," Patsey Michener, also from North Carolina, added. "Mother would laf sometime when I axed her 'bout him." These individuals may have had white fathers, but they either did not know for sure or deliberately withheld that information from their interviewers. When Michener's mother and siblings were sold away, she lost contact with the person who could verify her father's identity. Ryer Emmanuel's cautionary tale about how one "yellow" girl among the "heap of black chillun" on her Marion County, South Carolina, plantation provoked the wrath of the mistress speaks to the risks of revealing white paternity to young children. The mistress asked the girl who her father was, and the child, unaware of the consequences, repeated the name provided by her mother, leading to hostile treatment and distress for mother and child. The mother darkened her daughter's skin "wid smut, but she couldn' never trouble dat straight hair off her noway." Visible markers of white parentage might cause speculation and rumors, whereas concrete acknowledgment could be dangerous. Withholding information about paternity enabled mothers to protect themselves and their children and/or to cope with the trauma of sexual exploitation.[5]

The sexual dynamics of slavery and individual slaveholder behavior thus contributed to an indistinct and unevenly distributed number of fatherless families. These families were fatherless in actuality and often fatherless in memory. When enslaved and formerly enslaved mothers withheld information about paternity, some fraction likely did so strategically to protect themselves and their children. The FWP subjects, moreover, sometimes genuinely did not know the identity of their father or they echoed their mothers in suppressing that information, a continuing strategy of self-preservation. This further complicates the efforts to quantify the percentage of mixed-race people, and shows how sexual exploitation complicates efforts to categorize the enslaved family.

Slaveholder control of marriage and imposed mating systems on certain plantations also influenced family structures and limited father/child interaction. Mack Brantley only saw his father a few times and referred to himself as a "stole child" because his mother had a husband assigned by her master and was not "supposen to have children by my pa," who lived on a neighboring Alabama plantation. Other children knew only that their fathers lived on the plantation or nearby. On Mary Ingram's Louisiana plantation, men and women selected as breeders were not allowed to marry and their children "don' know any father." Ingram knew the identity of and had seen her father, who lived on an adjacent farm, but she had no substantive contact or relationship with him because he and her mother had been used as breeders and temporarily and forcibly paired. Ryer Emmanuel, enslaved in the Pee Dee region of South Carolina, indicated that individual slaveholder practices sometimes led to female-headed households. "We chillun used to ax us mammy whe' us come from en she say, 'I got you out de hollow log.' Well, just like I tell you, slavery chillun had dey daddy somewhe' on de plantation. Cose dey had a daddy, but dey didn' have no daddy stayin in de house wid dem," she related. "White folks would make you take dat man whe' if you want him or no. Us chillun never didn' know who us daddy been till us mammy point him out cause all us went in Massa Anthony Ross' name. Yes, mam, all us had a different daddy, so my mammy say."[6] Masters who engaged in forced pairing or breeding and who denied slaves choice in partners fueled the formation of emotionally matrifocal families and undermined the development of relationships and households that facilitated connections between fathers and children.

As Jeff Forret notes, masters who forcibly paired slaves for breeding purposes also contributed to disharmony in the quarters, "creating a breeding ground for domestic abuse."[7] Rose Williams, auctioned off in 1860, felt fortunate to be purchased along with her parents. Her father intervened with a potential buyer asking him to keep the family together, and this slaveholder decided Williams would serve well as a breeder. About a year later, when she was roughly sixteen years old, Rose's master placed her in the cabin of a slave named Rufus. After initially rejecting and fighting him off, she eventually acceded to the relationship when reminded of the purpose for which she had been purchased and threatened with separation from her parents. While it is impossible to know Rufus's feelings and motivations in this situation, David Doddington emphasizes Rose's description of Rufus as a "bully," and as an enslaved man "who expected his dominance to extend across the plantation." He points out that Rose believed Rufus favored the relationship, indicating that though the pairing was ordered by the master, Rufus may have colluded in this decision. Rufus may have feared punishment, and Thomas Foster uses the narrative as example of the sexual exploitation of men.[8] After freedom, Rose forced Rufus to leave and remained with her parents until they died. She never had another intimate relationship with a man. "De Lawd fo'give dis cullud woman," she finished her interview, "but he have to 'scuse me and look fo' some udder persons fo' to 'plemish de earth."[9] Completely lost in this discussion are Rose and Rufus's two children. Rose never talked about her children, and their presence is only discernable in the opening notes to the interview. The child born after freedom likely never knew a father. It is possible Rose was an attentive and loving mother, with her own parents serving as a positive model. However, it is reasonable to speculate about how her antipathy for Rufus affected her feelings toward her children. In addition, when Rose drove Rufus away after emancipation, she probably severed his contact with his children, something he may or may not have regretted. While much in this story remains elusive, one thing is clear—imposed management practices at times created two-parent households that did not emotionally function as cohesive families. Those decisions affected intimate relationships and parenting. Slaveholders forcibly created two-parent households just as they prevented the formation of others.[10]

Masters who dictated pairings to maximize reproduction adhered to a rough approximation of serial monogamy with sequential partners, while a few demanded that slaves take several concurrent partners. Some masters used men as studs, pairing them with multiple women and hiring them out to neighboring farms as breeders. Daina Berry argues that breeding created an enforced promiscuity that has been mislabeled as polygamy.[11] Whereas Berry and Thomas Foster see forced pairing and breeding as sexual abuse of women and men, David Doddington suggests that not all enslaved men saw themselves as victims in these situations, another example of varied responses to the oppression of slavery. He argues that many enslaved men conceived of intimate relationships through the lens of patriarchy and shared with white men a belief in male dominance over women. "The agency of black women could thus be limited by enslavers and enslaved men," Doddington writes.[12]

As Doddington shows, some enslaved men used sex to dominate men as well as women. Their children were likely to speak positively of these men if such behavior did not destabilize the informant's own family unit. Frank Adamson's father would not allow other enslaved men near his wife: "He sho' was a man; he run all de other niggers 'way from my mammy and took up wid her widout askin' de marster." Doddington uses this example to demonstrate masculine identity based on "supremacy over rivals."[13] Adamson clearly celebrated his father's manliness, but he linked it to defiance of the master as much as a position atop the hierarchy of enslaved men. For Adamson, to be a man meant resisting the master's authority and choosing and defending his own partner. That defiance, however, might come at the expense of enslaved women, who faced the control of master and husband. Adamson's family remained intact and was headed by his father after the war, and he lauded his father's sexual autonomy within the context of what appears to have been a monogamous marriage that worked to his benefit.

Doddington shows that men used as breeders sometimes exhibited a sense of pride and superiority. Here he uses the example of Jeptha Choice. Choice bragged about his physical attributes and the fact that being "in much demand for breedin'" meant lighter work and better treatment. Doddington argues that this admiring attitude, "implies a belief that sexually prolific men, even those outside of or alienated from community and kin, were not considered powerless or emasculated victims. Instead, these men embodied a particular type of manhood based on virility and dominance." He omits the fact that Choice then added, "later on we good strong niggers was 'lowed to marry" and jumping the broom in the presence of the master "married 'em for good."[14] Choice was not entirely clear, but he suggested that these men moved from unmarried breeder status to married, possibly with a single partner. Enslaved people often applauded sexual virility and accorded status to these men. However, it appears that they might also see this as a stage rather than a fixed or exclusive identity. I agree with Doddington's definition of sexual prowess as one of several masculine identities available to enslaved men, but I disagree that it meant a rejection of the provider and protector role.[15] Younger men who derived a masculine identity from sexual prowess might later choose (or not) to take on another masculine identity or they might merge identities and roles. Human beings are, after all, multidimensional.

FWP informants were more likely to speak admiringly of male sexual prowess if they were themselves male and if removed from or not overly adversely impacted by such sexual exploitation. Rias Body discussed several "stud bucks," including his older brothers, the "envy" of weaker men not chosen for such privileges, and competition among these men to see who could father the most children in a year.[16] Body was not talking about his own father, and born in 1846, and thus fifteen when the war began, he was probably still a shade too young to take on this role himself, but also at an age when the idea might hold some allure and shape his memories of slavery. More often, informants recalled male breeders in a more matter of fact manner. "My pappy have 12 chillun's by her an' 12 by Mary," Lewis Jones stated of his experience in Texas, starting an accounting with his mother. "Yous keep de count. Den dere am Eliza, Him have 10 by her, dere am Mandy, him have 8 by her an dere am Betty, him have five or six by her. . . . Dat am right. Close to 50 chillen. . . .'Tis dis away, my pappy am de breedin' nigger." These children lived on the same plantation, and Jones learned of his half siblings from his mother. His father seems to have settled down with his mother after the war, which may have affected his pragmatic tone. "Mammy and pappy and me stays," he said of his postwar life, and he took his father's name.[17] Being the child of the favored sexual partner made a difference. Ida Hutchinson claimed her grandfather was used as a breeder in Sumter County, Alabama, and fathered over fifty children. Having never met her grandfather and having benefited from his passing on valuable work skills to her own involved father, she discussed his sexual past in neutral terms, likening his treatment to that of livestock but avoiding acrimony. Although the interview conditions may have played a role and muted her response, informants more often adopted an informational tone when discussing a father who favored and then chose their mother and family unit in the postwar period, or when discussing breeding in abstract rather than directly personal terms.[18]

Others castigated sexual exploitation and slaveholders' deliberate attempts to profit off of the reproduction of enslaved people. "My pappy was used much as a male cow is used on the stock farm and was hired out to other plantation owners for that purpose," Barney Stone related, noting that his father visited his mother's Kentucky cabin on weekends. Stone had nothing more to say about his father and did not live with either parent after the war, though he was later reunited with his mother. His feelings about breeding may partially reflect the fact that he lost contact with his father following the war.[19] Elige Davison expressed bitterness at his role as a breeder. Davison's Virginia master "wouldnt let me have just one woman," a comment that suggests he would have preferred to have one wife, or at the very least, to make his own choices. "I dunno how many chilluns I have," he continued, indicating that his anger went beyond interference with mate choice. Davison also asserted that most enslaved children did not know their fathers, and separation after weaning also meant that few knew their mothers. Just as such imposed mating systems led to children who did not know the identity of or extensively interact with their father, it also resulted in fathers who did not know the identity of all of their children.[20] If some enslaved men accepted such sexual practices and the benefits they derived as among the select, others resented their own treatment and its implications for children and family. Forced pairing and breeding often destabilized families and family formation, and accounted for an unknown fraction of fatherless families. Not all children ended up fatherless in such cases, and the tenor of commentary on the sexual practices of slavery often reflected how one's own family was impacted.

Because forced breeding was relatively rare, a far greater number of former slaves lost contact with their fathers when slaveholders forcibly disrupted chosen relationships. The most common reason for not knowing one's father was that the master sold him away before a child grew old enough to remember him. "My pappy was sol' befo' I was born. I doan know nothin' 'bout him," Fanny Smith Hodges stated, in a familiar refrain across the South. "I never saw my father as he was sold before I was old enough to recognize him as being my father," George Womble added. John White noted that his mother "try to make it clear to me about my daddy." His father, who lived on another plantation and had permission to sleep in the cabin each night, suddenly stopped coming. She assumed he had been sold, but never knew for sure.[21] If White had an indifferent father who abandoned his family, they likely would have crossed paths with or heard about him, so they attributed his disappearance to slavery. The interstate slave trade, master migration, and hiring all took a heavy toll on enslaved families. Because masters were more likely to keep mothers and young children together for a longer period of time, the trade had a particularly destructive impact on fathers and their children.

While the interstate slave trade was most damaging, a slaveholder's decision to move destroyed existing abroad marriages, separating fathers from their families. Josephine Barnett's master relocated from Tennessee to Arkansas and refused to sell her and her mother locally. Her father's master also refused to sell, resulting in a broken family. "I never seen my papa after

I left back home," she stated. When her owners moved to Mississippi, Annie Love left behind a father in Virginia. At some point before they moved, he came to visit. "I remember one Sunday he come to see me and when he started home I know I tried to go with him. He got a little switch and whipped me. That's the onliest thing I can remember bout him."[22] In his attempt to instill discipline, and possibly even protect her from more severe punishment, Love's father left her with a bittersweet and fleeting memory. Abroad marriages increased the vulnerability of the enslaved family, leaving former slaves permanently separated from fathers at young ages and with only childhood impressions of these men.

An enslaved child might also lose a parent if that individual ran away, and men escaped at higher rates than women. "My father run away . . . before the Civil War," John Lynch recalled. "He lived in the woods till he nearly went wild. My mother fed him at night. I was twenty-one years old before I ever seen him."[23] Children with rebellious parents were more likely to lose contact due to sale or escape. A parent or parents who modeled resistance risked leaving children with no parental role model at all.

If the market and mobility frequently separated children from their parents, so too did high mortality caused by strenuous labor, physical punishment, and malnourishment.[24] Although slave narratives vary in length, form, and the time period of creation, they all tend to begin with the basic conventions of a chronological life history. When former slaves had greater paternal than maternal contact, the father assumed the early and central familial role in the narrative. John Jacobs, a fugitive writing on the eve of the Civil War, lost both parents, but spent a longer time with his father. "I have a slight recollection of my mother, who died when I was young, though my father made impressions on my mind in childhood that can never be forgotten," he remarked. As James Stith told his interviewer, "My father was named William Henry Stith, and I was a little tot less than two years old when my mother died. My father has called her name often but I forget it."[25] The adaptive nature of the slave family meant that while in general former slaves had more contact with their mothers, a sizeable minority knew only their fathers.

Slaves separated from one or the other parent retained a sense of family, whereas loss of both parents at an early age severed connections to kin, particularly for those children socialized by whites rather than relatives or surrogates within slave communities. Easter Brown was so young when sold along with the rest of her family that she had to be held up by an adult for bidding. "I don't 'member my real ma and pa, and I called Marster 'pa' an

Mist'ess 'ma', 'til I wuz 'bout 'leven years old," she stated. Despite this loss of kin, she knew her biological father exerted an indirect influence over her future. "Mist'ess wuz good to me," she recalled. "Pa begged her to buy me 'cause she wuz his young Mist'ess and he knowed she would be good to me."[26] Early sale deprived slave children of kin, family lore, and, for some, even a concrete place of birth. Adline Marshall's master told her that he brought her from South Carolina as a baby. "I reckon it's de truth, 'cause I never knowed no mama or no papa neither one." A slave trader left William Hamilton on a plantation saying he would collect him on the return trip, but he never reappeared. "Massa Buford says de trader comes from Missouri, but if I is born dere I don't know."[27] The slave trade alienated enslaved youth from their natal roots and identity by dispossessing them of their people and their place of origin.

When slaveholders removed children from their family orbit and raised them in the big house, they denied enslaved parents the opportunity to bond with their offspring and children the opportunity to know their kin, leading to confused allegiances and emotional detachment. "Pa was de boss for Marse Hamp. I don't 'member much 'bout him. My brother stayed in de cabin wid Pa and Ma, but I was all time up at de big house wid Mist'ess," Mahala Jewel related of her childhood in Georgia. After emancipation, her parents departed and Jewel chose to remain with her mistress's daughter.[28] Masters undermined the enslaved and later free family when they brought children into their homes as domestic labor. Whereas some young children removed from family and socialized in the big house might align with their owners, later in life John Williams's lack of connection to kin and community fostered feelings of isolation and alienation. Without a family, he struggled to define a sense of identity and belonging. "The reason I don't know who I am is that I don't remember my father and mother or any of my people," he told his interviewer. "When I got so I could remember anything I wus with the Williams family. Marster an' missus, an' their family are the only ones I ever looked upon as my people. They never told me who I wus. . . . I loved them but I realized I wus a nigger and knew that I could never be like them, and that I wus one to myself." Williams's dawning sense of difference from his former owners contributed to loneliness, as did their silence regarding his origins. Because he was so young at the time of emancipation, the other freedpeople on the plantation departed before he understood what was happening and before he could ask questions about his background. Silas Dothrum had a similar experience: "I don't know none of my kin people—father, mother, uncles, cousins, nothin'. When I found myself the white people had me." While slavery regularly destabilized and separated family and people responded by forming new ties and retaining memories that shaped their sense of self, these men serve as examples of how, in extreme cases, slaveholder decisions could utterly destroy the slave family physically and emotionally. Williams and Dothrum described themselves as a community of one. Both men mentioned the possibility that they might have had white fathers, underscoring the ways in which actual and suspected white paternity contributed to fatherlessness.[29]

Former slaves consistently identified having two parents as an ideal and consistently associated destruction of kinship with losing both parents. When informants discussed dislocation and fractured family ties, they lamented the loss of mother and father. To have both was preferable. To have neither parent removed them from their heritage. "I never had no father or mother; white folks raised me," another woman recalled. Her father was sold from Tennessee to Mississippi when she was "a little bittie girl," and then her mother died and the white family took her into the big house. "I was jus' throwed away," she declared, noting that her owners refused to allow her to interact with other slaves, denying her community after she had already lost kin. Having a memory of family, or even just a name, constituted knowing one's place in the world. All enslaved people lived with a sense of actual loss or potential and impending loss of family. Those separated from kin at a young age might have no concrete memory of loved ones, but they actively retained names and thus a sense of lineage and connection to a people.[30] They knew they came from somewhere and they knew they had a father and mother even if they no longer had physical contact with their parents.

Marriage, Multilocality, Household, and Constraints on Family

In a family unit not forcibly constructed or forcibly deconstructed by slaveholders, enslaved people faced a multitude of day-to-day pressures. As young men approached marriageable age, they confronted a central conflict in the life of an enslaved man. To become a husband and then a father, hallmarks of antebellum masculinity, underscored a bondman's powerlessness. That which defined him as a man, according to the standards of the dominant society, most revealed his lack of authority. Husbandhood and fatherhood highlighted the agonizing contradictions of the slave condition—to be a caretaker, to create and deepen human connections, enriched a person's life and yet further entangled them in a system that eroded their humanity. Despite the downsides, enslaved people embraced marriage and imbued it with meaning amidst a system that constantly destabilized their relationships.

Marriage represented one of the many dilemmas of slavery, as some men recognized the anxieties they would face as husbands and fathers and yet found the emotional ties of family life too beguiling to ignore. "It seems to me that no one can have such fondness of love, and such intensity of desire for home and home affections, as the poor slave," Thomas Jones argued. He "yearned to have a home," and he "did this, too, with a full knowledge of the desperate agony that the slave husband and father is exposed to. Had I not seen this in the anguish of my own parents?" Fellow fugitive Henry Brown admitted that "the slave is placed under strong inducements not to form a union of love," but as he approached adulthood he "began to think seriously of entering into the matrimonial state, as much as a person can, who can 'make no contract whatever,' and whose wife is not his." A few spurned marriage and the agonizing ties it created, but various factors usually wore down their resolve, including the attractions of companionship and the insistence of masters.[31] Enslaved men and women who tried to avoid marriage usually only succeeded if they ran away as teenagers.

Across the South, though slave marriage had no legal standing and existed at the whim of the master, certain conventions developed that led, with some exceptions, to a form of serial monogamy.[32] Marriage was sometimes a formality, and at other times occasioned a celebration organized by the master or the slave community.[33] Slaveholders exhibited a wide range of ideas and practices on the subject of slave marriage. Some recognized that kinship ties increased slaves' contentment and made them less likely to abscond.[34] Masters also wanted to increase their property, and stable families produced children. However, slaveholders tried to maximize their profits and minimize the autonomy of their human property, and they undermined family bonds that might encourage self-determination. Even those who espoused support of slave families in theory might renege on their stated principles under financial duress or incentives.

Because enslaved children followed the status of their mother and belonged to her owner, slaveholders differed on abroad marriages. Many hoped to restrict the mobility of enslaved men, keep them from developing a sense of independence, and prevent them from fathering or provisioning children who belonged to someone else. Unapproved unions incurred physical punishment, and men caught without a pass risked a beating by the slave patrol.[35] In the Upper South, where the interstate slave trade shifted the gender balance slightly in favor of female slaves, abroad marriages made economic sense. These marriages made less sense to individual planters in any region based on the sex ratios of their slave population, and masters approved abroad marriages based on their own needs and local circumstances. Slaveholders wanted to own the offspring of their male slaves, and they also worried about losing nonhuman property. Henry Bibb overcame obstacles in his quest to wed off-site in part because his owner "feared my taking off from his farm some of the fruits of my own labor for Malinda to eat, in the shape of pigs, chickens, or turkeys." One of the slave community's expectations of a father was that he provided for his family, if even only nominally, and slaveholder concerns about material provisioning underscore this convention. Abroad marriages usually resulted not from the choices of slaveholders, but from the limited options of enslaved people seeking to establish a family in the face of demographic constraints or as a means of exerting some independence.[36]

Choice over marriage and reproduction generated considerable tension between masters and enslaved men. John Jackson's master became "exceedingly angry" when he discovered Jackson's marriage to a woman on another South Carolina plantation, "because my children would not belong to him," and whipped Jackson every time he was caught making an unauthorized visit. Ordered to marry on-site, Andrew Jackson determined to escape, knowing the Kentucky master wanted "to enrich his plantation by a family of young slaves." Separation from family or refusal of permission to visit frequently induced escape attempts. John Anderson's new master would not allow him to visit his wife, now thirty miles away. "He wanted me to desert my wife and child, and become the father of children who should be his property." Anderson deemed this decision a "fair excuse for leaving him," and made his escape.[37] Enslaved men wanted choice over their relationships and resented efforts to limit options based on ownership of future children. Children, in the abstract and in the flesh, became a locus of conflict between masters and enslaved men negotiating marriage.

Masters who refused to approve cross-plantation relationships hoped to immobilize their labor force and exert control over and profit from reproduction. "Master would not allow his slaves to go off the place," Stephen Jordan recalled. In addition, no man over the age of eighteen or woman over fifteen could remain unattached. In an attempt to end the practice, Jordan's master allocated new partners to those in abroad marriages. "There was great sorrow on the place that day. Many of us had wives or husbands on neighboring plantations," Jordan recalled, including his assigned wife. "We were put in the same cabin, but both of us cried, me for my old wife and she for her old husband." Jordan used his literacy to write passes for men to secretly visit their wives on nearby Louisiana plantations. Jordan and his designated, older spouse lived in the same cabin, not as husband and wife, but rather as "son and mother."[38] This household was composed of husband and wife, but it functioned as a forced economic unit, and the members of the cabin remained emotionally invested in divided families located elsewhere.

That some enslaved men preferred abroad marriages speaks to their love of family and the emotional toll of emasculation. "I did not want to marry a girl belonging to my own place, because I knew I could not bear to see her ill-treated," John Anderson stated. Henry Bibb contrasted his early abroad marriage in Kentucky, "one of most happy seasons of my life," to the changes that occurred when purchased by his wife's master. "To live where I must be eye witness to her insults, scourgings and abuses, . . . was more than I could bear." Forced to witness physical and sexual abuse that he could do nothing to prevent, Bibb found his "happiness . . . all blasted, for it was sometimes a pleasure to be with my little family even in slavery. I loved them as my wife and child." Moses Grandy had a similar experience when purchased by his wife's owner in North Carolina. "No coloured man wishes to live at the house where his wife lives, for he has to endure the continual misery of seeing her flogged and abused, without daring to say a word in her defence," he wrote. "He is always liable to see her . . . stripped naked, and whipped before all the men." To live and work with family was a constant reminder of emasculation.[39] An abroad marriage reduced a man's direct confrontation with the intractable dilemmas of slavery and the conflict between duty to self and family, while still enabling him to act as a caretaker, but it also increased the vulnerability of a kinship unit by placing family integrity in the hands of two slaveholders.[40]

Men in approved abroad marriages had permission to visit their wives according to a schedule determined by the slaveholder, which could always be revised or revoked. Mobility represented another reason to favor such a union, despite its many drawbacks. While the previous examples came from fugitives writing from the vantage of hard-won freedom, some twentieth-century informants also expressed a preference for abroad marriage. "Slaves always wanted to marry a gal on 'nother plantation cause dey could git a pass to go visit 'em on Saddy nights," Tom Epps claimed of Virginia men's motives. In an institution that limited movement, legitimate travel had an appeal. If they lived in the same neighborhood, men usually visited their family twice a week, on Wednesday and Saturday nights, with consent to stay for the Sabbath and be back before dawn on Monday morning. Tom Woods's father in Alabama lived a mile away and had permission to spend every night with his family.[41] Men visited more infrequently, sometimes monthly or even yearly, if they lived further away.

If they could elude the patrollers, husbands made extra visits surreptitiously. John Anderson's Missouri master permitted him to visit his wife once a week. "I did not, however, care much for his orders, and I used to go almost every night," he noted. "My pappy was 'lowed de pass ever' two weeks fo' to come an' see him's fam'ly, but him sees weuns mo' often dan dat, 'cause him sneak off . . . ever' time him have de chance," Annie Row recalled of her childhood in Texas. Risking punishment to see their families created pleasure and anxiety, as wives and children savored extra family time, but understood the consequences of men being caught. "My father had to slip off at night to come and visit us," Marshall Mack stated of slavery in Virginia. "He'd oversleep hisself and git up running. We would stand in our door and hear him running over them rocks til he got home. He was trying to git dere before his master called him."[42]

Enslaved people expressed an abiding sense of family and home despite enforced physical separation. Parke Johnston, a man in an abroad marriage, "always spent Sunday at home." George Jackson identified his father's home as the Virginia plantation where his family lived rather than the plantation of his father's owner: "When my father wanted to cum home he had to get a permit from his massa. He would only cum home on Saturday." Sina Banks's father technically lived five miles away in Missouri, but "could come home often." Enslaved men and their children defined home as the mother's cabin. "Home" and place of residence were not synonymous. Dylan Penningroth argues that enslaved people in cross-plantation relationships "viewed the wife's house as the husband's primary residence," based on where they kept family property. "In spite of the masters' intentions, the flow of slave-owned property signaled that slave couples considered themselves to have one 'home,' though they had two cabins, with property at each."[43] When a committed father had a separate residence, abroad marriage could lead to emotionally intact and yet physically divided families. The majority of the members lived in a matrifocal household, but the family functioned as a multilocal kinship unit spread across two or more plantations.

Men in abroad marriages walked long distances to see their families. Fannie Berry described Christmas as the time in Virginia when "husbands hurry on home to see dey new babies." Allen Parker's father came once a week on Saturday nights and occasionally during the week, "as a slave did not mind a walk of ten miles after his day's work if he could have a chance to see his loved ones." Parker remembered having a compassionate father who attempted to maintain a family connection based on weekly visits. When his mother fell ill, Parker, by then also hired out, "obtained leave to be with her nights, as my father got leave to be with her three nights in a week and all day Sunday. At this time he lived about eight miles from my mother's cabin, and of course had to walk both ways every time he came to see her. Both my father and I were with mother when she died."[44] In such cases, distance failed to diminish affection or a sense of responsibility to kin. The enslaved family took a range of forms and shifted as children aged into productivity. Once he was old enough to be hired out, Parker was removed from a matrifocal household to become part of a multilocal kinship network divided among three residences.

Children in cross-plantation households across the South remembered their father's visits as special times. Robert Howard and his siblings "looked forward" to their father's Saturday night visits "with great joy, as they were devoted to the father," who had been hired out locally. Sarah Locke's family, also from Kentucky, had "big dinners" when their father visited on Wednesday and Saturday nights. Siblings Scott Hooper and Louise Mathews recalled that in general one woman cooked for all of the workers, but "once in awhile, a fam'ly would cook a meal in thar own cabin. My mammy does dat on Wednesday an' Saturday nights w'en father comes to see weuns," Hooper noted.[45] Residential household structure and a man's official place of residence did not necessarily determine the strength of emotional bonds between fathers and children, and family and household from Kentucky to Texas shifted and functioned differently depending on the day of the week.

A Fisk interview with a preacher who grew up in South Carolina, conducted by an African American fieldworker, highlights the difficulty of categorizing the enslaved household and family. The unnamed respondent discussed his father, Harry Green, who had a different owner and visited on Wednesdays and Sundays. The man had fond memories of these visits and described an emotionally cohesive family and shared parenting. "It was so joyful to see them together. He would always ask my mother if I had been a good boy. They smiled at me always and then turned away, either looking in the fire or at each other. I noticed that they always looked sad afterward but I didn't know why. I know now though that they were thinking of what might happen to me." When the son committed some transgression, his mother warned him that she would have his father whip him during the next visit, and his father did, in fact, handle discipline and punishment. Looking back on his early years, this informant viewed his father as the head of household despite the fact that he visited biweekly, noting his mother deferred to her husband and "wouldn't do anything without first asking him."[46] He portrayed a hybrid family that was matrifocal in household structure and seemingly patrifocal in function. A matrifocal household was not inevitably a matrifocal family. As discussed in the following chapter, Harry Green lived most of the week apart from his family and yet made a significant impact on his son's character and outlook on life. While we do not have the mother's perspective, her son clearly remembered his father as the family authority.

The conventions of abroad marriages reveal slaves' understanding of male roles. Men made visits and risked physical punishment from patrollers for both sanctioned and unsanctioned travel.[47] While reactions to abroad marriages varied and depended on the imposed constraints and personalities involved, sources from different regions and produced in different time periods show that children had fond memories of involved, visiting fathers, and indicate that many live-away fathers wanted and tried to be engaged in their children's lives. These were not fatherless families or fatherless children, nor were these single mothers, though they looked and lived that way much of the time. Categorizing one-parent households as one-parent families fails to account for lived experience, interpersonal relationships, and how some enslaved kinship units functioned.

Like abroad fathers, extended family, living on the plantation and nearby, complicates any assessment of the enslaved household and family. Ellen Claibourn's grandparents, manumitted in their old age, lived locally, and her grandfather, a traveling preacher, regularly visited. Claibourn and her siblings had an abroad father who lived on a neighboring Georgia plantation and visited two to three times per week and involved grandparents, which substantially increased the children's material provisions and enlarged their social network. "Every time he came to see us, granma sent us clothes and granpa carried 'em in his saddle bags," she recalled, adding that her grandmother filled her husband's beaver hat with ginger cakes.[48] Claibourn technically lived in a one-parent household, but she and her siblings had two involved parents, saw their father consistently, and received provisions prepared by her grandmother and delivered by her grandfather. This family functioned as a multilocal kinship network.

In extremely rare cases, the children of parents in abroad marriages lived with their father. "Pa would take me over to see mama every Sunday morning," Absolom Jenkins recalled his childhood in Tennessee. "We leave soon as I could get my clean long shirt and a little to eat. We walked four miles. He'd tote me. She had a girl with her. I never stayed over there much and the girl never come to my place 'cepting when mama come." Andy Nelson grew up in Texas and for a time lived with his father, and they visited his mother on the next farm each Sunday, but when "mah Daddy died . . . I musta been sold . . . cause I went ober with mah Mammay." Victoria Sims possibly went back and forth in Alabama: "I knowed papa's owners the best and I lived there heap the most. . . . I wasn't with mama much till after freedom."[49] Though anomalous, these cases underscore the adaptability and variation of the enslaved family.

If some enslaved people preferred cross-plantation marriages, most recognized that such arrangements had distinct disadvantages. "Dat was one of de hard parts of slavery, I thinks," Bill McNeil said of the fact that his father lived apart from his family in the South Carolina Midlands. George Sells felt fortunate to have lived with both parents, arguing that abroad marriages meant "sometime' de chillun ain't hardly git to know dey daddy." "They both b'long to old marster and bless God live on de same place in a little log house," Charley Watson similarly said of his parents and early childhood in the South Carolina Midlands. Those enslaved as children favored two-parent households and realized and regretted the fact that abroad marriages limited the paternal role and denied children regular access to their fathers. Husbands also yearned for a stable and involved family life. One ex-slave complained about needing permission to visit his family, telling his interviewer "he didn't enjoy the opportunity of being a help to his wife, only when his master saw fit for him to go see her."[50] This man resented interference in his relationship and his inability to consistently support his wife.

Because cross-plantation family networks required visitation rights, they also created the potential for and led to violence. After her father was sold away locally in Mississippi, Hannah Chapman remembered his clandestine visits. "My pa sho' did hate ter leave us. He missed us and 'us longed fer him. He would often slip back ter us' cottage at nite. Us would gather 'round him an' crawl up in his lap, tickled slap to death, but he give us dese pleasures at a painful risk," she stated. "When his Mars missed him he would beat him all de way home. Us could track him de nex' day by de blood stains." Vinnie Busby's father also endured abuse to see family. Denied permission to visit, "pa, he would keep a comin' to see us an' a takin' de beatins." Many enslaved men in unapproved abroad marriages loved their families more than they feared physical abuse, but such stories underscore the tremendous downsides and fragility of these unions. Millie Barber, from Fairfield County, in the South Carolina Midlands, described how the separation of her father from his family "caused some confusion, mix-up, and heartaches," particularly when he visited without a pass and was caught and whipped in front of his loved ones.[51] Such abuse may have undermined men's sense of self, which could then affect their interpersonal relationships. Jeff Forret argues that abroad marriages were vulnerable to internal as well as external violence. Based on court records from the South Carolina Upcountry, Forret shows that conflict arising from courtship and marital strife increased in areas with demographic constraints and higher levels of cross-plantation marriage. Abroad marriages decreased oversight over spouses, increasing incidents of adultery and retaliatory violence.[52]

Abroad marriages and parental death also left enslaved children susceptible to kin dislocation. A Fisk informant explained that her nonresident father visited nearly every week. After his wife died, "he come every two weeks to see me and my brother." During the war, the children's owner moved them, ending his visits, "and we cried and cried, and when any of the white people went down that way they would see pappy, and he would send messages to us by them." Their father managed to maintain communication despite a lack of physical contact. After Sarah Fitzpatrick's mother died, the mistress brought her into town, separating her from her father. "Ma' daddy, he wuked down on de plan'ation. He use'ta come to town ever 'Saddy an' come to de 'Big House' to see'mi." In addition, her mistress would take her along when she went to the Alabama plantation, "an' I'd git chance to see ma' daddy."[53] Fitzpatrick remained in contact with her father, but saw him only sporadically. After the war, when he returned from a stint in the Union army to find her, they were able to live together as a family. Abroad marriages and dispersed kin networks contributed to distant fathering, but it is important to avoid the assumption that this stemmed from men's irresponsibility and disengagement rather than the oppression of the system in which they lived.

Henry Bibb resented the fact that his daughter, though "nurtured and caressed by her mother and father," suffered when left with an abusive mistress while her mother worked in the fields. Bibb and his wife, Malinda, could offer their love, but little else because "the father and mother were slaves!" Bibb railed against his and his wife's powerlessness to protect their daughter, a condition they shared as human property and heightened by the couple's divided residence. When Malinda fell dangerously ill, they lost their second baby, and Bibb, who lived on a different farm and was thus unable to offer needed assistance, "was compelled to dig my own child's grave and bury it myself without even a box to put it in." Enslaved parents lacked authority, but they also lacked time with each other and with their children. Dylan Penningroth has defined the informal economy as "an economy of time," and this observation applies to family and parenting. Slavery enforced neglect and limited face-to-face contact between enslaved parents and their children and did so across regions and across household structures.[54]

Slaveholder attempts to undermine the bonds of slave families were sometimes deliberate, and at other times a matter of expediency. Some planters centralized childcare and removed enslaved children from their family at young ages, intentionally undermining kinship to facilitate eventual sale. "They tried hard to not let the negro know their children or children know who their father and mother was sos they wouldnt have such a time separating them," William Byrd claimed.[55] Other planters established a nursery in an effort to maximize labor, placing children under the care of an aged slave no longer able to do field work, at times assisted by older and/or disabled children. Such arrangements limited contact between parents and their children, making it more difficult for parents to bond with their children and to influence their character development and upbringing. "Sometimes it would be a week before I would see my mother and father," Needham Love recalled of his childhood on a Mississippi cotton plantation. Julius Jones and the other children on his Tennessee plantation were likewise cared for by an older woman while their parents worked. "I never did see my mother or father except on Sunday. I stayed in the house they did, but they left in the morning for the fields before I was awake and when they got back I was asleep." Both men described living in two-parent households, but household structure was only one component of family interaction. Labor regime and plantation social organization were also critical determinants of how a household could and did function. According to Steve Robertson, who claimed his siblings all had different fathers due to forced breeding, the children on his Texas plantation lived the entire week in the nursery, only going home to and seeing their mother on Sunday morning.[56] Such conditions meant that even if children lived with their mother and apart from their father, or like Love and Jones, lived in two-parent households, they had limited interaction with both parents. Removing the locus of childcare from the home and family dispossessed mother and fathers, though not necessarily equally.

Work schedules, as much as household composition and plantation organization, determined the degree of contact between parents and children. During the summer, Ella Washington's parents often returned from the fields in St. Mary's Parish, Louisiana, at around 10 P.M., and Victoria Lawson remembered falling asleep in Mississippi "out on de ground while looking at de moon in de heavens. Dis was when we's waiting for our folks to come from de field." Wes Brady recalled "crying for my mother," growing up in Texas because fieldworkers left the house before children awoke and returned after they were asleep, "so we generally didn't see our mammy till Sunday."[57] Sunday, the usual day for cross-plantation visiting, coincided with the day off, meaning that some children only saw or only spent quality time with their parent or parents once a week regardless of the structure of their household. Two-parent households often functioned similarly to abroad households, and living full-time with a parent did not guarantee that children would actually see them each day.

Because slaveholders controlled food, one of the basic ways that parents care for their children, they further reduced the authority and involvement of enslaved parents. A number of narratives commented on the practice of feeding enslaved children from troughs like livestock. The practice created an economy of scale, enabling slaveholders to feed large numbers of people at reduced expense. It also undermined kinship bonds by limiting each family's time and contact, and it was often calculated to instill a sense of debasement. Group feeding undermined a mother's control over nourishing her children and a father's role in provisioning his family. "Chillun was all fed up at de big house," Lina Hunter noted of her childhood in Georgia. "Deir mammies was 'lowed to come in from de fields in time to cook dinner for de menfolks, but dey didn't git deir chillun back home 'til atter supper."[58] Once again, centralized childcare interfered with the parental involvement of two-parent households.

Slaveholders prioritized production and reproduction, but not involved parenting. Nineteenth- and early-twentieth-century narratives, as well as interviews, describe encumbered parenting, including in two-parent households. James Pennington experienced "the want of parental care and attention. My parents were not able to give any attention to their children during the day. I often suffered much from hunger and other similar causes." Nat Love's father served as foreman and his mother as head cook and weaver, "so I early acquired the habit of looking out for myself." While they labored, enslaved parents had to leave their children to fend for themselves in a system that enforced neglect.[59] Mary Tate's parents left their infant behind during the day. One day, the master visited the cabins and became "annoyed at my crying and as punishment placed me in a fence corner. There was snow on the ground. Mother and father discovered me still crying." Enforced neglect and haphazard caretaking contributed to high childhood mortality.[60] When together with family, usually in the evening after a long day of toil, exhausted parents had little energy to devote to childcare. Household structure and residence patterns thus cannot fully account for paternal or parental involvement, which was also mediated by slaveholding practice, and conditions and interactions between masters and slaves on particular plantations.

Emasculation

The power and sexual dynamics of slavery put all slaves in an excruciating position. If they attempted to protect one another, they risked physical punishment or sale, separating them from loved ones. If they did nothing, they suffered the emotional trauma of witnessing abuse and their own inaction. Enslaved men keenly felt their inability to uphold masculine values by defending loved ones. "It is the chattel relation that robs him of his manhood, and transfers his ownership in himself to another," James Pennington remarked of slave status. Lack of self-ownership was only part of the problem. "My coloured brethren are . . . conscious of . . . the deep and corrupting disgrace of having our wives and children owned by other men—men, who have shown to the world that their own virtue is not infallible."[61] Denial of patriarchal prerogative and impotence to shield self and kin from physical and sexual abuse forced enslaved men to confront their own emasculation.

Fugitives from across the South argued that a husband and father unable to protect his loved ones resented his powerlessness more than he did physical abuse. "The hardest thing in slavery is not the work, —it is the abuse of a man, and, in my case, of a man's wife and children," Dan Lockhart insisted. "They were not punished severely, —but I did not want her whipped at all—I don't want any man to meddle with my wife." Louis Hughes remembered overhearing his wife's flogging in an adjoining room. "My blood boiled in my veins to see my wife so abused; yet I dare not open my mouth," Hughes said, "I was trembling from head to foot, for I was powerless to do anything for her." This initiation into one's impotence to protect loved ones began in childhood and was compounded by marriage and fatherhood.[62]

Having children increased the number of people an enslaved man felt it his duty to protect. "They would blindfold her and beat my poor child half to death," a former slave told an interviewer in the postwar period. "I tell you, my heart would bleed sometimes when I'd see how my child was treated. . . . I was not allowed to open my mouth." Men recently escaped from slavery, and men looking back from the latter half of the nineteenth century, detailed their emotional response to emasculation and their anger toward slaveholders. Men interviewed in the twentieth-century South addressed the issue more obliquely. According to Jordan Johnson, interviewed in Virginia by an African American fieldworker, "Husbands allays went to de woods when dey know de wives was due fo' a whippin', but in de fiel' dey dare not leave."[63] While he did directly not label it as such, Johnson described men's powerlessness, and though he did not explore their feelings, he indicated that they suffered. Johnson shared with nineteenth-century narrators an understanding that slavery denied men the power to protect those they loved.

Brothers, husbands, and fathers faced the intractable dilemma of balancing protecting self and defending kin. Seeing his sister flogged in Virginia by "a *professed* gentleman," Austin Steward declared, "The God of heaven only knows the conflict of feeling I then endured . . . at this outrage of manhood and kindred affection." Though young and strong, Steward had "to turn a deaf ear to her cries of assistance, which to this day ring in my ears . . . no hand of mine could be raised in her defence, but at the peril of both our lives." Eugene Genovese addressed the predicament of the enslaved: "If submission to outrage sometimes revealed cowardice, so did it often reveal a far greater strength than most men and women are ever asked—or ever should be asked—to display."[64] With direct action dangerous, self-control became essential to survival.

The awareness and experience of emasculation took a heavy emotional toll. Harriet Jacobs described men "so brutalized by the lash that they will sneak out of the way to give their masters free access to their wives and daughters," because the "torturing whip . . . lashes manhood out of him." Brenda Stevenson argues that constant fear of separation made some enslaved men emotionally guarded and stunted their relationships and negatively influenced their treatment of women. Enslaved women faced similar anxiety. While enslaved men had greater opportunity to perpetrate domestic abuse—and a number did—the violence of slavery affected the ability of some men and women to form healthy relationships.[65] Drawing on psychological literature, Nell Irvin Painter applies the concept of "soul murder" to the repercussions of slaveholder abuse, "which may be summed up as depression, lowered self-esteem, and anger." Painter avoids reiterating Stanley Elkins's thesis of slavery as utterly psychologically debilitating by discussing two critical factors, family and religion, that enabled slaves to survive.[66]

While the violence of the institution broke some slaves, resilient men retained a sense of self and manhood by directing their anger and humiliation outward, toward the oppressor, rather than inward. In addition to family and religion as critical factors in psychic survival, enslaved men's sense of honor helped to appease the wounds inflicted by the institution of slavery. Austin Steward could not defend his sister, an event that caused continued shame after he escaped, but he refused to consider her attacker a gentleman, highlighting the word "professed" to stress his sarcasm and slaveholder hypocrisy. In questioning the master's honor and morality, he implied that he himself better understood the meaning of family responsibility. In committing this "outrage of manhood and kindred affection," the slaveholder denied Steward access to masculine duty, but he did not make him feel inferior as a man. Jourden Banks recalled a time when his father rushed to help his wife and attend to her injuries. The master demanded he return to work or face a whipping. His father replied, "He would rather take it himself than to see his wife beaten." Banks's father did not prevent his wife's abuse. It took six weeks for his mother to recover and Banks called the master a "merciless human hog," defining him as an animal.[67] Formerly enslaved men knew that the institution of slavery suppressed their manhood. They also believed that it corrupted the masculinity, humanity, and honor of slaveholders.

White men might have a monopoly on concrete power, but they lacked morality and honor. Discussing how the master auctioned off his favorite sister and then lied about the details of her sale, Jourden Banks impugned his character, humanity, and manhood: "How was it possible for me to respect or even to fear such a being—I will not say man; but a being in the shape of a man? I could not—I could only despise him; and though I was in his power, yet I could not fear him; I should have felt my manhood degraded."[68] In her a book on black racial thought, Mia Bay argues that black intellectuals questioned white morality and in doing so challenged "the Anglo-Saxon as the manly ideal." According to African American writers, "Patient, long-suffering, and good, black people were a special redeemer race; whereas white people—or white men in particular . . . were brutal, domineering, and virtually irredeemable," she writes. "By vilifying whiteness, black male writers sought to reclaim their own status as men." For the fugitive African American community, patriarchal authority alone did not constitute manhood. Masculinity was defined by moral probity and how one used, or abused, power. Charles Thompson, referring to his Uncle Ben, argued that his master "wished to break Ben's spirit—his manhood, the God part of him."[69] Slaveholders might hold earthly power, but honorable masculinity was the province of God.

As enslaved people developed an understanding of the repercussions of retaliation, older children protected their fathers by avoiding situations that might compel a man to intervene or confront his own impotence. The master took Frank Hall "down into the brush and whipped" him, threatening to "kill him" should he tell his father, Samuel Hall. The slaveholder knew Samuel "so well that he feared to let me know that he had whipped one of my boys. Frank never told me about it until after we were up north, clear away from any danger."[70] Whether Frank worried more for himself or his father is unclear, but in concealing the incident he protected them both. Slaves learned to modify their demeanor as well as the information they shared with others. Frank averted the risk that his father, in anger, would strike back physically or verbally on behalf of his son. Self-control was a precaution that prevented an even further erosion of manhood or family separation. Dictating his memories decades later from Iowa, Samuel Hall juxtaposed the externally compromised masculinity of slaves with the master's cowardice. The slaveholder might hold the concrete power, but he feared his human property.

Witnessing the abuse of one's father could prove a decisive moment. James Pennington recalled an incident in which several men, including his uncle, came home late from visiting their abroad wives, "a grave fault." The master displaced his anger on Pennington's father, who had been uninvolved. "I was near enough to hear the insolent words that were spoken to my father, and to hear, see, and even count the savage stripes inflicted upon him." Pennington asked his readers, "How would you expect a son to feel at such a sight?" The incident "roused" the entire family, and "each member felt the deep insult that had been inflicted upon our head . . . we talked of it in our nightly gatherings." The slaveholder, in response, tried to "crush the spirit of the whole family." Although he did not escape for some time, Pennington later recognized this moment as pivotal, noting that, "In my mind and spirit, I was never a Slave after it." Seeing his father brutally beaten did not diminish Pennington's sense of his father's moral stature. In contrasting his father's actions on that "memorable" day with the "barbarous conduct" of the master, he "could not help . . . despising the proud abuser of my sire."[71] In vilifying their oppressors, former slaves found ways to celebrate their fathers and themselves despite the pervasive damage of the slave system to public masculinity. Pennington, writing in the late 1840s, and Hall, reminiscing in roughly 1910, lived in periods with different gendered expectations, and came from divergent class backgrounds. They both condemned slaveholder masculinity. Having power did not mean one had honor, and lacking visible power was not the same as lacking dignity.

Fugitives' discussions of their fathers in nineteenth-century slave narratives allow for an examination of the psychic repercussions of emasculation, particularly an inability to protect. When Josiah Henson's father attempted to defend his wife, the incident altered his character and led to his sale. Henson's father returned one day from the field "with his head bloody and his back lacerated. He was beside himself with mingled rage and suffering." The overseer had flogged Henson's mother and "my father sprang upon him like a tiger. . . . My father would have killed him but for the entreaties of my mother, and the overseer's own promise that nothing should ever be said of the matter." Once safe, the overseer reneged and Henson's father faced "one hundred lashes on the bare back, and to have the right ear nailed to the whipping-post, and then severed from the body." His father hid for a time, but was eventually "starved out." Formerly a "good-humoured and light-hearted man," Henson related, "from this hour he became utterly changed. Sullen, morose, and dogged, nothing could be done with him. . . . He brooded over his wrongs. No fear or threats of being sold to the far south—the greatest of all terrors to the Maryland slave—would render him tractable. So off he was sent to Alabama."[72]

It is impossible to know how Henson's father felt and what became of him. Did he resent his wife's saving his life and wish he had died upholding heroic masculinity, in which only those who resisted to the point of death were real men? He may have been sold to Alabama and started a second family, resuming the role of caretaker in a new setting. Or, based on this experience, he may have adopted an individualistic mode of masculinity, avoiding binding family and community ties that could yield further pain.[73] Regardless of his intentions, the incident illustrates the fact that an openly disaffected slave risked being sold. An individual unmoved by threats of sale and the use of familial love to compel a behavioral change was likely to be separated from kin. At least a few men faced with that trade-off must have chosen to display their antagonism rather than conciliate, even if they understood the consequences. And, for some men, losing family may have been preferable to having their loved ones see them humiliated or suffering the blow to their sense of self involved in appeasement. This need not have always been a conscious choice. A severely depressed man may have struggled to effectively modulate his outward demeanor and interactions with others. Depression also weakened the immune system. When his young North Carolina mistress married, Elijah Knox was subject to the dictates of her husband. A skilled carpenter, he was no longer allowed to live in town and hire his own time, and this separated him from his family and ended his efforts to purchase his children, an outcome that "added another link to his galling chain—sent another arrow to his bleeding heart." According to his son, John Jacobs, "My father, who had an intensely acute feeling of the wrongs of slavery, sank in to a state of mental dejection, which, combined with bodily illness, occasioned his death."[74] Unable to maintain his role as a provider and caretaker, Elijah became depressed and his mental state hastened his death.

Charles Ball's father similarly became melancholic after he lost nearly his entire family to the market. "My father never recovered from the effects of the shock, which this sudden and overwhelming ruin of his family gave him. He had formerly been of a gay, social temper," Ball related, but "after this time I never heard him laugh heartily, or sing a song. He became gloomy and morose in his temper, to all but me; and spent nearly all his leisure time with my grandfather." Unhappy with this shift in attitude, the master sold Ball's father. Before the trader could seize him, and warned by his own father, he made his escape from Maryland.[75] All three writers had vivid memories of fathers with whom they had limited contact. Did briefer contact with a man who modeled resistance in his own way have a greater influence on the character development of a boy like Henson, Ball, or Jacobs than spending a longer period with an accommodating father? All three stories demonstrated the difficulty of trying to balance caretaking and heroic resistance.

Because fighting back directly presented risks, caretakers offered to take physical punishment for loved ones, an indirect form of resistance that enabled men to partially uphold their sense of duty to protect. When the overseer prepared to whip Laura Bell's mother, an admirer, the man who eventually became her father, "comes up an' takes de whuppin' fer her. Atter dat dey cou'ts . . . till dey gits married." Lily Perry, also from North Carolina, recalled that her husband "uster hate ter see me git dem beatin's an' he'd beg me not ter let my mouth be so sassy, but I can't help hit. He uster take my beatin's when he could."[76] Unable to overtly defend his loved ones, a man might also minister to kin in the aftermath of physical abuse. Margrett Nickerson's Florida overseer beat her to hasten her work, and "At night my pa would try to fix me up cose I had to go back to work nex' day."[77] Such actions enabled enslaved men throughout the South to avoid direct confrontation with official power and to combine aspects of caretaking and heroic masculinity.

Bondmen, accustomed to controlling and concealing their anger, sometimes reached a breaking point and retaliated, risking their lives in the process. Charles Grandy discussed a Virginia man shot for attacking the overseer with a hoe after the overseer molested the man's wife "right fo' de slave's face." The overseer "kept shootin' 'till de man fell dead in his tracks. Nigger ain' got no chance." Sallie Carder's father died in Tennessee for defending his wife. "De overseer tied me mother to whip her and me father untied her and de overseer shot and killed him," she stated. William Anderson told of a slave, Branum Harris, who arrived late for work on a Mississippi cotton plantation after he and his wife stayed up all night attending their sick child. When ordered to stop for a whipping, the man cited his sick child and kept moving. The overseer "leveled his gun and shot him down."[78] Fatal outcomes convinced most men that the cost of insubordination and openly protecting loved ones were far too high to make this a typical mode of behavior.

Although they understood the dangers, enslaved men regularly refused to be whipped and/or fought back. Some leveraged their productivity to take such risks, whereas others no longer cared about the consequences.[79] Frederick Douglass retaliated against Edward Covey, a Maryland slave breaker to whom he had been hired. For Douglass, the struggle marked a "turning-point" that "revived within me a sense of my own manhood. . . . My long-crushed spirit rose, cowardice departed, bold defiance took its place; and I now resolved that, however long I might remain a slave in form, the day had passed forever when I could be a slave in fact. I did not hesitate to let it be known of me, that the white man who expected to succeed in whipping, must also succeed in killing me." Because Covey hired slaves, he could not kill Douglass without having to repay the owner, an expense he could not afford. Douglass believed Covey avoided calling the constable because his livelihood depended on his public persona as a slave breaker. "That reputation was at stake; and had he sent me—a boy about sixteen years old—to the public whipping-post, his reputation would have been lost; so, to save his reputation, he suffered me to go unpunished."[80] Surviving retaliation involved choosing the right target, good timing, and a willingness to flirt with death. A childless young man like Douglass risked his own life, but not the safety of or separation from his family, a factor that complicated the decisions and behavior of husbands and fathers.

Living in the North, a successful fugitive like Douglass could assume in his writing the mantle of the Self-Made Man.[81] As David Doddington points out, fugitive abolitionists equated masculinity with heroic action and drew stark comparisons between masculine resistance and feminine accommodation, shaming those who failed to resist as unmanly. When Lewis Clarke declared, "A SLAVE CAN'T BE A MAN!" he did not say a slave *is not* a man or that slaves lacked inherent manhood. Instead, he argued that the institution suppressed slaves' ability to exert their masculinity. In order to be men, they had to free themselves or die trying. Rebecca Fraser similarly uses Clarke and Douglass to argue that fugitives and free blacks believed only those who achieved freedom could be considered real men.[82] Frederick Douglass suspected and Lewis Clarke knew that he had a white father. Neither of these men who so vehemently linked masculinity to heroic action had enslaved fathers and thus neither had watched a black father grapple with the painful dilemmas of his role. Chapter 4 uses the narrative of Henry Bibb to show the ongoing pain of husbands and fathers who escaped alone. Bibb lived with the guilt of having left a wife and child in slavery, a guilt that he tried to explain away. The dominant society's ideals of manhood were difficult to achieve, even for those men who obtained liberty. The heroic example of Frederick Douglass rested on his having escaped prior to starting a family. In addition, Douglass had already been separated from his living relatives and dear friends, meaning that he did not have to worry about how his behavior would impact kin and community.

Douglass could exert his manhood by protecting self and did not face the added contradictions of the slave condition created by fatherhood. Each binding tie increased an enslaved man's vulnerability because his love of kin could be used against him. Bryant Huff's father left a Georgia plantation "in a fit of anger because one of his children had been whipped." Knowing how much he loved his family, the master jailed the man's wife and infant to lure him back. He returned, visited his wife, and was himself incarcerated. The following day, he and a son were sold to slave traders. For a husband and father to resist and demand his rights, or to stand up for his loved ones, was to risk removal from his family. To be a man in the sense of standing up for oneself or defending others could mean compromising or severing one's duty to family. Frederick Douglass constructed a narrative of masculinity in which he nurtured his own sense of self-worth. A committed father, regardless of the region, staple crop, or size of plantation on which he lived, had to think about how to take care of himself while taking care of others, and the institution of slavery placed those two imperatives in opposition. Open, dramatic resistance usually meant removal from family and community.[83]

Fortunate men escaped the potentially fatal consequences of defiant actions through sheer luck or the timely interference of others. Solomon Northup nearly died after fighting with his Louisiana master and believed that the fact that Tibeats owed a mortgage on him saved his life. The overseer rescued Northup from being hanged, using the mortgage as leverage. Northup slept in the big house that night, as those protecting him worried that Tibeats would return and murder Northup in the absence of white witnesses. "Why had I not died in my young years," Northup lamented, "before God had given me children to love and live for? What unhappiness and suffering and sorrow it would have prevented."[84] Fathers had to weigh the urge to die in defense of their honor against their love of kin. Northup recalled his contemplation of this quandary at a distance from his Northern, free family. Fathers of slaves knew their behavior could lead to abuse of kin and affected personal and family survival and that parenting often involved decisions about the individual versus the family or community. When a man chose to demonstrate self-control in the face of abuse, he had to sublimate his desire to overtly protect his loved ones to his desire to avoid sale and decide if his role as a protector meant direct intercession or remaining part of the family.

Men who watched their children sold away had to confront sorrow, anger, and their own powerlessness. Jourden Banks recalled his father's reaction to the sale of an older daughter. He realized he would likely never see her again, and also had to "endure . . . my other children weeping around me." The vocal grief of his other children reminded this father of his inability to safeguard the family's integrity. Banks's father requested that he be sold instead. "I rather you would sell me at once," he informed the master, "for I do not wish to witness the selling of my children." The slaveholder refused "unless you do some heavy fault," and Banks's father cogently responded, "Do you wish to tempt me to commit some crime?"[85] This enslaved father contemplated whether it might be preferable to engineer his own sale rather than stand by and suffer repeated blows to his family and sense of paternal duty.

Enslaved people lived in constant fear of the market and the dissolution of their families. As children, they worried most about losing parents.

Every time he saw slave traders come to the North Carolina plantation, Alex Woods "wus afraid my mother and father would be sold away from me." Adults feared the sale of or being sold away from spouses and children. Slaveholders used this ever-present fear and threat of sale to exert control. Cornelius Garner recalled an evening when noise from the quarters disturbed a Virginia master and his company. "Ole Marsa come clumpin' down to de quarters. Pick out de fam'ly got de mos' chillun an' say, 'Fo' God, nigger, I'm goin' to sell all dem chillun o' you'n lessen you keep 'em quiet.' Dat threat was worsen prospects of a lickin'. Ev'ybody sho' keep quiet arter dat."[86]

Henry Brown pointed out that he was never whipped and had ample food and clothing, but enslaved husbands and fathers measured their experience in far different terms. "More fearful by far than all the blows of the bloody lash, or the pangs of cruel hunger are those lashings of the heart," Brown said of having wife and "darling idols of my heart, my little children . . . snatched from my arms," a loss he called "more dreadful to all of us than a large number of lashes." Separation from family members epitomized the sorrow and cruelty of the peculiar institution. Heather Williams, in her exploration of the anguish and bitter memory of separation and enslaved and formerly enslaved peoples' denunciation of the inhumanity of slaveholders, calls the loss of family "a violation of the inviolate." The interstate slave trade removed numerous children, especially in the Upper South, from their parents, and fathers from their wives and children. "If the bond between mother and child mustered only the most limited protection, the relationship between father and child was not protected at all, except for a short time in Louisiana," Williams notes.[87] The market underscored and exacerbated the constraints on fatherhood, and men's reactions to family separation speak to their understanding of and struggle to fulfill paternal duty.

For an enslaved man, being forcibly parted from a wife or child entailed not only a sense of loss, but also a reminder of his emasculation and inability to protect his kin. Adelaide Vaughn told the story of her four-year-old mother being parted from her father in Virginia. "My grandfather was allowed to go a certain distance with her when she was sold away from him. He walked and carried her in his arms. Mama said that when he had gone as far as they would let him go, he put her in the wagon and turned his head away," she related. "She said she wondered why he didn't look at her; but later she understood that he hated so bad to 'part from her and couldn't do nothing to prevent it that he couldn't bear to look at her."[88] This is a good example of a woman who was fatherless, but not entirely so. She had no physical contact with her father after age four, and yet she remembered him. Vaughn's second-hand recitation of this incident indicates that the memory of this father was important to the family across generations. Her mother clearly believed that her father loved her and experienced anguish at their separation and his impotence to keep his family together. She attributed separation from her father to the cruelty of slavery rather than irresponsibility on his part. Through memory, fathering extended beyond physical presence. The anecdote also suggests that he turned his face so that his daughter would not see him cry. Later, from hindsight, she speculated about his feelings and developed a supportive understanding of his once seemingly inexplicable behavior. Already suffering, he did not need his daughter to see him doubly unmanned.[89]

To lose family to the market was a profoundly wrenching experience, though in their shock, many men reacted in an outwardly stoic manner.[90] Elisha Green purchased the freedom of several family members, but lost one son to sale. "I heard nothing more of John," he noted, "the sight of this act I thought would break the heart of my wife. . . . I considered it wicked and mean, not having the power to assist him in the least whatever. You can judge of my feelings at this time." Green emphasized his moral outrage and sense of powerlessness, but did not detail his emotional state, expecting a humane reader to understand.[91] Writing his narrative in the 1880s, Green described gendered responses to this loss. He saw his wife as immersed in grief, while he expressed grief suffused with anger and impotence. Achieving the freedom of several children did not mitigate a father's sense of loss if he failed to help them all.

When writing about or describing family separation, men found it difficult to translate their sorrow into words. "How I felt that day I cannot tell," William Grose noted. "I had never been more than twenty miles from home, and now I was taken away from my mother and wife and children." Abream Scriven, sold away from wife and children, penned a letter to his wife. "Give my love to my father & mother and tell them good Bye for me," he wrote. "If we Shall not meet in this world I hope to meet in heaven. My dear wife for you and my Children my pen cannot Express the griffe I feel to be parted from you all. . . . I remain your truly husband until Death."[92] Language seemed insufficient to convey the depth of their loss. Because the majority of slaves were illiterate, most suffered permanent dislocation and had no way to communicate with or leave their loved ones any lasting record of their feelings.

Literate fathers expressed their heartbreak at being separated from family in letters to people who could potentially facilitate contact with their kin. "For God sake let me hear from you all my wife and children are not out of my mine day nor night," Thomas Ducket wrote. James Skipworth, freed by his Virginia master and sent to Liberia, despaired over leaving his wife and children, owned by another slaveholder. "Thir is but one thing that I hate that I cant carry my Wife and Childreans," he told his former owner. Hezekiah Corpsen, freed along with several family members, delayed his trip to Liberia as he tried to raise money to buy a son who remained enslaved in Virginia. "To think of leaving this boy, so distracts my mind," he wrote. "I should have gone in October, but for this boy . . . his master allows him to visit us yearly, and stay for a few days. Believe me, sir, I long for this visit, and yet dread it, for we must part again; and then his grief, his tears."[93] Corpsen's letter offers a glimpse of how a complicated family division felt from the perspective of a father. He was free to leave the United States and slavery and yet could not bring himself to do so because that would mean leaving a son behind. He found the boy's annual visits excruciating. Those visits brought mingled joy and sorrow—the joy of reunion and the sorrow of its brevity. The hardest part was his son's emotional response to parting, which underscored the father's inability to rectify the situation and unite his family under one roof.

Even if they found themselves at a loss for words in the moment, the memory of separation remained etched in fathers' minds. In a dictated narrative published in 1902, Pharaoh Chesney recalled his anguish decades after being parted from family. "The saddest day in all my life came to me when I was told that my beloved wife and children must be taken one way, and that I must go another," he stated. "A more cruel blow could not have been given to me. I could not have felt worse if I had been told that we were all to be killed." Of his four children, he only knew what happened to one, and "of the other three I have never seen nor heard of since we were separated. I have contemplated making a search—like a mother partridge for her scattered brood—for them; but this life, though long, has been so full of all kinds of cares and duties that this supreme desire of my heart must go unsatisfied." A man did not forget his family even if he never saw them again, and Chesney defined searching for his family as his "supreme desire." Edward Baptist shows that men moved to the frontier by planter migration or the interstate slave trade, those he defines as caretakers, often bestowed on subsequent children the names of those they had lost to sale and death. A subsequent marriage, moreover, did not erase the pain of having been parted from an earlier family. Emotionally visceral accounts of separation entered family lore. "People held onto these memories," Williams writes, "because mixed in with the pain of separation was the love of the people who had been left behind."[94]

In their grief, enslaved fathers revealed the importance they placed on family and the desolation of separation. Reuben Madison called the sale of his two children, the "severest trial of my life . . . I mourned and cried, and would not be comforted." Enslaved people understood sale as permanent loss, and the lack of knowledge of a loved one's whereabouts and future could be as painful as the lack of contact. Lewis Hayden, writing in 1853 and discussing his children, stated, "I have one child who is buried in Kentucky, and that grave is pleasant to think of. I've got another that is sold nobody knows where, and that I can never bear to think of." Death at least had finality. After the death of the master, Reeves Tucker's family was included in the property division. "Mammy and all the chil'ren fell to his daughter, and Pappy was giv' to his son . . . what was fixing to move to Texas. Pappy begged so hard fer some of the chil'ren that finally they let me go with him. I never seed Mammy or any of my relations after that." This father facilitated the removal of his son from mother and siblings in order to maintain contact with at least one of his children, and the two men stayed together well after emancipation, with Tucker leaving his father's home only when he married.[95]

Thomas Jones had anticipated the loss of his spouse and three "bright, precious" children, having frequently "talked of this dreaded fate" with his wife. When his fears materialized, Jones felt "lonely and dreary," and "tempted to put an end to my wretched life." Sold to a trader, Charles Ball similarly "became weary of life." Ball "was distressed by painful dreams. . . . My little boy came and begged me not to go and leave him, and endeavored, as I thought, with his little hands to break the fetters that bound me. I awoke in agony and cursed my existence." When he arrived in South Carolina, Ball was assigned to a cabin occupied by a family of seven. Entering the cabin, Ball's escort "laid his hand upon the head of his naked child . . . and then turning to me, said, 'Did you leave any children at home?' The scene before me . . . caused my heart to swell until my breast seemed too small to contain it." Two men shared the commonality of their position and what it meant to be the father of slaves. In a simple question and gesture, Ball's housemate acknowledged what the arrival from the Upper South might be experiencing, as well as revealing his own anxiety. When they looked at their children, enslaved fathers saw not only their own love, but potential loss, and in that loss their own inability to protect themselves or their kin.[96]

Religion gave enslaved people a way to cope with separation, as heaven offered hope of eventual reunification with loved ones. "You're selling me to Georgy,/But you can not sell my soul,/Thank God Almighty, God will/fix it for us some day!" Sarah Thomas sang. Elizabeth Keckley had little contact with her father, who visited twice a year, at Easter and Christmas. For a brief time, her mother's master arranged for the family to live together, probably through hiring. When her father's owner moved shortly thereafter, he was permanently separated from his family, news Keckley called a "thunderbolt." The scene of her father's departure remained imprinted on her memory. Keckley's literate parents corresponded until her father died. "The most precious mementoes of my existence are the faded old letters that he wrote, full of love, and always hoping that the future would bring brighter days," she stated. "In nearly every letter is a message for me. 'Tell my darling little Lizzie,' he writes, 'to be a good girl, and to learn her book. Kiss her for me, and tell her that I will come to see her some day.' Thus he wrote time and again, but he never came. He lived in hope, but died without ever seeing his wife and child." Keckley copied one letter to his "dear biloved wife" in her book. "I hope with gods helpe that I may be abble to rejoys with you on the earth and In heaven," he wrote. "I am detemnid to nuver stope praying. . . . I hope to meet you In paradase to prase god forever. . . . I want Elizabeth to be a good girl and not to thinke that becasue I am bound so fare that gods not abble to open the way." For slaves deprived of family, religion offered hope of eventual reunion. Because distance did not diminish this man's love and longing for his kin, he fell back on the recourse available to him, appealing to higher power and a delayed reward. Keckley had a physical reminder in the form of letters, but most former slaves had only memories of those they lost to the market.[97]

Thomas Anderson's faith also provided succor when his children were sold away from Virginia, a common occurrence for enslaved families in the Upper South in the decades prior to the Civil War. "I have great cause to bless the Lord, for he has nursed me through all the journey of my life, and has been my comforter in distress, when trouble, like a gloomy cloud, has overshadowed me by the loss of three of my children—being taken from my bosom, sold and taken South," he lamented. "But here I got some consolation, reflecting upon Joseph being sold into Egypt. . . . In pray'r I liff up my eyes, that God might restore them again; but if not to meet again on this earth, that we may joyfully meet on that shore where parting, sighing, and selling will be no more. They were sold eleven years ago, and I have never heard from them since." Anderson invoked a typically maternal image, describing his children as a part of himself that had been "taken from my bosom." For people torn from family, hope of eternal salvation helped them confront the actual moment of parting and the ongoing pain in its wake. African American preachers in the Upper South told people that if they converted, they would "see their mother and father again. . . . All this would cause a person to pray."[98] Faith offered a way to make sense of and frame loss and memories, and had a particular appeal in an area marked by high levels of sale, migration, and hiring.

Whites usurped God's authority to justify slavery, whereas slaves conceived of God as a protector, an entity more powerful than masters who would ultimately punish slaveholding sinners. A former slave commented, "Now the poor slave when he is tied to the whipping post and whipped almost to death, he has no father to protect him, and no mother to protect him, and no one to fly to but his Heavenly Father. They have to bear patiently with their hard task masters, and live humble and faithful to God, and then at the end of the warfare God will richly crown them in heaven."[99] In an institution that regularly separated children from their parents, and in which young adults were especially vulnerable to sale, one significant appeal of Christianity was that it provided a father figure and defender in an institution that constantly undermined family stability and denied authority to earthly parents.

In God and Heaven, slaves always had a father and a home. "I'm going home to my loving Jesus, I'm going home to my loving Father," Liza White declared. Frederick Douglass never knew his father and met his mother only a few times before she died. While living in Baltimore, he found religion. "I was not more than thirteen years old, when, in my loneliness and destitution, I longed for some one to whom I could go, as to a father and protector," he wrote. J. Vance Lewis recorded the chorus of a slave song: "Before I'd be a slave, I'd be buried in my grave,/And go home to my Father and be saved."[100] When separated from kin or moved repeatedly, faith in God provided a constant in an unstable environment and a sense of comfort and shelter that could be carried internally and from place to place.[101]

In the conversion narratives gathered by Fisk University anthropology graduate student A. P. Watson between 1927 and 1929, formerly enslaved people discussed their visions of and conversations with God. God often called converts "my little one." One woman recalled, "A voice spoke to me,

'Come into Father's welcome home.'" And another reported, "He told me He was my Father and I was His child." When in need of guidance, another woman would "go to the telephone that is always in operation and ask the Father who is never too busy to answer." Christianity appealed to bondpeople in part because of the stress the institution of slavery placed on the family. Another informant associated his antipathy for life during slavery with his broken family. "I had neither mother nor father and I had just as soon been dead as alive." He continued to struggle with social isolation following emancipation, and when he converted, he prayed, "Lord, I have neither father nor mother, have mercy on me."[102] In an institution that so frequently separated slaves from their kin, God became a replacement parent.

Christian faith offered not just a hope of seeing loved ones again, but family reunification in a place devoid of slaveholders, a place with a real father who fulfilled his paternal responsibility, protected his children, and did not abuse his power. Slave Christianity defined African Americans as the chosen people of God, prioritized the Old Testament, and venerated patriarchal figures known for deliverance, such as Moses.[103] In addition, former slaves saw black preachers and religious officials as fathers. During her time teaching on the Sea Islands, Laura Towne commented on the revered status of church elders. "They call their elders in the church—or the particular one who converted and received them in—their spiritual father, and he has the most absolute power over them," she wrote. "These fathers are addressed with fear and awe as 'Pa Marcus,' 'Pa Demus,' etc." Masters positioned themselves as all powerful, but slaves did not see them as such, granting that role to God.[104] Slave conversion to Christianity, and the search for a moral father figure deserving of sincere rather than compelled veneration, represented a rejection of slaveholder paternalism.

"TO BE A MAN, and not to be a man—a father without authority—a husband and no protector—is the darkest of fates," John Jacobs summed up the status of the bondman. "Such was the condition of my father, and such is the condition of every slave . . . he owns nothing, he can claim nothing. His wife is not his: his children are not his; they can be taken from him, and sold at any minute. . . . A slave's wife or daughter may be insulted before his eyes with impunity. . . . To raise his hand in their defence is death by the law. He must bear all things and resist nothing."[105] The institution of slavery placed agonizing constraints on the slave husband and father. Ties that brought human connectedness and meaning simultaneously exposed him to greater abuse and reduced his ability and willingness to effectively respond to the mistreatment of self and kin. And yet, despite a system that enforced neglect of and limited contact with children, undermined a man's authority and ability to protect loved ones, and broke apart families, many enslaved fathers managed to exert influence over their sons and daughters. Enslaved men retained a strong sense of what it meant to be a father.

CHAPTER TWO

I Liked My Papa the Best

Enslaved Fathers

"A blessed thing it is for any one when they meet with sorrow and afflictions, to have a father's home to go to," an escaped former slave stated in 1845. After recounting the life-saving hospitality of a father and his widowed daughter on a freezing night, he then invoked the "Heavenly Father," using the concept of a father's home literally and figuratively. The ideal home was male headed, and the earthly father, like the divine father, served as a pillar of support for his children. Slaves and former slaves conceived of the role of the father as a protector and provider, a role they interpreted broadly by emphasizing emotional and spiritual as much as material sustenance.[1] Although slavery stripped men of authority and the slaveholder usurped the patriarchal role of provider, a significant number of enslaved men endeavored to uphold their vision of fatherhood. Despite the constraints on fatherhood, many former slaves had fond memories of and identified with their fathers. In their commentary on their fathers, children emphasized men's ability to survive, maintain their dignity, and support their kin in diverse ways.

In her study of identity among enslaved women in Virginia, Brenda Stevenson argues that women constructed a sense of self that was "overwhelmingly positive," "oppositional," and "heroic," and stressed devotion to family and community. Stevenson looks only at women's stories about themselves and other women, stating that men appear as marginal figures. In her discussion of Fannie Berry's tale about Sukie, a woman who changed the master's behavior by successfully fighting off a rape attempt, Stevenson never mentions that Berry heard the story of the auction block from an enslaved man.[2] Bondwomen were often tied to the plantation, and the story of Sukie's sale first came to them from the coachman, an enslaved man with limited mobility. He served as a vital link to the outside world, and his recounting of Sukie's behavior on the auction block indicates that he too probably relished her defiance. Sukie's story then took on immense importance to the women in this community who may have shaped it, through retelling, to fit their conception of self and moral standards.

The Virginia narratives collected in *Weevils in the Wheat* are an interesting study in family and identity. While in some narratives, as Stevenson notes, women occupy the central roles and men appear as bit players, there are counter-examples in which men take center stage and women are the marginal figures. This is true for male and female informants. Cornelia Carney, for example, focused on her father and only briefly mentioned her mother.[3] An examination of stories about fathers shows that slave communities valued self-determination, resistance, heroism, and dedication to family in men and women. Differing gender standards emerge, but the overlap in admired traits speaks to the greater fluidity of gender roles among enslaved people.

The Virginia narratives show that enslaved people were pragmatic and could base their identity on their mother, father, both parents, another relative, or a member of the broader community. In their interviews, informants discussed defiant behavior in men and women. At times, men and women identified solely with their mother, especially when an individual had a white father or lost contact with an enslaved father at an early age. If they had sustained contact, however, informants were eager to talk about and might identify more strongly with their father. Former slaves celebrated charismatic adults with whom they interacted as youth, and those role models could be male or female. Gender was less salient than the role model's personality and behavior. Informants also appreciated relatives and other adults who cared for kin and, at times, the broader community. Beverly Jones knew his mother and never mentioned his father, discussing a defiant uncle as a male role model. He also related stories of a rebellious woman, and his narrative is a good example of how identity formation among the enslaved was tied more to degree of contact and personality rather than to gender, though gender did mediate degree of contact. In terms of diverging gender standards, men and women engaged in insubordinate behavior, but women felt community sanction to stay near and care for kin and were less likely to run away. Men more often engaged in short-term and permanent flight and their children celebrated such behavior.[4] Anecdotes about men focus greater attention on skill, physical strength, ingenuity, and refusal to accept punishment, traits that enabled men to resist slavery and/or support their family.

Stevenson argues that although few women could overtly display rebellious behavior "for fear of severe retaliation," their tales, even when they discussed "fantastical deeds and attitudes," reveal that enslaved women "held great pride and esteem for those who did."[5] The same is true for stories of fathers. Even if and when they embellished, the way in which informants spoke of their fathers reveals the characteristics they admired. Slave communities articulated a robust vision of fatherhood and masculine duty that stood in opposition to their evaluation of slaveholders. The attributes former slaves most praised in their fathers, including rebelliousness, compassion and providing for family, physical strength, skill, and intelligence, often combined components of heroic resistance and the subtle resistance of caretaking. Informants also criticized men who failed to live up to these standards, admonishing fathers who behaved selfishly and who practiced the masculinity of domination, traits reminiscent of slaveholders. While informants criticized self-serving behavior, they countenanced individualistic action if it was in open defiance of slavery. Men contributed to their children's identity formation in different ways, including through dramatic action and the quiet resistance of supporting kin.

While not the only way to achieve manhood, heroic resistance represented the pinnacle of manly character in the eyes of many enslaved and formerly enslaved people. A man who escaped or died fighting back obviously could no longer interact with his children, but heroic fathers often continued to shape their children's identity. The vast majority of enslaved men, for whom dramatic resistance was not an option based on circumstance and/or choice, pursued a variety of masculine identities. Informants whose fathers had remained enslaved likewise discussed a range of admirable traits that reveal the multiple masculinities in slave communities. First and foremost, commentators praised caretaking men who invested in their children not just materially, but emotionally. Formerly enslaved people recognized the diverse ways in which men provided for and protected their children, but they articulated deepest praise for men who ideologically provisioned, a topic discussed in the following chapter. When evaluating their enslaved fathers, children highlighted defiant behaviors within slavery, including evading patrols, fighting back on a more limited scale, and protecting loved ones. Other admired traits included physical strength, ingenuity, industriousness, skill, and determination. All of these traits could be used to provide for family and, in some cases, to resist, but could also function as forms of accommodation. Slavery was messy, and children's observations of their fathers underscore this point. Enslaved fathers found different ways to be men, and their children found different ways to recognize them. Commentary on fathers often reveals combinations of identities and survival strategies rather than neatly demarcated masculine roles. When informants evaluated their fathers in twentieth-century interviews, the characteristics they most admired were those that enabled men to maintain dignity in an oppressive and capricious environment.

Of the subsidiary characteristics that earned commendation, informants most appreciated intelligence and ingenuity when used to defy slavery, but they also realized that such traits enabled men to provide for family within the system. Children of fathers who occupied trustee roles were most likely to be ambivalent in their assessments. They appreciated fathers who amply provided, as these families were often materially better off relative to the rest of the community, but trustees could also be prone to violence. Children of trustees were less effusive in their emotional evaluation of their fathers if these men turned the violence of their positions on their own family members. Former slaves might recognize aspects of masculinity and yet also believe those traits did not always make for a good father. Discussions of enslaved fathers stress family and neighborhood solidarity rather than broad solidarity within the slave community. A man who used his skill or a trustee role to protect and provide for family earned respect, whereas a man who earned privileges and then used them selfishly, or who perpetrated excessive violence on his family, was less praiseworthy.

Commentary on Fathers

The fieldworkers conducting interviews with former slaves in the late 1930s sought basic biographical information, but did not ask for specifics of family life. The FWP interviewers cared more about the interactions between slaves and slaveholders than enslaved parents and their children.[6] One Georgia interviewer noted that former slaves discussed parenting and then failed to provide supporting evidence. "Outstanding in their memories are the methods of rearing slave children and the amusements indulged in by their mothers and fathers," the writer stated, offering no explanation of "amusements." This comment indicates that subjects happily recalled such topics, but fieldworkers failed to seek clarification or include the information in written reports. Details about childrearing deviated from FWP goals and the standard set of questions, and the way in which such anecdotes emerge in the records reveals that interviewers steered their subjects toward topics they deemed important, such as plantation organization and work. Writers asked questions about folk culture, including children's songs and games, but not in the context of play with parents. As Karen Sánchez-Eppler notes, the writers had a "celebratory sense of what childhood should be like," which included disconnecting childhood games from the adult world.[7]

In the FWP narratives, commentary on ordinary interactions between enslaved parents and children often comes up in the context of other topics. "I heard my mother say when I was small Papa was bouncing me up and down. He was lying on the floor playing like wid me," Wash Ford recounted. "She looked up the road . . . and said, 'Yonder come some soldiers. What they coming here for?' Papa put me down and run. He hid. They didn't find him." In a story about his father eluding Confederate soldiers rounding up labor, Ford inadvertently provided a glimpse into an enslaved father's mundane involvement with his child. The next piece in the compilation, also an interview with Ford, makes no mention of his father lying on the floor and playing with his toddler. Because interviewers rarely pursued anecdotes about routine family life or asked questions that would more readily elicit such responses, they appear as asides to other queries. Mittie Freeman also grew up in Arkansas and also alluded to spending time with her father when she discussed the events surrounding the Civil War and emancipation. "The day freedom came, I was fishing with pappy," she stated. "Cannons was to roar every place when Richmond fell. Pappy jumps up, throws his pole and everything, and grabs my hand, and starts flying towards the house. 'It's victory,' he keep on saying. 'It's freedom. Now we'es gwine be free.' I didn't know what it all meant."[8] Although they were not probed about the emotional content of familial relationships, the brief comments FWP informants made in passing indicate that emotionally satisfying father/child relationships regularly developed within the constraints of slavery.

Despite the format and brevity of the interviews, formerly enslaved people managed to speak to their affection for their fathers. Delia Barclay revealed her attachment to her abroad father and the excitement surrounding his weekly visits when questions about life on the plantation triggered memory of a childhood accident. "Sunday was us bigges' day. On Sattidy night Marse Jack Bean he 'low my father a permit t' come t' see mudder 'n' us chillren. . . . I 'member one night he come 'n' I's so 'cited t' see him I run up d' po'ch 'n' got my big toe kotch in d' crack in d' step 'n' mos' pull it off. C'ose dat bre'k up d' merriment fo' w'ile but I soon git over it." Had she not chosen to discuss this event, she likely never would have divulged how she anticipated her father's visits. Sarah Pittman described her father, who died shortly after the Civil War ended, as "a wonderful man." Her parents lived apart in an abroad marriage in Louisiana. "On Saturday night he would stay with us till Sunday. On Sunday night he would go home. He would play with us." Pittman did not specify the content of their games, and her interviewer never followed up, but the succinct remark indicates that she and her siblings eagerly looked forward to their weekly visits with an attentive father. Will Adams lived with his father, but saw him only at night. "I 'members when I was just a walking good that Pa would come in from the fiel' at night and take me out of bed, dress me, feed me, then play with me for hours. Him being 'leader,' he was gone from 'fore day till after night."[9] After a full day, Adams's father took time to interact with his son, though, like Pittman, Adams never specified their activities. Cursory FWP commentary suggests that fathers and children saw play as an important element of their relationships.[10]

Abroad marriages limited the contact between a man and his children, but not necessarily their emotional bonds. Like Sarah Pittman, Oscar Rogers had fond memories of seeing his father each week in the South Carolina Lowcountry. "My father could get a pass and come to see us every Sunday providin' he didn't go nowhere else or stop long the road," Rogers recalled. "He came early and stay till bedtime. We all run to meet him. He kiss us all in bed when he be leavin.'" "I liked my papa the best," Lucy Key added of her childhood in Mississippi. "He was kind and never whooped us. He belong to Master Stamps on another place." While an abroad marriage, and the institution of slavery itself, could restrict an enslaved father's role in punishing his children, Key expressed affection for and identified her father as a caring individual. Despite the many disadvantages, an abroad marriage may have benefited this father, removing him from the day-to-day discipline involved in parenting. Richard Carruthers grew up in Texas and when discussing his father's weekly visits, he simply noted, "When my pappy come to see my mamma we talk and talk," suggesting a warm, open relationship.[11] Children favored emotional availability and connection even if a man lived at a physical distance, and these informants all had positive recollections of involved fathers despite not living with them on a full-time basis.

Among the constellation of attributes formerly enslaved children admired in their fathers, informants most appreciated caretakers; men engaged with and affectionate toward their families, regardless of region and household structure. "My fathaw was a great big man, with a mustache, and he looked lak a preachah, but he wasn't," Betty Coleman recalled. "I had the sweetest daddy that ever broke bread." While Coleman lived with both parents, Andrew Gill's father visited twice a week. "My daddy, he was a fine man an' treated us chullun jus' dandy," he stated.[12] In brief interviews, former slaves conveyed an understanding of masculinity that included and stressed attentiveness toward family.

While the FWP fieldworkers did not prioritize reminiscences of commonplace family life, a lack of substantive contact hindered detailed descriptions in longer narratives published in the nineteenth and early twentieth centuries. Mattie Jackson's father, who visited his Missouri family once a week, was sold further afield and then escaped when she was still a small child, "yet I can well remember the little kindnesses my father used to bestow upon us, and the deep affection and fondness he manifested for us." Though only seven at the time, Morgan Latta could "never forget" his father's illness and death prior to the Civil War. "Our loving father was so very dear to us." FWP informant Sarah Wilson also had vivid memories of a father she lost as a young child. "My father nebber cum wid us to Texas," she said of the division of her family, "but I 'member he uset to nuss me on his lap."[13] Impressionistic memories of fathers lost early in life underscored familial affection and appreciation of caretakers. Ex-slaves blamed slavery for limited or lost contact with fathers, believing these men loved them and would have remained emotionally invested had they been given that opportunity.

Although informants more commonly recalled the early nurturing of their mothers, some enslaved men who lost their wives assumed the full responsibility of childcare and headed one-parent households out of necessity. After her mother died of diphtheria, Martha Spence Bunton's father, who had been hired out, came back to care for his children and "was fathaw and mothaw to us." Bunton emphasized her father's ability to assume dual roles. "I remembah how on Sunday mawnin's when we didn't have nothin' to do, he'd git out ob bed in our log cabin, make a big fire, and tell us: 'Jiminy-cripes! Yo' chillun stay in yo' beds, I'll make de biscuits.' He would, too. I still laugh when I think about dem big rye biscuits. . . . Dey sure was big biscuits, but dey was good." Bunton also recalled her father remonstrating with the mistress on behalf of "his little chaps," because he worried about the lye soap she used to treat lice. Abraham Coker would think about his mother and "cry and cry" after her death. "Us boys and fathaw stayed on in de cabin and we sure was lonesome. Fathaw, who was a field worker, was good as he could be to us. Dat helped." Roxy Pitts's mother ran away, leaving Pitts and her baby sister. "Pappy had to raise dat little bitsy baby hisse'f. He tuk it en me to de fel' whar he workin', en kep' a bottle of sweeten water in he shirt to . . . gib de baby when it cry," she recalled. "Den Pappy he mai'ed Aunt Josie en dey had er whole passel er chilluns, en dey was my brudders en sisters."[14] Henry Picquet similarly raised his baby after his wife was sold. Unable to recover his spouse, he managed to redeem his infant daughter. "He bought the child, and brought it away," his second wife recounted. "It was about three months old, and he raised it on a bottle, work all day, and then worry with the child all night."[15] These men, even if they eventually remarried, were devoted and attentive single parents, willing to bottle-feed their infants, prepare food, and emotionally support their older children. Such one-parent households highlight the flexible, adaptive nature of the enslaved family and men's willingness to take on typically domestic duties in order to raise their children.

Members of slave communities, accustomed to loss of loved ones and the instability of the family unit, attempted to care for orphans.[16] Sarah Perkins's father, facing imminent separation, asked another enslaved man to look after his child. Perkins's mother died at her birth and then at the age of five her master moved to Texas. "Tom, my fathaw, told my uncle Tom Williamson, 'Tom, yo' take care of my baby.'" He also gave his child "his best hoss" for the trip. Perkins remained with her aunt and uncle after freedom. While blood relatives, often grandparents, aunts, uncles, and siblings commonly cared for children bereft of parents, non-kin, including men, contributed to this support network. Mingo White was separated from both of his parents at age four or five. "I was jes' a li'l thang; tooked away from my mammy an' pappy, jes' when I needed 'em mos.' The only caren' that I had or ever knowed anything 'bout was give to me by a frein' of my pappy," White recounted. "His name was John White. My pappy tol' him to take care of me for him. John was a fiddler an' many a night I woke up to find myse'f 'sleep 'twix' his legs whilst he was playin' for a dance for de white folks." At the urging of the boy's biological father, John White became Mingo White's surrogate father and "took me an' kep' me in de cabin wid him." Both Perkins and White ended up with a surrogate family at the behest of their biological fathers, men who interceded in an attempt to assure that their children received proper care. Louisa Gause's mother drowned crossing a South Carolina river on her way to visit her sick mother. Gause, an infant at the time, survived the accident and the boatman subsequently raised her. "My mammy, she been drown right down dere in de Pee Dee river, fore I get big enough to make motion en talk what I know. Dat how-come it be dat Pa Cudjo raise me."[17] As migration, the market, and mortality broke up enslaved families, new ones formed in their stead, and informants remembered dedicated and caring fathers who were not their blood kin.[18]

A constantly shifting family unit due to sale, death, and escape, coupled with required remarriage and at times forced breeding, meant that enslaved children regularly acquired stepparents. While more likely to criticize a stepfather than a biological father, many ex-slaves spoke highly of these men, noting that they cared for all of their children regardless of origin. Isiah Jeffries's mother had three "outside chilluns, and we each had a different father." After she married Ned, "den he jest come to be our Pa." The couple had four more children, and "Ned was as good to me as he was to his own chillun." According to Isabell Henderson, her stepfather, a preacher, "was good to me . . . better to me than my father was." Jacob Branch's master sold Branch's father and then bought and paired his mother with another slave who was a "good stepfather" and attentive to his new family despite not having any choice over the matter. Formerly enslaved children praised caretaking behavior and defined a man as their father based on how he treated others rather than on how a household formed.[19]

J. F. Boone managed to discuss his father at length by hijacking the interview. Boone started with the obligatory naming of both parents and then proceeded to focus on his father. "My father's name was Arthur Boone and my mother's name was Eliza Boone," he announced. "I am goin' to tell you about my father. Now be sure you put down there that this is Arthur Boone's son. I am J. F. Boone, and I am goin' to tell you about my father, Arthur Boone." Boone, born in 1872, discussed his father, and his father's memories of slavery, at length, commenting on cruel punishments, patrollers, and forced breeding. He mentioned his father's monetary worth, noting, "He was a mighty fine man and he sold for a lot of money. The slaves weren't to blame for that." After noting that his father fought for the Union and never received a pension, he ended the narrative, essentially entirely about his father, the same way he began, reiterating that he was his father's son.[20] Although Boone never described his personal relationship with his father, likely because he never received a question prompting him to do so, he made apparent his admiration for and thorough identification with the man.

Former slaves expressed their love and appreciation for their fathers by claiming to take after them. Betty Coleman described her father as "a gay ole feller," and recounted a story of him running from the patrollers in wooden-soled shoes. The family heard him coming from a distance and when he reached the cabin, he told his children he gave the patrol "plenty of heel-dust." Coleman framed a story of resistance in humorous terms, a form of subtext. When she commented that she "had the blood of my fathah," Coleman meant that she had inherited his defiant character. Nancy Thomas never met her father, but like Coleman she identified with him. "He died befo' I was bawn, dat is, he was shot to death 'cause he was so sassy and inderpendent. I take my sassiness f'om him."[21] Regardless of the accuracy of the story, Thomas believed that resistance to slavery led to her father's demise, and through a cherished memory of his personality, he continued to exert influence. Conceptions of fathers shaped and were shaped by conception of self. Even when denied physical contact, former slaves valued memories of their fathers and such memories contributed to their identity.

In likening themselves to their fathers, informants signaled their appreciation of rebelliousness and thereby critiqued slavery and the postwar racial order, even if only indirectly. In her study of the FWP, Catherine Stewart explores how "ex-slave informants revised white Southerners' master narratives by telling their own life histories." When constrained because they were being questioned by white Southerners, "their improvisations drew on black vernacular traditions, enabling them to tell stories of freedom and African American agency." In their interviews, informants used memories of rebellious fathers as a rebuke of slavery and Jim Crow. Discussing others enabled these individuals to seemingly distance themselves from such behavior and beliefs at the same time that they incorporated these memories into their sense of self. Willie Charleston opened his interview by announcing his similarities to his tough, taciturn father and ended it acknowledging his fear of the Ku Klux Klan. "I'm for the world like my daddy. He was light as I is. I'm jus' his size and make," Charleston remarked, before describing his father further. "My daddy was a feller of few words and long betwix' 'em. He was in the Old War (Civil War). He was shot in his right ankle and never would let it be took out." Although there were always exceptions, stories about defiant women often focused on verbal retaliation while stories about men emphasized physical actions. Betty Coleman and Nancy Thomas attributed their assertive personalities to paternal influence, which fit into this gendered pattern and may have been a less risky move for African American women in the Jim Crow South.[22] Charleston used a physical comparison to lay claim to his father's masculinity and fortitude, even as he disavowed open defiance in his discussion of the KKK.

Of the personal qualities that evoked admiration in their children, rebelliousness in an enslaved father ranked high. A defiant slave placed himself at considerable risk of being sold or killed as punishment, meaning that he would lose contact with his family. As a result, large numbers of children with bold fathers probably never knew these men well or at all. Charles Williams is a good example, having only heard his mother speak about his father. "Having a pappy in them days was sorter like Santy Claus is now," Williams noted, comparing fathers to a mythical provider beloved but never seen by children. "My mother tell me about my dady." Williams claimed his father ran after being threatened with a whipping and when tracked by bloodhounds, "he kill 6 or 7 of them hounds. . . . But they shot my dady and roll him in the river. I cin show you the very spot." Lewis Bonner claimed his father killed eighteen white men and then fled from a Texas plantation. "He ran away and stayed 3 years without being found. He come back and they was going to kill him, but he done killed 7 more before they could kill him." Similar to the likely embellished stories told by enslaved Virginia women and explored by Brenda Stevenson, children praised fathers who died resisting slavery, which reveals their feelings about the institution. According to Anne Clark, "My poppa was . . . strong. My father never had a lick in his life." When he refused to submit to a whipping, the master "shot my father down. My momma tuk him in the cabin and put him on a pallet. He died." A man who chose heroic resistance often died in the process, leaving his children without a father. Knowing or believing a father died standing up for himself offered solace and served as an ongoing source of pride. Even if unintended, heroic resistance thus contained an ongoing element of provisioning if and when memories of a man's personality and actions contributed to an individual's oppositional identity. "The reconstitution of 'family,'" Jennifer Fleischner writes in her study of women's slave narratives, "also takes place in the mind. We know that dead parents may remain 'alive' in the inner worlds of their offspring, sometimes resembling less what they may have actually been than what their children need (wish or fear) them to be."[23] Through memory, a father's influence could extend across time and space.

Rebellious grandfathers also earned praise. According to Marie Hervey, in Tennessee "they used to take pregnant women and dig a hole in the ground and put their stomachs in it and whip them. They tried to do my grandma that way, but my grandpa got an ax and told them that if they did he would kill them." Informants took pride in and recounted anecdotes of grandfathers with whom they had no contact because these men successfully escaped. Dave Lawson told a story in which his grandfather, facing the sale of his wife, subdued and bound the master and asked him to reconsider. When the slaveholder refused, the couple killed him by pouring boiling water down his throat. The sheriff "foun' Lissa an' Cleve settin by de door han' in han' waitin," and the authorities executed the couple, hanging them from the same tree. Even when formerly enslaved people never met their grandparents, they remained central to the family history and served as examples of suffering within and opposition to the institution of slavery.[24] Memory and family lore served as a touchstone for African American identity.

Regardless of the accuracy of the details, these stories reflect how informants chose to remember fathers and grandfathers who adopted the model of manhood based on heroic resistance. Children had limited contact with their fathers due to those traits, as men who fought back inevitably spent less time with their families. Frank Freeman's father refused to be whipped and "would fight," at one point running off and disappearing for four years.[25] Reacting to a cruel master and a brutal beating, Susan Hamilton's father managed to maneuver the master into the woods, tie him up, deliver an equal number of lashes, and then escape. Ishe Webb's father "killed his overseer and went off to the War."[26] Informants understood the trade-off between familial contact and a father modeling open resistance, and their stories underscore the intractable dilemma of balancing self-respect against preservation of the physical family unit.

Defining defiance of slavery and slaveholders as an important component of masculinity, ex-slaves writing or interviewed in the twentieth century celebrated their fathers' willingness to resist physical punishment. Sterling Brown claimed that his father "would never consent to be whipped by a master. He was manly to the core and would fight like a tiger when attacked. He had the distinction of whipping every overseer who tried his hand on him and was sold several times for the lone reason that he would not take a flogging without fighting back." Brown did not elaborate on the timing of these sales, which presumably occurred prior to his birth, and he avoided any mention of his father's direct interactions with slaveholders. When a white man attempted to sexually assault his daughter, Robert Ellett's father "jumped him and grabbed him in the chest," swearing he would kill him, successfully chasing him away. Ellett's father managed to combine caretaking and resistance to protect his child, but this was inherently dangerous and a difficult balance to strike. According to Ellett, who spoke to an African American fieldworker about his Virginia childhood, his father also announced he would die before taking a beating and Ellett imbibed this attitude, earning a whipping for refusing to call the slaveholder's sons, his playmates, by the title "master."[27] While defiance provoked physical consequences, these sons appreciated men who refused to meekly submit and defended themselves and their kin.

FWP informants celebrated their fathers' physical strength and fearlessness when men used such traits to resist punishment. Mary Gladdy recalled an enslaved man in a trustee position trying to administer a whipping and then seeking assistance from five other men when her father refused to submit to punishment. "All six of them couldn't 'out-man' my daddy! Then this foreman shot my daddy with a shot-gun, inflicting wounds from which he never fully recovered." The master had to obtain help when he wanted to whip Cornelius Garner's father, Remulus Garner. "Ole marse was 'fraid o' him himself 'cause paw was so stron'; so he called in de constable to whup him."[28] If men could not escape the degradation of slavery, they could make inflicting a whipping as difficult and costly as possible. A master, overseer, or foreman had to carefully plan when flogging a physically imposing enslaved man known for his willingness to fight back. If slaveholders prized physical size and strength as a potential financial asset, formerly enslaved people appreciated such attributes when used to undermine official power.

With open confrontation a recognized risk and an impossibility for most, enslaved people also admired men who defied authority indirectly. Sergio Lussana and Rebecca Fraser have discussed the importance of patrol evasion as a key aspect of masculine identity. A man who outsmarted or outran the patrols escaped punishment for traveling without a pass. "They never did whip my father because they never could catch him," Robert Farmer remarked, and Charlie Grant boasted that patrollers "tried four years to catch my daddy, but dey couln' never catch him. He was a slick nigger."[29] Cornelia Carney, discussing how her father outfoxed the authorities by living in the woods and making surreptitious visits when the master was at church, made a reference to Nat Turner and then denied any knowledge of the historical figure. "White folks was sharp too, but not sharp enough to git by ole Nat. Nat? I don't know who he was. Ole folks used to say it all de time. De meanin' I git is dat de niggers could always out-smart de white folks." Like animal tricksters, the less powerful could outwit those in authority, and men who eluded slave patrols served as concrete proof that those charged with controlling the slave population were not all-powerful.[30]

Former slaves admired a range of strategies men employed to express their discontent. "They had to be quiet wid him to get him to work. He would run to the woods. He was a fast runner," T. W. Cotton said of his father. Callie Elder claimed her grandfather "was so bad 'bout runnin' 'way Marse Billy made him wear long old horns," and Ellis Jefson credited his father with "a wild animal instinct," because the authorities "couldn't keep him out of the woods. He would spend two or three days back in there." Chronic truants remained enslaved, but their behavior disrupted the smooth functioning of plantations. The children of these men viewed being "wild," or the ability to survive beyond the plantation, as a positive trait that gave men a form of bargaining power. Richard Johnson's father regularly ran away and hid in a tree, refusing to come down even if treed by bloodhounds and the master threatened to shoot him. "Go ahead and shoot. You be de loser," he responded. Johnson claimed his father only relented when promised he would not be whipped and his son learned to employ similar tactics. "Dat wuz de way my daddy would hide when he would run away," he said of his own strategy.[31] A father who habitually spent time in hiding demonstrated his resistance to slavery at the same time that he necessarily removed himself from his family. Johnson's imitation indicates that a father might influence his children through behavior that limited his contact with them.

Children applauded their enslaved fathers' rebelliousness, and their distance from the events, and the fact that many had not witnessed such behavior firsthand, contributed to this stance. Walter Rimm recalled the dread his father's defiant behavior induced. "Ise sees my father git one whuppin'. 'Twarnt nothin' Ise could does 'cept stand dere an' cry." Seeing a parent flogged was traumatic. Nonetheless, as Rimm acknowledged the anxiety he felt every time his father ran away, he praised his father's fearlessness. Rimm mentioned another slave who was so afraid of a whipping he killed himself, contrasting this man with his father. "My father warn't 'fraid of nothin'," he proudly declared.[32] Men who ran, who refused to be whipped, and who fought back, all caused stress for their family members even if and as their loved ones celebrated such audacity.

While some enslaved men pursued a masculine identity through open or limited resistance, others focused on providing for family. David Doddington explores masculine identity tied to work and industriousness. According to Doddington, "Limited economic success led some black men to deliberately reject acts of rebellion against slavery." As an example, he discusses Israel Campbell, who worked within the system to pursue self-purchase, escaped only after being betrayed and sold, and then "stressed his desire to buy his family rather than encourage insurrection." This overlooks the fact that Campbell returned to a slave state intending to steal his three children out of slavery, and only when that risky endeavor failed did he opt to raise money to try to buy their freedom. In addition, the broader sweep of Campbell's life shows that he engaged in rebellious behavior as a youth before family life led to a period of stability. After Campbell ran away with several compatriots to deliberately ruin the master's crop, he was captured, jailed, and sold. In his new home, he took a fancy to a young woman and focused on courtship, marriage, and fatherhood. Campbell "took great pleasure" in his baby son and "was now as happy as I thought it possible to be in this world." The infant, named for Campbell's older brother, fell ill and died just before turning one, and Campbell lost his first wife shortly thereafter. In his anguish, Campbell resolved to become a better Christian in order to reunite with his departed loved ones.[33] "Rather than a dichotomy in which total rejection of slavery proved manhood while accommodation equaled emasculation," Doddington writes of multiple routes to masculinity, noting "hard work allowed enslaved men to prove manhood in a different form." However, family seems to have been the factor that most compelled men to compromise with their condition of bondage. Enslaved and formerly enslaved people praised hard work because industry and economic success enabled men to care for their dependents.[34]

While I agree with Doddington's assessment that enslaved men pursued a range of masculine identities and forged different paths to survival within slavery, these identities were not always distinct from one another. Enslaved men might also move through different identities, values, and priorities based on age, life-stage, context, and circumstance.[35] Caretakers prioritized their family roles, but that did not mean they always eschewed defiant behavior. Right before explaining his father's penchant for refusing to be whipped and fighting back against masters and overseers, Sterling Brown described him as a "boss mechanic" with a range of skills, "carpenter, blacksmith, wheelwright, and general utility man. So proficient was he in many ways that he was nicknamed and always called 'Handy.'" Given the opportunity, men could use their skills and ingenuity to seek freedom. Reverend C. W. B. Gordon's family escaped from North Carolina to Union lines in Virginia during the war, crossing a river in a dugout canoe his father fashioned from a tree. "This was a remarkable think for him to do," his son explained. "He used a broad ax and add [adz]. You see, you would have to have a good amount of mechanical ideas to know how to do this."[36] Children who respected and loved their fathers wanted to see them embody key attributes of masculinity, and when able they discussed a combination of admirable traits.

Other informants focused on and took pride in their fathers' skills and accomplishments. Skilled slaves often had greater value and increased privileges, including permission to travel and work on other plantations. If allowed to hire out, they could earn extra income enabling men to prosper within slavery and materially provision their kin. "He studied hard and became one of de bes' shoemakers in de state," Lorenzo Ivy said of his father. Ivy's father eventually hired his own time in Virginia and after the war set up his own shop.[37] Because skill could be conflated with class, pride in a father's talents may at times have reflected a sense of status and superiority.[38] Having a skill or trade offered greater opportunity to provide for one's family during and after slavery, and formerly enslaved people appreciated a combination of skill and determination in their fathers that enabled men to succeed and provide within slavery. A good father used his strength, ingenuity, and skill to model self-respect and to care for his family.

Children, especially male informants, were often most impressed by their fathers' mechanical versatility and the superior quality and enduring nature of the work they produced. "I was crazy to be as good a mason as my Daddy was," Neal Upson said of his choice of trade. "In Lexin'ton dere is a rock wall still standin' 'round a whole square what Daddy built in slavery time." John Elliott referred to his father as "the most highly prized Negro in the vicinity. He was a natural carpenter and builder. Often he would go to the woods and pick out trees for the job in hand. Some of the houses he built there are standing today."[39] Implicit in the commentary of children was the idea that their fathers, though enslaved, could outperform all others, including the slaveholders who depended on unfree labor.

William Heard commended his father's strength, skill, industriousness, and intellect. "He was a blacksmith by trade, and while he weighed only one hundred and forty pounds, he could use a sledge hammer as steadily and actively as a man weighing two hundred pounds, and shoe as many mules as any blacksmith in the county." He lacked formal education and "did not know figures at all, yet he could give a bill for lumber as accurately as a master mathematician." Nat Love referred to his father as "a man of strong determination, not easily discouraged, and always pushing forward and upward, quick to learn things and slow to forget them, a keen observer." Former slaves respected men who, despite being unschooled, learned quickly and thereby defied the intellectual deprivation of enslavement. David Doddington argues that informants who appreciated their fathers' efforts as providers adopted slaveholders' "discourse of industry and energy," but also employed such "rhetoric to highlight the abuses and hypocrisy of enslavers," attributing enslaved men's achievements to their own "hard work, honesty, or responsibility, rather than paternalistic benevolence."[40]

Henry Gladney's evaluation of his father, William, combined the themes of physical strength and skill, and touched on limited rebelliousness. "Pappy was-called 'Bill de Giant,' 'cause him was so big and strong," he stated. "They have mighty bad plantation roads in them days. I see my pappy git under de wagon once when it was bogged up to de hub and lift and heft dat wagon and set it outside de ruts." As a blacksmith, William made and fixed a range of tools, and his position and skills enabled him to take some behavioral risks, including guarding his wife against the sexual encroachment of and fighting with other enslaved men, and avoiding a flogging by threatening to run away. The master relented for fear of losing his blacksmith. Similarly, Eugenia Weatherall called her father "as smart as they make them" and a gifted worker who could manufacture a range of items and tools. "He wasn't scared of nothing either. He never was afraid of the overseers whipping him cause he was known to be the best shot any where in the country and they was scared if they hurt him he would get them."[41] Skills or a trade generated profit for the slaveholder and increased a man's value, and gave him some leverage, allowing some to push back against the institution that quantified skill in market terms. Even in the absence of skill, physical strength had similar paradoxical qualities in that it both increased a man's value as a slave and gave him the wherewithal to be able to fight back, which could then decrease his market value and yet inflate his stature in the eyes of his kin and community. Neither of these men engaged in dramatic, heroic resistance, but their children presented them as skilled, industrious, and fearless within the confines of slavery.

Some formerly enslaved people commented on a different type of talent, remembering their fathers and grandfathers as herb doctors and practitioners of conjure and emphasizing healing skills and spiritual authority. The services of Gus Smith's grandfather, "an old fashioned herb doctor," were in high demand in the white and black community. "Lots of cases dat other doctors gave up, he went and raised them. He could cure anything." In addition to achieving literacy, George Bollinger mentioned his father's otherworldly aptitude. "My pappy wuz a smart man. He could read and write," he related. "An' he had de power, my daddy did. He cud break a 'Hoodoo' spell, an' he cud tell things dat happened wen he diden see it."[42] As with accounts of mechanical skills, ex-slaves relished the idea that oppressed people excelled in their chosen trade, gained knowledge, and outperformed those with education and advantages.

In addition to masculine identity tied to work, David Doddington discusses enslaved men in trustee positions. Although such roles often made these men unpopular and placed them at odds with the rebels, trustees derived a sense of masculine identity and self-worth from their positions. Enslaved people linked physical strength to authority and saw authority as proof of manliness. While always subordinate to the white power structure, trustees "held a degree of autonomy and independence not available to others in bondage." Enslaved men had different responses to such roles, with some attempting to support the community, while others were "motivated by the psychological benefits of superiority as much as material gain." Access to resources enabled them to use trustee positions to achieve the masculine role of provider/protector, which then exacerbated community divisions.[43] Whereas Doddington emphasizes positive recollections of male trustees as "patriarchal figureheads," I believe children had mixed reactions to such men. Trustees regularly had the power to discipline, and Doddington calls "the use of violence against other slaves . . . the most controversial aspect of managerial roles." As a form of justification, some trustees "refashioned their activities in upholding bondage as evidence of their virtue as honest and honorable men." Children, he argues, similarly rationalized their fathers' violence in disciplining other slaves and saw such positions as a sign of their father's "talent and skill."[44]

When men used their authority and privileges to support their family, even at the expense of the broader community, children praised their fathers as providers.[45] When men behaved selfishly, or when they turned violence on family members, children expressed ambivalence or criticized these men. Informants thus discussed the advantages of their fathers' roles as well as the more problematic outcomes. Nancy Williams had positive and negative things to say about her father, a "big strong" and also "mean" man with "plenty temper" who defied and nearly killed the overseer. The master then dismissed the overseer and installed Williams's father in that position due to his reputation as an industrious worker with "plenty sense." She appreciated her father as a provider and his access to money as the plantation banker, which eased slavery for her family. However, she also candidly detailed his extreme reaction to her abrogation of his authority. Williams once stole money from her father, and as he prepared to beat her and counseled her to admit her sin or suffer eternal damnation, she lied. Her father then carried her to the meat house, hung her in a guano bag, smoked her with a pile of burning tobacco, and "whup me somepin awful." When the other slaves heard her yelling and crowded around, he warned them about theft, threatening to kill anyone who disobeyed. Williams's narrative revolved around her religious faith, a trait she shared with her father, and which his severity reinforced. Fearing for her soul, Williams stopped lying and "never stole from nobody else," after this experience. While her father dominated her memory of family, and it is clear she respected and feared him, she was ambivalent about him, a feeling compounded by the fact that her family initially prospered and then suffered economically in the postwar period after he died. Although Williams's father provided materially and he taught her a valuable lesson about honesty, he does not emerge from the narrative as an affectionate or beloved man. Williams benefited from her father's accommodation, but when she identified heroic behavior within slavery, she looked elsewhere, discussing the torture, death, and defiance of a devout enslaved man on a neighboring plantation.[46]

Robert Young offered a mixed evaluation of his father, a man who served as a driver, helped whip the other slaves, and earned special privileges, including access to whisky. Young described his father's manly size and strength, and identified him as the only slave on the plantation allowed to work his own patch and sell the proceeds. Yet he never mentioned his father buying provisions or treats for his family, only that he sold his cotton "fo' hisself." Young's father accompanied the master to war and returned home with another woman expecting to keep two wives, whereupon his mother "run him an' de gal off an' we didn't never heah no mo' from him atter that." While Young was impressed with his father's masculinity and status on the plantation, he did not portray him as a good father, but rather as an individualist who appears to have shown minimal concern for his family.[47]

If rebellious fathers won widespread admiration, commentary on men complicit in the institution of slavery was far more varied. Jeptha Choice noted that on his plantation the black driver was called "'nigger traitor' behin' his back," an attitude that could influence childrens' feelings about fathers who occupied positions of authority within the plantation hierarchy. Sarah Benjamin said little about her father, but pointed out that he served as a driver and "done all de whippin." Because her mother died and "my daddy didnt try to get me back," after emancipation, thereby failing as a protector, Benjamin was indentured, achieving freedom only when she ran away at age sixteen. Former slaves often found it difficult to identify with a man who represented the power structure of slavery. Writing in the late nineteenth century, Peter Randolph had complicated memories of his father, a driver on a neighboring plantation. During weekly visits, "my father would often tell my mother how the white overseer had made him cruelly whip his fellows, until the blood ran down to the ground. All his days, he had to follow this dreadful employment of flogging men, women, and children, being placed in this helpless condition by the tyranny of his master." Randolph continued, "I used to think very hard of my father, and that he was a very cruel man; but when I knew that he could not help himself, I could not but alter my views and feelings in regard to his conduct." When Randolph was about ten years old, his father died, and while he did not specify when his feelings shifted, age and experience with slavery probably offered perspective, enabling Randolph to better understand his father and the constraints he faced.[48]

Mose Davis, speaking to an African American interviewer, denounced his father's affiliation with slaveholders at the expense of his own kin. "My daddy was so crazy about the white folks and the horses he drove until I believe he thought more of them than he did of me." Davis "was made to live in his father's cabin," but expressed a preference for and desire to live with his field hand mother and siblings, who had a separate cabin. Martin Jackson "rebelled" against slavery and his father's accommodating attitude. Jackson constantly ruminated on escape. "I could have done it easy, but my old father used to say, 'No use running from bad to worse, hunting better.' Lots of colored boys did escape and joined the Union army, and there are plenty of them today still drawing a pension for deserting the Confederacy." Jackson's father was aware of his son's hesitation and "would rub my fears in deeper."[49] If he believed he protected his son from potential death while "always counseling" him, he certainly failed to promote his son's self-determination. Jackson's feelings about his father were tied up with his regrets over his own indecision and weakness in the face of danger. Unlike former slaves who honored fathers for inspiring defiance and hope for freedom, discussed in the following chapter, Jackson resented his father's compliance with the institution of slavery.

Although far more former slaves had no memory of or positive things to say about their fathers, they readily expressed disappointment or hostility when a man failed as a caretaker. Criticism of enslaved and formerly enslaved fathers reinforces the qualities children most appreciated and their vision of a father's basic duties. Henry Jenkins and his brother spurned their father's name after he "took up wid another woman after freedom, and my brother and me was shame of him." Sexual arrangements during slavery could be excused, but children were less forgiving in freedom and based on the impact such behavior had on their own family. Thomas Cole, likewise, rejected the name of his "bad hornery no count" father. He indicated that his father was a womanizer, but never fully explained why he disliked the man. Jane Sutton distanced herself from her father during and after slavery. "He jest come on Saddy night and we don't see much of him. We called him 'dat man.' Our mammy tol us we ought to be more respectful to him cause he wuz our daddy, but we don't keer nothin' bout him. He never did bring us no candy or nothing." Limited contact enforced by an abroad marriage may have contributed to her feelings, but she indicated that he made no effort to win the affection of his family and he failed to provide even tri-fling gifts, one consistent expectation of a visiting father. After emancipa-tion, her father came to collect her and when she refused to leave, he had the sheriff intervene. Sutton ran away twice and returned to her mother and siblings, who lived with her former mistress. Sutton clearly disliked her father and wanted to live with her mother. A song Sutton included in her interview, "Husband Don't You 'Buse Me," offers a potential clue, sug-gesting that her antipathy stemmed from domestic abuse.[50] For the for-merly enslaved, a poor father was abusive, neglectful, and/or avoided his duty to provide for and protect his family, traits associated with slaveholders. As Christopher Morris notes, "Surviving recollections of violent husbands and fathers are unrelentingly negative. A violent mother could represent opposition to male authority—patriarchy—and thus to slavery. A violent father or husband, however, recalled the master."[51]

Several informants condemned their fathers' physical violence. George and Steve Weathersby both mentioned their father's harsh treatment of his kin. "He wuz mean to us chillun an' 'specially to ma. He made hit powerfully hard on us all," George recalled, noting that his mother worked all day and then endured abuse at night. Their mother returned to a former master to escape her husband, and not surprisingly, the couple remained separated after freedom.[52] Zenie Cauley admired her industrious preacher father and disparaged his postwar replacement. When her father died, her mother re-married "that man," who beat the children and "wouldn't let us go to school. Had to work and just live like pigs." Similarly, Callie Shepard noted, "I had my tribulations after my ol' dada die. He was good to us little childer," working in his spare time to earn extra money. "But my nex' dada was a man mighty rough on us."[53] Both women criticized abusive stepfathers who failed as providers in freedom, comparing them to diligent, caring enslaved men.

Paternalism

Slave communities' understanding of fatherhood and paternal duty shaped slaves and ex-slaves' response to the ideology of paternalism. According to Eugene Genovese, planter paternalism "protected both masters and slaves from the worst tendencies inherent in their respective conditions." Geno-vese argued for the existence of a precapitalist world in which planters treated their slaves as extended family and "paternalism created a tendency for the slaves to identify with a particular community through identifica-tion with its master." Historians have since rejected this understanding of master/slave relations, pointing out that white Southerners adhered to a paternalist ideology but they were not paternalists in their behavior, in that they were motivated by profit rather than altruism. Paternalistic ideology provided a set of rationalizations and enabled whites to deceive themselves into believing that their self-serving actions were a form of benevolence toward their perceived dependents. Walter Johnson refers to slaveholder paternalism as "a way of imagining, describing, and justifying slavery rather than a direct reflection of underlying social relations."[54] Paternalism, a component of and like masculinity, had a public definition that applied only to white men. Paternalism and masculinity shaped slaveholders' self-conception, and both qualities involved a public performance that masked the actual conduct of masters and slaves within the institution of slavery.

Whites publicly erased paternal control by African American men, but enslaved people respected fatherhood in their own way. "We called our fathers 'daddy' in slavery time," Jerry Hinton stated. "Dey would not let slaves call deir fathers 'father.'"[55] The "father" of the plantation was the slaveholder. Slaveholders conceived of and defined themselves as father figures, but for formerly enslaved people, a good master was one who behaved like a father, upholding paternalism in his actions and not just his rhetoric. "I loved him as well as I did my daddy," James McLean said of his former owner. "He taught me to be honest, to tell the truth, and not to steal anything." Betty Bormer claimed that the ex-slaves from her plantation mourned the death of their kind master shortly after emancipation. "All us cullud fo'ks cry like 'twas our pappy dat am daid. He was de blessed man." Similarly, Andrew Moody likened a good master to a biological parent: "Cunnel Floyd he treat us good as if he's us father 'r' mother. No we didn' suffer no 'buse."[56] Just as a parent was supposed to care for their children, a benevolent master eschewed abuse. Rather than directly call a master father, all three individuals expressed their appreciation by comparing how they felt about their master to how they felt about their own father. A good master approximated, but did not replace, a black father.

The highest commendation for a slaveholder was to compare him to one's actual father and to imply that he achieved the vision of paternal duty valued and privately practiced by slave communities. Calvin Moye referred to his Georgia master as "one of the best men that ever breathed." Moye considered his parents "lucky ter be with a good Maser . . . and gets to keeps der chilluns and raise dem." His parents raised all seven of their children "under the same Maser." Furthermore, when their owner died, "we all cried bout him dyin like we would had he been our own daddy." A good master avoided separating enslaved families, allowed parents to raise their own children, and inspired comparison to a biological parent because he actually cared for his slaves. Former slaves' statements were calculated to appeal to white fieldworkers, and yet they managed to appropriately praise slaveholders and subtly prioritize and elevate their own fathers and conception of paternal duty. Catherine Stewart argues that FWP informants, when constrained by the presence of a white Southern interviewer, found ways to "tell a free story within the confines of the master narrative." As Stewart notes, "They hid in plain sight." These examples show how ex-slaves "turned the racial hierarchy of the Lost Cause on its head," with "strategic counternarratives" that their audience did not understand.[57] Informants signaled who and what values were important to them. They simultaneously paid lip service to paternalism while actually elevating their own fathers and their community's vision of honorable manhood.

While the FWP respondents, interviewed in the Jim Crow South, felt compelled to commend their former owners, antebellum fugitives with greater latitude to speak their minds at times expressed affection for former masters. David West, interviewed in Canada, called slavery a "disgrace" and slaveholding an affront to God that could not be justified according to his reading of the Bible, but he admitted that he "loved" his master. He saw his master as a "good" man, but he did not go so far as to compare him to a father. Instead, he condemned paternalistic rationalization as a form of inherited sin. "It is a common remark that they have a right to hold the slaves, because they were given them by their fathers, —justifying their own sins by those of their fathers: would it excuse them for stealing or drinking, to say that their fathers were thieves and drunkards?" Other fugitives dismissed paternalistic attachments. "There never can be any affinity of feeling between master and slave, except in some few isolated cases," Charles Ball concluded.[58] Because slaveholders saw their slaves as property and a financial investment and good fathers saw their children as human beings and an emotional investment, in the minds of former slaves the two roles seldom overlapped.

When slaves developed fondness for their masters, they did so because those owners upheld the vision of fatherhood prized by the slave community. Israel Campbell initially viewed his master with affection and chose to pursue self-purchase rather than to escape. "We were more like father and son than master and servant. He would most always consult me about his general business, and I would always ask his advice of whatever I was about to do." This relationship soured when the slaveholder, falsely believing

Campbell intended to escape, had him jailed. "I had strong thoughts about taking old master's life, or injuring him in some way, for the wrong he had done me; but the good spirit always got the better of such designs and always thwarted my plans." Richard Allen's master had qualms about slavery and allowed him to purchase his freedom. "He was what the world called a good master. He was more like a father to his slaves than any thing else." Ex-slaves defined a good master as one who approximated their vision of a good father, a man who provided for and protected his dependents. When Allen and his brother bought their freedom, "We left our master's house, and I may truly say it was like leaving our father's house. . . . I had it often impressed upon my mind that I should one day enjoy my freedom; for slavery is a bitter pill, notwithstanding we had a good master."[59] For slaves and former slaves, the ultimate gift a father could provide was freedom, so a father-like master was one who enabled slaves to achieve liberty, something that happened only rarely.

Not surprisingly, individuals most likely to refer to a former owner as a father were those who had been emancipated. Liberians writing to their former owners sometimes addressed their letters to "Dear Father." One man expressed gratitude that he had ended up "in the hands of one who has been a father to me instead of a cruel possessor. When I was young and foolish you took me . . . from my father and mother into your own dwelling and brought me up as a Son instead of a servant. I ofton thought hard of it at the time but now I find it was for my own benefit," he wrote, noting that his master taught him the value of "truth and honesty." It should be noted, however, that because they had relatives and friends still in slavery, manumitted Liberians had an incentive to maintain positive relations with their former owners and these letters likely contained a performative aspect. Lewis Chambers served as the headman on a Maryland plantation and eventually bought his own liberty. After living for a time in the North, he reassessed his attitudes toward his former owner and felt he better understood the condition of slaves. Though he had once "thought more of him than I did of my own father," he came to resent the fact that his master had "deceived me. He used to reason me out of going to see my own father."[60] Slaves did occasionally identify with their owners, an outcome achieved by removing individuals from the influence of their kin and separating them from contact with the culture and values of their neighborhood and community.

If a father's most important roles were caretaker, provider, and protector, a consummate father gave his children freedom. "I feel that Abraham

Lincoln was a father to us," Reverend Squire Dowd declared. "We consider him thus because he freed us." During the war, a freedman echoed this sentiment, telling Northern teacher Laura Towne, "Lincoln died for we, Christ died for we, and me believe he de same mans."[61] Ex-slaves attributed their spiritual freedom to Christ, and some attributed their political freedom to Lincoln. Slaves' conception of paternal duty and provisioning meant that few masters lived up to their ideal of fatherhood, because few were true caretakers. Walter Johnson discusses slaves' attempts to manipulate paternalistic promises to forestall sale and separation, arguing that such appeals "implied no internalization of slaveholder paternalism."[62] Paternalistic attachment on the part of slaves was uncommon because slaveholding violated slaves' definition of honorable manhood and paternal duty. Masters imagined and described themselves as father figures, but they did not act as such. When assessing fatherhood, former slaves cared about moral integrity and actual behavior rather than rhetoric and overt power.

IN THEIR INTERVIEWS AND MEMOIRS, formerly enslaved people discussed a range of commendable traits, strategies of survival, and expressions of masculinity in their fathers and grandfathers, sometimes assessing these men from firsthand experience and sometimes based on stories they heard from others. Children of men who died in slavery were more likely to relate anecdotes of dramatic resistance, whereas children of men who outlived slavery told stories that combined aspects of more limited resistance and caretaking. Others focused on their father as a masculine provider. In their evaluation of their fathers, former slaves revealed how much the institution of slavery shaped their conceptions of paternal duty. Informants' celebration of their fathers drew on the experience of bondage, emphasizing rebelliousness, physical strength, skill, industriousness, intelligence, and, above all, a willingness to care for and support family. This vision mirrored American definitions of manhood, and yet in their criticism of failed fathers, former slaves articulated shared values rooted in the African American experience that diverged from the dominant culture. In the eyes of ex-slaves, a bad father acted like a slaveholder. A good father was the opposite of the immoral, abusive, and selfish slaveholder. He provided for his kin and cared for his dependents.

CHAPTER THREE

Blasphemous Doctrine for a Slave to Teach
Provisioning

In 1864, in the midst of the Civil War, runaway slave John Dennis wrote to Secretary of War Edwin Stanton. Dennis had reached Union lines, and he asked for assistance freeing his children. After losing his wife, possibly to sale, Dennis was the sole parent of "three Children and I being a Slave At the time Could Not do Anny thing for the poor little Children for my master. . . . Carry me some forty mile from them So I Could Not do for them and the man that they live with half feed them and half Cloth them & beat them like dogs & when I was admited to go see them it use to brake my heart." Dennis politely requested help securing his family, listing the names of the white men who held them. "I want to get the little Children out of Slavery," he concluded, noting his ambition to then "rase a Shool" to educate them.[1] Hired out, separated, allowed only occasional visits, and unable to properly care for his children, Dennis's letter nonetheless reveals his aspirational conception of his role and his condemnation of slaveholder paternalism. When slavery fractured the household and family, men like Dennis adapted by attempting to serve as primary caretaker, a responsibility he took seriously. He lamented his inability to feed and clothe his children and shield them from abuse. The onset of war enabled Dennis to express hope that he could give his children the ultimate good a father could offer: freedom. In a short letter, Dennis enumerated the wide range of resources, emotional, material, and ideological, that enslaved men wanted to provide for their children.

A good father provided for his family. For enslaved fathers, provisioning came in numerous forms, including straightforward material resources, such as food and clothing, or less tangible goods such as advice and spiritual counsel. Often unable to provision in a direct manner, a role appropriated (though not always upheld) by the slaveholder, enslaved men found ways to support their children that involved intangibles, ideological and cultural goods over which the master, despite efforts at complete dominance, exerted little control. Enslaved men, lacking overt authority, engaged in covert caretaking. Their influence over their children was often subtle, indirect, and hidden from the dominant society.

Material Provisioning

Lawrence McDonnell, Kathleen Hilliard, Dylan Penningroth, David Doddington, and Jeff Forret have highlighted the contradictions of the informal economy. While licit and illicit economic activity offered some advantages and could serve as a form of individual defiance of paternalism, market participation also further enmeshed enslaved people in bondage and created material and status disparities in the quarters that incited internal conflict and undermined community cohesion. Because "masters restricted slaves' access to time much more than they restricted their access to land," Penningroth defines the slave economy as "an economy of time."[2] The centrality of time magnified the importance of kinship, and enslaved people accumulated property through their social networks.

Enslaved families worked collectively, using the economic opportunities available to them, which varied regionally and locally, to supplement rations, earn extra cash, and accumulate property.[3] Some kin groups fared better than others, a function of demographics as well as work ethic. Individuals without a strong family network, especially single mothers with young children and orphans, fared the worst.[4] Henrietta King's mistress tempted the undernourished orphan with a piece of candy and then beat her so viciously when she took the bait that she suffered permanent impairment. "I was hungry," King recalled. "Ain't had a father workin' in de fiel' like some of de chillun to bring me eats—had jes' little pieces of scrapback each mornin' throwed at me from de kitchen." King associated her hunger with her lack of a social network, wishing she had a father to provide for her and offer basic protection. Slaves without family connections faced heightened material and social deprivation.[5]

Historians have documented enslaved men's efforts to materially support kin and defined the provider role as one of the key models of masculine identity across the South. Bondmen had greater access to activities that enabled them to obtain, produce, or trade for resources, and greater opportunity to earn cash for skilled labor because such labor was defined as men's work, whereas women's work, even when it involved considerable skill, was defined as domestic labor and devalued.[6] Within the quarters, enslaved men and women had gendered expectations of female domesticity and dependency, and male provisioning and authority over households. Despite the difficulties and often impossibility of putting such beliefs into practice, David Doddington argues that enslaved people believed "men *should* be economic figureheads if possible, and this was important to their gendered sense of self."[7]

Enslaved people viewed provisioning as a male responsibility even as women made critical, often more substantial, contributions to family subsistence.[8]

During slavery, an attentive father provisioned his family materially, obtaining extra food and clothing, and manufacturing household items, efforts that earned respect from children and the broader community.[9] Informants recalled resident and coresident fathers contributing to basic subsistence and supplying resources withheld by slaveholders. Dr. Solomon Hicks saw his father only once every two weeks, and yet emphasized his dedication to family. "My father was one of the unsung heroes as he labored this way for forty-seven long years to secure a little for his family. He was a basketmaker and would work far into the night," Hicks said of his father's nearly five decades in slavery. Enslaved men without a way to earn income provided with their own labor. "My Pa uster come evy Sadday evenin' to chop wood out uv de wood lot and pile up plenty fur Ma till he come agin," Nancy Settles remembered. "On Wensday evenin' pa uster come after he been huntin' and bring in possum and coon. He sho could get 'em a plenty." Settles's father, visiting the South Carolina cotton plantation twice a week, provided extra calories in the form of meat, as well as the means by which her mother cooked plantation rations and heated the cabin. Across the South, enslaved men took advantage of available opportunities to contribute to their kin and households.[10]

Fathers with the skill and wherewithal to hunt earned particular praise across the South because they supplemented bland rations and their children were less likely to go hungry.[11] Hunting was an activity that boys could share with their fathers. "My daddy used to hunt rabbits and possums. I went with him and would ride on his back with my feet in his pockets," George Henderson recalled. In order to hunt, however, men needed skill, time, and permission, meaning that those with especially demanding masters were less likely to engage in such activity. John Jackson's father built a pen to trap wild turkeys and Jackson constructed a fish trap, but the slaveholder destroyed these contraptions, arguing fish and fowl were "too good for niggers." Access to hunting varied by master rather than by region and, when allowed, enabled men to substantially augment the caloric intake of their family and community. Nicholas Proctor argues that in hunting and sharing game, enslaved men "assumed the patriarchal mantle of provider," and engaged in a "surreptitious usurpation of slaveholder power."[12]

Informants spoke fondly of fathers who used their earnings to treat their children. Julia Frances Daniels grew up in Georgia and contrasted the material deprivation of the postwar period with her father's provisioning during slavery. "We goes on about the same," she said of freedom, "'cept they dont never seem to be no money like when my pa used to take a chicken to the town and bring back sweets and little bright things for us chilluns." Archie Fennels's father was allowed to keep the proceeds of his garden plot on a Texas farm. "My daddy he go in to town an' buy marbles an' t'ings. Sometime' he 'low us to hab a li'l money," Fennels remembered. "One time us buy 15 cents wuth of pep'mint candy." Mose Smith also grew up in Texas, but lived apart from his father. Smith similarly recalled that "Father worked out for extra money and every Saturday night he come over and give each of us children a nickel."[13] Smith and his siblings bought candy or a tin of sardines in town. All of these informants recalled being well provisioned with food and/or clothing by their masters, enabling their fathers to save or use extra money for small indulgences. Although slaves could not legally own property, modest accumulation through the informal economy was widespread, and enslaved people protected their claims with public pronouncements and display.[14] Giving or spending small amounts of cash on children enabled men to signal their paternal engagement and publicly perform, within the quarters, their masculine role as provider.

A man in an abroad marriage felt it his duty to arrive for his visits with offerings for his family, an expectation broadly shared by slave communities. "Papa would come home on Saturdays an' he would bring food wid him," George White recalled of his Virginia childhood. Delia Barclay's father visited his family in Texas once a week, and "alays brung sumpthin' fo' all he little shavers w'en he come t' stay ober Sattidy night 'n' Sunday. He brung us sweet 'taters 'n' sweet gum t' chew like chewin' gum is now." Parke Johnston told his interviewer that abroad husbands in Virginia spent the week amassing gifts, and when a man had kind owners "sometimes contributions were levied on all the white family." Johnston earned extra cash and assisted fellow slaves whose parsimonious masters and overseers left them with little means to provision their family. "He always brought us some little present, such as the means of a poor slave would allow—apples, melons, sweet potatoes, or, if he could procure nothing else, a little parched corn, which tasted better in our cabin, because he had brought it," Charles Ball wrote of his father's Saturday night visits in Maryland.[15] Abroad fathers brought treats or luxury items not included in plantation rations. While these men did not substantially feed their kin, their children appreciated the effort, seeing such gifts as an expression of their fathers' affection.

Even men who rarely or never saw their family members attempted to provision and acknowledge their children in whatever way they could. Katie

Phoenix was sold away from her parents as a child, but her father lived nearby: "My father made shoes. He would send mine over to me." Ida Fluker rarely saw her father, and while she had little to say about him as a person, she had a distinct memory of his gifts. "Every Christmas they let him come to see mama, and he'd bring me and my sister a red dress buttoned in the back," she recalled. "I 'member it same as if 'twas yesterday 'cause I was crazy 'bout them red dresses."[16] Both of these fathers, one in Texas and the other in Alabama, unable to provide food or other support, tried to help clothe their children.

Slaves risked punishment by stealing food to augment meager rations, and men felt particular social pressure to resort to theft to care for kin. Whereas enslaved people stridently censured and policed theft from one another, they morally sanctioned theft from the master, which represented a response to need, form of resistance, and illicit market activity.[17] Informants' stories incorporating theft reveal how those ex-slaves often blurred the lines between different forms of admirable masculine activity, preferring to remember their fathers as resisters and providers. Sarah Ford's father, a chronic truant, stole his own body and labor and then provisioned his family while in hiding, sneaking home at night to leave food and clothing for his wife and daughter, a form of reverse theft. A skilled tanner, he hid with a German family and "he tans hides on de sly like, an' day feeds him an' lots of mawnin's when we opens de door of our cabin, on a shelf jes' above de door is food for mamma an' me an sometime store clothes. No one knows whar it come from an' no one see papa, but dere de stuff was." Though the authorities believed her mother was feeding her runaway father when they caught him with "meat and stuff," Patsey Southwell, also raised in Texas, disagreed. "I t'ink it the other way, I t'ink he was gittin' and sen'in' her stuff."[18] These women celebrated fathers who combined resistance with caretaking. Though the actual direction of exchange remained murky, Southwell assumed her father continued to provision even after running away, which suggests that children who loved their fathers wanted to see them embody multiple masculine roles.

Ford's narrative mentions all of the masculine traits admired by children—resistance, ingenuity, skill, industry and success in work, providing, and protecting. Because her father "had spirit," he was regularly punished, but he was never sold due to his reputation as the best tanner in the area. He repeatedly ran away, evaded tracking dogs, and according to Ford could have escaped to freedom. Yet love of family always brought him back. Ford contrasted her father's heroism, even within the confines of slavery, to the actions of "Uncle Big Jake," an enslaved driver. "One time durin' night time he brung mamma an' me a dress," Ford said of another clandestine visit. Angered by this blow to his authority, Uncle Jake threatened to whip Ford's mother, "iffen she don't tell him whar papa is at." Ford's mother insisted she had no idea, and her husband returned just in time to save her from being flogged. He then spent three days in chains and was tortured with hot grease, leaving permanent scars on his back, during which time his wife gave birth to a second child.[19] Provider and rebel were not mutually exclusive identities.

As Dylan Penningroth notes, the informal economy "directly boosted the formal economy of the plantation, and that is why so many masters allowed it." Offering economic incentives to slaves served as a management tool, saved money, and increased profits. Masters' inadequate provisioning shifted some of the burden and expense of feeding and clothing their human property to their own slaves and those of their neighbors. "The slaves' economy did much for African Americans, but it also helped prop up the white-dominated formal sector while offering little chance of transforming Southern society as a whole," Penningroth writes. Slaves could not legally own property or access credit, and they struggled to gain more time, the commodity they most needed to amass property. This led to "painfully slow, incremental accumulation," which "suited masters just fine because masters were only interested in reducing their expenses, not in seeing their slaves become wealthy."[20]

As enslavers demonstrated the hypocrisy of paternalism, caretakers attempted to provide for wives and children denied adequate material resources.[21] When slaveholders stinted rations, fathers felt increased pressure to provide for their kin. Doing so taxed their resources and ingenuity, but enabled them to feel morally superior to slaveholders. Lunsford Lane's wife, sold to a new owner in North Carolina, received insufficient food and clothing and "now I was compelled to draw from my slender resources to make up what was deficient." Despite the professed religiosity of the new master, he worked his slaves tirelessly and barely fed them. "Almost every article of clothing worn either by my wife or children, especially every article of much value, I had to purchase, while the food he furnished the family amounted to less than a meal a day," Lane remarked. "So that, both as to food and clothing, I had in fact to support both my wife and the children, while he claimed them as his property and received all their labor."[22] Lane's union is an excellent example of an abroad marriage and multilocal family network in which the husband amply provided. Although Lane and his wife lived in separate households, he largely fed and clothed his family.

Slaveholders benefited from the labor of their own or other men's slaves when enslaved husbands provisioned their family members. Writing and reminiscing from the viewpoint of freedom in the antebellum North, Lane identified himself as the better provider, a mark of nineteenth-century masculine duty, and yet he underscored how the unfairness of the situation further trapped him in bondage. Being a good husband and father threatened to deprive him of the chance to earn liberty. Lane hoped to purchase his own freedom, and the need to spend his "scanty earnings" supporting his family undermined that goal. "Dark despair possessed my soul, respecting my freedom," he recalled. "I was a slave, a husband, the father of two children, a family looking up to me for bread . . . and I penniless." Acting as a devoted father and husband meant deferring his own desire for freedom because his labor, and that of his wife and children, profited a slaveholder who privately abrogated paternalistic duty.[23]

The institution of slavery deprived enslaved men of their manhood in multiple ways, as the economic greed of slaveholders shaped their interactions with and treatment of their labor force. A particularly tightfisted master, in his drive to economize, often set up a situation in which male slaves could outdo him. Masters might consider themselves the paternalistic authority, but former slaves subtly mocked them by pointing out that slaveholders failed to support the women and children supposedly in their care. When slave narratives discussed provisioning, they often implicitly posed the question: Who was the better man? The lowly slave who attempted to care for his kin and neighbors after long hours of toil for another, or the self-important master who starved his charges? Lunsford Lane identified the catch-22 slavery imposed on bondmen. Being a responsible husband and father reinforced his status as less than a man. He outperformed his wife's stingy master, but understood that his caretaking behavior contributed to the power structure that oppressed him, which curbed his sense of moral righteousness.[24] Paternal duty and the attempt to provide for kin, like that of trying to protect them, brought men face to face with the painful contradictions of slavery. Taking care of others reduced men's opportunities to seek their own freedom, and in materially provisioning kin and community, men economically supported slaveholders and thus their own oppression.

Faced with a similar realization, George Henry made a different decision, prioritizing freedom and his refusal to aid a slaveholder above remaining with his family. Henry worked as a sailor, and returning home one day, expected his wife to serve him dinner. "I supposed I had a wife and a home. I sent for her to get me some supper," he recalled. "Just as she got my supper pretty well under way, her mistress sent for her, and said she must wait upon her first." He recognized that, "I had neither wife nor home. I made up my mind then and there. I had two children by her, a girl and a boy. I said to myself, madam you may have your woman and her children. I will never work myself to death to raise children for your use." Henry determined to escape, telling no one of his plans, and eventually reached Philadelphia, leaving his slave family behind. Unlike many men who expressed emotional pain after escaping alone, Henry openly acknowledged his reasoning. He did not want his labor to maintain a slaveholder, even if that labor involved caring for kin. A wife and children who legally belonged to another person were, to Henry, "your woman and her children," and not his own.[25] Supporting them meant supporting slavery. Henry represents the opposite response to the catch-22 of slavery and paternal duty. He exerted his manhood by focusing on himself and refusing to provision enslaved family members.

Patriarchal authority and legal marriage mattered, and as a free man, Henry became a devoted husband, father, and provider to his second family. After escaping, Henry married a widow with two young children. He and his wife lost two babies as infants, and Henry endeavored to care for his stepchildren, who he referred to as his children. "I found prejudice so great in the North that I was forced to come down from my high position as captain, and take my whitewash brush and wheelbarrow and get my living in that way," he stated. "But I was determined to work, knowing it was my living, and I had to support a wife and two children." While Henry's comments on his enslaved family seem callous, his insistence on standing up for his rights made him an involved father in freedom. In 1855, he became politically active on "the subject of public school rights." He paid high taxes, yet found "my children debarred from attending the schools, for which I was taxed. So a few of us got together and resolved to defend ourselves against such an outrage."[26] Individualized manhood in the context of slavery did not mean a person would continue that behavior in freedom.

Slaveholders often manipulated enslaved men's sense of responsibility and love of family for economic gain. Proslavery rhetoric posited that slaves had weak social connections and they easily formed new attachments and forgot the old. These attitudes justified the market and the frequent disruption of family ties. "Another trait is the want of domestic affections, and insensibility to the ties of kindred," proslavery writer William Harper claimed of slaves. "They entertain less regard for children than for parents, to whose authority they have been accustomed to submit." Because paternalists deemed themselves the ultimate father figure, they believed slaves' meaningful attachments were to the master. Harper argued that slaves should not be pitied for the inability to legally marry, as this released them from the anxieties of marriage, including the obligation to support offspring. Proslavery ideology recognized only white masculinity, failed to account for the internal plantation and family economy, and dehumanized bondmen, defining male slaves as childlike and less than men. However, in their actual behavior, slave owners recognized, and used to their own advantage, enslaved men's abiding affection for their kin and practice of paternal duty within the quarters. James Smith's mother's frequent pregnancies made her "not very profitable as a servant," so when the guardian of his underage master hired out all of the slaves to the "highest bidder," she was "let out to the lowest one that would support her for the least money." His father, "though a slave, agreed to take her and the children and support them for so much money." This arrangement enabled the master to reduce the costs of materially maintaining a slave family. The master eventually profited from any children produced without having to invest in their upkeep until they reached a marketable age. For a time, Smith's father headed a household, kept his family together, and supported his children, whom he raised for the master, but like all slaves, they remained vulnerable to sale, especially as they grew older and more valuable. "The first cruel act of my master, as soon as he became of age . . . was to sell one of my mother's children," Smith recalled.[27] Enslaved couples could use their fecundity as a bargaining chip, but that strategy might only delay the breakup of their family.[28] Within the confines of the quarters, enslaved men were able to take on the attributes of and fulfill the duties of fatherhood if doing so provided a financial benefit to the master.

Particularly unscrupulous and enterprising slaveholders went beyond trying to save money on upkeep and defrauded enslaved men by exploiting their familial devotion. Henry Brown, a skilled slave who worked in tobacco processing in Richmond, Virginia, worried about the impending sale of his wife, Nancy, who had a different owner. A white man named Samuel Cottrell approached Brown and claimed that he wanted to buy Nancy, but he lacked sufficient funds. "If I would let him have fifty, to make up the price, he would prevent her from being sold away from me," Brown said of the proposition. Though wary of "being fooled out of my money," Brown agreed after Cottrell professed religious intentions. Cottrell purchased Brown's family and "that very same day he came to me and told me, that my wife and children were now his property, and that I must hire a house for them and he would allow them to live there if I would furnish them with everything they wanted, and pay him 50 dollars, a year; 'if you don't do this,' he said, 'I will sell her as soon as I can get a buyer for her.' I was struck with astonishment to think that this man, in one day, could exhibit himself in two such different characters." After Brown had his family "comfortably situated," Cottrell demanded that Nancy do his laundry. Brown now paid for rent, hiring his wife's time, and supplying all of his family's needs, "and she had to do his washing beside." Despite the unfairness of the situation, the couple "felt ourselves more comfortable than we had ever been before," because they finally lived together. Brown paid Cottrell for Nancy's hire, "whenever he called for it—whether it was due or not." Though he understood Cottrell was "bent on robbing me," Brown had no choice but to comply, as the man owned his wife and children. Eventually, Cottrell sold the family to a slave trader and then, on the pretext of a debt, proceeded to take "everything which he could find in my house and carried it off to be sold."[29] Cottrell targeted Brown because he had the known ability to earn money and he loved his family, characteristics of manhood, and yet a slave had no public and legal standing as a man, and thus no possible recourse when cheated.

With the power structure aligned against them, male slaves' only comfort was their sense of honor and moral superiority, but a feeling of righteousness did not prevent one's family from being abused or sold. Emancipation enabled former slaves to engage in what Catherine Stewart calls "strategic counternarratives about the black experience of slavery and emancipation." Writing in the twentieth century, Sam Aleckson related the story of a man who following the war took care of his former mistress. The master, Tom Bale, returned home "broken in health and fortune" and went abroad to try to revive his finances, leaving his family "reduced from affluence to poverty." The former coachman, London, found work as a teamster and each week left food for his penniless mistress, "bought with his own money, from the same exclusive establishment where she formerly dealt." Tom Bale died overseas, and London brought provisions to the white family until his former mistress died. A formerly enslaved man thus became the provider when a white man abandoned his family. If told from a white perspective, this anecdote would emphasize the undying loyalty of former slaves. Told from London's perspective, the story represents a reversal of roles and power and a freedman fulfilling a paternal obligation to needy women and children, despite having been "much abused" by the white family while enslaved.[30]

Ideological Provisioning

In addition to their pursuit of profit, enslavers attempted to coopt enslaved masculinity to bolster their mastery and to reinforce obedience. When Jourden Banks threatened to run away from Virginia if the master sold another sibling, his owner "came to the conclusion, that my father had spoiled me, by talking to me and making me believe that I was treated badly. This is very common in such cases. A slave mother or father is expected to impress upon their children the necessity of strict servility to the master . . . otherwise they are blamed for any spirit or desire manifested by their children for relief." Banks replied that he reached his own conclusions and "that the blame need not be laid on my father." Slaveholders acknowledged a father's role if and when it served the master's interests and in an attempt to solidify white dominance. In other words, this master recognized an enslaved man's authority over his family in order to use it against him and further emasculate him. The master manipulated the concept of paternalism to enhance his own paternalistic authority. Paternalism included assumptions of male control of households, but African American men were not allowed to threaten white power and could only exercise the attributes of masculinity within the bounds of the quarters and if in doing so they provided some gain to the slaveholder. Through ideological provisioning, however, enslaved men managed to exert a hidden influence over their children. If material provisioning was limited by imposed constraints and a double-edged sword that profited the master, ideological provisioning gave fathers another way to care for their loved ones and a form of indirect power. Stephanie Camp argued that "the secret life of slave cabins offers glimpses of the practices and ideologies that lay behind the development of visible slave resistance." Historians have examined family life in the quarters and open resistance, but have less often explored the links between these realms. "Individual slaves' political consciousness was never inborn but always learned; it was acquired in places of work, such as the field, and places of anguish, such as under the lash," she wrote, "and it was developed in the home."[31] Material provisioning was public performance of masculinity in the quarters, but ideological caretaking often took place quietly, within the intimate spaces of the father/child relationship.

Enslaved parents faced difficult choices. They endeavored to instruct their children in survival skills that would benefit the individual and group, but how to do so reflected a range of approaches and personalities. How did one teach a child how to defer to slaveholder authority without crushing their spirit? Was imparting a sense of humanity and confidence risky or ultimately useful? Enslaved people learned early that their interactions with whites could affect not just themselves, but their loved ones. Parents understood that children's behavior had potentially far-reaching consequences, including physical abuse, diminished resources, and sale and separation. Parenting, like many aspects of slavery, placed enslaved men and women in a double bind—they had little authority over their children until those children broke the rules, in which case they could be held responsible.[32]

Training children to adopt and present an outward demeanor that mollified the white power structure was a harrowing responsibility. This usually involved learning when and how to mask their true feelings. "I will admit that slaves are sometimes cheerful; they sing and dance, as it is politic for them to do. I myself had changed owners three times before I could see the policy of this appearance of contentment," John Jacobs explained. "My father taught me to hate slavery, but forgot to teach me how to conceal my hatred. I could frequently perceive the pent-up agony of his soul, although he tried hard to conceal it in his own breast. The knowledge that he was a slave himself, and that his children were also slaves, embittered his life, but made him love us the more."[33] Emotional attachment to children intensified the pain associated with an inability to safeguard them or exercise direction over their lives. It also made teaching them to hide their feelings, modify their reactions, and carefully choose their words quite problematic. Jacobs's father, Elijah, struggled to model this behavior for his children precisely because he cared so much about them. Public emasculation fueled Jacobs's affection for his father and heightened the private, internal nature of Elijah's fatherly influence. Banks narrated and Jacobs wrote from the vantage point of antebellum Northern domesticity and fugitive abolitionism. Both men presented their fathers as devoid of sanctioned power, and yet a powerful emotional presence in the lives and minds of their children.

Enslaved parents lacked ultimate authority to discipline or to protect their children. Lucretia Alexander complained of being whipped once by the overseer on her Mississippi plantation. "He aimed to kill me but I got loose. He whipped me about a colored girl of his'n that he had by a colored woman." The overseer, Phipps, had a biracial daughter, Martha Ann Phipps, who stole a pair of stockings Alexander received as a gift from her mistress. In response, Alexander "beat her and took them off of her. She ran and told her father and he ran me home. He couldn't catch me, and he told me he'd get me. I didn't run to my father. I run to my mistress, and he knew he'd better not do nothin' then." Outranked, the overseer bided his time, later catching Alexander on her way to run an errand. She again eluded him. "I got away and went back to my old mistress and she wrote him a note never to lay his dirty hands on me again. A little later her brother . . . came there and ran him off the place."[34] Alexander explicitly noted that she went to her mistress rather than her father, because she knew who had authority vis-à-vis the overseer. Her father, himself a slave, had no power to defend her.

Alexander's pragmatic decision enabled her to escape a whipping from the overseer and ultimately got him fired, but in telling her story, she also exposed her father's inability to protect her or himself. Despite her tacit recognition of the emasculating nature of slavery, Alexander expressed pride in her father's rebelliousness. She was unable to recount his family history because he moved around so much. He was sold five times, the last placement resulting in her birth. "Wouldn't take nothin'," she declared. "So they sold him. They beat him and knocked him about. They put him on the block and they sold him 'bout beatin' up his master." In addition, she appreciated her father's secret religious services, where the slaves could get "some real preachin'." The mistress purchased Alexander's father at a high price, in spite of his reputation for running away, as a favor to Alexander's mother. Perhaps realizing that her story about her run-in with the overseer compromised the father she so admired, Alexander defended him, adding, "My father was an old man when Phipps was an overseer and wasn't able to fight much then."[35] She left unspoken the fact that her decision protected him. She managed to outsmart white authority without inducing or risking a confrontation between her father and the overseer that could end in physical punishment and even greater humiliation for him. Her tale revealed the limits of his authority, but her actions prevented him from facing his powerlessness directly. This story exemplifies the complexity of fatherhood within slavery. An overseer attempting to defend his mixed-race daughter ran up against the authority of the mistress. In this scenario, slavery emasculated two fathers of enslaved children—one white and one black. In a highly patriarchal society, mistresses had little power compared to their husbands, but they trumped a slave and a white overseer.

Enslaved youth coming of age experienced a harsh awakening when they realized the limits of parental protection and the extent of their own oppression. Jacob Stroyer hoped to become a hostler, having accompanied his father in his duties around the barnyard. After being thrown by a horse on his first day of training, he received a beating from a white groom. "This was the first time I had been whipped by any one except father and mother, so I cried out in a tone of voice as if I would say, this is the first and last whipping you will give me when father gets hold of you." Stroyer ran to his father, "but soon found my expectation blasted, as father very coolly said to me, 'Go back to your work and be a good boy, for I cannot do anything for you.'" He then found his mother, who approached the groom and earned herself a whipping. The groom then took the boy back to the stable and delivered "a severe flogging." This cruel treatment continued, and Stroyer announced that he intended to fight back. His father counseled against it, for his own self-preservation as well as the good of the family. If he retaliated, his father warned, the groom "will say that your mother and I advised you to do it, and it will make it hard for your mother and me, as well as for yourself." Stroyer's father urged, "You must do as I told you, my son; do your work the best you can, and do not say anything." The boy protested, arguing that he had done nothing wrong. His father replied, "I can do nothing more than to pray to the Lord to hasten the time when these things shall be done away; that is all I can do."[36] Caretaking has been obscured because it was often subtle and indirect. Lacking legal agency, enslaved fathers invoked spiritual agency. Unable to take direct action, many enslaved fathers channeled their leadership and influence through religion and a higher power.

Stroyer discovered the arbitrary nature of slavery and his parents' powerlessness. His mother, distraught over her son's injuries, determined to go to the master, but her husband delivered a similar warning, telling her that even if the master intervened, the groom "may revenge himself through the overseer." He told his wife, "You would gain nothing in the end," again urging prayer and expressing his belief that freedom would come for his children even if he did not live to see it. Although he could not physically shield his son, his faith did provide solace. "When father spoke of liberty his words were of great comfort to me, and my heart swelled with the hope of the future," Stroyer noted. Breaking his father's rule about early bedtime, the family stayed up late as his parents discussed this dilemma. They prayed together, his father pleading, "Lord, hasten the time when these children shall be their own free men and women." Though he had not directly protected his son, Stroyer trusted his father's leadership, youthfully expecting freedom to arrive in a matter of weeks rather than a long six years later.[37] Stroyer's father steered a careful course. He did not overtly fight back, but he encouraged his children to believe in and desire freedom, itself a form of indirect and ideological resistance.

Like Lucretia Alexander and her story about the run-in with the overseer, Jacob Stroyer discussed both his esteem for his father and his father's public impotence within the institution of slavery. Stroyer published his narrative in 1885, whereas Alexander was interviewed in the late 1930s. Though written or collected at two different times, and though Alexander responded to questions, the two presented similar portraits of enslaved fathers. Stroyer could take the time to provide detail and craft a depiction of fatherhood within slavery, and while he discussed public emasculation he also emphasized his father's dignity and private influence. Alexander recalled an incident from her life, realized it revealed her father's emasculation, and quickly added a rejoinder to uphold his honor. She implied that he would have defended her if he could have, stressing intent over lack of authority. Alexander and Stroyer acknowledged that their fathers could not provide physical protection, and yet they both gained a sense of inspiration and metaphysical guidance from these men. Unable to openly defend their children, enslaved fathers tried to safeguard loved ones through less visible and more ideological means.

Understanding the trials of slavery informed children's love of and respect for emasculated fathers. After being separated from his family and sent to Wilmington, North Carolina, Thomas Jones "providentially met my dear old father," while running an errand. The enslaved man selling produce asked him about his background and after a series of questions, he "took me in his arms, hugged and kissed me, and said 'You are my own child!'" His father asked where he lived and when Jones pointed to the house, his father said, "When I sell my load I will come up there and bring you a melon; you go home." His father needed to accomplish his own work and probably wanted to avoid detaining his son. Jones returned to his mistress and related the story. She reacted positively and asked him to finish his work quickly so as to be ready when his father arrived. "I watched for him anxiously," Jones recalled. "I suppose I went to the gate fifty times before he came." Later that day, he saw the cart approaching, and hurried to tell his mistress, who told him to welcome his father. "I ran with all my might, threw the big gate wide open, and said, 'My mistress says come in.'" Mistress Anna said, "'My boy says you are his father.' 'Yes, ma'am, he is my child; I have been sold away from him over three years.'" After disparaging "this selling business," the mistress declared, "'I will try and treat your child kindly. He has been a good boy since he has been with me. If he behaves well, I will treat him well.' My father turned to me, placed his hand on my head, and said, 'My boy, hear what your mistress says? Now I want you to be a good boy . . . and when she tells you to do anything, do it just as quick as you can. I will come and see you as often as I can.'"[38] Mistress Anna gave Jones's father permission to visit whenever he came into town.

Thomas Jones felt fortunate to reconnect with his father and emphasized his own palpable excitement. That father and son needed permission from the mistress did not dampen his mood. She mediated their interaction, made possible future meetings, and offered kind treatment to her slave conditional on his obedience. In her presence, an enslaved father reinforced the need for his son to follow orders, because he could hardly do otherwise and hope to visit again. Mistress Anna made the hierarchy clear, using a father's counsel to boost her own authority, telling Jones, "Now you must be a good boy. You heard what your father said." Jones's father did, however, offer his son one piece of advice that had amorphous meaning, particularly for the mistress. He counseled his son that he must not "neglect" his nightly prayers, thereby invoking a higher power. Only Jones knew the content of those prayers. Enslaved fathers attempted to nurture their children's sense of self-worth using ideas, a medium over which slaveholders had little control. The influence of enslaved fathers was concealed from masters, but understood by children, and the protection they offered was indirect and often couched in religious terms. Regularly separated from their children and unable to intervene in their lives on a daily basis, when possible, enslaved fathers attempted to father from a distance and offered what they could provide: life lessons and counsel.[39] While access to provision grounds and skilled labor varied regionally, a father's willingness to emotionally invest in his children and to ideologically provision was less geographically bounded and encompassed even situations with limited physical contact.

Due to age, grandparents were more likely than parents to have reduced labor, and often had more time to spend with children. Isiah Jeffries's grandfather never called him by his nickname, "kaise I was named atter him, and he too proud of dat fact to call me any nickname. I stayed wid him at his house lots atter I started working fer de marster, kaise he showed me how to do things." Grandfathers taught children a range of lessons and skills. Older men who had learned to navigate the slave system also provisioned children with advice calculated to help them survive. "My grandfather . . . he would tell us things! To keep the whip off our backs," Austin

Grant recalled. Frank Bell remembered a time when his grandfather, normally a taciturn man, picked him up and revealed his feelings about slavery. "'Son,' he say, 'I sho' hope you never have to go through the things your ole grandpa done bin through.'"[40]

Like the proverbial "mammy" who raised white children, enslaved men had official childcare roles on plantations. Abram Sells's great-grandfather had charge of all the children, black and white, on his Texas plantation. "He was too ol' to do any kin' 'r' wuk 'n' he was jes' 'pinted to look atter all de li'l 'uns 'n' teach dem how to wuk. Us all jes' strung 'roun' atter him, w'ite 'n' black, watchin' him potter 'roun' 'n' listenen' to him tell how t'ings ort to be run 'roun' dat place." The children obeyed because if they failed to do so, "sump'n bad was sho' to happen to us. He allus hab he pocket full 'r' t'ings to conjure wid."[41] In an interview highlighting her father, Charity Moore indicated that he spent time with and instructed white children. "Don't you 'member my pa Isaiah Moore?" she asked her interviewer. "Course you does! He was de Uncle Remus of all de white chillun 'round dese parts. He sho' was! I seen him a settin' wid you, Marse Johnnie, Marse Boyco, and Dickie Brice, in de back yard many a time. You all was askin' him questions 'bout de tale he was a tellin' and him shakin' his sides a laughin'. He telled all them tales 'bout de fox and de rabbit, de squirrel, brer tarrapin, and sich lak, long befo' they come out in a book."[42] Whether or not her father had an explicit job as a caretaker of white children, he interacted with them and in some measure contributed to their upbringing.

If male caretakers helped maintain plantation discipline, they also engaged in informal and clandestine provisioning of enslaved children. Charity Moore did not delve into the content of her father's stories for his white audience, but she did discuss in detail a tale he told the black children in Fairfield County, South Carolina. "White folks, my pa had Bible tales he never told de white chillum," she announced. While Moore's opening commentary disarmed her visitors, whom she obviously knew, by painting a stereotyped picture of a jovial Uncle Remus entertaining the white children, the Bible tales "he told the colored chillum" suggest he deliberately attempted to instill a radical and yet hidden sense of racial pride. Moore's father told the black children that the "fust man, Adam, was a black man. Eve was a ginger cake color, wid long black hair down to her ankles. Dat Adam had just one worriement in de garden and dat was his kinky hair." Adam could play with Eve's hair, but she could not reciprocate. The devil gleefully took note of Adam's sadness as Eve's hair grew longer, disguising himself as a serpent and "de Prince of light" to tempt Eve. The devil told Eve she could cure Adam's melancholy by convincing him to take a bite of an apple, "and in a night his hair will grow as long, be as black, and as straight as your'n." Eve bit into the apple and presented it to Adam. "While he was eatin' it, and takin' de last swallow of de apple, he was 'minded of de disobedience and choked twice. Ever since then, a man have a 'Adam's Apple' to 'mind him of de sin of disobedience," Moore continued. "Twasn't long befo' de Lord come alookin' for them. Adam got so scared his face turned white, right then, and next mornin' he was a white man wid long hair but worse off than when he was a nigger." In Isaiah Moore's interpretation of the Bible, the first man was black and the fall from grace created whiteness as secondary to and a devolved form of blackness.[43] White people might have straight hair, but they were "worse off," the result of disobeying God and falling for the devil's tricks.

Human corruption stemmed from Eve, an individual tainted by white blood. Eve was susceptible to Lucifer in the guise of an angel, thinking to herself, "A prince, he'll be a king someday." The devil flattered Eve, appealing to her vanity and her striving. "Of course, one of your beauty will one day be a queen," he insisted, before he addressed her dejection and its solution. Eve represented the corruption and immorality of white blood. In this story, original sin derived less from Eve's gender and more from her partial whiteness. Charity Moore implicitly commented on and condemned the sexual dynamics of slavery and the class pretensions of mixed-race people.[44]

William Dusinberre, in his discussion of paternalism, writes: "An indispensable witness in any paternalistic portrayal of slavery was the docile elderly black dependent, wholly reliant in old age on the goodwill of a white person for economic support and privileged treatment, who told the white people what they thirsted to hear."[45] Charity Moore is a good example. Her white Southern interviewer stressed the ex-slave's dependence on the son of her former owner, and Moore made obligatory remarks about the kindness of the white folks. Like her father, Charity Moore never left her former owners and lived on "the goodness and charity of Mr. Brice," in a small house on his property. Moore's story, however, indicates that her self-perception and the perception of her white neighbors diverged significantly. "I wonder sometime in de winter nights, as de north wind blows 'bout de cracks in de house, if pa is warm and in Abraham's bosom," Moore mused. "But I knows pa; he's 'umble. There's so many white folks in dat bosom he'll just be content to lie in Isaac's bosom or maybe de prophet Isaiah's, for who he was named." Moore had absorbed her father's teachings. If white people, even in Heaven, took up too much room and demanded top billing, she believed her father would carve out his own sacred space. Moore indirectly contrasted her father's morality and humility with Eve's vanity. In both her recounting of her father's Bible story, and her meditation about her father in Heaven, Charity Moore's subtext was that white people might believe themselves superior, but black people knew better, a lesson imparted by her father. To be white, or part white, was, like Eve, to be morally deluded.[46] Her white audience probably failed to recognize her meaning.

Though circumscribed by the emasculating conditions of slavery, enslaved men engaged in cultural and ideological provisioning private to the family and quarters. More so than material provisioning, ideological provisioning could be concealed from white authorities and enabled men to care for their children on their own terms. Through cultural and ideological provisioning, men could pursue the survival and dignity of themselves and their kin and community. Isaiah Moore was at once a preacher and father, a religious leader and caretaker whose Bible stories taught his daughter and other enslaved children about religion and the history of their people, and which encapsulated an underlying theme of resistance and black self-worth.

William Becker argues that the black preacher "symbolized self-assertive masculinity and integrity for the slaves who watched and heard him," and represented a form of continuity, echoing the centrality of the priest and father in African societies. The slave preacher was an American adaptation of male performance, cultural transmission, and leadership.[47] The duties of enslaved preachers toward their flock, their spiritual "children," corresponded to the ideal role of fathers. Leadership positions in Southern evangelical churches gave enslaved men one of several routes to masculine identity and achievement. However, within the institutional church, white evangelicals controlled enslaved preachers and limited their religious authority. Restrictions in the wake of the Nat Turner revolt in 1831 made it harder to use the church as a path to public masculine action and recognition.[48] According to Reverend Ishrael Massie, Virginia slaveholders and patrollers targeted the black preacher for abuse because "he wuz de leader of de meetin'," and thus a dangerous example of influence and expertise. A Kentucky informant agreed that preachers faced increased scrutiny and abuse because "they thought preachers were ruining the colored people."[49] White authorities attempted to intimidate and weaken the men who most represented and embodied an overarching father figure in slave communities.

Other informants echoed Charity Moore, discussing an enslaved father figure who served as a neighborhood caretaker and purveyor of ideas. A. C. Pruitt never met his own father, but "Dey was a ol' man name' Peter Green on de place. Ev'ry evenin' us chillen hatter go to he cabin and he spen' de evenin' teachin' us prayers. He git us all 'roun' him in a circle and teach us to count and says us prayers and t'ings like dat." Though a shoemaker and not a recognized preacher, "he jes' tuk dat much interes' in de chillen to try to teach dem sump'n'." Thomas Cole recalled that an older man on his Alabama plantation, Uncle Dan, "would read de Bible ter de rest of us and tell de meanin of it."[50] In the face of constant stress and the instability of the family unit, slave communities adapted. Older men served as mentors and religious guides and helped shape the lives of children, teaching agency through knowledge and prayer.

Religion offered fathers a tool to teach their children self-respect and survival and to navigate the dilemmas of authority within the institution of slavery. Charlie Grant's mistress threatened a whipping because he failed to behave in church and when she asked, "Who made you," he responded, "Papa made me." She asked again and received the same, unsatisfactory answer. "I sho thought I was right. She took de Bible en told me God made me. I sho thought papa made me en I go home en tell." Grant's father accused him of "cuttin up in church," and "told me dat God made me. Say he made Miss Lizzie en he made everybody." Grant escaped a beating and his father managed, even if he did not say so directly, to imply that his son was equal to Miss Lizzie in the sense that God made them both. His father admitted God outranked him, but he simultaneously and subtly undermined the absolute authority of the mistress by presenting both earthly father and mistress as subservient to God.[51] Slave preachers and caretaking fathers shared common goals of challenging the white power structure and instilling a sense of dignity.

Caretaking and religiosity overlapped, and former slaves writing or interviewed in the antebellum period, the late nineteenth century, and the early twentieth century credited their fathers with providing spiritual guidance and modeling religious devotion. "Father could neither read nor write, but had a good head for figures and was very pious," W. B. Allen stated. "His life had a wonderful influence upon me, though I was originally worldly—that is, I drank and cussed, but haven't touched a drop of spirits in forty years and quit cussing before I entered the ministry."[52] Morgan Latta, who also joined the ministry, recalled that his father "taught us say our prayers at night. He always would have a family prayer every Sunday morning, and every Sunday night." Mandy Jones's father held prayer meetings in the family cabin, and "ever night we said our prayers at my daddy's knee." A father might inspire religious faith in a child even in the absence of sustained physical contact. Sold away from her parents, Adeline Hodge had a single memory of her father: "When I war a li'l chile, he met me on a log by him an' prayed, an' I knows dat war whar de seeds ob religion war planted in my min'."[53] Denied access to earthly and direct power, enslaved fathers often transmitted influence through a higher power, imbuing leadership with a humility they believed slaveholders lacked.

Religious advice gave enslaved fathers a way to nurture their children's moral well-being in hopes of eventual spiritual freedom. As he courted a young woman and prepared to marry, Will Dill's father advised, "Son don't you never cut that woman across the back, for as sure as you do, that cut will be against you on Judgment Day." Such advice also gave fathers, who were powerless to prevent dislocations, an incorporeal gift to offer their loved ones. "My kind old father consoled and encouraged my mother all he could, . . . while praying, shouting, crying, and saying farewell," Charles Thompson recalled of the breakup of his family as the plantation's seventy-five slaves were apportioned among six white heirs. Thompson and his two siblings, his mother, and his father ended up in three separate lots. His father then told him, "Be a good boy, and God will be father and mother to you. If you will put your trust in him and pray to him, he will take you home to heaven . . . where parting will be no more." Thompson's father, known as Old Uncle Jack, had a "fatherly feeling for all" and consoled the assembled slaves and "spoke words of comfort to all of us before we were parted."[54] An enslaved man could not prevent family or community division, but he could speak to a form of power beyond the control of slaveholders, and he could envision a time and place without the buying and selling of human merchandise. If a father could not give his children an intact family or even his own physical presence, he could try to give them hope and nourish their sense of self-worth.

While Sergio Lussana overstates male solidarity and resistance, he makes an astute point about enslaved men's structural role in disseminating "subversive ideas," due to their greater mobility and access to jobs that provided proximity to information and allowed them to move between social spaces. Lussana notes that men often passed on ideas and information when they made visits to their cross-plantation families, but because his focus is on a homosocial world and not on family life, he never explores fatherhood as a conduit of ideological provisioning. Noting that scholars have tended to equate masculinity with open rebellion, Lussana "reconceptualizes male resistance to slavery by shifting attention from the visible, organized, collective world of slave rebellion to the intimate, hidden, and private world of enslaved men."[55] An integral part of that hidden world was men's relationships with and influence on children.

Cultural provisioning included telling stories for purposes of entertainment and instruction. Sabe Rutledge's parents used trickster tales to keep their children awake and working at their winter task. "We four chillun have to pick seed out the cotton. Work till ten o'clock at night and rise early! Mudder and Father tell you story to keep you eye open!" In Rutledge's example, Brer Partridge, the smaller, weaker animal, outsmarted Brer Rabbit to win a bet. Charlie Cooper's African-born father told stories of his former home, insisting that he came from "the most care free and happiest people that ever was on the face of the Globe." Parents' and grandparents' memories of Africa made an impact on children. "I often prayed that some day I would be like my grandparents free to roam and go where I pleased," Parilee Daniels stated.[56] Hearing such stories enabled young people to envision and believe they deserved freedom.

Enslaved children turned to their fathers when they sought reassurance or had questions about the world. When Caroline Wright believed she saw a ghost, "I hollers to my pappy, 'Pappy, wake up, dere's a haint.'" Mollie Edmonds was frightened not by a ghost, but by the arrival of Union soldiers on her Mississippi plantation. "I was so scared I ran to my pa and wouldn't turn loose of him for nothing. He tells me 'taint nothing to be scared 'bout it means that freedom done took place." Even within an institution that limited men's public authority, enslaved children looked to their fathers for protection. They also sought answers and information. William Rose accompanied his father on a trip to town to pick up the mail on the day a train full of Union soldiers passed through. Rose found the men fascinating and quizzed his father about their laughing, singing, and joking about eating dinner in hell. "They been in de army 'long time," his father replied. "They don't study hell anymore." When another ex-slave had a vision he did not fully understand, he similarly sought his father's counsel. "I told my daddy about it and he said it was God."[57] Like young people across time and space, enslaved children expected their fathers to interpret, inform, and protect.

A critical aspect of parenting involved teaching children to survive in a hostile and arbitrary world. Many enslaved parents taught their children to appear outwardly compliant and inwardly yearn for freedom. "Our parents used to tell us that we would not be always slaves. It made me feel glad to think that I would be free some day," John Quincy Adams commented. His parents encouraged his quest for literacy but taught him to seek knowledge covertly. "When I would hear any one reading I would always go and stand around and listen. They often asked me what I wanted. I would always say 'nothing,' but go and tell my father and mother, and they would say, 'try to hear all you can, but don't let them know it.'" An enslaved man who managed to acquire literacy, despite laws against teaching slaves to read and write, prioritized transmitting that knowledge to his children. "Our father had endeavoured to bestow upon both of us some rays of intellectual light, which the tyrant could not rob us of," John Jacobs said of the instruction he and his sister received.[58] Part of paternal duty involved passing down skills and wisdom in hopes of preparing children for a better future.

Children internalized the counsel and behavior of fathers who encouraged resistance. Jourden Banks discovered his degraded status when he "grew too strong" for the master's son. The white boy complained to his father every time Banks defeated him in their games. The master called both boys to him, slapped Banks, and had his son "do the same," attempting to train authority into his son and docility into his slave. Banks informed his own father, who "told me not to take a blow from Alexander, for the more I did take, the more I would have to take." Banks had "imbibed" the "spirit of my father," and followed these instructions. "It was more natural for me to obey my own father than to obey Alexander's father," he explained. "So I carried out my father's plan, and punished Alexander more and more severely each time he attacked me." The master then decided to send his son off to school and Banks to the field. Based on these interactions, Banks discovered the unfairness of bondage, but his father taught him to stand up for himself, a lesson he applied throughout his life. Banks scoffed at bodily threats, proclaimed his readiness to die, and "liked to tell a man what I thought." At one point, faced with a whipping, he fought back, beating the overseer and master with a stick, an event that precipitated his escape on the eve of the Civil War.[59] Despite his limited public authority, an enslaved father who had earned his children's respect could exert a far greater influence on their character development than the master.[60]

A man might realize that resistance increased the chances of being separated from loved ones and still urge his children to employ such tactics. Peter Robinson was cheated in an arrangement with his master to purchase freedom and sold. As he bid farewell to his family, his parting advice to his son encouraged defiance. "William, never pull off your shirt to be whipped," he instructed. "I want you to die in defense of your mother; for once I lay in the woods eleven months for trying to prevent your mother from being whipped." William Robinson later acted on his father's advice. When he saw the slaveholder kicking his prostrate mother, Robinson "knocked him

down with the ax handle," and ran. After his recapture, Robinson anticipated a flogging. The master "locked the door, then demanded me to pull
off my shirt. I had not forgotten the promise I made my father, so I fully
made up my mind to fight him until I got a chance to jump out of the window." However, when he spied a pistol, Robinson "reluctantly pulled off my
shirt." Although Robinson could not at that moment fully act on the advice
of a man from whom he had been permanently separated, his father remained a defining influence in Robinson's life and outlook on slavery.[61]

Successful fugitives honored fathers who taught their children to yearn
for and value freedom. Harriet and John Jacobs attributed their resistance
to their father, Elijah Knox. Harriet opened her narrative with a discussion
of her father, the man who shaped her sense of self-worth. Elijah, a skilled
and sought-after carpenter, had permission to "manage his own affairs," so
long as he paid his mistress $200 a year. "His strongest wish was to purchase
his children," she explained, "but, though he several times offered his hard
earnings for that purpose, he never succeeded." Despite his inability to purchase their freedom, his desire and attempts to do so, and his relative independence, had a profound impact on his children. Elijah died with his wish
to provide liberty for his children unfulfilled, but he left them with a deep
loathing of the injustice of slavery and the belief that they deserved better.
"He left us the only legacy that a slave father can leave his child, his whips
and chains," John Jacobs reminisced. "These he had taught us to hate, and
we resolved to seek for liberty, though we travelled through the gates of
death to find it." When her father died, Harriet reported her master and
mistress's antipathy toward him. "They thought he had spoiled his children,
by teaching them to feel that they were human beings. This was blasphe-
mous doctrine for a slave to teach; presumptuous in him, and dangerous to
the masters." Jennifer Fleischner emphasizes the close relationship between John and Harriet Jacobs, the interconnections between their narratives, and "their overlapping memories of their father," in the siblings'
thirst for liberty and eventual escape. "Ultimately, it is Jacobs's ability to
integrate her father's memory into her conception of self that enables her to
run from slavery," she writes.[62] From the standpoint of slaveholders, ideological provisioning was particularly threatening. A man who fed his
children built up the master's property. A man who fed them notions of autonomy put cracks in the edifice of slavery.

In the fugitive accounts of John Brown and Frederick Douglass, surrogate father figures occupy a pivotal role, particularly in nurturing notions
of freedom. After being separated from his natal family, John Brown met

and worked with John Glasgow, an older, formerly free British sailor kidnapped and sold into slavery in Georgia, who became a sort of surrogate father and rescued the young man from his despair. Sergio Lussana discusses the relationship between Brown and Glasgow as an example of deep friendships between enslaved men, often developed in the context of sex-segregated labor gangs, that helped these men survive bondage. While I certainly agree with Lussana's assessment of the "subversive" nature of this relationship and the impression it made on Brown, I see Glasgow as a surrogate father as well as a friend. Brown grieved for his parents and Glasgow for his wife and children, and these two men of different ages forged a strong bond. Glasgow "used to tell me not to cry after my father and mother, and relatives, for I should never see them any more. He encouraged me to try and forget them, for my own sake, and to do what I was bidden." From his mentor, Brown learned survival skills and about the world beyond the plantation. "He said I must try, too, to be honest and upright, and if I ever could get to England, where he came from, and conducted myself properly, folks would respect me as much as they did a white man," Brown continued. Glasgow's "kind words . . . gave me better heart, and inspired me with a longing to get to England, which I made up my mind I would try and do some day." Glasgow stimulated in his young friend a desire to escape, and when he eventually succeeded, after several attempts, Brown acknowledged this critical guidance. "To John I owe a debt of gratitude for he it was who taught me to love and to seek liberty." In freedom, Brown settled in England and sought to locate Glasgow's lost family.[63]

At the age of thirteen, Frederick Douglass, who never knew his biological father and had limited contact with his mother before she died, found religion and, for a short time, a surrogate father in a "good colored man named Charles Lawson." Lawson became "my spiritual father and I loved him intensely, and was at his house every chance I could get," Douglass recalled. "When I would tell him, 'I am a slave, and a slave for life, how can I do anything?' he would quietly answer, 'The Lord can make you free.'" Following Lawson's teachings and even after he lost physical contact with the man, Douglass always prayed "that God would, of His great mercy, and in His own good time, deliver me from my bondage." Whether through direct advice or by channeling authority through a higher power, the ideological provisioning of fathers, biological and surrogate, convinced children they deserved a better life. Historians have emphasized the performative nature of gender identity and especially masculinity, but some aspects of paternal caretaking were not meant for public display.[64]

Fathers frequently urged their children to seek freedom, especially if an impending sale meant family separation. Charles Ball's grandfather fortuitously overheard the constable and an overseer discussing his son's sale. Owing to his physical strength, several men concocted a plan to surprise and seize Ball's father before he became aware of the transaction, and Ball's grandfather happened to eavesdrop on their conversation. That night, he hastened the three miles to his son's cabin, "aroused him from sleep, made him acquainted with the extent of his danger, gave him a bottle of cider and a small bag of parched corn, and then enjoined him to fly."[65] Walter Hawkins, learning he had been sold, went straight to his father, who "burst into tears." The two "talked and wept," and Hawkins's father suggested, "Boy, run away."[66] Both fathers understood that they would likely lose contact with their sons in any case, so the risk of flight made sense. One of the most dreaded costs of failure, removal from family, was already a given.

Some fathers went beyond advising their children to flee and substantially aided them in the process of gaining liberty. Friday Jones, who himself fought back against his master when denied permission to visit his family, had a daughter with a similar disposition. During the war, she refused to let her master whip her and when he trapped her in a corn crib and ordered another slave to help, "she whipped them both, flung the door open, and left," hiding in the woods. Knowing that she would be sold, Jones went and managed to find her. He wrapped her in blankets and drove through the night, taking an indirect path, because he worried about being caught and arrested. Jones arrived in Raleigh, North Carolina, at daybreak and "astonished" his wife and the other children. The family "wanted to know what I was going to do with her," he recalled. "I replied that I was going to keep her for awhile in my stable loft." Jones took considerable risk and hid his daughter for two years. She emerged when the Union army arrived. In that time, she became ill, and twice "her mother had said she could not live; to turn her loose in the road and let them take her, for they would ruin me. Bless my wife! I will never meet a woman that I will love as I love her. I said, 'I shall not turn her loose, madam, if she dies I intend to bury her.'" His pragmatic wife believed death was imminent and saw no reason to sacrifice the entire family, but Jones refused to give his daughter up and she survived slavery and the war.[67]

Unable to immediately free his child, Jared Franklin made arrangements for her eventual emancipation and traveled a considerable distance to retrieve her when her indenture ended. A Dunkard, a member of an antislavery religious group, purchased Franklin and promised to free him if he served "faithfully for ten years." Franklin's wife, Ann, also owned by a Dunkard, gained her freedom once she earned back her purchase price. This master then moved to Ohio, and rather than sell the couple's daughter before he departed, he "agreed that if Jared would allow him to take her with him at the end of six years he would set her free." When her term of service ended, Franklin "went for her a distance of five hundred miles, walking all the way, and accompanied by his daughter also walked the whole distance back, except fifteen miles which they rode in a farmer's wagon—a journey of a thousand miles on foot, performed under the feeling of paternal love."[68] Caretakers went to great lengths to see their children achieve liberty.

A PREACHER INTERVIEWED ABOUT religion by an African American fieldworker in the late 1920s provided an unusually detailed account of his interactions with and observations of his father, Harry Green. Green visited his family on an adjoining South Carolina plantation twice a week, on Wednesday and Sunday. His son listed several attributes that typically earned praise, describing his father as "a powerful man," a "good carpenter," and an involved family man. This unnamed informant's memories depicted a father who provided in several ways, materially and ideologically. During his visits, Harry Green gave his son lessons from a spelling book he purchased as a gift. "I kept it for years and years," the man recalled. "I was always glad for him to come because he could read a little and he taught me about all that I ever learned out of the Blue Back Speller. I was anxious to learn."[69]

The narrative emphasized Harry Green's religious guidance. "My father started me off to praying. Every Wednesday night when he came to see us, as soon as it was time for us to go to bed he always called me to him and made me kneel down between his knees and say my prayers," the son recalled. He also noted that his mother deferred to her husband on matters of discipline, and before administering punishment, his father always "told me to pray because he was going to whip me. . . . He took me up on his knees and told me that I must be a good boy and that I must honor and obey my mother or God wouldn't love me." While the preacher remembered his father as successful in work, and a man who "could do anything," he accentuated the life lessons imparted and credited his father with inspiring his religious career. He also underscored his affection for his father, an indication of the contours of their relationship. "I loved my father. He was such a good man. . . . I sometimes think that I learned more in my early childhood about how to live than I have learned since."[70]

When the son reached the age of roughly twelve to fourteen, and heard he would be sold away from his parents, his mother fainted. "My father came over and they prayed and sang over me. He gave me this advice." Harry Green knew freedom was coming and urged his son to come back and find them, "but whatever you do, treat people right; respect the old; go to meetings; and if you never more see us in this world, meet us in heaven." Enslaved fathers often focused on the concept of the afterlife, a space beyond the reach of slaveholders. This man included in his interview a tableau of his father's biweekly visits. "He used to sing a song all the time when he came to see mamma. The song was, 'Jesus, my all, to heaven has gone.' He would sing that and my mother would almost shout. I used to watch them when they sat and talked."[71] The narrative highlights the qualities former slaves most admired in a father as well as the fact that a man who lived most of the week apart from his family could be highly involved in family life and mold his child's character. The interview touched on Harry Green as compassionate, physically strong, a skilled carpenter, head of household, and a man who provided for his son in multiple ways, including education and religious and moral guidance. Children most appreciated ideological provisioning, the intangibles men could provide regardless of local conditions.

A more expansive definition of providing reveals caretaking behavior, a subtle form of resistance, internal to enslaved families and communities. Enslaved people adapted their material, cultural, and ideological provisioning to fit the environment in which they lived and the local limitations they faced. While committed enslaved fathers certainly attempted to provide for their children materially, with that role circumscribed, they found alternate ways to provide that were less visible to and under the control of slaveholders, including guidance, inspiration, and religious counsel. A good father provisioned his children in the ways available to him, and he taught his children to develop a sense of self-worth and humanity, and to hope for a better future.

CHAPTER FOUR

This Great Object of My Life
Purchase and Escape

The ultimate good an enslaved man could provide for his loved ones was freedom, something few could hope to accomplish. In the rare cases where a man had the opportunity to earn cash for skilled labor and purchase his own freedom, many then attempted to raise the requisite funds to buy family members. More widely available as a potential avenue to freedom, and more dangerous, was escape. To flee with family, and especially young children, significantly reduced the chances of success, and failure risked separation and sale. As a result, men most often escaped alone, though a few managed to defy the odds and abscond with kin. In calculating and timing escape attempts, and in their response to achieving liberty, men revealed the paramount importance they placed on family.

Considering an escape attempt forced enslaved men to confront the pervasive dilemmas and painful contradictions of fatherhood and slavery. To abscond and be free was to become a man, but a lone fugitive had to be willing to relinquish his role as husband and father. Standing up for oneself meant forsaking duty to kin. As with so many aspects of their lives, the structural constraints of slavery alienated men's responsibility to self from responsibility to kin. Seeking freedom brought care of self into conflict with the desire to care for others. The only men who overcame these constraints were those who escaped prior to having a family, those who purchased an entire family, or those who escaped with kin. Those who failed, including lone fugitives, lived with an enduring sense of loss. In failure and in the infrequent cases of success, former slaves' words, choices, and actions as they sought to free self and family underscore the centrality of kinship and slave communities' enduring conception of paternal duty.

Purchase

After the death of his master, Amanda Smith's father earned his mistress's trust running the plantation. As a reward, she allowed him to work to purchase his freedom, which he did at night, after completing his daily labor. "He had an important and definite object before him, and was willing to sacrifice sleep and rest in order to accomplish it. It was not his own liberty alone, but the freedom of his wife and five children," Smith related. "For this he toiled day and night. He was a strong man, with an excellent constitution, and God wonderfully helped him in his struggle. After he had finished paying for himself, the next was to buy my mother and us children." When able, slaves purchased themselves and then attempted to purchase family members. Self-purchase required a combination of skill, favorable placement, luck, initiative, and a master willing to negotiate. Enslaved people in the Upper South, where hiring out was common, and those living in or near urban areas across the South more often had such opportunity. Some women purchased husbands, children, and other relatives, but with greater access to skilled labor and self-hire, enslaved and free black men were more likely to purchase family members.[1]

Men with skills and permission to hire their time endeavored to free themselves and then their wives and children.[2] They next had to make choices about the order in which they purchased kin. Working to save the money required considerable effort and time, leaving members of the family vulnerable to sale in the meantime, and the actual transaction usually involved incurring debt. One strategy involved purchasing children in order of their age, possibly because older children had higher market value and their owners were thus more likely to sell them for the profit. However, because younger children were less valuable, they were easier to obtain, and their masters might be willing to negotiate an attainable price.[3] With limited access to material and financial resources, and at the whims of the owners of their loved ones whose permission they required, even in the rare cases when they had ample money, men and women attempting to purchase family members faced difficult choices.[4]

Stephen Whitman examines the shift from slave to free labor in Baltimore, arguing that slavery was eclipsed not due to the inevitable march of capitalism, but rather a confluence of factors. By 1830, four-fifths of blacks in the city were free, the largest free black population in the nation. Because slaves could easily flee due to Baltimore's location, masters used negotiated and gradual manumission and term slavery as a labor management strategy, making concessions to slaves to ensure uninterrupted production. Slaves also shaped who became free. Whitman argues that black families made decisions about order of purchase based on price. Younger children were easier to free and manumitted in greater numbers, and girls were more likely to benefit from immediate manumission because they were less expensive than boys. In addition, a black family had to weigh the advantages of purchasing a son and benefitting from his labor to assist in the purchase of other kin, or purchasing a daughter and thereby ensuring that her children would be born free. However, across the South, enslaved and free families also made decisions or faced obstacles based on sexual concerns, which complicated price.[5]

Buying yourself and your family was in some ways less risky than attempting to escape, which could end in physical punishment and sale if caught, or even in death. But purchasing freedom necessitated the right conditions and the agreement and good will of one's owner. It also necessitated the owner upholding the bargain, making it a tenuous undertaking. Purchase took time and frequently ended in profound disappointment when an owner swindled a slave out of hard-earned money, or sold family members before enough money had been amassed. And, if enslaved family members had different owners, this compounded the difficulties. Slaves had to calculate the potential advantages and risks of various plans to try to achieve freedom. A man who managed to purchase himself and then tried to do the same for his family members typically faced years of toil and tied himself to a particular location to remain near enslaved kin. Taking on debt also left him and his family beholden and vulnerable to the white men who provided financing or security. "The workings of manumission helped generate new forms of dependency in which former slaves became enmeshed," Whitman writes.[6] In addition, the interstate trade in the nineteenth century drove up prices, making self-purchase more expensive, and as Southern states suppressed free black communities, manumission became an increasingly difficult process.[7] Because remaining in the South to be close to and attempt to liberate family members put a man at greater risk of reenslavement, caretaking compromised personal safety and opportunities. A man who endeavored to uphold paternal duty by provisioning freedom through purchase often became further entrapped in the slave system.

Calvin Schermerhorn explores the ambivalence of the market through enslaved people's networking strategies to forestall family separation, defining African American families as the "fuel" driving the market revolution. "With tragic irony, enslaved people sought to use the changing market that was responsible for slavery's new commercial vitality to defend themselves from market-made separations," he writes. As they negotiated the market and attempted build a web of "patrons and allies," and accumulate resources, "most enslaved people chose family over freedom."[8] The attempt to purchase freedom for one's kin often dominated a man's life and demonstrated how the institution of slavery placed individual concerns at odds with caretaking and family integrity. The Reverend Noah Davis published a narrative in 1859 for the express purpose of raising "SUFFICIENT MEANS TO FREE HIS LAST TWO CHILDREN FROM SLAVERY. Having already, within twelve years past, purchased himself, his wife, and five of his children, at a cost, altogether, of over four thousand dollars." Davis detailed a long quest to purchase his family, as well as the significant assistance he received from his congregation and benevolent white friends. After he became a preacher and his master gave him permission to travel and earn funds for self-purchase, Davis's "white Baptist friends in Baltimore" offered an "appointment as missionary to the colored people of that city," and help paying the remainder of his debt to his master. This prospect created a dilemma because it meant liberty, but entailed leaving his enslaved family. "I began to think, how can I leave my wife and seven small children, to go . . . a distance of more than a hundred miles from them," he wrote. "I thought my children would need my watchful care, more now than at any other time." His wife and children belonged to a widow who "had always given me the entire control of my family." Davis discussed the matter with his master, accepted the offer, and began traveling back to Virginia three to four times per year to see his family. Davis had already been in an abroad marriage, and now visited more infrequently. His children lived in a divided household, but like the children of many such marriages, had two involved parents and a father who provided from afar.[9]

After Davis's first year in Baltimore, his wife's mistress "agreed to sell to me my wife and our two youngest children," giving him a year to raise the fixed price of $800. "The sun rose bright in my sky that day; but before the year was out, my prospects were again in darkness," he said of the strain of collecting such a large sum. "Now I had two great burdens upon my mind: one to attend properly to my missionary duty, the other to raise eight hundred dollars." Davis managed with a combination of money he raised outright, bonds, and loans from friends. When he returned to Virginia to collect his wife they faced "feelings commingled with joy and sorrow — sorrow at parting with five of our older children, and our many friends; and rejoicing in the prospect of remaining together permanently in the missionary field." Thrift with his salary combined with his wife's day work, and hiring the children, enabled the family to slowly repay their loans.[10] Davis did not choose the order in which he purchased his children. He started with the youngest because their mistress agreed to sell them along with their mother.

The older children had higher market values, and Davis scrambled to purchase each one as they faced sale in Virginia. Their ages compounded the financial challenges, and with each proposed sale, Davis again went through the anxious and time-consuming process of raising money and taking on increased debt, first purchasing his oldest daughter and then his oldest son. Davis stated, "I have been necessarily much hindered in my own labors, from pecuniary embarrassments, arising from the sale of my children, who were left in Virginia—two daughters and three sons." In 1856, the mistress of the three remaining slave children died, triggering the sale of her estate. The thought of purchasing three people at once in such a short time nearly caused Davis to give up: "I felt very certain that my daughter, about whom I felt the greatest anxiety, would sell at auction for more money than I could get any of my friends in Baltimore to give for her; and I saw no way to do any thing for the two boys." When the court postponed their sale, giving him more time, he regained some hope of redeeming his children. At the auction, Davis's two sons, aged twenty-one and seventeen, sold for far less than their sister. After the sale, the slave trader "agreed to let my friends have her, for me, for eleven hundred dollars." His friends supplied a bond for the amount and he immediately began raising money, printing circulars and traveling throughout the North. Ultimately, another friend made up the difference when he failed to raise the full amount in the allotted time, and after a year of fundraising, he was able to secure his daughter. He concluded with the hopes that sale of the narrative would allow him to purchase his two sons. "Having, through the aid of a kind Providence, been enabled to pay for my daughter, I have felt it my duty to turn my attention toward redeeming my word to my last children now in bondage." Davis never said so explicitly, but his worries about his daughter, her significantly higher price than two young men, and his relief at leaving her with friends he trusted while he raised funds implied sexual concerns.[11] The constant struggle to purchase their children meant that Davis and his wife were unable to amass any property as free people. Raising money to buy those still enslaved compromised the couple's ability to materially provide in the present and build future assets for themselves and the children they had freed.[12]

Davis, following the lead of his own father, chose a mode of masculinity based on caretaking. The family's path to freedom can be traced back to Davis's father, who served as head miller for his Virginia master and enjoyed "many privileges," including that of "keeping his children with him, until they were old enough to put out to such trades as they might choose." As a favored slave, Davis's father had an intact family and his children learned valuable skills, with Davis apprenticing as a shoemaker before embarking on his church career. Davis's father also introduced him to religion. "My father could read a little, and make figures, but could scarcely write at all. His custom, on those Sabbaths when we remained at home, was to spend his time in instructing his children, or the neighboring servants, out of a New Testament, sent him from Fredericksburg by one of his older sons," he recalled. "Such was the esteem I had for my pious father, that I have kept that blessed book ever since his death, . . . and it was the first New Testament I read, after I felt the pardoning love of God in my soul." His father's religious teachings shaped the remainder of Davis's life. When the master sold the mill, he freed Davis's parents, and "allowed them to maintain themselves, by cultivating as much ground on the farm as they needed." Davis thus had an example of freedom in his own parents.[13] The ability to sustain a cohesive family life over two or more generations created material and social stability that aided in efforts to attain liberty. The caretaking approach to masculinity applied across class, region, and urban and rural areas.

Due to the popularity of slave narratives in the antebellum North, publishing an autobiography served as a means of raising money to purchase family members, and pecuniary interests motivated several writers. Israel Campbell, like Noah Davis, hoped to use the proceeds of his autobiography to purchase his children from Kentucky. Though he had the good fortune to "come into the promised land," he declared his "mission" unfulfilled because three children remained enslaved. "I see the oppressor's rod becoming heavier, and the shackles becoming tighter and tighter around them, and my heart yearns for them," he wrote. Campbell offered his readers a trade, information about his life in slavery for their financial assistance in freeing his children, "to this end I expect to devote the proceeds of the sale of this book."[14] Reverend Davis lived in Baltimore and remained on good terms with the owners of his children and tied to the institution of slavery, factors that moderated his commentary, whereas Campbell fled to Canada and penned a decidedly abolitionist narrative.

Israel Campbell addressed what Noah Davis only implied: that fathers at times prioritized the purchase of teenaged daughters because of their vulnerability to sexual assault. Before his escape, Campbell bought his time from his master and served as a traveling preacher. He had the opportunity to flee, and friends encouraged him to do so, but he demurred, telling them he intended to purchase freedom. His master agreed to the plan, and also agreed to allow him to purchase his children. "Maria, my oldest daughter, was a sprightly girl, with black eyes and black curly hair. I then intended buying her first," he noted. After this plan failed and his master, fearing an escape attempt, jailed and then sold him, Campbell fled to Canada. As he endeavored to raise money to buy his children from afar, he worried most about his daughter. "I have three children there to-day exposed to the lash, the chains, and the assaults of ruffians day after day. And when I think over things that are now transpiring, and think that I have a lovely daughter, eighteen years old, with no father to protect her, no mother to guide and advise her," he continued. "My spirit cannot rest." While he skirted direct mention of rape, Campbell's reasoning behind his plan to first purchase his daughter became clear in his discussion of forced amalgamation, which he denounced as the "most disgraceful" aspect of slavery. Shortly after his escape, Campbell returned once to the South in a failed bid to rescue his children. He went back North, sought an education and trained for the ministry, opting to use his writing to accumulate "a fund for the liberation of my children." He concluded, "Never, under God's blessing, do I intend to lay down in quiet until this great object of my life is accomplished."[15] Campbell removed himself from his children in securing his own liberty, and he endeavored to uphold his paternal duty by raising money in the hopes of freeing them.

Men with families usually planned to first free their wives and then their children. Liberty for a woman meant that her subsequent children would be born free, placing an upper limit on the number of enslaved people in an immediate family.[16] After his master died, his mistress allowed him to hire out, and Lunsford Lane started a tobacco business with his father that enabled him to save enough money to purchase freedom. He then bought a house and made plans to purchase his family. He intended to first buy his wife, figuring that her earnings would help them jointly save to redeem the children. His wife's owner agreed to sell the entire family, and Lane made an arrangement that involved accruing substantial debt. "I gave Mr. Smith five notes of five hundred dollars each, the first coming due in January 1840, and one in January of each succeeding year. My family were thus transferred into my own possession, with a written obligation to give me a bill of sale when I should pay the notes." Despite a stressful financial position, "We now, to our exceeding great joy, found ourselves living in our own house."[17]

In the nineteenth century, as Southern states became increasingly hostile to free blacks, slaves and freemen attempting to purchase their own liberty or that of relatives faced legal as well as financial hurdles. Because Lunsford Lane's freedom had been secured through a petition in New York, a local citizen charged him with moving to North Carolina, a state that legally debarred the immigration of free blacks. Even with legal assistance from white friends, his bid to remain in residence failed. "My secret enemies in Raleigh reasoned that I must hereafter be looked upon as a free negro, from another State." Lane attempted to maintain a low profile, but free black men were threatening, especially those trying to augment the free population. Lane and two other former slaves trying to purchase family members were required to move out of state, as the "the Legislature determined to make it clean sweep of this troublesome class of citizens."[18] Lane prepared to leave his loved ones and hoped to raise enough money to purchase and take at least one child with him, but after traveling in the North he collected the funds to free his entire family.[19] As they departed for Boston, his mother's mistress was moved by Lane's emotional reaction to leaving friends and home and allowed the old woman to accompany her son with the promise of later payment.[20] While Lane prevailed, legal records reveal the obstacles enslaved people faced as they attempted to purchase freedom for themselves or kin. A newly manumitted individual forced by state law to move had to leave behind family and community, and those who remained in the South to be near family placed their own freedom in jeopardy.[21]

African Americans who purchased kin often relied on white assistance, which gave these financiers leverage over free and enslaved families. White men fronted money, vouched for a man's character, and attested to his high likelihood of repaying loans.[22] When their master faced financial ruin, Elisha Green purchased his wife and children with the help of his Maysville, Kentucky, church community. Several of his family members were sold at a sheriff's sale, and a white citizen "went my security." White churchmen pooled resources and bought the family for $850, and the court allowed Green to choose where they would be hired out. "They told me to go and make the money and pay it in 'bank calls,' but if I could not do this, none of them would trouble my family." This group of white men navigated the legal system, and with his earnings as a preacher Green slowly repaid them.[23] While this kept his kin from being sold away, it did not mean they all lived together or that Green had full control over his children, as the members of his family were hired out, placing them largely under the power of white employers.

Because he had not paid for their purchase outright and he remained in debt, Green only nominally owned his family members. Green continued to preach at churches in the area and struggled against continued challenges to his ability to protect his loved ones and exert his authority over a family scattered among multiple households. Amanda, the one child he did not own, "got a pass and came home to me." Her owner then sued Green for "harboring slaves." Next, his daughter Maria, unhappy with her living situation, arrived at his doorstep. "I asked her what was the matter. She said that she had left home and was not going back any more." Her employer insisted that Green return Maria. "I told her I would do no such thing, but if Maria wanted to come she could do so," he responded. "Then said they if she does not she will have to leave the state. I told them very well; I would never send her back." Maria's employer used state laws requiring the departure of free blacks as a threat. Green had to find a new employer, again calling on the assistance of his white friends to settle the dispute. In terms of its daily existence, Green's family was physically divided but emotionally intact, and in order to sustain those multilocal connections, he had limited options and limited mobility. Because freedom remained insecure, even with proper papers, those with the financial ability and free of entangling debt brought their family North after securing their liberty.[24]

Unscrupulous whites could take advantage of slaves' and free black men's love of kin and their desire to stay in the South in order to free those family members. As Calvin Schermerhorn notes, "Slaveholders' financial interests were the submerged shoals on which the best strategy could founder." Charles McMullin, a free black man in Kentucky, borrowed money to purchase his enslaved son and then had to sue for control of his child. According to the court proceedings, the white lender was motivated not by benevolence, but "was solely actuated by a desire to secure the debt which Charles McMullin owed, and to make profit on his money."[25] Lenders could profit from a black man's love of family and sense of duty, making finding trusted white patrons essential to securing freedom.

It took most formerly enslaved people years to free an entire family, and in the meantime death, debt, and financial collapse could disrupt the plan. In a case from Tennessee, a free mother sued to formally emancipate three children. Her deceased husband, George Porter Sr., had purchased his freedom. He then bought his wife and emancipated her, and they legally married. They had six children who had been born in slavery, whom the couple purchased and freed one at a time. Before they completed this process, the master gave the three still-enslaved children to his brother, Thomas Porter. Porter allowed the family to live together, assuring George that he could work to purchase the rest of his children. Thomas Porter then died without a will and his slaves were sold to pay his debts. The three children in question were sold at auction and purchased by their father with "sixty dollars . . . and a note . . . for . . . $990." George Porter could only come up with a fraction of the payment, and this purchase led to financial "embarrassments." George Sr. died without a will, without having emancipated his last three children, and "hopelessly insolvent," as a result of purchasing his entire family. His wife sued to free the three children, an action the court supported, because at this point the Civil War had made emancipation a reality. The outcome would have been different had this case occurred earlier.[26]

The financial challenges of purchasing the freedom of kin were considerable, but other factors beyond an enslaved person's control included the attitudes of the master. Edmond Kelley's Tennessee owner provided a pass to travel and preach out of state, including in the North. After securing his own freedom, he hoped to purchase his family. In his 1851 narrative, written in response to requests from patrons helping him raise funds, Kelley included correspondence with the owner of his wife and children. The letters reveal how slaveholder paternalism could help and hinder efforts to achieve liberty via purchase. James Walker at first resisted the idea of selling Kelley's family. He cited their considerable market value, and then invoked his own paternalistic self-image, insisting that, "no price . . . could be offered by anyone that would induce them to be the slaves or servants of any but my own family." Dolly, "the mother of your wife, was my nurse, took the tenderest care of me when I was an orphan child." As a result, Walker and his wife and children felt an "attachment" to Dolly and her children and grandchildren that led to "treatment . . . altogether different from what is ordinarily termed slavery." Walker felt himself to be such an exemplary master that he did not believe the term slaves applied. "Although they occupy the position of servants to me and my family, they in reality, in the tie of affection and regard for their comfort and happiness which exists, are not slaves at all," he argued. Instead, the enslaved family "stand next in my affections to my own wife and children and children's children. The affection I believe to be mutual."[27]

Because Walker had a paternal regard for his slaves and felt they loved him in return, Kelley's query about purchasing his family elicited disbelief and defensiveness. Walker had a difficult time imagining that his slaves would want to leave his home and an even harder time imagining that a former slave could care for them as well as he did. He questioned Kelley's ability to provide, emotionally and materially. "Now, if you could command the means to pay for and emancipate them," he asked, "could you provide and place them in a happier and more comfortable condition than they now are, and have every guarantee of remaining?" He would not consider selling the family until he had an answer. "I much doubt your ability to make the change you desire beneficial to them, if I were even voluntarily to emancipate them. This I shall not do for the simple reason that I believe doing so would not benefit them," he added.[28] Because freeing his slaves would prove detrimental to them, Walker demonstrated his love for them by keeping them enslaved. He saw the scheme as Kelley's, because he could not fathom the idea that his slaves might want their own freedom. How could they, if they were so well treated? When Kelley asserted his own prerogatives as a father and husband and proposed purchasing his family, he challenged the slave master's conception of himself as the benevolent patriarch.

Ultimately, however, the request was less about Kelley and his family, and more about the slaveholder. After insisting freedom would not benefit the enslaved family, Walker then discussed his own needs. "My family are accustomed to and must have servants. Servants to whom they are attached, and who are truly attached to them, are invaluable," he wrote. "Servants who are raised up in a family, perfectly honest and upright, attached to those who are their owners and protectors, are a necessary part of a family, not conveniently dispensed with, not calculated to promote the happiness and welfare of either owner or servants, unless under the existence of unusual circumstances." Walker even questioned whether Kelley had bettered his own life through freedom. "Perhaps you have," he admitted, "but the effect may be different if you could accomplish what you wish in relation to your wife and children." Walker doubted an African American man's ability to capably look after his own affairs, let alone take care of others. In the end, Walker agreed to consider the proposal if Kelley could raise the requisite $2,800 and "satisfy me that you have the further ability of providing comfortable support for them, and will inform me of the fact." In the absence of such assurances, Walker told Kelley he could live with his family as "a free man with your wife and children nominally slaves."[29] As Walker adjusted to the idea that a former slave could adequately serve as father and provider, market considerations remained ever present. In Walker's estimation, his slaves provided more than labor. They had sentimental value and would be difficult to replace. Paternalistic regard thus justified their high market value, making Kelley's task more complicated and more expensive.

Five months later, Walker decided he would grant Kelley's request if Kelley could raise the requisite funds. Paternalism shaped his initial incredulity, but it also contributed to his change of heart. He cared for his slaves, so their potential freedom deserved reasonable deliberation. He delayed in responding because his daughters had been in New Orleans, and he needed to discuss the matter with them. The Walkers decided that if Kelley could "raise the money required," Kelley's wife, Paralee, and all of her children but one, Dolly, "may go free." He could not provide a definitive answer about Dolly because he had given the slave to his daughter, "to raise her up as she chose. She is very fond of her and has raised her more like she was her child than as a servant . . . and without her consent I cannot promise to let her go." Walker and his wife felt the entire family should remain together, and he promised they would "use all our persuasion" to convince her. If Annie refused, he would "make a fair and liberal deduction" from the total amount owed. Walker deferred to his own daughter, and in doing so, placed extra hurdles between Kelley and his child. Walker reiterated that he would "part with Paralee and her children with great reluctance," but felt he could not deny them the opportunity to achieve freedom. "I cannot refuse it," he said.[30] Two days later, he wrote again to say that Annie decided "she cannot be so selfish as to keep Dolly for her own personal gratification." If Kelley could raise the money, as well as cover their travel expenses, he could have his family.[31] The entire negotiation underscores the deep connections between paternalistic planter ideology and market concerns. An enslaved man, in this case a recently freed man, was allowed to exercise his paternal duty if and when those actions provided economic benefit to the master. In order to actually take over as patriarchal head of household, moreover, Kelley had to remove his family from the South. The slaveholder profited economically from this transaction, and the price he imposed undercut the biological father struggling to exert authority over his family. The considerable financial cost of acquiring his family increased the difficulty of caring for them in freedom, a vicious cycle encountered by men who purchased the liberty of kin.

A paternalistic and kindly master might be swayed with the right fiscal incentives, but purchasing kin became particularly complicated when sex was involved. A master might refuse to sell a woman he intended to keep for himself, or the inflated price of a slave might make it exceedingly difficult to redeem her. After he escaped and became a minister in New York, James Pennington recalled a visit from "an aged coloured man" who exhibited "anxiety bordering on despair." Though free, this man's wife and children remained enslaved in Maryland, and six of his children had been sold after an escape attempt, including two daughters. Pennington included an extract of a letter explaining why the girls were being held at a much higher price than their four brothers, and why agents acting on behalf of their father could not convince the traders to lower that price. "The truth is, and is confessed to be, that their destination is prostitution," one of the agents admitted, "of this you would be satisfied on seeing them: they are of elegant form, and fine faces."[32] The sexual dynamics of slavery lurked as a constant backdrop and influenced a range of transactions, including purchase of self and family.

While most men with the means first purchased themselves and then their wives, unmarried men sought to free other kin. John Meachum purchased his own freedom and then went to find his father, an enslaved preacher who had been left behind when the master migrated. "It seemed to me, at times, though I was seven hundred miles from him, that I held conversation with him, for he was near my heart," he recalled. "I went to Virginia, and bought my father." The two men had a "joyful meeting," Meachum found religion and was baptized, and after saving enough money, they walked to Kentucky to reunite with the rest of the family. Although mostly intact, Meachum considered his family incomplete without his father. After married men purchased wives and children, they next sought to free parents and grandparents.[33] For caretakers, duty to family began early in life and extended to multiple generations.

An enslaved man with the means and opportunity might purchase relatives first if he could not at that time secure his own freedom, or if such a decision better served family integrity. Caretaking within slavery regularly involved balancing individual needs and desires against the good of the family. Thomas Jones, an urban slave in Wilmington, North Carolina, who hired his own time and lived relatively independently, purchased his wife before he liberated himself because he realized this would ensure the freedom of any future children. Jones lost his first family, a wife and three young children, when their mistress moved to Alabama. Following his re-marriage, with help from a friend, he bought his second wife. "We had before determined to try to accomplish this enterprise, in order that our dear babes might be free. Besides, I felt that I could not bear another cruel separation from wife and children," he explained. "So we made a box, and, through a hole in the top, we put in every piece of money . . . that we could save from our hard earnings." Jones buried the box to keep it safe from patrollers, and with their earnings and a loan, he eventually "became the owner of my wife." They had a single child before she became free, and "that child is still in chains," Jones lamented, underscoring their reasoning. Jones bought his wife while he remained enslaved so that their children would follow her condition, a decision based on the anguish of having already lost one beloved family. Because Jones later purchased houses in the name of a white man he believed to be a friend, and noted, "a slave cannot hold property," he likely made a similar arrangement with his wife. In 1848, another friend warned Jones that "some white men were plotting to enslave my wife and children again," and he moved to protect their status. A lawyer informed him "they were not safe, unless emancipated by a special act of the Legislature," something this friend could not accomplish due to prevailing prejudice against manumission, so Jones bargained with a ship captain to secretly take his wife and three free children north. Jones stayed to sell his property, was defrauded by the white man whose name appeared on the deeds, and made his escape.[34] This order of purchase depended on having trustworthy white friends and a slave's ability to successfully escape, itself an uncertain and dangerous proposition.

Without access to banking and lacking a secure way to save and protect money, purchasing one's own family members served as a way to prevent separation and an investment that enabled enslaved and free blacks to keep a financial cushion in the form of slave property. Slaves could be quickly converted into cash or used as collateral in an emergency.[35] Stephen Whitman notes that some free blacks in Maryland chose to purchase their children and then to delay manumission to adulthood as a way to protect those children from indenture. One way to guard against indentures was to use the legal benefits of slaveholding. Owning slaves, even kin, also "undercut the presumption of being propertyless and thus a suitable target for the binding out of one's other children." Keeping children as slaves thus operated as a "conscious defensive strategy to avoid white control," and Whitman shows that free blacks delayed the manumission of their children at higher rates in counties where indigent indenture had become "virtually an all-black institution." Scholars such as Carter Woodson initially argued that free blacks became slaveholders in order to protect family integrity and as a response to restrictions on manumission, particularly if freeing family members would require them to leave the state, whereas Larry Koger, Michael Johnson, and James Roark have more recently defined free black slaveholding as an example of accommodation to white values. Koger characterizes free black ownership of slaves in South Carolina as a commercial undertaking that was exploitative rather than benevolent, and mirrored white standards and behavior. Johnson and Roark agree that while many free blacks owned family members, slaveholding increasingly included non-kin. In a hostile world, owning slaves was the best way for free blacks to establish respectability, and served as "a kind of social and economic insurance, a shield against the full force of white oppression." Johnson and Roark see both a buy-in to white values as well as a form of opposition. "Free Negro slaveholding was compelled by family considerations," they write. "Most of their slaves were not family members, as Woodson argued, but they were, black masters hoped, the means by which family members could remain free."[36]

Whitman complicates this debate, seeing a combination of both interpretations in Maryland, in that free blacks most often owned their own kin, but they made an "instrumental" rather than forced decision to delay manumission.[37] Slaveholding functioned as a way to safeguard assets by giving free blacks a property buffer recognized by white society and that protected their status, which also ultimately and paradoxically protected the family unit and offered flexibility in a precarious environment.[38] If debt threatened free status, holding slaves, even kin, operated as a sort of savings account. Being able to sell a slave quickly meant that free families could ensure that the most productive family members with the highest earning capacity remained free and able to work to keep the greatest number safe. Parents might also have sold children with the hope that with hard work they could redeem them again in the future. Adjusting to the financial and legal realities of the Old South did not necessarily signify an acceptance of white oppression. Rather than emphasize the good of the individual or the community, free black slaveholding was a strategy meant to assure the survival of a particular, atomistic family.[39]

Men unable to buy their wives or children instead tried to arrange a sale to a local master with a humane reputation. An enslaved man with regular income might also negotiate with a slaveholder to hire his wife and children on an annual basis. This gave him greater influence, but not ownership or absolute authority, as his kin remained susceptible to sale. In the years prior to emancipation, Friday Jones hired his wife and several of his children. "Mary was nearly a young woman; I watched over her," he said of one daughter. Because he knew he could not intercede directly, he had a white friend "hire Mary for me—I took her away from Mrs. Martin's by paying a big price for her. No matter how much they asked for my wife and children, I paid it."[40] Although hiring reduced their control, slaveholders employed the practice because it was lucrative, an example of how enslaved men were allowed to privately exhibit masculinity, including aspects of paternal duty, if this worked to the economic advantage of a master.

Facing numerous obstacles, many slaves failed or only partially succeeded in their goal to purchase the freedom of self and kin. James Holmes's father, a blacksmith and carpenter in Georgia, bought his own freedom and then that of his wife, "and as many of the chillun as he could. Some of dem old Masta wouldn't sell. He could not buy me 'cause dey done give me to young 'Miss Virginia." Isaac Griffen bought himself, his wife, and one child. "I left eight children in bondage, who undertook to escape," he told his antebellum interviewer in Canada. "The oldest got here; the others were retaken, and sold in Texas." Thomas Johnson's free father was unable to purchase his wife and son because their Virginia master refused to sell: "My father died when I was nine years old, he left money for me to purchase my freedom when I became a man, but the money got into other people's hands." Even if a man had the resources, a master had to agree to sell. Trusting money to white patrons was a dubious undertaking that enabled the unscrupulous to profit off of a man's love of kin. Robert Glenn's parents unsuccessfully attempted to influence his sale. His father, who hired his own time and had money saved, "got the consent and help of his owners to buy me," because a slave could not legally own property. This enraged the trader, who "cursed my father saying, 'you damn black son of a bitch, you think you are white do you? Now just to show you are black, I will not let you have your son at any price.' . . . They had to stand and see the speculator put me on his horse behind him and ride away without allowing either of them to tell me goodbye."[41] Slaves and free blacks had to negotiate not only structural, but ideological obstacles, carefully attempting to exercise their paternal duty without publicly threatening paternalism.

A plan to purchase freedom could be easily derailed by a deceitful master. Slaves depended on the honesty of masters in what were often verbal agreements.[42] Even a literate slave able to read and sign a contract had little legal standing compared to a slaveholder, who could and did violate their word. Slaveholders benefited from a self-purchase arrangement because slaves felt motivated to work harder and it promised immediate monetary gains for people generally short of cash. When a quest to purchase freedom ended in betrayal, failure cost time, money, health, and often that which motivated a man in the first place: their family. Peter Robinson earned considerable wages and tips guiding a tugboat in the Wilmington, North Carolina, harbor. He nonetheless worked out a payment plan with his master because he did not want to raise suspicion or invite theft by trying to purchase his freedom in a single lump sum and his goal was the freedom of his entire family. Despite this caution, he was arrested and sold and thus robbed of what he had already paid, his chance at liberty, and his family. William Robinson and his siblings never learned of their father's fate. Allen Allensworth, also looking back on slavery from the early twentieth century, blamed duplicity for his father's untimely death. Establishing a "transportation business," in Louisville, Kentucky, his father planned to purchase freedom for himself and then his wife and son. After making the second of three installment payments, his master sold him to another man. The new master agreed to similar terms, but he lost what he had already paid and had to begin anew. "Levi started out the second time to purchase his freedom; but the shock of disappointment and the extra hard work brought on physical prostration; after a brief illness, all worn out, sad and heart-broken, he died," his son recounted. "His new owner claimed his teams for the remaining debt."[43] Broaching the subject of self-purchase was risky. Slaves understood that a master could easily take advantage of their desire for freedom and their love of family to make a sizeable profit. Because of the power differential, an enslaved or even free black man who entered into such a bargain took a risk that he might lose more than just his labor and his money.[44] Whites manipulated enslaved men's conception of paternal duty to deny these men full attainment and practice of patriarchal privilege.

Dimmock Charlton twice attempted to purchase his own freedom and both times his masters defrauded him, taking his money and selling him and his family. After a third master allowed him to buy his freedom, he went north and endeavored to liberate his kin. He succeeded in freeing a granddaughter whose mistress brought her to New York. In the midst of his suit to gain legal custody, he became embroiled in a dispute with the Philadelphia Anti-slavery Society, and his narrative was the result of friendly members defending his character against a defamatory article in the *National Anti-slavery Standard*, accusing him of collecting money under "false pretences," and of being "entirely unworthy of confidence." Drawing on interviews, the 1859 narrative discussed Charlton's efforts on behalf of his granddaughter, noting that he "removed her to Canada, to prevent what he feared, her re-capture." In addition, he "steadfastly declined to bind his little girl to one of the members of the Anti-Slavery Society, who had been interested in her emancipation, and this decision, and his removal of her to Canada," caused friction. Charlton admitted that he had in fact "threatened to shoot a colored man sent to prevent his removing her—if he dared to lay a hand upon her."[45] Charlton may well have been a difficult personality, and he clearly caused tension when he defended his granddaughter. His story highlights the importance of a fugitive's relationships with the antislavery community. A man who escaped was not free of the white power structure. Positive interactions, code for displaying some level of obsequiousness and softening public masculine assertion, could help a fugitive solicit aid in locating and purchasing his family. In order to recover his role as a father, a fugitive might need to make sacrifices, including individual pride and un-regulated patriarchal authority.

Fugitives who purchased relatives after escaping made arrangements via correspondence or agents, sending money south. A runaway eager to locate and free loved ones faced several challenges, including the inability to find and then go to kin directly without endangering his own liberty. Moses Grandy purchased his freedom and then traveled the world as a sailor. Once he had amassed some savings, he worked through agents to purchase the family members he could locate. When he purchased his wife, "I dared not go myself to fetch her, lest I should be again deprived of my liberty, as often happens to free coloured people." Because enslaved people "have no family name of their own by which they can be traced," Grandy had "little hope" of finding his missing children. "If born free (and white), Grandy might have risen by talent and have become a successful businessman," Calvin Schermer-horn argues. "Instead, he spent his life's fortune buying relatives scattered about the South." In the late 1840s, Northern friends and congregants of Jermain Loguen, "overcome by his love for his mother," raised money to purchase her from Tennessee. Her master, however, refused to sell unless Loguen, a fugitive, also paid for himself, a concession to slavery Loguen refused to make.[46] To free his mother meant acknowledging the slavehold-er's ownership and rebranding his achievement of liberty as a crime. Even from a distance, a master attempted to turn a profit and degrade a man's sense of self-possession and familial control.

Escape

Purchasing freedom was not an option for slaves who had no means of earning money or a master who refused to sell. This might favor an escape attempt, leading to yet another set of difficult calculations. Escaping alone, though challenging, offered the highest chances of success, but meant leav-ing family and friends. Escaping with kin most quickly achieved freedom for an entire family, but was extremely risky. Involving more people in an escape plan upped the chances of accidental or purposeful betrayal. Travel-ing with children or the elderly slowed the group's progress and risked re-capture. Running away with a spouse increased the likelihood of failure and fleeing with children made escape far more logistically difficult and further reduced the chances of success.[47] A man who successfully escaped with his family provided the ultimate good, freedom, but more often, he escaped alone. A father who escaped alone had to confront the painful dilemma of whether to prioritize his individual conscience or his duty to family.

The different constraints on enslaved men and women, including gender norms in slave communities, contributed to rates and types of escape. Stephanie Camp argued that slaveholders built "geographies of containment" on plantations, restricting the mobility of slaves, especially women. Masters issued passes authorizing movement for work and family visitation overwhelmingly to men. In addition, enslaved men had greater access to the types of skilled work that allowed for some mobility. In their study of runaway slaves, John Hope Franklin and Loren Schweninger use over two thousand advertisements to construct a profile of the runaway. They emphasize the diversity of those who absconded, but note that "the great majority of runaways were young men in their teens and twenties." The outline was remarkably similar in the earlier and later periods of the study, with men comprising 81 percent of runaways and a mean age of twenty-seven. Many younger men had yet to marry or start a family, making the decision easier. In addition, men were more likely to be sold alone, and many chose to flee when they felt they had little to lose. Women had children at younger ages, limiting their opportunity to become fugitives. Most women who attempted to escape permanently did so when young and unencumbered.[48] Childbearing impinged on a woman's opportunities to run away and gender standards further tied her to the plantation. "Community sanctions against women abandoning their children normalized female dedication to the family and were another pressure that limited the number of women who could escape to the North," Camp wrote. Far more slaves engaged in truancy, or temporary absenteeism, than attempted to reach the North, and truancy was particularly common in women.[49] All slaves faced the tension between duty to self and duty to kin, but gender standards within slave communities meant that while women might experience internal turmoil over the decision to escape, they faced different external expectations about rebellious behavior.

The decision to try to abscond was easiest for unmarried slaves, but even they had to weigh potential freedom against the hardships of the journey, the consequences of being caught, fear of the unknown, and the difficulty of leaving loved ones and the familiar. Slaves were deliberately kept ill-informed about the wider world, and trained to be risk averse. "I sometimes wonder, that a slave, so ignorant, so timid, as he is, ever makes the attempt to get his freedom," Lewis Clarke observed. "Without are foes, within are fears." Another successful fugitive, Henry Bibb, articulated the quandary family men faced when considering escape. In addition to fear of capture, death, and sale, "my strong attachments to friends and relatives . . . twined about my heart and were hard to break away from," he wrote. "But I had counted the cost, and was fully prepared to make the sacrifice. . . . I must forsake friends and neighbors, wife and child, or consent to live and die a slave."[50] For Bibb, to love oneself meant leaving loved ones.

Deciding to run away involved a set of calculations that went beyond the individual, as family bonds and community ties could link a person to their home even if they loathed slavery. James Pennington faced "perplexing thoughts," as he weighed an escape attempt. "I distinctly remember the two great difficulties that stood in the way of my flight: I had a father and mother whom I dearly loved, —I had also six sisters and four brothers on the plantation. The question was, shall I hide my purpose from them?" Pennington felt troubled not just about leaving those he loved, but the repercussions of his actions. "How will my flight affect them when I am gone? Will they not be suspected? Will not the whole family be sold off as a disaffected family," he worried. Running away could end in severe physical punishment, death, or sale for those directly involved, but also had ripple effects.[51] Family members might be blamed, especially if they knew about or abetted the flight. To tell loved ones exposed them to greater peril, and to escape without a proper farewell was painful. Pennington's parents, in creating a cohesive family environment, unwittingly complicated their son's quest to obtain liberty.

A man planning to escape alone faced the emotional pain of leaving loved ones and deliberations about how much information to reveal, especially to his children. After escaping from jail and going into hiding, Israel Campbell arranged to speak with his oldest daughter. A friend brought her to the hiding place and asked "if she could keep from telling the white people." Campbell hesitated to see her for fear she would reveal his whereabouts. "I was afraid, as all children will do, that she would be so glad to see me, and run off and tell master and mistress. But she said, 'Not for my life will I tell.'" The two had a joyful reunion, and he told her "that I was going to start for Canada pretty soon now; and that when I got free, I would go back for her. I told her that she must be a good girl and obey every body in all that is right." Campbell chose to meet with his eldest child and not his two younger sons, "for she was the only one large enough to remember what I might tell them." Campbell traveled with another fugitive to Canada, where he found his brother. William Webb's father informed his children of his plan to escape.

"He called his children about him . . . and told us to remember what he had taught us, and how he had tried to bring us up right, and he told us all to mind our mother."[52] Slaves feared purposeful and accidental betrayal, even by kin, so they had to make calculated choices about how much information to share. Hiding one's intentions meant departing without saying farewell.

Escape presented a dilemma in that a man might feel impelled to run away because he despised his own powerlessness, but in taking the initiative, he abandoned his family and responsibility to kin. For many antebellum fugitives, escape was an expression of manhood.[53] As with other aspects of slavery, men faced a conflict between exerting and defending their individual masculinity and, in doing so, cutting themselves off from their duty as husbands and fathers.[54] For some men, resentment over the treatment of not just themselves, but family members, induced escape. "It seemed hard when I had earned any money to have to carry it to another man, when my wife needed it herself," Elijah Perkins complained to his antebellum interviewer. "I have left a wife and five small children. I had a good wife, and, if I could, would have her and the children here this minute. I never heard of a man running away from slavery to get rid of his wife."[55] A successful escape meant complete separation from those people a man loved but could not adequately provision or protect.

Escape attempts motivated by the agony of seeing abuse and the inability to intervene speak to affection for family. In 1844, Henry Bibb wrote to his master to explain his decision to abscond. "To be compelled to stand by and see you whip and slash my wife without mercy, when I could afford her no protection, not even by offering myself to suffer the lash in her place, was more than I felt it to be the duty of a slave husband to endure," he wrote. "This kind of treatment was what drove me from home and family." Men's urge to protect kin came into glaring conflict with the realities of the slave condition, which impelled flight. The abuses of slavery promoted individualistic action, something former slaves deeply resented. Fugitives blamed slaveholders for denying them the ability to uphold their vision of paternal duty. Because the institution of slavery compartmentalized different aspects of masculine responsibility, making it impossible to achieve them all, men who escaped prioritized individual resistance, interpreting caretaking in a personal and global rather than local sense. To escape was to resist slavery, which might have negative consequences for a particular family, but had potentially positive consequences for the broader family: the African American community writ large. If these men could no longer take care of their enslaved family, they consoled themselves with the thought that they could take care of themselves and, as abolitionist activists, their race.[56]

Some men left their family because they loved them, one of the agonizing contradictions of the slave condition. Dan Lockhart ran away because he could no longer bear seeing his wife and children whipped. "I could not stand this abuse of them," he commented, "and so I made up my mind to leave." He informed his wife, who feared his recapture. Lockhart told his mistress his father was sick and she gave him permission to visit. "I got up and dressed myself to leave. One of my little children came to me when I had stepped out. Said I, 'Jane, where are you going?' 'Daddy, I'm looking for you.' My feelings were very tender at the time," he recalled. "I took her up in my arms, and carried her and laid her back in the bed with her mother and the other little child, Julia. I sat down and waited till they were all asleep; I then got up . . . said 'Farewell!' and started on my journey." A man who reached the North knew he might never see his loved ones again, nor did he have any easy means of communication. "My mind being uneasy," Lockhart wrote to a friend to inform his wife of his safe arrival, "and assuring her of my continued affection. My old master got hold of this letter, and so pursued me with two officers," forcing Lockhart to move to Canada.[57]

When interviewed in Canada in the 1850s, men who escaped alone or with other men expressed profound grief even as they savored their freedom. "I felt, when free, as light as a feather—a burden was off of me. I could get up and go to my work without being bruised and beaten," Isaac Griffen remarked. "The worst thought was for my children,—what they might have to go through. I cannot hear from them." "Liberty I find to be sweet indeed," Henry Atkinson similarly remarked, right after discussing the anguish of leaving his family and his belief he would never again see his wife and child. Knowing one's family members remained enslaved, and not knowing what became of them, clouded a fugitive's contentment and left him with an acute and ongoing sense of loss. "I left a wife and three children, and three grand-children,—I never expect to see them again in this world—never," Christopher Nichols added. David West believed life in Canada would be ideal if only he had his family with him: "My family are perpetually on my mind. I should be perfectly happy if I could have my wife and the four children." "There is only one thing to prevent me being entirely happy here, and that is the want of my dear wife and children," Jackson Whitney wrote to the Kentucky master from whom he had escaped. Whitney invoked a sense of religious guilt and asked that his former master send his wife and children to Canada, "thus preparing to meet your God in peace," and avoid eternal damnation.[58] Whitney impugned the morality of slaveholders, but the master still held the earthly power. A father who achieved liberty without his family did not escape the pain associated with separation. He might be free of slavery, but he was not free of its corrosive shadow.

Because most slaves were illiterate and communication involved dangers on both ends, fugitives had few options for contact with enslaved loved ones. "It is three years ago that I left my family, and I don't know whether they are dead or alive. I want to hear from them," said William Brown. Even when slaves managed to escape with a few family members, they invariably left kin in the South. Mrs. Frances Henderson missed her parents, telling her interviewer, "I like liberty, and if Washington were a free country, I would like to go back there, —my parents were there." While fugitives praised the North and Canada, ultimately, what they most appreciated was liberty, and what they most missed was family.[59]

For men who wanted to escape in part to exert control over their lives and family, a solution was to try to escape with loved ones. "One absorbing purpose occupied my soul—to gain freedom, self-assertion, and deliverance from the cruel caprices and fortunes of dissolute tyrants. Once to get away, with my wife and children, to some spot where I could feel that they were indeed mine—where no grasping master could stand between me and them," Josiah Henson declared. Families did manage to escape, but traveling in a group, and especially with children, complicated the attempt, and failure could end in separation and a worse situation.[60] While women were accustomed to hard labor, men had greater opportunity to acquire outdoor skills that could aid in an escape. Because men almost always did the visiting in an abroad marriage, they also had greater experience moving beyond the confines of the plantation, though few slaves had extensive geographic knowledge.

Traveling with young children involved the greatest hardship and risk. "I brought my wife and three children with me," Henry Morehead told his interviewer. "I left because they were about selling my wife and children to the South. I would rather have followed them to the grave, than to the Ohio River to see them go down. I knew it was death or victory." Faced with separation, and with little to lose, Morehead and his family became fugitives. "I was longer on the road longer than I should have been without my burden: one child was nine months old, one two years old, and one four," he continued. "The weather was cold, and my feet were frostbitten, as I gave my wife my socks to pull on over her shoes. With all the sufferings of the frost and the fatigues of travel, it was not so bad as the effects of slavery."[61] To escape with a baby or toddler meant carrying an extra burden and keeping them quiet so as to avoid detection. Even young children capable of walking could not travel as fast or far each day as adults.

Escaping as a family involved considerable peril, anxiety, physical exertion, and more extensive preparation. "I felt energy enough in my own breast to contend with privation and danger," Josiah Henson noted, and had he been single, "knowing no tie of father or husband, and concerned for my own safety only, I would have felt all difficulties light in view of the hope that was set before me. But, alas! I had a wife and four dear children." In order to escape on foot with his family, Henson had to plan ahead. He first had to convince his wife, who was "overwhelmed with terror." She "besought me to remain at home, contented." Henson, however, knew his master intended to sell him and saw escape as his only chance of keeping the family intact. He told his wife he would run away and take all the children "except the youngest," rather than be "forcibly torn from her," and she relented. "The chief practical difficulty that had weighed upon my mind, was connected with the youngest two of the children. They were of three and two years respectively, and of course would have to be carried. Both stout and healthy, they were a heavy burden, and my wife had declared that I should break down under it before I had got five miles from home." Henson had his wife construct a knapsack "large enough to hold them both, and arranged with strong straps to go round my shoulders." He then "practised carrying them night after night, both to test my own strength and accustom them to submit to it," which his children deemed "fine fun." On the appointed night, Henson asked permission for their oldest son, who slept in the master's house, to visit his mother. The family traveled by night from Kentucky, hiding by day, surviving hunger, thirst, and wild animals. Henson often left them hidden in the woods to scout ahead and procure food. "When my feet first touched the Canada shore," he recalled, "I threw myself on the ground, rolled in the sand, seized handfuls of it and kissed them, and danced around, till . . . I passed for a madman."[62] Thomas Jones, who escaped from North Carolina after sending his nominally free family north when he heard rumors that white men intended to sell them as slaves, called reuniting in freedom with his wife and children "the happy hour of my life."[63]

Families with young children were far more likely to make and succeed in the attempt to escape if they lived in the Upper South and were often compelled to run by impending separation. Samuel Ward owed his freedom to his parents' escape from Maryland, an event precipitated by his mother's approaching sale. "Said she to my father, 'we must take this child and run away.' . . . As is the case in other families where the wife leads, my father followed my mother in her decision." Escape from the Upper South also diversified the travel options, particularly for men with access to horses and carts. Henry Garnet's father "got permission of his master to attend the funeral of a friend" and instead "procured a covered wagon," and drove his wife and two children from Maryland to Delaware where they met up with abolitionists. Such travel might draw attention to a party, making it practical only over shorter distances.[64]

Because a man who lost his family felt he had nothing to lose, separation or looming separation from family inspired many escape attempts. "The first thing that occurred to me, after the cruel separation of my wife and children," was to try to obtain freedom, Henry Brown recalled. "Those reasons which often deter the slave from attempting to escape, no longer existed . . . for my family were gone, and slavery now had no mitigating circumstances, to lessen the bitterness of its cup of woe." "I came away because I was standing in fear of being separated from my wife and children," George Ross told an interviewer in Canada. "I got my family all away." Slaves desired freedom, Ross insisted, but "the great difficulty is to get families off." He believed that men could escape more easily, and many refused to try if they could not bring their wives and children.[65] Caretaking tied men to slavery just as it pushed others to flee.

Kinship ties kept many slaves from absconding, and a number made their escape only after losing family. "I had a great wish for liberty when I was a boy. I always had it in my head to clear. But I had a wife and children," George Johnson stated. "However, my wife died last year of cholera, and then I determined not to remain in that country." David West also escaped after his master died and he learned he would be sold. West had hired out, "was treated well," and admitted he likely would have stayed if circumstances had not shifted. "I did not believe that slavery was right, but as I was born there, and had a family there, I tried to content myself to remain, and should probably have done so, but for the dread of being sold south. My only trouble is about my wife and family. I never should have come away but for being forced away."[66] The fact that love of family deterred many from attempting to flee, and loss motivated others to take the risk, demonstrates how intensely slaves valued family and the ways in which kinship ties shaped their decisions, lives, and sense of identity.

Many fugitives, facing a sense of emptiness and isolation without kin, devoted themselves to finding and freeing loved ones. The most daring risked their safety to return and attempt to free loved ones, while most raised money to try to purchase family members or engineer their escape, soliciting logistical and financial aid from Northern contacts.[67] When able, fugitives wrote to family members to remain connected, expressing their mingled joy and sadness.[68] Henry Bibb escaped from slavery and then returned for his wife and daughter more than once, leading to his own reenslavement. "They well knew that my little family was the only object of attraction that . . . would induce me to come back and risk my liberty," he wrote of his first failed attempt. Because he "felt it to be my duty, as a husband and father, to make one more effort," Bibb went back to Kentucky. This time Bibb was betrayed and captured, and his family sold to New Orleans. Though he believed he could have escaped the boat, Bibb stayed "for the sake of my wife and child who was with me. I could see no chance to get them off, and I could not leave them." Bibb eventually made it back to the North, where he spent several years searching for his wife and daughter and raising money to secure their liberty, but he never again saw his family. He finally gave up when he heard his wife was living as a concubine to a new master.[69] In his attempt to uphold his responsibility to family, Bibb's dogged pursuit of liberty for his wife and child made their situation worse rather than better, as his actions led to their removal further south and away from home, the familiar, and extended family.

Justifying his decision to abandon hope of reunification, Bibb focused on his former wife. For Bibb, the absence of a legally recognized marriage to Malinda did not negate the significance of the union in his eyes. A contract "voluntarily assumed" could only be voided by one of the partners, and Malinda "relinquished" their marriage when she consented to cohabitate with a subsequent master. Bibb insisted that he blamed slavery and not Malinda for this situation, but as Heather Williams notes, "His words belied the fact that he held her responsible." Williams argues that he worried about the reaction of his abolitionist audience and endeavored to assure them that Malinda, rather than he, had ended their marriage.[70] Bibb implicated both slavery and his former wife because to do otherwise would be to admit that his own attempts to free her, though undertaken with noble intentions, led to her situation and made him complicit in her degradation. To absolve himself and his own sense of guilt, he implied that Malinda likely accepted her role as a concubine. Conspicuously absent in the entire discussion is

Bibb's daughter, Mary Frances. To admit he had failed as a husband would be to admit he failed as a father, and so the culpability fell on Malinda. Heroic resistance in the form of escape did not enable a man to fully achieve antebellum standards of masculinity if and when he left loved ones behind. Publishing and lecturing about their lives then forced these free men to confront the ways in which slavery continued to impinge on their manhood.

David Doddington argues that fugitives presented men as protectors of "helpless female dependents," in their effort to stake a "claim for black masculinity and ability to integrate into a patriarchal republican society." He uses Henry Bibb as an example and later cites Bibb as a runaway who acknowledged the painful need to leave loved ones in order to achieve liberty and become a man.[71] He never addresses Bibb's return trips, unsuccessful efforts to free his family, and subsequent internal guilt. Heroic masculinity and providing were not always separate identities, and men often faced turmoil in attempting to achieve and reconcile these competing visions of manhood. Enslaved men certainly fought against the dehumanization of slavery, but those who remained slaves, and even those who managed to escape, never fully escaped the ongoing struggle inherent in trying to bridge these aspirations that slavery so brutally partitioned.

Not all runaways headed north, as many men absconded in an effort to return to or find family members from whom they had been separated, stories highlighted in the FWP narratives. When their master moved from Mississippi to Texas, Millie Ann Smith's mother and siblings were separated from their father, but "Pappy run off and come to Texas and begged Master in to buying him so he could be with his wife and chil'ren." Wash Ingram's father, "a fightin' man," ran away and found work gold mining in Virginia. However, when he heard that his wife had died and his three sons had been sold, Ingram's father followed and overtook his sons en route to Texas, and returned himself to bondage. The loss of a mother left the father as the sole caretaker and he adjusted his role and life accordingly. As Ingram recalled, "He come and fin' me and my brothers. Den he jine Master Ingram slaves so he can be with his chil'ren."[72] In the minds of some enslaved men, duty to and love of family outweighed individual freedom.

Other men ran off and hid locally in order to remain near family. Constant beatings caused Sarah Ford's father to disappear from his Texas plantation on more than one occasion. "One time papa run away an' is gone for a whole year. Dat's de time he runs off to Mexico. He sure look like a monkey when he gits back, — his hair all standin' straight up on his head, an' his face all covered up with long hair," she recalled. Ford believed her father could easily have escaped permanently. "He sure was mighty good to mamma an' me though, an' de only reason he would come back was to see us. He knew he was gwineter get a whippin', but he'd come back jes' to see us anyhow. Dey never could cotch him when he runs 'way, 'cause papa too smart for 'em." A slaveholder in Mississippi told Frederick Law Olmsted that men who ran away could be easily recaptured: "They almost always kept in the neighbourhood, because they did not like to go where they could not sometimes get back and see their families."[73] In Louisiana, where there were a high number of single men in the slave population, runaways were less likely to hide out locally because they had no wives and children to tie them to the area.[74]

Charles Ball, kidnapped and sold away from his family, eventually made his way from Georgia back to Maryland. "My heart yearned for my wife and children, from whom I had now been separated more than four years." An experienced hunter, Ball's ability to subsist in the forest was critical to his escape. After a long journey and a brief recapture, Ball reached his wife's cabin. His children "had forgotten me. When I attempted to take them in my arms, they fled from me, and took refuge under the bed of their mother." Ball then faced the reality of his status as a fugitive: "I passed the night, with my children around me, oppressed by a melancholy foreboding of my future destiny. The idea that I was utterly unable to afford protection to and safeguard my own family, and was myself even more helpless than they, tormented my bosom with alternate throbs of affection and fear." Ball hid, worked for wages, and eventually purchased land. His decision to remain in Maryland, motivated by his desire to be with his family, ultimately proved unwise. When his wife died, he remarried and had more children. After a decade of "happiness and comparative ease," a relative of his former master located Ball and had him arrested. He escaped again, this time to Philadelphia. When Ball returned to Maryland to sell his farm and collect his family, he discovered that his wife and children, all freeborn, had been kidnapped and sold. "It was the most dreadful of all the misfortunes that I ever had suffered," he declared. Ball returned to Philadelphia "without the least hope of ever again seeing, my wife and children."[75] Love of family caused men to compromise their hard-won freedom. Calvin Schermerhorn provides a detailed accounting of Charles Ball's seemingly "counterintuitive" choices and actions throughout his life, undertaken in an effort to keep his family intact and safe. Ball had many opportunities to escape slavery as an individual, and "each time he acted as a father, as a husband, and as someone with a stake in the status quo, even though agents of that status quo had kidnapped and brutalized him."[76]

When slaves escaped, white authorities closely watched, interrogated, and incarcerated family members in an attempt to gather information or lure escapees back. Despite proslavery rhetoric, slaveholders expected slaves to feel and exhibit concern and affection for kin. After William Green escaped from Maryland, "they even went down to my father's to see if I had been there. They believed he knew of my whereabouts, but the old gentleman knew nothing about it."[77] Actions belied the claims that slaves formed only transitory attachments.

ALTHOUGH THE PERVERSE INCENTIVES of slavery encouraged individuals to behave selfishly and devalue community, slaves resisted and cherished family above all else. Prioritizing family was a means of survival, but could exacerbate the anguish of enslavement and further enmesh individuals and the families in the institution. Skilled slaves who purchased their own freedom often remained in the South and tied to slavery in an effort to free family members, and their love of kin gave white owners and lenders increased leverage over the slave and free black communities. Slave narratives also show that love of family impeded flight and influenced who ran, where they went, and the timing of escape attempts. Large numbers of young men escaped because they had fewer family entanglements holding them back. Married men who escaped with family members provided the ultimate good a father could give his children: freedom. The husbands and fathers who fled alone, many after losing family to sale, some because they could no longer stand their own impotence in the face of abuse, found the fruits of freedom bittersweet. Love of liberty never fully erased the pain of leaving behind family and one's paternal duty.

CHAPTER FIVE

Tuckey Buzzard Lay Me
Slavery, Sex, and White Fathers

Shortly before the Civil War, Jermain Loguen published a narrative of his life in which he made a stark claim about fatherhood and slavery. "It is the condition of the mother . . . that makes the slave," he noted. "As to the progenitor on the male side, he is rarely known as the father in fact, never in law. The slave has no father." As the child of a white slave trader who sold his black family, Loguen had bitter experience with slavery and paternity. Frederick Douglass, who never knew the identity of his white father, agreed: "Slavery does away with fathers, as it does away with families . . . and its laws do not recognize their existence in the social arrangements of the plantation. . . . The order of civilization is reversed here."[1] Slavery warped what Douglass saw as the natural human order in which paternity determined a child's lineage and social status and the family coalesced around the patriarch. Whereas those with enslaved fathers regularly spoke of these men with admiration despite the emasculation of the system, slaves with white parentage often felt fatherless.

Both men addressed a central feature of slavery and the power dynamics of the institution. Jennifer Morgan discusses *partus sequitur ventrum* (offspring follows belly) and the 1662 Virginia Act that linked heredity and race through maternal reproduction and the bodies of black women. "When racial slavery depended on the transformation of lineage into embodied inheritance, black women could not be allowed to produce kinship," she writes, exploring "the violence done when economic structures supersede kinship, and when enslaveability displaces maternity."[2] According to Morgan, "for black women, maternity wrenched parenting out of the realm of the domestic and into the marketplace." If the status of the enslaved mother determined the status of her children, an enslaved man lost the "patriarchal ability to confer status through his person." White men, meanwhile, could father children with enslaved women and each child inherited her bondage and "was transformed from kin to property."[3] White paternity existed along a continuum between the home and the market, often blending the two. White men could bequeath their status to free children by white women, or exploit the bodies of enslaved women to generate property. White fathers of slaves owned their own children as commodities, meaning that they were simultaneously erased as fathers and reified as paternalists.

Hortense Spillers pinpoints white paternity of slaves as a fundamental aspect of the "dehumanizing ungendering" of slavery. "Under conditions of captivity, the offspring of the female does not 'belong' to the Mother, nor is s/he 'related' to the 'owner,' though the latter 'possesses' it, and . . . often fathered it, *and*, as often, without whatever benefit of patrimony." Sexual exploitation created "a dual fatherhood . . . comprised of the African father's banished name and body and the captor father's mocking presence."[4] In fact, multiple fatherhoods developed and persisted within slavery even as, according to nineteenth-, twentieth-, and twenty-first-century normative definitions of the role, fatherhood could not exist for enslaved people. All enslaved children were legally fatherless, but as earlier chapters have shown, many children recognized and loved their enslaved fathers, and those separated from kin early in life believed they had a father. If enslaved fathers had no bearing on the status of their children, they often played an influential emotional and spiritual role in their children's lives and conceptions of self. Enslaved fathers could be physically present, or present in the mind, but they had no external legal or patriarchal standing. White paternity of slaves again points to a social experience in which normative notions of paternity rarely existed, and only did so when a handful of these men violated the legal strictures that defined their enslaved offspring as property. Of the causes that led to emotional and physical fatherlessness for enslaved individuals and families, white parentage was one, if not the, most significant factor.

Catherine Clinton defines slavery not simply as a labor regime, but "a means of sexual and social control." Early colonial statutes governing interracial sex "provided errant males with an *incentive* to prefer slave women as illicit partners." White women could use the courts to sue for financial support of illegitimate children, whereas enslaved women could not. Prior to the Civil War, miscegenation laws stigmatized interracial liaisons. Such relationships had no legal standing and the parties involved lacked property or inheritance rights. While interracial sex was common, and commonly ignored, Southern law policed the boundaries of respectability and marriage and enforced a rigid racial hierarchy.[5] White men could not be accused of or charged with rape for having sex with an enslaved woman, making consent a moot point. The law thus financially incentivized illicit sex with enslaved women and imposed no criminal impediments. Sexual access to slaves inevitably produced children, and these children were commodities white men had no legal obligation to support.

According to former slave Jack Maddox, "white men got plenty chilluns" by enslaved women. "They didn't ask them. They just took them." Rosa Maddox agreed: "Seems like some of them had a plumb craving for the other color. Leastways they wanted to start themselves out on the nigger women." White men could use enslaved bodies for sexual initiation, gratification, and experimentation, or to express their dominance, and could do so without fear of penalty. "From the masters' point of view, slave women were perfect women, for slaves existed to fulfill their masters' wishes. The sexual availability of enslaved women was a function of their powerlessness in society," Nell Irvin Painter writes.[6] Longer-term sexual relationships with slaves also made sense to white men. A white wife entailed a negotiation and affiliation with in-laws, the expense of setting up a proper household, and the need to educate and provide for heirs.[7] For white men not yet financially or emotionally ready to marry, or who had no desire to remarry, a concubine offered companionship. A wife could not be sold. A slave could be, as could her children.

A master could satisfy his sexual appetites and desire for dominance and turn a profit at the same time. Mollie Kinsey accused slaveholders of selling their own children "lak herds uv cattle," identifying the crux of white paternity of slaves. Legally and socially, a white man could produce enslaved children without incurring the encumbrances and duties of fatherhood.[8] Slave communities looked upon white paternity of slaves quite differently. In the opinion of former slaves, few aspects of slavery underscored the moral hypocrisy of white Southerners and the abdication of honorable manhood like the sexual exploitation of enslaved women and the refusal of most white fathers to acknowledge and take responsibility for their own children.

The sexual dynamics of slavery created a substantial mixed-race population, as masters, sons and relatives of masters, overseers, and patrollers all fathered children by enslaved women.[9] Many white men ignored, sold, or abused their enslaved offspring, others gave them preferential treatment but kept them as slaves, and a few manumitted their enslaved concubines and children. Former slaves' feelings about their white fathers varied considerably and depended on a range of factors, including the degree and nature of contact, how the father treated his illegitimate children, the circumstances leading to a person's birth, and the reaction of slave communities. The reaction of the local slave community was a complex interaction with, and often response to, mixed-race identity. White fathers who defied Southern conventions and freed their children earned the highest praise and those who abused and sold their progeny elicited the most scathing criticism. Informants expressed admiration for the handful of white fathers who openly acknowledged their children and provided freedom and education. They had ambivalent to negative reactions to white fathers who offered a privileged status on the plantation but not manumission. Finally, a significant number of informants despised their cruel, neglectful white fathers. Antebellum narratives, late nineteenth-century autobiographies, and twentieth-century interviews share consistent evaluations of white fathers, revealing former slaves' enduring conceptions of paternal duty across time and space.

Slave Narratives and White Paternity

Sexual abuse, like family separation, overshadowed enslaved peoples' lives. Abolitionist authors used the ubiquity of sexual assault and enslaved men's inability to protect their daughters to arouse the indignation of Northern fathers. "Fathers! . . . In your own land are thousands of daughters, as lovely, as much beloved, as yours, whose parents cannot protect them," Peter Randolph declared. "They must look tamely on and witness their degradation; they must behold them become the spoiler's prey, and presume not to utter one word in their behalf. Why? They are SLAVES! . . . Ah, father! could you see your daughter in such a situation and not cry aloud for vengeance?"[10] Fugitives focused on sex because they believed the argument would gain traction in the fight against slavery and because this line of criticism reflected their deepest anger toward predatory white Southern manhood.

Former slaves understood that sex functioned as a means of gratification, a tool of control, and as a method of physical and psychological warfare. Describing his master's intimidation, William Ward told an African American interviewer, "One day he tol' me dat if my wife had been good lookin', I never would sleep wid her again 'cause he'd kill me an' take her an' raise chilluns off'n her." The assault on the slave community included the exploitation of women's bodies, the disruption of the family, and the reproduction of children as a commodity. Masters presented the greatest threat, but slaves also had to worry about their owners' sons and relatives, overseers, patrollers, and slave traders. When Samuel Hall noted that patrollers "out to keep the negro in his place would often be the father of some of these children," torn from their mothers and sold, he defined sexual violence as a weapon of dominance, targeting women's self-possession, men's ability to protect, the stability of the family, and all slaves' emotional well-being.[11] African American men usually faulted the perpetrators rather than the victims of sexual assault and enumerated the collateral damage inflicted on men and children. Those who had lived bounded lives could relate to the powerlessness imposed on others.[12]

In interviews and autobiographies, former slaves described the Old South as morally depraved to the point of sporadic incest. George Fortman related a complicated story about his "unsatisfactory birth" in Kentucky and the fact that his father and grandfather were one and the same. Jacob Aldrich accused his white grandfather in Louisiana of having "chillen by his own chillen." Mattie Curtis's North Carolina master kept all the "yaller gals in one quarter," with access limited to himself, his sons, friends, and the overseers. The resulting children grew up and themselves entered the "yaller quarter" and then had "more chilluns fer her own daddy or brother. . . . Day say dat a heap of dem is halfwits."[13] Although they could do little about white sexual activity, slaves policed their own. Enslaved people throughout the South had more relaxed standards concerning consensual premarital and extramarital sex than whites, but they had strict notions of appropriate partners.[14] Several FWP narratives related Oedipal stories of family members separated and later unknowingly married through force or choice and only then realizing the identity of a relative, often due to a distinguishing scar. Such tales enabled informants to condemn slavery in that family separation could unwittingly lead to what they saw as unnatural relationships.[15] Though rare compared to other forms of sexual exploitation, white Southerners facilitated incestuous relationships by refusing to define their enslaved offspring as part of their family and establishing a rigid demarcation between legitimate and illegitimate sexual relations.

Former slaves denounced the treatment of mixed-race children and the white fathers who shirked paternal responsibility and willingly enslaved and sold their own offspring.[16] "No man with one grain of soul could sell his own flesh and blood!" William Mallory declared. "These men will all be rewarded for their deeds and misdeeds . . . on the last great day when the trumpet shall sound." William Anderson called slaveholders "white fiends in human shape" who flogged women "until they yielded" and sold their own "cousins, brothers, sisters, sons, and daughters. . . . Men who will do these things are capable of committing the most atrocious crimes." Both men defined slaveholders' willing traffic in their own blood as devoid of more than just honor and feeling, defaming them as subhuman, soulless brutes. Mia Bay shows that black intellectuals promulgated a "distinctly male image of the white race as overly brutal and predatory" and cast African Americans as a "morally superior redeemer race."[17] Black communities cared about the moral exercise of power. A man with authority, if he was a good father, used that power to support kin and community rather than to abuse or in the service of self.

While Mallory and Anderson wrote from the safety of the North prior to and after the Civil War, enslaved people expressed similar sentiments, albeit in more measured terms. A slave named Virginia, jailed and awaiting sale by her former white partner, wrote to Rice C. Ballard, a slave trader, seeking his intervention. At the very least, she believed she deserved to choose her own buyer. "What is still harder [is] for the father of my children to sell his own offspring yes his own flesh & blood," she wrote. "Is it possible that any free born American would hand his [character] with such a stigma as that . . . to sell his child that is his image."[18] Virginia appealed to paternal duty, indicating that concubines, though sometimes aligned with white men, shared slave communities' definition of honorable fatherhood. She found it unfathomable that a free man would forsake his responsibility to kin. African American narrators stressed the sexual dynamics of slavery precisely because the behavior of these white men so unambiguously deviated from their conception of what it meant to be a father and patriarch.

White Southerners and Miscegenation

Miscegenation varied regionally, with a higher level of race mixing in the Upper South and increasing rates in the South as a whole as the Civil War approached. "I am surprised at the number of fine-looking mulattoes, or nearly white-coloured persons, that I see," Frederick Law Olmsted said of his travels in Virginia. Whereas in the colonial and early national period many planters freed their offspring, leading to a largely mulatto free black population, this practice declined in the nineteenth century.[19] Social mores changed with the advent of proslavery ideology, and legal constraints on manumission made the process increasingly difficult. In the 1850s, "slavery was becoming whiter, visibly so and with amazing rapidity," Joel Williamson argues. "White people were enslaving themselves, as it were in the form of their children and their children's children." A rise in interracial sexual contact was accompanied by a rise in the number of enslaved mulattos and a full-scale attack on the rights of the free black population. The enslavement of those with white blood caused some debate, but ultimately proslavery ideologues pushed the one-drop rule as justification for enslaving partially white persons.[20] With the closure of the international slave trade and the western expansion of the plantation complex seen as politically and economically critical, Southerners felt they needed more slaves.[21]

The burgeoning mulatto population forced white Southerners to confront the uncomfortable topic of interracial sex. Deborah Gray White argues that by labeling black women promiscuous Jezebels, Southerners absolved white men of responsibility. Black women "tempted men of the superior caste," and their loose morals obviated the need for and existence of force. Mistresses also invoked the Jezebel image to rationalize the actions of their husbands and to blame the victims, but it proved less useful when countering abolitionist charges of the moral depravity of slavery. As a result, Southerners pushed a dual image of black women, and as proslavery ideology solidified, "the image of the Jezebel excused miscegenation, the sexual exploitation of black women, and the mulatto population," while the Mammy served to "calm Southern fears of moral slippage."[22]

White fathers rationalized the enslavement and often sale of their own progeny by invoking proslavery ideology, which denied that these children were part of the white family. White men's paternity of slaves was normalized and yet veiled, in that Southern social conventions demanded that men not openly acknowledge mulatto offspring, and thus illicit sex, but they did not treat their paternity as in any way abnormal. White men who engaged in sexual contact with black women suffered no legal, social, or ethical repercussions as long as they observed basic rules of decorum. The relationship, even if long term, had to appear "casual," and men had to maintain utmost discretion. "Transcendent silence was the proper policy," Bertram Wyatt-Brown writes. A man must never acknowledge his illicit affairs or the rumors they generated, and he could keep a concubine without eliciting disapproval as long as she remained in her place as a slave.[23] Most white men responded to fathering slaves by hiding their paternity and avoiding paternal responsibility.

White men had good reason to hide or downplay their relationships with and paternity of slaves, as those who abrogated the rules of discretion and the racial order faced public shame in a culture obsessed with honor.[24] While most proslavery writers avoided the topic of interracial sex, William Harper believed slavery ensured white men's and women's purity by providing men with a sexual outlet that occasioned "impropriety" but rarely led to "vice." Harper never addressed the glaring fact that casual liaisons might produce children. Amalgamation was a notion he and other proslavery writers could not stomach. Whites "would suffer deterioration from such intermixture" with an inferior race. "What would be thought of the moral conduct of the parent who should voluntarily transmit disease, or fatuity, or deformity, to his offspring?" Harper queried. "Is he not criminal who would desecrate and deface God's fairest work; estranging it further from the image of himself, and conforming it more nearly to that of the brute?" White men might at times "overcome the natural repugnance, and find transient gratification in intercourse with females of the other race. But this is a very different thing from making her . . . the companion of bosom and hearth. Him who would contemplate such an alliance . . . we should esteem a degraded wretch." Another proslavery writer, Henry Hughes, similarly vilified amalgamation, insisted intermarriage must remain illegal to ensure racial "purity," and labeled mulattoes "monsters."[25] The response to mixed-race people was to pretend they did not exist and, when they somehow appeared, to ignore their paternity and class them with slaves. Biracial children were uneasily swept under the rug so long as they remained enslaved and in their inferior social sphere.

Few white men left records of their sexual involvement with enslaved women. South Carolina planter James Henry Hammond was an exception. In 1839, Hammond took as a concubine an eighteen-year-old mulatto slave named Sally, whom he had purchased along with her one-year-old daughter, Louisa. When Louisa reached the age of twelve, Hammond initiated a sexual relationship with her, fathering children by both, and, in essence, fathering children with a child. The two women and their children shared a cabin. Carol Bleser, editor of Hammond's diaries, points out the rarity both of Hammond's acknowledgment of his sexual indiscretions and the fact that his heirs never destroyed the evidence. The relationship with Louisa caused a rupture in the white family, and Hammond's wife, Catherine, left her husband for a time.[26]

Hammond revealed how a white father perceived his enslaved offspring, and how he rationalized their status to himself and others, in a letter to his oldest white son, Harry:

In the last will I made I left to you, over and above my other children, Sally Johnson the mother of Louisa and all the children of both. Sally says Henderson is my child. It is possible, but I do not believe it. Yet act on her's rather than my opinion. Louisa's first child *may* be mine. I think not. Her second I believe is mine. Take care of her and her children who are both of *your* blood if not mine and of Henderson. . . .

I cannot free these people and send them North. It would be cruelty to them. Nor would I like that any but my own blood should own as Slaves my own blood or Louisa. I leave them to your charge, believing you will best appreciate and most independently carry out my wishes in regard to them. Do not let Louisa or any of my children or possible children be slaves of Strangers. Slavery *in the family* will be their happiest earthly condition.[27]

While it is rare to have a white father's open justification for enslaving his children, his treatment of them existed along the standard continuum of slaveholder behavior. Numerous informants recalled the uneasy status of mixed-race children. Some fathers sold their mulatto children quickly, whereas others, like Hammond, adopted a condescending and doubly paternalistic attitude toward them. They were of his blood, but not fully part of the white family. They were black, and thus servile, and without a doubt to remain enslaved, as would their descendants. Hammond clearly believed he was doing these children, his children, a favor. To free them and send them north would be a disservice to them, a "cruelty." They would remain slaves "*in the family*," and would thus be protected from their own inferiority. In Hammond's mind, to protect them, to provide a good life, was not to emancipate them, but to ensure that they were never owned by "Strangers." Masters could not emancipate concubines and their own children without undermining proslavery dogma, so they had to find a way to excuse, especially in their own minds, their ownership of blood. Those excuses buttressed the larger framework of proslavery thought.

As Bleser points out, Hammond's attitudes toward his own children enable us "to better understand his unquestioning acceptance of slavery."[28] As master and patriarch (in this case biological father and plantation head), it was his job to provide for and ensure the happiness of his dependents. These particular dependents, being part black, needed the guidance of their supposed superiors. Any treatment of them, kind or unkind, could be justified as being for their own good. This letter exudes Hammond's deluded sense of his own benevolence, the hallmark of slaveholder paternalism, and his failure to realize that his actions and decisions benefited himself and his white family and not his slaves. The combination of paternalism and paternity can, therefore, elucidate the proslavery argument more broadly. If it was this easy to apply paternalistic logic to one's own blood, it was even easier to apply it to the general mass of slaves. Many white fathers sold their children to rid themselves of the embarrassment. Others physically abused their offspring, possibly an expression of self-directed anger at sexual behavior they perceived as debased. They punished their own lack of self-control by displacing abuse onto others. Many, like Hammond, could neither fully welcome their enslaved children into the family, nor fully deny them a subservient place within it. Planters expected their slaves to revere them as father figures as part of the paternalistic ethos. Proslavery ideology held that slaves had fleeting attachments to their own family, and instead their loyalty and abiding affection were for the white "family." In their minds, paternity would complement and deepen that feeling. If all slaves already loved their master more than their own spouses and children, then having a father as a master concentrated their natural loyalties. To be owned by kin would be "their happiest earthly condition." Hammond never considered that his slaves might resent their bondage, nor did it dawn on him that white parentage might complicate their feelings toward self, slavery, and slaveholder.

White men felt the need to maintain the public and private distinction, even in the case of decades-long relationships. Augustin Macarty had children by at least three different concubines and lived with one of them, Celeste Perrault, for nearly fifty years. When white relatives challenged Macarty's will emancipating and leaving property to favored slaves, the court established that Macarty privately recognized his son, Patrice Macarty, by Perrault, but argued that he did not lawfully recognize Josephine Macarty, a daughter by his first concubine. "In his correspondence with Patrice . . . he . . . invariably addresses him as *mon ami*. That correspondence is full of affection and although he knew . . . he was Patrice's father, he never could bring himself to speak or to write the humiliating truth."[29] Macarty supported his son economically and his letters spoke to intimacy, but he never openly announced his paternity.[30]

Though few white men publicly acknowledged their paternity of slaves, the information was usually well known or at least suspected in the quarters. Madison Hemings called his mother "Mr. Jefferson's concubine" and identified Jefferson as the father of all four of Sally Hemings's children. Hemings remembered his father as a kind man, but "he was not in the habit of showing partiality or fatherly affection to us children. We were the only children of his by a slave woman. He was affectionate toward his white grandchildren, of whom he had fourteen." Thomas Jefferson's enslaved children performed only "light work," learned trades, and knew they would be freed at age twenty-one. "We were free from the dread of having to be slaves all our lives long, and were measurably happy," Hemings recalled.

Jefferson provided for his illegitimate children, but he never openly admitted his paternity and treated them differently than his white descendants. Israel Jefferson, another Jefferson slave, also called Sally Hemings a "concubine," showing that her status was understood in the quarters even as Jefferson maintained an absolute public silence.[31] Thomas Hughes, a mixed-race slave owned by his half-brother, approached his wealthy white father and asked to be purchased and freed. Though his father did not deny paternity in private, "to all my entreaties he turned a deaf ear, and in public would not speak to me." While some masters practiced this private acknowledgment and public denial, others engaged in full disavowal. John Boggs's Maryland master attributed his illegitimate offspring to Irishmen living on his plantation, "but everyone knew they were his. They were as much like him as himself."[32] A slaveholder who hid his paternity of slaves protected his reputation and honor with his white peers. That did not stop his illegitimate children from recognizing his hypocrisy, nor did it protect him from the moral judgment of the slave community.

Court cases show that a remarkable number of white fathers, even when they intended to emancipate their enslaved children, waited until after death to do so. When men violated the code of silence on interracial sex by leaving property to concubines and offspring or freeing them in their wills, they often provoked virulent anger and legal challenges from white heirs. This went beyond a loss of property. As Bertram Wyatt-Brown notes, such wills caused "exposure to public criticism," by bringing an illicit, secret affair into the open with the consequences falling mainly on the living family members rather than the deceased perpetrator.[33] Some white fathers may have hesitated to emancipate their offspring in states that legally encumbered the process and required free persons of color to leave after being freed. Taking a concubine and/or child to another state to manumit them meant that they could not return to the place of their birth as a free person.[34] A white man who chose to liberate his slaves by taking them to a free state had to move with them if he wanted to remain in daily contact with his black family.[35]

Samuel Townsend of Alabama left a will manumitting and bequeathing considerable property to his ten mixed-race children by five different enslaved women. Sharony Green cites possible reasons why Townsend did not free them before his death, including frugality and his need for "companionship" during his life. "Given the near-universal racism of nineteenth-century white American society, both South and North, Townsend probably concluded, quite reasonably, that his children were better off under his watchful eye and protection in Huntsville than they would be as freedpeople in an overwhelmingly hostile environment in the North," Green writes. Based on the "hardships and racism" they encountered in freedom, she argues, "his apprehensions were warranted."[36] The desire to retain the companionship of enslaved concubines and children probably motivated many of these men, as did concern for the well-being of their kin. However, delaying manumission until after death also suggests that white fathers could not entirely overcome their paternalistic attitudes. A man worried about his children's transition to freedom stood a better chance of exerting influence over that process if he manumitted them during his lifetime when he could offer direct emotional and financial support. These concubines and children would face a hostile world in any case, and to free them by will meant that they would do so without the presence of a father. White men who liberated their children in their lifetime showed a greater willingness to challenge social conventions, accept possible damage to their reputations, and make sacrifices on behalf of certain slaves.[37]

Legal proceedings offer only indistinct clues about planters' reasoning or the emotional content of relationships, but they do indicate that many slaveholders hesitated to free their offspring while they themselves were alive.[38] It seems that many of them could not escape the notion that their slaves, including their own children, could or should function without oversight. It also suggests a lurking fear that these concubines and children had ambivalent attachment and would not only leave, but would also thrive without a master. That scenario threatened the entire bedrock of paternalistic, proslavery ideology. If your own child showed no or little affection, how might the rest of the slaves really feel? When white men wanted to free their sexual partners and children, delaying manumission until after death enabled them to escape the public fallout and inherent contradictions that their fond feelings for slave property exposed. Waiting until after death to offer freedom was simultaneously generous and self-serving, and it involved an element of cowardice. A slaveholder might justify the decision as being for the protection of his concubine and children, but the person he most protected was himself.

In his study of miscegenation, contested wills, and "illegitimate" heirs in the antebellum South, Bernie Jones notes that as part of the public record, wills brought illicit sex into the open, and when white men attempted to manumit or transfer property to favored slaves, their actions violated and threatened the racial order. In the nineteenth century, states restricted manumission in response to the abolitionist movement and growing sectional tensions and in an attempt to curb the growth of the free black population. Because white relatives regularly and successfully challenged wills, they were a precarious means of liberating slaves or transferring an inheritance. Courts ruled on wills based on manumission laws, which varied by state. Jones argues for the "significance of geography upon the litigation," showing that men were more likely to achieve their goals if they took or sent favored slaves to a free state.[39]

The handful of white men who openly acknowledged their relationships to slaves and who wanted to provide for those individuals in their wills faced several obstacles, including state laws that sought to stem manumission rates, finding an executor they trusted, and anticipating the behavior of white relatives. Slaveholders willing to admit to paternity often distinguished between "natural" offspring and their legitimate descendants, showing that even if they loved their mixed-race children, they recognized the burdens of enslavement and illegitimacy.[40] Men who wished to leave property to and/or manumit slaves had a higher rate of success if they took concrete steps while alive. To wait until after death placed power in the hands of executors and resentful white heirs. The way to ensure manumission and transfer of property was to move slaves out of the South and free them prior to one's death, a step few men took. Such an action required resources and planning, and necessarily involved losing valuable property.

White men who had the foresight to manumit slaves in free states but then brought them back to the South jeopardized that freedom. Affection for kin and the desire to avoid separation seems to have at times led people, white and black, to make poor decisions that could lead to reenslavement, although the risk varied by state. Mississippi went beyond other states and banned attempts by slaveholders and executors to bypass manumission laws, making it illegal, after 1842, to leave instructions in a will intended to secure emancipation of a slave or slaves, "or to direct that any slave or slaves shall be removed from this state for the purpose of emancipation elsewhere."[41] In 1826, Elisha Brazealle took his concubine and son, John Munroe Brazealle, to Ohio to emancipate them and then the three returned to Mississippi. Brazealle willed his property to John, "acknowledging him to be his son." The court refused to recognize the Ohio emancipation documents and invalidated the inheritance, calling the will "pernicious and detestable." "The contract had its origin in an offence against morality. . . . But above all, it seems to have been planned . . . with a fixed design to evade the rigor of the laws of this state," the court continued, ruling that because "the validity of the deed must depend upon the laws of this state . . . John

Munroe and his mother, are still slaves." Under Mississippi law, John would not have been granted property in any case, but he and his mother lost their freedom because they returned to the South.[42] Illicit relationships, though deemed immoral, were tolerated as long as a white man lived. His death placed mixed-race children in peril.[43]

Slaveholders who freed their concubines and children were successful when they transported those individuals to a free state. James Brown died without "lawful issue," but he owned a mulatto woman named Harriet, who had two sons, "Francis and Jerome, whom the testator claimed to be his sons." According to his will, James Brown wanted his land and other slaves sold, his debts paid, and the remainder deposited in a bank account for his sons. Brown's brother, John Brown, sued to overturn his brother's bequests. James Brown had taken Harriet, his sons, and two other children to Cincinnati to emancipate them and settled them in Indiana. Brown "wished them to be with him," and at some point his sons "returned to Mississippi, contrary to his wishes. . . . His object in sending them out of the State was to prevent his relatives from forcing them into slavery." A witness noted that Francis "called Brown 'father.'" After Brown died while visiting his family in the North, the executor "wrote to Francis, advising him not to come to Mississippi." The court ruled the will valid because the money could be transferred without the individuals stepping foot in Mississippi, where they could not live as free people.[44] James Brown realized that his white relatives might attempt to reenslave his children and wisely chose to establish their liberty before his death. The proceedings provide hints of strong bonds between Brown, Harriet, and their sons. Manumission laws made it difficult for affectionate mixed families to remain intact unless they all chose to relocate to a free state. White men who fathered slaves had to choose between ensuring freedom and, if they wanted stay in the South and maintain a livelihood as a planter, daily contact with kin.

Another white father, Jonathan Carter, willed his daughter to a close friend, Joseph Barksdale, and intended that she be treated as white. According to the will, Harriet, a twelve-year-old "yellow girl, nearly white," was to live in Barksdale's house "as a free white person, and in no way to be treated as a slave, but . . . to be fed from his table . . . and to be clothed from the store." In this case, the court ruled that all of Carter's slaves be sold, and Barksdale appealed. Based on the "tenor" of the document and "the evasive statements in the answer to the petition," the court decided that Harriet was Carter's daughter and invalidated the will. "No court certainly would lend its aid to enforce rights predicated upon immorality of the grossest and most dangerous kind—dangerous, because the example of a negress, or mulatto, brought up in the . . . style specified . . . would necessarily exert a most baleful influence upon the surrounding negro population." Carter's will shows that some white men may have hesitated to admit paternity not out of a lack of affection or fear for their own reputation, but because they worried such declarations would harm their children and nullify their bequests.[45] Regardless of the care these men exercised in wording their wills, the best way to assure freedom was not to wait until death, but to bring favored slaves to a free state and directly oversee their transition to liberty.[46]

White paternity created legal and social problems, especially as it became difficult to easily identify a person's racial background. To grant respectability and status to a slave or the descendant of a slave endangered the social order. When slaveholders fathered slaves, they exercised their dominion as masters and multiplied their human property, but that property served as a visual reminder of the troubling paradoxes of the institution. Only a few white fathers defied Southern social standards to uphold paternal duty and provision their mixed-race children with freedom or property, and an array of impediments meant that those few who tried sometimes failed. When former slaves assessed their white fathers, the men who provided freedom emerged as the rare examples of honorable paternity. A white man who freed enslaved concubines and children prior to his death had to relinquish some control over them and rely on bonds of affection rather than ownership. Evaluations of white fathers thus underscore how enslaved and formerly enslaved people idealized paternal duty based on support and emotional connection rather than physical domination.

Evaluating White Fathers

Sexual exploitation came up repeatedly in the twentieth-century interviews conducted by African American fieldworkers. The respondents differed on how white men treated such children, with some noting that masters whipped and sold their own offspring, and others recalling preferential treatment. "They would make women do that. Some of them would treat these children better, and some of them wouldn't," one woman concluded. "White men who would have children by slaves would treat them just like the rest," another man added. "They mighta liked them a little better, but they didn't want to show it."[47] Others recalled masters who sold their children, "just like he would any others. Just since he was making money."[48] Depending on the behavior of the father, white parentage could have advantages or disadvantages, dramatically increasing or decreasing the likelihood of sale and abuse.

Former slaves expressed a range of feelings about white fathers that largely depended on how those fathers treated their enslaved children. Some informants made neutral or ambivalent assessments of their white fathers, others articulated sheer hatred, and a few expressed admiration and affection. The variety of attitudes was shaped by interactions with white fathers and the different ways these men responded to fathering slaves. Interactions with white fathers also influenced and were influenced by self-identity. A considerable number of white fathers utterly disregarded their enslaved offspring and their own paternity, treating such children as they would any other slave. Those embarrassed by their presence, urged by bitter white relatives, or eager to profit, sold their enslaved offspring. Others dispensed preferential treatment but not freedom, and a tiny minority challenged Southern social conventions and publicly acknowledged and legally emancipated their enslaved children.

White men who ignored their enslaved children, providing little beyond genetic material, contributed to a significant number of fatherless individuals and families within slavery. "My mother died when I was real young, and I had no father," Rosa Hardy recalled. "Pike Sutton was mother's master. He was my old grandfather. . . . Tove Sutton was his son and my father." Hardy outlined the Tennessee family tree, but because her biological parent displayed no interest in her, she considered herself functionally and emotionally fatherless.[49] Bob Benford knew that he had a white father, but he lacked further information, including a name: "I don't know nothin' bout my father. They said he was a white man." Interviewed in Canada after escaping, Williamson Pease also had limited knowledge of his paternity and no reason to withhold information. "I do not know who my father was, but have heard that he was a white man. My mother was called there a mulatto. I passed for a white man when among strangers."[50] White paternity greatly increased the likelihood that an enslaved child would not have a father in their life.

When mothers withheld details about their children's parentage as a survival strategy, individuals with mixed parentage had incomplete knowledge about their origins. Orleans Finger named her mother and her stepfather, but "my real father, I don't know. My mother never told me nothin' bout him. . . . I can't tell what I don't know." In a parenthetical note, the interviewer identified Finger as "apparently octaroon or quadroon," indicating that her unknown father was likely white. "I dunno my father's name as I was a stray found in the woods," William Byrd similarly remarked. "I'se always believed my master was also my father, but I never did know, cause my mother, she would never tell who my father was." Sophie Belle learned about her father from her aunt. When a French doctor stopped by her workplace after emancipation, "my Aunt Jane said to me, 'he is your papa. That is your papa.' I saw him many times after that." Belle never mentioned interacting with this man, nor did she indicate if he was aware of their connection.[51] These individuals never knew the motivations behind their mothers' silence, leaving them with limited family history.

White parentage also blurred the family lineage going back a generation. Informants guessed at the background of their parents but avoided a delicate topic if it remained unspoken. They understood that light skin usually meant white blood in the family and the implications of such ancestry. "Mama was darker than I am. My father was brighter than I am. He likely had a white father. I never inquired. Mama had colored parents," Charles Anderson commented. Bell Williams remembered a similar reserve on the part of his parents: "Mother was darker. Papa was light—half white. They didn't talk in front of children about things and I never did know. I've wondered." Men and women could be equally reticent about sharing information related to illicit sex. "Mother was light," Hettie Mitchell explained. "She said she had Indian strain (blood) but father was very light and it was white blood but he never discussed it before his children. So I can't tell you." The sexual dynamics of slavery left many informants with an imprecise sense of their family history and their family members' experiences in slavery. Fugitive authors made similarly vague statements about anonymous white fathers. When Frederick Douglass's mother died unexpectedly, she left him "without the slightest intimation of who my father was." Douglass knew only that he had a white father. "The opinion was also whispered that my master was my father; but of the correctness of this opinion, I know nothing."[52] Douglass grew up fatherless and never spent a long enough time with his mother to know if she would have eventually shared sensitive details about her life.

Former slaves continued to be evasive on the subject of white paternity decades after emancipation, and several FWP informants stonewalled or bristled when asked about their fathers. Spart Quinn's interviewer knew Quinn's master was his father, having learned this from another source, but Quinn was "very sensitive about answering personal questions," and would not provide a name, saying simply, "I can't tell who my father was." Ed Barber and Louis Fowler knew the identity of their white fathers and chose to keep names hidden. "Dat's not a fair question when you ask me who my daddy was," Barber replied. "Well, just say he was a white man and dat my mother never did marry nobody, while he lived. I was de onliest child my mother ever had." Fowler called attention to his red hair and light skin and turned the questioning around: "Who does yous think my father was? Yous don't know, ob co'se, but I's know 'cause on dat plantation am a man dat am over six feet tall an' his haiah am red as a brick."[53] Fowler indicated that his looks alone should have made his parentage obvious and the interviewer should have politely avoided the topic. Barber may have felt the same way. Because they failed to elaborate, it is hard to know if they felt ashamed of their parentage, they were trying to protect themselves or others, or if they knew uncomfortable details about the circumstances of their origins that they did not want to discuss. Cryptic interviews also make it impossible to gauge the tone of the interactions, if any, between fathers and children.

Respondents hesitated to share names of white fathers, particularly if they still lived in the vicinity of their enslavement. Minnie Davis knew the identity of her one mulatto brother's father but refused to divulge that information. "I know who his father was, but of course you won't ask me that. I wouldn't want to expose my own mother or the man who was Ned's father." Bill Reese told his interviewer, "My mother's owner was also her own father, and for that reason I'd rather not tell his name. You know things like that was common in slavery time. . . . He was kind to me, and she was kept on duty in the big house as a maid. She didn't' have to do field work." Informants were protective of their loved ones and this was a thorny subject in the Jim Crow South. Concealing such information also protected people who were still alive. Candis Goodwin admitted to her African American interviewer that she had a white "brother libin' ret on dis here street; one dem toof doctors. . . . Cose he's white! But tain' knowd round here dat I's his sister. 'Twould ruin him. He's a nice man, though. Uster to go see my son an' his wife lots o' times."[54] Goodwin likely would not have revealed this information to a white fieldworker, and the anecdote did not appear in the official version of her narrative sent to the Library of Congress from Virginia. Her commentary indicates that the two families interacted, but maintained a public facade of disavowal. Goodwin had no desire to ruin the reputation of her half-brother and potentially cause difficulties in her own life.

Ex-slaves were more candid about sexual exploitation and white paternity in the presence of African American interviewers, indicating that they underreported and sanitized family history when speaking to white fieldworkers. Ishrael Massie told his interviewers, "I can tell ya a mess 'bout reb times, but I ain't tellin' white folks nuthin' 'cause I'm skeer'd to make enemies." Massie's most bitter memories of slavery involved the sexual violation of enslaved women, men's impotence to intervene, and the resulting disruption of the enslaved family. "Did de dirty suckers associate wid slave wimmen? I call 'em suckers—feel like saying something else but I'll 'spec ya, honey. Lord chile, dat wuz common. Marsters an' overseers use to make slaves dat wuz wid deir husbands git up, do as dey say. Send husbands out on de farm, milkin' cows or cuttin' wood. Den he gits in bed wid slave himself. Some women would fight an tussel. Others would be 'umble—feared of dat beatin'. What we saw, couldn't do nothing 'bout it. My blood is bilin' now." Even as he modified his language, Massie referred to the abusers as debased and inhuman. Massie's firm belief that God would punish white people for "terrible, terrible times" was directly related to the sexual violence of the institution and slaveholders' abrogation of paternal duty. "When babies came dey ain't exknowledge 'em. Treat dat baby like 'tothers—nuthing to him. Mother feard to tell 'cause she know'd what she'd git. Dat wuz de concealed part." To hide behind notions of propriety meant that white fathers left enslaved women alone with the repercussions of interracial sex. In Massie's opinion, a real man took responsibility for his actions and for his children. Former slaves differentiated between those who had power and those who had honor. Predatory white men used their power to forcibly reproduce slaves, making them immoral and dishonorable as men and as fathers. While antebellum authors more often and openly discussed the gulf between power and honor, Massie's invective shows that twentieth-century informants also made such arguments when they felt safe with their audience.[55]

Talking about white paternity caused discomfort even with African American interviewers, further suggesting that ex-slaves responded differently to white fieldworkers. Two Virginia informants called sexual abuse the shame of whites, again invoking the idea of slaveholder dishonor. "Well, I reckon I oughter tell dat, but it ain't my shame," Alice Marshall responded when asked about her father. "'Twas ole massa Jack Nightingale. . . . He's my father. Chile, dat was ev'y day happenin's in dem days." Virginia Shephard's accounting of her family history unfolded similarly. "My mother was a slave and my father—well the fact is so evident you can' dodge it. It's their stamp an' not ours; therefore I don't blush when I tell you this part of the story." She explained that a white physician hired her mother and she ended up with a baby. "I don't know how your going to write that, but it's just the same true." Annie Wallace, meanwhile, would not disclose her parentage to a white fieldworker. "I didn't have no father," she insisted. According to the writer, "her son again elucidated that her father was a Mr. Fields, a white man of the neighborhood but she was ashamed to say so."[56] For Wallace, having a white father meant she had no father, at least in the presence of a white person. Without further information, it is impossible to know if she was ashamed of her father as an individual, his behavior, the way he treated his daughter, her mother, or other slaves, being biracial, or a combination of factors. Informants' feelings about their parentage and parents influenced how they reacted to questions about kin. Because most interviews started with a brief family history, this line of questioning may at times have negatively affected the remainder of the narrative, especially for those who preferred to suppress information about a white father.

Having white fathers they never knew, or with whom they never extensively interacted, intensified formerly enslaved peoples' attachment to and identification with their mothers. "I was born of a slave mother; I am told that my father was white. I know nothing of a father's counsel, and . . . I am what I am by the grace of God and my mother's prayers," Lloyd Ray declared.[57] Charley Stewart knew, interacted with, and resented his white father. "Dey usta say dat I wuz de very picture of my mother. I don't guess I look anything like my daddy," Stewart claimed. "He never did anything fer me anyway—but tried to kill me one day when he beat me wid a buggy trace. When freedom come my mother wuz glad enough to leave him. I saw him once or twice after the war, and he said, 'Howdy, Charley!' and went on. He never give me nothing."[58] Stewart used physical resemblance to affiliate with his mother and distance himself from an abusive white father, his former master. White fatherhood fueled emotional matrifocality by creating a greater number of households and families that were fatherless in structure and function. Charley Stewart and his mother, who served as the cook, were the only slaves of Robert Stewart on a rented Alabama farm. Stewart never specified if they lived in a separate cabin or in the house with Robert Stewart and his white wife and children. Regardless of the makeup of the household, Charley and his mother comprised a female-headed family of two and felt no emotional connection to the master. During slavery, this was a fatherless family even as the father and patriarch was physically present on the same farm and possibly lived under the same roof. There was a stark contrast between an enslaved father who lived apart from and yet was invested in and appreciated by his kin and a white father who lived on the plantation and refused to acknowledge or emotionally engage with his children.

Those who only knew about a biological father in the abstract and benefited from having an involved black stepfather could assess their white fathers more dispassionately. "I do not even know his name," Booker T. Washington said of his father in his 1901 autobiography. "I have heard reports to the effect that he was a white man who lived on one of the near-by plantations. Whoever he was, I never heard of his taking the least interest in me or providing in any way for my rearing. But I do not find especial fault with him. He was simply another unfortunate victim of the institution" of slavery.[59] Washington had never been owned or sold by his white father, making him less likely to denounce a man with whom he had no concrete experience, and he blamed slavery rather than the individual for his nameless father's failure to provision. He grew up with a stepfather, meaning that he was fatherless only in the abstract and in memory, and he purposed that memory to fit his conservative postwar political vision.

While many former slaves never met their white fathers, others had a basis for a more substantive evaluation. After the War of 1812, planters moved into the western areas of the cotton South, working to establish stable farms before they brought white families to the frontier or married. In the interim, a number of these men took enslaved concubines.[60] According to a man who had purchased his own freedom, mid-nineteenth-century "Cincinnati was full of women, without husbands, and their children. These were sent there by planters from Louisiana and Mississippi, and some from Tennessee, who had now got fortunes, and had found that white women could live in those States. In consequence, they had sent their slave-wives and children to Cincinnati, and set them free."[61] Louisa Picquet related the family history of the man she married after she was freed and moved north. Like her, he had a white father, but his father took an interest in his children and lived openly with their mother. His children belonged to him, "but he never uses them as slaves. They are his children." In Picquet's mind, treating a person as a slave was antithetical to paternal duty. When this planter married a white woman, he sent his illegitimate family to Cincinnati and freed them because "it would be unpleasant for them all to stay there together."[62]

Sharony Green focuses her study of black-white relationships on Cincinnati, the favored destination of many white men who freed their concubines and children. The city, and the state of Ohio, offered a supportive community and educational facilities, but free blacks also faced prejudice in the labor market. Cincinnati was well placed for Southern white men who intended to maintain contact with or periodically visit their black family.[63] In 1850, mulattos comprised 54 percent of the adult free black population in Cincinnati, the highest proportion in the North, and higher than all but the deep South, where 76 percent of the free black population was mixed race. In addition, the free black population contained a high proportion of children, women outnumbered men, and women headed 30 percent of all households.[64] A considerable number of these women and children had been relocated and manumitted by slaveholders. The financial support of white patrons enabled certain free blacks to live well, and form part of the black middle class, while others struggled to survive. "Many members of the nineteenth-century black bourgeoisie had their roots in miscegenation: mixed race men and women who had access to privilege and whose white benefactors manumitted them, provided funds for their upkeep, and made it possible for them to learn trades," Bernie Jones writes. This status and financial backing generally came at the expense of the still enslaved.[65]

While conscientious white fathers freed their children and provided an education or vocational training, a few went beyond emancipating their families and leaving them, fatherless, in a free state.[66] "My father carried my mother to Pennsylvania before I was born and set her free. Then he carried her back to Montgomery, Alabama, and all her children were born free there," Betty Johnson related. "We had everything that life needed. He was one of the biggest planters around in that part of the country." Johnson's father provided for and educated his children. "We were always supported by my father. My mother did nothing at all except stay home and take care of her children. I had a father that cared for us. He didn't leave that part undone. He did his part in every respect," she continued. "He sent every child away to school," including sending one to Yale. Johnson saw this man as an ideal father because he provided material and emotional support, treated her mother like a legal wife, and educated his children, preparing them for the future. Josiah Settle's father "was devoted to his children and their mother," freeing them and settling them in a home in Hamilton, Ohio. He then lived with them during the summers and spent the rest of each year on his Mississippi plantation.[67] A good white father provided freedom and material support and, ideally, an emotional presence.

Formerly enslaved people were more likely to have positive feelings about white fathers who freed them or did not own them in the first place. Ralph Kates's father purchased and freed Kates's mother from her Tennessee master and "was always good to all of us." Though he left after the Civil

War, he "often visited us and brought gifts and money to the children." The interviewer stressed that Kates was "proud of Thomas Cates, his white father who was never his master," and especially thankful that he "gave his family freedom from a tyrannical master."[68] Thomas Cates combined several traits of a good white father. He was not the master, and he provided freedom and material support.

Their status as property, however, left slaves vulnerable even when a white father took an interest in them.[69] Eliza Potter, a free black resident of Cincinnati, told of a white man in St. Louis who purchased a "housekeeper," with whom he had two "acknowledged daughters." When he "took suddenly ill and died, without having made any preparation for his daughters or secured their freedom," assuming they would enjoy the rights available to legitimate children, he miscalculated. His brothers took control of the estate and sold all three women.[70] "While a great majority of such men care nothing for the happiness of the women with whom they live, nor for the children of whom they are the fathers, there are those to be found, even in that heterogeneous mass of licentious monsters, who are true to their pledges," William Craft said of slaveholders who kept concubines. "But as the woman and her children are legally the property of the man, who stands in the anomalous relation to them of husband and father, as well as master, they are liable to be seized and sold for his debts, should he become involved." Like other abolitionist fugitives, Craft denigrated the morality, humanity, and masculine honor of the majority of slaveholders sexually involved with enslaved women. As an example of the few with integrity, Craft cited his wife's aunt, purchased by a "humane and wealthy gentleman," and treated as a wife. This man cared for and educated his children. "On the father being suddenly killed it was found that he had not left a will." As the family made "preparations to leave for a free State," an unrelated white man heard the story, swore he was a relative of the deceased, and sold the family back into slavery. Well-meaning white fathers undermined their own efforts to take responsibility if they failed to legally manumit enslaved kin and remove them from the South and then experienced a financial setback or unexpectedly died.[71]

Debt, death, and white family politics could upset the comfortable world of favored concubines and mixed-race children, even when freedom had been verbally promised or included in a will. After his kidnapping, Solomon Northup encountered one such woman and her children in the trader's pen. Eliza's wealthy master, Mr. Berry, had a falling out with his white wife and set up a separate household where he lived with Eliza, fathering a daughter and promising eventual emancipation. After a life of "luxury," Eliza and her two children became the property of Berry's white daughter, who sold them to a trader. When sold in New Orleans, the anguished Eliza begged her new master to buy her daughter, but the trader refused to sell. "There were heaps and piles of money to be made of her, he said, when she was a few years older. There were men enough in New-Orleans who would give five thousand dollars for such an extra, handsome, fancy piece as Emily would be." When white men fathered biracial women and failed to secure their freedom, they set up the potentiality for the sale of daughters into the sex trade. Postponing manumission to avoid the expense or hassle was dangerous.[72]

Martha Gowens, interviewed in Canada in the 1850s, had a controlling white father and master who freed his enslaved family members as long as they abided by his wishes. While a father had the wherewithal to disown a child, a slaveholder's power over freedom heightened his absolute control. Free children could anger their father and lose their inheritance but still retain their liberty. Enslaved children of white fathers risked much more. Gowens's father "liberated all the children he had by my mother, and one other slave woman, with one exception—that was a daughter whom he had educated and put to the milliner's trade. . . . But he found she had two children by a white man. This so enraged him, that he carried her and her two children back to his farm, and put her to work in the field, and there, he said, she was to die." The young woman's white partner tried to purchase her, but "her father would neither let him have her nor his children." Her lover offered substantial sums of money and even proposed trading five adult slaves for one woman and two children, "but my master told him . . . if he ever set foot on the farm again, he would blow his brains out. So, I suppose, they are slaves yet, and will be: for their mistress never was disposed to sell; she would rather keep them and punish them, on account of his having so many wives."[73] By violating her father's standards, this woman lost her chance at freedom and had to suffer the wrath of the white mistress.

Gowens had ambivalent feelings about her father. "Keep on the right side of him, and he was very kind," she noted. She also claimed that he kidnapped "my mother and her cousin's family," despite knowing they were "entitled to their freedom." When she was twelve, and shortly before he died, Gowens's father brought her from Mississippi to Cincinnati. "He charged me to marry neither a white man nor a black man: if I should, he would take me back south, and put me on the farm." After her guardian stole her tuition money, Gowens moved to Canada and lost contact with her mother, who "married a colored man against my father's consent. For this reason, she remains a slave to this day." Gowens's father had a white wife and several enslaved concubines, and he expected them all to accept his polygynous living arrangements. In pursuing a relationship of choice, Gowens's mother, like the daughter discussed above, relinquished the possibility of emancipation. As long as these women remained property, the master exercised power over their lives, labor, and relationships. "I have known many owners to have two or three colored women for wives, and when they got a white wife, keep all. If the slave woman would not comply she would be whipped," Gowens elaborated. "Some of the masters have their slave children's hair shaved off, so that people need not notice that they favor them." These planters kept harems, exercised sexual domination over concubines and daughters, and abased their enslaved children to avoid the appearance of partiality.[74] Mixed-race children could be provisioned with freedom and still vacillate in their feelings about a white father if he callously wielded his power, practiced the masculinity of domination, and failed to exhibit compassion.

While a handful of men liberated their enslaved children, a greater number of white fathers charted a middle course, giving their illegitimate offspring special favors, but not going so far as to free them. "He was my mother's father as well as her master," J. H. Curry said of his grandfather. "He used to come to our house and he would give mama anything she wanted. He liked her." Henry Pettus claimed that his father, "a sort of foreman," and the son of his master, "never did do much." Because her father was the son of his Alabama master, Amanda Ross's family experienced preferential treatment. "They didn't never whip none of my father's children," Ross noted. "If we done something they thought we ought to been whipped for, they would tell father to whip us, and if he wanted to, he would; and if he didn't want to, he wouldn't."[75] White parentage often led to fatherless families, but it could also have the opposite effect, particularly in the next generation, enabling this mixed-race man to exert limited patriarchal authority over his family. White parentage also led to trustee status for favored mulatto men.

Mixed-race children who received privileged treatment from their fathers did not fear abuse and sale to the same degree as other slaves. Winger Van Hook and his siblings were never sold, and "Ole Marse say dat's his youn'uns an' dey gwine lib at he home 'twel he died."[76] "She was a white man's girl. She never had so much bad luck as we dark skin children," Bessie Lawson said of a half sibling. "They treated the mulatto a little better than they did the other slaves," John Hunter similarly argued. "You know you would have more respect for your own blood. My Aunt Rena was half sister to my father. They had the same mother but different fathers and they always gave her a little better treatment than they give him. They didn't sell her."[77] These fathers tacitly acknowledged their enslaved children, but stopped short of full and public acceptance.

This group of white fathers granted their enslaved offspring reduced labor and material benefits and kept them off the market, but their children remained property. Aaron Lyons told his African American interviewer that Louisiana masters coerced enslaved women and then used "their children as free slaves, but not allowing them to leave the plantation." These children were "allowed choice marriages," sometimes educated, and their mothers "were given better treatment after the children were born." Lyons's description of mixed-race children as "free slaves" highlights their precarious status. Despite better treatment, they were still slaves, subject to the whims of their father.[78] According to Harriet Daves, her father, her mother's master, never legally married and he "loved my mother and he said if he could not marry Mary he did not want to marry." Her father also acknowledged his paternity. "My father was good to me. He would give me anything I asked him for." Daves "distinctly" recalled a time when a white girl made a disparaging comment and "my white father took exception telling her I was his child and that I was as good as she was." It appears, however, that he did not provide freedom. After emancipation, Daves's mother "told my father she was tired of living that kind of life, that if she could not be his legal wife she wouldn't be anything to him," and took her two children from Missouri to Kansas.[79] Daves had positive memories of her father, but because her mother chose to leave when free to do so, possibly a reaction to antimiscegenation laws, Daves lost contact with him. It is possible that Daves's father intended to liberate his family and the war intervened. In any case, it seems that the relationship between her parents meant different things to the two people involved and, regardless of the level of affection, rested on a power imbalance.

Daves's mother is a good example of the fact that planters who waited to manumit favored slaves by will may have done so due to legitimate fears that their concubines and children would leave them. Lewis Bonner married a woman whose father was her master. "He wanted to own her, but she sure didn't return it. He kept up with her till he died and sent her money jest all the time. Before he died, he put her name in his will and told his oldest son, who is white, to . . . keep up with her. . . . He would visit us, even after we moved to Oklahoma from Texas." In this case, a white father continued to provide for and seek connection to his offspring, but the affection in the relationship was one-sided. Bonner's wife felt ashamed of her white parentage. "When our grandchillun would visit us, they would call my wife 'Old White Woman', and sure made her feel bad."[80] While the details of the relationship are unknown, Bonner's wife did not identify with her white father.

Former slaves had complicated reactions to white fathers who treated them well and yet represented the system of slavery. In his 1855 narrative, William Grimes described his father, "one of the most wealthy planters in Virginia," as "a wild sort of man, and very much feared by all his neighbors." His father had two legitimate sons and two sons by enslaved women. Grimes and his mother had a different owner, so his father did not double as his master. Grimes claimed his father shot at least two white men and was "acquitted on the ground of insanity." Grimes lived about a mile from his father's home "where I went frequently, to carry newspapers, &c. He always used to laugh and talk with me, and send me to the kitchen to get something to eat. I also at those times, saw and played with his other children. My brother, the mulatto, was sent to school, and I believe had his freedom when he grew up. My father, I have no doubt, would have bought and freed me, if I had not been sold and taken off while he was in jail." Because he never lived with his father and was sold away and never knew how his father would have treated him later in life, Grimes retained his childhood fascination with the man. This fugitive simultaneously disparaged slavery, noting that he was born a slave "in a land boasting its freedom, and under a government whose motto is Liberty and Equality," and admired the bravery of a father willing to arm his slaves and resist arrest.[81]

Although they realized they had privilege relative to other slaves, mixed-race individuals understood that they did not have the same status as white children, leading to ambivalent feelings about white fathers and grandfathers. William Thompson's white master and father "used me kindly, but gave me no instruction at school."[82] The author of Newell Ensley's life sketch reported "it was always a problem how he could be a grandchild with his white playmates, who too were grandchildren of the same old man, and be treated so differently, and why he must say 'Old Mass' while his mates said lovingly 'grandpa.'" James Calhart James was born after the mistress died and his mother became housekeeper. James and his mother lived in the "servant's quarters of the big house enjoying many pleasures that the other slaves did not." His father "told mother when I became of age, he was going to free me, send me north to be educated, but instead I was emancipated."

James noticed the disparity between his own existence and that of other slaves. "During my slave days my father gave me money and good clothes to wear. I bought toys and games," he said. "My master was my father; he was kind to me but hard on the field hands who worked in the rice fields." James's ambivalence toward his father stemmed from his hatred of slavery.[83] Taking an enslaved concubine after the death of a mistress enabled a planter to sidestep the expense of setting up another white wife and household. He could avoid entanglements with a new family of in-laws or fathering a second family of legitimate heirs. James lived in the servants' quarters of his father's home, but is unclear if his mother and father functioned as a family. Like many enslaved concubines and their children, James and his mother formed a family embedded within a white household. His narrative speaks to the need to assess family composition based on emotional relationships and not on household structure. This appears to have been a family that was matrifocal and yet not matrilocal, an effect caused by white paternity.

Many former slaves abhorred slavery and slaveholders, but they had some measure of appreciation for their own fathers, especially if those men did not own them. In his 1845 narrative, Lewis Clarke expressed more sympathy for his nonslaveholding white father than his slaveholding grandfather. Clarke sarcastically noted that his grandfather, Samuel Campbell, "was considered a very respectable man among his fellow robbers—the slaveholders. It did not render him less honorable in their eyes, that he took to his bed Mary, his slave, perhaps half white, by whom he had one daughter," Clarke's mother, Letitia Campbell. Clarke's father married Letitia on the promise of her father that she would be freed in his will. Clarke believed Campbell "was as good as his word, and that by his will my mother and her nine children were made free. But ten persons in one family, each worth three hundred dollars, are not easily set free among those accustomed to live by continued robbery." His black family believed the white heirs destroyed the will. Lewis's brother Milton had more to say about their father. When Samuel Campbell died and the white heirs auctioned off the slave family, "my venerable old father" was "roused by this outrage. . . . 'He had never expected,' he said, 'when fighting for the liberties of this country, to see his own wife and children sold in it to the highest bidder.' But what were the entreaties of a quivering old man, in the sight of eight or ten hungry heirs?" Neither son offered detail about their father, possibly because he died shortly thereafter, and both had far more to say about their mother and siblings, with whom they strongly identified.[84]

Milton likely had warmer feelings toward their father due to a divergence in their subsequent treatment at the hands of white relatives. White paternity created complicated reactions in mixed-race slaves. When having a white father incurred the wrath of his legitimate relatives, ill treatment embittered mixed-race slaves toward their white ancestry and strengthened their black identity. The Clarke family was divided after the grandfather's death, and Milton and Lewis ended up with different white aunts. Only one of the grandfather's white children, "to her everlasting honor," protested the auction of their sibling, arguing, "Letty is our own half sister, and you know it; father never intended they should be sold." This kind aunt, Judith, ended up with Letitia and three of her children, including Milton, and until her death she mitigated the abuses they suffered at the hands of her cruel husband. "She was the only one of all the family that I was ever willing to own, or call my aunt," Milton stated, pointedly calling his white kin "the" rather than "my" or "our" family. Lewis went to another aunt, Mrs. Banton, who, "as is common among slave holding women, seemed to hate and abuse me all the more, because I had some of the blood of her father in my veins." According to Lewis, no slaves faced more abuse than those who shared blood with white women, especially "the children of their own husband; it seems as though they never could hate these quite bad enough." When a visitor mistook one of Lewis's sisters for Miss Campbell, his mistress displaced her fury on Lewis, deciding, "She would fix me so that nobody should ever think I was white." On a particularly hot day, "she made me take off every rag of clothes, go out into the garden and pick herbs for hours—in order to burn me black. When . . . I came in she gave me a severe beating on my blistered back."[85] Abuse perpetrated by white relatives and based on being biracial alienated young enslaved people from their white blood.

White fathers regularly sold concubines and children to mollify wives and to rid themselves of visual reminders of their own illicit behavior. "Men do not love those who remind them of their sins, . . . and the mulatto child's face is a standing accusation against him who is master and father to the child," Frederick Douglass observed. "What is still worse, perhaps, such a child is a constant offense to the wife." Louisa Picquet's mother was "forbid to tell who was my father," but did so anyway. The injunction did little good. "I looked so much like Madame Randolph's baby that she got dissatisfied," and mother and daughter were sold. Elvira Boles's mistress sold her "'cause she don want me there. . . . Ise a child of the marster." When sold as babies and toddlers, former slaves' conceptions of their white fathers were shaped by what their mothers told them, often and understandably quite negative, and the reality of having been trafficked by a parent. Ruth Allen referred to her father and former master as "the ol' devil," and stressed her mother's lack of consent. When she was about three and the white family realized "I was goan 'a be much whiter and even better lookin' than his own chilern by his own wife, they sold me and my mammy, an' got rid of us for good."[86] Jealous white wives demanded the sale of their husband's illicit partners and mixed-race children.

Slaveholders also sold their own children to remove them from vindictive mistresses. "My daddy was a white man, my master. His wife was so mean to me that my master sold me to keep her from beating me and kicking me and knocking me 'round. She would have killed me if she could have got the chance," Augustus Robinson reported.[87] Moses Roper's mistress nearly killed him because he resembled her husband: "She got a large club-stick and knife, and . . . went into my mother's room with full intention to murder me," but his grandmother "caught the knife and saved my life." Roper accused his father and master of "disposing of me," and the six-year-old was first given to a white relative and then sold. "My resembling my father so much, and being whiter than the other slaves, caused me to be soon sold . . . several hundred miles from my mother."[88] If white parentage at times proved advantageous, at other times it increased the likelihood of abuse and separation from kin and community.

Lacking power relative to their spouses in the rigid patriarchy of the Old South, mistresses frequently displaced their anger on their husband's victims, and as a visual reminder of the unfettered power of white men, biracial children became a target of such animosity. "She is never better pleased than when she sees them under the lash, especially when she suspects her husband of showing to his mulatto children favors which he withholds from his black slaves," Frederick Douglass remarked. "The master is frequently compelled to sell this class of his slaves, out of deference to the feelings of his white wife." Douglass argued that it could be more humane to sell one's children than to have to flog them, watch others do so, or unintentionally increase their abuse at the hands of other white relatives through perceived favoritism. Sarah Wilson learned only after her mistress died that she was the daughter of the master's son, and that was "why old Mistress picked on me so. . . . Then I knowed why Mister Ned would say, 'Let her along, she got big big blood in her,' and then laugh." William Grimes was the son of a neighboring planter, and yet his own master "was very fond of me, and always treated me kindly. This made my old mistress, his wife, hate me; and when she caught me in the house, she would beat me until I could hardly stand."[89] Though her husband was not his father, this white wife resented a mulatto child, possibly based on personal experience or fear of what had or might transpire in her own home.

White wives unable to act on their antagonism had to tolerate their husbands' indiscretions. Henry Ferry discussed a Virginia master who never had children by his wife, a woman who was "pow'ful jealous of Martha an' never let her come near de big house, but she didn't need to 'cause Marsa was always goin down to the shacks where she lived. Marse John used to treat Martha's boy, Jim jus' like his own son, which he was. Jim used to run all over de big house, an' Missus didn't like it, but she didn't dare put him out."[90] The presence of the master restricted the options of the mistress, underscoring the fact that favorable treatment for mixed-race children depended on their father remaining alive, solvent, and willing to extend his support. In this case, polygyny practiced by the master created a matrifocal household with a visiting white father who lived on the plantation.

While some white mistresses unleashed their bitterness on their husband's victims, others treated illegitimate children as source of profit or even with affection. "Southern women often marry a man knowing that he is the father of many little slaves. They do not trouble themselves about it," Harriet Jacobs argued. "They regard such children as property, as marketable as the pigs on the plantation . . . passing them into the slave-trader's hands as soon as possible, and thus getting them out of their sight." Jacobs mentioned two "honorable exceptions," who convinced their husbands to free slaves they had fathered.[91] Jacobs presented slavery as an abrogation of antebellum domesticity, warping the priorities of white men and women. Because former slaves judged masters who sold their own children as dishonorable, they looked favorably upon the few white women who persuaded these men to uphold paternal duty.

Another small subset of wives, rather than urge their husbands to sell or free their enslaved offspring, gave them a favored status on the plantation. Stephen Jordon's mistress "used to love me like her own children. In fact, my old master was my own father; but, of course, the thing was kept a sort of a secret, although every body knew it. . . . I was raised about the white folks' house." Jordon carried his half siblings' books to school, "and they taught me every lesson they learned, so that when I was about fourteen or fifteen years old I could read and write as well as any of them." Jordon never commented on his father or his mother's treatment. This comfortable upbringing ended when the plantation and slaves "were seized and sold," to pay debts. His mistress, "sorry to part with me and a little pet calf she had raised . . . had us kept until the last . . . but old master's debts could not be met after every thing else had been sold, so the calf and I had to be sold." As property, Jordon was expendable.[92]

When the father was not their husband, white women found it easier to vent their anger over racial mixing. Annie Burton learned about her father, a local planter, from her mistress. "I only saw my father a dozen times, when I was about four years old; and those times I saw him only from a distance," Burton recalled. When he rode by, Burton's mistress "would take me by the hand and run out upon the piazza, and exclaim, 'Stop there, I say! Don't you want to see and speak to and caress your darling child?'" He never stopped, but "would whip up his horse and get out of sight and hearing as quickly as possible. My mistress's action was, of course, intended to humble and shame my father. I never spoke to him, and cannot remember that he ever noticed me, or in any way acknowledged me to be his child."[93] Overlooking how this behavior might affect Burton's feelings, the mistress used an enslaved child to express her discontent with the sexual liberties white men exercised within the institution of slavery.

A white woman resigned to her husband's sexual practices might sympathize with enslaved women. "She was never angry with my mother. She knew a slave had to submit to her master," George Fortman said of the Kentucky mistress who treated mother and son kindly. Other white women feared their husbands, making them unhelpful resources for targeted slaves. Annie Young's aunt tried and failed to resist. "Old Master tried to have her and she run off out in de woods," but when caught by bloodhounds, "he knocked a hole in her head and she bled like a hog, and he made her have him. She told her mistress, and mistress told her to go ahead and be wid him 'cause he's gonna kill you. And he had dem two women and she had some chillun nearly white."[94] Polygynous mating created a complex milieu for the resulting legitimate and illegitimate children.

Fathering slaves generated more property for the estate but complicated family dynamics. White children, like wives, had a range of responses. Some expressed jealousy and abused their enslaved siblings, leading to disparities in conduct by different members of the slaveholding family. Legitimate kin often felt threatened by an emotional connection between a white father and his enslaved offspring. Loyd Ford's white sons refused to fulfill the provisions of their father's will, revealing their contempt for their mixed-race half siblings. A man's recognition of his illegitimate children did not grant them status in the eyes of white relatives. Though treated well by his master and father, James Calhart James faced animosity from his white half siblings. "They treated me fairly good at first . . . until they realized their father was my father, then they hated me." Frederick Douglass discussed William Wilks, rumored to be the son of his master and favored by his father. His white half-brother resented their "striking resemblance," and convinced his father to sell William.[95] The pressure to maintain social appearances and entreaties from a legitimate child led a father to sell an illegitimate son he initially attempted to protect.

White siblings resented enslaved mixed-race children who compromised the reputation of the family. Half white sisters envious of attractive slave girls insisted that they be sold. Doc Daniel Dowdy recalled the sale of his cousin Eliza to a slave trader in Georgia. Because visiting white suitors regularly noticed and commented on Eliza's beauty, her half-sisters "decided to get rid of her right away," and Eliza's master and father deferred to their wishes. When Eliza was stripped for sale in the presence of her father and she and her aunt cried, the "master told 'em to shet up before he knocked they brains out."[96] For young white women, a slave like Eliza embodied the real indiscretions of their own father and the possible indiscretions of their future husbands. Selling a biracial person who resembled white relations enabled white Southerners to rid themselves of visual reminders of the inconsistencies of slavery and to pretend that racial categories made logical sense.

Other siblings and white relatives treated mixed-race children with familial regard. Earvin Smith's father gained basic literacy from his half-brothers in South Carolina: "My father got pretty good training. He got it from his brothers and that's how he learned to keep such good records." In the estate division, William Troy's father fell to his half-sister when his father and master died. She "had taken a liking to my father. My father then commenced making boots and shoes, and became a first-class workman," hiring out his time and eventually purchasing his freedom. Mixed-race men could be less threatening to white women because the sexual double standard meant that they did not have the same potential to undermine white marriages. Another man's troubles increased after he purchased his freedom. "I had been well used as a slave, for my mistress was my aunt," but as a free man, he became "an object of jealousy to the white mechanics, because I was more successful in getting jobs." He relocated his family from Kentucky to Cincinnati to escape such abuse.[97] White workingmen and relatives lashed out at slaves and free blacks who destabilized their social and economic status.

While responses to racial mixing varied by individual, on a broader social and ideological level, Southerners found mulatto men frightening because in the minds of whites, partial whiteness insinuated some degree of masculinity. White parentage reinforced enslaved women's status as sexual objects, whereas the same heritage in men might upset the sex and gender hierarchy. Bertram Wyatt-Brown argues that Southerners considered mulatto women less problematic than men due to concerns that mixed-race men would be alluring to white women and exhibit a sense of pride and independence unbecoming in a slave and destructive to the institution. "The whiter a man is, the lower down they keep him," Lewis Clarke insisted. Light-skinned women commanded higher prices on the slave market as sexual objects, whereas fair skin often decreased prices for men, who were seen as a flight risk. Eliza Overton's aunt had two children by her master, and "one of them was so white that Mr. Jones couldn't sell him for a slave." Light skin enabled men to pass as white during escape attempts, but because white women traveled with chaperones, it did not offer the same benefit to women, yet another way in which the sexual climate of slavery complicated enslaved women's lives and options.[98]

If white parentage sometimes proved advantageous, it often had serious drawbacks, and the cruelty of fathers, mistresses, siblings, and fellow slaves alienated biracial individuals from their white heritage and solidified their black identity. Interviewed in Canada in the 1850s, Francis Henderson remembered being persecuted because he had a white paternal grandfather: "On that plantation the mulattoes were more despised than the whole blood blacks. I often wished from the fact of my condition that I had been darker. My sisters suffered from the same cause. I could frequently hear the mistress say to them, 'You yellow hussy! you yellow wench!'" William Wells Brown deemed his "fair complexion" a "great obstacle to my happiness, both with whites and blacks, in and about the great house. Often mistaken by strangers for a white boy, it annoyed my mistress very much." One visitor said to the mistress, "Madam, I would have known that he was the doctor's son, if I had met him in California, for he is so much like his papa." The mistress pointed out Brown's status as slave and "the major begged pardon for the mistake. After the stranger was gone, I was flogged for his blunder." Brown had trouble with fellow slaves as well, and on some plantations, the local slave community shunned mulattos as untrustworthy and associated with whites. Mary Peters explained how light skin benefited some and cursed others even within a single community. "There was a light brownskin boy around there and they give him anything that he wanted.

But they didn't like my mother and me—on account of my color. . . . They tell their children that when I got big enough, I would think I was good as they was. I couldn't help my color. My mother couldn't either."[99] When individuals associated being part white with rejection and abuse, this affected how they felt about their fathers and their mixed ancestry.

Social ostracism within slave communities also fueled negative feelings about a person's own white parentage as well as former slaves' assessments and treatment of one another. Dora Franks knew her father was the young master. "My mammy always told me dat I was hissen," she related. "Lawd, it's been to my sorrow many a time cause de chillen useter chase me around and holler to me, 'Ole yellow nigger!' Dey diden treat me very good either." Franks spent most of her time in the big house with the mistress, widening the social gulf between her and the other slaves. Lizzie Williams recalled a mulatto girl named Emily who lived in the big house, was "treated jes like she white," and taught to read by her mistress. "But Emily have de saddes' look on her yaller face cas' de other niggahs whisper 'bout her pappy."[100] While these two girls received favorable treatment from white mistresses, other biracial children faced abuse from whites and blacks.

Slave communities exhibited diverse responses to mixed-race children and more often ostracized children born of relationships perceived as consensual. When slaves asked questions about the parentage of children with lighter skin, they evinced more than idle curiosity—they were assessing the potential threat to themselves, their loved ones, and their community. "Who's yuh pappy? Who's yuh pappy?" fellow slaves asked Candice Goodman when she visited a neighboring plantation. "Ah jes' say 'Tuckey buzzard lay me an' de sun hatch me' an' den gwan 'bout my business. Cose all de time dey knows an' ah knows too dat Massa Williams was muh pappy." Those questioning Goodwin already knew the identity of her father, and in fact she learned about her parentage from fellow slaves. They wanted to know if she and her mother openly claimed his paternity, as this helped to determine their status and level of acceptance within the slave community.[101] Goodwin protected herself from potential abuse, and likely protected her mother, by never publicly acknowledging her white father. Enslaved people tested Goodwin's allegiance to the slave community, and her response clearly signaled her black identity by invoking the turkey buzzard, one bearer of black children in African American folklore.[102] Lucy Galloway was born as result of her mother's forced sexual relationship with the master. "She tole me atter I got older who my daddy wuz but tole me not tell anybody," Galloway explained. "De chillun used to ask me who my daddy wuz but I jes' tole dem I didn't have no daddy."[103] Mothers withheld information from young children as a survival strategy, and children collaborated with their mothers to maintain that silence.

A denial of one's white father, however, did not always deflect mistreatment, particularly from black relatives. Patience Avery's mother in Virginia always told her that the turkey buzzard laid her and the sun hatched her, and on the sole occasion that she met her white father, she refused to interact with him and insisted she had no father. In the postwar period, after her mother and grandmother died, Avery lived with her uncle and suffered abuse from her aunt, who resented Avery's white parentage. "I'll tell you 'bout dis terrible part o' my life," Avery recounted. "You see I was treated cruelly 'cause I was dis white man's chile. Ev'y thing de other chillum did dey would put it on Patience. I was a po' motherless chile." Avery's aunt underfed and whipped the young girl. While negative commentary on a grandparent is exceedingly rare, Mandy Billings believed her maternal grandfather treated her poorly because of her white father. "The hardest treatment I had was my grandfather's, Jake Nabors. Look like he hated me cause I was white—and I couldn't help it."[104] A range of people, black and white, displaced their anger over miscegenation on mixed-race children, despite the fact that these individuals had no control over the actions of slaveholders and in many cases had never met or substantively interacted with their fathers.

Former slaves who expressed hostility toward their white parentage did so for a number of reasons, including the unequivocal cases of being sold, betrayed, or abused by their father. How an ex-slave felt about slavery also influenced their response to having a white father and the man himself, and privileged status could induce more positive memories of slavery.[105] On the other hand, having a white father could intensify abuse, and this, in turn, induced negative perceptions of one's father and white heritage. Antebellum fugitive and author Francis Fedric believed slavery imposed particular "degradation and hardship" on biracial children: "To know that it is their own fathers who are treating them as brutes, especially when they contrast their usage with the pampered luxury in which they see his lawful children revel, who are not whiter, and very often not so good-looking as the quadroon."[106] Identity complicated commentary on white fathers, just as feelings about one's father and white relatives could affect self-identity.

A white overseer as a father had potential upsides and downsides. Because they lacked the resources to establish and keep a white family in comfort, some overseers took enslaved concubines. However, overseers seldom owned slaves and thus had no power to protect or free their offspring. A former slave with an Irish foreman as a grandfather noted that "he had to whip his children and grandchildren just like the others." Like masters, they at times developed affection for enslaved kin. "My fathah was good and when we got freedom he took us all and moved to another fahm," Louise Neill recalled.[107] Other overseers terrorized enslaved women and showed little concern for the children they produced.[108] Overseers also had a reputation for brutality. James Watkins loathed his overseer father: "My father's name was Amos Salisbury. . . . He was a cruel and severe disciplinarian, and has often punished me very severely, never recognising me as his son." When his father died, Watkins recalled "how glad I felt at having got rid of such a cruel overseer."[109] When an overseer fathered children by enslaved women, he might anger the master and hasten his own dismissal, leaving his children with little to no knowledge of or contact with their father.[110]

Depending on their father's response, having white parentage could significantly increase or decrease the likelihood of sale. Because mulatto children were regularly sold for a variety of reasons including profit, the demands of white wives and siblings, and a man's desire to evade responsibility for his actions, having a white father amplified the chances that a mixed-race child would be separated from what little family they had. Mixed-race people were thus especially vulnerable to social isolation. Though his sale removed him from the orbit of a wrathful mistress, Moses Roper resented his father, adding the following verse to one of his narratives: "'Twas a father who fettered my limbs with these chains, Sold, — nor one parting blessing bestowed." Selling their illegitimate offspring enabled white fathers to take the easy way out. These men preferred to unload their own progeny rather than deal with the convoluted family dynamics their actions created.[111] Masters who showed little compunction about trafficking in their own blood violated what former slaves considered to be a basic paternal duty.[112] In selling their enslaved offspring, two contradictory forces of masculinity came into play: prowess in the market economy on the one hand and domestic responsibility on the other. White paternity of slaves thus provides yet another example of the paradoxes of the slave South.

While they disparaged men who sold their own blood, former slaves reserved particular venom for fathers who physically abused their enslaved offspring. "I couldn't tell you nothing 'bout my daddy, 'cept they said that Tom Bias was my father," Annie Osborne said of her Georgia master. Osborne's mother and brothers never discussed her parentage, possibly because her "mother was skeered of old Tom Bias as if he was a bear. . . .

We was treated just like animals and beasts in slavery time. Some owners treated the stock better than old Tom Bias handled my fo'ks." She recounted an incident when he "grabbed me and hit me 'cross the eye with a leather strap and I couldn't see out my right eye for two months. He is dead now, but I is gonna tell the truth 'bout the way we was treated." The author of a dictated narrative of an escaped slave, published in 1863, detailed brutality at the hands of her master and father. Dinah was regularly flogged on her father's orders, and he also dictated her marriage and chose her partner. Dinah gave birth to fifteen children, including four sets of twins, many stillborn, and served as a wet nurse to her master's younger children. The master sold a surviving daughter and threatened to sell Dinah's son, "in order to raise money to educate" his legitimate children. After her escape, Dinah was sometimes "kept awake by frightful dreams, in which she fancies she is being tortured over again." Josephine Howell discussed her mother's experiences. "Her own papa bought her when she was eight years old. . . . When she got to be a young maid he forced motherhood up on her."[113] A slaveholding father who bought, sold, and abused his own children failed in his paternal duty to protect his kin.

Memories of a white father's abuse remained acute decades later. In his 1937 interview, J. W. Terrill described being tortured by his father, also his master. After removing him from his mother at six weeks old, Terrill's master eventually gave his son to his sister to be raised. "She was good to me, but befo' he let her have me he willed I must wear a bell till I was 21 year old, strapped 'round my shoulders with the bell 'bout three feet from my head in steel frame. That was for punishment for bein' born into the world a son of a white man and my mammy, a Negro slave," Terrill related. "I wears this frame with the bell where I couldn't reach the clapper, day and night. I never knowed what it was to lay down in bed and get a good night's sleep till I was 'bout 17 year old, when my father died and my missy took the bell offen me." Terrill recalled being "strapped to a tree and whipped like a beast by my father, till I was unconscious, and then left strapped to a tree all night in cold and rainy weather." Terrill's mistress treated him fairly well when his father was absent, but she was only allowed to feed him cornbread, water, and sweet potatoes, "and jus' 'nough of that to keep me alive. I was allus hungry." Terrill's father also verbally abused his son, telling him "I wasn't any more than a damn mule." When his father died, a man he believed "would have kilt every one of his slaves rather than see us go free, 'specially me and my mammy," Terrill obtained relief. "I sang all day, 'cause I knowed I wouldn't be treated so mean. When missy took that bell offen me I thinks

I in Heaven 'cause I could lie down and go to sleep. When I did I couldn't wake up for a long time and when I did wake up I'd be scairt to death I'd see my father with his whip and that old bell. I'd jump out of bed and run till I give out, for fear he'd come back and git me." Terrill's father continued to haunt him and years of mistreatment left damaging psychological scars.[114]

Former slaves who felt betrayed by their fathers had little love for these men and rejected their white ancestry. Isaac Johnson's white father treated his enslaved mother "as a wife and she, in her innocence, supposed she was such." However, Yeager's open cohabitation with a slave "resulted in social ostracism." He "felt the social cut keenly and concluded to sell out and leave that part of the country. He advertised his farm and stock for sale," including his four illegitimate children, ages two to nine. Yeager neglected to tell his family, and thinking he had gone to New Orleans to sell his horses, "we remained waiting patiently his return, till about two months thereafter, when the sheriff came and took us all" to a slave pen where the family members were auctioned off separately. Johnson and his mother and siblings did not realize that "my own father had brought all this change to us, that we were sold by his orders and the three thousand three hundred dollars we were sold for went into his pockets less the expenses of the sale. He sold his own flesh and blood." In "ignorance of the true situation I mourned for him in common with my mother and brothers, and sat through that night bewildered." The experience of being abandoned and deceived in a cowardly manner by a man he had loved deeply affected Johnson's sense of identity. In freedom, Johnson distanced himself from his father and took his mother's name. "Any man of the South who is a descendant of a slave holder who upheld the system of American slavery, ought to blush with shame for his degraded origin," he declared. "I have in me the blood of one such, on the side of my father, and to me, my poor black negro mother shines as an angel in comparison to a devil, and, if I could, I would willingly draw from my veins every drop of that white blood that goes pulsing through my body received by way of my father. It is the only stain I have, received from the laws of nature, of which I am ashamed, while on the other hand, I am proud of my negro blood." Johnson referred to his father as a "devil" and to his white inheritance as "degraded" and a "stain." Publishing his narrative in 1901, he echoed antebellum denunciations of slaveholder perfidy, inhumanity, and immorality, contrasting the dishonor of his white father with the honor of his mother and her race.[115]

Informants and authors who never met or had limited contact with their white fathers adopted similar attitudes and dismissed these men based on their feelings about slavery. Once free, William Wells Brown chose a new name. "I resolved on adopting my old name of William, and let Sandford go by the board, for I always hated it. Not because there was anything peculiar in the name; but because it had been forced upon me," he commented. "And as for my father, I would rather have adopted the name of 'Friday,' and been known as the servant of some Robinson Crusoe, than to have taken his name. So I was not only hunting for my liberty, but also hunting for a name." Brown felt no connection to his white father, a relative of his master. When a kind Quaker who aided in his escape informed him "thee has become a man, and men always have two names," Brown "told him that he was the first man to extend the hand of friendship to me, and I would give him the privilege of naming me." The Quaker gave him his own name, but because Brown insisted on keeping the name "William," he became William Wells Brown, after his "first white friend, Wells Brown."[116] Brown identified more strongly with this "civilized human" who helped provision him with liberty than the biological father whose behavior left him enslaved. These individuals actively dissociated themselves from their white progenitors, men who represented a reviled institution and who dishonorably failed to fulfill their paternal duties.

As formerly enslaved authors reflected on their life experiences, they crafted a narrative about their parents, black and white. In the first published iteration of his autobiography, Frederick Douglass acknowledged that due to his limited contact with his mother, he "received the tidings of her death with much the same emotions I should have probably felt at the death of a stranger." In a later version, Douglass forged a sense of kinship with his mother despite having only met her on the few occasions when she walked twelve miles to visit him at night. Douglass realized that she attempted to bond with him even if it failed to inspire his affection at the time. On the other hand, he never knew the identity of his white father, though he suspected his master, a man he interacted with for a greater portion of his life. When surveying his past, Douglass felt regret over his mother, whereas he considered the mystery of his father a symptom of slavery. "To me it has ever been a grief that I knew my mother so little, and have so few of her words treasured in my remembrance," he wrote. He also made an effort to learn more about her, discovering she was the only literate slave in that area of Maryland. Douglass pointedly chose to identify with his enslaved mother and to reject his putative white father. "That in any slave State a field-hand should learn to read is remarkable, but the achievement of my mother, considering the place and circumstances, was very extraordinary," he continued. "In view of this fact, I am happy to attribute any love of letters I may have, not to my presumed Anglo-Saxon paternity, but to the native genius of my sable, unprotected, and uncultivated mother—a woman who belonged to a race whose mental endowments are still disparaged and despised." Douglass lamented not knowing his mother and her forefathers, but he did not feel a similar sense of loss when it came to his white father. As Douglass endeavored to reestablish the primacy of the patriarchy denied to slaves, he invoked a nameless lineage and a connection to a line of kin extending through his mother. Arguing that emancipated slaves would not "flock to the north," he insisted, "we want to live in the land of our birth, and to lay our bones by the side of our fathers; and nothing short of an intense love of personal freedom keeps us from the south."[117]

Attitudes toward the institution of slavery and postwar race relations informed feelings about white fathers. An informant from Virginia fathered by the master's oldest son recalled being treated well and having an "easy time compared to some." Nevertheless, he despised slavery and did not mince words when discussing his father, something he felt comfortable doing with an African American fieldworker. "I was riding on a street car long after freedom and I passed the cemetery where my father was buried. I started cussing—'Let me get off this damn car and go see where my God damn father is buried, so I can spit on his grave, a God damn son-of-a-bitch,'" he railed. "I got no mercy on nobody who bring up their children like dogs. How could any father treat their child like that? Bring them up to be ignorant like they did us. If I had my way with them all I would like to have is a chopping block and chop every one of their heads off. Of course I don't hate them that is good. There are some good white folks. Mighty few, though."[118] Preferential treatment did not mitigate the fact that this white father neglected his paternal responsibility by keeping his children enslaved, treating them as inferior, and denying them an education and opportunity to better themselves. A father who had power and resources, and yet refused to fully support his children, epitomized the depravity of slavery, slaveholders, and white people. When able to safely express their opinions, former slaves, writing and reminiscing decades apart, emphasized the immorality and disgrace of white men who fathered slaves and yet failed to act as fathers.

Assessments of white fathers were complicated by and in turn complicated the identity of mixed-race individuals. As the sexual exploitation of enslaved women and white paternity of slaves created a sizeable mixed-race population, how those children felt about their fathers shaped their conceptions of themselves and their place within the local community. Whereas some rejected their whiteness, others embraced it, believing their white blood made them better than other slaves, and, in freedom, the rest of the black community. Delia Thompson appreciated the fact that her light complexion earned her a posting in the big house and proximity to the white family. She announced that her paternal white grandfather, a man she possibly never met, was "no poor white trash," and referred to her family as the "colored aristocracy of de town."[119] Claiming an affinity with a nameless white grandfather indicated she inherited that attitude from her father or chose to use her white ancestry to reify her own conceptions of class.

Masters' preferential treatment of concubines and their own children led to "classes of slavery," and some favored slaves reinforced this status. Slave communities, meanwhile, often regarded concubines and their children warily and considered them outsiders. Mary Reynolds's master returned from Baton Rouge with a mulatto seamstress, "dressed in fine style," and built the woman a house removed from the quarters. "This yellow gal breeds so fast and gets a mess of white younguns. She teaches them fine manners and combs out they hair." One day, two of these mulatto children went to the big house and tried to use an outdoor playhouse. The master's legitimate son objected, telling them it was for white children only. "But I ain't no Nigger, we aint no Niggers 'cause we got the same dada you got. . . . The one which is your dada is our dada and he comes to see us every day and fetches us our clothes and things from town," they responded. The white mistress overheard this exchange and questioned the children, and Reynolds noted that the enslaved boy insisted, "He is our dada and we calls him dada when he comes down to our house to see our mama." While the master established the concubine's difference by placing her house away from the quarters, this woman appears to have held herself aloof from the other slaves and passed her sense of superiority to her children. Because they called the master "dada," and he visited daily and brought gifts, her children considered themselves better than slaves and equal to the white children. However, they quickly learned that while they shared a father, they did not share the status of their white half siblings, and instead occupied an uneasy, and probably lonely, middle ground. The relationship between the master and mistress soured after this incident, and though the "seamster" remained, her children "don't go down the hill no more to the big house."[120] Reynolds referred to the children as "white," indicating that this slave community viewed them as a class apart. Recognizing class divisions initiated by slaveholder behavior, however, did not mean that slave communities bought into the idea of black inferiority. As for the mixed-race children in

Reynolds's story, the white children looked down on them, the mistress objected to their presence, and the slaves talked about them behind their backs. These children had only each other, their mother, and a father who owned and could sell them at any time. This atomistic family, already sequestered as a result of the master's actions, further isolated themselves from a community. Polygynous mating on the part of the master created a matrifocal household with a visiting white father who lived on the plantation. Because the children appear to have identified with their father and the status of the family derived from proximity to and identification with him, it is difficult to define this as a matrifocal family.

Class pretensions stemming from miscegenation led to social isolation, as slave communities rebuffed the ideology of those who set themselves up as superior. Alexander Robertson exemplified the loneliness of mixed-race individuals who chose to identify with their white father. While his brother knew the identity of his black father, Robertson knew little about his white father. His mother "and de white folks never tell me who my father was. I have to find out dat for myself after freedom, when I was lookin' 'round for a name. From all I hear and 'pear in de lookin' glass, I see I was half white for sure, and from de things I hear, I conclude I was a Robertson which have never been denied." Robertson took the name of his unknown father's white family. After freedom, he initially farmed with his mother and stepfather, but branched out on his own after he "tired of workin' for a plum black nigger." Robertson ended his narrative by cataloging the hardships of being mixed race: "You have no idea de worry and de pain a mulatto have to carry all his eighty-four years. Forced to 'sociate wid one side, proud to be related to de other side. Neither side lak de color of your skin." Robertson took pride in his partial whiteness, but realized he was not accepted into or by white society. Instead, he had to spend his life among people he condescendingly considered beneath him. Robertson distanced himself from the black community, a community suspicious of the white heritage he celebrated.[121] In this case, adopting the model of individualized manhood seems to have stemmed from identification with white parentage rather than a desire to forsake all community ties, though it had that effect.

Class stratification in slave communities was highly correlated with the sexual exploitation of enslaved women. Brenda Stevenson argues that the response of mixed-race children to their own identity and status, as well as how the slave community viewed them, was "complex and contradictory." Some mulatto individuals perceived themselves as superior, whereas others felt a sense of shame and rage derived from the exploitation of their mothers and their own poor treatment. In addition, while the slave community also saw in mixed-race children a visible reminder of their own oppression and vulnerability, at times, light skin was accorded increased status and the neighborhood took on class and color stratification.[122] For black communities, practical acceptance of class divisions based on color was not the same as an ideological acceptance of notions of superiority and inferiority.

Michael Gomez uses folklore and the discussion between "Tad" and "Yellow Jack" in the story "A Yellow Bastard" to explore mixed-race identity and the black perspective on race mixing. Expressing pain over being rejected by whites and not fully accepted by blacks, Yellow Jack "had an identity without location." The response of the black community was ultimately based on the identity and self-definition of mixed-race individuals, and those "who sought acceptance within the African American community would quickly find it." Gomez discusses the black community's "rejection of claims to superiority by those of mixed race. But an even greater offense is the hypocritical denial of blackness."[123] Lucy Chase, a Northern contraband camp volunteer, for instance, recalled the reactions of African American workers to a mixed-race assistant, Ary. The young woman earned a swift reprisal when she "boasted of her white blood and all the others became at once enraged." Individuals like Ary were more likely to identify with and tout their white heritage if they had a positive relationship with their white father. Ary claimed her father "loved her as well as he did his other children," and would have given her freedom and property had he lived and the Civil War not intervened. Ary believed her white parentage made her better than those with darker skin, but her coworkers disagreed.[124]

White men fathered enslaved children who then grew up to realize they were somehow different and who struggled to find a sense of belonging and a place in the world. Adline Marshall reported that her unmarried master kept a black concubine. "Dat's de reason why dere is so many 'No Nation' niggers 'round now. Some call 'em 'Bright' niggers, but I calls 'em 'No Nation' niggers, 'cause dat what dey is, — dey ain't all black and dey ain't white, but dey is mixed. Dat comes from slave times and de white folks did de wrong, 'cause de blacks get beat and whipped if dey don't do what de white folks tell 'em to."[125] Marshall addressed coercion and lack of consent, and blamed whites for race mixing and the confusion it created. She also stated that while mixed-race individuals were not white, they were not "all black." As Gomez argues, the black community left open the possibility that mixed-race people could find acceptance if they chose to embrace their blackness. White society provided no such opportunity, defining anyone with visible or known African blood as black. Belonging thus centered on self-identity, and those who saw themselves as superior due to their lighter skin removed themselves from potential community. White society was exclusive, whereas black communities, though cautious, offered a greater chance of inclusion.

Raised in the big house and denied knowledge of his family, John Williams had an existential crisis. "I don't know who I am nor what my true name is," Williams responded to the question about background. He took his former owners' name because he had no other choice, but felt his "true" name derived from his unknown enslaved kin. Asked about his parentage, Williams responded, "I have nothing to say about being partly white, I leave that to your imagination, I have thought about it a lot. I don't know." Because he was so young at the time of emancipation, Williams grew up knowing only the family of his former owners. "They never told me who I wus. . . . I loved them but I realized I wus a nigger and knew that I could never be like them." Reared by the white family, Williams knew he did not fit in, and he sought but never uncovered information about his origins: "I have asked thousands of questions trying to find out who my people are but no one has ever told me who I am or who my people are." Williams's sense of loss and isolation stemmed from not knowing his black family. While he grew up without either parent, Williams was likely fatherless because his biological progenitor was white. Unlike Williams, Robert Grinstead knew his parents, but he too felt a sense of dissimilarity as the only child of a bachelor master and a concubine. "When I was large enough to pay attention to my color and to that of the other slaves I wondered to myself why I was not black like the rest of the slaves," he recalled. William Byrd suspected that his master, a man he deemed cruel, was his father, but did not know for sure. While he had an enslaved family, he never felt truly incorporated. "I'se always out of the family life because they knew I was just half brother to them," Byrd said of his siblings.[126] White paternity complicated the identity formation and family and neighborhood integration of enslaved mixed-race children, leading to social isolation, at the individual and family level, that could be chosen and/or externally imposed.

A number of mixed-race individuals saw their own existence and their light skin as evidence of the moral corruption of slavery. Ethel Daugherty's interviewer noted that she attributed the "sin of mixed races" to slavery, and "she herself is very sensitive over the fact that her eyes are blue." Daugherty took comfort in the thought "that through no fault of hers she is not a full-blood," and she advised her children to "stick to their color always." Another informant similarly disparaged the immorality of racial mixing and slaveholders by calling attention to his own physical appearance. "You see me right here, de sin of both races in my face, or was it just de sin of one? My Marster was my father," Jack Johnson declared. Amy Patterson, the child of her master, called slavery "a curse to this nation . . . which still shows itself in hundreds of homes—where mulatto faces are evidence of a heinous sin and proof there has been a time when American fathers sold their children at the slave marts of America." Patterson denounced her father, branding the degradation of her mother and other enslaved women "the greatest crime ever visited on the United States. It was worse than the cruelty of the overseers, worse than hunger, for many slaves were well fed . . . but when a father can sell his own child, humiliate his own daughter by auctioning her on the slave block, what good could be expected where such practices were allowed?"[127] Johnson, interviewed in South Carolina, hedged, while Daughtery and Patterson were interviewed in the North. All three mixed-race individuals traced their resentments over the "sin" and "curse" of slavery to white men who fathered slaves. Patterson was most direct and detailed, accusing white men who sexually exploited slaves and then willingly trafficked their own children of rank dishonor and moral degeneracy.

Many black observers associated mixed ancestry with the disgrace of predatory white paternity. Ryer Emmanuel argued that the sexual practices and unchecked power of slaveholders created the "different classes today" in the twentieth-century black community. "Yes, mam, dat whe' dat old stain come from." James Childress felt "glad he is not a mulatto but a thorough blooded negro." "There is no white blood in me; not a drop," John Little similarly announced. Robert Cheatham's interviewer recorded that he "says it is proof of the honor of his and his forefathers' masters that their blood was never mingled together to produce a mixed race."[128] Honorable white men refrained from sexual contact with enslaved women, and such contact, in the eyes of former slaves, represented a sin and dereliction of paternal duty.

IN A FICKLE MARKET ECONOMY that could promise glittering opportunity and yet easily lead to financial ruin, sex with slaves enabled white men to indulge their carnal desires and patriarchal prerogatives without multiplying their responsibilities. A slave concubine provided physical and often emotional companionship without the encumbrances of legal marriage. Keeping concubines in addition to a legitimate wife and family or raping slaves offered sexual gratification and the attainment of the pinnacle of white male power. Not all white men forced sexual attentions on their slaves, but those who did so, and the fancy trade their behavior fueled and perpetuated, reproduced the oppression of slavery and produced a visible reminder, in the form of mixed-race children, of the availability and ubiquity of illicit sex. When a white man fathered enslaved children, he had the option of abjuring paternal responsibility and instead employing paternalistic prerogative, which allowed him to abuse or sell them with impunity. When white fathers sold their enslaved offspring, they unleashed two contradictory forces of masculinity, as market expertise came into conflict with family duty.

In his book, *My Father's Name*, Lawrence Jackson traces his family history, addressing the impact of slavery and its aftermath, including the difficulty presented by frequent name changes. He discovered a marriage license for his grandmother's grandparents or great-grandparents that provided no name for the father, and instead "substituted a squiggly line." Jackson writes, "I suppose if you got Booker T. Washington's marriage certificate, or Frederick Douglass's, they too would have squiggly lines in place of their father's name. How does the fact of their unknown fathers make these African American heroes different from men like my enslaved ancestor, Richard Waller, who was not famous, not even completely literate, but who would have had a fundamentally different sense about his human connection to the past? His father was not a squiggly line but a black man like himself. It's the same way for me . . . and for my sons. We knew our fathers." In the search for his own past, Jackson poignantly confronts secretive white paternity.[129] One of the many consequences of slavery is broken family trees that leave children, and then subsequent generations, with no knowledge of an ancestor.

Regardless of why and how white men had sex with slaves, their actions created a host of consequences. In another of the many contradictions of slavery, sexual contact often led to feelings of affection. White fathers of enslaved children exhibited a range of reactions to their offspring. A handful emancipated sexual partners and children, others bestowed special treatment but not freedom, and still others flogged and sold their children as they would any other slave. How mixed-race children felt about their white fathers also varied and depended on the treatment they received, the treatment of their mothers, and their interactions with white kin and the local slave community. How they felt about their white fathers also influenced and was influenced by how they felt about themselves. The most unreservedly positive commentary on white fathers came from those few who had been manumitted. Others, usually those accorded privilege, expressed ambivalence. Many had nothing good to say. These reactions underscore the definition of paternal duty espoused by enslaved and formerly enslaved communities across time and space, from the decades prior to the Civil War through the 1930s. A good father protected and supported his children and an ideal father provided freedom. In that context, a few, but very few, white fathers met the standard. White men who abused and sold their own flesh and blood violated slaves' conception of what it meant to be a father. Masters who fathered slaves, therefore, compounded a sense in black communities of white male immorality and dishonor.

CHAPTER SIX

Mortifications Peculiarly Their Own

Rape, Concubinage, and White Paternity

Sexual violence complicated enslaved women's feelings about and reactions to their own children. Most of these women, in a remarkable demonstration of mental resilience, disassociated their love for their children from their antipathy toward the fathers. In rare cases, traumatized women rejected children produced through violence. Furthermore, mixed-race children might adopt negative feelings about and toward their white father in solidarity with their black mother. Relationships that involved some level of consent or acquiescence, even if they began in coercion, could yield quite different responses from concubines and children. For mixed-race women who aligned with their white fathers or sexual partners, children served as a concrete tie to white men who could provide material and other benefits.

Catherine Clinton calls concubinage a "built-in subculture within the slaveowner's world." Nell Irvin Painter argues that the South "more or less concealed slave wives, who represented an open secret that polite people pretended not to see." Concubinage took several forms, with some white men establishing serial relationships with multiple enslaved women, and others keeping concurrent partners, often including white wives, and maintaining polygynous mating arrangements. The discussion of African cultural retention and polygamy surrounding slave breeding and enslaved men and women with multiple partners overlooks the fact that the most obvious form of polygyny in the Old South was the slaveholders who simultaneously kept a white family and a black concubine and her children, sometimes under one roof. Ethel Daugherty discussed concubinage with her FWP interviewer, who reported that "many of the well-built girls were taken by the master into his house and kept similar to Mormonism." White men also established long-term quasi-marriages with enslaved women, and these were most likely to lead to bequests of freedom and property. While many white men in such unions developed affection for their enslaved concubines and children, these relationships started in and were based on a fundamental imbalance of power.[1] White men's ability to rape enslaved women without legal or financial penalty, and the incentives that favored enslaved women as illicit sexual partners, shaped the relationships of limited consent that developed. Enslaved women were always susceptible to sexual assault, and this informed their decisions and the costs and benefits associated with those choices.

Concubines underscore the contradictions of slavery. Illicit sex was not supposed to exist or lead to affection, but both happened regularly. How concubines felt about their position is harder to assess, given a dearth of first-person sources. Observers accused these women of purposely seeking and engaging in relationships with white men and then flaunting a sense of superiority over fellow slaves. Some women did use the advantages offered by physical beauty and/or light skin to carve out lives of reduced labor, material benefits, and the potential reward of freedom for themselves and their children. Enslaved girls and women had a range of reactions to concubinage and some used sex strategically.[2] However, defining these relationships as consensual, although some undoubtedly involved high levels of affection, is problematic because enslaved women started from a place of circumscribed options and relative powerlessness. They might have made different decisions if free or under different circumstances. As Annette Gordon-Reed writes, "Enslaved women practically and legally could not refuse consent." There could be no full consent in a legal climate where white men who had sex with slaves could not be accused of or charged with rape.[3] As a result, it is more accurate to refer to such relationships as proceeding from limited consent, defined as agency without full consent. Some of these women made choices and took an active role in shaping their lives and relationships, but because of the power differential, there was rarely or never the possibility for full consent.[4] The level of consent in these relationships influenced how women felt about their children. Partially consensual relationships enabled enslaved women to exert a small measure of control and sometimes leverage in being able to positively impact the lives of their children. The wills discussed in the previous chapter reveal the reasons black women may sometimes have chosen, through limited consent, to enter into relationships with white men: inheritance of property and freedom. However, as Bernie Jones points out in his study of contested wills, promises could always be broken, making it difficult to discern if and when these women acquired any power.[5]

In his discussion of the market in fancy maids, usually light-skinned women sold for sex, Walter Johnson notes that the high prices paid for these slaves were a matter of public record. Men who purchased a fancy "showed that they had the power to purchase what was forbidden and the audacity to show it off. To buy a 'fancy' was to flirt publicly with the boundaries of acceptable sociability." Buying a fancy enabled white men to combine market prowess and sexual prowess. Southerners understood what was happening, but no one openly acknowledged illicit sex, referring to slaves purchased as sexual objects as cooks or seamstresses. As part of this "double discourse," Johnson argues, "There was a polite way of describing things and another way of seeing them."[6] Despite the polite facade maintained by white men and women, the sex trade existed and reproduced itself as enslaved women had the children of white men.

Edward Baptist uses the fancy trade as a window into the group identity of slaveholding men and "why and how some white men identified rapes and slave sales as conjoined and essential parts of their very selves." Two defining facets of the Old South, the slave market and sexual violence, combined in the fancy trade. "Sexual fetishes and commodity fetishism intertwined with such intimacy that coerced sex was the secret meaning of the commerce in human beings, while commodification swelled its actors with the power of rape," Baptist writes. In choosing and selling these women, traders gratified the tastes of buyers, and while Southerners liked to blame the slave trade and sexual exploitation of enslaved women on lowly traders, slaveholders and traders jointly commodified African Americans and commodified sex. Usually mulatto, often themselves the children of slaveholders, fancy maids "embodied a history of rape" in the antebellum South. White men who purchased a fancy "pleasured themselves with bodies marked by the past of their own power as a class; they had sex with their own histories." The power to sexually violate and dominate slave women was a fundamental part of white Southern men's identity and another example of the fiction of planter independence.[7]

The extent of concubinage and sexual violence in the South, therefore, points to how fathering slaves took on different shades of meaning based on the sex of the children. Fathering biracial daughters set up the potentiality that those girls would become part of the cycle of sex and slavery, and the daughters of concubines were more likely to enter sexual relationships with white men based on some level of consent. A white man who sold his own offspring likely sold his daughters into the sex trade, underscoring how deeply imbedded rape was in the market economy and in the role of white planters as *fathers*. The act of rape connected the private realm of the Southern home to the market. White fathers who willingly sold their own children also demonstrate how cold market relationships negatively affected the family and the home. In his proslavery treatise and condemnation of the North, *Sociology for the South, or the Failure of Free Society*, George

Fitzhugh declared the incompatibility of the values of the home and "domestic affection" with the individualism of free trade and the market. In doing so, he blatantly ignored white paternity of slaves.[8] A handful of slaveholders also purposely raised mixed-race women for the fancy trade, understanding full well that they sold for high prices. Fathering slaves and selling daughters on the slave market and for sex perpetuated the exploitation of the slave system.

The sexual regime of slavery, and particularly concubinage, led to adultery and secrecy, which Painter defines as "toxic to marriages, families, and, ultimately, society." Adultery adversely affected white relationships and white children and contributed to a "pathological" society. White mistresses deplored interracial sex, but felt most threatened by concubinage, and especially mixed-race women and girls. Concubines and their children represented a danger to the racial order. In her journal, mistress Ella Thomas voiced fears of the usurpation of white wives by mulatto women. Emancipation heightened such worries. If concubines gained the right to legally marry, they could upend the social hierarchy and usher in racial equality.[9] White women's fears affected their reactions to and treatment of mixed-race women and children. As a result, concubines often found themselves caught between the sexual demands of white men, the contempt and abuse of white women, and the mistrust of fellow slaves. Some concubines identified with a slave community, whereas others were individualists, prioritizing their own well-being and advancement and that of their children above allegiance to community or race. If white women eschewed the bonds of gender in order to cement their racial and class status, some concubines saw themselves as a class apart and ranked class above gender and race.[10]

Calvin Schermerhorn discusses the strategies some enslaved women used to shield themselves and their children from the market as they manipulated the category of the fancy. "Domestic workers' networks of protection were forged across lines of color and class, gender and generations, and framed in terms of sentiment," he argues, detailing several "enduring domestic partnerships" between white men and enslaved women. At least two of his main examples passed as white at some point in their lives, and he never explores how being mixed race created a potential opportunity, and yet also set these women up for sexual exploitation and made them more likely to align with white partners across racial lines. He uses domestic workers as an example of the lack of a common identity and broad solidarity among enslaved people and their prioritization of family over race. Whereas Schermerhorn emphasizes the importance of place and local conditions, I see the status of the overwhelming majority of these women as the daughters of slaveholders as a critical factor in their decisions and a defining component of the environment and boundaries that shaped their lives. By the mid-nineteenth century, most women sold as fancies were the children of white men. They could sometimes maneuver that designation to their advantage, but they were also encumbered by the status into which they had been born, were classified by others, and regularly sold. The earlier actions of their fathers gave them an opening they could exploit, but also entrapped them.[11]

Concubinage highlights the difficulty of categorizing the slave household and family and demonstrates how white paternity, and fathers, mothers, and children's responses, led to a range of family outcomes. White fathers could be physically present and emotionally absent. When white fathers ignored or abused their children, mixed-race children identified more strongly with their mother. A concubine and her children at times formed an embedded family within a white household, identifying with each other and not with the father, magnifying matrifocality. White men's polygyny led to the existence of enslaved families that were emotionally matrifocal and yet technically not matrilocal. White family members sometimes took and raised mixed-race children, and thus disrupted the enslaved family and erased the mother. When a white father showed interest in his enslaved children and they identified with him in order to derive material benefits and freedom, they strengthened white patriarchy and marginalized the enslaved mother.

Sexual Violence and the Sex Trade

Slaves and former slaves tracked the paternity of children born of sexual assault, information they passed to their offspring. In most cases, mothers accepted and loved children produced through force. Alice Bratton's white father raped her mother, a former slave whose husband had recently died. Bratton had no direct contact with her father, and knew of him through her mother's warning about the dangers of sexual assault. "My pa was a white man," she noted. "He was a bachelor, had a little store, and he overcome mama. . . . Mama told me how she got tripped up and nearly died and for me never to let nobody trip me up that way."[12] The brevity of these interviews offer glimpses of how a sexual history affected the mother-child relationship, but no concrete answers. Bratton's mother never remarried, but it is impossible to tell if this was related to an ensuing distrust of men. Bratton also only hinted at something she might not have fully understood. In saying that her mother almost died, she suggested a brutal incident. Bratton's mother cared enough about her daughter to try to protect her from a similar fate by using her own experience as a cautionary tale.

As Jeff Forret convincingly shows, enslaved women cared deeply about their reputations and "staked a claim to a form of sexual honor familiar to antebellum Southern white women, despite the many obstacles the institution of slavery erected in fulfilling that vision."[13] Not surprisingly, given this honor culture, informants were more open about rape and the problematic paternity of their children with other African American women. Nancy Anderson related the memories of her friend, Jane Peterson, who "come to visit me nearly every year after she got so old. She told me things took place in slavery times." Peterson "had two girls and a boy with a white daddy." The master ordered her to collect eggs in the barn, and "she was scared to go and scared to not go. He'd beat her out there, put her head between the slip gap where they let the hogs into the pasture. . . . She say, 'Old missis whip me. This ain't right.' He'd laugh." Anderson detailed recurring rape, something that might have been harder to do if she had been discussing her own history. Peterson lived in the master's Virginia house, and "bore three of his children in a room in the same house his family lived in." As soon as she heard of emancipation, Peterson "took her children and was gone, she said. She had no use for him. She was scared to death of him. . . . She was so glad freedom come on before her children come on old enough to sell. Part white children sold for more than black children. They used them for house girls."[14] Peterson feared her master, but loved her children, and in order to keep her family intact, she removed her children from their father and the threat of sale, and the implicit threat of the sex trade for her daughters, as soon as the opportunity arose. Some mixed-race individuals had no contact with their fathers because their mothers took bold action to escape abuse. Peterson and her children are an example of an enslaved family embedded within a white household. Her children lived under the same roof as the man who produced them, but though her master fathered her children, Peterson did not consider him a father to her children. White paternity created complicated family and household structures that were emotionally matrifocal, but that were not technically matrilocal.

Sharing painful sexual information with strangers proved more challenging than talking about a friend's experiences. The fieldworker who interviewed Mary Peters struggled to elicit the story of her mixed parentage, obvious in her appearance. "She is very reticent about the facts of her birth," the interviewer noted. "The subject had to be approached from many angles and in many ways and by two different persons before that part of the story could be gotten." Eventually, Peters related the basic details of her mother's rape, an account that revealed she had no way of knowing the exact identity of her father: "My mother's mistress had three boys, one twenty-one, one nineteen, and one seventeen. Old mistress had gone away to spend the day one day. Mother always worked in the house. . . . While she was alone, the boys came in and threw her down on the floor and tied her down so she couldn't struggle, and one after the other used her as long as they wanted for the whole afternoon. Mother was sick when her mistress came home. When old mistress wanted to know what was the matter with her, she told her what the boys had done. She whipped them and that's the way I came to be here." Because her mother was "about" fifteen when Peters was born, she was likely fourteen when this incident occurred.[15] Gang rape and then sale of mother and baby meant that Peters was undeniably fatherless. Peters's protectiveness toward her mother, and the fact that when nearly sold separately her mother cried and convinced a buyer to purchase her infant, suggests a strong bond between the two despite the violence that led to her birth.

In some cases, however, the indignity associated with white paternity led enslaved and formerly enslaved women to reject children produced through rape. Henrietta Smith noted that there had once been other children in the family. "My great-grandmother was considered pretty when she was young," she stated. "Her master would take her out behind the field and do what he wanted. When she got free, she gave both of her children away. She had two children by him—a boy named Eli and a girl named Anna. She didn't want them 'round her because they reminded her of him." While some enslaved women considered their children their own regardless of how they felt about the men who sired them, for others, the violent acts of the father tainted women's emotional response to their children. Emancipation offered women the opportunity to escape reminders of violence and abuse by leaving their children. Fannie Tatum's mother abandoned her children after freedom. Exactly why she left is unclear, but the fact that her master fathered her daughters may have contributed to her decision. "My mother ran away and left my sister and me when we was three and five years old," Tatum recalled. After their mother left, their master and father had both girls bound to him until age twenty-one. Tatum's mother may have been unfit in any case, but the abysmal treatment the two girls endured from their own father during their indenture offers testament to his character and the harm he likely inflicted on their mother. "I never slept in a bed until I was twenty-two years old," Tatum continued. "They kept my hair cut off like a boy's all the time. . . . I was treated like a dog."[16] Rape damaged women and had radiating repercussions for their children. For Tatum, white paternity destroyed any semblance of family, and she grew up without a mother and with a man she accused of treating her more like an animal than a human being.

Fannie Tatum had good reason to despise her father, whose cruelty she experienced firsthand, but other former slaves, in solidarity with their mothers, expressed loathing for white fathers they had never met and knew little about. "I hate my father," Hannah Travis declared. "He was white. I never did have no use for him. I never seen him because Mama was jayhawked from the place. I never heard my mother say much about him either, except that he was red-headed. He was my mother's master. My mother was just forced. I hate him." Abbie Lindsay suggested that sexual assault motivated her father's postwar choice of a surname, a reference to the town of Summerville, Alabama. "My father was an overseer's child. You know they whipped people in those days and forced them. That is why he didn't go by the name of Watts after he got free and could select his own name." In his decision to adopt a certain name, Lindsay's father spurned his white paternity. Morgan Ray rejected a white father he knew, the master's son. "When my mothah was only 13 years old, John done took advantage of her at de point of a gun. I was the result. . . . My mothah nevah did forgive my pappy for what he done to her, or I either. Long after de war my daddy offered to give me 25 acres of his land for my very own. I wouldn't take it then, and I wouldn't take it now." Ray celebrated his mother's defiance. After she physically punished Ray and his father found out, he had the overseer administer a brutal whipping. "It took three men to lick her dat time," Ray proudly noted. "She was high spirited and hard to boss."[17] Even in coming to his son's defense and trying to belatedly provision, this white father could not earn his son's allegiance. Sexual violence often reinforced the bonds between children and their mothers as male and female informants upheld the sexual honor of enslaved women and denigrated white men. Rape thus fueled matrifocality across a range of household structures.

Caring for their children and exhibiting their resilience, however, did not erase the fact that women carried with them shame and resentment as a result of sexual abuse. Elizabeth Keckley briefly discussed her "suffering and deep mortification." A "fair-looking" young woman, she attracted attention, and "for four years a white man—I spare the world his name—had base designs on me." She did not directly mention, but implied the use of force. "I do not care to dwell upon this subject, for it is one that is fraught with pain. Suffice it to say, that he persecuted me for four years, and I—I—became a mother." Keckley understood that when sexual assault led to reproduction, despised circumstances and paternity caused emotional difficulty for mother and child. "The child of which he was the father was the only child that I ever brought into the world," she continued. "If my poor boy ever suffered any humiliating pangs on account of birth, he could not blame his mother, for God knows that she did not wish to give him life; he must blame the edicts of that society which deemed it no crime to undermine the virtue of girls in my then position." Though she did not want to have a child and had no affection for the father, Keckley loved her son. She later purchased his freedom, as well as her own, and they eventually went north, where she worked as a dressmaker for Mary Todd Lincoln. When her son died fighting in the Civil War, she called the loss "a sad blow," and visited his battlefield grave in Missouri.[18] Even in the case of a long-term concubine, a woman with children by different men might display favoritism based on the father. One ex-slave noted that her master never legally married and instead kept a mulatto concubine. Phyllis had several children by the master, but also "one boy that wuz nigger black. His daddy was a nigger man. When she wuz drunk er mad she'd say she thought more of her black chile than all the others."[19] If fellow slaves noticed her behavior, her children probably did as well. How this contributed to their sense of self and feelings about their paternity is unknown.

Illicit sex went beyond domination and gratification of carnal appetites and generated profit, creating an incentive to produce, raise, and sell enslaved children. Those familiar with the market knew that mixed-race children meant "immense profit." "No difference was it his own flesh and blood—if the price was right!" John White declared of masters willing to sell their children. It was in the "pecuniary interest" of "licentious" masters to keep slave concubines, Henry Brown explained. "Their progeny is so many dollars and cents in their pockets . . . and mulatto slaves command a higher price than dark colored ones." Charlotte Martin, interviewed nearly a century later, similarly noted that the "products of miscegenation were very remunerative. These offsprings were in demand as house servants."[20] Mixed-race individuals were regularly sold and purchased as domestic workers, placing them at higher risk of sexual abuse and reinforcing the cycle of sex and slavery.

Because mulatto women were especially vulnerable to the sex trade, the consequences of white parentage varied according to the sex of the child.

Mixed-race women sold as fancy girls consistently brought the highest prices on the slave market, meaning that white men realized the consequences of siring illegitimate daughters. "The slave pen is only another name for brothel," John Brown declared. According to William Craft, slaveholders understood that they could maximize financial gain by selling mulatto daughters into the sex trade. "It is a common practice for gentlemen (if I may call them such), . . . to be the fathers of children by their slaves, whom they can and do sell with the greatest impunity; and the more pious, beautiful, and virtuous the girls are, the greater the price they bring, and that too for the most infamous purposes." James Pennington, also a fugitive writing from the antebellum North, argued that slaveholders "raised" mixed-race women "for the express purpose of supplying the market of a class of economical Louisiana and Mississippi gentlemen, who do not wish to incur the expense of rearing legitimate families." Francis Fedric offered a specific example. A master of his acquaintance "sold his own daughter, a quadroon, to a gentleman of New Orleans," who "wanted her to be housekeeper for him . . . for he had no wife." Addressing the taboo subject of mulatto children born to white women, Harriet Jacobs observed, "In such cases the infant is smothered, or sent where it is never seen by any who know its history. But if the white parent is the *father*, instead of the mother, the offspring are unblushingly reared for the market. If they are girls, I have indicated plainly enough what will be their inevitable destiny."[21] Jacobs identified how the sexual abuse perpetrated by white fathers connected the home, the market, and the sex trade. Rape and concubinage intimately linked paternity and paternalism.

White blood became a double-edged sword for mixed-race women. It increased the chances of sexual coercion, but could also lead to opportunities for women able to manipulate concubinage as a survival strategy.[22] The status of slaves enabled white men to compel sex by offering rewards and not just by threatening punishments, and the understanding that concubines might potentially gain from sexual liaisons with white men created space for women to use their bodies as a tool and men to win compliance through promises they had no intention of keeping. Enslaved women who tried to use sexual relationships strategically often discovered that masters sold even favored concubines and willingly peddled their own offspring. Former slaves maligned the honor of white men who purchased concubines, keeping them as consorts as a matter of convenience until they legally married or another slave piqued their interest. William Wells Brown related the history of Cynthia, "a quadroon, and one of the most beautiful women I ever saw," who was purchased by a bachelor. When Cynthia refused his "base offers," he threatened to "sell her as a field hand to the worst plantation on the river," wore down her resolve, and "established her as his mistress and housekeeper at his farm." The master later married a white woman and sold Cynthia and their four children. Common law marriages provided companionship until white men were financially and socially ready to marry. Many white men deemed the children of such relationships an expendable source of revenue.[23]

Concubinage of a female relative, even one's own mother, however, could complicate reactions to sexual exploitation if the relationship provided advantages. The master's son told Victor Duhon's mother "he gwine shave her head iffen she don' do like he tell her. Atter dat she was his woman 'til he git marry to a w'ite lady." Like many Southern men, Duhon's father began his sexual life with an enslaved concubine and then moved on to a legal marriage. Duhon grew up in the big house and had limited interaction with other slaves, including his mother. "You know Missus Duhon she was r'ally my gramma. She was sho' good to me," he recalled. His mother eventually married an enslaved man on a neighboring Louisiana plantation and had more children. After the war, Duhon stayed with the white family. Raised apart from a slave community, Duhon identified more with his white grandparents than his mother. Anthony Christopher's family benefited from his sister's relationship with their Texas master. "Dey didn't bother mama and pappy none, though, and dat's 'cause Deenie, what was my sister, was Marse Patton's gal. He wasn't married and he keeps Deenie up to de big house." Christopher never commented on Deenie's feelings or how the relationship started, but it is possible she accepted this situation as a way to remain near and to shield her family.[24]

Regardless of how they evolved, most sexual relationships between white men and enslaved women started with coercion, and many began in outright violence.[25] Rape enabled white men to dominate enslaved women, dispirit enslaved men, and break down the resistance of both. Rape and sexual exploitation present another set of paradoxes within slavery. As an act of violence and domination, rape is fundamentally dehumanizing, and yet, in a perverse way, the white perpetrators recognized the humanity of slaves.[26] To say that a rapist recognizes the humanity of his or her victim, however, provides little solace to those suffering intimate violation. Enslaved women and girls who resisted faced physical punishment that often shattered their defiance. "The slave girl is reared in an atmosphere of licentiousness and fear," Harriet Jacobs declared. If a white man could not win compliance with bribery, "she is whipped or starved into submission." Jacobs managed to evade the demands of her master, but she could not maintain her chastity indefinitely, and unable to marry the free black man she loved, she ended up in a relationship with another white man, who fathered her two children. "Resistance is hopeless," she concluded. The sexual dynamics of the institution defined Jacobs's experience in slavery. "When they told me my new-born babe was a girl," she said of her second child, "my heart was heavier than it had ever been before. Slavery is terrible for men; but it is far more terrible for women. Superadded to the burden common to all, *they* have wrongs, and sufferings, and mortifications peculiarly their own."[27] Jacobs's parents both had a degree of white heritage and her liaison with a white man perpetuated the cycle of mixed-race women as sexual objects.

Mulatto girls learned at an early age that they faced a life of sexual exploitation and their choices must be assessed in that context. When she was fourteen, Louisa Picquet's master made sexual overtures that she averted when the sheriff arrived and seized his slaves to pay outstanding debts. "I was glad when I heard I was taken off to be sold," she recalled, "because of what I escape; but I jump out of the fryin'-pan into the fire." Picquet was separated from her mother and brother and sold to Mr. Williams, a divorced father from New Orleans, as a concubine and housekeeper. "He said he was getting old, and when he saw me he thought he'd buy me, and end his days with me. He said if I behave myself he'd treat me well: but, if not, he'd whip me almost to death." At around fifty, he was significantly older than the teenaged slave and Picquet described him as threatening, jealous, and possessive, not allowing her to leave the house, even to attend church.[28] Isolated in his home, she had no community and no protection.

Louisa Picquet had four children in New Orleans, and though she acknowledged Mr. Williams as the father, she defined them as her children. "He never let on that he was the father of my children," she said of his public persona. In fact, there were two sets of children in the house, or as Picquet put it, "My children and his. You see he had three sons." If he went out and she fell asleep and was slow to wake and let him in when he knocked, "he'd come in and take the light, and look under the bed, and in the wardrobe, and all over, and then ask me why I did not let him in sooner." Picquet and her children lived in a two-parent household that sheltered two distinct families, and she maintained her emotional distance from the man with whom she was forced to live. Picquet is yet another example of how white paternity could create emotionally matrifocal families located within patriarchal, patrilocal white households. Picquet disliked her controlling master, and "after a while he got so disagreeable that I told him, one day, I wished he would sell me . . . because I had no peace at all. I rather die than live in that way. Then he got awful mad, and said nothin' but death should separate us; and, if I run off, he'd blow my brains out. Then I thought, if that be the way, all I could do was just to pray for him to die." Her prayers were eventually answered, and Williams informed Picquet that he expected to die.[29]

As part of his planning for death, Williams made preparations to provide for his enslaved family. If she promised to go to the North, "he would leave me and the children free." Ever controlling, he gave Picquet instructions about how to proceed. "He told me how to conduct myself, and not to live as I had lived with him, with any person. He told me . . . not to let any one know who I was, or that I was colored. He said no person would know it, if I didn't tell it; and, if I conducted myself right, some one would want to marry me, but warned me not to marry any one but a mechanic—some one who had trade, and was able to take care of me and the children." Did he care about her future and ensuring the freedom of his children, or was he trying to keep them away from another slaveholder in New Orleans, or a mixture of both? When he died, Picquet "didn't cry nor nothin', for I was glad he was dead; for I thought I could have some peace and happiness then. I was left free, and that made me so glad I could hardly believe it myself." Williams's brother evicted her from the house and threatened to re-enslave her, so she sold her possessions and took her two living children to Cincinnati. Regardless of Williams's motives, he seems to have been fonder of Picquet than she was of him. In the North, she met and married another former slave and they had three children. She also located and eventually purchased the freedom of her mother.[30] Louisa Picquet is a good example of how many mixed-race individuals focused their familial love on their mothers, their children, and, when able, their African American spouses.[31] She felt no emotional connection to the white father who sold her and doomed her to the fancy trade, and she tolerated Mr. Williams.

Christie Farnham, in a discussion of female-headed slave households, emphasizes women's ability to manage without men. The sexual dynamics of slavery fueled this trend, with concubines often forming female-headed families embedded within white households. Bondwomen whose children had white fathers, particularly fathers they detested and who had forced them into a relationship, tended to view those children as their own. Lucy Galloway's mother told her that her master was her father, but that she should keep this information to herself and when asked "jes' say dat she wuz 'my mammy and daddy bof'."[32] The white man provided paternity, but he was not a father, certainly not in an emotional sense. For black concubines who never identified with their captors, their perception of their children as having a single parent fostered psychological self-reliance. Louisa Picquet eventually married and created a combined family, but only after making her own way north with her children. Sexual exploitation thus exacerbated matrifocality of household and family, as it increased the number of enslaved children with a disengaged or absent father. Concubines also had to fend for themselves in the face of social and legal practices that systematically denied them family rights and inheritances. If a white man died intestate, his legal wife automatically received one-third of his estate as dower. Concubines lacked such legal privileges. At times, white fathers named the mothers of their illegitimate children in their wills in order to identify them, but did not acknowledge the children as their own. Significant bequests to the children, or the testimony of a witness, might suggest or reveal paternity. This indicates that these men distanced themselves from fatherhood and supports the idea that African American matrilineal descent in the antebellum South was often a by-product of white paternity, propagated even in the wills of white men who attempted to provide for their concubines and children.[33]

Many concubines dissociated their love of their children from their distaste for the men who violently produced them. Lucendy Hall discussed a slave girl "overpowered" by her master who gave birth to his daughter. Forbidden to whip the concubine, the mistress nonetheless instigated abuse, and the child's "hair was kept cut short because they did not want it to be long like the mistress' little girl's hair." Although she had greater freedoms than other slaves, she did not lead a happy life. "This slave had liberty to go where and when she pleased; lived in a room of the white people's house," Hall reported to her African American fieldworker. "However, she despised her master because he was the father of her child." The young woman loved and endeavored to protect her child, and viewed the little girl as her own. Her hostility to her master stemmed from sexual abuse and powerlessness to resist.[34] Fathering slaves created convoluted household dynamics, and Hall described another instance of an enslaved woman forced to live in the big house who saw herself and her child as a discrete, matrifocal family within a white, patrilocal, and patriarchal household.

While Louisa Picquet had no way to refuse a relationship with a master who purchased her as a sexual companion, Harriet Jacobs avoided becoming Dr. Norcom's concubine, but she could not escape entanglements with white men altogether. Norcom destroyed Jacobs's hope of marrying a free black man, and then informed her of his intention to "build a small house for me, in a secluded place," to outfox his hypervigilant wife. Jacobs made a difficult choice to enter into an affair with another white man, Samuel Sawyer, and asked her readers to judge her by a set of standards commensurate with the institution that severely constrained her options. "I wanted to keep myself pure; and, under the most adverse circumstances, I tried hard to preserve my self-respect; but I was struggling alone in the powerful grasp of the demon Slavery." Denied the opportunity to marry, and realizing she could not maintain her virginity for long, Jacobs's relationship with Sawyer represents a form of limited and strategic consent made under duress. "It seems less degrading to give one's self, than to submit to compulsion," she argued. Jacobs also believed "nothing would enrage" Norcom "so much as to know that I favored another; and it was something to triumph over my tyrant even in that small way." She calculated that Norcom, in his anger, would sell her and that Sawyer would purchase her, "and I thought my freedom could be easily obtained from him."[35] Though she correctly predicted that Sawyer would purchase her, Norcom refused to sell.

Jacobs's two children by Samuel Sawyer, according to the laws of slavery, became the property of her tormentor, Dr. Norcom.[36] When Norcom sent her to the plantation to break her resistance, Jacobs, hoping to trigger the sale of her children, ran away, hiding in a cramped attic garret of her grandmother's house for seven years. Norcom jailed her brother and children in an effort to lure her back. Finally, tricked into thinking he was selling them out of state, Norcom sold her brother and children to a slave dealer representing their father. Describing her children's return to their great-grandmother's home, Jacobs revealed her ambivalence about their father: "The father was present for awhile; and though such a 'parental relation' as existed between him and my children takes slight hold of the heart or consciences of slaveholders, it must be that he experienced some moments of pure joy in witnessing the happiness he had imparted." She appreciated his having rescued them from Norcom, but called them "my" children. Sawyer was "the" rather than "their" father, and while she believed he had good intentions, she did not fully trust his emotional investment. Later, from her hiding place, she fretted about her children's freedom, taking a tremendous risk to speak to Sawyer. "He had not emancipated my children and if he should die, they would be at the mercy of his heirs," she reasoned. Jacobs faced a "new and unexpected trial" when Sawyer married and his wife took a liking to the children, even when informed of "his relation to them." Jacobs knew that her children could be sold at any time unless legally emancipated.

Jacobs and Sawyer decided to send the children north when Norcom threatened to invalidate their sale. "So, then, after all I had endured for their sakes," she lamented, "my poor children were between two fires; between my old master and their new master!"[37] Jacobs preferred Sawyer to Norcom, but ultimately he was a master and she distrusted all slaveholders, even in matters relating to their own flesh and blood.

After finally securing her own freedom and that of her children, Harriet Jacobs lived with her daughter in Boston. Before Louisa departed for boarding school, Jacobs "resolved to tell her something about her father," a task for which she "had never been able to muster sufficient courage." Jacobs worried that if she unexpectedly died, her daughter "might hear my story from some one who did not understand the palliating circumstances." When Jacobs mentioned her "great sin," Louisa asked her to stop. "But, my child, I want you to know about your father." Louisa responded, "I know all about it, mother," and continued: "I am nothing to my father, and he is nothing to me. All my love is for you. I was with him five months in Washington, and he never cared for me. He never spoke to me as he did to his little Fanny. I knew all the time he was my father, for Fanny's nurse told me so; but she said I must never tell any body, and I never did. I used to wish he would take me in his arms and kiss me, as he did Fanny; or that he would sometimes smile at me, as he did at her. I thought if he was my own father, he ought to love me. I was a little girl then, and didn't know any better. But now I never think any thing about my father. All my love is for you."[38] After repeated urging on the part of Jacobs, Sawyer freed his enslaved children, but he never bestowed on them the same attention he gave to his white daughter, Fanny. Without her mother's vigilance, Louisa would have remained uneducated and indentured to a Northern branch of the Sawyer family. Though he provided manumission, Sawyer treated his white and black children differently, and his lack of emotional warmth and public acknowledgment affected his daughter, who identified with and gave her love to her mother.

The frequency of sexual exploitation within slavery raises the question of consensual relationships between white men and black women. "Some did it because they wanted to and some were forced. They had a horror of going to Mississippi and they would do anything to keep from it," one informant told her African American interviewer. "Of course the mixed blood, you couldn't expect much from them." These women weighed sex with white men against the fear of separation from home and kin, fear of the unknown, and hard labor. Betty Brown knew her father was an Irishman, and also knew he had a white family, "but mah mammy say he like huh an' she like him." Consensual relationships did exist, but the records indicate that black women made pragmatic decisions from a position of powerlessness. Given the constraints they faced, these relationships cannot be defined as fully consensual, making limited consent a more accurate description. Harriet Jacobs serves as a prime example. Her liaison with Samuel Sawyer was the best of a limited set of unpalatable alternatives. In addition, when survival depended on making concessions to an owner, what might seem like a consensual relationship often began with force. "My boss made me have a child for him," Matilda Shepard told her interviewer, offering no further detail.[39] Many women faced a choice between violence and compliance.[40]

It is difficult to find first-person examples of enslaved women who willingly entered relationships with white men. Scholars have documented the dearth of sources illuminating the feelings of black women. "So much of the inner life of black women remains hidden," Darlene Clark Hine writes. "Rape and the threat of rape influenced the development of a culture of dissemblance."[41] As a result, comments on concubines' behavior and motivations come from observers, including their children. "Dem yaller wimen was highfalutin' too, dey thought dey wus better dan de black ones," Mattie Curtis said of concubines. "Some of them thought it was an honor to have the marsa, but I didn't want no white man foolin' with me," another woman added.[42] Former slaves believed that mixed-race women more readily assented to relationships with white men and that these women considered themselves superior.

The fact that white men at times willed slave property to their concubines and illegitimate children fueled distrust between these individuals and slave communities. A Tennessee master willed four slaves to a concubine and his "publicly acknowledged" daughter Emily. When he sold two of those slaves before his death, Emily brought suit for compensation, signifying that she felt entitled to the slaves or the proceeds of that property. Free black hairdresser Eliza Potter traveled extensively and commented on black slaveholders in Natchez, Mississippi, and New Orleans. She found fault with mixed-race women who achieved social status through relationships with white men, describing one slave mistress in New Orleans as "the most tyrannical, overbearing, cruel task-mistress that ever existed; so you can see color makes no difference, the propensities are the same, and those who have been oppressed themselves, are the sorest oppressors." When white men purchased mulatto women as housekeepers and concubines, Potter argued that they then treated the household slaves with contempt.[43] Mistrust of concubines influenced a slave community's response to their children.

Whereas Sarah Ford called her master's concubine "uppity over de slaves," not all of these women had an antagonistic relationship with slave communities. Anna Coffee's North Carolina master sent his mixed-race children to schools and churches where they passed as white. His concubine, Miss Patsey, served as mistress of the plantation and treated everyone kindly, and though she kept it secret from the master, the slaves believed her to be an "abolitionist at heart." Alice Freeman reported that her white father in Missouri treated his concubine as a wife and "contrary to the accepted practice of ostracism in a case like this," she and her mother and siblings "were accepted and respected members of the society of the vicinity." Freeman's father educated his five children, and because he gave them land as they came of age, she claimed that they were the "envy of the negro population." How the local slave community actually felt is unknown, as is the timing of their freedom. Freeman, who sold her land and moved west after the Civil War, would not reveal her father's name.[44] Freeman never elaborated on her mother beyond noting her "stunning" beauty, but her narrative hints at a certain level of consent, at least in the eyes of the daughter.

The mixed-race daughters of planters were more likely to voluntarily enter sexual relationships with white men if they had positive relationships with their fathers and identified with their white heritage. White men who at least privately acknowledged and accorded special privileges to their enslaved children, therefore, paradoxically increased the chances that their daughters would become concubines. Concubinage bred further concubinage by enlarging the pool of enslaved women white men found alluring. Lucy and Sarah Chase, volunteers from Massachusetts, worked in a wartime contraband camp with a number of freedwomen. One assistant named Ary announced a sense of superiority derived from having a white father. She spoke frequently of her father's "affection" and his intention to leave her the "largest share" of his property. Ary had also been the sexual partner of her white cousin, a man she referred to as "Young Master," who fathered her deceased baby. "He would not let me have anything to do with colored men; he said they weren't good enough for me," Ary reported. In the Chase sisters' retelling and the quotes they attributed to Ary, this relationship appears to have involved a high degree of consent, stemming in part from Ary's identification with her white father and reinforced by a conscious strategy on the part of white men to keep her sequestered from black men and a slave community. When the other workers angrily rejected Ary's color-based snobbery, she responded by mentioning her dead baby. "'Well, how near do you think my child was to being white?'" she asked, citing his white grandfather and father. "'Well,' said one, 'just tell me how many folks it takes to make a white person?' Ary was obliged to answer, 'One white man and one white woman.'"[45] Ary loved and missed her baby as a mother, but having a child with a white man also gave her greater proximity and claim to whiteness.

In addition, concubines seem to have been aware that white men often favored their children above their sexual partners. The child of a concubine and her master, Harriet Daves recalled that her father would give her anything she asked for. "Mother would make me ask him for things for her. She said it was no harm for me to ask him for things for her which she could not get unless I asked him for them."[46] The children of slaveholders became leverage that enslaved women used to secure their attachment to men who had the power to dispense material support and, in rare cases, manumission. Depending on the circumstances, mixed-race children could remind their mothers of violence and trauma, or they could represent a potential avenue to improved conditions.

Published in 1956, Pauli Murray's family history exposes the lonely life of the slave concubine and the complicated identity of a mulatto child. Though not a first-person account, the story is nonetheless revealing. Murray explored the background of the woman who helped raise her, her grandmother, Cornelia Smith Fitzgerald. The story began with Harriet, a beautiful mixed-race woman purchased as a personal maid for Mary Ruffin Smith, the daughter of a North Carolina planter. As Harriet matured, Mary's two brothers became obsessed with her and savagely whipped and chased off Harriet's free black husband, Reuben Day, the father of her oldest son. The other slaves "kept their distance," and Murray speculated that while the enslaved women sympathized with Harriet, they realized that her predicament "might save their own skins for a while." Black men avoided her, making it impossible she would find another slave or free black husband. Sidney Smith beat Harriet into submission and repeatedly and violently raped her, leading to the birth of Cornelia. He left Harriet alone after a beating from his own brother, Francis. Following the birth of Cornelia, Francis initiated a sexual relationship with Harriet, and this time she did not resist. Murray lacked access to her great-grandmother's feelings, but she suggested that Harriet was "resigned," and mentioned her "wretched loneliness." In addition, Francis offered some security from the "predatory" brother. However, Murray does not sugarcoat this emotionally "distant" long-term relationship, referring to Harriet as a "mere pawn."[47] Harriet had three more daughters by Francis.

Harriet had five children by three different men, relationships of choice, force, and limited consent. Her oldest son, Julius, was neglected and raised in the slave quarters as his mother fulfilled her responsibilities in the big house. Mary Ruffin Smith, faced with her brothers' disgrace, chose to honor her blood and raised the four half-white girls in the big house, becoming their de facto parent. Murray's description of their upbringing paints Harriet as a figure consigned to the background, a woman who lacked authority over or even much involvement with her children. The girls occupied an ill-defined status, so often the station of mulatto children related to the master's family. "The Smiths were as incapable of treating the little girls wholly as servants as they were of recognizing them openly as kin," Murray wrote of her grandmother's childhood. The white family "carefully preserved a thin veneer of master-servant relationship," the girls remained enslaved, and Francis's three daughters called him "Marse."[48] Murray presented a convoluted household that cannot be easily categorized. The four girls lived with or near both of their parents, three of them interacted uneasily with their white father, and they all seem to have had an attenuated connection to their mother.

Murray inherited and recorded a complex appraisal of her great-grandfather, Sidney Smith. On the one hand, Murray noted that after his involvement with Harriet and run-in with his jealous brother, he became the "outcast" of the family, "took to drinking and brooded his life away." On the other hand, Murray's grandmother Cornelia clearly appreciated her father. He flouted Southern convention and openly acknowledged his daughter, something his brother refused to do and much to the shame and embarrassment of the white family. Cornelia "adored" her father, the man who "instilled in her that she was inferior to nobody." Murray called Sidney Smith a "contradictory little man," who even began to flirt with antislavery views. In the end, Murray chillingly detailed Sidney's sexual violence, and yet did not entirely condemn this man to whom she in part owed her own existence.[49]

While Murray's book is most useful for the views of Cornelia Fitzgerald toward her father, it also highlights the isolated existence of the enslaved concubine. Former slaves often accused these women of adopting an air of condescension and of setting themselves apart, and some undoubtedly did. However, their treatment by the slave community contributed to their social isolation. Over the weeks that Sidney Smith visited Harriet's cabin, he nailed her door shut from the inside to prevent her escape, and the other slaves overheard her anguished cries. No one intervened, which is understandable given that to do so would have invited physical retaliation and would not have rescued Harriet. This raises the question of how the local slave community, even if sympathetic, interacted with Harriet when they knew what was happening and what had happened and knew that they themselves had not and could not help her in any way. In addition, many sexual captors physically removed concubines from community, keeping them in a room in their own home or in a cabin separated from the quarters. In such a situation, a concubine had few confidants, especially if she lived under the roof of a white mistress who reviled her. Her children became her social world, and Murray makes it clear that Harriet's children looked not to her for guidance, but to their white aunt. Murray never met Harriet, but her description of "wretched loneliness" seems more than apt, and a fitting description of the life of the enslaved concubine.[50] Mixed-race children raised by white relatives were more likely to identify with their white heritage, further isolating their mothers.

Slave communities tended to shun enslaved women who voluntarily, or seemed to voluntarily, engage in sexual relationships with white men.[51] Their children more often faced rejection by slave communities. Social ostracism could create a feedback loop, in that a woman initially coerced into a relationship might then make the choice to affiliate with her white captor or a later partner because it offered her a social network, and her children might make the same choices based on their social distance from other slaves, which further widened the gulf from a black community. Enslaved men often avoided these women as a matter of their own mental and physical self-preservation, white men kept them separated, isolated, and dependent, and white women and children spurned them. Nell Irvin Painter enumerates the possible psychological repercussions of rape, including isolation, lack of trust, "self-hatred, anger, and identification with the aggressor," all highly applicable to concubines. These women and their children were deeply enmeshed in the structural and actual violence of the slave system.[52]

Josephine Boyd Bradley and Kent Anderson Leslie's account of Amanda America Dickson, the mulatto daughter of a wealthy Georgia planter, contains echoes of Murray's family history. In 1849, David Dickson raped a twelve-year-old slave, Julia, who belonged to his mother. The authors use the African American Dickson Family Oral History, legal records pertaining to Dickson's contested will, and newspaper articles to piece together the life story of Amanda, an "elite mulatto 'lady,'" who "was both protected and trapped." According to the family history, Julia "never forgave" Dickson for raping her at such a young age, and she exacted her "revenge" by becoming his housekeeper and exerting control over his household. Despite her resentment, Julia chose to remain on or near Dickson's plantation even after emancipation, possibly out of a desire to stay with her oldest daughter. Shortly after Amanda was weaned, the baby was taken from Julia and raised by her white grandmother. Treated as a member of the family, and "adored" by her father, she nonetheless remained enslaved until 1864. Following the war, Amanda married a white veteran with the help of her father, who took the couple to Baltimore to evade Georgia's antimiscegenation laws. After having two children, she left her husband and returned to her father. Bradley and Leslie address the numerous unanswered questions about Amanda's identity, but note that she called herself an "orphan" following her father's death, despite having a living mother. When he died, David Dickson left his estate to Amanda, bringing his secret "outside" family into the public eye, and though challenged by his white relatives, the will stood. Amanda moved to Augusta, Georgia, married a mulatto man, and died a wealthy woman. While Amanda appears to have identified with and appreciated her father, Julia remains more enigmatic, an admitted rape victim who "never allowed herself to be erased."[53]

The story told by Pauli Murray and that of Amanda Dickson share the similarity of a white man raping a young girl and then doting on the resulting child, indicating that men often demonstrated greater emotional concern for and granted higher status to their children than their sexual prey.[54] In cases of divergent treatment of mother and child, some children allied and identified with their fathers, especially if they had been taken out of their mother's care and raised by white relatives. If concubinage and white paternity at times strengthened matrifocality, women's self-reliance, and children's identification with mothers, it could also have the opposite effect. Disinterested and absent white fathers reinforced matrifocality of household and family, whereas Bernie Jones argues that in cases of involved white fathers, black mothers were often effaced. Mixed-race children, in an effort to try to secure bequests of property or freedom, had to align with their father. "The legal system forced the enslaved women's children to minimize or deny their black mothers," Jones writes, "for to claim rights through their father's wills they had to present themselves as if they had no other parent."[55] White paternity of slaves thus had divergent outcomes, in that it contributed to fatherlessness and emotionally matrifocal families, and in a small number of cases, the marginalization of black mothers.

Using newspaper accounts and trial records, Melton McLaurin details the life of Celia, a teenaged slave executed in 1855 in Missouri for the murder of her master, Robert Newsom. After purchasing her at age fourteen as a concubine, Newsom raped Celia on the trip home, establishing the basis of their relationship. Celia eventually had two children who lived with their mother in a matrifocal household, and their white father visited the cabin at night. Celia kept an emotional distance from Newsom, and her actions indicate that she did not consider him part of her family. Despite being set apart from the other slaves in her own cabin, Celia managed to start a relationship with an enslaved man named George. Pregnant and faced with an ultimatum from George, Celia attempted to end the sexual demands of her master. While fending him off, she ended up killing Newsom and then burning his body to hide the crime. Celia revealed her hostility toward the white family when she offered Newsom's white grandson a reward to unknowingly clean his grandfather's ashes out of her fireplace. His demands created the crisis, but Celia received no support from George. Questioned about his missing master, George saved himself and implicated Celia, who initially denied any knowledge of Newsom's whereabouts, but threatened with loss of her children, eventually confessed. Realizing that whites believed he had assisted in the murder, and depending on Celia's continued denials of his involvement to keep him safe, George ran away. Alone in her ordeal, Celia was tried, convicted, and, after giving birth to a stillborn child, executed by hanging.[56] Though few instances of sexual abuse ended in a dramatic murder, Celia nonetheless exemplifies many aspects of the life of a concubine. Purchased young and alone, continually abused, and isolated from a community, Celia lacked social support and had no means of defending herself. Her children tied her to her captor, made escape unlikely, and gave Newsom and then the white authorities investigating his death leverage over her behavior and movements. Her involvement with George proved painful and fateful. George's impotence to protect her led to his threat to break off their relationship that ultimately caused her downfall. Even when she tried to establish a relationship of choice, Celia remained alone. She fought back and killed her tormentor, but at the price of her own life, and at substantial and unknown cost to her two mixed-race children, who lost both parents.

While concubinage could lead to rewards, it was a precarious existence. Regardless of the level of affection they gave and received and the degree of agency they exerted, concubines faced similar confining circumstances. Some, like Celia and Louisa Picquet, were purchased alone and explicitly as sexual companions. Others, like Julia and Harriet, were pursued on the plantation or in the household where they lived, places they could not escape.

Slaveholders often targeted adolescent girls, with many between the ages of twelve and fifteen at the time of their sexual initiation. In grooming a concubine, white men exhibited the classic behaviors of domestic violence, isolating these women and possessively reinforcing their dependency.[57] Piquet's master threatened to blow her brains out should she attempt to leave him. Slave communities, even when sympathetic to their plight, often compounded the isolation of concubines and their children by treating them with a degree of suspicion and caution. And at times, white family members, including white women, took and raised mixed-race children, further complicating allegiances and further alienating concubines from a social network.

Damaged Families

Sexual exploitation of women and the fathering of mixed-race slaves interfered with slaves' family life. Some men pragmatically accepted the fact that their wives, through no choice of their own, produced their master's children. Jacob Green fell in love with a mulatto woman on a neighboring plantation who told him she "had already had a child to her master in Mobile, and that her mistress had sold her down here for revenge," with the baby sold separately. Green ended up marrying another woman chosen by his master. "My master told me I must marry Jane," he noted. Five months later, Jane gave birth. "I then asked who was the father of the child, and she said the master, and I had every reason to believe her, as the child was nearly white." Green did not choose his partner and she bore the master's son, but "not withstanding this we lived happily together, and I felt happy and comfortable, and I should never have thought of running away if she had not been sold." After six years together and two of their own children, Green returned to find his entire family gone, an event that fomented his desire to escape. Green did not provide much detail, but it appears that he acted as a father to all of his wife's children, including his own and that of the master. The master's new wife "made a condition that all female slaves whom he had at any time been intimate with must be sold, and my wife being one was sold with the children." A white woman's jealousy and caution led to broken slave families, but the master's sexual practices created the problem and caused significant collateral damage.[58]

When white fathers disregarded their paternal duties, some black men pragmatically endeavored to care for enslaved children regardless of biological parentage. Harriet Jacobs discussed an enslaved woman denied permission to marry a man of her choice. The woman had a mixed-race child, "of course not acknowledged by its father. She claimed that the black man who loved her would have been proud to acknowledge" the baby. Other enslaved men reacted to the sexual dynamics of slavery with antagonism and recrimination. Jacobs mentioned another man being whipped, possibly for having argued with his wife and "accused his master of being the father of her child. They were both very black, and the child was very fair." The master sold both slaves, she for having "forgotten that it was a crime for a slave to tell who was the father of her child."[59] In this case, white paternity and the presence of a mixed-race child led to conflict between husband and wife and the emotional and physical dissolution of a family.

The enslaved family faced internal as well as imposed pressures. Although reported at lower rates compared to rape by white men, domestic violence and sexual coercion existed in the quarters, with black overseers and drivers especially prone to committing sexual violence.[60] "A fraction of enslaved husbands committed violent acts upon family members to exercise physical domination in the slave cabin, enforce their vision of domesticity, or grasp at some semblance of patriarchal control over their wives and children otherwise denied them under the system of slavery. But the more formidable sets of challenges to slave unions were external," Jeff Forret writes.[61] Informants criticized enslaved men who internalized a model of masculinity based on dominating others, a recapitulation of slaveholder behavior. A man's approach to masculinity and whether he assumed the role of caretaker or practiced domination determined how he treated those around him, and, in turn, how they perceived him. Male caretakers might commiserate with enslaved women, but victims of white sexual abuse often confronted their emotional burdens alone.

Ishrael Massie discussed how sexual exploitation and white paternity undermined trust and relationships in the quarters, but he directed his wrath toward the oppressors rather than the victims. He told the story of a man sitting "wid de baby in his arms—rockin' away," when he realized what he thought was his infant looked different than the couple's other children and resembled the overseer. His wife, fudging the timing of the child's conception, fooled him into believing it was his own. "De pint I'm at is, she wuz feard to tell on overseer den," Massie noted. Worried about physical retaliation, the woman lied to her husband. Women suffered sexual abuse and then the strictures of silence, isolating them from potential comfort and support. Despite his simmering resentment at his own and all enslaved men's powerlessness, Massie understood this woman's dilemma and validated her fears.[62] Enslaved men could be sensitive to the predicament of sexually victimized women and still realize that involvement with them presented risks. Sexual abuse at the hands of white men increased the likelihood that an enslaved woman would be socially isolated from and even within her neighborhood and community.

Slaves' relationships may have been impaired by not only visceral anger, but also emotional withdrawal. The psychological ramifications of physical and sexual abuse vary, but can include depression, disrupted sleep, a sense of isolation, a damaged sense of self-worth, trouble establishing relationships and interacting with others, and sexual dysfunction.[63] Sis Shackelford recalled her mother's reaction to the interest of a local planter, who wanted to buy her but did not want the children. "He was a bachluh you know an' he need a 'oman," Shackeford explained. "Mama jes' sits roun' jes' as sad an' cried all de time. She was always nice lookin' an' we all knew what de old Marse Greene want." Shackelford's mother escaped concubinage when the planter purchased another woman, but her response to the prospect of such a life and potential separation from her children highlights the anxiety wrought even by the prospect of rape. Lewis Hayden's mother was flogged and jailed when she refused to become her new master's concubine. "She began to have crazy turns," Hayden recalled. "When she had her raving turns she always talked about her children." His mother made more than one suicide attempt and her hair turned entirely white.[64] Fear of rape and actual sexual assault affected the targeted women, spouses, and enslaved children.

If sexual exploitation and white paternity damaged the black family, former slaves argued that it also had pernicious effects on the white family.[65] Mistresses' anger over their husbands' indiscretions led to infighting. A fellow slave informed Henry Brown "that his master and mistress lived very unhappily together, on account of the maid who waited upon them. She had no husband, but had several yellow children." Though an atypical response in a social system where failed marriage could destroy a woman's reputation, Henry Watson had a master whose wife left him and returned to her family because she discovered "that he had made a wife of one of his slaves." Mary Reynolds's mistress confronted her husband when she realized he had fathered multiple children by a mulatto seamstress he installed on the plantation, threatening to leave and return to her father, but she never followed through. "Missus didn't never leave and the Marster bought her a fine new span of surrey horses. But she don't never have no more chillun and since that time ain't so cordial with the Marster."[66] Mixed-race children frequently grew up in an environment of secrecy, jealousy, and recrimination.

Divorce proceedings indicate that sexual infidelity with slaves caused discord in white households and dissolved marriages.[67] White wives objected to concubines and the potential inversion of power they represented, and for many the proximate cause of discontent was the arrival of a mixed-race baby. A Tennessee wife who filed for divorce cited "the birth of a mulatto child." Another aggrieved wife made a rare admission of white paternity to incite acrimony among the white children toward their father, telling them "that Hester's child was their sister."[68] In this case, a mixed-race child became a pawn in the white family's power struggle.

Informants described rancorous couples and cruel, unhappy white women, but many also noted that these women were themselves victims and subject to the whims of their husbands, even as they, in turn, victimized slaves. "His wife stood in great fear of him. She presided over his household, but neither inspired nor enjoyed his respect," Anthony Burns said of one master. "He kept a harem of black girls, and took no pains to conceal the fact from his wife," and then sold his offspring and their mothers "without compunction." Based on her experience with a lecherous master and his bitter, unsympathetic wife, and the frequent quarrels that her presence incited, Harriet Jacobs cautioned Northern women who might entertain "romantic notions" of marrying a slaveholder. "To what disappointments are they destined! The young wife soon learns that the husband . . . pays no regard to his marriage vows. Children of every shade of complexion play with her own fair babies, and too well she knows that they are born unto him of his own household. Jealousy and hatred enter the flowery home, and it is ravaged of its loveliness." Jacobs argued that the institution corrupted everyone involved. "Slavery is a curse to the whites as well as to the blacks. It makes the white fathers cruel and sensual; the sons violent and licentious; it contaminates the daughters, and makes the wives wretched. . . . Yet few slaveholders seem to be aware of the widespread moral ruin occasioned by this wicked system. Their talk is of blighted cotton crops—not of the blight on their children's souls."[69] When white men sexually exploited slaves, their dishonorable behavior undermined paternal duty not only to any mixed-race offspring they produced, but also to their white children, family, and society. In Jacobs's eyes, these men failed as paternalists and patriarchs and as fathers.

The ability to rape enslaved women with impunity was central to white male identity and the mechanisms that maintained slavery. The social and legal climate of slavery created an inducement to favor enslaved women as illicit sex partners, and a number of white men acted on those incentives. Enslaved women's constant vulnerability to assault also formed a backdrop that affected the more consensual relationships that developed between white men and enslaved women. Harriet Jacobs, for instance, entered a relationship with a white male neighbor in an effort to avoid being raped by her master. Some enslaved women responded to the conditions of slavery by using sex and companionship to gain favorable treatment, material rewards, and, at times, even freedom. Their feelings about the white fathers of their children influenced women's feelings about their mixed-race children. Regardless of how enslaved women reacted to and tried to manipulate concubinage, social isolation was one fundamental aspect of the experience of sexual exploitation.

Sexual abuse and white paternity also created complicated family structures and responses in mixed-race children. Children tended to identify with the person or persons who reared and emotionally invested in them. Children raised by victims of sexual assault who formed emotionally matrifocal families, sometimes embedded within white households, often identified solely with their mother and rejected their white father. Mixed-race children of involved white fathers, or those taken from their mothers and raised by white relatives, might align and identify with their white heritage, especially if they could secure freedom or financial bequests. White paternity thus had a range of outcomes, including the opposite results of promoting matrifocality or effacing the enslaved mother and reinforcing the white patriarchy.

White men's power to rape enslaved women was central to slavery as an institution, and threats that undermined that power then shaped postwar race relations. After the Civil War, as Diane Miller Sommerville shows, rape law became "race neutral." For the first time, African American women could make rape charges, and though they mainly brought complaints against black men, white men could now be charged with the rape of black women. As white Southerners lost trust in the court system during Reconstruction, their perceptions of the law shifted. Southern whites increasingly favored extralegal vigilantism, which contributed to the rise of lynching. "The relationship of law to Southern society was forever altered, and the newly recast rape laws were at the center."[70] During slavery, with the white male patriarchy in control, enslaved men accused of rape received trials and were often exonerated or pardoned. "With the demise of slavery, however, and the enfranchisement of black men, whites began to conflate politics and sexuality and to associate newly won black political rights with black manhood," Sommerville writes. Postwar Southern whites became fixated on the idea of black men raping white women.[71] With the rape of black women now a possible risk, stoking a fear of the potential black male rapist became a way to reassert white supremacy.

CHAPTER SEVEN

My Children Is My Own
Fatherhood and Freedom

In a commentary addressed to his former owner and published in 1855, Frederick Douglass outlined the meaning of freedom for a father, calling his four children "perfectly secure under my own roof. There are no slave-holders here to rend my heart by snatching them from my arms, or blast a mother's dearest hopes by tearing them from her bosom. These dear children are ours—not to work up into rice, sugar, and tobacco, but to watch over, regard, and protect, and to rear them up in the nurture and admonition of the gospel—to train them up in the paths of wisdom and virtue, and, as far as we can, to make them useful to the world and to themselves." Douglass felt it was his duty to provide moral and religious guidance and set his children on a path of future promise. "A slaveholder never appears to me so completely an agent of hell, as when I think of and look upon my dear children," he concluded. Freedom enabled men to protect and provide for their family, and antebellum fugitives contrasted their conception of honorable fatherhood with the base immorality of home-wrecking slaveholders.[1]

Douglass wrote from the perspective of a man who had been free for almost two decades and attained a measure of success. Writing a decade later, having only recently achieved freedom in the aftermath of the Civil War, Jourdan Anderson laid out a nearly identical vision of masculine duty and condemnation of slaveholder paternalism. In a sarcastic reply to a letter from his former master, who wanted Anderson to return to the plantation, Anderson revealed his understanding of paternal duty and the meaning of freedom. Besides asking his former master to forward back wages as a sign of good faith, Anderson discussed his apprehensions about returning to the South, noting that all of his children attended school and his son showed signs of becoming a preacher. "In answering this letter please state if there would be any safety for my Milly and Jane, who are now grown up and both good-looking girls. You know how it was with poor Matilda and Catherine. I would rather stay here and starve, and die if it comes to that, than have my girls brought to shame by the violence and wickedness of their young masters," Anderson wrote in an open acknowledgment of the sexual degradation of slavery. "You will also please state if there has been any schools opened for the colored children in your neighborhood, the great desire of my life now is to give my children an education, and have them form virtuous habits." Like prewar fugitives, Anderson saw it as his responsibility to protect his children, provide moral guidance, ensure they received a proper education, and prepare them for a respectable future. He defined slavery as the sins of the white patriarchy enacted on a long-suppressed and emerging black patriarchy. "We trust the good Maker has opened your eyes to the wrongs which you and your fathers have done to me and my fathers, in making us toil for you for generations without recompense. Here I draw my wages every Saturday night, but in Tennessee there was never any pay-day for the Negroes any more than for the horses and cows. Surely there will be a day of reckoning for those who defraud the laborer of his hire."[2] Freedom brought with it the hallmarks of manhood: earning pay for one's labor and safeguarding and providing for one's family.

After escaping in 1827, Anthony Chase wrote a letter of explanation to the man who had hired him: "I don't take this step mearly because I wish to be free but because I want to do justice to myself and to others and also to procure a liveing for a family a thing that my mistress would not let me do." One vital component of being a man was providing for family, and seeking liberty meant not diminished cares but rather greater responsibility. Over a century later, Susie Hawkins remembered and related to her FWP interviewer her father's comments about slavery, freedom, and his own ambitions for the future, hopes that revolved around his children. "I done heerd my pappy say how dey faired; he wuz glad when we wuz freed, kaze he say he allus want to raise his chilluns free citizens en give em as good as eddication as he could."[3] Freedom empowered former slaves to not only feel like men, but to act on their aspirations and sense of masculine duty. The actions, decisions, and concerns of free fathers reveal their hopes, ideals, and understanding of paternal obligation. Regardless of how and when they achieved liberty, most formerly enslaved people prioritized family. They also faced ongoing challenges, though the specifics varied. Prewar fugitives, men who escaped to Union lines during the Civil War, and emancipated freedmen encountered discrimination and violence that compromised their ability to fully assert patriarchal privilege and status. Fugitives and freedmen parented their children, despite numerous obstacles, as a form of survival and ongoing resistance to oppression. Their experiences highlight the continuing limitations of normative definitions of family and fatherhood in the context of African American history.

Antebellum Freedom and Fatherhood

Men who achieved freedom prior to emancipation commented on their sense of self-possession and ability to establish a stable and enduring family life. "I served twenty-five years in slavery, and about five I have been free. I feel now like a man, while before I felt more as though I were but a brute," William Grose described his life in Canada after escaping in 1851. Freedom meant enjoying "the rights and privileges of any other man," including "living with my wife and children." Fugitives and manumitted slaves hoped that freedom would enable them to establish male-headed households and patriarchal status. "Every man has a right to wages for his labor; a right to his own wife and children," Henry Bibb declared.[4] However, antebellum fugitives, including those fortunate enough to flee with kin, confronted social, legal, and economic challenges. They arrived in a foreign place with few to no connections and had to find shelter and a means of support. Men who arrived with dependents faced added pressure to earn an adequate living so as to provide for kin.

Fugitives worried about their physical safety, and the threat of kidnapping or recapture added a baseline anxiety to their economic stress. The draconian Fugitive Slave Act passed as part of the Compromise of 1850 uprooted runaways and destabilized free family life. With kidnapping and slave hunters an incessant concern, many runaways and free blacks moved regularly and stayed armed and vigilant, protective measures that undermined economic stability.[5] Those with the resources looked to Canada and England as safer places to raise a family. William and Ellen Craft escaped from Georgia to Boston, but eventually fled to England after the passage of the act, and celebrated "this truly free and glorious country; where no tyrant, . . . dare come and lay violent hands upon us or upon our dear little boys (who had the good fortune to be born upon British soil)."[6] With limited economic opportunity, most fugitives lacked the means to make such a move and continued to raise their families under a cloud of anxiety.

Prior to the Fugitive Slave Act, free blacks in the North had long faced legal, social, and employment discrimination that intensified over the course of the nineteenth century and undermined the efforts of fathers to act as head of household and uphold their vision of paternal duty. As the social and legal encumbrances on free blacks increased, so too did the pressures on husbands and fathers.[7] Northern racial attitudes and discriminatory indenture practices compromised a free black father's status and ability to care for, protect, and fully control his family members. Losing control over the labor of his dependents, moreover, made it more difficult for the family to accumulate property. J. C. Brown discussed the reaction of the free black community to an 1804 Ohio black law requiring "every colored man . . . to give bonds in $500 not to become a town charge, and to find bonds also for his heirs." Such laws financially disadvantaged free blacks and enmeshed them in a web of economic subservience. Brown and others formed a "Colonization Society, of which I was President," and sought "an asylum for ourselves, our wives, and children," in Canada. Brown considered escaping the discriminatory laws of the United States an integral part of raising his children. "Our children growing up in this country, and not having the fear of any white man, and being taught to read and write, will grow up entirely different from their fathers," he declared, "and will be more able to set good examples to the rising generation."[8] In the minds of free black men, parenting was a significant aspect of self-improvement and racial progress.

Free black parents in the antebellum North worried about kidnapping and abusive indentures for all members of the family, but particularly children. Even former slaves who had been granted or purchased their liberty remained vulnerable to kidnapping, as did those born free. Free blacks commonly earned money by hiring out, a form of wage labor that presented risks. Deceitful employers at times sold contracted laborers, especially children, for fixed terms or worse, to kidnappers and slave catchers. Both of Henry Jackson's parents had been slaves in New York, but he was born free. His father hired him to an employer until the age of twenty-one, and this man took Jackson south and illegally sold him as a slave. Such concerns limited the economic options of free black families. Slave catchers also targeted children. When slave catchers captured his two children in Ohio in the 1830s, Lewis Williamson spent six years tracking them down, whereupon he proved their free status and repatriated them. Because he could not legally testify in the South, Williamson had to relinquish his farm to repay a white neighbor to testify on their behalf.[9] Keeping a kin unit intact and ensuring the continued freedom of its members often left a free black family impoverished, and fathers continued to grapple with painful choices. Prior to the Civil War, free black fathers struggled against impediments that eroded their patriarchal authority and ability to prosper and accrue property, which then impinged on their capacity to provide for and protect their kin. Although discrimination, poverty, indenture, and kidnapping made it difficult to achieve white, middle-class gender conventions, black men endeavored to uphold their conception of paternal duty.[10]

The Civil War

As the escalating tensions between North and South in the 1850s erupted in Civil War, African Americans throughout the United States understood that the conflict had potentially momentous consequences for their own lives and the institution of slavery. While the war created opportunities and ultimately led to emancipation, it also increased instability throughout the South. The feasibility of escape to Union lines varied by region and shifted over time, and in the chaos of armed conflict, the tension between duty to self and duty to family took on heightened urgency. The wartime decisions of caretakers often revolved around kin, with enslaved people choosing to run or wait based on the external conditions and calculations about family cohesion and reunification.

Slaves who took matters into their own hands and attempted to reach Union lines found that federal authorities, starting with designating runaways as contraband of war, prioritized military-aged men as labor and later as soldiers. As enslaved people moved to take ownership of their lives and families, Union policy offered escaped men a path to citizenship through military service. Stephanie McCurry has pointed out that the "heroic narrative of black soldiers" as the locus of emancipation overlooks the experience of the majority of enslaved people and the "slave insurgency" within the Confederacy carried out by women and men. Inside Union lines, because federal policy fixated on men of military age, the solution to the arrival of women and children was to define women as wives and dependents, and marriage emerged as a central feature of emancipation policy.[11] Throughout the evolution of emancipation policy, Union authorities recognized and ideologically bolstered freedmen's patriarchal status, and yet logistically and materially undermined their practical authority and ability to provide for kin.

As word of Union policy spread, entire families arrived inside Union lines, indicating that parental obligations and kinship ties had earlier impeded flight. Enslaved people saw the war as a chance to escape with kin, and made those attempts in greater numbers.[12] Mary Barbour's parents seized the opportunity afforded by the war to flee as a family. "One of de fust things dat I 'members wuz my pappy wakin' me up in de middle o' de night, dressin' me in de dark, all de time tellin' me ter keep quiet. One o' de twins hollered some an' pappy put his hand ober its mouth ter keep it quiet," she recalled. They hurried to a hidden wagon, "pappy totin' one of de twins an' holdin' me by de han' an' mammy carryin' de udder two." Union forces had destroyed the North Carolina plantation where her father resided, and in the chaos he stole a cart and mules, escaped, and went to collect his family on another farm. They traveled to New Bern, where her father manufactured boots for the army, "an' we gits 'long pretty good." Calline Brown's father heard rumors of freedom, disappeared for a week, and then came back in the middle of the night, and the family quietly gathered their belongings, swaddled the baby, and slipped away. The boat her father had found was so small he had to take them across the river "two at a time, but we all made it over before daylight caught us."[13] The war enabled freedpeople, including committed fathers, to unite, relocate, and free their families.

Although the war reduced the distance slaves needed to travel in order to obtain freedom, fleeing remained a dangerous undertaking, and failed escape attempts could end in death or mutilation.[14] As a result, some simply bided their time waiting for the war to end. Walter Rimm's father had earlier tried and failed to arrange an escape for his entire family. During the war, his owners worried he would flee but he never tried, "'cause he wants to carry his fam'ly w'en he goes 'way." William Davis's father, anticipating a Union victory, also stayed put in Tennessee. "I know papa say de Yankees gwinter win 'cause dey is always marchin' to de South, but you don't see none of de South soldiers marchin' to de North. 'Course he didn't say dat to de white folks, but he sure say it to us."[15] Wartime strategies varied, and for caretakers who lived in intact households, avoiding the risk of separation made sense.

After the 1863 Emancipation Proclamation authorized the recruitment of black troops, free and enslaved men saw military service as a way to actively contribute to the destruction of slavery and to become men. Free black men in the North enlisted, and formerly enslaved men joined in significant numbers as they escaped to Union lines and Union forces pushed deeper into the South. By the end of the war, approximately 179,000 black men had served in the Union army, comprising a tenth of Union manpower.[16] "I can remember when my father went away to war to fight for freedom," Laura Thompson stated. Omelia Thomas expressed pride in her father's military service. "He was fighting for our freedom," she declared. "He wasn't no Reb. He'd tell us a many a day, 'I am part of the cause that you are free.'"[17] To provision a child with freedom was the ultimate act of a devoted parent, and African American fathers considered military service a means to that end.

Among their motivations for fighting, many recently enslaved men viewed military service as way to free family members. Samuel Hall served in the

Union army and along with a band of soldiers went back to the plantation to liberate his family. Eliza Suggs's father likewise fled and enlisted hoping he could bring his regiment to his home to free his family, not realizing that a private had little influence over military movements. Unable to reach his family during the war, he obtained help from his captain and brought them north after the conflict ended.[18] Joseph Harris wrote to a general asking for a "small favor." He provided directions to the plantation where his family resided and asked that troops "take a way my Farther & mother & my brothers wife with all their Childern," and bring them to Union headquarters. "I wishes the Childern all in School," he added. Similarly, Aaron Oats penned a letter to military authorities to "respectfully ask for the liberation of my Wife and children." As a soldier "willing to loose my life for my Country," he felt entitled to such a privilege.[19] Runaways who enlisted expected reciprocity from the Union military in the form of freedom for their kin.

Just as slaveholders manipulated enslaved men's love for their families, Union authorities used familial incentives to recruit black men into the army in the border states. Because the Emancipation Proclamation did not apply to Union slave states such as Kentucky, and the army needed manpower, Congress eventually granted freedom to men's wives and children, a strategy that dramatically upped enlistment. Men from these areas comprised nearly a fifth of the Union's black military power, and enlistment rates were highest in the loyal slave states because military service was the sole route to freedom prior to the Thirteenth Amendment.[20] Secretary of War Edwin Stanton argued in favor of such a policy: "The liberation of wife and children from slavery, and placing them under the protection of the law as free persons, would relieve persons enlisting from great anxiety in respect to the conditions of those whom they love and desire to protect." Union authorities wanted to secure men's military service, whereas freedmen who escaped alone longed to reconnect with and felt anxious about paternal duty and their still-enslaved families.[21]

Runaways who enlisted worried about mistreatment of their enslaved kin as punishment for the actions of husbands. Family members inside Confederate lines often faced added abuse, including the practice of using children as hostages to prevent further escapes. "You do not know how bad I am treated," one enslaved woman explained in a dictated letter. "Our child cries for you. Send me some money as soon as you can for me and my child are almost naked." She added a postscript, requesting that her husband "sind our little girl a string of beads in your next letter to remember you by." Martha Glover resented her husband's decision to run away and enlist.

"They abuse me because you went & say they will not take care of our children," she wrote. "You ought not to have left me in the fix I am in & all these little helpless children to take care of. . . . The children talk about you all the time. I wish you could get a furlough & come to see us once more." Letters from enslaved wives, as well as army officials, became fodder in the Congressional debate over the enlistment measure. For Glover, however, the concerns were personal, and she pointed out that in doing his duty to country, her husband had forsaken his duty to family. A man receiving such a letter, though now free, faced a continuation of the painful conflicts of slavery. He could not stand up for himself without undermining his obligation to protect his family. Realizing that his service as a soldier jeopardized his family, George Washington unsuccessfully requested a discharge to go and care for his wife and children, who had been turned out by their master.[22] Slaveholder abrogation of paternalism further destabilized the paternal duty of African American soldiers. When slaveholders purposely abused or neglected the enslaved kin of black Union soldiers, they unleashed white resentments over emancipationist policy, and their actions emasculated soldiers even as fighting represented an expression of manhood.

During the Civil War, particularly in areas insecurely occupied by the Union army and marked by shifting lines, slaves who fled to Union encampments were preoccupied with retrieving their loved ones, a risky undertaking. Sam Marshall took a wagon to collect his children, and a Union official reported that he had been arrested, beaten, and barely escaped alive. Archer Alexander escaped with the help of a white employer and then devoted himself to freeing his family. "We've been married most thirty years, and we'se had ten chilluns, and we want to get togedder mighty bad," he remarked. Alexander's reunification with his wife "brought peace of mind," and he then found two daughters and learned his son "had served and died in the cause of freedom. 'I couldn't do it myself,' he said, 'but I thank the Lord my boy did it.'" The narrative reveals a freedman's love for and single-minded focus on reuniting his family.[23]

When runaways escaped with kin and enlisted, they did so with the belief that Union officials would provide for their family. "Our wives are now cared for by our government," George Thomas said of Camp Nelson, a contraband camp in Kentucky, "and we feel like men, and are determined to be men, and do our duty to our government honestly and faithfully." The ability to serve honorably and without distraction was predicated on security for one's family. When they were paid less than white soldiers, these men objected to the insult to their masculinity, but another paramount concern was the impact on their duty to family. Unequal pay left their kin vulnerable. "My poor wife at home is almost starving. When I was at home I could make a living for her and my two little ones; but now that I am a soldier they must do the best they can or starve. It almost tempts me to desert," one man threatened. "Men have families at home, and they looking to them for support."[24] Union policy defined freedmen as patriarchal heads of household and wives and children as dependents, but the failure to adequately pay African American soldiers or provide for their family members, meant that these men found it difficult to impossible to uphold paternal duty while they defended the Union cause. As during slavery, men were allowed to exhibit traits of masculinity when in doing so they provided benefit to those in power, but black manhood remained burdened and subordinate to white manhood.

Fugitives who arrived at Union lines with kin discovered that the authorities, while eager to enlist men as soldiers or military labor, showed far less concern for the well-being of their dependents, who lived in squalid camps plagued by material shortages and abusive labor contracts. African American soldiers protested against reduced rations, starvation, and abuse, comparing conditions in contraband camps to slavery. Soldiers on Roanoke Island resented the forced indenture of their sons, demanding that their children be enrolled in school. The summary eviction of families from Camp Nelson in 1864 aroused indignation among black soldiers. Women and children being "thrown out without any protection or home" violated these men's understanding of paternal responsibility. Joseph Miller brought his family with him to Camp Nelson because his master refused to support them should he enlist. On the day of their eviction, his wife and children were ordered to leave their tent despite the "bitter cold." Miller objected, arguing that this move "would be the death of my boy," then recovering from illness. Cognizant of his military duty, Miller followed as far as allowed and went back that evening. "I found my wife and children shivering with cold and famished with hunger," he reported. "My boy was dead. . . . I Know he was Killed by exposure to the inclement weather." Miller walked several miles back to camp and returned the next morning to bury his son. "I dug a grave myself and buried my own child."[25] Freedom did not end the intractable dilemmas men had faced in slavery, as military obligations came into conflict with duty to family.

Black soldiers confronted racism, unequal pay, abusive treatment of themselves and their families, poor medical care, and higher disease mortality, and yet military service often had a profound impact on these men and enabled them to act on and display their conceptions of honorable fatherhood. Jim Cullen argues that soldiering provided a "powerful sense of agency over their own lives and responsibility for their families." Former slave and Union soldier Spotswood Rice wrote a letter to his daughter's owner in 1864 that illustrates paternal duty as a key motivation for military service. Rice wrote to a slaveholder named Kitty Diggs:

> I received a leteter from Cariline telling me that you say I tried to steal to plunder my child away from you now I want you to understand that mary is my Child and she is a God given rite of my own and you may hold on to hear as long as you can but I want you to remembor this one thing that the longor you keep my Child from me the longor you will have to burn in hell and the qwicer youll get their for we are now makeing up a bout one thoughsand blacke troops to Come up tharough . . . and when we come wo be to Copperhood rabbels and to the Slaveholding rebbels for we dont expect to leave them there root neor branch. . . . I want you to understand kittey digs that where ever you and I meets we are enmays to each orthere I offered once to pay you forty dollars for my own Child but I am glad now that you did not accept it Just hold on now as long as you can and the worse it will be for you . . . my Children is my own and I expect to get them and when I get ready to come after mary I will have bout a powrer and autherity to bring hear away and to exacute vengencens on them that holds my Child you will then know how to talke to me I will assure that and you will know how to talk rite too . . . this whole Government gives chear to me and you cannot help your self.

In this extraordinary document, a recently enslaved man released pent up anger and spoke to a former master in a tone and language dangerous before the war. Rice commented that he was happy that Diggs had refused his attempt to purchase his child, because payment would have been a concession to legal slavery and he now had the power, in the form of the Union army, to defend and claim his family. As a father, Rice also believed he had God on his side. His paternal rights outweighed the purported rights of the slaveholder, and he stressed his belief that to deny a man control over his "own" child invited eternal damnation. As a soldier, Rice could assert his authority over his children and fight back against an immoral system that deprived him of full humanity and denied him patriarchal control over his labor and family.[26]

Rice wrote not only to his daughter's owner, warning her of his plans, but also to his two still-enslaved daughters, Mary and Caroline, reminding them "I have not forgot you and that I want to see you as bad as ever . . . be assured that I will have you if it cost me my life." As he did in the letter to Diggs, Rice expressed outrage at the idea that a man could steal his own children, arguing, "God never intended for man to steal his own flesh and blood."[27] Rice pledged that he would do everything in his power, even if it ended in his death, to reunite the family. In Rice's eyes, a father had a duty to protect his kin, and a man's flesh and blood rightfully belonged under his care and authority.

The daughter Spotswood Rice referred to, Mary Bell, commented extensively on her father in her FWP narrative. She confirmed that "an old maid named Miss Kitty Diggs" owned her, her mother, two sisters, and three brothers. Her father belonged to a planter on a neighboring farm and visited his family twice a week. Spotswood Rice thus exemplifies a highly committed father within an abroad marriage. Rice's children lived most of each week in a one-parent, matrifocal household, but this was a two-parent family with patrifocal elements. According to his daughter, Rice undermined his owner's Missouri plantation during the war even before he joined the Union army. The owner's son had taught him to read, and when emancipation came, Rice read the proclamation to the other slaves, angering his master because the news "made dem so happy, dey could not work well, and dey got so no one could manage dem." Rice's owner, who depended on his skilled slave, realized freedom was imminent and promised Rice a house for his family if he agreed to stay on after emancipation and manage the tobacco business and to use his community standing to convince the other slaves to remain as well. Bell said her father agreed in order to mollify the master, but he had no intention of staying. Six months later, he "taken eleven of de best slaves on de plantation, and went to Kansas City and all of dem joined the U. S. Army." The patrollers attempted to retrieve them, but "de officers said dey were now enlisted U.S. Soldiers and not slaves and could not be touched." Though Mary Bell did not discuss exactly how she and her mother and siblings reunited with her father, she noted that she never attended school until she came to St. Louis, "when Abraham Lincoln was assassinated." At that time, her father "was a nurse in Benton Barracks and my mother was taken in washing and ironing." In addition, at least two siblings were among the valuable slaves her father guided to the Union army, and "one of my brothers was killed in de Civil War."[28] Rice's assertiveness and defiance influenced fellow slaves, including his sons.

Spotswood Rice's letters underscore his love for and determination to reconstitute his family. Mary Bell's narrative reveals how an enslaved child returned that affection and how an involved father could shape the attitudes and future of his children. Bell's narrative focused on her father and exudes the tremendous respect she had for him. Bell married a soldier and her son followed in the footsteps of his father and grandfather, serving in the Philippines. At the time of her interview, she was an army widow receiving a pension. "I love army men, my father, brother, husband and son were all army men," she declared. "I love a man who will fight for his rights, and any person that wants to be something." In a similar case, a white officer removed children from continuing enslavement or indenture based on the intervention of their father. "A negro soldier *demanded* his children at my hands. I endeavored to test his affection for them, when he said: 'Lieut., I want to send them to school; my wife is not allowed to see them;' I said they had a good home' said he: 'I am in your service; I wear military clothes; *I want those children*; they are my flesh and blood,'" Col. George H. Hanks testified.[29] Both this unnamed man and Spotswood Rice used military service to demand their rights as fathers, and supplementary documents show that Rice's actions and character had a lasting impact on his daughter.

If military service and war facilitated the reunification of some families, it also undermined others. A considerable number of freedpeople lost their fathers during and to the Civil War. African American men who fought for the Union died in camps and hospitals and on the battlefield at higher rates than white soldiers. "He served in de War three years and never came home," John Pope said of his father. "He died right at the surrender." R. C. Smith's father ran, joined the Union army, and also died at the end of the war. "He died with pneumonia. Never got to enjoy his freedom after he fought so hard for it."[30] In their effort to end slavery, black soldiers offered up their lives, leaving their families with a sense of pride but also with a significant economic and emotional loss.

Enslaved men taken to war by Confederate masters as personal body servants or used as forced military labor also suffered high mortality.[31] According to Cella Perkins, "Pa went to war with his master and he never come back to mama. . . . She didn't never know if he got killed or lost his way back home." When a father was taken to the front or ran away during the war and never returned, it was impossible to know if he had intentionally abandoned his family or perished. For Aleck Woodward, "de saddest day of slavery time" occurred when Union soldiers took his father away, never to be seen again. Men who ran to the Union lines frequently disappeared.

Many likely died attempting to escape, or working or fighting for the Union. "He run off and went on with the Yankees," Ellis Jefson said of his father. "We think he got killed. We never heard from him after 1863."[32] In the confusion of wartime, some people ran away and had no intention of reestablishing contact, and many died and their families never knew what happened. The chaos of war created possibilities for escape, mobility, and military service, but also caused tremendous dislocation and loss of life.

Emancipation and Family

At the end of the Civil War, with universal emancipation a reality, freedpeople entered a new phase in their lives. The first priority of many formerly enslaved people was to try to put their families back together, and they frequently made decisions about exercising their newfound mobility based on calculations about finding or being found by kin. The quest to find lost loved ones started during the war and continued long after the conflict ended. African Americans sought their children, parents, siblings, and other friends and relatives. Mattie Curtis's parents "tried to find dere fourteen oldest chilluns what wus sold away, but dey never did find but three of dem." Multiple sales and name changes increased the difficulty of locating lost kin, but even after decades of separation, freedpeople searched for missing family members. "It was thirty years before my pa knew if we was still living," Nancy Gardner noted. "Finally in some way he heard dat I was still alive, and he began writing me. . . . Well, my pa started out to see me and on his way he was drowned in de Missouri River, and I never saw him alive after we was sold in Memphis." After a "long and persistent search," Lucy Delaney found her father near Vicksburg and arranged a "joyful reunion," though she could not convince him to live with her permanently.[33] Formerly enslaved people found it difficult to articulate the elation of reconnecting with family members, before and after emancipation. Robert Glenn called finding his parents, years after the war, "the happiest period of my entire life."[34]

Although such searches continued for decades, the most intense period of family reconfiguration happened in the immediate postwar period. Forcibly separated spouses had usually remarried, leading to a period of readjustment as people made choices about how to rearrange and stabilize family relations. Of his two wives in slavery, Lewis Brown's father chose the one with whom he had children. "He was the father of nine children. He had two wives. One of them he had nine by, and the other one he had none by. So he went back to the one he had the nine children by," Brown related. It is impossible to know if Brown's father favored one woman over the other or if he felt a duty to his children or both. Freedpeople had to make difficult choices based on pragmatism and desire, and decisions about reconstructing families often took into consideration the needs of children.[35]

In the aftermath of the war, Laura Spicer and her former husband grappled with the implications of his remarriage. He sent agonized responses to her letters, noting that each one "tears me all to pieces." He still loved Laura and their children, but he also cared about and felt an obligation to his new family. When Spicer initiated contact, asking him to return, she created an intractable dilemma for which he had no satisfactory solution. He asked her to send "some of the children's hair in a separate paper with their names," and hoped she would "marry some good, smart man that will take care of you and the children." He concluded one letter with a message to his children: "Tell them they must remember they have a good father and one that cares for them and one that thinks about them every day."[36] Some children lost the chance to reconnect with caretaking fathers because these men had to choose one family over another.

In many cases, freedpeople with more than one family simply remained in place, a decision that may have reflected greater attachment, practicality, inertia, or a combination of factors. Virginia Bell knew her father had been sold to Louisiana and away from a previous family, but she had no idea what happened to them, "'cause when we was freed he stayed with us." Searching for lost kin was costly and time consuming and could lead to dead ends or difficult decisions, and some people may have opted to avoid the potential pitfalls. Like Bell's father, many former slaves never discussed their reasoning with their children. Ann Hawthorne's family, when moved to Texas, left their abroad father behind. After the war, their former master went back to Georgia to find him, "but he done raisin' up anudder family dere and won't come." Sometime later, and not long before her mother died, "den he come. Some of de ol'es' chillun 'member dey daddy and dey crazy for him to come and dey mek up de money for him."[37] Hawthorne offered no further information, and she may not have had any. Did his other wife die? Were those children grown and gone? Did he stay to care for his second family and only then return to his first? Did he come back to his aged first wife and children because he longed to see them or because he was down on his luck and needed a place to live?

Emancipation facilitated both the reconstruction and dissolution of family units. A number of informants lost their parents during the war, as the conflict enabled parents to run away if they had no desire to care for their

My Children Is My Own 239

offspring or wanted to escape intolerable living situations. While women deserted children in the midst of and aftermath of war, more typically, fathers left and children remained with their mothers, or their father stayed on the plantation and other family members moved. "Daddy, hims goes back" to Louisiana to "de Marster's place. Dat am de last weuns heah ob him," Fred Brown commented. Sylvester Brooks's Alabama master told his former slaves they could stay and work for a share of the crop. "Dey all stayed but two, an' I am sorry dat one of de two wuz my daddy, he lef' my mammy wid six chillun an' never cum back." Losing contact meant that many children never fully understood the motivations of parents who departed. Sim Greeley's father, kidnapped from Virginia, returned to his place of origin and Greeley "would not go." Push factors included leaving a cruel master and pull factors included searching for one's roots or returning home.[38] Reconnecting with family could entail leaving family. With incomplete information it is impossible to know which men opted to renounce family ties and which men chose to leave a specific family to return to another.

When a master had paired a couple against their wishes, freedom offered a chance to escape a coerced, loveless marriage. "My papa went on off when freedom come," Linley Hadley noted. "Mama never seen him no more. I didn't neither. Mama didn't care so much about him. He was her mate give to her." Hadley understood the nature of her parents' relationship, and an earlier expression of pride in her father's strength and cunning suggests positive memories and a lack of resentment that he opted to leave. John Matthews's mother left his father, her much older assigned husband, for a younger man, and Matthews split his time between his parents. "Some times I stayed wid my pappy an' some times I wus wid mammy."[39] As forced households disbanded, children found themselves in an array of reconfigured family structures.

Disputes over how and where to live in freedom contributed to family realignment. William Stevens ended up with his father when his mother chose to follow her former owners from Alabama to Texas, because "they treated her so nicely." Stevens's father "wouldn't follow. He said she thought more of them than she did him. He kept me with him. He married ag'in." Complications arose when couples intended to stay together, but disagreed on a place of residence. Matilda Poe was briefly separated from her mother because her parents had divergent reactions to emancipation. "Master told us we was free. Mammy she say, 'Well, I'm heading for Texas,'" Poe recalled. "My pappy wouldn't leave old Master right then but old Master told us we was free to go where we pleased, so me an' pappy left and went to Texas where my mammy was." Adeline Willis and her husband continued to maintain two households for a time because she refused to leave her former owners. "Lewis . . . wanted me and the chillun to go on over to his white folks' place with him, an' I wouldn't go. . . . So we kept living like we did in slavery, but he come to see me every day. After a few years he finally 'suaded me to go on over to the Willis place and live with him." The desire of adult partners to find and/or live with their own parents also placed pressure on marriages. Charlie Meadow went back and forth between his parents until they eventually lived together. "My pa stayed at de Meadow plantation. I went wid my maw, but I also stayed wid my pa and his ma some," he recalled. "Atter dat, when ma's maw died she went back to pa." This multilocal kinship network included extended family in both households. For many formerly enslaved children, household and family structures remained in flux and defied easy categorization in the immediate postwar period. Though only allowed one legal marriage, household arrangements occasionally varied as former slaves navigated the postwar world and the complex family relations inherited as a legacy of slavery.[40]

When marriages ended, children more often stayed with their mothers, but a significant number lived with their fathers, especially if their mother passed away. As they had during slavery, caretaking men assumed responsibility for children when former spouses died. "First I lived with Mother and then when she died my Father took me," Emma Sanderson told her interviewer. "He died when I was about 15. By that time I was old enough to look out after myself."[41] In an economically challenging environment, some separated couples decided who would raise the children based on ability to provide and access to resources.[42] And, as families realigned, some fathers demonstrated their interest in maintaining contact with and supporting children even if they lived in different households. Laura Ray's parents separated after freedom, but her father "would allus come back to see us and helped sell the cotton in the fall." Similarly, Martha Everette's mother took all of her children and left while her father stayed on the plantation, "but he'd come ter see us."[43] In freedom, the black family remained highly flexible as a matter of choice and survival and in order to ensure that children had caregivers.

In the aftermath of the war, freedpeople had two immediate goals, to find and secure their family and to find a means of support. As Rebecca Grant explained, locating family members could be a grueling process. "First, my mother and de young chillun, den I got back. My uncle, Jose Jenkins come to Beaufort and stole me by night from my Missus. He took me wid him to his home in Savannah," she stated. "When my father heard that I wasn't wid de others, he sent my grandfather, Isaac, to hunt me. When he find me at my uncle's house, he took me back. We walked all back—sixty-four miles." Emancipated with few resources, former slaves began to build new lives, starting with building households. Freedpeople drew upon their own ingenuity, and until the collapse of the final three Reconstruction state governments in 1876, took advantage of whatever backing they could obtain from institutional sources. As African Americans attempted to reconstitute and support their families, they faced the ongoing repercussions of slavery, a lack of material resources and aid, the ideological and logistical limitations of the Freedmen's Bureau, and the intransigence of former slaveholders.[44]

Committed fathers saw freedom as a chance to assert patriarchal status and collect their family members. Children similarly realized that emancipation invested their parents with newfound authority. After freedom, Hannah Austin's mistress ordered her to play with the white children. "I did not go but politely told her I was free and didn't belong to anyone but my mama and papa," Austin recalled. "As I spoke these words my mistress began to cry." A slaveholder lost not just property, but power to command the obedience of someone else's children. For dependent children, liberty meant parental control as much as it meant self-ownership. "I sho remember when freedom come here. Remember when my boss told me I was free," Aaron Ford stated. "My father come dere en say he wanted his boys. Boss called, 'Aaron, come here, your daddy wants you.' . . . I felt like a new man." Ford interpreted his burgeoning sense of masculinity through the hierarchy of his own family. Children's responses to freedom demonstrate how deeply their identity revolved around kin and being or becoming part of a family. When she learned she was free, Margaret Nickens immediately responded, "If I still have a mother and father I wants to go to dem." Even the white community, which quickly moved to blunt the impact of emancipation, interpreted freedom for enslaved children as transferring authority from the master to the parent. Daniel Phillips remembered when his master informed him he was free. Phillips asked what that meant and "He say, 'Dat mean you can live with you mammy and you pappy, and what you makes you kin keep.'"[45]

Looking back on the end of slavery decades later, informants felt fortunate when freedom meant the return of an absent father and family reunification. Irene Robertson and Malindy Smith remembered their fathers coming home from the war. Robertson's father left to fight for the Union, "but he come back to us," and when Smith's mother saw her husband walking up the road, "she tore out to runnin' towards him an' us kids right in behind her." Isaac Rodgers's father "went way ter de war, en de day he come back wuz er happy day fer sho'."[46] Informants also recalled family reunification after longer periods of separation. Nettie Henry's father had been moved, "but after de War he come back to us, walked most all de way frum Texas." William Curtis's father had been sold away. When freedom came, he and his mother and siblings stayed on the Georgia plantation, "and after a while my pappy come home to us. Dat was de best thing about de war setting us free, he could come back to us." In Charlie Huff's case, he and his mother and siblings went to locate his father. "We come to Arkansas as soon as we could after freedom," he recounted. "We wanted to find pa."[47] Emancipation meant an end to sale and forced separation and a chance to live together as a family.

Those in cross-plantation marriages or dispersed locally moved to assemble the family. Duncan McCastle had minimal contact with his abroad father until after emancipation and celebrated emancipation because it allowed for the consolidation of a forcibly divided family. "Dat wuz a joyous day when we could all be together," he stated. Freedom had the same meaning for Tom Wilcox: "We lived fer each other, but my pappy belonged ter one man an' my mammy ter another one an' so we wanted ter be all together." Laura Thompson remembered that her Kentucky family heard of freedom and "we all got our things together right away and went over to the Straders where our father was."[48] Emancipation meant that an emotionally two-parent, multilocal kinship network could become a two-parent, nuclear household.

Consolidation of the kin unit involved not just spouses in abroad marriages, but gathering those hired out to different farms or sold away. Following the announcement of emancipation, "I remember that the first thing my father did was to go down to a plantation where the bigger children was working, and bring them all home, to live together as one family," Julia White recalled. Sue Lockridge's father similarly collected and relocated his children: "My daddy he tek he wife and all he chillen. . . . My daddy hab a time findin' my big sister, Mimi, 'cause de ol' marster done hire her out to wuk for somebody else." Ishrael Massie's sister had been sold away and he did not see her again until after freedom when "my father went after her."[49] These postwar actions demonstrate that the physical form of the households in which they lived often diverged considerably from enslaved people's emotional conception of family.

Many FWP informants recalled that their fathers came to fetch them after emancipation. Those too young to fully understand the exact meaning of the events of the war marked the arrival of freedom by the arrival of their father and unification of their divided family. "Ise don't know nothin' 'bout when freedom comes," Hannah Mullins recalled, "but Ise knows de time 'cause my pappy comes aftah me an' weuns all lives togedder in de cabin 'stead of me aliving in the Marster's house." Emma Weeks had a similar response to questions about the timing of emancipation: "I don't remembah de day when I was set free, but I do know dat pappy come over one day and got mammy and her chillun, and took e'm over to his cabin. . . . So, I reckon dat was de day we was set free."[50] Mollie Scott's mother had ten children, her father only the one. Her mother died during the war, and after the fighting ended, her father arrived on the Georgia plantation to claim her. "White folks hated fo me to leave. . . . They said he take me off and let me suffer or die." Contrary to these fears, "I had plenty when I stayed at my fathers an we worked together all the time. When he died I married." Cheney Cross's former owners also tried to prevent her departure, promising to provide an education, but her father insisted on taking his child.[51] For caretaking fathers, claiming their children and their patriarchal rights was one of the first steps in exercising their liberty.

A father might encounter resistance from children apprehensive about leaving the familiar. "After de war wuz over my pa, he comed up to our house an got my ma an all us chillen an carries us down to his marster's place. I didn't want ter go cause I loved my mistis," Susan Matthews admitted. However, her father's hard work paid off "an we helped him an in a few years he bought a little piece of land an he owned it till he died." Securing the loyalty of children who had been raised in the big house could be difficult, particularly if those children felt little connection to their kin. Henry Johnson had been removed from his family in Virginia at such a young age, "I never even saw my mother and father until I was in my twenty's." After emancipation he noticed a "colored man kept watching me so much I got plum scared." That man introduced himself as Johnson's father, and he was reunited with his family. After much "rejoicing," during which his mother killed her only two chickens to celebrate his arrival, Johnson's family took precautions. "My father and brothers would go to work every day and leave me at home with my mother for over a year. They would not trust me to work, feared I would run off cause I didn't no nothin' 'bout them. Hadn't even heard of a mother and father." Johnson's father and brothers worked long hours for a pittance, indicating that losing his wages compounded the family's hardship. Slaveholder practices that undermined the enslaved family continued to cause problems in freedom.[52] The desire to promote family unity could compromise economic gains just as the struggle to purchase kin had worsened hardship during slavery.

While some children denied the opportunity to bond with kin during slavery had confused loyalties, claiming allegiance to the white family could be calculated. After her mother died and she and her brother were separated from their father, one young woman orchestrated family reunification after hearing about emancipation. She counseled her younger brother to slip away, find a courthouse, and obtain a pass, and provided directions to their father's house. "I knew right where pappy lived. I told him after he got to a certain place anybody would tell him where pappy lived." She learned that he succeeded, and "my pappy was sure glad to see him." She then waited, knowing her father would come for her, and one day, when she heard his voice, "I was the happiest child you ever heard of." Despite internal elation, she hedged about leaving in front of the white family, and "poor pap just burst out crying." While her motives are not entirely clear, it seems that she pretended to be conflicted so as to maintain the possibility of future employment. She lived with her father until Christmas, then hired out, and remained with her father, though not always under the same roof, until she married.[53]

Regardless of their allegiance, establishing authority over children was a challenging process, as whites immediately acted to undermine emancipation by apprenticing freed children, which complicated postwar black family life. Former slaveholders used labor contracts and apprenticeship to bind emancipated children to white families and to disrupt and control the black family, depriving freed families of vital labor and income and reducing their mobility. With a child or children apprenticed, black families were stuck. Controlling the labor of children ensured a stable supply of adult labor.[54] Whites moved to secure the labor of older children, leaving freed parents to care for the younger ones who could not economically contribute and thereby intensifying the poverty of black families. Apprenticeship codes allowed for the binding of orphans, and in the Reconstruction South, the Freedmen's Bureau conflated poverty with orphanhood and regularly refused to recognize the kinship claims of ex-slaves. Freedmen's Bureau agents often aided in the process of binding black children to white employers, leading to numerous disputes over children. African Americans viewed apprenticeship as abusive and preferred to hire their children out, but they did attempt to use the practice in the struggle to survive. In her study of postwar Virginia, Catherine Jones writes, "As figures around whom adults articulated and promoted visions of the postemancipation future, children were at the heart of Virginia's varied reconstructions."[55] Apprenticeships and indentures meant that many free families remained multilocal kinship networks divided among several households. In hiring out, apprenticing, and restraining the movements of former slaves, whites erected barriers to unbroken black households, which then undermined the status of the head of household.

Following the Civil War, emancipated parents and other relatives struggled to exert authority over black children. Henry Walton's mother died when he was three or four following a brutal whipping. After the war, his mistress had him bound to age twenty-one, but "when Papa . . . came home from the War . . . this court order was nullified and I was free." In 1866, a man named Comas attempted to take charge of his thirteen- or fourteen-year-old son, Henry, when his former wife, from whom he had separated, died. A court described Comas as "a man of good character for honesty, industry and morality, and abundantly able to support his family." When Henry was erroneously bound out to a white man because he appeared to be an orphan, his father sued. Another recently freed father protested against his children being indentured by an Orphan's Court without his or his wife's permission and the refusal of their employers to release the children upon his request.[56] Freedmen believed they had a right to dictate the placement and lives of their family members, but they found they had to appeal to federal authorities for help in securing their children. If freedom gave black men patriarchal privilege in theory, actually exerting those rights proved difficult, as black masculinity remained subordinated to and bounded by white masculinity and power. The masculine hierarchy survived slavery and remained a fundamental aspect of the American social, economic, and political landscape.

Disagreements over labor often revolved around children, and by extension a man's ability to exercise patriarchal prerogative. Georgia Johnson remembered her father's dispute with his former master. "Pa and Marster had a fallin' out, 'cause Marster wouldn't have no settlement wid 'im. He just wouldn't give my Pa no money. Marster said us younguns still b'longed to 'im and dat us had evvything us needed, and could git anything us wanted at his store," Johnson recalled. "But my Pa said he didn't wanter take up evvything he wukked for in trade." Johnson's father believed freedom entitled his entire family to wages and he wanted authority over his children and their labor. The family moved repeatedly, experiencing disappointment in several states. Former masters demanded the labor of black children at reduced or no wages, believing that contracting with the head of household gave them control of dependents, whereas freedmen endeavored to exert independent authority over their family members. Apprenticing black children also functioned to tie adults to their former plantations. As they had during slavery, whites recognized freedmen as head of household when they could use that position for their own advantage and subsume its power.[57]

In addition to external stress, some African American families experienced internal discord. Freedmen attempted to assert status as head of household, which was not always a positive development for freedwomen if and when men adopted a model of masculinity based on domination rather than caretaking. Some women refused to accept a new form of bondage in place of the old, a factor that contributed to marriage realignment. Amy Dru Stanley argues that enslaved and freedpeople favored marriages of "mutual dependency," but after emancipation some men exerted their liberty by assuming the mantle of authority of the master and did so by physically abusing and controlling their wives. Many freedwomen affirmed their own self-ownership by resisting this transfer of mastery from slaveholder to husband, and a few avoided marriage altogether.[58]

White Southerners and federal authorities preferred to negotiate contracts with and perceived men as heads of household.[59] As African Americans endeavored to strengthen the family unit, they also attempted to strengthen the position of the family head. When families remained intact or, in the case of an abroad marriage, coalesced in one place after the war, they often followed the father's lead. Lorenzo Ivy's father felt indebted to a Virginia slaveholder who had prevented his family from being separated. "Father said he could never do enough for his master for buying us," Ivy explained. At the end of the war, "Father made us all stay." "My papa stayed with his old miss and master after freedom until he died and he just died in 1918, so we all stayed with him too," Mose Banks stated. Freedmen weighed where to settle the family or hire its members based on past experiences and present circumstances. "The Wades wasn't so good to their slaves," Cat Ross noted. "When freedom was declared, Papa come and got me and Mama and took us on over to his place." George White's father refused to hire his children to their mother's former master because he had abused his slaves. Freedmen also sought greater safety through mobility. Scott Hooper's father moved the family to Fort Worth when Ku Klux Klan activity increased. "Father don't lak to leave Marster's place but him gits so 'fraid something am gwine to happen to his fam'ly. . . . He 'cides to leave de country." As fathers attempted to protect and provide for their kin they moved their families around, searching for more favorable conditions in a bleak postwar environment.[60]

My Children Is My Own 247

The decision to move was not without risk. Informed of emancipation, Frank Williams's father opted to leave despite the offer of wages. His master, loath to lose a skilled worker, tied Williams's father up, beat him, and left him there for days in an effort to change his mind. Williams stayed with his father and gave him water. When this intimidation failed, the former master tried to blacklist Williams's father and challenged him to find work elsewhere, assuming "my daddy would have to come back to him so's his family woulden starve to death." The family moved, "and all of us worked hard at fust one thing and then another. . . . We finally saved up enuf to buy dat little farm." This former master used violence and a man's responsibility to care for his family to attempt to compel postwar employment.[61] As they had during slavery, former slaveholders manipulated men's love of and desire to provide for kin in order to control labor.

Children struggled to establish their liberty if they had only one or no parents to advocate on their behalf, and being fatherless aggravated such hardships. As Mary Farmer-Kaiser notes in her study of the Freedmen's Bureau, "Black mothers who attempted to retain custody of their children without the support of husbands or fathers encountered formidable obstacles."[62] Eva Martin's father died before her birth and because her mother worked in the field, she was taken into the big house. "Dey raise me up hard 'cause I didn' had nobody to proteck me," she stated. At freedom, her mother was compelled to sign an indenture, and that was "how dey hab us stay slave. . . . Sometime' I t'ink 'bout dat and my heart breaks. I work hard and ain't git nuthin'." As ex-slaveholders exerted dominion over African Americans and their labor, families headed by women were most susceptible to abuse and most likely to live in white households.[63]

Orphans experienced a particularly precarious postwar existence. Mary Overton, sold away from her parents at age four, remembered that she "stayed wid my white folks a long time after we was made free. I didn't have no where to go." After emancipation, Sally Foltz lived in the big house, but when they could no longer afford to keep her, she was "turned loose." She "didn't have no people, brothers or sisters or anybody, so I just stayed round with first one then another. Sometimes I didn't have a dress to wear and plenty of times I was hungry." Katie Darling's mother died during slavery and her father was taken to war by his master and then ran away. The choices of men who sought individual freedom during the war had costs for the children they left behind. Darling worked for her former owners for six years following emancipation, and "mistress whip me after the War just like she did before." She was not truly free until her brother found her. Peter

Brown also suffered until his aunt, uncle, and sister discovered him, arranging a more favorable work placement. His parents had both died of cholera, and after the war, "I fell in the hands of some mean people. They worked me on the frozen ground barefooted. My feet frostbit."[64] Relatives formed extended and combination households when parents could or did not choose to reconstitute families, and black communities attempted to shelter and care for orphans.[65]

Having white parentage exacerbated adversity because it left freed children vulnerable to abuse and often effectively left them orphaned. Catherine Slim had a white father and a mother who died when she was an infant. During the war, Slim was "bound out by de court to Marse Barley and Miss Sally," where she worked incessantly for no pay and endured whippings. Alice Moore Davidson also had a white father and a deceased mother. "I had to work hard after slavery," she recalled, "'cause I was never with no kinfolks down here." Silas Dothrum knew nothing about either of his parents, but heard rumors that he had a white father. His master's family raised him, and after freedom he was bound to whites, a situation he likened to bondage. Rachel Fairley's mother lost guardianship of her sister's two children, fathered by the master, and they ended up indentured to their half siblings. Because their own mother could not speak for them, and they had no publicly known father, these children were easily exploited. The refusal of so many white fathers to acknowledge their illegitimate offspring contributed to these children's status as actual or seeming orphans.[66] White parentage increased the number of fatherless individuals and being without a father intensified postwar hardship.

While light skin sometimes provided benefits during slavery, having white parentage in the postwar period left many mixed-race children without a father figure to help support the family or negotiate on their behalf. Annie Burton and her siblings had a white father, a neighboring planter who never acknowledged his illegitimate offspring. Her mother quarreled with the mistress and ran away during the war. "My mother came for us at the end of the year 1865, and demanded that her children be given up to her. This, mistress refused to do, and threatened to set the dogs on my mother." Burton's mother sent word to her children with a friend and they climbed through the fence to escape. When the master's sons arrived and "demanded that the children be returned. My mother refused to give us up." Burton's mother suggested they take the issue to Union military headquarters, and "the young men left, and troubled us no more."[67] Because she temporarily left her children, her owners believed she had relinquished them, making the slaveholder the de facto parent. Southern whites maneuvered to deny liberty to freed children, those individuals least able to fully exercise and defend their newfound status. Burton's mother stood up for herself and her family, but her story demonstrates that children without a father to speak for them faced additional obstacles beyond those they shared with all emancipated children. Although white authorities consistently undermined black men, a patriarchal society accorded men greater respect than women. In a society that associated childhood with dependency, whites took advantage of black children with missing or compromised parents, especially fathers, to claim continued ownership of their lives and labor. Former slaves with biological white fathers, but fortunate enough to have involved black stepfathers, had a comparative edge.[68]

During Reconstruction, former slaves in the Mountain South faced limited mobility, inadequate Freedmen's Bureau coverage, vagrancy and indenture laws that pushed many into debt peonage and poverty, high levels of racial violence, and circumscribed educational opportunities, a multiplicity of stressors that negatively impacted family life. Wilma Dunaway finds that in 1870 "more than two-fifths of all black Appalachian family units were headed by one parent, in a majority of instances the mother." Over 25 percent of children lived apart from their families as labor in white households.[69] Multilocality remained a feature of postwar African American family life as a result of unfavorable external conditions.

While conditions varied by state and locality, freedpeople across the South faced white supremacist violence that contributed to mortality and family instability. Sarah Whitmore witnessed her father being shot and killed in Mississippi "direckly after the war by a white man. . . . A Rebel scout." Lina Pendergrass's father disappeared in South Carolina and was presumably killed by the Klan: "They took my daddy. . . . Us nebber did see pa no mo'." Amos Lincoln did not know who murdered his father, who had staked a squatter's claim to one hundred acres of government land in Louisiana. "Ma tuk d' chillen t' Shady Bayou t' gran'par atter dey kill my pa. Nobody was big 'nuf t' run d' place." A family composed mainly of young children needed adult labor to survive and maintain a functioning farm. Will Burks's father had a run-in with the Klan in Tennessee that left him alive but permanently injured. "Ku Klux come to our house and took my papa off wid em. Mama was cryin'," Burks related. "My papa died wid knots on his neck where they hung him up wid ropes. It hurt him all his life after that. . . . He was laid up a long time."[70] Violence that intimidated, maimed, or killed adult freedmen left families without critical support in the short and long term.

Freedmen who demanded their rights jeopardized their personal safety. George Fleming's "bullheaded" father voted Republican in South Carolina "in spite of hell." He insisted on casting a ballot, and "dat's when my daddy got kil't. He had already been shot in de leg befo' dat, and dey called him 'cripple Bill'." In his interview, Fleming made positive comments about slavery, perhaps a calculated response conditioned by his father's death.[71] As during slavery, a rebellious father might teach his children to stand up for themselves, but he also risked his life and his ability to protect them even as his political activity was designed to advance the position of his people. The intractable dilemmas of slavery carried over into the postwar period, and men continued to face a conflict between standing up for self and duty to family.

The Klan in Arkansas killed Betty Brown's grandfather, a man she proudly described as educated, "smart," and a "good mayor," simply because he held office. "Ku Klux'ers said dey wuz zen' gonna have no 'nigguh' mayor," she explained. "So dey tuk him out and' killed him." "My papa was charge' wid bein' a leader," for counseling African Americans about voting "for Grant's fus' 'lection. De Klu Klux wanter whip him. He hafter sleep in a hol-ler log eb'ry night," Lorenza Ezell recalled. The Klan, also in South Carolina, targeted Jane Wilson's father for preaching over the body of a man they murdered. "The Ku Klux came to kill my father for doing this, but they never caught him." Easter Campbell's father fought for the Union and came back to Kentucky armed. "De Ku Klux cum after him one night en he got three of dem wid dis pistol, nobody eber knowed who got dose Kluxes." As with the slave patrols, children relished their father's ability to elude or out-smart the Klan.[72] Despite the danger these men invited and faced, family members admired and celebrated their courage.

Identity

Among its other outcomes, emancipation entailed choosing last names, and approaches to naming speak to how fathers, known and unknown, good and bad, informed identity.[73] While naming could be a matter of conve-nience, it was more often a conscious choice. In the immediate postwar pe-riod, the majority of freedpeople moved to establish a patriline. For some, the chosen name honored a man who was present and who provided for his children. A few used a name to reject an abusive master, white father, or neglectful enslaved father.[74] In various forms, the choice was a way to honor spiritual freedom from slavery and to refuse a history inscribed by masters' naming of slaves. Through their choice of name, former slaves wrote their own history that pointed to a true lineage, heritage, and family.

After emancipation, many former slaves adopted names they already used and frequently kept hidden from whites. Choice of surname reflected freedpeople's attempt to shape their own families, connect to kin, and distance themselves from former owners. Carrie Bradley Logan Bennet's father strategically chose his postwar surname based on his desire to locate missing kin. "When freedom come on, I heard pa say he thought he stand a chance to find his folks and them to find him if he be called Bradley." As they celebrated freedom, families changed their names in accordance with their own history. "Before they were free, every colored man took the name of his master, but afterwards, I took my father's name," George Woods remarked. Ellis Bennett simply stated, "Ah tell da man to change mah name to mah father's name." "After 'mancipation papa stop calling himself Jacob Baldwin and called himself Jacob Brown in his own pa's name," Rebecca Brown Hill said. These names might ultimately derive from a slaveholder, but former slaves cared about the connection to their own family line.[75] Some took the name of a father they never met and from whom they had been separated. James Wiggins learned of his family history from others. "Peter Brooks, one of the oldest colored men in the county, told me that my father's name was Wiggins." He also learned that his literate father ran away after being punished for writing passes for other slaves and died in Philadelphia trying to save money to purchase his wife. To take the name of a biological father established a connection to a family heritage even in the absence of concrete memory or contact.[76]

Choices of surnames reveal how freedpeople conceived of their male ancestors and family history, and the hybrid nature of the enslaved and free family. William Robinson's family never again saw their father after he was sold, but they continued to honor his memory. Robinson claimed that his father had been a prince in a South African tribe and a missionary aunt later learned of his history. At a postwar reunion, the family voted "to discard all other names and hereafter answer to our father's name, which meant Robinson," he wrote. "I am prouder of my father's heathen name than of all the professed christian names that I was compelled to acknowledge while a slave. I pray God that none of us who bear the name of our father will ever bring dishonor to it." Based on the research and leadership of a woman, the members of the family chose to honor their male lineage. Jacob Stroyer's father, born in Sierra Leone, died before the Civil War, and his family made a similar decision. "Father had a surname, Stroyer, which he could not use in public. . . . He was known only by the name of William Singleton . . . his master's name. . . . The title Stroyer was forbidden him, and could be used only by his children after the emancipation of the slaves." These stories indicate that a family could reunite in freedom and coalesce around a living mother, but a physically absent father might remain central to the family history.[77] Families that looked and functioned as matriarchal on a practical level could strongly identify with and feel an emotional and spiritual connection to an absent father. Such families combined matriarchal and patriarchal elements and speak to the importance of avoiding normative definitions of household when evaluating African American families.

For many former slaves the choice of name had direct meaning and the caretaking father was the object the name signified or, as discussed in chapter 5, a white father was the object the name repudiated. Freedpeople honored the name to honor the true father, a means of transcending the master-slave relationship. To honor a name was a way to acknowledge that the power of the *paterfamilias* (owner) was not total, that the *pater vero* (true father) was the provider of things that the slaveholder either could not offer or were more valuable and cherished, even if those things were immaterial or indirect. To take a father's name, including the name of a father one had never met, was to say my father was not my master, or conversely, my master was not my father. In this way, the father became a symbol, whether consciously or not, of resistance.

FREEDOM REPRESENTED AN ESCAPE FROM the oppression of bondage, and freedpeople celebrated the end of abuse, forced marriage, sale, and separation. Freedmen and women also realized what they gained, and they rejoiced in their ability to assume long-suppressed obligations. Individuals exhibit a range of reactions to change, but historians have detailed the consistent efforts of freedpeople to reconstitute their families and exert agency over their lives and livelihoods in the face of discrimination, violence, and dispossession. Postwar and post-Reconstruction conditions undermined the aspirations and patriarchal authority of African Americans, but many of these men persevered. As freedpeople formed households, children with committed fathers had a comparative advantage, whereas those without fathers often faced an even greater struggle to survive. Although the promise of emancipation remained incomplete, caretakers used their newfound freedom to assert their paternal rights.

CHAPTER EIGHT

Good to Us Chillun

Provisioning in Freedom

Freedmen entered a new phase of their lives armed with strong conceptions of paternal duty, but they lacked the resources to easily establish and exert patriarchal authority. After they reconstituted their families, caretaking men attempted to protect and support their kin, paternal prerogatives undermined by a lack of education, property, and economic opportunity. The collapse of Reconstruction governments meant that these men tried to uphold paternal responsibility in a hostile world that denied them basic civil rights and where African Americans who amassed any property or spoke up became the targets of racial violence. Burdensome tax policy and debt peonage trapped freedpeople in a cycle of poverty, and yet men continued to parent their children as a form of survival and resistance.[1]

Born in 1864, Mary Davis's memories of her father stemmed entirely from the postwar period. "Oliver Burleson was my poppa," Davis stated. "He was a tall black man. Oh, Lawd, he was good to us chillun. He was a lovin' man to us."[2] Though she offered few details, Davis described her father as a hard worker and indicated that the family produced ample food. Positive and negative commentary on free fathers reveals the enduring and adapting conceptions of ideal fatherhood in African American communities. Caring engagement remained central to the definition of a good father, and with survival now dependent on pooled family resources and labor, material provisioning, industriousness, and group-oriented leadership took on added importance. A responsible father materially supported his family and prioritized his childrens' education and future, whereas a neglectful father was physically abusive and an inadequate provisioner. Following the war, freedpeople willingly worked long hours and relinquished their pay to their fathers as heads of household so long as these men modeled diligence and each child's earnings contributed to the collective well-being of the family. A violent man who beat his family members or selfishly appropriated the labor and income of his dependents for his own good was no better than a slaveholder and abrogated his paternal duty. To abuse when you had the power to protect was dishonorable and inexcusable. A compassionate man with the right intentions, even when limited by the harsh Jim

Crow environment, could maintain his dignity and earn the abiding respect of his children.

Postwar Hardship

As they had when enslaved, caretaking men considered it their duty to provide for their families. If able, those with young children sought skilled or wage labor. Louis Hughes's "first effort as a freeman was to get something to do to sustain myself and wife and a babe of a few months," including renting a home and finding a job driving a carriage. After freedom, Elisha Green first collected all of his children, who had been hired out to various employers, and then turned his attention to supporting his family. "In order to pay for my house and clothe my family I must, of necessity, get to some trade," he reasoned, so he learned to whitewash. "In going around to whitewash I would get hold of many chairs that needed bottoms. . . . My four girls, my son and myself would at times be working on a chair apiece."[3] In the postwar period, families pooled resources and worked collaboratively, making leadership, cooperation, and the labor of older children crucial elements of economic success.

Basic survival was especially difficult for African American families with children too young to earn wages or make substantial household contributions. Lucius Holsey, a former house slave with few marketable skills, described the decade after the war as "a terrible struggle to keep our heads above the wave." Facing "suffering and almost starvation," he and his wife depended on their garden "and often at night when the moon was shining, she and I would put the little ones to bed, and work until twelve o'clock." The former master wanted another man to remain in his employ in St. Louis and offered wages, but announced that his wife and six children were unwelcome. This informant moved his family, and "my wife and I went to work at anything we could get to do and raised our children."[4] Postwar labor conditions created incentives for individual action, but caretakers prioritized family.

In the immediate postwar period, with the South ravaged by warfare and denuded of resources, fathers sheltered and fed their children in any way they could. Ann Matthews's mother died of disease during the war. After the war, her father "went back in de woods en built us a saplin house en dobbed hit wid mud." He then disappeared for two weeks. "One nite sumbody knocked at de do'er en hit wuz mah daddy en he had two sacks ob food, en de urthur chilluns got up en we et a big meal." Paternal duty often meant trying to stave off hunger. "I'se have seen the time when I never had anything to eat, and my big bunch of children crying for bread," Eli Davison recalled. "Use to, we could live in this country if we did not have money as the woods was full of wild game, but we can't do that anymore." Foraging options became increasingly limited as Redeemer governments legally restricted African American access to hunting and fishing, another means of forcing freedpeople into employment in white homes and controlling labor, which then destabilized family cohesion and patriarchal control.[5]

Freedpeople exited slavery with minimal property, leaving them with little but their labor and ingenuity. In this disadvantaged position, men struggled to provide for their families and establish their authority. Family members, accustomed to the paternalistic practices of slavery, sometimes compounded the problem by favoring the support of the former master, those with a monopoly on resources, over that of the husband or father. Sarah Harris recalled her sense of loss after her family entered Union lines in North Carolina during the war and had to live on military rations. "Our white folks give us good things to eat, and I cried every day. . . . I would say, 'papa le's go home, I want to go home. I don't like this sumptin' to eat.' He would say, 'Don't cry, honey, le's stay here, dey will sen' you to school.'" In trying to provide opportunity and ultimately a better life, a subtlety a hungry and homesick child failed to grasp, Harris's father had to contend with his daughter's disappointments. Shortly after emancipation, Van Moore's abroad father traveled to Galveston, Texas, to visit his family, "'cause he wants to take us back wid him. He rid all de way on a mule, carryin' a wallet what was thrown over de back of de mule like a pack saddle." The pack contained "a coon an' possum an' some corn dodger, 'cause he thought we wasn't gettin' plenty to eat." Moore's mother rejected the offerings. "Mamma she give one look at de stuff, an' say, 'you, Tom, I'se stayin' right here wid old Mis' Cunningham, an' we has white folks eats', an' den she throw de whole mess away." Moore lacked access to his father's feelings, and failed to comment on his reaction, but his mother's preference for the food provided by former slaveholders undermined her husband's well-meaning and hard-fought attempt to support his family. As the mistress's economic fortunes ebbed, however, "we move back to Crosby an' mamma an' papa live together again."[6] Caretakers endeavored to provide materially and to establish paternal prerogatives and authority, interrelated goals undermined by the ongoing repercussions of slavery and the postwar environment.

Losing or being abandoned by a father amplified the economic adversity of free families. Mary Mitchell associated the departure of her father with her mother's postwar struggles: "My father ran away and left my mother with all the children to raise." Lewis Jefferson recalled going hungry after "my pappy left my mammy an' tuck up wid a nudder woman, an' I wus de oldest uf five chilluns, an' we had a hard time." Morgan Latta's father died right before the Civil War, leaving a wife and thirteen children. "Soon after the war, my oldest brother was drowned, leaving the responsibility of supporting the family on my shoulders," Latta recounted in his 1903 autobiography. Deprived of adult male labor, the family struggled to survive and often went hungry. Without a father to offer protection or negotiate more favorable labor contracts, white employers physically abused Latta and his younger siblings. "My mother being a widow, people whipped us as they pleased. We had no father to care for us. I have cried many a day and said that God had forsaken us as a family. We worked hard, but seemed to realize very little." Freedpeople people recognized that a two-parent household had better prospects in the postwar period.[7] The loss of adult labor and a male head of household to handle contracts made sharecropping more difficult and reduced the opportunities for income from wage labor.

Postwar hardship, malnutrition, and poverty led to high mortality, leaving many freed children and adolescents without a parent at a critical juncture in their lives, and forcing young people to become heads of household. After the war, Nat Love's father "decided to start out for himself" and rented twenty acres. "We were at this time in a most destitute condition . . . without food or money and almost naked, we existed for a time on the only food procurable, bran and cracklins." At night, after completing the farm work, his father made brooms and mats with help from his sons, and during the winter, when agricultural labor eased, "we started to try to learn ourselves something in the educational line. Father could read a little, and he helped us with our ABC's, but it is hard work learning to read and write without a teacher." Just after they planted their second crop, "father took sick and died. . . . This was a stunning loss to us just at a time when we most needed a father and husband's help, counsel and protection." Love "took on the leadership, and became head of the family." Next, his brother-in-law died, and then his sister, and Love ended up in charge of his two nieces. Love found a job, and just as his own father had attempted to provide a rudimentary education, Love did the same: "With so many at home to provide for, my wages did not last long, but out of my three dollars I bought each of the children a book. The rest went for provisions and clothing."[8] As Love's life story illustrates, committed fathers, in their effort to provide for kin, were especially vulnerable to disease and early death.

Freedpeople emerged from slavery in poor health, and many worked themselves to death trying to support their families. Several informants remembered fathers who intended to care for kin, but who died after breaking ground to plant, or after one or two crops. "My father come for us and told us that us wuz free and not to be scared of nobody," Janey Landrum recalled, "but he died before he made the second crop." Dorsey Scott's father moved to his wife's place, and "'sists on me comin' home too. He am 'tending' to start a home fo' weuns, but he dies befo' he gits to do it." Mary Gibson's father died of pneumonia at age thirty-eight and the loss still affected her decades later. "I was only about eleben years old when he died, but I cry about it now," she related. "Pappy was good to his chillun. He fed us enough. . . . . If pappy was livin' now I wouldn't want for anything. He sure was a hahd worker. He had leased some land near where we lived and he was tryin' to build a house fo' his fambly. Oh, he was a noble man."[9] In an attempt to fulfill paternal duty, many men succumbed to disease and overwork, leaving their family bereft of a father.

Freedwomen also experienced high mortality, and in a continuation of the adaptations to loss seen during slavery, involved fathers assumed responsibility for their children. When Emma Ray's mother died, her father was left with nine children to support, including a baby. Separated during the war, the family reunited when the conflict ended, and then in 1868, Ray's mother, who "had been worked hard as a slave," fell ill. Prior to her death, Ray's mother asked that her husband not "separate the children, but to let them 'work out' and always keep a home for them," a request he honored. The family's subsistence required labor from the older children, and Ray's father attempted to negotiate favorable placements. When Ray ran away from her employer, "my father told me I should not have left, but as I cried and was afraid of the doctor, who swore at me, father said perhaps he could find another place for me." Despite material deprivation, he insisted that his children carry themselves with pride. "As poor as we were, our father did not allow us to beg, especially for something to eat. He told us it was a disgrace to beg. He thought it better to go hungry than to beg, and if he saw a person, especially a white person who had been free all his life, begging, he would say, 'I can't see how persons that have had their liberty all their lives need to come to such want.'"[10] African American fathers imparted values and life lessons they deemed important, and freedmen continued to distinguish between power and honor, a comparison unfavorable to white people.

Families suffered the greatest privation when they lacked adult labor, so the death of either parent hurt. Looking back on her life from the 1920s, Ray noted that "conditions grew brighter and better as we children grew older. The boys were old enough to leave school and work. My older sisters went into service, and my father would collect their wages. Our rations became better." The eldest daughter acted as "a mother to us" and, at age fourteen, "could do a woman's work." Ray's sisters in domestic service brought home leftover food. "All the ex-slaves did not fare as hard as we, having mothers to help them shoulder the responsibilities; but my father's was a lone man's struggle, with nine motherless children, and it was also a struggle to pay for our home." Ray's father provided moral counsel, education for at least his sons, and a home that kept the family together even as they hired out to different employers. With only one older child to care for, Joe Bouy's father had greater flexibility and after the war, "ma mammy had died, an me an' pappy trable roun de country wukin'."[11] Men with large families and young children could not use constant mobility as a lifestyle and labor strategy.

Caretaking men made sacrifices to support and educate their children, directing the fruits of their own labor into an effort to create a better future for their kin. Like Emma Ray's father, former Union soldier Bill Simms made a vow to his dying wife. "She had had to work hard all her life and she said she didn't want her children to have to work as hard as she had, and I promised her on her death bed, that I would educate our girls." Both attended Ottawa University in Kansas, "the oldest one being the first colored girl to ever graduate from that school." The fact that she "bought me my first suit of clothes I ever had" speaks to her appreciation. Martha Bunton's father also became a single parent after his wife died during slavery. "After slavery, fathaw sent us to school. . . . Dat's why I kin read and write. . . . I wanted to go to school so I could work and help fathaw." Bunton had positive memories of a man she loved, but who was probably an alcoholic. "He was drinkin' a lot now," she continued. "But he was good to us." If a storm blew in after the children left for school, "we'd be on our way home and way down de road, we would see somethin' comin' along dat looked lak a elephant. It was fathaw wid a bundle ob coats fo' us to wear. . . . Oh fathaw was good to us."[12] Bunton owned the home where she gave her interview and her sister lived next door, houses situated on land originally purchased by their father, a man who managed to care for and keep his family intact in the transition from slavery to freedom and beyond.

When freedmen and women failed as caretakers, due to their own choices or overwhelming economic pressures, relatives often raised children. Grandparents were central figures in this network of care. Minksie Walker admitted that when his first wife died he gave his two children to their grandmother, "and I have never seen dem since." Jim Franklin, unlike more committed fathers, could not handle childcare following his first wife's death: "W'en she die, I's jes' crazy, and lef' and follow' the tuppentime wuks on Wes'. I lef' the six chillen wid us folks," including his sister, uncle, and mother.[13] Cornelius Holmes's mother sought help from her father when her husband died. "When freedom come, my pappy was dead," Holmes related. "Mother . . . give me to my grandpap. . . . I stay dere 'til I 'come twenty-one." After freedom, George Gilliam's grandfather "came to Florida after his children and grandchildren," when he heard that Gilliam's mother was living with a "no good" man. He removed his grandchildren from a cruel step-father, taking them all home with him. The older children walked and the youngest rode in the wagon, and with stops to make money to buy food, the trip to Alabama took a year. Grandparents also enabled a parent to temporarily cede custody as they worked to regain their financial footing. After his wife died, leaving him with three children too young for farm work and medical and funeral bills, Calvin Moye accepted his parents' offer to take them. He continued to pay for food and he purchased their clothing in an arrangement reminiscent of cross-plantation networks during slavery. He later moved to town and reclaimed his children, eventually seeing them all married and settled.[14] Extended family remained an essential source of support in an environment marked by malnutrition, poverty, and high mortality.

Multigenerational households and multihousehold extended families allowed African Americans to care for children and the elderly and maintain a labor force large enough to protect assets.[15] Jason Miller's mother died when he was "'bout turnin' into 16 years old and my daddy never marry no more. He owns 'bout 15 acres and de house we lives in and he rents more land close to us. We 'most always has plenty to eat and wear." When his father became too old for labor, "me and my wife and our two chillun was livin' wid him." Miller's father insisted on retaining legal ownership of the property. "He never turn over de home nor de lands to me while he was livin' and I follow right in his tracks." Miller owned his South Carolina home and his own son and family lived with him, as he had with his father. "I now owns de farm and is still boss dere," he noted, arguing that he had seen cases where a man relinquished control and "de head of de house become no more pow'ful than a child and . . . get sent to de poorhouse, to boot." Both men had been slaves, though Miller only as a child, and slavery conditioned the father to safeguard his authority and property, a lesson he passed down to his son.[16] In Miller's 1930s worldview, the oldest adult man was rightful head of household, but time in slavery and life experience in Jim Crow America had taught him and his father that the position and concrete power were not always coupled.

African American families in the postwar period relied on the labor of every able-bodied member, and while former slaves acknowledged the critical economic contributions of older siblings, many credited their fathers with maintaining family cohesion. John Adams's family fled to Union lines in 1862 and his father eventually purchased property in Pennsylvania and "then we all got places to work at," a common family strategy of combining farming and hired labor. "He now farms for himself," Adams said of his father in his 1872 narrative, "and I think a man works much better for himself than he can for another man for nothing. . . . If my father had been working for himself no doubt all of his children would have been well educated and had good trades."[17] Slavery and postwar conditions compromised his father's ability to provide opportunity, but not his desire to see his children well placed. A father with the right paternal intentions could maintain his dignity in the absence of ideal outcomes. As they had during slavery, children appreciated engaged, supportive men and they understood the constraints under which their fathers labored and lived.

Looking back on their own role as fathers, informants were forthright about the sacrifices and grueling work needed to stay afloat and support a family during the postwar period. "I wecked night and day fer ter take care of my family an' ter school my children," Charlie Turner stated, including a long list of the jobs he had held during his life. "I did a little ov everthing fer to comfort my family." According to Morgan Ray, "Work and raisin' a fambly wuz about all I knew 'cept on Sundays. Den I allus found time to go to church." When asked about postwar politics, Tob Davis demurred and focused instead on his responsibilities as a father. "De white fo'ks tries to stop weuns, an' dey did," he said of voting. "Ise don't want to fuss, Ise wo'ks hard an' cares fo' my fam'ly." Children also recognized the all-consuming and unsung nature of a man's obligations to family. "He farmed all his life," Lewis Brown said of his father. "He raised all his children and got wore out and pore."[18] Caring for family meant a life of unremitting labor and little public reward.

Neglectful Fathers

Jim Crow conditions and the psychological damage of slavery undermined some men's aptitude as fathers. John Smith cited the negative example of slaveholder behavior and claimed his father "believed in whuppin like de white folks did. He cut de blood out of me wid a switch an' scarred me up an' I left him." At age twenty-one, Smith returned and repaid his father "for every day I was away from him from de time I ran away at 16." After the two men reconciled, Smith attributed his long life to paying this "just debt" to his father. "Daddy said before he died I had done more for him dan de other chilluns. He whupped me too much but atter all he was my father an' I loved him an' paid him all I owed him for de time I was away."[19] Smith's ambivalent assessment of his father combined bitterness over excessive physical violence with sense of filial duty to contribute to the family economy.

While former slaves understood the postwar conditions that made it difficult for their fathers to succeed economically, they resented men who refused to work or unfairly appropriated older children's wages. "My daddy wuzn't no good—wouldn't work," Gus Alexander noted, adding that his mother passed away and his father later died in prison, so he took care of himself from the age of eight. Gus Jackson's father hired him out after emancipation. "Until I was twenty-two years ole my father collected my wages. I never got a penny of it," he stated, adding that his white employer "done more for me dan my own daddy done." Children expected to help subsidize the family, but they also expected to share in the proceeds. A father who behaved like a slaveholder, exploited his children's labor, and took care of self rather than others shirked his paternal duty.[20] In the postwar period, a patriarch controlled his dependents' labor. A good father worked with and for his children and emotionally invested in them. To treat them solely as a financial asset was to become like an enslaver. Former slaves thus denounced men who were individualists, but whose individualism took different forms. Alexander's father abandoned his family. Jackson's father retained his family ties, but he failed as a caretaker because he embraced a vision of masculinity based on domination rather than reciprocity.

Children criticized men who failed to thrive in freedom due to their own personal foibles or their inability to overcome the oppression they faced. Unlike the intelligent, skilled, industrious, and determined men of positive accounts, these men made poor decisions and squandered opportunities. "Pappy didn' have good sense, he jes' kep' movin' from place to place twel he died," Annie Coley related.[21] Bill Reese's father trained as a barber and eventually ran his own "first-class" shop, but Reese had to take over and support the family after the war when his father became a "heavy drinker." Jeff Bailey's father "drank hisself to death." Because her father was indolent, Martha Richardson's mother supported the family. "If my daddy had worked and saved lak my mammy, we would be 'way head of what we is, and my brudders say so, too. But we fond of our daddy, he so good lookin' and all."[22] Even a well-liked father earned reproach if he failed to exert himself to provide for his kin. In an unforgiving environment that required collective action to achieve basic survival, children expected a responsible father to put family needs ahead of individual needs.

One of the most complete and complex appraisals of a formerly enslaved father comes from Theodore Rosengarten's interviews with Nate Shaw (Ned Cobb), an Alabama tenant farmer. Born in 1885, Shaw never experienced slavery, but his father was fifteen when freed, and slavery figured prominently in Shaw's assessment of the man. Shaw's unvarnished portrayal of a man he resented, and yet grudgingly loved, shows how deeply the institution of slavery could affect an individual personality and influence a father-son relationship. Despite being born twenty years after the end of the Civil War, slavery continued to shape Nate Shaw's life. Shaw's vision of his role as husband and father, in many ways a reaction to and against his father, was affected by the ongoing repercussions of slavery and a postwar racial climate that recapitulated bondage. Shaw was candid and raw in his criticism of his father, a womanizer who beat his wives and children. Few individuals dominated his recollections so much as Hayes Shaw. Nate Shaw provided his family history, comparing himself physically to his father: "Hayes Shaw was my daddy. He was just about my color or maybe a shade darker; he was dark. He was a kind of rawboned, slender man like I am." He expressed pride that as a young boy, his father trusted him to ride into the hills to collect his grandmother, indicating that he wanted to please Hayes.[23]

In Nate Shaw's eyes, Hayes failed to uphold the central tenets of fatherhood and paternal duty. He overworked and physically abused his wives and children and in doing so he failed in his responsibility to provide for and protect them. Nate Shaw faulted his father for the fact that his mother, who died early, would "be in the field workin like a man, my daddy out in the woods somewhere huntin." Hayes Shaw's violence countermanded a man's responsibility to care for his kin. "I didn't see no cause for it," Nate said of the abuse suffered by his mother and then stepmother. "I don't expect it ever come up in my daddy's mind what his children thought about it or how they would remember him for it, but that was a poor example, to stamp and beat up children's mothers right before em." When Nate Shaw described Hayes beating his wife with a bullwhip, he underscored his father's socialization in slavery. "He was just careless with us like a brute," Nate added of his father's handling of his children.[24] When former slaves criticized bad fathers, they compared them to slaveholders, invoking the most negative example they had of abdication of masculine responsibility. A man who abused when it was within his power to protect behaved like a slaveholder, and in so doing violated black communities' sense of paternal duty.

Nate Shaw also criticized his father's inadequate provisioning. He resented his father's failure to send him to school because Hayes depended on his son's labor and did not want to contribute to the teacher's salary. However, every time Nate Shaw criticized his father, he tempered his commentary. Hayes Shaw failed to work hard enough as a farmer and overworked his family, but his skill as a hunter and fisherman often kept them from starving. He failed to provision an education and send his children to school, "but it wasn't entirely my daddy's fault that I didn't get an education," Nate added, in a denunciation of the postwar racial climate. Though he never forgave Hayes for his domestic abuse, Nate Shaw blamed many of his father's defects and failures on slavery. "He was imprisoned in slavery for fifteen years—slavery were equal or worser than prison, but both of em bad and the poor colored man knows more about them two subjects than anybody." Hayes Shaw never overcame the psychic injuries inflicted by slavery, but equally important, he was broken by Jim Crow oppression. "Slavery just taught the colored man to take what come and live for today. And the colored man held his children back as he held hisself," Nate concluded. Hayes Shaw "wasn't a slave but he lived like one. Because he had to take what the white people gived to get along. That much of slavery was still hangin on."[25] Hayes Shaw emerges in the interviews as a flawed man who never had a chance to succeed in an environment that constantly knocked him down.

Even as he criticized his father, Nate Shaw remained with and near him, supported him, and continued to seek his approbation. "I reckon my daddy was scared I'd leave him, so he held me down. Of course, I don't blame no man for not wantin his children to get away from around him," Nate Shaw noted. Hayes hired his son out and then took his earnings, "and he et up my wages as fast as I worked." Nate considered this treatment "just like slavery," but he refused to run away. "I . . . knowed it was wrong to run away from him." In addition, he took his father's beatings longer than necessary, knowing that if he fought back, Hayes would displace his frustrations on the younger children. In many ways, Nate Shaw became the father figure, protecting his siblings and half siblings, and providing for his own and his father's family. When Hayes accused his son of working too hard, even as he benefited from the fruits of that labor, his words "fretted me," Nate recalled. "Me knowin my duty for my family's sake and wantin to comply with my duty." Despite his feelings about Hayes and his father's failure to model self-respect, Nate still wanted his approval and found his criticism stung. When his sister Sadie died, Nate rescued her three sons from a neglectful stepfather. He then divided the boys with Hayes, allowing his father to determine who would live where. In the process, Hayes revealed his ability to consider the needs of others, taking the younger boys and giving Nate the oldest so as to reduce the labor of and impact on Nate's wife. The two men agreed that the boys should make regular visits between the homes to maintain their ties.[26] Hayes Shaw was abusive, but he understood the importance of kinship.

Nate Shaw openly detailed his father's abuses and shortcomings, but he also acknowledged what he learned from Hayes. He learned practical skills like how to cut ties and make baskets, but of greater import, "I learnt years ago to keep my tongue still. But I also learnt to obey the white man. I aint quit that yet in some ways. My daddy told me, many a time, to obey the white man, do what he tell you to do and avoid trouble; and also, even my daddy's ways and actions told me that. My daddy stood back off of white folks considerably. . . . He was born and raised in slavery habits." Nate Shaw recognized the importance of this lesson for survival and yet could never fully stomach his father's appeasement. He appreciated his father's advice to "always . . . treat people with care and respect," but he chafed against his father's unwillingness to stand up for himself. Nate Shaw told of how Hayes had been shot by a white man and never spoke out against the perpetrator. Instead, he waited for the bullet to work its way up near the surface of the skin and cut it out with a pocketknife. Hayes would not fight back against white or adult black men, and instead took out his anger on those under his control and unable to fight back: his wives and children.[27]

Nate Shaw also reacted to the negative example of his father, commenting on how his father's relationships with women exemplified the opposite of what he wanted in life. Nate refused to marry before he could support a wife and children. "I want a woman what wants to stay with me until I die or I'll stay with her until she dies—let death part us." Self-respect enabled Nate Shaw to establish relationships of mutual respect with others. As a young, married man, when his father came himself or sent smaller children for food and Nate essentially fed his own and his father's younger children,

Nate took exception to any disrespectful treatment of his wife. "That was my wife," he explained. "She was the same as me—flesh and blood; that woman was a whole person." While Hayes Shaw partially exemplifies a model of masculinity focused on sexual performance, he avoided flaunting his extramarital relationships. His wives knew about his womanizing, but Nate "never did know my daddy to boast about his outside children in front of his wives." Rather, Hayes Shaw seems to have been unable to exert self-control and form meaningful relationships, possibly as a result of his own low self-esteem. Nate Shaw's manner of interacting with his children was also a rejection of his father's example. If he detected a developing behavioral problem, "then it was time for me to talk to em. But I did not put a bridle on em like my daddy did to me; it wasn't necessary. . . . I never did have to whip em much at all. We talked to our children and they was very eager to obey our rulins. They was well cared for by me and their mother."[28] Nate Shaw disagreed with the way his father employed corporal punishment. For Nate Shaw, a whipping should instill discipline, not serve as a cover for and retaliation against a man's own degraded status.

Nate Shaw was never a slave, but his experience shows how black sharecroppers faced many of the same challenges as enslaved fathers. "It wasn't freedom really," Nate Shaw said of emancipation and its aftermath. "Had to do whatever the white man directed em to do, couldn't voice their heart's desire. That was the way of life that I was born and raised into." Nate Shaw insisted on defending himself, and Rosengarten sought him out precisely because of his involvement with the Sharecropper's Union. But Shaw's principled stand incurred a high cost. After confronting a sheriff's posse in 1932, Nate Shaw spent twelve years in prison, during which time his family struggled to survive. Of his conversations with Shaw's children, Rosengarten writes, "While they acknowledged his courage they were invariably critical of his stand. For they had lost their father for twelve years and watched the task of raising a large family during hard times take its physical toll on their mother." Nate's youngest daughter referred to his pride as "the white man in him."[29] Like enslaved fathers, black men in the Jim Crow South confronted intractable dilemmas. To publicly demand one's rights, to resist, was to risk removal from and hardship for one's family. To be a man could mean compromising one's duty as a father. Nate Shaw might dislike his father's accommodating behavior, but Hayes never ended up in prison for over a decade.

While incarcerated, Nate Shaw came to a more nuanced understanding of his father's character. In prison, "if you aint guilty but they decide you is, you goin to suffer," Shaw reflected. "I think of my daddy's words—he had a whole lot of good in him and good logic. He done wrong things—I don't say he committed no crimes. . . . And he had his own theories and he always said, 'When you in Rome, you got to take Rome's fare.' Well, that's very truthful, because you got no way of helpin yourself when you land in prison. You got to obey orders." Long before he ended up in prison, Nate Shaw was with his father when Hayes died. When he heard about his father's final illness, Nate rushed to his side. "I visited him, I hauled him to the doctors, and the evenin he died . . . where was I at? Sittin down in a chair and me only, right by his head." Nate Shaw refused to leave, keeping the flies off the dying man with a peach tree brush. Hayes Shaw's last words were an exhortation to pray. "I told him, Papa, I will. I will." Though Nate Shaw was not religious at that point, in the aftermath of his father's funeral he repented. Even in death, his father continued to exert influence. As Nate Shaw reflected on his memories of his father, many profoundly negative, he still felt bereft in his loss: "Now I didn't have a mother or father livin in the whole world. I was on my own, lookin out for myself."[30]

Being ensconced in a social network did not make a man a good father, and in the estimation of his children he succeeded or failed based not only on external factors, but on the mode of masculinity he adopted within a family structure. Choosing to be a father did not mean a man chose to be a caretaker. Hayes Shaw failed as a husband and father because he had internalized a hegemonic model of masculinity based on dominating his dependents. As an African American man in the post-Reconstruction South, he had power over black women and children, which he exerted through physical violence. Nate Shaw, meanwhile, was a good father who failed his family due to imposed constraints. He endeavored to take care of kin and community, and yet he ran into trouble when a public assertion of defiance landed him in jail. Combining heroic resistance with caretaking had steep consequences that could remove a man from those he sought to support. Slavery may have ended, but black men in the Jim Crow South had to continue to hide their practice of manhood. The private exercise of masculinity could include domestic abuse so long as that violence was internal to the community and did not threaten white masculinity and the racial hierarchy. If the white masculine ideal of dominance and the African American masculine ideal of caretaking had different outcomes and meanings for black children, the white community cared primarily about preventing the public performance of black masculinity.

As Nate Shaw detailed, any African American man who accumulated property in the Jim Crow South became a target. "Whenever the colored man prospered too fast in this country under the old rulins, they worked every figure to cut you down," Nate Shaw stated. "I seed my daddy cleaned up twice; everything he had they took away from him." After twice being defrauded of his crop by unscrupulous whites and "stripped of everything he had . . . he never did prosper none after that." Oppression broke some less resilient individuals. In the late nineteenth and early twentieth centuries, men like Hayes Shaw saw little reason to toil to get ahead when they knew their labor and earnings would likely be appropriated.[31] Nate Shaw was highly critical of his father, but he also believed that growing up enslaved and the postwar environment damaged his father's prospects and psyche. Even under ideal conditions, some people in any population fail to thrive as parents due to character or lack of interest, and a few abandon, neglect, or abuse their children. Slavery and Jim Crow imposed added burdens. Hayes Shaw was a present but deficient father who kept his family together and yet abused those weaker than himself. It is impossible to disentangle Hayes Shaw the man from the oppressive environment in which he was raised and lived.

The experiences of Hayes and Nate Shaw demonstrate why African American fathers would choose to conceal their postwar efforts, authority, and any successes they achieved. To demonstrate one's ability to provide was to invite white animosity and violence. To be a good father meant remaining hidden from public view. As Edward Blum notes, in early twentieth-century Jim Crow America, African American men realized that "having their manhood recognized was a knotty problem. Masculinist power, such as in the form of champion boxer Jack Johnson, frightened and infuriated whites." In addition, as Craig Friend points out, Southern masculinity was "performed publicly, but African American men were restricted from public venues in which they could compete against and join with white masculinity."[32] In the twentieth century, multihousehold extended families and male leadership that was internally recognized, but not externally publicized, helped African Americans survive in part by distributing material and human resources in a world where flaunting or concentrating such assets could unleash a racist backlash.[33]

Responsible Fathers

Families worked together to survive in a postemancipation world that denied freedpeople upward mobility, opportunity, and social and political rights. "Me and my father stuck—stuck close as a lean tick to a sick kitten,"

Felix Haywood announced. T. W. Cotton framed the accomplishments of his father and family by emphasizing the fact that freedpeople started with nothing: "Father never got no land at freedom. He got to own 160 acres, a house on it, and some stock. We all worked and helped him to make it. He was a hard worker and a fast hand." Postwar subsistence was a group effort that required adult leadership and children's labor. "He wuz smart and got plenty of work to do, so we got on all right," Elizabeth Finley said of her father and postwar experience in Montgomery, Alabama, "but we had to all wuk hard." Like Cotton, she noted that emancipated slaves "never did git nothing. . . . We wuked hard for whut we got." Silas Nelson's father and his sons worked as a team. "My pa riz up four boys. Us had four mules and hauled dirt to Graniteville evey day. . . . I helped my paw evey day when I was young with everything."[34] Cohesive families with conscientious fathers had better economic outcomes.

Informants looking back on their postwar lives appreciated hardworking fathers who fed and supported their kin, enabling the family to achieve a measure of self-sufficiency. Immediately after emancipation, Sarah Ford's former master announced that everyone on the plantation could stay and work for wages with the exception of her father, a chronic truant and "bad influence." Undaunted, Ford's father borrowed a wagon and team and moved his family. "Mamma an' papa an' me hire out 'cause I was a big girl an' stron, an' we has a patch our own, too, what we makes a crop on, an' dat was de fust time I ever see money. We has a cabin what papa built an' a corn crib out in de back, 'cause we raise our feed, too, an' we sure was happy 'cause de bright light had come an' day wasn't no more whippin's." A diversified economic strategy combined hired labor and home production. "Pa cut down trees an' built us a log cabin," Georgia Telfair recalled. The family kept livestock, gardened, and dried fruit for the winter and had plenty of food. When not in school, she and her brother "wukked in de fiel' wid pa." Smokey Eulenberg praised his "industrious" father, who "worked hard and saved his money and in a couple of year he bought a team and we moved to a little place."[35] Formerly enslaved people from across the South defined postwar success in terms of material abundance, property ownership, and the kin unit's independence from former masters, and families that managed to prosper were usually two-parent households with one or more older children.

The survival of sharecroppers depended on every member of the family contributing. Because able-bodied men had the most earning power, prosperous family units had a male head of household. The death or absence of a patriarch compromised contract negotiations and often forced a family to move.[36] In this climate, large families with multiple older children fared best, and freedmen who managed to purchase land were better able to achieve self-sufficiency, something their children understood. Betty Powers's father purchased unimproved land with no buildings, "so weuns all pitches in an' fixed a cabin." The large family worked "lak beavers" to make a crop. "Weuns watched it grow lak 'twas little chil's, 'cause it all b'longed to weuns. 'Twas ours." Powers, at age twelve, was the youngest of twelve children, and she "tooks care of de house while mammy wo'ks wid de tudders, doin' de outside wo'k." Pooled labor and property enabled African American families to establish an economic footing in the postwar period, and when fathers modeled diligence and distributed resources fairly, children willingly contributed to the family economy. "I'd rather work in the field any day as work in the house. . . . I didn't make my living by rascality. I worked like my father raised me. Oh, I haven't forgot how my old father raised me," Hattie Hill announced. Another former slave remembered that after emancipation, "my father took charge of me. He told me I was free but as long as I was under the roof of his house he was boss." This father gave each of his sons their own tobacco patch to instill the value of independence.[37] Informants continued to assess their fathers based on how these men wielded the power they had, praising those who displayed judicious leadership. As African American fathers moved to establish themselves as heads of household, children respected patriarchal authority so long as these men took care of the family and treated their dependents fairly.

A father could impart life lessons in the behavior he modeled and the choices he made. For Archie Millner's father, moving away from the Virginia plantation where he had been enslaved was a statement of self-possession rather than a comment on past treatment. "Soon as freedom come, father took us boys cross de county line to Freetown an' fixed up a shack on de edge of de woods," Millner recounted. The old master visited and begged them to return, offering up the overseer's house. Millner's father listened and then declined. Although their former master insisted that Miller's father should come see him if he ever needed anything, "pa never would go back. He . . . felt better workin' fo' hisse'f." Millner's father sent his son a longer distance to have corn ground, "rather dan use Brown's mill," at no cost. Despite having to pay for this service, "pa said it made him feel like a free man to pay fo' things jus' like anyone else." Isaac Rodgers noted that many people stayed on the plantation, "but father en me made us er little shack, en I raised melons en sold em."[38] Rodgers's immense pride in earning money for the first time indicates that his father allowed him to keep some or all of the proceeds.

Children who transitioned from slavery to freedom with an intact and supportive family frequently remained with their parents until they married. Bryl Anderson, after tenant farming for a time with his father and siblings in Virginia, decided to marry and set out on his own. "I gave my father all I had accumulated to establish another place for the family, saw them situated an' told my father that I was going away." Anderson viewed his father as the head of household to whom he owed his labor, and he bought his independence from the family using saved wages. Henry Anthony moved from North Carolina to Arkansas with his wife and children only after his parents passed away. "We stayed round close and farmed and worked till they died." Fannie Moore and her siblings had a similar life cycle, farming as a family "till de chillun all grown an' mammy an' pappy both die then we leave."[39] Parents who cared for their children inspired life-long family allegiance.

Because black communities considered it a father's primary duty to provide for his children, informants praised the masculinity of those who supported large families. Despite their meager earnings, Robert Shepherd was proud of the fact that he and his wife "raised our nine chillun, give 'em plenty to eat and wear too and a good roof over der haids." Henry Blake and J. H. Beckwith both had fathers who married twice and raised two sets of children, and both had been born to the first wife. Beckwith's father had at least fifteen children, sent the two oldest to college, and taught his son a trade. Lula Jackson's father, her mother's second husband, "raised all his children and all his stepchildren too."[40] As they started their own families, moreover, several informants remembered being married in their father's home. "You know I had a pretty fine wedding 'cause my pappy had worked hard and commenced to be prosperous," Alice Alexander explained. "I sho did have smart weddin'," Maria Jackson added. "My Daddy seed to dat."[41] Part of a father's duty was to provide for his children until they established their own household and to see them properly ushered into adulthood.

Even more so than observations of slavery, evaluations of fathers in the postwar period celebrated industry, skill, and a man's willingness and ability to provide for his family. "My fadder was a wukkin' man. He help buil' de big customs house," Mary Johnson stated of her family's time in New Orleans. "He put he name upon de top of de customs house and it dere to dis day. . . . My pa holp buil' de hospital, too." Mary Wilson identified her family as "one of the first Negro-land owners in Portsmouth," Virginia. "My father builed his own house . . . and it still stands with few improvements." Children took pride in the enduring accomplishments of their fathers as slaves and freemen.[42] While commentary on formerly enslaved fathers varied slightly based on class status, the traits children most admired transcended class. The children of sharecroppers and farmers respected a father who produced ample food, whereas the children of tradesmen touted their fathers' mechanical ability and access to wages. They shared an appreciation of skill, diligence, perseverance, and duty to family. Most important, they admired self-sufficiency, even if men, families, and households achieved this goal in different ways. "My daddy was one of those Negroes what made plenty fo' his chillun ter eat. He wuz one of dem farmers what never need a store only in a great while," Sallie Smith stated. August Smith's father "raised his own sheep and cotton, and from this my mother made our clothes." His father also built a sorghum mill, and "every part of the mill was handmade, with home made tools."[43] To be self-reliant in the postwar period was to avoid dependency on white landowners, employers, and merchants. If rebelliousness outranked other masculine attributes during slavery, industry and skill took on increased prominence in the postwar period and represented ongoing resistance.

An ideal father took care of his family materially and set them on the path to self-sufficiency by providing for their education and/or passing on vital economic skills. J. H. Beckwith praised his multitalented father as "a mechanical talent" and "somewhat of a genius." His father learned to read and write after emancipation, and took his son on as an apprentice. "I used to be called the best negro journeyman carpenter between Monroe, Louisiana and Little Rock, Arkansas," Beckwith declared, highlighting not only his own achievements, but his shrewd and adept father. Beckwith used his interview to discuss racial uplift and the habit of self-improvement his father instilled in his children. Men who learned a trade in slavery often taught their sons, giving them an economic advantage. James Bertrand told his interviewer that he "never did do any sharecropping. I am a shoemaker. I learned my trade from my father." Aaron Nunn's father purchased two hundred acres, built a house for the family, and then passed his blacksmith shop to Nunn, who passed it on to his own son.[44] Teaching children a skill or leaving them property helped to ensure that the family would remain self-supporting.

Postwar evaluations of fathers emphasized hard work, skill, and material providing. With slavery and masters' rationing ended, men's material offerings and ability to support a family no longer had a tinge of accommodation.

What a man and family produced was entirely based on his and their own labor and diligence. In addition, with education a legal possibility, though often violently opposed by white Southerners, a father's willingness to provide educational opportunity took on greater importance in memories of freedom. Regardless of these shifting concerns, the mode of fatherhood most celebrated by children of formerly enslaved men contained a strong undercurrent of moral masculinity and selfless, family-centered leadership.

Education

As part of the responsibility to prepare children for the future, once they had established themselves economically, formerly enslaved fathers prioritized education, a goal shared by men throughout the nineteenth and into the twentieth century. "Let the father not forget that he is accountable before God for the raising of his children," abolitionist minister and former slave John Meachum argued in an 1840s address, invoking the duty of "Colored Citizens" to provide their children with "industry and good education."[45] Fugitives in the antebellum North, however, faced discrimination and segregation in education as in other realms of life. "I cannot say they are in a free land," Thomas Jones related, "for, even here, in the city of Boston, where, I am told, is kept the old cradle of liberty, my precious children are excluded from the public schools, because their skin is black. Still, Boston is better than Wilmington, inasmuch as the rulers of this place permit me to send my children to any school at all." Austin Steward attempted to provide his children with an education for their own edification and as a career path. "This beloved daughter, I had spared no pains nor money to educate and qualify for teaching," Steward wrote of an older child. Based on past "trials and difficulties," he had his daughter trained so that she could "not only . . . provide for her own wants, but . . . teach her younger brothers and sisters, should they be deprived of the advantages of a good school." Frederick Douglass encountered such prejudice when he attempted to send his daughter to a local seminary. "They were not allowed in the public school in the district in which I lived, owned property, and paid taxes," but instead forced to attend "an inferior colored school." Through "considerable agitation," Douglass managed to overturn this policy.[46] For many antebellum fugitives, the struggle for civil rights was intertwined with taking care of and assuring a better future for their children.

Samuel Ward, whose parents escaped from Maryland with their young son around 1820, remembered following "my dear father up and down his garden, with fond childish delight. . . . There he first taught me some valuable lessons—the use of the hoe, to spell in three syllables, and to read the first chapter of John's Gospel, and my figures; then, having exhausted his literary stock upon me, he sent me to school." Decades later, after various careers, "teaching law, medicine, divinity, and public lecturing," Ward noted, "I am glad to hasten back to what my father first taught me . . . the tilling of the soil, the use of the hoe." Ward credited paternal guidance with having shaped his pursuits, outlook, and the arc of his life. Vance Lewis's father, who died shortly after the Civil War, influenced his son's identity and career trajectory. The plantation community elected Lewis's father as judge, charged with handling disputes, "because he bore the name of being the most level-headed Negro on the place," and Lewis eventually pursued a career as a lawyer. Shortly before his father died, he chose the site of the schoolhouse, which Lewis regarded as his father's "monument."[47] Two fathers, in different time periods and places, and one whose time with his child was limited, made a lasting impression.

In the postwar period, a significant number of freedpeople, like prewar fugitives, believed that education represented opportunity. Many freedmen made a concerted effort to ensure that their children received an education, a challenging undertaking in a period marked by white violence against black schools.[48] When F. H. Brown's father purchased property, "he built a church and built a school, and I went to school on our own place." Neal Upson's sister had learned enough from her young mistress to teach, and her father built an extra room on the house as a school. Similarly, Mary Wilson started a school in the family home. "After two years my class grew so fast and large that my father built a school for me in our back yard. I had as many as seventy-five pupils at one time."[49] With education for African Americans a tenuous prospect in the postwar South, some freedmen established their own small schools, another manifestation of the drive toward self-sufficiency.

Former slaves recognized educational attainment as a fundamental element of future success. "My brothers and sisters all did well in life," Julia White declared. "Our parents always insisted we had to go to school. It's been a help to me all my life." When his former master wanted to hire his daughter as a domestic, Ambrose Headen replied, "I always thought that if ever I was free I would educate my children; if 'twas not for that, sir, I would accommodate you." As a slave, Headen had resented providing labor as part of his master's subscription to a new school, "when I could have no privilege of educating my own children." With emancipation, "God has turned things about," and three of his children had graduated from the school he helped build, with the fourth nearly done. Headen expressed pride that all four were accomplished scholars, adding, "I love to think of my son down in Selma preaching." In the decades following the Civil War, education emerged as a cornerstone of racial uplift.[50]

Providing children with educational opportunities required parental sacrifice. "Us wuked mighty hard to raise 'em and give all of 'em a good education," Ike Derricotte related, giving his wife joint credit. "Dat was somepin us couldn't have when us was growin' up and I'm thankful to be able to say dat us was able to send 'em all to college."[51] Perry McGee "went naked, barefooted, and hungry and send my daughter to school." Charles Williams gave his son a "first Class Education," refusing to allow him to "work for me," or anyone else. "His learning made me felt grand. I went in patches and rags for to educate My Boy." Williams defined his son as "a better man than I was, and *I has been a Man among Men.*" Williams's son, who spoke three languages, died at age twenty-six, a source of profound grief for his father, who took solace in the fact that "he died all right with His Lord." While the exact parameters of Williams's sense of manliness are unclear, his masculine identity certainly included work, providing for kin, and religion. These men hoped their children would grow up with broader horizons and expanded prospects compared to their formerly enslaved parents. "I have raised all of my children, educated them, then college, those who wanted it," William Johnson noted. "I've helped grandchildren and now I help to educate great grandchildren."[52] Paternal obligation to family and the future did not stop with children.

Because children and teens with an involved father were more likely to attend school and/or learn a trade in the transition from slavery to freedom, freedpeople with missing fathers were at a disadvantage. Bob Benford had an unknown white father and never attended school "a day in my life," due to the need to "help mammy work."[53] Mose Hursey's father died after the war, and though his teacher declared he "learned the fastest of any boy she ever see," his mother removed him from school "'cause she needed me at home to 'tend the other children so's she could work." Perry Madden "made the fifth grade before I stopped. My father died and then I had to stop and take care of my mother."[54] An oldest child, even if they had a living and present father, might also be denied an education if their labor was essential to family survival. "I never went to school. I was the oldest chile my father had out a sixteen and I had to work," J. N. Brown recalled. "We had a kinda hard time."[55] With families dependent on the earnings and production of adults, the death or absence of a father threatened subsistence, necessitated adjustments, and heightened the importance of the labor of older children.

When criticizing the shortcomings of their fathers, informants faulted those men whose single-minded focus on remunerative labor led to a failure of imagination on the benefits of an education. Ida Fluker acknowledged her father's drive, but felt that he overworked his children. "I never went to school but about two weeks," she recalled. "My papa was hard workin'. Other folks would let their chillun rest but he wouldn't let his chillun rest." "My ambition was to be a teacher, but daddy always kept me busy in the fields," Clarissa Scales added. "Daddy was a good fahmer, and dat's all dat he knowed. He always told me dat it was enough learnin' fo' me if I could jes' read and write. He never even had dat much." Ann Matthews was less sympathetic and ran away because her father would not allow her to attend school. "Said he needed me in de fiel wors den I needed schul." These men ranked immediate gain above future earning potential and self-improvement. Most believed their fathers lacked an understanding of the value of education rather than that they wanted to impede their children. "My father neglected his own education as well as his children," Menellis Gassaway reflected. "He could not read himself. He did not teach any of his children to read, of which we in later years saw the advantage."[56] George Washington Rice, however, believed "Pappy wouldn't let me learn to read and 'rite fer fear I leave home."[57] Resistance to change and the need for control could cloud a man's judgment. Once again, informants expressed a decided preference for a model of masculinity based on caretaking rather than dominance.

Fathers' failure to comprehend the personal and economic benefits of an education caused intergenerational conflict. Irving Lowry's father placed his son in school, but believed "work stood first in importance, and schooling was something to attend when farm work was over." Lowry ran away and found a railroad job. His father "waited patiently till the month was ended," and arrived to collect the minor's wages, the patriarchal prerogative of head of household. Realizing his father would do this every month, Lowry "willingly returned" home. At this point, his father compromised and allowed him to go to school. Booker T. Washington had less success convincing his stepfather, "one of the keenest disappointments that I ever experienced." Because he had been working for wages, "my stepfather had discovered that I had a financial value," and refused to release him from work.[58] Young people eager for knowledge clashed with fathers and stepfathers responsible for ensuring household subsistence.

Educating African American youth in the postwar South had direct costs in the form of reduced family income while they remained in school, and children who benefited from future-oriented parenting felt the need to repay their fathers in some manner. "Having been sent to school all this time by my father . . . I thought it was no more than right that I should do something," George Stephens explained. Stephens worked as a schoolteacher and gave part of his earnings to his father, and "in this way I helped my father to build a house, and sent my sister to the Hampton Normal School." Stephens felt he had made himself "a good and useful man."[59] Stephens used his learning to reward his father's investment, as well as pay it forward by assuming responsibility for his sister's education. His definition of masculinity included assuming a share of his father's paternal duty, and to be useful meant going beyond self-improvement and supporting others.

Caretaking

Caretakers savored the accomplishments of their kin, proudly listing in nineteenth- and twentieth-century autobiographies and interviews their children's skills, professions, and educational attainment. Two of James Smith's daughters graduated from Norwich Free Academy, "qualified themselves for future usefulness," and had become "successful as teachers." His son practiced "the trade of his father." Sterling Brown detailed the lives, education, and careers of his offspring and took "pleasure in the fact that all our six children grew up, were educated and settled at their task as good citizens." After William Towns discussed the career paths of his nine living children he concluded, "I feels sati'fied 'bout my chillun now. Dey seems to be able to make a livin' for they se'ves pretty well."[60] When describing their children, former slaves accentuated the importance of vocation and self-reliance.

African American fathers provided food and labor, but they also imposed discipline designed to keep their children safe and morally upright. "Once when I was a big boy I got drunk and pa whipped me so hard I never got drunk no mo' till I was married," Bob Young admitted. Josephine Bristow's father punished his children to teach them honesty and right from wrong: "Sho meant what he say. Wouldn' never whip you on Sunday though." Nellie Smith's grandfather denied her permission to go to events or places he deemed inappropriate for a "decent" girl. Paternal duty included enforcing strict rules of conduct. "I've tried to advise my chillun an teach 'em the foundation an right principles of livin'," James Polk noted.[61] Fathers considered it their responsibility to provide moral guidance in order to prepare their children for respectable adulthood. The masculine identity associated with honorable fatherhood included an important element of moral rectitude. In the late nineteenth and early twentieth centuries, and especially for the emerging middle class, the defining features of African American masculinity included fatherhood, religion, and resistance.[62] Just as the black preacher led his flock, the black father supported his children and prepared them, often through schooling or training for a trade, to be self-supporting. Fatherhood and religion remained deeply interconnected.[63]

African American fathers' reputation as exacting disciplinarians reflected the unforgiving nature of life in Jim Crow America and the fact that the actions of one individual could be detrimental to the collective good of the family. When Calvin Moye's son had financial trouble that affected his family's ability to eat, Moye paid his son's debt, "to keeps him out of trouble and I tole him right dar dat he had been raised better dan dat." Moye warned his son he would not bail him out again, though he admitted to his interviewer that this was a falsehood, but it was a lie that worked: "He ain't got into any mo' trouble since dat time." George Brown managed to buy property, the goal of many freedmen, but he lost his land when his son needed aid. "I owned one farm, forty-nine acres, but my boy got into trouble and I had to sell it."[64] African Americans had few external avenues of support and relied on their kinship and community networks. A father who placed family above assets risked losing whatever gains he accrued if and when a family member required his assistance. In a world with a narrow to nonexistent margin of error where mistakes could be devastating and few people had the luxury of second chances, ex-slaves remembered their fathers as morally uncompromising men.

Caretaking fathers' advice, and their moral and physical discipline, was aimed at survival. "Daddy always tried to tell us to tend to our own business, and how to go through dis world. He sure did make us behave and he would whoop us if we didn't," Irella Walker recalled. Living in Louisiana, Della Fountain's parents worried about her brother's behavior. "My brother Joe felt mighty big after freedom and strutted about." When her brother "started to git smart" with a white man, "father told him he'd break his neck if he didn't go on home and keep his mouth shet. Father finally had to whup Joe to make him know he was black. He give father and mother lots of concern, for dey was afraid the Ku Kluxers would git him." While black communities prized resistance, fathers made pragmatic decisions about instilling such values, training their children to be mindful of how they presented themselves to the white world. Allen Manning counseled his children to be cautious in their public demeanor: "I always tried to teach my children to be respectful and act like they think the whitefolks they dealing with expects them to act."[65] Fathers taught their children to hide their true feelings when interacting with white people. Like enslaved fathers, freedmen had painful but critical lessons to teach their children about survival in post-Reconstruction America, lessons that could mean the difference between life and death. Slavery had ended, but the agonizing contradictions of parenting while enslaved remained a reality in Jim Crow America.

Fathers advised against overt and risky displays of resistance, but they celebrated emancipation within black communities. Men shared their feelings about and appreciation of freedom with their children. "Daddy said he wus proud o' freedom, but wus afraid to own it. Dey prayed fer freedom secretly," Susan High remarked. "Pappy 'splains it all to me," George Austin said of the meaning of freedom and Juneteenth.[66] Freedom had many meanings, but one of the most significant for committed fathers was the ability to keep their family intact and protect their children. When asked by a white interviewer about whether or not he preferred slavery to the present, Jacob Thomas hedged. He first stated he did not know and then added, "Dar's dis much fer bein' free, I has got thirteen great-gran'chilluns an' I knows whar dey everyone am. In slavery times dey'd have been on de block long time ago." Daniel Lucas also circuitously critiqued slavery by comparing his past to his children's future: "I is thankful they ain't none of my children born slaves and have to remember all them terrible days when we was ruled by the whip—like I remember it, just like it was yesterday."[67] Freedmen were thankful for their own liberty, and thankful that their children would grow up free of the physical brutality of bondage.

As caretakers aged, many reaped the benefits of years of labor and responsibility and lived out their lives in intergenerational households. "It's pretty nice being with my daughter," James Baker told his interviewer. "She's good to me. I loves my granddaughter." "My daughter has taked keer of me ever since I not been able to work no more," Boston Blackwell added.[68] Willis Woodson moved between the homes of his seven children, and "I helps dem all when I stays wid dem." Joe Barnes assisted with childcare: "I live wid one of my gran' chillen. I sorter helps look atter dey chillen. . . . Dat 'un you hear cryin', dat's de baby I's raisin' in dere." George Jackson simply said, "My chillun are my best friends and dey love me."[69] Black communities had a strong sense of reciprocity, and adult children cared for parents who had invested in their upbringing. Sylvia Durant's retelling of her father's childrearing advice summarized this sense of mutuality: "Pa always say dat you couldn' expect no more from a child den you puts in dey raisin. Pa say, 'Sylvia, raise up your chillun in de right way en dey'll smile on you in your old age.'" In black communities, social support emanated from the family. Sam Kilgore, when asked the standard questions about family history, expressed regret that he had no children, despite more than one marriage. "Ise never dat lucky," he reflected.[70]

The lives and concerns of caretakers focused on kin groups, and these men sought to maintain family unity, memory, and a connection to and between ancestors and descendants. Solomon Hicks's father outlived his mother by eight years, and "he requested me to keep the younger children together," an appeal his son honored. Ike Derricotte showed his interviewer his wedding coat and the pen he had used to ask his wife of fifty years to marry him: "I'm keepin' de coat and pen for our chillun."[71] Several informants named their fathers as the keepers of family history who recalled or recorded, usually in a family Bible, the birth dates or ages of their children.[72] Freedpeople kept alive the memory of their departed relatives. Anthony Lacy wanted, in old age, to remain near "whar fadder and mudder die' and be bury." Johnson Thompson's mother died in Texas, and when the family moved following the war, "pappy took us children to the graveyard. We patted her grave and kissed the ground . . . telling her good-bye." One of Cornelia Winfield's treasured possessions was a wardrobe her father built using every plank of wood on which a deceased member of the family had been laid out.[73] Former slaves cherished family history, and engaged fathers played a role in transmitting that history from generation to generation.

Formerly enslaved men who wrote autobiographies at the behest of and/ or for the benefit of their children revealed the centrality of fatherhood in their lives and conception of self. "I dedicate this book to my children and grandchildren," Peter Bruner stated in his 1918 narrative. "I have given the actual experiences of my own life. I thought in putting it in this form it might be of some inspiration to struggling men and women."[74] Paternal duty extended beyond the kin group and encompassed racial uplift. FWP informants realized they could use the interview experience to convey their story to future generations. Martin Jackson, who affectionately referenced his "thirteen children and . . . big crop of grand-children," asked for a written copy of his interview. "Maybe some of my children would like to have it," he explained.[75] Children born in freedom, likewise, often recorded the life story of their fathers as a form of recognition and motivation for others. Sarah Early published a biography of her father in 1894 and invoked the themes of provisioning and compassion prominent in the writings of and interviews with African Americans from the early nineteenth century through the 1930s. Her formerly enslaved father was "always a bountiful provider for his family, always solicitous for their well-being, and careful to supply all of their wants." Reverend Early "was an affectionate father, indulgent to his children, even in their mature years."[76] A good father provided for his family in multiple ways, offering material and emotional support, a lifelong responsibility.

IN AFRICAN AMERICAN FOLKLORE, the steel driver John Henry embodies the multiple masculinities admired in black communities. John Henry was revered for his strength and skill with a hammer, his role as a provider, his sexual virility, and his heroic resistance. According to legend, John Henry won a race against a steam-powered hammer and then died of overexertion. He became arguably the most famous African American cultural hero, with stories widely disseminated as early as the 1880s. The ballad is the most recorded folk song in American history. Among his other masculine attributes, songs present John Henry as a father, provider, and protector and reveal the African American ideal of honorable fatherhood. "Got a wife and child/ Waiting for me at de fire./ If I don't work/ Ain't no way dey can smile." Following his victory, "John Henry told the captain/ Just before he died,/ Only one favor I ask of you:/ Take care of my wife and child/ Take care of my wife and child." John Henry is morally upright, dutiful, and focused on caring for his family. When his wife hears of his death, she cries, "Lord, there is one more good man done fell dead." The tale likely resonated with communities accustomed to the early demise of men who overworked themselves trying to care for kin. Tunnel crews often lived apart from their families, and the John Henry songs also present lonesome men who worried about their distant loved ones.[77]

To celebrate John Henry was to celebrate African American fatherhood and to recognize the burdens under which these men operated as well as the continuing flexibility of the black family. Children and fathers understood that caring for and supporting a family in the Jim Crow landscape meant unremitting toil, and they believed their reward lay in producing self-reliant children. African American communities tended to hide successes, a form of self-preservation in an environment where any black man who publicly accumulated property or masculine prestige became a target for racial violence. Such a life left these men largely invisible, and it is their own commentary and that of their children that illuminates the quietly heroic efforts of African American men as fathers.

Epilogue

Justifications for slavery and actual treatment of slaves regularly diverged as ideology encountered avarice, the market, and the complexity of human interactions. "To succeed both as an economic and social system, New World slavery constantly had to balance and reconcile the contradictory requirement of patriarchy and the market," Robert Olwell argues. "Slavery could not long survive in a social order based entirely upon market relations. Similarly, a perfectly patriarchal slave society would not be economically profitable."[1] Masters envisioned themselves as benevolent patriarchs, but patriarchy coexisted uneasily with market considerations. The contradictory nature of the slave system extended to the practice of masculinity, and many slaveholders willingly undermined the rhetoric of slavery for personal gain. Within the plantation sphere, black men often had limited space to exercise traits of manhood and masculine authority if in doing so they profited or appeared to profit the master. Masculine authority exercised by black men had to be subsumed by the white male patriarch, and masculinity in the slave South took on a public/private dichotomy.

White society defined enslaved men and freedmen in the late nineteenth and early twentieth centuries as less than full men and denied them the ability to publicly perform masculinity. Within the constraints imposed on them, black men paradoxically had flexibility in privately expressing manhood. As a result, African Americans have long had a range of options for masculine identity within their communities, even as black manhood has been externally curbed and regulated. Enslaved men could be men in relation to other slaves so long as they remained subordinate and obedient to white men, and this arrangement enabled some enslaved men to dominate black women and children to compensate for their broader emasculation compared to whites. It also created the space for hidden forms of masculine practice based on supporting kin and community and seeking comfort by bringing comfort to others. Caretaking was and is one critical mode and ideal of masculinity within black communities. Where caretaking has not been recognized is outside African American communities—the media continues to stereotype black men as absent from family, distorting the historical and ongoing diversity of the African American experience.

Although unable to fully access or act on their ideals, slave communities articulated a robust notion of the meaning and central duties of paternity. The institution of slavery divested enslaved men of patriarchal privilege and standing, but slaves invested fatherhood with meaning and importance. Fugitives and former slaves writing in the antebellum period and the late nineteenth and early twentieth centuries, and informants interviewed in the late 1930s, defined a father as a provider and protector. What a man could provide and how he could protect varied based on local conditions and shifted over time. Across different periods, however, children most appreciated an emotionally engaged father who ideologically provisioned. The basic and broad definition of paternal duty remained consistent because enslaved and freedpeople faced similar and ongoing challenges. Based on their understanding of fatherly duty, furthermore, former slaves accused white men of immorality and dishonor, denouncing white men who fathered and then abused or sold their own children, a violation of paternal obligation.

By telling the story of the quiet, unseen, and heroic efforts that enslaved and then freedmen undertook to be fathers, this book offers a counterpoint to the dominant narratives about the pathology of the African American family and the absent black father. Slavery was undoubtedly destructive to family, masculinity, and paternity. Men were more likely to be sold as individuals away from their kin, though all slaves lived with the threat of separation. The institution of slavery placed agonizing constraints on the enslaved husband and father. In this emasculating environment, the easy choice was to abdicate responsibility. Modern studies of PTSD and trauma show the variation in human resilience and vulnerability in the face of stress, and slavery was no different.[2] Not every enslaved man attempted to act as a father. Many more tried to care for their children, despite the barriers erected by the system, and failed or only partially succeeded. What is notable, given the constraints they faced, is how many former slaves commented on the positive impact their father made on their lives and sense of self.

In the 1830s, a slaveholder offering advice on proper plantation management argued that "a perfect understanding between a master and a slave is that the slave should know that his master is to govern absolutely, and he is to obey implicitly. That he is never for a moment to exercise his will or judgment in opposition to a positive order." The master was "guardian and protector of his slaves," and they in turn were to demonstrate "unconditional submission."[3] Slaves labored for the master, physically producing and embodying wealth, but were never supposed to think or act independently.

Individualism, one hallmark of American culture and politics, belonged solely to white people. Jordan Peele's brilliant 2017 horror film *Get Out*, with rich white people appropriating black bodies and shunting black consciousness to the "sunken place," draws on and illuminates this ongoing history.

For white Southerners, the ability to think freely most unambiguously defined manhood, and mental dependence justified enslavement. "The African negro is physically a man, mentally a child—treat him as such," a Georgia planter advised in 1860. In his 1935 history of Reconstruction, W. E. B. Du Bois quoted a Louisianan who observed that in the post–Civil War period, Southern whites were "more hostile to the establishment of schools" for former slaves than they were to the idea of African Americans "owning lands."[4] This comment fits into a long history of actual and assumed ownership of black bodies and white fears of sovereign black minds. As white Southerners grappled with the aftermath of emancipation and moved to keep African Americans socially, legally, and economically shackled, a black man working his own land was preferable to a man who reasoned for himself.

After emancipation, legal, economic, and social discrimination and racial violence continued to impede the ability of men to fulfill paternal duty to provide for and protect family. "Son, we never would get out of debt and could not tell much difference in freedom from slavery time," John Mosely remarked. "Our wages was terribly low, that is when we got pay, as lots of them beat us all together out of what little we did make," Charlie Sandles added. "The negro has had a hell of a hard time getting to where he is now because everything has been against the negro."[5] Emancipation enabled men to reconstitute their families and attempt to negotiate the terms of their own labor, but full freedom and justice remained elusive. The postwar racial climate, and the strict enforcement of a racial and masculine hierarchy, continued to undermine normative visions of fatherhood.

If burdens persisted, so too did the critique of immoral, predatory white manhood. "The Ku Klux and the Paddyrollers was all around and doing meanness," Lu Lee told her interviewer. "They were just as ornery and mean as the policemen are now. They never did nothing that amounted to nothing in they life so they think they is smart big mens when ten of them jump on pore nigger and beat the life out of him."[6] Lee's commentary included a critique of postwar class politics, disparaging the poor white men who colluded with elites to bolster white supremacy. Poor whites were willing to forego potential class solidarity and the opportunity to make economic gains in favor of a rigid racial hierarchy. The elite accorded working-class men and women access to "whiteness" in return for their needed assistance in keeping African Americans subjugated.[7] Lu Lee realized that violence emasculated black men, but she defined a succession of white enforcers of the racial order as the ones truly lacking masculinity. Black communities retained a sharp distinction between those who had power and those who had honor.

Each time the police shoot an unarmed black man, we face the ongoing and often fatal repercussions of stereotypes rooted in slavery and Jim Crow and the monolithic image of black men as criminal and the black family as pathological.[8] Police officers facing an African American man see only a looming threat and not a brother, son, husband, or father, a man embedded in a family and community. Reports rationalize and explain deadly encounters by noting that officers felt endangered, or they mistook some other object for a weapon, because a weapon is expected. In encounters with the police, black men are hypermasculinized, but at other times, and in relation to social and economic roles, they are emasculated. According to the contemporary media narrative, white men are men when it comes to authority and power and they are boys when such a description exonerates their bad behavior or mistakes. Black men are boys when it comes to authority and power and men when such a definition incriminates them and exonerates others. During slavery, in its aftermath, and continuing today, black men are men only when it suits the needs of the white power structure. In addition, they are only allowed to be men in restricted ways—as a stock representation and threatening figure. They are not allowed to be men of positive action. Black men are not supposed to fight back, and to do so, or be accused of doing so, is to invite and justify retaliatory and lethal force.

The dominant image of black men portrays them as individuals only loosely connected to a kinship or social network and devoid of job, career, profession, or vocation. On one end of the age spectrum, a twelve-year-old like Tamir Rice is seen as a dangerous thug and not as a child and a student. On the other end of the age spectrum, an adult like Terence Crutcher is seen as a dangerous thug and not as a father. The image infuses our culture, and influences policing and police responses to situations involving black men.[9] The image denies the young their childhood by labeling them grown men, and yet they are never allowed to mature into fathers or productive members of society. Older men are never presented first or foremost as fathers and providers, which is a further denial of their full manhood. Black men are compressed into a single, static group—they are seen as lone individuals (though lacking individuality) peripheral to family, a vision based on our society's definition of the black family as a matriarchy, and the black father as ineffectual and missing. If connected to a group, black men are defined as gang members. This image does a disservice to and fails to account for a past and present range of personal experience and family structures in black communities.

In the case of a perpetrator of public gun violence, the narrative is reversed. A study of media coverage of 219 mass shootings between 2013 and 2015 shows that white shooters are often portrayed as mentally ill and as victims of unfortunate circumstances beyond their control, a sympathetic rendering that deflects blame. A black perpetrator of gun violence, meanwhile, is usually presented as an inherently violent "thug." While a white man who performs public violence that violates the social contract is seen as a troubled individual, a black man who performs public violence represents his community and race.[10]

Penning a powerful letter to his son in the wake of recent police shootings, Ta-Nehisi Coates defines modern police brutality against African Americans as a "heritage and legacy" of slavery. His missive shows how black men continue to modify their behavior due to the threat of white violence, how that pervasive apprehension is as much or more about kin as it is about self, and how it influences parenting. "I feel the fear most acutely whenever you leave me," Coates writes, invoking the mingled love and dread of previous generations. "I saw it in my own father, who loves you, who counsels you, who slipped me money to care for you. My father was so very afraid. I felt in the sting of his black leather belt, which he applied more with anxiety than anger." Attitudes and stereotypes inherited from slavery, including a persistent vision of manhood and the masculine hierarchy, have real world, destructive outcomes. Such stereotypes directly affect how American society handles masculinity and treats certain men. "You are a black boy," Coates tells his son, "and you must be responsible for your body in a way that other boys cannot know. Indeed, you must be responsible for the worst actions of other black bodies, which, somehow, will always be assigned to you."[11]

Racial categories are tied to Americans' ideas about class and social mobility. Media narratives tend to assign to black men, more so than white men, self-inflicted states of poverty, and failure of mobility teeters on the slippery slope of race rather than structural factors. In her 2015 book, *Blaming the Poor*, Susan Greenbaum picks apart the Moynihan Report, highlighting the defective data and reasoning and showing how Moynihan's misguided ideas have been used to fault and punish the poor for their own situation, enabling Americans to avoid confronting the deeper problems caused by systemic racism. The report and its ideas continue to negatively impact policy decisions, fueling mass incarceration and the criminalization of African American youth. Greenbaum stresses how Moynihan's ideas have and continue to entrench stereotypes of African Americans. These attitudes then justify indifference and hostility to the poor and policies that exacerbate rather than alleviate poverty.[12] Damaging stereotypes of masculinity, inherited from slavery and reinforced by the Moynihan Report, continue to undermine black men and African American communities.

In a study of contemporary nonresident African American fathers, Jennifer Hamer discusses the history and current social standards that contribute to an enduring and false image of black fathers as uninvolved. In part, Americans define a good father as a resident father. Despite a negative perception of live-away black fathers, she argues that many take their role and responsibilities seriously. The tenacious image of the black family as matriarchal, moreover, obscures the practice and experience of fatherhood in black communities. Lora Bex Lempert writes that due to "inattention to the significant roles of African American men in their families and communities, the complex contributions of men in African American families have been effaced." A range of socioeconomic factors impinge on the black family, including drug addiction, homicide, disproportionate incarceration, excess mortality from chronic disease, neglect, and abuse, and Lempert explores how "other fathers," including grandfathers and other relatives, men who remain involved in their family from the confines of prison, and community members, all contribute to child rearing.[13] Just as the institution of slavery regularly separated men from their families, structural impediments, including the criminal justice system, continue to fracture the black family. High rates of incarceration inflict a modern form of family separation, and as during slavery, black communities adapt. Left out of the narrative entirely are significant segments of African American communities—two-parent households in various forms (including two fathers), resident fathers, and single fathers.

The nation has made significant progress in race relations, but old attitudes persist. Although black men can now openly perform masculinity, they still face restrictions in white spaces. Many white Americans react to public displays of African American masculine expression with fear and animosity. White America remains particularly uncomfortable with overt and unregulated black action, and individuals who push against these implicit boundaries incur a backlash. The response to NFL players kneeling during the national anthem in 2016 to protest police violence exemplifies this unease, especially when masculine provisioning involves ideas, an arena that is difficult to control. Players can labor for the coach, the owner, the fans, and team, making money for themselves in the process, but revealing independent thought is beyond the pale. Alt-right trolls who tried to tank the Rotten Tomatoes scores of the 2018 action film *Black Panther* ahead of its release similarly saw the movie as an ideological transgression of the racial hierarchy. Both cases show that it is still better that black people own land than that they envision and demand a better future. For those who equate citizenship with whiteness, demonstrations of autonomous black citizenship must be contained and subordinated to white citizenship.

The favorite new insult of the alt-right and white nationalists is to call a white man a "cuck," a reference to a cuckold and sometimes short for a sellout cuckservative. In the view of the alt-right there is no man weaker or more demeaned than one whose wife cheats on him with a black man.[14] The term speaks to white male insecurity, fear of black men (and women), and the desire to reestablish and solidify control over African Americans and women in the post-Obama world. It also reveals white men's resentment that they no longer have a guarantee of masculine superiority and can no longer violate black bodies with absolute impunity. For a significant subset of white Americans, sense of self is predicated on being at the apex of a racial and gender hierarchy. Challenges to that hierarchy are perceived as challenges to their status and way of life. Black Lives Matter is especially threatening because police are the group that can still perpetrate deadly violence on black bodies without fear of negative repercussions. As a result, and even if they do not fully realize it (and some clearly do), for many white Americans, the police and the criminal justice system form a critical bulwark against the further erosion of white supremacy.

The election of Barack Obama in 2008 precipitated the resurgence of white supremacist activity. Obama's political rise depended in part on a denial of his blackness. "To understand Obama, analysts needed to give him a superpower that explained how this self-described black man escaped his assigned corner," Ta-Nehisi Coates writes. "That power was his mixed ancestry." The repudiation, however, could not entirely elide the fact of Obama's presidency and eight years of the public performance of black masculinity. Coates compares the rise of President Donald Trump to the nation's retreat from the promise of emancipation and the collapse of Reconstruction in 1876, arguing that the nation had once before achieved a "transracial spirit," and once before "promptly retrenched in the worst part of itself. To see this connection, to see Obama's election as part of a familiar cycle, you would have had to understand how central the brand of white supremacy was to the country." The age-old custom of white Americans viewing their rights as inversely proportional to the status of African Americans endures. Trump's obsession with undoing every part of the Obama legacy no matter how small, and regardless of the consequences, is a manifestation of white masculinity endeavoring to push black masculinity back into a subservient place.[15]

Notes

Abbreviations

AS   George P. Rawick, ed. *The American Slave: A Composite Autobiography: Supplement, Series 1 and Series 2*. Westport, CT: Greenwood, 1977, 1979.

SNC   Slave Narrative Collection, *Born in Slavery: Slave Narratives from the Federal Writers' Project, 1936–1938*. Federal Writers' Project, Library of Congress, Manuscript Division, National Digital Library Program, Vols. 1–17.

Introduction

1. See Jean Fagan Yellin's biography of Harriet Jacobs for further information on Elijah, who was born on the plantation of Dr. Andrew Knox and likely the son of an enslaved woman, Athena, and a neighboring nonslaveholding white farmer, Henry Jacobs. Jacobs, *Incidents*, 17; Yellin, *Harriet Jacobs*, 7, 14.

2. Baptist, "The Absent Subject," 137. On race and masculinity, see Nelson, *National Manhood*; McCurry, *Masters of Small Worlds*; Roediger, *Wages of Whiteness*; Baptist, "'Cuffy,' 'Fancy Maids,' and 'One-Eyed Men.'"

3. Johnson, *Soul by Soul*, 93, 102.

4. Countering scholars who claim that it made economic sense for slaveholders to amply provide, Wilma Dunaway argues that Mountain South masters had an incentive to inadequately feed and clothe their slaves, leading to higher levels of malnutrition and mortality than in the Lower South. Dunaway, *African-American Family*, 86–97, 100–113, 273, 282; Fogel and Engerman, *Time on the Cross*, 5, 109–126.

5. See Brenda Stevenson's discussion of dysfunctional white families in Loudoun County, Virginia. Stevenson, *Life in Black and White*, 108.

6. Despite proslavery rhetoric that claimed masters only sold slaves under duress, Michael Tadman shows that "the great majority of sales to the trader were not involuntary or reluctant." Planters sold for profit and not just due to death or debt. Slaveholders could break up families and "still see themselves as paternalists—since they could deceive and flatter themselves with the view that only they, the whites, really worried about black families." Tadman, *Speculators and Slaves*, 117, 217, 113, 111; Schermerhorn, *Money over Mastery, Family over Freedom*, 4; Baptist, "'Cuffy,' 'Fancy Maids,' and 'One-Eyed Men,'" 1636; Johnson, *Soul by Soul*, 107–108, 111; Dusinberre, *Them Dark Days*, 107. On white attitudes towards separation of enslaved families, see Williams, *Help Me to Find My People*, 90–116.

7. Moynihan, "The Negro Family," 47, 16. On the "fatherless matrifocal" family, the report quoted Thomas F. Pettigrew. The critique of African American family life as pathological has never accounted for contemporary sociological and ethnographic evidence showing that black fathers spend more time with their children than do white fathers. In 2014, a Centers for Disease Control study found that 70 percent of black men surveyed reported bathing, diapering, dressing, or helping their children use the toilet on a daily basis, as compared to 60 percent of white fathers. Jones and Mosher, "Fathers' Involvement with Their Children."

8. In his discussion of antebellum evangelical religion and violence, Jeff Forret notes that white church leaders "imposed strict limitations upon the performance of black masculinity," and "carefully guarded against individual bondmen from becoming too religiously powerful." Forret, *Slave against Slave*, 319, 323.

9. Du Bois also commented on the absent mother, arguing she was frequently a concubine of the master or overseer. E. Franklin Frazier's earlier work defined the slave family as matrilocal but also discussed the slave father as a provider. He later emphasized the fundamental weakness of the family. Daniel Geary argues that Frazier focused on adaptation and the "heterogeneity of black family modes based on time, place, and social class." Geary contends that Moynihan misused Frazier's work: "Since Moynihan's lacked Frazier's attentiveness to heterogeneity, he could more easily be read as saying that 'disorganized' Negro families were *the* Negro family." Stampp, *Peculiar Institution*, 344; Du Bois, ed., *Negro American Family*, 49, 21; Moynihan, "The Negro Family: The Case for National Action"; Frazier, "The Negro Slave Family," 198–259; Frazier, *The Negro Family*; Geary, *Beyond Civil Rights*, 60; Spillers, "Mama's Baby, Papa's Maybe," 74.

10. West, *Chains of Love*, 109. Herbert Gutman argued that "slave behavior and slave belief were not always congruent." John Blassingame added, "While the slave father could rarely protect the members of his family from abuse, he could often gain their love and respect in other ways." Gutman, *Black Family*, 31; Blassingame, *Slave Community*, 191; White, *Ar'n't I a Woman?*, 120.

11. Whereas for Herbert Gutman slave families "derived their inner strength from a cumulative slave experience with its own standards and rules of conduct," Genovese argued that masters favored a stable slave family to further their own social control. Robert Fogel and Stanley Engerman focused not on internal agency, but on the capitalistic decisions of slaveholders to reach comparable conclusions, arguing that masters had an interest in promoting stable slave families. Genovese, *In Red & Black*, 113, 112, 114; Gutman, *Black Family*, xxii–xxiii, 261; Fogel and Engerman, *Time on the Cross*, 127–128.

12. Gutman explored a range of "adaptive slave practices." He argued that most children grew up in two-parent households, but noted that, "*all* slave marriages were insecure," and thus "cannot be characterized as stable." Gutman, *Black Family*, xxii, 153; Jones, *Labor of Love*, 32; Berlin and Rowland, *Families and Freedom*, 7–9; Fogel's more recent work posits that two-thirds of all slaves resided in two-parent households. Fogel, *Without Consent*, 69, 142–150, 178–182.

13. On the 1970s tendency to overstate slave agency, see Kolchin, *American Slavery*, 137–138; Stevenson, *Life in Black and White*. In his study of the origins and reactions to the report, Daniel Geary argues that "Moynihan's analysis of matriarchy, largely shared by liberal intellectuals and civil rights leaders, asserted that black women emasculated black men." Geary, *Beyond Civil Rights*, 68.

14. West, *Chains of Love*; Berry, *Swing the Sickle*.

15. "The myth of the stable nuclear slave family was derived from analysis of conditions that are representative of only a small minority of U.S. slaves," Dunaway writes (272). She defines a small plantation as having nineteen or fewer slaves. Dunaway, *African-American Family*, 1, 2, 3, 14, 54, 270, 271. According to Stephen Crawford, plantation size most significantly affected slaves' quality of life, with a higher incidence of female-headed households, more exacting punishment, higher levels of malnutrition, and increased fertility in the case of smallholdings. Crawford, "Quantified Memory"; Steckel, "Peculiar Population," 738–739. Ann Malone also challenges the literature on the stable, nuclear family, arguing that historians "analyzed only the composition of simple families rather than that of the entire community." Malone, *Sweet Chariot*, 254. While Gutman argued for a preponderance of two-parent households, his own data shows regional variation. Gutman, *Black Family*, 129, 45, 58, 131, 132, 135. West finds 34 percent of slaves mentioned abroad marriages in her South Carolina sample and argues that Crawford and Malone undercount abroad marriages and thus overemphasize female-headed households. West, *Chains of Love*, 44, 48, 49.

16. Pargas concludes that "a typical American slave family surely did not exist" (205). In Fairfax County, Virginia, soil exhaustion led to a shift from tobacco to grain production and slaveholding size decreased and workload increased. Between 1810 and 1860, the slave population declined by 47 percent, leading to a high rate of family division. In the affluent rice-producing area of Georgetown District, South Carolina, nearly half of the enslaved population lived on plantations with over a hundred slaves. The task system led to a relatively stable family life. The

quality of family life in St. James Parish, Louisiana, a developing sugar region, fell in between. An imbalance in the sex ratio left as many as a third of all men unable to find suitable mates. Risk of family division also varied regionally. Virginia had the highest rates of family disruption, South Carolina the lowest, and St. James Parish fell in the middle. Pargas, *Quarters and the Fields*, 204, 4, 15, 45, 72, 118, 119, 123, 140, 161, 183, 191; Malone, *Sweet Chariot*, 18. JoAnn Manfra and Robert Dykstra find that 35.3 percent of broken slave marriages in Dinwiddie County, Virginia, were ended by force. Manfra and Dykstra, "Serial Marriage and the Origins of the Black Stepfamily"; Stevenson, "Distress and Discord," 105.

17. In her comparison of Georgia's Wilkes and Glynn counties, Daina Berry shows a greater number of abroad marriages in the Upcountry due to smaller holdings, and more stable families on the large holdings of the Lowcountry. Different crops (rice and cotton) and labor organization (gang labor and task labor) affected family structure, involvement in an informal economy, rates of hiring, and family separation. Lowcountry slaves were more likely to be sold in groups, whereas Upcountry slaves were more likely to be sold as individuals, leading to higher rates of family division. In his study of three regions in South Carolina, the Low-, Middle-, and Upcountry, Larry Hudson Jr. also shows that rates of abroad marriage varied based on plantation size, as well as demographic and material conditions. Plantation size and labor regime affected access to economic opportunity, and family economic activity influenced family structure and stability. Berry, *Swing the Sickle*, 54, 88–100, 106, 108–109, 112, 125, 128; Hudson, *To Have and to Hold*, 142–143, 179–180.

18. The experience of enslaved people varied not simply due to region and crop, but based on the conditions imposed by particular owners. Berry, *Swing the Sickle*, 71, 72; Hudson, *To Have and to Hold*, 142–147; Dusinberre, *Them Dark Days*, 414.

19. West, *Chains of Love*, 5; Malone, *Sweet Chariot*, 5, 252, 258. While scholars generally agree that the ideal was a two-parent household, Stevenson sees the extended family as the "norm," and ideal. Stevenson, *Life in Black and White*, 325, 160.

20. Referring to the neighborhood by the fictitious name, "The Flats," Stack writes, "a resident in The Flats who eats in one household may sleep in another, and contribute resources to yet another. He may consider himself a member of all three households." She highlights the problematic nature of government statistics used in the Moynihan Report, arguing that many of the households defined as single mother were in fact multigenerational, contained father figures, and engaged in communal child rearing. She discusses the "elasticity of residence patterns" and the "structural adaptations of poverty." Stack, *All Our Kin*, 31, 71, 126. In her book about contemporary African American "live-away" fathers, Jennifer Hamer explores the long history of negative images and how standards of the ideal father as coresident continue to impact the black community and inaccurately portray black men as uninvolved parents. Hamer, *What It Means to Be Daddy*, 31, 20, 24–26.

21. Townsend refers to the focus on residential household structure as "narrow and distorting," pointing out that in Botswana, men generally establish households late in life, and "paternity and marriage precede coresidence with wife and children." He also discusses both biological and "social" fathers. Townsend, "Men, Migration, and Households in Botswana," 405, 420, 406, 407, 417, 413. Anthropologists have long referred to the matrilineal Mosuo of Southwest China as the sole human society without husbands and fathers. Based on two years of fieldwork, Mattison et al. recently showed that the Mosuo do in fact recognize fatherhood, measuring paternal efforts in coresidential households in terms of "direct care and monetary investment in their children." Children live in the mother's household. A man visits his partner's home at night, returning to his mother's household in the morning. This voluntary engagement leads to augmented resources and positive outcomes for children. Such residential patterns parallel cross-plantation marriages in slavery, though Mosuo men do not require passes and can visit each night. This work reinforces Townsend's study and shows that a narrow focus on residential household will miss the depth and complexity of family life and fathers' investment in their children. Mattison et al., "Paternal Investment and the Positive Effects of Fathers among the Matrilineal Mosuo," 591–610. In a 1981 review article of studies in Africa,

Jane Guyer similarly notes the "serious criticisms of the use of classificatory terms like 'patrilin-eal,' 'matrilineal,' . . . as too static and simplistic." Guyer argues that "a household approach can hide relationships between domestic groups," and the concepts of lineage and household both "share the problem of implying a single explanatory context." Guyer, "Household and Community in African Studies," 88, 101, 104, 121.

22. Agresti, "Household Composition," 257.

23. The analysis of Arditti et al. counters the myth of migrant fathers as missing. Men send remittances to and stay involved with their children through weekly calls. The migrant family is flexible and family members accord these men respect and recognize their willingness to make sacrifices in order to provide economic support. Arditti et al., "Fathers in the Fields: Father Involvement among Latino Migrant Farmworkers," 537–557; Coltrane et al., "Complexity of Father Involvement in Low-Income Mexican American Families," 179–189.

24. Marsiglio et al., eds., *Situated Fathering*, xi–xiv; Lamb, "The History of Research on Father Involvement," 23–42; Doherty et al., "Responsible Fathering," 277–292.

25. "Researchers into past family life should be careful not to mistake variable situation-related patterns of household composition with more stable, normative ones," Barbara Agresti writes. Agresti, "Household Composition," 257. Scholars also tend to approach the family as neolocal, meaning that when a couple marries they form a new and distinct household, and that is not the rule across space and time, even in Northwestern Europe. Stem households, where one son marries and remains with his parents, eventually inheriting the property, enable families to keep landed property intact. This means that households shift and spend some frac-tion of time as extended family household structures. Hammel and Wachter, "Primonuptiality and Ultimonuptiality," 113–134.

26. Tadman, *Speculators and Slaves*, 153; Johnson, *Soul by Soul*, 17, 7, 187, 215.

27. Stevenson, *Life in Black and White*, 222, xii, 251, 256. In her article, "Distress and Discord in Virginia Slave Families, 1830–1860," fathers have slightly more stature. Because they were denied authority and the role of provider, Stevenson argues "while slave fathers had a signifi-cant presence in the consciousness of their children, mothers obviously were much more phys-ically and psychologically present in the children's lives" (108). Conditions did limit paternal contact, but Stevenson conflates matrifocal household structure and degree of daily contact with family function and the emotional content of relationships. Economic conditions in Virginia led to a preponderance of smallholdings, but there may also have been African cultural retentions that favored a female-centered family. Michael Gomez argues that due to regional ethnic concentrations, many Akan speakers, people generally from matrilineal societies, ended up in Virginia and Maryland. Gomez, *Exchanging Our Country Marks*, 105, 107, 110.

28. Multilocality is a concept applied to modern families, including in cases of divorce or commuter marriages. Wood et al., "A Residential Perspective on Multi-Locality."

29. For a discussion of exogamy among slaves, see Gutman, *Black Family*, 88–94. Dylan Penning-roth refers to cross-plantation arrangements as "split-residence households." Penningroth, *The Claims of Kinfolk*, 105.

30. When constrained by the demographic conditions of the area and/or specific plantation, enslaved people attempted to marry as close by as possible, preferably on a neighboring farm. Even in regions with conditions favorable to the formation of two-parent households, the age and sex ratios of specific plantations varied. Pargas, *Quarters and the Fields*, 117, 143–144, 152–154, 156–157, 159, 163–164, 168, 170; West, *Chains of Love*, 11, 45. Stevenson argues that hold-ing size was not the main determinant of abroad marriages in Loudoun County, Virginia, where plantations of all sizes tended to have skewed sex ratios. Small farms skewed female, whereas mid- to large-sized farms skewed male. Even though the sex ratio in the county as a whole was close to even, the conditions on each plantation led to high rates of abroad marriage. Stevenson, *Life in Black and White*, 208, 215, 219.

31. Slaveholders could and did revoke visitation rights. Despite these marriages being "dou-bly precarious," Larry Hudson Jr. argues that family was so important that enslaved people took the risk if they had limited options. Hudson, *To Have and to Hold*, 176.

32. Blassingame, *Slave Community*, 164. Abroad marriages facilitated men's mobility and left women tied to the plantation, a drawback when it came to escape. Berry, *Swing the Sickle*, 59; White, *Ar'n't I a Woman?*, 76.

33. Dunaway, *African-American Family*, 285; Pargas, *Quarters and the Fields*, 92. Stevenson argues that enslaved people often chose these unions for a variety of reasons including exogamy, a desire to expand their social connections, the need to distance themselves from abuse of kin, and a retention of African cultural patterns. Men gained mobility, an important aspect of manhood, and women gained "greater domestic power." Stevenson, *Life in Black and White*, 231, 230, 232. Whereas Stevenson sees some female-headed households as a choice, West sees female-headed households as broken households. West, *Chains of Love*, 56.

34. I agree with West that slaves usually entered such unions out of "practical necessity," but some chose abroad marriages (11). West, *Chains of Love*, 44, 45, 49, 50, 59. When faced with local hiring, slaves were most concerned about maintaining family connections and securing the right to visit kin. Martin, *Divided Mastery*, 46, 52.

35. Modern commuter marriages in which partners maintain two residences can similarly function and be perceived by the children as two-parent families. In addition to dual-career commuter couples, there are different forms of LAT (living apart together) partnerships. These forms of multilocational family living are most often the result of labor market constraints, but some couples with shorter commutes choose to maintain separate residences. Such arrangements, regardless of causation, appear in statistics as one-parent or one-person households. There are also modern two-parent families where a job requires travel or long absences, including military deployment, commercial fishing, and long-haul trucking. All of these living arrangements can create stress and reduce children's time with a parent, but they also underscore the need to look beyond full-time household residence when evaluating family life. Reuschke, "Living Apart Together over Long Distances"; Forsyth, "Socio-Economic Factors Affecting the Rise of Commuter Marriage"; Zvonkovic, "Family Work and Relationships."

36. Christie Farnham sees the female-headed slave family as a response to the constraints of slavery as well as a "redefinition of certain West African cultural forms" that emphasized the lineage and kin group rather than a conjugal pair. Claire Robertson argues that matriarchal and matrifocal family structures were not among the African cultural continuities in the New World, but emerged from poverty. According to Robertson, "matrifocality characterizes contemporary African-American families more than it did slave ones." Farnham, "Sapphire?," 83, 69–72, 81; Robertson, "Africa into the Americas?," 20; Stevenson, *Life in Black and White*, 222–223, 326. In Georgia, Berry finds that because slaveholders assigned cabins and distributed rations and garden plots to women, slave families "developed matrifocally," and yet "fathers found ways to raise their children." Berry, *Swing the Sickle*, 73. Ann Malone identifies a tendency towards matrilocality in antebellum Louisiana, but sees the slave family as coming closer to equality rather than being matriarchal or patriarchal. Malone, *Sweet Chariot*, 258–259. Suzanne Lebsock finds that over half of free black families in antebellum Petersburg, Virginia, were headed by women, a situation she sees as an adaptive response to the oppressive legal and social environment. Single women retained control of their property, whereas married women did not. Lebsock, *Free Women of Petersburg*, 90. Michael Johnson and James Roark disagree, arguing that many of these women were probably married to enslaved men and could not afford to buy their freedom, meaning that rather than rejecting legal marriage, they could not achieve it. Johnson and Roark, "Strategies of Survival," 92.

37. Calvin Schermerhorn calls the enslaved family "simultaneously exceptionally strong and incredibly vulnerable." Schermerhorn, *Money over Mastery, Family over Freedom*, 206. Ann Malone describes the "mutability and yet constancy of Louisiana slave household organization," and calls the slave family "far more diverse and adaptable than previously believed." Malone, *Sweet Chariot*, 5. While I disagree with her treatment of fathers, I agree with Stevenson's broad conclusions on the family as "a diverse phenomenon, sometimes assuming several forms even among the slaves of one community" and the fact that this diversity was "a measure of the slave family's enormous adaptive potential," and a key to its survival. Marie Schwartz

calls the slave family "a flexible institution." Stevenson, *Life in Black and White*, 324–325; Schwartz, *Born in Bondage*, 208, 46; Blassingame, *Slave Community*, 151.

38. Malone, *Sweet Chariot*, 7–8, 18; Berry, *Swing the Sickle*, 70. "Matrifocality, polygamy, single parents, abroad spouses, one-, two-, and three-generation households, all-male domestic residences of blood, marriage, and fictive kin, single- and mixed-gender sibling dwellings — these along with monogamous marriages and coresidential nuclear families, all comprised the familial experiences of Virginia slaves," Stevenson writes in *Life in Black and White*, 160–161.

39. "Building a flexible family structure was a secondary strategy, and most enslaved people lived with a mix of distant and close relatives along with nonblood relations such as adopted children," Schermerhorn continues. Penningroth, *The Claims of Kinfolk*, 89, 90, 108; Schermerhorn, *Money over Mastery, Family over Freedom*, 91. Wayne Durrill, examining Somerset Place Plantation in Washington County, North Carolina, finds a range of household structures, "nuclear, stem, extended." Durrill, "Slavery, Kinship, and Dominance," 15–16.

40. Michael Tadman discusses "lifetime and regional cycles of separation" in which the risk of forcible family separation varied by place and life stage. In the Upper South, couples faced a high chance that their first marriage would be broken up, that risk decreased as they aged, and then they faced the "the increasing chance that their growing children would be sold away from them." As children aged, their chances of being separated from their parents increased. Ann Malone refers to a "pattern of destruction, reconstruction, and dispersal," as the family reacted to external pressures. Tadman, *Speculators and Slaves*, 173, 46, 169, 171; Malone, *Sweet Chariot*, 114, 17, 48, 68; Dunaway, *African-American Family*, 272. Loss was not just due to sale. In his study of three rice-growing plantations in South Carolina and Georgia, William Dusinberre notes of Gowrie plantation, "child mortality devastated these families, so that the most common nuclear grouping was a husband and wife with *no* surviving children." Dusinberre, *Them Dark Days*, 84.

41. "Whether we are hunting for two-parent families, female-headed, nuclear, or otherwise, our very hunger to find structure in nineteenth-century black families tends to obscure some of what is most fascinating about them: their ability — even eagerness — to change as they pursued their interests," Penningroth writes. Penningroth, *The Claims of Kinfolk*, 190. Gutman used plantation records to show that the slave family must be studied over a long period and not just a particular moment in time. Gutman, *Black Family*, 96–97.

42. When forced to return to the plantation near Edenton, North Carolina, Elijah was separated from his older children as well as from his new, free wife, Theresa, and their baby son, Elijah. Yellin, *Harriet Jacobs*, 7, 11, 14, 18.

43. The two men who take care of her are her brother John Jacobs, and her Uncle Mark, identified in the narrative as Philip. "Slave narratives, in addition to their more obvious function as protest narratives, often serve as memorials for lost lives and loves" (112), Fleischner writes. Fleischner, *Mastering Slavery*, 64, 6, 91, 92, 113.

44. Whereas scholars initially rebutted the Moynihan Report by presenting the slave family as patriarchal, more recently historians have come to differing and often-opposing conclusions. According to Jacqueline Jones, slave marriages functioned on "reciprocal obligations," and "women and men worked together to support the father's role as provider and protector." Jones comes down on the side of equality, but argues that slaves' lack of power "rendered virtually meaningless the concept of equality as it applies to marital relations." Deborah Gray White and Emily West note a gendered division of labor and yet both consider the slave family highly egalitarian. West stresses "a profound sense of solidarity between enslaved partners." Jones, "'My Mother Was Much of a Woman,'" 258, 253, 258; Jones, *Labor of Love*, 42, 36; White, *Ar'n't I a Woman?*, 158; West, *Chains of Love*, 11, 70, 91, 101; Cashin, "Black Families in the Old Northwest," 455. In response to those who suggest equity, Darlene Clark Hine calls the sexual division of labor "decidedly unequal." Hine, "Lifting the Veil," 225; Dunaway, *African-American Family*, 163–166.

45. As Darlene Clark Hine notes, "the black woman bore primary responsibility for reproducing the slave labor force and for ensuring the continuation of the black race during and after

the demise of slavery." Hine, "Lifting the Veil," 224; White, *Ar'n't I a Woman?*, 159; Camp, *Closer to Freedom*, 37.

46. Wilma King also considers men and women as parents. Schwartz, *Born in Bondage*, 53; King, *Stolen Childhood*. Elsewhere, however, she writes, "abroad marriage, work schedules, and other separations generally precluded the presence of slave fathers." King, "Suffer with Them Till Death," 149. In her book on contemporary "live-away" black fathers, Jennifer Hamer discusses the history of nonresident fathers and concludes, "throughout American history, black men attempted to parent their children." Hamer, *What It Means to Be Daddy*, 51.

47. Johnson, *Soul by Soul*; Gross, *Double Character*.

48. White, *Ar'n't I a Woman?*, 110; Jones, *Labor of Love*, 12, 14, 35.

49. "Despite their travails, many enslaved parents demonstrated an unfailing love for their offspring and socialized them to endure slavery by paying deference to whites while maintaining self-respect," King writes. She calls this "a major act of resistance" that "equipped children to defend themselves on the psychological battlefield." King, *Stolen Childhood*, 94, 67–68; Schwartz, *Born in Bondage*, 47.

50. Proslavery literature presented black family attachments as transitory and easily replaced. Proslavery writers also insisted that family separations rarely occurred and when they did, slaves did not feel the loss deeply. Slaves' enduring attachments were to the slaveholding family. Frederickson, *The Black Image in the White Mind*, 56–66; Tadman, *Speculators and Slaves*, 212–216. "Despite the self-serving proclamations of proslavery propagandists, many enslavers expected and relied on enslaved men to play important roles in domestic economies, often with assumptions about masculinity in mind," David Doddington writes. Doddington, *Contesting Slave Masculinity*, 100; Genovese, *Roll*, 489.

51. Friend, "From Southern Manhood to Southern Masculinities," x. Following the early nineteenth-century expansion of white male suffrage and the democratization of honor, all white men were defined as citizens. Ariela Gross shows that when marginalized groups used the legal system to claim whiteness and thus citizenship, in ensuing racial identity trials "judges gave special weight to the civic performance of white manhood." Whiteness was equated with citizenship and a public performance of "civic acts and displays of moral and social character," that defined the racial and social hierarchy, a concept that outlived the demise of slavery. "The connection between racial identity and fitness for citizenship," Gross writes, "remains potent today in discussions about culture, affirmative action, and 'the end of racism.'" Gross, *What Blood Won't Tell*, 49, 296, 297.

52. As Rebecca Fraser notes, enslaved men did perform their masculine identities within their own social world. For enslaved men in the Upper South, eluding slave patrols contained an element of "performing their masculinity in front of their peers." Men were able to "enhance their own masculinity through group solidarity and camaraderie." Fraser, "Negotiating Their Manhood," 85, 86, 88.

53. West, *Chains of Love*, 81, 101. Deborah Gray White writes, "Female slave bondage was not better or worse, or more or less severe, than male bondage, but it was different." Women faced higher levels of sexual abuse, and childbearing and childrearing shaped their experience within slavery. White, *Ar'n't I a Woman?*, 89, 90, 23; Jones, *Labor of Love*, 28.

54. Berry, *Swing the Sickle*, 119; Stevenson, *Life in Black and White*, 222; Williams, *Help Me to Find My People*, 32. Louisiana law forbade selling mothers away from children under the age of ten, and an 1829 extension of the *Code Noir* prohibited the importation of such slaves. Although slaveholders and traders could and did break this law by labeling children as orphans, its existence speaks to the greater concern, at least in paternalistic rhetoric, with avoiding separating mothers, rather than fathers, from children. Johnson, *Soul by Soul*, 122–123.

55. The interregional slave trade accounted for at least 60 percent of antebellum movement of slaves, with older children and young adults especially vulnerable. Tadman concludes, "Any broad theory of master-slave relationships in antebellum America must either take careful account of family separations or rest upon treacherous foundations." Tadman, *Speculators and*

Slaves, 133, 112, 211; Gutman, *Black Family*, 146, 148–149, 319; King, *Stolen Childhood*, 107; Johnson, *Soul by Soul*, 22, 23.

56. Fleischner explores "identity and identification" and self-conception in women's slave narratives, including memory of lost fathers. Fleischner, *Mastering Slavery*, 29, 30.

57. Using census reports, Eugene Genovese identified the mulatto population in 1860 at 13 percent, and Fogel and Engerman place the number slightly lower at 10.4 percent, an increase from 7.7 percent in 1850. They combine the urban rate of 20 percent with rural rates of 9.9 percent to reach the figure of 10.4 percent based on a larger rural population. Genovese, *Roll*, 414; Fogel and Engerman, *Time on the Cross*, 132.

58. White, *Ar'n't I a Woman?*, 34; Jennings, "Us Colored Women Had to Go though a Plenty," 65, 66; Baptist, "'Cuffy,' 'Fancy Maids,' and 'One-Eyed Men,'" 1619–1650; Clinton, *Plantation Mistress*, 221–222. For a discussion of sexual exploitation of enslaved men and the problem of consent, see Foster, "Sexual Abuse of Black Men," 459–460. West argues, based on the South Carolina narratives, that a "significant minority of masters sexually abused their slave women." West, *Chains of Love*, 131. Slave women were "exceptionally vulnerable to rape, and sexual harassment by whites occasionally extended to the most vicious sadism. Their slavery thus had a psychophysical dimension that male slaves did not experience," David Geggus writes of Saint Domingue in an argument that applies to New World slavery more broadly. Geggus, "Slave and Free Colored Women in Saint Domingue," 265.

59. Fifteen percent of Appalachian narratives in Dunaway's sample discussed interracial sex, and most "involved acts of male force or physical violence." Slaves on smallholdings had a higher likelihood of white parentage, one in ten female-headed households resulted from sexual exploitation, and 5 percent mentioned concubinage. Dunaway, *African-American Family*, 120, 121, 127. Joel Williamson discusses a "massive increase" in the number of enslaved mulattoes from the 1850 to 1860 census and the higher rates of race mixing in the Upper South. Williamson, *New People*, 63. Damian Pargas argues that in 1850 mulattos made up 22 percent of the slave population in Fairfax County, Virginia, and in 1860 that had increased to 30 percent. In Georgetown District, South Carolina, meanwhile, mulattos were a mere 0.5 percent of the slave population in 1850 and 1.3 percent in 1860. Pargas, *Quarters and the Fields*, 158.

60. Enslaved women and men were more apt to face sexual abuse if they worked in close proximity to whites. Foster, "Sexual Abuse of Black Men," 454; Berry, *Swing the Sickle*, 44.

61. In his analysis of slave narratives, Paul Escott notes, "Although no one will ever be able to quantify the amount of interracial sex in the Old South, it is apparent that it occurred often enough to produce substantial numbers of mulatto children." Escott and Thelma Jennings find that 12.26 percent of former slave women mentioned interracial sex (Jennings used a sample of women). Both also point out that this is likely an undercount. Escott shows that former slaves were more or less willing to discuss race mixing based on the sex and race of the interviewer. Escott, *Slavery Remembered*, 46; Jennings, "Us Colored Women Had to Go though a Plenty," 60. Many informants were reticent to discuss the topic or lacked complete information, and visual cues could be misleading, leading to underreporting. Using the slave narratives to quantify racial mixing is also problematic due to the overrepresentation of house slaves and those from large holdings, which would skew the results in opposite directions. Using census data presents similar problems if and when people unknowingly or purposely misreported. Furthermore, masters reported on their own slaves. The census did not include a separate category for mulattos until 1850, and at that point census takers made determinations based on visual evidence, which was not always diagnostic. Gutman noted gaps in the registers of several plantations, where births list no father in the space normally allotted for his name. These cases may indicate abroad marriages, or may have been the result of sexual contact between enslaved women and white men. West notes that slave narratives provide a "*minimum estimate*" of such sexual contact. West, *Chains of Love*, 127; Gutman, *Black Family*, 59, 117; Williamson, *New People*, 24.

62. "Miscegenation is a prime example of the failure of quantification," Clinton writes. Stevenson, "Distress and Discord," 112; Clinton, *Plantation Mistress*, 220, 221; Clinton, "Southern Dishonor," 58.

63. Spillers, "Mama's Baby, Papa's Maybe," 66, 80, 72; Davis, "Reflections on the Black Woman's Role in the Community of Slaves," 4, 5, 14, 15; Wallace, *Black Macho and the Myth of the Super-Woman*, 16, 23, 91; Geary, *Beyond Civil Rights*, 68, 122.

64. For a discussion of conflict in the slave community, see Forret, *Slave against Slave*; Griffin, "Contest and Competition in the Folklore of Slaves," 769–802.

65. For a discussion of the shift to the Self-Made man, see Michael Kimmel, *Manhood in America*, 13–42; Friend and Glover, eds., *Southern Manhood*, x, xi. "Slaveholders' domination over their chattel—slaves' dishonor—contributed to the construction of Southern white men's senses of honor and mastery," Forret states. "The result was a paradox: in fashioning an identity as self-assured, independent men, slaveholders were highly dependent upon their slaves." Forret, *Slave against Slave*, 285.

66. David Walker's appeal exemplifies this conception of manhood. The model of heroic resistance was the male version of the tragic mulatto. In both cases, to achieve the pinnacle of masculinity or femininity was concomitant with death. The slave could not remain alive and be a proper man or woman. Fugitive former slave Henry Highland Garnet encouraged men to engage in heroic resistance. "You had better all die—*die immediately*, than live slaves." Baptist, "The Absent Subject," 137, 138; Henry Highland Garnet, *A Memorial Discourse*, 1865, in Sterling, ed., *Speak Out in Thunder Tones*, 165; Doddington, *Contesting Slave Masculinity*, 20–48.

67. Hine and Jenkins, *Question of Manhood*, 57.

68. Fraser argues that fugitives equated manhood with heroic resistance, but with such a model unattainable for most, enslaved men in the Upper South "defined their masculine ideals within the parameters of the experience of slavery." She calls on historians to "broaden the terms of what we define as 'heroic'" and to move "towards a more inclusive definition of the African American masculine ideal during this period." She shows that enslaved men expressed their manhood by providing for and protecting family and community members, and through group solidarity. Fraser, "Negotiating Their Manhood," 88, 80, 78, 79, 81, 84, 85.

69. "Although depicted as objects stripped of claims to masculinity, many enslaved men stubbornly demonstrated through acts of caretaking and dignity that they believed that their own lives and identities mattered, and that they had choices and will" (147), he states. Baptist, "The Absent Subject," 147, 155, 151, 152, 154.

70. Doddington uses James Day's praise of his father's work ethic and skill as a blacksmith as an example of industrious manhood, and here, as elsewhere, uses the son's commentary as a stand-in for the father's sense of identity (89, 90). Lussana, *My Brother Slaves*, 6, 52; Doddington, *Contesting Slave Masculinity*, 90, 215, 88, 126, 120, 49, 50.

71. The focus on enslaved solidarity "can negate discussions on gendered power dynamics within black communities and neglect the ways in which expressions of black male dominance have affected black women" (130). Doddington, *Contesting Slave Masculinity*, 127, 128, 199, 82, 163, 131, 132. Whereas bell hooks and Daniel Black argue that enslaved men developed a sense of manhood based on sexual prowess and phallocentrism became a "'manhood substitute' in place of black husbandhood and fatherhood," Doddington sees sexual prowess as one of many masculine identities and traces the overlap with white conceptions of male sexuality. Black, *Dismantling Black Manhood*, 127, 126; hooks, *Black Looks*, 94.

72. Forret sets out to "plumb the ways in which the condition of slavery itself bred violence" (7). Slave-on-slave violence undercuts the idea of community solidarity promoted by many scholars, and yet such acts "also contributed to the creation of the very communities that sustained slaves," Forret concludes. "When slaves fought over what they valued, they revealed the senses of fairness, justice, honor, and pride that they relied upon to persevere against and resist the terms and conditions of bondage" (395). Violence also marked enslaved people as profoundly Southern. Forret, *Slave against Slave*, 19, 25, 288, 295, 296, 312.

73. Forret traces the African roots of these ideas as well as the ways in which bondage shaped honor culture among the enslaved: "Slaves could maintain their own sense of honor without simply replicating white codes." Forret, *Slave against Slave*, 288, 295, 294, 296. Doddington similarly argues that gendered identities were not built solely "in opposition to white social

norms." Doddington, *Contesting Slave Masculinity*, 19, 10 199, 214. Joshua Rothman shows that although Southern whites generally did not recognize a slave's honor, as that would recognize their manhood, they at times acknowledged that slaves had honor among themselves. Rothman, *Notorious in the Neighborhood*, 161; Wyatt-Brown, "Mask of Obedience," 1249.

74. "Enslaved men understood that their sense of honor had its limitations within the constraints of Southern white society," Forret writes. Forret, *Slave against Slave*, 313, 289, 291, 292, 293, 315, 330, 331. In detailing the different ways in which enslaved men saw themselves as masculine, Lussana, Doddington, and Forret add complexity to older views of manhood within slavery.

75. Use and eventually misuse of John Blassingame's seminal work, *The Slave Community*, influenced this trend. For a discussion of this unrealistic portrait of "the idyllic slave community," see Kolchin, "Reevaluating the Antebellum Slave Community," 601. On divisions within the family, see Stevenson, "Distress and Discord in Virginia Slave Families, 1830–1860"; Morris, "Within the Slave Cabin: Violence in Mississippi Slave Families." On discord created by the informal economy, see McDonnell, "Money Knows No Master," 37; Penningroth, *The Claims of Kinfolk*, 8; Hilliard, *Masters, Slaves, and Exchange*, 2, 120.

76. As Forret points out, people fight over that which they most value, making violence a fascinating window onto the culture and lives of the enslaved. "This study asks readers to accept, if not necessarily embrace, the totality of bondpeople's humanity," he writes. Forret, *Slave against Slave*, 26, 7, 3, 6, 19, 25, 214; Penningroth, *The Claims of Kinfolk*, 192, 88, 6. On the idea of neighborhood, Forret builds on the work of Anthony E. Kaye, "Neighbourhoods and Solidarity in the Natchez District of Mississippi."

77. Forret discusses "unflattering and unconventional forms of agency." Forret, *Slave against Slave*, 8; Johnson, "On Agency;" Schermerhorn, *Money over Mastery, Family over Freedom*, 24, 132; Doddington, *Contesting Slave Masculinity*, 213, 214.

78. See chapter 6 for a discussion of how this social isolation, while sometimes a choice, was often foisted upon women as a result of structural violence and social ostracism. Schermerhorn, *Money over Mastery, Family over Freedom*, 18, 52, 207, 210.

79. Doddington, *Contesting Slave Masculinity*, 198.

80. Calvin Schermerhorn examines several cases of fathers' thorough identification with and focus on family. Schermerhorn, *Money over Mastery, Family over Freedom*.

81. Rothman, *Notorious in the Neighborhood*, 139–145; Forret, *Slave against Slave*, 290.

82. David Doddington writes, "Wider cultural values embedded across the slave South, as well as commonalities of bondage, shaped people's constructions of manhood, and these similarities outweighed experiential differences stemming from regional issues such as crop type, demographic patterns, and social structures." Doddington, *Contesting Slave Masculinity*, 16.

83. Kimmel discusses the social construction of manhood, the importance of context, region, class, age, ethnicity, and sexuality, and the need to "speak of *masculinities*." Kimmel, *Manhood in America*, 4.

84. In his discussion of violence and enslaved women's sense of honor, Forret explores "a blurring of the boundaries between 'masculine' and 'feminine' in slave society. Compared to whites, gendered expectations of proper conduct among slaves were relatively less sharply differentiated." David Doddington discusses the "fluidity of gender" in his study of enslaved masculinity. Forret, *Slave against Slave*, 342; Doddington, *Contesting Slave Masculinity*, 2, 9, 214; Cashin, "Black Families in the Old Northwest," 455.

85. Davis, "Reflections on the Black Woman's Role in the Community of Slaves," 8, 7; Cashin, "Black Families in the Old Northwest," 458, 462, 463.

86. This book focuses on heterosexual contact and relationships, but this does not presuppose sexual preference. A man's attractions did not determine his commitment as a father.

87. Only a few men admitted to abandoning their children in the FWP interviews, and the records are biased in favor of caretakers. Drew, *North-Side View of Slavery*, contains antebellum interviews in Canada with men who escaped alone and discussed the decision to leave family behind. See chapter 4, 198–200.

88. This book was in part inspired by clues about enslaved families in the manuscript sources of slaveholders. However, because archival sources from white Southerners do not address the questions in which I am most interested, I cut such sources from the book. For example, Katherine Polk Gale, in her reminiscences of the Civil War, commented on her father's "faithful servant," Altimore, and how his return from the front "reunited" him with his "dear ones," including his mother, wife, and son, Taylor. While Gale hinted at Altimore's love for his kin, there is no way to evaluate his feelings about his son, Taylor's feelings about his father, or their conceptions of paternal duty. Katherine Polk Gale, "My Recollections of Life in the Southern Confederacy, 1861–1865," 66.

89. Egypt was a researcher at the Social Science Institute at Fisk University. *God Struck Me Dead*, iii; *Unwritten History of Slavery*, iv.

90. Where possible, I have included the name of the respondent. Not surprisingly, given the race of the interviewers, these informants emphasized the brutality of the institution. Cade, "Out of the Mouths of Ex-Slaves," 294–337.

91. Yetman, "The Background of the Slave Narrative Collection," 534–553.

92. I reference both collections rather than relying solely on Rawick's volumes, because the Slave Narrative Collection (*SNC*) can be accessed with an Internet connection, whereas the published and digitized volumes require institutional access.

93. Escott, *Slavery Remembered*, 6, 7, 9, 10, 11; Woodward, "History from Slave Sources," 470–481; Blassingame, "Using the Testimony of Ex-Slaves," 85. Individual interviewers created variance, but there is also variance in the focus of the questions and tenor of responses by state.

94. Emmaline Kilpatrick was interviewed by her former master's granddaughter, an example of what Paul Escott calls "coercive situations." *SNC*, Georgia, pt. 3, 4:9; Escott, *Slavery Remembered*, 8.

95. Rawick, *AS*, supp., ser. 2, Texas, pt. 4, 5:1904; Escott, *Slavery Remembered*, 9. Ben Simpson "was afraid to tell the truth about his life as a slave, until assured that no harm would come to him." *SNC*, Texas, pt. 4, 16:27.

96. Woodward, "History from Slave Sources," 481; Escott, *Slavery Remembered*, 13, 16. Blassingame cautioned about the bias, in many states, toward interviewing the "most obsequious" former slaves and the fact that the advanced age of the respondents skewed the sample toward the long-lived, who may have been treated better as slaves. Blassingame, *Slave Testimony*, li.

97. Sánchez-Eppler, "Remember, Dear," 28, 30, 29. Stephanie Shaw reframes the sources as "American narratives of the Great Depression," to examine the toll the era took on aging African Americans. Shaw, "Using the WPA Ex-Slave Narratives to Study the Impact of the Great Depression," 629, 655.

98. Charity Moore, for instance, lived on the property of her former master's son, knew her interviewer, and had the requisite positive things to say about the white family, and yet she extensively praised her father and subtly commented on his attempts to instill racial pride. Positive commentary on a former owner and biological father often existed side by side, with subjects prompted to speak of masters and choosing to speak of kin. This means that the interview process probably inhibited the quantity but not the quality of commentary on kin. *SNC*, South Carolina, pt. 3, 14:205–209.

99. "To criticize slavery without seeming to criticize the masters was the delicate problem presented to every FWP respondent interviewed by a Southern white interviewer," William Dusinberre writes. "The standard response was to deflect the blame onto the shoulders of the black drivers, or of the poorer whites." Many former slaves attributed brutality to overseers or neighboring masters so as to avoid critiquing former owners. Dusinberre, *Them Dark Days*, 420, 419.

100. Gender-specific labor patterns meant that men often worked with men and women with women, so a greater number of male respondents may increase commentary on fathers. West finds that more men mentioned separation from fathers. West, *Chains of Love*, 148.

101. Blassingame, *Slave Testimony*, xliii–lvii. Donna J. Spindel, using the psychological literature, argues that historians need to address the problems of memory in the narratives. Spindel, "Assessing Memory: Twentieth-Century Slave Narratives Reconsidered," 247–261.

102. The content and order of the questions often led the editors to "craft narratives that concluded with a note of reconciliation rather than one of anger, pain, or rebellion." Musher, "Contesting 'The Way the Almighty Wants It,'" 11, 5.

103. Blassingame's comparison of Peter Bruner's FWP interview and longer autobiography shows that he omitted much information in his FWP interview, including a discussion of his parents. Blassingame, *Slave Testimony*, lvii.

104. Perdue et al., *Weevils*, xvii, xxxvii, xxxix.

105. I counted ninety-eight of the narratives, omitting ten informants who were born free, thirty-seven narratives that made no mention of family because they are too short, fragmented, and/or focused on a specific anecdote, and five from informants who grew up in states other than Virginia or West Virginia. Another six informants mentioned a family member but did not discuss either parent and the fragments are too short to determine whether or not the individual had any contact with a parent (under fifteen lines). I retained ten narratives that mentioned the mother briefly or in passing, but are too truncated to determine whether or not these individuals knew their fathers. Nine narratives mentioned only the father, five of which are under twenty lines. Given the legal and social realities of slavery it is safer to assume that someone who mentioned only the father also knew their mother, but that assumption cannot be reversed and it is ultimately impossible to tell. The fact that many short narratives discuss only one parent is a good indication of incomplete information. A small fraction of short narratives that only mention the mother are from individuals who probably knew their father but failed to mention him. Of the ninety-eight used, forty-three (44 percent) mentioned both parents. Of these, two mentioned both parents, but offered hints that the father was white. The living situation is often fuzzy, but ten informants discussed clear or likely abroad marriages. Seven (7 percent) informants were separated from both parents due to death or sale or likely separated from both parents. Several longer narratives made no mention of parents, but it is unclear how the separation occurred. One provided hints at possible white parentage. Five (5 percent) were separated from the father due to sale and stayed with the mother or stayed with her for a longer period of time. Twenty-six (27 percent) informants did not discuss their father, including nine narratives that are too short to fully determine family relationships. Four of the twenty-five (15 percent of those who did not discuss the father) offer hints that the individual had a white father. Nine (9 percent) informants did not discuss the mother, and again many are too short to determine if she was present. In one case she appears to have been missing. A total of seventy-four (75 percent) had contact with their mother, while fifty-two (53 percent) had contact with their enslaved father. Eight (8 percent) narratives discussed white fathers. A total of 15 percent clearly identified or hinted at having a white father. Perdue et al., *Weevils*. My analysis differs slightly from that of Brenda Stevenson. She finds 42 percent of respondents discussed regular interactions with their fathers as compared to 82 percent who discussed their mothers. Stevenson, "Distress and Discord," 108.

106. Stewart explores the background of FWP state employees. White Southerners, many members of neo-Confederate organizations, envisioned the project as a way to glorify the Lost Cause, celebrate slavery as a benign institution, and strengthen white supremacy. These goals framed how they conducted interviews and influenced their demeaning descriptions of informants. Stewart, *Long Past Slavery*, 6, 199, 200, 201, 202, 218, 47, 51, 52, 53, 55, 208, 210.

107. Virginia had the most African American employees, at 20 percent of its writers. Stewart, *Long Past Slavery*, 134, 137, 133, 127. Because attempts to represent black vernacular were problematic and necessarily depended on white interpretations, the federal office attempted to standardize how writers transcribed dialect. The federal office realized the pitfalls of transcribing dialect, but concerns about salability, especially worries that Standard English would not appeal to a commercial audience, won out. Dialect reinforced ideas of racial inferiority, and "very often the use of phonetic spelling resulted in stereotypical depictions of African Americans as provincial folk people, whose racial difference was embodied in their speech." The standardization elided class differences and "'Race' became the defining linguistic feature in the Ex-Slave Project's adoption of literary renderings of the black vernacular," giving the

impression that all former slaves had the same speech patterns. Dialect in the FWP narratives emerged as a "literary means of racial 'othering.'" Stewart uses "black vernacular" in reference to African American oral traditions and "Negro Dialect" in reference to FWP output. She also explores how the guidelines could bias how an interviewer heard an informant, gave them a template to use when writing up the interviews, and led writers and state offices to feel the need to explain away any departure from the formula (79, 85, 86, 88, 89).

108. Stewart, *Long Past Slavery*, 202, 242, 243, 221. Mia Bay explores informant evasions: "Interviewer bias complicates rather than invalidates the vast collection of evidence." Bay, *The White Image in the Black Mind*, 115.

109. The autobiographies overrepresent the "exceptional" slave. Blassingame, *Slave Testimony*, xli.

Chapter One

1. Black, *Life and Sufferings of Leonard Black*, 7.

2. Human resilience to trauma varies in any population. Peres et al. suggest that because hopelessness is a strong risk factor for PTSD, researchers should explore spiritual beliefs as a framework for intervention and helping individuals cope with trauma, thus reducing vulnerability and increasing resilience. Slaves seem to fit this modern hypothesis, as many handled the physical and emotional abuse of slavery through shared values, family, and religion. Peres et al., "Spirituality and Resilience in Trauma Victims," 343, 344–348; Bonanno, "Resilience in the Face of Potential Trauma," 135–138.

3. Escott, *Slavery Remembered*, 43–46; Jennings, "Us Colored Women Had to Go though a Plenty," 60, 61, 48–52; Jones, *Labor of Love*, 34–35; hooks, *Ain't I a Woman*, 39; Sutch, "The Breeding of Slaves for Sale," 173–210; Berry, *Swing the Sickle*, 77–84.

4. SNC, Arkansas, pt. 5, 2:284; North Carolina, pt. 1, 11:177; Arkansas, pt. 3, 2:92, 88. Patterson was a slave near Paducah, Kentucky, and as a four-year-old was moved to Arkansas with his mother to keep them away from Union soldiers. Coggin had no siblings and his mother married after the war. He never specified her marital status as a slave, a clue to possible white paternity.

5. SNC, North Carolina, pt. 2, 11:156, pt. 2, 11:119; South Carolina, pt. 2, 14:14. Revealing such information violated the rules of social discretion and put slaves at risk for punishment and sale. In addition, the slave community more often ostracized women who appeared to or voluntarily had sex with white men, and this affected treatment of her children. This information could be painful, perilous, or both. Schwartz, *Born in Bondage*, 45.

6. SNC, Arkansas, pt. 1, 2:241; Rawick, AS, supp., ser. 2, Texas, pt. 4, 5:1848; SNC, South Carolina, pt. 2, 14:23; Rawick, AS, supp., ser. 2, Texas, pt. 3, 4:1341, pt. 6, 7:2563.

7. Forret, *Slave against Slave*, 269, 348. Stevenson discusses "marital discord" as a result of forced mating. Stevenson, "Distress and Discord," 118.

8. "Enslaved men sometimes found support from white male enslavers in enforcing dominance over enslaved women" (131), Doddington writes. Doddington, *Contesting Slave Masculinity*, 169, 168, 128; Foster, "Sexual Abuse of Black Men," 457. While we do not know how Rufus felt about the master's demands, Virginia Yarbrough described a forcibly paired couple colluding to fool the master. Sad to see her whipped after she refused him, the man offered to sleep on the floor so long as she would not reveal their arrangement. The master assumed she was infertile and allowed her to interact with the man she favored, and she then had children. Rawick, AS, supp., ser. 2, Texas, pt. 9, 10:4295–4296.

9. Williams purposely never married. "Aftah w'at I's do fo' de marster, I's never wants any truck wid any man." Williams had complex feelings about her former master, a combination of gratitude that he rescued her from being separated from her parents, and resentment that he forced her to "marry" a man she despised. As Doddington writes, her refusal "implies the degree to which some enslaved people considered their oppression along gendered lines as well as racial ones." Rawick, AS, supp., ser. 2, Texas, pt. 9, 10:4123, 4119–4123; SNC, Texas, pt. 4,

16:176, 178, 174; Doddington, *Contesting Slave Masculinity*, 169; King, *Stolen Childhood*, 119, 149.

10. "The old master picked out a wife for you, and you would git a whipping if you didn't stay with her; whether that was the one you liked or not," one man recalled. *Unwritten History of Slavery*, 222; Watson, *Narrative of Henry Watson*, 18; SNC, Arkansas, pt. 2, 2:195.

11. Berry, *Swing the Sickle*, 83. Because "the main factor involved was the desire on the part of the Master to rear negroes with perfect physiques," Henry Buttler called Virginia slave marriages "a farce." Rawick, *AS*, supp., ser. 2, Texas pt. 2, 3:555; Escott, *Slavery Remembered*, 45; Jennings, "Us Colored Women Had to Go though a Plenty," 48–52. One ex-slave accused a Tennessee slaveholder of running "a farm of slaves" and breeding for sale. During his travels in the "slave-breeding States" of the Upper South, Frederick Law Olmsted noted that Southern whites often discussed breeding for profit and the value of enslaved women as a "brood-mare." *Unwritten History of Slavery*, 18:1; Olmsted, *Cotton Kingdom*, 1:58, 57, 59. On slave rearing for profit, especially in the Upper South, see Bancroft, *Slave Trading*, 68, 208; Stampp, *Peculiar Institution*, 245–246.

12. Because enslaved men took the initiative in courtship they might also ask for certain partners. Doddington, *Contesting Slave Masculinity*, 149, 131, 132, 134, 147, 152. For a discussion of breeding and sexual abuse of men, see Foster, "Sexual Abuse of Black Men," 455–456. Berry argues "forced breeding in the slave quarters manifested itself as an indirect form of rape where *powerless* enslaved males and females became the victims of reproductive abuse to which they did not *willingly* give their consent." Berry, *Swing the Sickle*, 79.

13. SNC, South Carolina, pt. 1, 14:14; Doddington, *Contesting Slave Masculinity*, 155, 150, 154; Forret, *Slave against Slave*, 245, 248, 250.

14. Choice was born in 1835 near Henderson, Texas. He had no children from his legitimate marriages, but did have "outside" children and attributed this to the "old days" being different from the present. Again, it is not clear if any of these children were born after marriage or slavery, though they might well have been. Rawick, *AS*, supp., ser. 2, Texas, pt. 2, 3:709, 713; Doddington, *Contesting Slave Masculinity*, 159.

15. On status in the quarters based on sexual virility, see Forret, *Slave against Slave*, 245; Stevenson, *Life in Black and White*, 241; Doddington, *Contesting Slave Masculinity*, 164, 162.

16. Doddington makes an excellent point that the "light-hearted tone" used by many informants should be contrasted with the "harrowing descriptions" of enslaved women in such exploitative situations. Men were more likely than women to use such a tone, and women were more likely to use matter-of-fact language when discussing other people and not their own experiences. Rawick, *AS*, supp., ser. 1, Georgia, 3:68, 69; Doddington, *Contesting Slave Masculinity*, 160, 161, 159, 166.

17. Andrew Boone's father was assigned multiple partners in Wake County, North Carolina, "an' no udder man wus allowed to have anything to do wid em.'" Though Boone's father had children by several women, after emancipation he lived with Boone's mother until she died and then he remarried. Father and son lived and worked together. Rawick, *AS*, supp., ser. 2, Texas, pt. 5, 6:2109, 2111, Texas, pt. 2, 16:239; SNC, North Carolina, pt. 1, 11:136, 137. Zeno John's parents did not stay together after the war, but he remained in contact with his father. Though John did not know the specifics of his parents' relationship, he discussed it in the context of breeding. He praised the elder Zeno as "much of a man," and recounted that his father, prior to his death, claimed to have seventy children, grandchildren, and great-grandchildren. John's parents both became sharecroppers, and though he provided little detail, he appears to have lived with his mother and worked with his stepfather, and it is possible his mother left his father. Born and raised in Louisiana, John was quite young at the end of the Civil War and at the time of the dissolution of his parents' relationship. Rawick, *AS*, supp., ser. 2, Texas, pt. 5, 6:1950.

18. Hutchinson's grandfather appears to have favored her grandmother, and her narrative suggests that a man could be used as a breeder and be devoted to what he considered to be his primary family, but she had no direct knowledge of his feelings and recounted what she had

heard from his son. *SNC*, Arkansas, pt. 3, 9:370, pt. 1, 2:210–211; Rawick, *AS*, supp., ser. 2, Texas, pt. 7, 8:3332, pt. 6, 7:2616.

19. Stone fought for the Union army, and later became a preacher and devoted family man. *SNC*, Indiana, 5:186, 188.

20. Doddington uses Davison as an example of some men's resentment of sexual exploitation, but he does not explore how these feelings could be related to children. Rawick, *AS*, supp., ser. 2, Texas, pt. 3, 4:1116; Doddington, *Contesting Slave Masculinity*, 146; Jennings, "Us Colored Women Had to Go though a Plenty," 50–51. Ambrose Douglass earned a whipping for trying to reject a forced pairing and order to produce a child with this woman. *SNC*, Florida, 3:10.

21. *SNC*, Mississippi, 9:68; Georgia, pt. 4, 4:179; Oklahoma, 13:322; North Carolina, pt. 2, 11:317; Williams, *Help Me to Find My People*, 32.

22. *SNC*, Arkansas, pt. 1, 2:109; pt. 4, 2:290; Perdue et al., *Weevils*, 161; Rawick, *AS*, supp., ser. 2, Texas, pt. 4, 5:1809; *SNC*, Texas, pt. 3, 16:262; South Carolina, pt. 2, 14:207.

23. *SNC*, Arkansas, pt. 4, 2:307, pt. 4, 2:207.

24. Compared to the general slave population, Dunaway finds that slaves in the Mountain South were 1.4 times more likely to die due to inadequate provisioning of food and clothing, malnutrition, overcrowded housing, poor sanitation, and occupational hazards. Dunaway, *African-American Family*, 85–113, 273.

25. Jacobs was ten when he was taken from his father's home and eleven when his father died. Jacobs, "A True Tale of Slavery," 85; *SNC*, Arkansas, pt. 6, 2:239; Mississippi, 9:22; Edwards, *From Slavery to a Bishopric*, 28.

26. *SNC*, Georgia, pt. 1, 4:136, 137, pt. 2, 4:305; North Carolina, pt. 2, 11:343.

27. Rawick, *AS*, supp., ser. 2, Texas, pt. 6, 7:2577; *SNC*, Texas, pt. 2, 16:106.

28. *SNC*, Georgia, pt. 2, 4:318, 320; Schwartz, *Born in Bondage*, 104, 126. The slave trade in the Upper South created numerous orphans who were often raised by white families, leading to neglect and emotional distance from kin and community. Slaveholders believed that the ideal way to train house servants was to bring them into the big house at an early age. Stevenson, "Distress and Discord," 105–106.

29. *SNC*, North Carolina, pt. 2, 11:391, 392; Arkansas, pt. 2, 2:185, 187. According to Heather Williams, decades after the Civil War the language of those searching for lost kin shifted, increasingly invoking the hope of finding "my people," rather than specific individuals. African Americans sought a "sense of history and identity," as well as "a sense of having come from somewhere and someone," even if they had never met those relatives. Williams, *Help Me to Find My People*, 193.

30. *Unwritten History of Slavery*, 181, 182, 188; Williams, *Help Me to Find My People*; West, *Chains of Love*, 19; Dunaway, *African-American Family*, 83.

31. Even after the wrenching loss of his first family, Jones felt he "could not live in utter loneliness any longer," and remarried. He eventually freed his second family and escaped from North Carolina. Jones, *Experience and Personal Narrative of Uncle Tom Jones*, 23, 25; Brown, *Narrative of Henry Box Brown*, 23, 47, 24, 25; Blassingame, *Slave Community*, 164; Cade, "Out of the Mouths of Ex-Slaves," 303; Brown, *Narrative of William W. Brown*, 87, 86.

32. Farnham, "Sapphire?," 73–74. This section focuses on heterosexual relationships, the dominant form within slavery. However, form should not assume sexual preference or sexuality in all cases. Some unknown number of nonheterosexual men and women had children within slave marriage.

33. Some masters allowed slaves to marry in church-sanctioned ceremonies, but most avoided church weddings. Such unions forced Southern churches to confront the dilemmas created by separation and remarriage. Blassingame, *Slave Community*, 168–171. Scholars have noted the variation in slave marriage ceremonies. See Gutman, *Black Family*, 273–277, 283; Jennings, "Us Colored Women Had to Go though a Plenty," 53–54; Berry, *Sweet Chariot*, 57–59. For a discussion of courtship and marriage rituals, especially as they changed over time and the connections to West African cultural patterns, see West, *Chains of Love*, 20–34.

34. Gutman, *Black Family*, 286. "One thing that distinguished a 'good master' from a bad one in the slaves' eyes was his attitude toward marriage," Thelma Jennings writes. Jennings, "Us Colored Women Had to Go though a Plenty," 53.

35. West, "The Debate on the Strength of Slave Families," 232–233; *Chains of Love*, 50–53; Williams, *Help Me to Find My People*, 61–63. Groups of white men organized to control the slave population and prevent escape and unauthorized travel, and slave patrols acted as a police force that enforced discipline on the slave population. Hadden, *Slave Patrols*.

36. Bibb, *Narrative of the Life and Adventures of Henry Bibb*, 40; Pargas, *Quarters and the Fields*, 204–205; Jennings, "Us Colored Women Had to Go though a Plenty," 46. Emily West notes that slaves formed abroad marriages based on circumstances, but that they also sometimes chose such unions, an example of "a desire . . . for autonomy from their owners." For some, abroad marriages were about exercising choice over marriage partner. They were also critical in enabling slaves to cope with local sales. West cites marriage and choice over partner as an example of the "social space" between masters and slaves. West, *Chains of Love*, 45, 39, 54, 73, 150, 158; Stevenson, *Life in Black and White*, 232.

37. Jackson, *Experience of a Slave in South Carolina*, 21–22; Jackson, *Narrative and Writings of Andrew Jackson*, 8; Twelvetrees, *Story of the Life of John Anderson*, 134; Thompson, *Biography of a Slave*, 21–31; West, *Chains of Love*, 28–30.

38. Jordan had two children on another plantation. His new wife had no children. Albert, *House of Bondage*, 106–107, 108, 109; SNC, Georgia, pt. 2, 4:296. Isaac Martin's master preferred that his slaves marry on-site or on the farms of his two sons. SNC, Texas, pt. 3, 16:56.

39. Twelvetrees, *Story of the Life of John Anderson*, 129; Bibb, *Narrative of the Life and Adventures of Henry Bibb*, 41, 42, 43; Grandy, *Narrative of the Life of Moses Grandy*, 25, 28; Pickard, *Kidnapped and the Ransomed*, 161–162; Blassingame, *Slave Community*, 164. Pargas, in reaction to Blassingame, argues that enslaved people in Fairfax County, Virginia, preferred to marry on-site when able. Pargas, *Quarters and the Fields*, 149.

40. Brown, *Narrative of Henry Box Brown*, 48, 53; SNC, South Carolina, pt. 3, 14:209.

41. Perdue et al., *Weevils*, 89; SNC, Oklahoma, 13:355; Georgia, pt. 1, 4:62.

42. Twelvetrees, *Story of the Life of John Anderson*, 131; Rawick, *AS*, supp., ser. 2, Texas, pt. 7, 8:3369; SNC, Oklahoma, 13:212. One informant noted that in some abroad marriages, children never saw their fathers. Cade, "Out of the Mouths of Ex-Slaves," 304. Allen Crawford's father was stranded at his family's cabin by an unusual snowfall and needed help from his wife's master to get back to his master's plantation. Perdue et al., *Weevils*, 75.

43. The tendency to keep the bulk of family property at the wife's cabin "strengthened black women's control over property" (105), Penningroth continues. Blassingame, *Slave Testimony*, 491; SNC, Ohio, 12:45; Rawick, *AS*, supp., ser. 1, Oklahoma, 12:17; Penningroth, *The Claims of Kinfolk*, 103, 104, 105, 106; Hudson, *To Have and to Hold*, 63.

44. Perdue et al., *Weevils*, 49; Parker, *Recollections of Slavery Times*, 8, 79, 36, 40. Allen Parker's mother was hired out to a different employer each year in Chowan County, North Carolina, and when he was old enough, Parker was hired out separately. Parker recalled at least one time when his father then visited both his wife and son. On the hiring of enslaved children, see Martin, *Divided Mastery*, 59.

45. SNC, Indiana, 5:105; 5:128. Mathews called Tom Hooper her stepfather, and may have been Hooper's half sibling. Rawick, *AS*, supp., ser. 2, Texas, pt. 4, 5:1800, pt. 6, 7:2603.

46. The informant was not named, though he did identify his father. *God Struck Me Dead*, 19: 148, 161, 166.

47. West argues that cross-plantation marriages speak to slaves' understanding of men as "protectors and risk-takers." West, "The Debate on the Strength of Slave Families," 238, 236–37.

48. Grandmothers often occupied a central place in the lives and memories of former slaves. Fed poorly by her master and mistress, Harriet Jacobs depended on her grandmother. "I was indebted to *her* for all my comforts, spiritual or temporal." SNC, Georgia, pt. 1, 4:186; Jacobs, *Incidents*, 19, 12; Parker, "The Freedman's Story," 153.

49. Jenkins's family, at that point with eight children, lived together after emancipation. *SNC*, Arkansas, pt. 4, 2:48, 49; Rawick, *AS*, supp., ser. 2, Texas, pt. 6, 7:2892; *SNC*, Arkansas, pt. 6, 2:161. While husbands usually made visits, other family members could also obtain passes.

50. *SNC*, South Carolina, pt. 3, 14:164; Rawick, *AS*, supp., ser. 2, Texas, pt. 8, 9:3494; *SNC*, South Carolina, pt. 4, 14:188; Cade, "Out of the Mouths of Ex-Slaves," 307.

51. Rawick, *AS*, supp., ser. 1, Mississippi, pt. 2, 7:382, pt. 1, 6:310; *SNC*, South Carolina, pt. 1, 14:39.

52. Forret believes that the percentage of cross-plantation marriages in the Upcountry must have been higher than the 34 percent Emily West estimated for South Carolina as a whole. Sergio Lussana argues that abroad marriages increased the importance of male friendships, as men denied regular contact with family bonded with other men, and he suggests that cross-plantation residential patterns may have exacerbated feelings of distrust toward women. Forret, *Slave against Slave*, 238, 246, 247, 255; Lussana, *My Brother Slaves*, 99–112.

53. The young woman and her brother reunited with their father after the war, likely in Tennessee. Henry Baker's father lived on another Alabama farm, and after his mother died "all de rest ub de boys en gals on de plan'ation had mothers en fathers 'cep me." *Unwritten History of Slavery*, 18:61, 61–62; Blassingame, *Slave Testimony*, 639, 640, 642, 644, 655–656.

54. Bibb, *Narrative of the Life and Adventures of Henry Bibb*, 42, 43, 118; Penningroth, *Claims of Kinfolk*, 47. Mothers working in the field had a set number of times per day when they could come in to nurse their babies and incurred a whipping if they lingered. Pickard, *Kidnapped and the Ransomed*, 121–122; *SNC*, Arkansas, pt. 2, 2:32, pt. 2, 2:225; Olmsted, *Cotton Kingdom*, 2:177. An inability to spend time with their infants caused emotional stress and made it harder for enslaved mothers to bond with and win the emotional attachment of their children. White, *Ar'n't I a Woman?*, 112–113; Schwartz, *Born in Bondage*, 43. Nell Irvin Painter discusses insecure attachment and chronic depression among enslaved children as a result of neglect. Painter, *Soul Murder and Slavery*, 14. See Sarah Hrdy for a discussion of the importance of breast-feeding for mother-child bonding and infant health and survival. Hrdy, *Mother Nature*, 137, 140–141, 144, 162–163. William Johnson, emancipated by his master and probable father in 1820, became a successful barber in Natchez, Mississippi. Johnson and his free black wife, Amy Battles, had eleven children. In late 1841, Johnson worried about his son, Richard. "He is very Sick and has had several Fitts or Spasems which So alarms me, I remained all the Evening at Home, Did not go to the Shop," he wrote. After two weeks of vigilance and visits by physicians, Johnson reported his relief and gratitude to God for his son's recovery. Had he and his wife been enslaved, they would have lacked the time and resources to offer such care. Johnson, *William Johnson's Natchez*, November 27, 30, December 6, 16, 1841.

55. Byrd grew up in Texas. Rawick, *AS*, supp., ser. 2, Texas, pt. 2, 3:576, pt. 2, 3:864.

56. *SNC*, Arkansas, pt. 4, 2:294; Rawick, *AS*, supp., ser. 1, Mississippi, pt. 3, 8:1215, supp., ser. 2, Texas, pt. 7, 8:3332; King, *Stolen Childhood*, 13, 14. Damian Pargas argues that centralized nurseries improved childcare and that being related to some of the children enabled caretakers to fulfill their obligations to kin. Pargas, *Quarters and the Fields*, 74, 75, 81–83.

57. Brady mentioned his father, but it is unclear if he lived with the family. Rawick, *AS*, supp., ser. 2, Texas, pt. 9, 10:3970, supp., ser. 1, Mississippi, pt. 3, 8:1304, supp., ser. 2, Texas, pt. 1, 2:400, pt. 2, 3:537.

58. Hunter indicated that her parents and grandparents all lived on the same plantation. *SNC*, Georgia, pt. 2, 4:254-55, Oklahoma, 13:111, 13:356; Cade, "Out of the Mouths of Ex-Slaves," 300; Rawick, *AS*, supp., ser. 2, Texas, pt. 4, 5:1920; Schwartz, *Born in Bondage*, 80, 82.

59. Pennington, *Fugitive Blacksmith*, 2; Love, *Life and Adventures of Nat Love*, 7; King, *Stolen Childhood*, 17; Schwartz, *Born in Bondage*, 4; Dunaway, *African-American Family*, 68; Jennings, "Us Colored Women Had to Go though a Plenty," 58; Owens, *This Species of Property*, 41–42.

60. Rawick, *AS*, supp., ser. 1, Indiana and Ohio, 5:212. Poor nutrition leading to low birth weights as well as illness and child death placed a heavy emotional burden on enslaved parents.

King, *Stolen Childhood*, 12; Dunaway, *African-American Family*, 141, 273; Steckel, "A Peculiar Population," 728–737; Kiple and Kiple, "Slave Child Mortality," 284–309. High infant mortality, twice that of white women, resulted from hard labor, malnutrition, disease, attenuated breast-feeding, and seasonal patterns of conception and childbearing. Steckel, "Women, Work, and Health under Plantation Slavery in the United States," 55–56; Cody, "Cycles of Work and Childbearing," 61–78; King, "Suffer with Them Till Death," 149–150.

61. Pennington, *Fugitive Blacksmith*, xii, xiii.

62. Lockhart escaped from Virginia. Hughes lived on a plantation in Mississippi. Drew, *North-Side View of Slavery*, 49, 211; Hughes, *Thirty Years a Slave*, 97, 99; Brown, *Narrative of William W. Brown*, 16; SNC, South Carolina, pt. 2, 14:311.

63. Albert, *House of Bondage*, 66–67; Perdue et al., *Weevils*, 160.

64. Steward, *Twenty-Two Years a Slave*, 96, 97; Genovese, *Roll*, 485; Clarke and Clarke, *Narrative of the Sufferings of Lewis and Milton Clarke*, 74. The experience of slavery, Daniel Black notes, "forced enslaved African American men to disassociate manhood and the ability to defend oneself." Black, *Dismantling Black Manhood*, 110.

65. Jacobs, *Incidents*, 68; Stevenson, *Life in Black and White*, 242. "As much as enslaved men aspired to fulfill this vision of masculinity, bondage circumscribed their ability to conform to that model of manhood," Jeff Forret writes of the protector role. "Violent behaviors at times filled the void." Forret, *Slave against Slave*, 263, 254.

66. Painter draws on the work of Leonard Shengold. Painter, *Soul Murder and Slavery*, 7, 21, 23; Shengold, *Soul Murder*; Elkins, *Slavery*.

67. Pennington, *Narrative of Events of the Life of J. H. Banks*, 32.

68. Pennington, 28. William Dusinberre discusses narrators' sense of being "dishonored" within the institution of slavery. Dusinberre, *Them Dark Days*, 424.

69. Bay writes that in critiquing white men as "hypermasculine," black intellectuals "held up their own race's religious and moral virtues" to redefine ideal masculinity (109, 222). Bay, *The White Image in the Black Mind*, 110, 54, 111; Thompson, *Biography of a Slave*, 28.

70. Hall and Elder, *Samuel Hall*, 37.

71. Pennington, *Fugitive Blacksmith*, 5, 7.

72. Henson, *Autobiography*, 14, 15, 16.

73. Baptist, "The Absent Subject," 155–158.

74. Jacobs was eleven years old when his father died. Jacobs, "A True Tale of Slavery," 86.

75. After Ball's mother and siblings were sold and his father escaped, only Ball and his grandfather remained in the area. Ball, *Fifty Years in Chains*, 12.

76. SNC, North Carolina, pt. 1, 11:101, pt. 2, 11:165; Genovese, *Roll*, 484–485. See chapter 4 of Fraser, *Courtship and Love among the Enslaved*; Fraser, "Negotiating Their Manhood," 84. David Doddington discusses men helping with or assuming the heavier aspects of women's labor, and Jeff Forret describes men defending loved ones from slights and insults in the quarters, a form of "enslaved male chivalry." Doddington, *Contesting Slave Masculinity*, 97; Forret, *Slave against Slave*, 304.

77. Celestia Avery's pregnant grandmother was tied to a tree in Georgia and whipped for praying. Afraid to approach her in daylight, her husband waited until dark and "cut her down." She then "crawled on her knees to the woods and her husband brought grease for her to grease her raw body." Louisa Adams cared for her father in the aftermath of physical abuse: "I have greased my daddy's back after he had been whupped until his back wuz cut to pieces." SNC, Florida, 17:253; Georgia, pt. 1, 4:25, 24, North Carolina, pt. 1, 11:5.

78. Perdue et al., *Weevils*, 117; Rawick, *AS*, supp., ser. 1, Oklahoma, 12:97–98; Anderson, *Life and Narrative of William J. Anderson*, 25; SNC, North Carolina, pt. 2, 11:103, South Carolina, pt. 2, 14:36; Genovese, *Roll*, 484–485; West, *Chains of Love*, 71; Rothman, *Notorious in the Neighborhood*, 136. Louvinia Pleasant's father intervened on behalf of his pregnant wife, stopping her beating by attacking the overseer's horse with a hoe. A favorite with the master's son-in-law, he escaped punishment. He also wisely chose to attack a horse rather than a human. Rawick, *AS*, supp., ser. 2, Texas, pt. 7, 8:3100.

79. Bruner, *A Slave's Adventures toward Freedom*, 16; Campbell, *An Autobiography*, 113, 114, 116; Drew, *North-Side View of Slavery*, 163–165; Hall and Elder, *Samuel Hall*, 30, 34; Thompson, *Life of John Thompson*, 26; SNC, Indiana, 5:162.

80. Douglass, *Narrative*, 72–73. Walter Johnson refers to slave breaking as a "fantasy of mastery embodied in the public subjugation of another" and a "technology of the soul." Johnson, *Soul by Soul*, 107, 106.

81. Kimmel, *Manhood in America*, 13–42.

82. Blassingame, *Slave Testimony*, 152; Doddington, *Contesting Slave Masculinity*, 21, 22, 23, 31, 36, 39, 43, 44, 47; Fraser, "Negotiating Their Manhood," 76, 77, 78, 88.

83. Huff's father told his mother to "wait for his return, whether it be months or years. She grieved over his departure and refused, although urged, to marry again." He came back during the war without Huff's brother, who had died shortly after being sold. SNC, Georgia, pt. 2, 4:239. Martha Harrison lost her father when he was sold from Tennessee to Mississippi after he killed the overseer with a hoe. *Unwritten History of Slavery*, 18:116, 119.

84. If Tibeats killed Northup, he would owe that debt to Northup's former master, a man who arranged for Northup to be hired out after he escaped another attack, this time involving a hatchet. Northup, *Twelve Years a Slave*, 125, 106, 115, 123, 133, 135, 139, 144, 153.

85. Pennington, *Narrative of Events of the Life of J. H. Banks*, 19, 19–20, 20, 18. The separation of children from parents had ripple effects on the slave community. Gutman, *Black Family*, 148.

86. Woods's father's first wife had been sold, and he was a child of the second wife. Knowing that one of his parents had lost a family member possibly increased his anxiety, as did the fact that the master's brother was a slave speculator. Woods and his siblings lived in a two-parent household, but at least one member of the cabin had directly experienced family dislocation. SNC, North Carolina, pt. 2, 11:417; Perdue et al., *Weevils*, 104; Williams, *Help Me to Find My People*, 121. Wilma King stresses the widespread emotional "trauma" of selling or hiring children away from their families and the anxiety of knowing that risk of sale increased as children aged. Part of parenting was preparing children for potential separation. King, *Stolen Childhood*, 104, 102–103; Schwartz, *Born in Bondage*, 90, 156, 163, 164, 166, 171.

87. Brown made his escape from Virginia shortly after losing his family. Brown, *Narrative of Henry Box Brown*, 12–13, 55; Williams, *Help Me to Find My People*, 190, 32.

88. SNC, Arkansas, pt. 7, 2:9; Blassingame, *Slave Testimony*, 169. "Nothing demonstrated his powerlessness as much as the slave's inability to prevent the forcible sale of his wife and children," John Blassingame wrote. Blassingame, *Slave Community*, 174.

89. "Paying attention to the special situation of enslaved children serves to accentuate both the logic of childhood and the logic of slavery," Karen Sánchez-Eppler writes. As a four-year-old, Vaughn's mother was not fully able to comprehend her father's behavior. Sánchez-Eppler, "'Remember, Dear,'" 41.

90. Women were more likely to trade on gender conventions to vocally express their sorrow and attempt to sway the conscience of slave owners to forestall family division. While emotional scenes often incurred a brutal response, women hoped that their punishment might be less severe. A distraught woman appeared less threatening and was less likely to be summarily killed or shackled by a trader for challenging white authority. Traders chained men in coffles and secured women with ropes because they believed women were not as likely to attempt escape. Johnson, *Soul by Soul*, 36, 60. Williams argues that because some women also reacted stoically to the sale of a spouse, gender does not fully account for varied reactions to separation. According to Williams, enslaved people more often vocally protested the sale of children, possibly because they believed they might be able to influence the owner, whereas they felt little hope in the face of broken marriages. Williams, *Help Me to Find My People*, 87–88.

91. Emancipation came only a couple of years later, but Green was unable to locate his son. Green, *Life of the Rev. Elisha W. Green*, 10, 21.

92. Grose was sold from Virginia to New Orleans. Drew, *North-Side View of Slavery*, 83; Abream Scriven, Savannah, to Dinah Jones, Sept. 19, 1858, in Starobin, *Blacks in Bondage*, 58; James Phillips to Mary Phillips, Richmond, June 20, 1852, in Blassingame, *Slave Testimony*, 96.

93. Ducket's family failed in an escape attempt from Maryland and ended up being sold. Ducket was implicated and sold to Louisiana. Thomas Ducket to Bigelow, Feb. 18, 1850, in Blassingame, *Slave Testimony*, 89. After James Skipworth died, his cousin Maltilda, wrote to their former master and discussed James's desire that "you will take good care of his children and bring them up in fear of the Lord." The letters of the Skipworths, a family emancipated and sent to Liberia by colonizationist John Hartwell Cocke, underscore a deep attachment to family. The letters span decades, and the Liberians regularly asked for news of and to be remembered by loved ones still in the United States, and expressed a strong desire that more of their kin would be allowed to join them. Matilda Skipworth to John Hartwell Cocke, Feb. 22, 1861, in Miller, *"Dear Master,"* 120, 42, 52, 55, 83, 125, 133; Hezekiah Corpsen to the Editor of the Journal of Commerce, Dec. 4, 1851, in Blassingame, *Slave Testimony*, 94; James Henry to "Dear Sir," in Starobin, *Blacks in Bondage*, 162.

94. Chesney was from Tennessee. Chesney, *Last of the Pioneers*, 26; Baptist, "The Absent Subject," 148; Williams, *Help Me to Find My People*, 195–196, 77–80; SNC, Indiana, 5:169.

95. Madison was enslaved in Virginia, Kentucky, Mississippi, and Louisiana. Blassingame, *Slave Testimony*, 185, 697; Rawick, *AS*, supp., ser. 2, Texas, pt. 9, 10:3891, 3894.

96. Jones, an urban slave in North Carolina, hired his time and eventually freed his second family. Jones, *Experience and Personal Narrative of Uncle Tom Jones*, 23, 24, 25; Ball, *Fifty Years in Chains*, 30, 31–32, 114. "I could never look upon the dear child without being filled with sorrow and fearful apprehensions, of being separated by slaveholders," Henry Bibb said of his daughter. Bibb, *Narrative of the Life and Adventures of Henry Bibb*, 44.

97. Keckley's father was moved when his master left Virginia. Rawick, *AS*, supp., ser. 1, Mississippi, pt. 5, 10:2107; Keckley, *Behind the Scenes*, 23, 25; George Pleasant to Mrs. Agnes Hobbes, Sept. 6, 1833, 26–27; John Boston to "My Dear Wife," Jan. 12, 1862, in Berlin et al., eds., *Free at Last*, 30; Williams, *Help Me to Find My People*, 41–44; Fleischner, *Mastering Slavery*, 99, 107. One former slave "promised my father on his deathbed that I wouldn't dance no more." He counseled her to pray so that they could meet in heaven. *God Struck Me Dead*, 19:26.

98. Anderson, *Interesting Account of Thomas Anderson*, 5–6; *Unwritten History of Slavery*, 149–150, 319.

99. Aaron, "The Light and Truth of Slavery," 4; Raboteau, *Slave Religion*.

100. Rawick, *AS*, supp., ser. 1, Alabama, 1:445; Douglass, *Life and Times*, 110; Lewis, *Out of the Ditch*, 10. In his study of black liberation theology, James Cone wrote, "Because black families were brutalized and broken by slavery and oppression, God became the stabilizing and liberating force in their lives. Thus in prayer, God is often referred to as 'mother for the motherless' and 'father for the fatherless.'" Cone, *God of the Oppressed*, 143.

101. Writing to his still-enslaved mother from Liberia, Peyton Skipworth responded to the news of his father's death with religious resignation. He counseled his mother to do the same, noting his father had gone to a "better world." He did not "greave after my father," because he accepted the Lord's will and expected they would meet again. The news of his Cousin Charles's death was a greater blow due to doubts that he had made his peace with God. Religion offered those separated from loved ones the hope of future reunification. Peyton Skipworth, Monrovia, Liberia, to Lucy Nichels, May 10, 1838, in Miller, *"Dear Master,"* 68.

102. *God Struck Me Dead*, 19:11, 24, 95, 209, 108, 130, 123, 102; Levine, *Black Culture and Black Consciousness*, 33–35.

103. Levine argued that in their folklore, slaves viewed Christ as a second Moses. Levine, *Black Culture and Black Consciousness*, 50. "It was instilled in me many a time: the bottom rail will come to the top someday," Nate Shaw said of his postwar understanding of the Biblical message. Rosengarten, ed., *All God's Dangers*, 7.

104. Towne, *Letters and Diaries*, 162; Levine, *Black Culture and Black Consciousness*, 34; Rawick, *AS*, supp., ser. 1, Mississippi, pt. 2, 7:797.

105. Jacobs, "A True Tale of Slavery," 85; Fleischner, *Mastering Slavery*, 69.

Chapter Two

1. Aaron, "The Light and Truth of Slavery," 3, 4. Lawrence Levine noted the propensity of African American folktales "to celebrate the father as the family's chief protector and provider." Levine, *Black Culture and Black Consciousness*, 97, 94, 95, 396.

2. Stevenson, "Gender Convention, Ideals, and Identity," 169, 170, 172, 174, 179.

3. Fannie Berry, Stevenson's main example, represents one extreme within the narratives. Perdue et al., *Weevils*, 66–67.

4. Perdue et al., *Weevils*, 181–185, 66–67.

5. Stevenson, "Gender Convention, Ideals, and Identity," 171. Lawrence Levine discussed celebration of resistance in men and women. Levine, *Black Culture and Black Consciousness*, 391–397.

6. In the supplementary volumes from Mississippi, ex-slaves regularly mentioned their fathers. However, because the questions focused on plantation jobs, they discussed their father's role and labor but rarely commented on how they felt about him or the quality of the relationship.

7. *SNC*, Georgia, pt. 2, 4:346; Sánchez-Eppler, "'Remember, Dear,'" 35, 36.

8. Ford believed his father hid because Confederate soldiers forced enslaved men to "go wait on them and fight too." Freeman's terse description of her father as a "stern man, and honest," suggests he may not have been particularly emotive. He did, however, keep his family together and succeed as a farmer after the war, and he inspired loyalty. Her brothers "learned shoemakers trade. . . . But when pappy died, them boys give up that good business and tuck a farm . . . to make a home for mammy and the little chilluns." *SNC*, Arkansas, pt. 2, 2:324, 327, 2:348, 350.

9. As headman on a Texas plantation, Adams's father may have done less physical labor. Rawick, *AS*, supp., ser. 2, Texas, pt. 1, 2:156–157; *SNC*, Arkansas, pt. 5, 2:351; Rawick, *AS*, supp., ser. 2, Texas, pt. 1, 2:11. On abroad fathers as active family men and the strong bonds in these relationships, see Berry, *Swing the Sickle*, 73; Hudson, *To Have and to Hold*, 175; West, *Chains of Love*, 57. I disagree with Stevenson that men in abroad marriages were uninvolved in family life and with Dunaway who describes such fathers as "absent shadows." Stevenson, *Life in Black and White*, 222; Dunaway, *African-American Family*, 67.

10. "I 'members him well," John Collins said of the father he lost during the Civil War. "He was a tall black man, over six feet high, wid broad shoulders. My son, John, look just lak him." While Collins never discussed their personal relationship, his description indicates that his father had a playful disposition and he revealed his understanding of how a man ought to interact with children. "Daddy used to play wid mammy just lak she was a child. He'd ketch her under de armpits and jump her up mighty nigh to de rafters in de little house us lived in." Collins grew up in South Carolina and indicated that his parents had different owners. *SNC*, South Carolina, pt. 1, 14:224–225. Wes Brady's paternal grandfather "showed us chil'ren how the Indians march round the camp-fire," Brady recalled. "That was 'bout all we done on Sunday, playing Indian." Rawick, *AS*, supp., ser. 2, Texas, pt. 1, 2:397.

11. *SNC*, Arkansas, pt. 6, 2:70, pt. 4, 2:199; Rawick, *AS*, supp., ser. 2, Texas, pt. 2, 3:636. John Watts's interviewer noted that some of his earliest memories were of his father's visits, but provided no examples. Rawick, *AS*, supp., ser. 1, Georgia, 4:635. "Father often visited us," Allen Parker stated, "and did what he could to make us all happy. Though of course we saw much less of him than most children see of their father." Parker, *Recollections of Slavery Times*, 40.

12. Rawick, *AS*, supp., ser. 2, Texas, pt. 2, 3:837, supp., ser. 1, Mississippi, pt. 3, 8:841. Nat Love called his father "a loving husband and father." Love, *Life and Adventures of Nat Love*, 18. Francis Fedric commented on enslaved fathers: "The affection of the men for their wives and children would be noticed by any one. The men never, if possible, allow their wives to carry the young ones, but are always delighted to have them in their arms." Fedric, *Slave Life in Virginia and Kentucky*, 25.

13. Latta's father came down with pneumonia and died a week later. Jackson, *Story of Mattie J. Jackson*, 5; Latta, *History of My Life and Work*, 116; Rawick, *AS*, supp., ser. 2, Texas, pt. 9, 10:4216. Austin Steward described his father as "a kind, affectionate husband, and a fond, indulgent parent." Steward, *Twenty-Two Years a Slave*, 126.

14. One version of Pitts's story takes place in the immediate postwar period, whereas in the supplemental version her father died during the war. Rawick, *AS*, supp., ser. 2, Texas, pt. 2, 3:522, 523, pt. 2, 3:742–743; *SNC*, Alabama, 1:316; Rawick, *AS*, supp., ser. 1, Alabama, 1:295–296.

15. Picquet's wife was purchased as a concubine. Picquet used money provided by his white father, a slaveholder who freed his slave concubine and children. Mattison, *Louisa Picquet*, 27.

16. Owens, *This Species of Property*, 192, 210. Stevenson argues that with a high number of absent fathers, other enslaved men contributed to the socialization of children. However, she does not consider the contributions of uncles and grandfathers as part of enslaved people's conception of fatherhood. Stevenson, *Life in Black and White*, 222, 251; Stevenson, "Distress and Discord," 107. After Charles Ball lost his mother and siblings to the market, and his father, facing imminent sale, ran away, "my grandfather was the only person left in Maryland with whom I could claim kindred. He manifested all the fondness for me that I could expect from one so old." Ball's grandfather was allowed to visit his grandson regularly and occasionally bring Ball to his own cabin. Later, when Ball was sold south, he thought of his wife, children, and grandfather. Ball, *Fifty Years in Chains*, 15, 31.

17. Perkins was not entirely clear if her Aunt Polly and Uncle Tom were related to her mother, or if she referred to them in kinship terms. Rawick, *AS*, supp., ser. 2, Texas, pt. 7, 8:3072, 3074; *SNC*, Alabama, 1:413–414, South Carolina, pt. 2, 14:107. Mollie Vance and her siblings were raised by an uncle after their parents died. Rawick, *AS*, supp., ser. 1, Mississippi, pt. 5, 10:2142. On fictive kin and surrogates, see Gutman, *Black Family*, 154, 223; Williams, *Help Me to Find My People*, 40.

18. Edward Baptist discusses Joe Kilpatrick, an enslaved man sold away from his family, who, in his new home, adopted and raised a young boy, George Jones, who had been separated from his parents at age five. Later, when Jones was grown, he named his daughters after the two girls his surrogate father had lost so many years earlier and whom he never met. The story reveals reverence for the memory of lost kin, and the transmission of such lore to adopted family. Baptist, "The Absent Subject," 136.

19. *SNC*, South Carolina, pt. 3, 14:17, North Carolina, pt. 1, 11:391; Rawick, *AS*, supp., ser. 2, Texas, pt. 1, 2:406, pt. 3, 4:1210. In contrast, Lulu Wilson compared her treatment to that of her half siblings. "My step paw never did like me, but he was a fool for his own young'uns," she recalled. After the war, "he tramped over half the world gathering up them younguns that they had sold away." A good father displayed compassion for his family, something Wilson's stepfather did only for his biological children. Rawick, *AS*, supp., ser. 2, Texas, pt. 9, 10:4195. Dylan Penningroth stresses that among enslaved people, "kinship could be created; people could start life as strangers and *become* family." Those moved in the slave trade, many teenagers, had to "make kin," in their new homes. Penningroth, *The Claims of Kinfolk*, 87, 88.

20. Boone's father told him stories about forced breeding. "I don't know for certain that my father was used that way or not. I don't suppose he would have told me that." Because he then made the comment about his father's worth he clearly suspected this could have been the case. *SNC*, Arkansas, pt. 1, 2:210, 211. Rochelle Ward, born in 1847, similarly guided her interview, stating, "I want to tell about paw," and then relating her father's stories of slavery. Rawick, *AS*, supp., ser. 1, Oklahoma, 12:360.

21. Fellow slaves informed Thomas that she was lucky, because "a child dat is bawn after her pappy's death kin cure people," by blowing into the mouths of babies. Thomas and the slave community turned her father's death into a source of strength. Rawick, *AS*, supp., ser. 2, Texas, pt. 2, 3:839, 840, pt. 8, 9:3808.

22. Stewart, *Long Past Slavery*, 228; *SNC*, Arkansas, pt. 2, 2:8. David Doddington discusses Robert Falls's comparison of his own reaction to slavery with that of his father, who consistently fought back until sold to a slaveholder he could abide. I see Falls's commentary as a form

of signaling. He used stories about his father to critique slavery, and by extension, the postwar racial order. When Falls announced, "if I had my life to live over, I would die fighting rather than be a slave again," he registered his discontent while placing hypothetical rebellious behavior safely in the past. Doddington, *Contesting Slave Masculinity*, 21, 22, 33. Leo Mouton was also guarded in his comparison to his father. In the immediate postwar period, Mouton's father, who died when his son was nine, served as an informal teacher to the children on a plantation near Lake Charles, Louisiana. "I had a head like popper. I was apt," Mouton announced. "Lot's 'r' times he's teachin' d' bigger chillen how t' speak 'n' talk 'n' sich, 'n' I's too little but I be listenin'." He also claimed his creole father, who died before Reconstruction ended, was the only African American man in the area allowed to sit on a jury. Mouton never had the opportunity to attend school. Rawick, *AS*, supp., ser. 2, Texas, pt. 6, 7:2811.

23. Fleischner notes that Harriet Jacobs remembered "her idealized, virtuous mother" and "her idealized, rebellious father." Rawick, *AS*, supp., ser. 2, Arkansas, 1:201, supp., ser. 1, Oklahoma, 12:69, supp., ser. 2, Texas, pt. 2, 3:735; Fleischner, *Mastering Slavery*, 30, 88.

24. *SNC*, Arkansas, pt. 3, 2:231, North Carolina, pt. 2, 11:50, 48–49, Missouri, 10:299, Maryland, 8:29, South Carolina, pt. 2, 14:145.

25. *SNC*, North Carolina, pt. 1, 11:321, pt. 2, 11:287. Monroe Brackins's father ran off after a whipping. When he returned he was "wild." Rawick, *AS*, supp., ser. 2, Texas, pt. 1, 2:379.

26. Searchers believed Hamilton's father had drowned because his tracks ended at the river, but a white man later recognized him in New York. Webb's family had been enslaved in Georgia. *SNC*, South Carolina, pt. 2, 14:233, Arkansas, pt. 7, 2:77.

27. Brown's father was the illicit child of a white mother and enslaved father and highly skilled. Sterling N. Brown, author of this narrative, was a minister and divinity school professor and the father of Sterling A. Brown, poet, Howard University professor, and from 1936–1939, Editor on Negro Affairs for the Federal Writers' Project. Ellett, enslaved in Virginia, escaped sale under the provisions of a will that stated that certain slaves, including his part-white father and his father's children, could not be sold out of the white family. Brown, *My Own Life Story*, 7; Perdue et al., *Weevils*, 84, 85.

28. Rawick, *AS*, supp., ser. 1, Georgia, 3:261; Perdue et al., *Weevils*, 102; Rawick, *AS*, supp., ser. 2, Texas, pt. 8, 9:3784; Ball, *Fifty Years in Chains*, 13; Doddington, *Contesting Slave Masculinity*, 46.

29. *SNC*, Arkansas, pt. 2, 2:271, South Carolina, pt. 2, 14:175; Rawick, *AS*, supp., ser. 1, Georgia, 3:7–8; *SNC*, North Carolina, pt. 2, 11:396, pt. 1, 11:69, Arkansas, pt. 5, 2:42. Outrunning and outsmarting slave patrols represented one important part of masculine identity and a "fundamental expression of enslaved men's self-confidence" in the Upper South, Fraser writes. Fraser, "Negotiating Their Manhood," 86; Lussana, *My Brother Slaves*, 75–85.

30. Carney is a good example of how ex-slaves use signifying and subtext even with African American interviewers. Perdue et al., *Weevils*, 66; Stewart, *Long Past Slavery*, 202, 221. Charles Joyner discussed trickster tales as "symbolic inversion of roles," and a way for enslaved people to experience "vicarious victory over oppression." Joyner, *Down by the Riverside*, 180, 178, 172–195; Levine, *Black Culture and Black Consciousness*, 115, 106–113.

31. *SNC*, Arkansas, pt. 2, 2:39, Georgia, pt. 1, 4:310, Arkansas, pt. 4, 2:44; Rawick, *AS*, supp., ser. 2, Texas, pt. 5, 6:2043, 2045, pt. 2, 3:944. For other examples of defiant grandfathers, see Rawick, *AS*, supp., ser. 1, Mississippi, pt. 2, 7:427, supp., ser. 2, Texas, pt. 1, 2:165–166.

32. Rawick, *AS*, supp., ser. 2, Texas, pt. 7, 8:3312, 3313.

33. Campbell and his wife were baptized together, and he began to want to preach. He hoped to reunite with his departed mother, son, and wife. Doddington, *Contesting Slave Masculinity*, 103, 104; Campbell, *An Autobiography*, 64–65, 40, 41, 49, 53, 57, 108–109.

34. Doddington's argument about male trustees, in which he contrasts heroic resistance with "a different view of manhood centered on the family," applies more broadly and also fits some of the men he argues formed an identity through work. Doddington, *Contesting Slave Masculinity*, 122, 75.

35. "Enslaved men performed their masculinity in different ways in different places, but they could not fulfill every role, in every space, for every person," he writes. While this is true, it

overlooks the ways in which enslaved fathers, and the children who commented on them, regularly mixed different elements of masculine identity. Doddington, *Contesting Slave Masculinity*, 213.

36. Brown, *My Own Life Story*, 7; Perdue et al., *Weevils*, 110; South Carolina, pt. 2, 14:6–7. "Some men viewed their family roles as more important to survival and self-respect than engaging in rebellion or resistance that seemed futile," Doddington writes. Doddington, *Contesting Slave Masculinity*, 74.

37. Perdue et al., *Weevils*, 152; SNC, Arkansas, pt. 2, 2:169, 170, pt. 4, 2:132, Texas, pt. 3, 16:184; Rawick, *AS*, supp., ser. 1, Mississippi, pt. 1, 6:123. Sergio Lussana discusses skilled work as a way to provision family, achieve respect as a provider, and bond with and pass on valuable skills to sons. Lussana, *My Brother Slaves*, 40–44.

38. A skilled slave, often in a managerial position, was more likely to maintain an intact, or largely intact, family. Favored slaves were often allowed to discipline and provision their children differently than field hands. West finds that favored slaves were slightly more likely to live in two-parent households. West, *Chains of Love*, 106. William Dusinberre shows that this varied by plantation. Status and skill did not protect Gowrie slaves from separation or improve their children's survival, but at Chicora Wood, there was a "network of privilege" that benefited favored slaves. Dusinberre, *Them Dark Days*, 349, 87, 91, 176.

39. SNC, Georgia, pt. 4, 4:66–67, South Carolina, pt. 2, 14:3, Alabama, 1:174; Rawick, *AS*, supp., ser. 1, Mississippi, pt. 3, 8:1029–1030, supp., ser. 2, Texas, pt. 3, 4:1056, 1057, pt. 9, 10:4007.

40. "Some enslaved and formerly enslaved people depicted men's labor as indispensable, reversing the emasculating notion of dependency," Doddington adds. Heard, *From Slavery to the Bishopric*, 23; Love, *Life and Adventures of Nat Love*, 18; Rawick, *AS*, supp., ser. 2, Texas, pt. 4, 5:1479, supp., ser. 1, Georgia, 3:330; Doddington, *Contesting Slave Masculinity*, 113, 114, 120. Mary Church Terrell was never a slave, but her parents had been. "Although my father never went to school a day in his life . . . he was unusually intelligent and thoughtful and reasoned exceedingly well. He learned to read by constantly perusing the newspapers," she wrote. Terrell, *A Colored Woman in a White World*, 6.

41. Gladney's father mate-guarded, refusing to allow other enslaved men near his wife and breaking another man's leg. SNC, South Carolina, pt. 2, 14:129; Rawick, *AS*, supp., ser. 1, Mississippi, pt. 5, 10:2214, 2215.

42. Smith's grandfather mastered "a secret charm, handed down from generation to generation," called "blowing fire," in which he "blew on de burn and de fire and pain was gone." Only one family member could possess the secret and he passed it on to Smith's Aunt Harriet, an example of flexibility in gender roles within slave communities. SNC, Missouri, 10:330, 331, 10:40. George White called his father "a kinda doctor too like his master, an' papa knowed all de roots," noting that he once healed a woman his master predicted would die. Perdue et al., *Weevils*, 310; Rawick, *AS*, supp., ser. 1, Oklahoma, 12:322, supp., ser. 2, Texas, pt. 8, 9:3491; SNC, Texas, pt. 3, 16:268; Jackson, *Experience of a Slave in South Carolina*, 7.

43. Trustee positions were held mainly by men. Abolitionists criticized these men as morally compromised and used them as a foil to the heroic rebel. Doddington, *Contesting Slave Masculinity*, 52, 69, 60, 61, 64, 70, 71, 72.

44. Doddington sees such responses as an indication that parents passed this attitude on to their children. Doddington, *Contesting Slave Masculinity*, 73, 76, 78, 81, 80.

45. Doddington states that "enslaved people might refashion the divisive system of rewards used by enslavers to strengthen small-scale loyalties, often familial-based, at the expense of more expansive models of solidarity." Doddington, *Contesting Slave Masculinity*, 74.

46. Williams may also have related the story of a woman named Aunt Cissy and her vocal opposition to slavery. Cissy informed the master that he could never sell her child who had died and gone to heaven. However, editorial notes indicate that this story may have been misattributed. Williams also mentioned being beaten by her mother, a figure who barely appears in the narrative. Perdue et al., *Weevils*, 317, 315–323. Doddington uses the example of Nancy Williams to

show "links between honesty, identity, and standing in the community, even in the application and use of violence." Doddington, *Contesting Slave Masculinity*, 78, 79. Some slaveholders allowed enslaved people to discipline their own children, especially men who served as drivers or headmen. Blassingame, *Slave Community*, 178; Rawick, *AS*, supp., ser. 2, Texas, pt. 7, 8:3162.

47. Rawick, *AS*, supp., ser. 1, Mississippi, pt. 5, 10:2409, 2411. Doddington notes, "Young's perception of his father was not harmed by this acquiescence to disciplinary violence." Young did not appear to be particularly bothered by his father's position, an attitude likely fostered by his own status as a favored slave with a room in the big house. Doddington, *Contesting Slave Masculinity*, 71, 72.

48. Randolph said little about his father, but his death increased the family's hardship, indicating that he had helped provide. "When my father died, he left my mother with five children," he noted, "and mother had no one to help take care of us." Their master underfed his slaves, and his mother "used to get a little corn, without his knowledge, and boil it for us to satisfy our hunger." Rawick, *AS*, supp., ser. 2, Texas, pt. 2, 3:708, pt. 1, 2:255, 259, 257; Randolph, *From Slave Cabin to the Pulpit*, 16. "Enslaved people could hate or resent black male trustees yet still feel they were manly," Doddington writes. "Attributes associated with enslaved masculinity were not always laudable expressions of triumph and solidarity and the violence inflicted by enslaved trustees helped them forge identities as men others dare not cross." Doddington, *Contesting Slave Masculinity*, 87.

49. As the coachman, Davis's father had an easier life. He also had access to and liked to drink alcohol. *SNC*, Georgia, pt. 1, 4:265, 269; Rawick, *AS*, supp., ser. 2, Texas, pt. 4, 5:1905, 1904–1905, 1908.

50. Jenkins and his brother did keep a middle initial to represent their father's name, Dinkins. *SNC*, South Carolina, pt. 3, 14:24; Rawick, *AS*, supp., ser. 2, Texas, pt. 2, 3:784, supp., ser. 1, Mississippi, pt. 5, 10:2084, 2092, 2086, 2091. Dunaway argues "one of every five of the Appalachian ex-slaves reported that they were indifferent towards their fathers. A few Appalachian slave children rejected their fathers, defining them as strangers to whom they owed no allegiance." It is unclear how she defines indifference and its causal factors. As explored in chapter 1, removal from parents and socialization by whites could lead to alienation from kin, and this applied to mothers and fathers. As for rejection, Dunaway cites the example of Sutton, an anomalous comment on a father among the entirety of the FWP narratives. Dunaway, *African-American Family*, 79, 78. Sutton's narrative was revised by fieldworkers in a way that altered meaning. The revised interview indicated Sutton ran away to return to her mistress rather than her mother and siblings. Musher, "Contesting 'The Way the Almighty Wants It,'" 16.

51. Morris, "Within the Slave Cabin," 272.

52. Rawick, *AS*, supp., ser. 1, Mississippi, pt. 5, 10:2232, 2233, 2243, pt. 5, 10:2246. "Enslaved men sometimes exerted control over their families through the abuse of their offspring," Jeff Forret writes, noting that such men "were not recollected fondly." He also found two cases of enslaved men who "recoiled from impending fatherhood," and killed pregnant women, one then committing suicide. Forret, *Slave against Slave*, 261, 262, 266, 357–358; Morris, "Within the Slave Cabin," 272.

53. Cauley grew up in North Carolina. *SNC*, Arkansas, pt. 2, 2:4, 3; Rawick, *AS*, supp., ser. 2, Texas, pt. 8, 9:3508.

54. Slaveholders could purchase a "paternalist fantasy in the slave market," Johnson writes (109). Genovese, *Roll*, 6; Johnson, *Soul by Soul*, 111, 107–108; Tadman, *Speculators and Slaves*, 218–219; Dusinberre, *Them Dark Days*, 356, 359–360, 367–368, 416.

55. *SNC*, North Carolina, pt. 1, 11:429. Another informant, who grew up in Tennessee, recalled that slaves "couldn't say papa; they had to say 'daddy' and 'mammy' and when they got free they started saying 'papa' and then the white people started saying 'daddy.'" *Unwritten History of Slavery*, 18:5.

56. *SNC*, North Carolina, pt. 2, 11:86; Rawick, *AS*, supp., ser. 2, Texas, pt. 1, 2:344, pt. 6, 7:2722.

57. Rawick, *AS*, supp., ser. 2, Texas, pt. 6, 7:2818, 2859; Stewart, *Long Past Slavery*, 228, 217.

58. Drew, *North-Side View of Slavery*, 89; Ball, *Fifty Years in Chains*, 218; Bruner, *Slave's Adventures toward Freedom*, 48.

59. After he was sold, Campbell escaped from a different master and made his way to Canada. Campbell, *An Autobiography*, 124, 160, 172; Allen, *Life, Experience, and Gospel Labours of the Rt. Rev. Richard Allen*, 6, 7.

60. W. W. McDonogh to "Dear Father," J. McDonogh, Oct. 7, 1846, in Starobin, *Blacks in Bondage*, 179; Blassingame, *Slave Testimony*, 412.

61. Towne added that another former slave could not sleep "for thinking how sorry she is to lose 'Pa Linkum.'" *SNC*, North Carolina, pt. 1, 11:268; Towne, *Letters and Diaries*, 162; Philadelphia, *Press*, April 11, 1865 in Sterling, ed., *Speak Out in Thunder Tones*, 362.

62. Michael Tadman, discussing strategies of appeasement on the part of slaves, similarly writes that "the dominant tendency seems to have been an adjustment to power relationships rather than a basic accommodation of ideas and values." Stevenson argues that enslaved women evaluated white women according to their own standards, coming away with a "disrespect grounded in slave women's beliefs about appropriate female behavior." Based on their conception of masculine duty, slave communities articulated a similar disrespect of white men. Johnson, *Soul by Soul*, 36; Tadman, *Speculators and Slaves*, 10; Stevenson, "Gender Convention, Ideals, and Identity," 183.

Chapter Three

1. John Q. A. Dennis to Edwin M. Stanton, July 26, 1864, in Berlin et al., *Free at Last*, 120–121.

2. The ambivalence of the internal economy applied to slaveholders as well as slaves. McDonnell, "Money Knows No Master," 37–39; Hilliard, *Masters, Slaves, and Exchange*, 7, 9, 10, 16, 37, 67; Penningroth, *The Claims of Kinfolk*, 49, 47, 6, 8, 46, 55, 77, 82, 173, 191–192; Doddington, *Contesting Slave Masculinity*, 89–126; Hudson, "All That Cash," 77, 78, 80, 83, 84; Wood, *Women's Work, Men's Work*, 186–187. Forret details the violence in the quarters that erupted over property: "Although positive in many respects, the internal economy also prompted conflicts disruptive to the harmony and solidarity of the slave quarters." Forret, *Slave against Slave*, 203, 202, 207–235.

3. Economic opportunities included garden plots, overwork, skilled work, and hiring out, and kin groups utilized the labor of children. Penningroth, *The Claims of Kinfolk*, 50, 51, 53, 83, 84; Hudson, *To Have and to Hold*, 1, 31, 32, 48, 53, 55; Pargas, *Quarters and the Fields*, 88, 89, 91, 97–98, 100, 104, 105.

4. In South Carolina, enslaved families with fewer adult full-time residents struggled to amass property. The economies of large, productive families offered a buffer against the vagaries of slavery and contributed to family stability. Extra food improved health, protecting against illness, and larger kin groups could better navigate the death of family members. Hudson, *To Have and to Hold*, 58, 69, 78, 79, 140, 183, 184.

5. Her face beaten to a "soft pulp," King was unable to eat solid food for the rest of her life. Perdue et al., *Weevils*, 191. Karen Sánchez-Eppler uses King as an example of the need to approach the FWP narratives and slavery from the perspective of children. "The mistress wielded conventional emblems of childhood happiness as physical weapons," and King then used those emblems as "rhetorical weapons" to critique "the perverse cruelty of this mistress and of the slave system as a whole." Sánchez-Eppler, "'Remember, Dear,'" 41. Though rarely whipped, as a child Frederick Douglass had no parents to help provide, and he "suffered much from hunger, but much more from cold." Douglass, *Narrative*, 27.

6. West, *Chains of Love*, 89–91; Dunaway, *African-American Family*, 163, 164, 166; Hudson, *To Have and to Hold*, 73. Enslaved and free black men had more opportunities to perform skilled labor. Marks, "Skilled Blacks in Antebellum St. Mary's County, Maryland," 227–251; Doddington, *Contesting Slave Masculinity*, 100.

7. Rebecca Fraser discusses material provisioning and masculine identity in the Upper South. Doddington, *Contesting Slave Masculinity*, 97–98, 92, 101, 124; Fraser, "Negotiating Their Manhood," 81; Forret, *Slave against Slave*, 207–208, 264–266; Blassingame, "Status and Social Structure in the Slave Community," 137–151.

8. Doddington, *Contesting Slave Masculinity*, 97, 99. The John tales, in which John's theft and the master's unsuccessful attempts to catch him feature prominently, indicate that slaves saw provisioning as a male responsibility despite women's crucial role in the material upkeep of households. Joyner, *Down by the Riverside*, 188–189; Levine, *Black Culture and Black Consciousness*, 127, 390–391.

9. Doddington, *Contesting Slave Masculinity*, 101–102, 105, 107; Lussana, *My Brother Slaves*, 42–43.

10. Hicks grew up in Kentucky. His mother put the children to bed before his father's visits, but Hicks recalled peeking out from under the covers and seeing his father unloading bread from his bag and "then to my delight I saw him hand out a jug of milk." Rawick, *AS*, supp., ser. 1, Indiana and Ohio, 5:85, 84, Georgia, pt. 3, 4:233; Rawick, *AS*, supp., ser. 2, Texas, pt. 5, 6:2036–2037, supp., ser. 1, Mississippi, pt. 5, 10:2076. Despite being "crippled up with rheumatism," Sina Banks's father, who lived on a neighboring Missouri farm, made and sold brooms, using the proceeds to "buy things for mother to use in our cabin." Rawick, *AS*, supp., ser. 1, Oklahoma, 12:17. Even in areas where conditions limited their involvement in family life, enslaved men made contributions to household economies. For examples of ex-slaves in the Virginia Narratives who indicated that their fathers added considerably to the family economy and possibly at higher levels than women, see Cornelius Garner, 102, Lorenzo Ivy, 152, Ishrael Massie, 211, George White, 310, and Nancy Williams, 316–317, in Perdue et al., *Weevils*.

11. In her article on slave masculinity in the Upper South, Rebecca Fraser writes that "hunting and fishing were also fundamental features of enslaved men's sense of themselves as providers—both materially and emotionally." Fraser, "Negotiating Their Manhood," 81. Sergio Lussana notes children's appreciation of fathers who hunted, but emphasizes hunting as a homosocial group activity that enabled men to perform masculinity and pass on their skills to younger men. Lussana, *My Brother Slaves*, 71–74.

12. *SNC*, Kentucky, 7:5, Georgia, pt. 3, 4:267; Jackson, *Experience of a Slave in South Carolina*, 30; Proctor, *Bathed in Blood*, 157, 158.

13. Rawick, *AS*, supp., ser. 2, Texas, pt. 3, 4:1026, pt. 3, 4:1335, supp., ser. 1, Oklahoma, 12:276. Sampson Willis's father worked his cotton patch by moonlight, and "all ways had some money and he'd give us chillun a few nickels to spend." The bulk of the money, $900, was hidden, guarded by the family, and used to buy a farm after freedom, land Willis eventually inherited. Rawick, *AS*, supp., ser. 2, Texas, pt. 9, 10:4165, 4163.

14. Money was different and generally hidden. Penningroth, *The Claims of Kinfolk*, 91–96; Forret, *Slave against Slave*, 212.

15. Perdue et al., *Weevils*, 310; Rawick, *AS*, supp., ser. 2, Texas, pt. 1, 2:156–157; Blassingame, *Slave Testimony*, 491; Ball, *Fifty Years in Chains*, 12.

16. Rawick, *AS*, supp., ser. 2, Texas, pt. 7, 8:3084; *SNC*, Arkansas, pt. 2, 2:322, 323.

17. Sergio Lussana argues that men used theft to provide for family and community, and such activity earned respect from others and imparted a sense of satisfaction and self-worth. Lussana, *My Brother Slaves*, 85–97; Henson, *Autobiography*, 26. Theft internal to the quarters could cause discord and even violence. Forret, *Slave against Slave*, 211, 214, 215, 216, 221, 222, 229; Hilliard, *Masters, Slaves, and Exchange*, 103–107, 110, 130; Lichtenstein, "'That Disposition to Theft, with Which They Have Been Branded.'"

18. Rawick, *AS*, supp., ser. 2, Texas, pt. 3, 4:1366, pt. 8, 9:3715. A few FWP narratives mention men who hid and fed their families in caves. Regardless of the veracity of such stories, they indicate what former slaves valued. A man who stole his family and hid them in a cave was simultaneously engaging in heroic resistance and acting as a provider and protector. *SNC*, Georgia, pt. 2, 4:14, 15, Georgia, pt. 1, 4:24. Moses Grandy discussed his family members, including his brother-in-law, provisioning a runaway sister who hid in the forest. Her husband some-

times slipped away to spend the night with her and she bore three children in her den before being caught. Grandy, *Narrative of the Life of Moses Grandy*, 54.

19. Rawick, *AS*, supp., ser. 2, Texas, pt. 3, 4:1363, 1366, 1367.

20. "Masters who skimped on rations for their own workers ended up forcing slaves on neighboring plantations to siphon off their earnings," Penningroth writes (56). Penningroth, *The Claims of Kinfolk*, 55, 77, 57, 78, 191; Wood, *Women's Work, Men's Work*, 186.

21. Peter Still built his wife a cabin, furnished it, and provided food, clothing, and other "comforts" to make up for a neglectful master. Pickard, *Kidnapped and the Ransomed*, 199, 117, 141; Ball, *Fifty Years in Chains*, 78; Arkansas, pt. 4, 2:191–192.

22. Hawkins, *Lunsford Lane*, 28. "Legal and managerial restrictions hemmed slaves in at every turn, and more ominously so did the spending habits of their masters. Overmatched though they were, bondpeople imposed paternalist judgment on the choices masters made," Kathleen Hilliard writes. Hilliard, *Masters, Slaves, and Exchange*, 68.

23. Lane eventually freed himself and his family. Hawkins, *Lunsford Lane*, 30; Lane, *The Narrative of Lunsford Lane*, 11, 12. Fraser explores how "the enslaved and the slaveholder negotiated the boundaries" of their performance of masculinity. When slaveholders encouraged the internal economy, doing so offered economic benefits because they controlled the products, an outcome that ultimately upheld their masculine self-identity and conception of paternalism. "Slaveholders and enslaved men negotiated particular boundaries with each other in order that they might both prove their masculine credentials." Fraser, "Negotiating Their Manhood," 81, 83.

24. In his discussion of honor and enslaved men, Forret notes that these men "understood that their sense of honor had its limitations within the constraints of Southern white society." Forret, *Slave against Slave*, 313.

25. Henry never referred to the children as his son and daughter. Henry, *Life of George Henry*, 33–34, 45. David Doddington writes, "Some enslaved men fashioned the labor they performed into evidence of manhood, but others resented any compromises with slavery or with enslavers that might be required by such activities, emphasizing the superior virtues of resistance instead." Doddington, *Contesting Slave Masculinity*, 102–103.

26. Henry commented on the importance of educating girls, indicating he objected to slavery and not being beholden to a mistress. Henry, *Life of George Henry*, 62, 63, 67, 56, 57.

27. Being a favored slave did not protect Smith's father from losing a child to the market. Harper, *Memoir of Slavery*, 36, 29; Smith, *Autobiography of James L. Smith*, 4, 13.

28. Peter Brown's father "stole" his wife and hid her in the woods for a time. Because she was a "fast breeder" who gave birth to three sets of twins, the master agreed to relieve her of work if she returned. *SNC*, Arkansas, pt. 1, 2:311, 312, North Carolina, pt. 1, 11:238. For masters who rewarded fertile women with reduced labor and/or material benefits, see Cade, "Out of the Mouths of Ex-Slaves," 307; White, *Ar'n't I a Woman?*, 100.

29. Brown, *Narrative of the Life of Henry Box Brown, Written by Himself*, 36, 37, 38, 42; Brown, *Narrative of Henry Box Brown*, 50. See Calvin Schermerhorn for a more detailed discussion of Brown and the failure of his work and church networks. Though Brown managed to borrow a small sum from a church friend and reclaim his material property, he could not prevent the loss of his family. Cottrell's profit, Schermerhorn writes, "was partly the result of Nancy and Henry Brown's reproductive successes." Schermerhorn, *Money over Mastery, Family over Freedom*, 159, 137–140, 158–162. Hannah Plummer's father hired his own time and lived with his family on the plantation of his wife's owner. This master called him "a high-headed fellow and said he was livin' on his lot and in his house and that he didn't do anything for him, and that he ought to keep up his family." *SNC*, North Carolina, pt. 2, 11:178.

30. Stewart discusses ex-slaves using their FWP interviews to revise the standard narrative of slavery and emancipation, adopting duties once solely the province of the slaveholder, and acting as "protector, guardian, and provider." Using examples from men's narratives, Stewart shows how "the Confederate theme of the faithful slave who won't leave the plantation even after emancipation is reconfigured, as these former slaves literally take the master's place, becoming surrogate husbands to their former mistresses" (226). Although this anecdote deviates

somewhat from the scenes explored by William Andrews in an article about postbellum reunions between former slaves and slaveholders, in that London never left the South, it contains similar elements. "By demonstrating the moral leadership in such reunions, the former slave comes before the reader of the postbellum slave narrative as an active agent in the reconstruction of the South, not as the white man's burden so often portrayed by New South politicians," Andrews writes. Aleckson, *Before the War, and After the Union*, 106, 106–107; Stewart, *Long Past Slavery*, 228; Andrews, "Reunion in the Postbellum Slave Narrative," 12.

31. Pennington, *Narrative of Events of the Life of J. H. Banks*, 23, 23–24; Camp, *Closer to Freedom*, 94.

32. Hudson, *To Have and to Hold*, 54.

33. John S. Jacobs, "A True Tale of Slavery," 85, 85–86; Yellin, *Harriet Jacobs*, 7. "I am a father," Thomas Jones wrote from the perspective of an enslaved father, noting "feelings of unspeakable anguish, as I have looked upon my precious babes, and have thought of the ignorance, degradation, and woe which they must endure as slaves." Jones, *Experience and Personal Narrative of Uncle Tom Jones*, 8. As Wilma King notes, enslaved parents endeavored to teach their children the "balance between social courtesies to whites and their own self-esteem." King, *Stolen Childhood*, 71. Marie Schwartz argues that enslaved children "learned to negotiate between acts of submission and selfhood, between the worlds of commodity and community, as they grew to adulthood." Nell Irvin Painter discusses the emotional damage inflicted by teaching children to suppress their anger. Schwartz, *Born in Bondage*, 18; Painter, *Soul Murder and Slavery*, 15.

34. "Phipps went with a colored woman before he married his wife," Alexander noted. *SNC*, Arkansas, pt. 1, 2:35, 36. Children learned to parse the social hierarchy of the Old South as a matter of survival, and they often manipulated paternalism to their own advantage. In doing so, they could deliberately and inadvertently undermine the limited authority of their parents. "Obviously, slaves sometimes internalized prevalent racist views which created tension within their families and communities," Brenda Stevenson writes. Stevenson, "Distress and Discord," 112. Marie Schwartz notes that enslaved children had to please parents and masters, and "the task of maintaining their children's allegiance was daunting to slave couples, whose resources were meager." Schwartz, *Born in Bondage*, 78.

35. *SNC*, Arkansas, pt. 1, 2:33, 35, 37, 34.

36. Stroyer, *My Life in the South*, 19, 20, 22–23; Schwartz, *Born in Bondage*, 2; King, *Stolen Childhood*, 116.

37. Each time he suffered a setback, including a serious injury caused by a horse, Stroyer's mother became extremely upset. "Father did not show his grief for me as mother did, but he tried to comfort mother all he could" (27). When emancipation came, Stroyer's father had died, but his mother lived to enjoy freedom. Stroyer, *My Life in the South*, 23, 24, 37.

38. Jones, *Experience of Rev. Thomas H. Jones*, 74, 74–75, 75.

39. Jones, 76. See Albert Raboteau, *Slave Religion*, 308–309, for a discussion of prayer as a form of resistance to slavery. John Irvine, hired out as a youngster, had permission to visit his parents' cabin once a week. His father would return him to work on a horse so he could stay longer, "giving the boy good advice all along the road." Simmons, *Men of Mark*, 997.

40. Jeffries's grandfather also paid him a quarter for his work, money he used to buy chewing tobacco. *SNC*, South Carolina, pt. 3, 14:18; Rawick, *AS*, supp., ser. 2, Texas, pt. 4, 5:1537; Perdue et al., *Weevils*, 26; *SNC*, South Carolina, pt. 2, 14:75; Rawick, *AS*, supp., ser. 2, Texas, pt. 4, 5:1822.

41. Rawick, *AS*, supp., ser. 2, Texas, pt. 8, 9:3485, pt. 3, 4:1423, supp., ser. 1, Oklahoma, 12:17; Schwartz, *Born in Bondage*, 70. George Washington Brooks helped raise the white children and was known in his Missouri community as "the shepherd of the flock." Rawick, *AS*, supp., ser. 1, Missouri, 2:152. For a discussion of the image of the mammy, see White, *Ar'n't I a Woman?*, 46–61; Genovese, *Roll*, 360–361.

42. Moore clearly knew her white interviewer. Moore mentioned her mother and twelve siblings, but focused her narrative on her father. *SNC*, South Carolina, pt. 3, 14:205. Charles Joyner noted that Brer Rabbit stories might be shared with whites, but slaves kept certain folklore,

such as John tales, to themselves. Joyner, *Down by the Riverside*, 189. When whites called older men "Uncle," the term connoted nurturing, but not authority. Whites saw this title as a token of affection, but it spoke to limited power. However, as with many aspects of slavery, titles had different meanings for enslaved people and white people. Herbert Gutman discussed how enslaved people, unable to use forms of address such as "mister," taught their children to call adults "uncle" and "aunt," which expressed respect and "invested non-kin *slave* relationships with symbolic kin meanings and functions." Gutman, *Black Family*, 217, 216–222. The Uncle Tom image presents the black man as a kindly helper rather than as authoritative father. Richardson, *Black Masculinity and the U.S. South*, 3.

43. She also showed a catechism, dated 1840, owned by her father and proudly noted that he knew the contents "from cover to cover." *SNC*, South Carolina, pt. 3, 14:205, 206, 207; Levine, *Black Culture and Black Consciousness*, 85; Bay, *The White Image in the Black Mind*, 122. For another example of a story about the origin of the world in which all people were initially black, see Levi Pollard, in Perdue et al., *Weevils*, 233. In Pollard's tale, people heard about a lake that would wash away their skin color. As the water became increasingly murky, some emerged mulatto. See Cone, *God of the Oppressed*, 133–137, for a discussion of black Jesus.

44. *SNC*, South Carolina, pt. 3, 14:206.

45. Dusinberre comments on the "bitterness" that lurks beneath the surface of "suitably polite remarks" in FWP interviews gathered by white Southern fieldworkers. Dusinberre, *Them Dark Days*, 418, 363. "Southern paternalism led white collectors to comfortably assume they were in charge of these exchanges," Catherine Stewart remarks. Stewart, *Long Past Slavery*, 97.

46. Before her father died, when asked by his former master's son, "Is dere anything I can do for you Uncle Isaiah?" her father responded, "Take care of Charity." *SNC*, South Carolina, pt. 3, 14:205, 208, 207. Charles Joyner wrote, of slave folklore, "Throughout the animal trickster tales runs the reminder that overweening pride, literally hubris, often leads to a tragic fall." Moore's father injected the same concept into his Bible stories. Joyner, *Down by the Riverside*, 182; Levine, *Black Culture and Black Consciousness*, 96.

47. Becker, "The Black Church: Manhood and Mission," 324; Raboteau, *Slave Religion*, 231–239. Michael Gomez argues that scholars have missed the African origins of the black preacher, who most resembled the West African *griot*, or storyteller, and played an important role in shaping African American folklore. Gomez, *Exchanging Our Country Marks*, 280–281.

48. Forret, *Slave against Slave*, 320, 321–323.

49. Perdue et al., *Weevils*, 208; *Unwritten History of Slavery*, 18: 122; *SNC*, Oklahoma, 13:234.

50. Green grew up in Louisiana. Rawick, *AS*, supp., ser. 2, Texas, pt. 7, 8:3203, pt. 2, 3:801; Blassingame, *Slave Testimony*, 659–660.

51. *SNC*, South Carolina, pt. 2, 14:174. Mary Reynolds's family attended a secret church where a black preacher "told us that a day would come when Niggers only be slave of God." Rawick, *AS*, supp., ser. 2, Texas, pt. 7, 8:3290.

52. *SNC*, Georgia, pt. 1, 4:12. Amanda Smith decided to "pray and lead a Christian life" after an illness and her father's professed concern "about my soul." Likewise, James Smith's father, in the postwar period, called his children to his deathbed, "bade us all farewell," and announced that the "one thing that troubled him" was that none of his children "professed religion." After that day, Smith declared, "I commenced to seek the Lord with all my heart, and never stopped till I found Him." Smith, *An Autobiography*, 43, 42; Smith, *Autobiography of James L. Smith*, 14; Thompson, *Life of John Thompson*, 48; Jeter, *Pastor Henry N. Jeter's Twenty-Five Years Experience with the Shiloh Baptist Church*, 15; Baptist, "The Absent Subject," 151, 152.

53. Latta, *History of My Life and Work*, 116; Rawick, *AS*, supp., ser. 1, Mississippi, pt. 3, 8:1231, 1233, supp., ser. 1, Alabama, 1:186; *SNC*, North Carolina, pt. 1, 11:429; Rawick, *AS*, supp., ser. 1, North and South Carolina, 11:95, 11:112. Susan Forrest's father "teached me how to shout," and Lou Austin, discussing spirituals and clandestine worship, said, "My Daddy shore could make it ring." Rawick, *AS*, supp., ser. 2, Texas, pt. 3, 4:1379, pt. 1, 2:130.

54. Thompson was nine years old when he and his two sisters were separated from their parents in Mississippi. *SNC*, South Carolina, pt. 1, 14:323; Thompson, *Biography of a Slave*, 20. Lizzie

Williams recounted the lyrics to a spiritual "my pappy used ter sing in de fiel'," which expressed the hope "I'll meet my mothah and fathah dar." *SNC*, North Carolina, pt. 2, 11:395.

55. Lussana, *My Brother Slaves*, 132, 9, 18, 125, 128–130, 135.

56. Cooper grew up in Louisiana. *SNC*, South Carolina, pt. 4, 14:67–68; Rawick, *AS*, supp., ser. 2, Texas, pt. 2, 3:920, pt. 3, 4:1029; *SNC*, Oklahoma, 13:48; Levine, *Black Culture and Black Consciousness*, 87, 369.

57. Rawick, *AS*, supp., ser. 2, Texas, pt. 9, 10:4282, supp., ser. 1, Mississippi, pt. 2, 7:664; *SNC*, South Carolina, pt. 4, 14:49; *God Struck Me Dead*, 19:39. During his first train ride following the war, Charlie Meadow sat between his father's legs "and dat de best ride dat I ever had and I'll never forget it." Startled by the train's speed, he "held on tight to my daddy's knees." *SNC*, South Carolina, pt. 3, 14:179. Fathers also offered lessons for everyday life. Irella Walker's father taught his children how to "rub tallow, fried meat grease, or any other kind ob grease into our hard shoe leather" to soften their plantation shoes. Rawick, *AS*, supp., ser. 2, Texas, pt. 9, 10:3934.

58. Adams, *Narrative of the Life of John Quincy Adams*, 6; Jacobs, "A True Tale of Slavery," 86; Drew, *North-Side View of Slavery*, 110; Arter, *Echoes from a Pioneer Life*, 14; Blassingame, *Slave Testimony*, 618; *SNC*, Alabama, 1:384, Indiana, 5:211. George Skipworth, in a letter to his master, a man who provided his slaves with educational opportunities, professed pride in his children's intellectual progress. George Skipworth to John Hartwell Cocke, April 15, 1845, in Miller, *"Dear Master,"* 168. Literacy represented one component of enslaved men's provisioning in the Upper South. Fraser, "Negotiating Their Manhood," 84.

59. When he said he did not care if he died, Banks echoed words he had heard his father utter when defending his wife from a whipping. He also detailed his father's frank interactions with his master. Pennington, *Narrative of Events of the Life of J. H. Banks*, 10, 11, 44, 19–20, 32, 48, 62, 63.

60. Enslaved women also engaged in ideological provisioning. One informant's father had a garden, raised chickens, and went on nighttime pig "hunting" trips. He kept a storehouse under the cabin, prepared meals, ran a clandestine "little restaurant," and had permission to take the wagon to town each Sunday to sell his goods, which his daughter insinuated were regularly resold to the people from whom he had pilfered them. In this two-parent household, her father was the material provider, especially of food, but she learned to have a "backbone" from her mother, defining her father as the more "timid" personality and her mother as the force in the home. Tangible and intangible contributions and internal family dynamics varied as much based on personality as household structure. *Unwritten History of Slavery*, 19:285, 286, 284.

61. Robinson was sold after this incident. He eventually fought for the Union, serving in the Mass. 54th and Indiana 28th. Robinson, *From Log Cabin to the Pulpit*, 24–25, 29, 39–40, 117. "The memory of his father guided him as he established his neighborhood status and sense of self worth," Calvin Schermerhorn says of William Robinson. In another instance of paternal influence, Schermerhorn argues that Solomon Bayley provided his two daughters with "a compelling example of character." Calvin Schermerhorn, *Money over Mastery, Family over Freedom*, 105, 40.

62. Jacobs, *Incidents*, 11, 18–19; Jacobs, "A True Tale of Slavery," 86; Fleischner, *Mastering Slavery*, 65, 7, 84, 113. Enslaved parents "taught their youngsters how to tolerate inhumane acts and degradation while maintaining their humanity and keeping their spirit intact." King, *Stolen Childhood*, 68.

63. Glasgow also cared for Brown after a vicious flogging, another characteristic of a father figure. "He gave Brown hope—a reason to live," Sergio Lussana writes. "The story of Brown and Glasgow shows how friendship provided men with a buffer against the brutal features of enslaved life." Lussana, *My Brother Slaves*, 114, 113; Brown, *Slave Life in Georgia*, 23–24, 44, 168.

64. Douglass, *Life and Times*, 111, 112. Waldo Martin calls Lawson "a much-needed father figure and role model," and Calvin Schermerhorn labels him a "religious mentor" to Douglass. Martin, *The Mind of Frederick Douglass*, 20; Schermerhorn, *Money over Mastery, Family over Freedom*, 83, 84. On the performative nature of masculinity, see Doddington, *Contesting Slave Masculinity*, 3, 4; Lussana, *My Brother Slaves*, 6.

65. Ball never saw his father again. Ball, *Fifty Years in Chains*, 14, 13. While working in the big house, Susan Broaddus overheard the master talking about selling two male slaves. She memorized the names and ran and told her father, who counseled her to return to the big house and say she had never left. The next day the two men went missing. Perdue et al., *Weevils*, 55.

66. Hawkins's father had purchased his own freedom, but his children remained enslaved. Though his father urged him to escape, neither father nor son knew where he should go, as neither had ever traveled any distance. With help from free friends and kind strangers, Hawkins made it to Philadelphia and reunited with a brother who had escaped earlier. Edwards, *From Slavery to a Bishopric*, 49–50, 66, 123.

67. Jones, *Days of Bondage*, 11–12, 14, 15. Strong-willed parents socialized strong-willed children. Ellen Cragin claimed that neither of her parents would easily accept a whipping. When the master "cut sores" on her father's back that he took to his grave, and then rubbed salt in his wounds, her father threatened, "'when you do it again, I'm goin' to put you in the ground.' Papa never slept in the house again after that. They got scared and he was scared of them. He used to sleep in the woods." After the war, when Cragin's second husband slapped her, she retrieved her gun, nearly killed him, and drove him away permanently. SNC, Arkansas, pt. 2, 2:43, 48.

68. *Sketch of Henry Franklin and Family*, 1, 2.

69. The interview did not provide the informant's first name. *God Struck Me Dead*, 19:148, 161, 147, 166.

70. *God Struck Me Dead*, 19:148, 161.

71. After attending church, his parents would discuss the sermon. *God Struck Me Dead*, 19:162, 166, 149.

Chapter Four

1. Smith, *An Autobiography*, 18; Albert, *House of Bondage*, 125; Simmons, *Men of Mark*, 294. When her master moved to St. Louis and prepared to hire out her aged mother to defray his debts, Elizabeth Keckley volunteered instead, establishing a reputation as an accomplished dressmaker. Living in an urban area and being allowed to hire her time enabled Keckley to capitalize on her skill. When she proposed to buy herself and her son, her master at first refused, but later changed his mind. Keckley purchased their freedom with the help of loans from "my lady patrons," whom she worked diligently to repay. Two of Moses Grandy's daughters earned the price of their freedom working on steamboats. Women who purchased enslaved kin, however, often came into money as concubines and through inheritance from white men. Keckley, *Behind the Scenes*, 63, 45–46, 49, 55; Grandy, *Narrative of the Life of Moses Grandy*, 46, 48; Arkansas, pt. 5, 2:306. Free black and enslaved men had greater access to skilled labor. Marks, "Skilled Blacks in Antebellum St. Mary's County, Maryland," 227–251. For examples of self-purchase and purchase of family members, see Blassingame, *Slave Testimony*, 98, 385, 388–391, 394, 431, 439–440, 469.

2. "Self-hire offered the greatest opportunities for using hiring in the service of family integrity," Jonathan Martin writes. Laws against self-hire were seldom or only laxly enforced, and despite complaints about the practice, owners pursued self-hire because it was so lucrative. A slave who hired his or her own time had to find work and pay the owner a set amount, usually per month. This arrangement had benefits, offering mobility and greater opportunity to attain literacy. Such individuals often rented a home and lived on their own. But there were serious drawbacks. It could be difficult to find work and meet financial obligations to the master, and skilled slaves often experienced the resentment of white workers. Martin argues that the lives of such slaves should not be romanticized, and that they "did not consider themselves quasi-free." Martin, *Divided Mastery*, 68, 178, 161, 163–164, 166, 168, 172, 176, 183–185. Charles Dew argues that industrial slaves could better provision kin and negotiated greater control over their families, giving them a sense of "personal dignity and individual initiative." Dew, "Disciplining

Slave Ironworkers in the Antebellum South," 223. Although enslaved people attempted to use the practice to their advantage, Calvin Schermerhorn calls hiring "more perilous than advantageous," underscoring the "psychic and spiritual" costs of long periods of family separation that often resulted from labor contracts. Schermerhorn, *Money over Mastery, Family over Freedom*, 79, 80. Kathleen Hilliard defines self-purchase and purchase of kin as "the ultimate act of consumption," noting that such practices highlight "the contradictions inherent in slavery, and required a good bit of mental gymnastics by both defenders and critics of the institution." Hilliard, *Masters, Slaves, and Exchange*, 155, 157.

3. Informed that his fifteen-month-old daughter "was dying of neglect," because her mother was overworked, and that her master, believing she would die, would sell the baby, Ella Shepard's father, a man who had purchased his own freedom, immediately traveled from Nashville, Tennessee, to Mississippi and paid $350 for his child. He went back for his wife, but the master would not sell. Blassingame, *Slave Testimony*, 611.

4. "The agony of dealing with such choices can only have been increased by the knowledge that children or siblings might be sold out of the state, never to be seen again, even as free members of the family struggled to generate cash to buy them out," Stephen Whitman writes. Whitman, *Price of Freedom*, 123; Hilliard, *Masters, Slaves, and Exchange*, 163–165.

5. Whitman, *Price of Freedom*, 1, 61–63, 67, 74, 98–103, 115, 120–121, 124, 132–135, 160–163; Rockman, *Scraping By*, 6, 34–35, 60–61, 233–234.

6. Slaveholders in Baltimore maintained slavery by specifying the term slavery, for long time periods, of children and grandchildren born to term slaves. In addition, after 1830, prejudice in Baltimore hardened, making it more difficult for free blacks to obtain skilled work. Whitman argues that the economic dependency of free blacks, exacerbated by their efforts to free themselves and family members, fueled such racist attitudes. In his study of labor in Baltimore, Seth Rockman notes that free blacks and slaves attempting to purchase their own freedom or that of family members had added economic burdens compared to working-class whites that prevented them from being able to emerge from poverty and made it impossible to accumulate property. Whitman, *The Price of Freedom*, 5, 28, 122–123, 140, 165; Rockman, *Scraping By*, 60–61, 113–114, 167, 184–185.

7. Larry Koger argues that free blacks in South Carolina who purchased family members usually freed them, but after 1820, private manumission ended and the process required legislative approval from both houses of the assembly. Because debt could incur the seizure of property, free blacks worried their children would be sold to pay their debts, and they started using deeds of trust and secret trusts to free kin, or had a trusted white acquaintance hold the title to loved ones. Koger, *Black Slaveowners*, 45–68.

8. "Slaveholders, in turn, chose money over mastery," he continues. The combination of networking strategies and the "intensifying market economy," militated against slave rebellion (20, 208). Schermerhorn, *Money over Mastery, Family over Freedom*, 4, 3, 19, 20, 23, 141, 206, 209, 210; Deyle, *Carry Me Back*, 6.

9. Davis, *Narrative of the Life of Rev. Noah Davis*, 3, 31, 26. After 1806, manumitted former slaves in Virginia had to leave the state within a year. Maryland did not have a similar law until after Nat Turner's rebellion, but the 1832 Act Relating to Free Negroes and Slaves was not enforced in Baltimore. Rockman, *Scraping By*, 34, 249–250. See Calvin Schermerhorn's discussion of Solomon Bayley's use of patrons in the Methodist Church to attempt to protect his family and to rent and eventually purchase his wife and children, a long process with many setbacks, including being cheated. Schermerhorn points out that although Bayley lived and worked away from his loved ones, for a time visiting only at Christmas, he did so in an effort to keep the family together and in an attempt to free his kin. "Bayley was not an individual actor," Schermerhorn writes. "He saw himself fundamentally as a Christian, husband, and father." Schermerhorn, *Money over Mastery, Family over Freedom*, 31, 35, 24–40.

10. Davis, *Narrative of the Life of Rev. Noah Davis*, 37, 40–41, 42. Free blacks struggled to accumulate property due to efforts to free family members. Whitman, *Price of Freedom*, 124.

11. "The girl was of course left in the hands of these gentlemen, in, whom I had the most implicit confidence," he wrote (59). Davis, *Narrative of the Life of Rev. Noah Davis*, 54–55, 57, 58–59, 71, 70.

12. Calvin Schermerhorn writes that Solomon and Thamar Bayley "exhausted their family's savings and borrowed against future income to buy or rent relatives," using up all of their credit and savings and having to apprentice their daughters. Schermerhorn, *Money over Mastery, Family over Freedom*, 38, 40.

13. His parents died in 1826 and 1831. Davis, *Narrative of the Life of Rev. Noah Davis*, 9, 11, 10, 12, 14.

14. Campbell, *An Autobiography*, iii, vi. Peter Still, who had been kidnapped near Philadelphia and sold in Kentucky as a young boy, purchased his freedom, went north, and reunited with his birth family. He then attempted to free his enslaved family, and a narrative about his life raised funds for this endeavor. Peter asked his sons to avoid marriage while he worked on securing their freedom. His oldest son, encouraged by the master, started a family. Young Peter's wife died, but one baby survived, and when Still redeemed his family, they had to leave his grandson behind. Pickard, *Kidnapped and the Ransomed*, 262, 213, 221, 232, 231, 248–250, 257, 260, 343, 348, 368, 373. Another such narrative, published in 1828, related the story of Abduhl Rahhahman, known as Prince, who had been kidnapped from "Tombuctoo." When a man recognized him in Mississippi, Prince earned his freedom, and subscriptions emancipated his wife. Friends in New York published the narrative to raise funds to free Prince's five children and eight grandchildren and return the family to Africa. Gallaudet, *Statement with Regard to the Moorish Prince*, 3, 4; Abdul Rahhahman to R. R. Gurley, Monrovia, May 5, 1829, in Blassingame, *Slave Testimony*, 18.

15. Campbell's wife had died. In his critique of slavery, Campbell wrote, "The system of amalgamation is another wrong which slavery enforces upon the slave. It is no uncommon thing to see among a company of children one black and another half-white by the same mother; and should the colored husband say any thing, he is whipped or sold. I have known instances where a man would have children by his slave-woman, and then his legitimate sons would have children by his own slave-daughters" (284). Campbell, *An Autobiography*, 121, 286, 284, 260, 103, 113, 211, 212, 241, 248, 259.

16. If older children started families, their parents then endeavored to liberate grandchildren. Various relatives contributed to the expensive and time-consuming process of trying to free the entire family.

17. Hawkins, *Lunsford Lane*, 86, 50, 84. Lane complained about the price of his family. "This seemed a large sum, both because it was a great deal for me to raise; and also because Mr. Smith, when he bought my wife and two children, had actually paid but five hundred and sixty dollars for them, and had received, ever since, their labor, while I had almost entirely supported them, both as to food and clothing. Altogether, therefore, the case seemed a hard one, but . . . I was entirely in his power." Lane, *Narrative of Lunsford Lane*, 23, 24–32.

18. "I had, ever since obtaining my freedom, endeavored so to conduct myself as in no way to become obnoxious to the white inhabitants, knowing as I did their power and . . . hostility," he noted. "Two things I kept constantly in mind. First, to make no display of the little property or money I possessed. . . . Secondly, I never appeared to know half so much as I really did." Hawkins, *Lunsford Lane*, 87, 99, 98–99. Jerry Moore's father, who purchased his own freedom, was not allowed to interact with slaves and "had to have a guardian who was 'sponsible for his conduct till after surrender." Texas, pt. 3, 16:122. Following Nat Turner's revolt, slave states moved to limit manumissions and the rights of free blacks. Rockman, *Scraping By*, 248–250.

19. Upon returning to pay his debt and release his family, Lane was arrested for supposedly giving abolitionist lectures in the North, tried and acquitted, and then kept in jail for his own safety when an angry mob formed. In their hurried departure from Raleigh, Lane had to abandon his property. Hawkins, *Lunsford Lane*, 139, 145–159.

20. "The emotions experienced at the moment of parting from my friends almost unmanned me, and I cried like a child," Lane stated. He later arranged for his father's freedom. Though he

abandoned assets and arrived in the North penniless, Lane felt thankful to have kept his family intact. "When my feet pressed the pavements of Philadelphia, with my family around me, consisting of nine dependent beings, with my money nearly expended, and with nothing to depend upon but my two hands, I still felt happy; I felt as though I was in a new world." Hawkins, *Lunsford Lane*, 158, 161, 159, 196; Lane, *Narrative of Lunsford Lane*, 33–52.

21. *Lewis v. Simonton*, 8 Humphreys 185, December 1847, Catterall, *Judicial Cases*, 2:534–535. See Bernie Jones for a discussion of the hardships imposed on free blacks when states required newly freed people to relocate. When Kentucky manumission laws tightened in the 1850s, a free black man with an enslaved spouse could no longer free her because if he did, she would be required to leave the state. If he kept her as a slave, she could be sold to pay any debts he incurred. Jones, *Fathers of Conscience*, 94. "It was the certain separation from family that affected many slaves' choices with regard to freedom," Kathleen Hilliard writes. Hilliard, *Masters, Slaves, and Exchange*, 164, 162–166. Schermerhorn argues that "within a hierarchy of values, the enslaved chose family over freedom," though with freedom rarely an option, the choice they faced was often "between family or not-family." Schermerhorn, *Money over Mastery, Family over Freedom*, 210, 90.

22. Whitman argues that white men who acted as security for or lent money to slaves purchasing themselves or family members out of slavery benefited from a "simple, secure, and risk-free type of loan." If the enslaved individual failed to pay the debt on time, the lender could demand longer terms of service or sell the slave, who could not testify and thus had no legal recourse. Lenders also had leverage over and could mortgage any children, who served as collateral. Whitman, *Price of Freedom*, 127, 124–125, 128–129.

23. One son had been sold south and was lost to the family. Green had previously purchased his own freedom. Green, *Life of the Rev. Elisha W. Green*, 10–11, 13, 14.

24. Green, *Life of the Rev. Elisha W. Green*, 19, 21, 20, 15. Angie Boyce's father bought himself and his wife and baby and sent his family to Indiana. They were arrested and returned to Kentucky, though once they showed their free papers they were allowed to proceed. Boyce's mother kept the papers hidden, even in jail, for fear they would be stolen. Caroline Hammond's free father purchased his wife and children but had to send them to Pennsylvania via the Underground Railroad when the master died and his wife refused to honor the deal. SNC, Indiana, 5:21, Maryland, 8:19, 20.

25. After being manumitted in Kentucky, Levi Bennet purchased his four children on annual installments. When he was unable to make payments, his former master's son abducted and enslaved the three older children. Schermerhorn, *Money over Mastery, Family over Freedom*, 98; *Craig v. Mullin*, 9 Dana 311, May 1840, 348; *Jones v. Bennet*, 9 Dana 333, May 1840, Catterall, *Judicial Cases*, 1:349.

26. *Porter v. Blakemore*, 2 Coldwell 556, December 1865, Catterall, *Judicial Cases*, 2:582.

27. James Walker to Rev. Edmond Kelley, Feb. 24, 1850, in Kelley, *Family Redeemed*, 9, 6, 8.

28. Walker to Kelley, 9, 9–10.

29. Walker to Kelley, 10.

30. James Walker to Rev. Edmond Kelley, July 27, 1850, in Kelley, *Family Redeemed*, 10, 11. "A master considering manumission might be moved by benevolence, egalitarian principles, fear for his soul, desire for gain, or all of the above," Whitman writes. Whitman, *Price of Freedom*, 96.

31. Kelley's church in New Bedford helped him publicize his quest and collect funds. Paralee and the four children arrived in New York in May 1851. James Walker to Rev. Edmond Kelley, July 29, 1850, in Kelley, *Family Redeemed*, 11, 12, 17, 18. Hannah McFarland called her free father "de richest Negro in South Carolina," and yet he could not buy his wife. He purchased his three children for "$1,000 apiece." Her mother's owners did allow her to "come home ever night." SNC, Oklahoma, 13:210.

32. The girls, aged fourteen and sixteen, had a combined price of $2,250, which Pennington's congregation helped raise. Pennington, *Fugitive Blacksmith*, viii, x, ix.

33. The master emancipated his mother and siblings, and Meachum's father moved them to Indiana. Meachum married a slave and eventually purchased the freedom of his wife and children. Meachum, *An Address*, 3, 4, 5; Anderson, *Life of Rev. Robert Anderson*, 38, 39, 42.

34. Before escaping, Jones purchased his wife and also hired his mother and father. "I had the privilege of buying my father's time from the task-master, after he became old and decrepit, paying $50 annually. I could not do this myself, but was obliged to employ Mr. Owen Fennel, a Baptist deacon, to hire him for me. In this way I secured his liberty. While he was twenty miles from me I could not take care of him when he was sick, but after he was removed to my house I could attend to his wants." He also walked eighty-five miles to his old master's home, and convinced him to release his aged mother. Jones, *Experience and Personal Narrative of Uncle Tom Jones*, 26, 27, 28; Jones, *Experience of Rev. Thomas H. Jones*, 76; O'Neal, *Life and History of William O'Neal*, 35, 37, 42.

35. Gavin Wright calls slavery "a set of property rights," and "a form of wealth and a basis for credit and exchange," and Seth Rockman discusses slavery "less as a labor system and more as a property regime—that is, as a legally protected way of investing, storing, transporting, and bequeathing wealth." Wright, *Slavery and American Economic Development*, 2, 6; Rockman, *Scraping By*, 6.

36. Whitman, *Price of Freedom*, 137, 136; Johnson and Roark, "Strategies of Survival," 101, 94, 95; Woodson, "Free Negro Owners of Slaves in the United States in 1830"; Koger, *Black Slaveowners*, 2, 80, 101.

37. Whitman, *Price of Freedom*, 139, 136–138; Johnson and Roark, "Strategies of Survival," 88–102; Rockman, *Scraping By*, 184.

38. Seth Rockman calls slaves "a highly fungible form of property," broadly used as collateral for loans. Slaves could be converted into cash faster than real estate, and "it was the prospect of *convertibility* that defined the 'chattel principle.'" Rockman, *Scraping By*, 234, 235.

39. "Those in the best place to accumulate property were also the most likely to be sold and thereby have their plans undermined," Schermerhorn writes of the market strategies of the enslaved. He also observes that kin networks "pooled resources to buy or rent other slaves not for their productive value but, put in economic terms, for consumption, because they were related. The antebellum period, then, saw a shift towards enslaved families as property holding corporations, even if they lacked civic standing to hold property legally." Schermerhorn, *Money over Mastery, Family over Freedom*, 142.

40. Jones, *Days of Bondage*, 10; Mary Crane's grandfather convinced his master to buy his son. He also helped the master, who was short on cash, by providing an extra $25 he had saved, enabling the master to meet the purchase price. *SNC*, Indiana, 5:10.

41. Rawick, *AS*, supp., ser. 1, Mississippi, pt. 3, 8:1044; Drew, *North-Side View of Slavery*, 284; Johnson, *Twenty-Eight Years a Slave*, 1; North Carolina, pt. 1, 11:330; Henry, *Autobiography of Rev. Thomas W. Henry*, 56. On the auction block at age fifteen, Delicia Patterson informed a judge with a reputation for cruelty that she would kill herself if he purchased her. "So he stepped back and let someone else bid for me. My own father knew I was to be for sale, so he brought his owner to the sale for him to buy me, so we could be together. But when father's owner heard what I said to Judge Miller, he told my father he would not buy me, because I was sassy, and he . . . did not want one that was sassy. That broke my father's heart, but I couldn't help that." *SNC*, Missouri, 10:271.

42. Martin, *Divided Mastery*, 174; Grandy, *Narrative of the Life of Moses Grandy*, 17, 21, 18, 38, 40. In Baltimore, where manumission by deed remained legal and widely used, slaves often purchased their freedom in installments, and their manumission would not be registered until the final payment had been made. The death of the master could disrupt such an agreement. Verbal contracts for gradual manumission left slaves more vulnerable than written contracts. A slaveholder who freed an individual by deed had to identify the slave, testify that they could earn their own living, set a date for freedom, and obtain signatures from two witnesses. The slave, by law, had to be age forty-five or younger. Whitman, *Price of Freedom*, 95, 98, 105, 109; Rockman, *Scraping By*, 239–240.

43. Robinson, *From Log Cabin to the Pulpit*, 11, 16, 17, 23; Alexander, *Battles and Victories of Allen Allensworth*, 11, 12. See Calvin Schermerhorn for a longer discussion of Peter Robinson. Robinson had permission to travel to and work in California. Rather than escape, he abided by

his arrangement with his master because he hoped to free his entire family. He was arrested and sold on his second Christmastime trip home to North Carolina to visit his family and pay his master, who then pocketed the significant hiring fees and sale price. Robinson's devotion to family made him an easy target to cheat. "Robinson was first and foremost a father and husband, and he used his weak ties to protect those relationships that mattered most rather than to accrue benefits as an individual," Schermerhorn writes. Schermerhorn, *Money over Mastery, Family over Freedom*, 94, 95, 96.

44. See Whitman, *Price of Freedom*, 119–122, for a discussion of how slaveholders used children and other kin to exert control over parents and perpetuate slavery. Schermerhorn discusses slaveholders' strategies to motivate enslaved people and then cheat them of their earnings, knowing they would work harder to try to free family members. Schermerhorn, *Money over Mastery, Family over Freedom*, 36, 98.

45. Charlton, born in Africa, was captured and enslaved as a boy, but when the British took the slave ship, he ended up in England, where he was given the name John Bull and became a ship hand. He was then taken prisoner during the War of 1812, and a judge in Savannah, Georgia, changed his name to Dimmock Charlton and sold him into slavery. "Caution," *National Anti-slavery Standard*, Nov. 27, 1858; Cox, ed., "Narrative of Dimmock Charlton," 1–2; Dimmock Charlton, Blassingame, *Slave Testimony*, 325–338.

46. As an example of an enslaved man who lost family to the forces of the market and also used his market opportunities to try to locate and "gather them up again," Schermerhorn discusses Moses Grandy at length. Grandy eventually managed to purchase his own freedom after being cheated twice. He then turned his attention to trying to locate and purchase his family, "an endeavor that would occupy him for the rest of his life." When Grandy wrote his life story in an effort to raise more money, six of his children had been sold. "His life's resources went into the pockets of slaveholders who were happy to cheat him and sell his children" (64, 78, 97). Grandy, *Narrative of the Life of Moses Grandy*, 42, 49, 50, 44, 46; Schermerhorn, *Money over Mastery, Family over Freedom*, 79, 63–83; Loguen, *Rev. J. W. Loguen*, 380, 381–387.

47. Franklin and Schweninger, *Runaway Slaves*, 62, 63, 65, 66.

48. Women rarely left the plantation and were frequently assigned evening tasks. Camp, *Closer to Freedom*, 16, 20, 28, 31, 33; Franklin and Schweninger, *Runaway Slaves*, 210, 212, 233; White, *Ar'n't I a Woman?*, 70–71. Commenting on slave songs and folklore of the trade, Walter Johnson notes that the "emblematic slave was male, and those left behind to mourn and remember him were women and children." Johnson, *Soul by Soul*, 43.

49. Camp, *Closer to Freedom*, 37, 35, 44–45; White, *Ar'n't I a Woman?*, 70–71, 74; King, "'Suffer with Them Till Death," 160; Franklin and Schweninger, *Runaway Slaves*, 98–103.

50. Clarke, *Narrative of the Sufferings of Lewis Clarke*, 34; Bibb, *Narrative of the Life and Adventures of Henry Bibb*, 47. "I had . . . friends that I loved almost as I did my life," Frederick Douglass wrote, "and the thought of being separated from them forever was painful beyond expression. It is my opinion that thousands would escape from slavery, who now remain, but for the strong cords of affection that bind them to their friends." Douglass, *Narrative*, 106.

51. Pennington's family was fine until he sent a letter that ended up in the wrong hands. They were then sold. Pennington, *Fugitive Blacksmith*, 12. Solomon Bayley, removed from Delaware, ran back to his wife, traveling with another runaway. Both men were "hunted like partridges" and his companion was killed. Bayley, *Narrative of Some Remarkable Incidents in the Life of Solomon Bayley*, 6.

52. Campbell's wife was dead, and his delay in starting for Canada stemmed from the difficulty of leaving his children rather than concern for his own safety. "I had made up my mind that I was going to try for either liberty or death this time, and intended killing any one who should undertake to stop me," he wrote. Once he reached Canada, he wrote a letter to his friends in the South, asking them to read it to his children and promising, "I will come back if I live." He tried and failed to return to the South to collect them, and began to work on raising money to purchase their freedom (172, 210, 209). Campbell, *An Autobiography*, 159, 160, 161, 175, 203; Webb, *History of William Webb*, 4. Pierce Harper's father came to where he was hired

out to say farewell prior to a successful escape: "He say he want to tell me goodbye 'cause he was going to run 'way in a few days an' go to de North, but not to tell nobody." Rawick, *AS*, supp., ser. 2, Texas, pt. 4, 5:1644.

53. Baptist, "The Absent Subject," 145.

54. Black, *Dismantling Black Manhood*, 125; Gutman, *Black Family*, 264. John Jacobs chose to escape while his sister, Harriet, was in hiding. Fleischner refers to "John's dilemma—self-interest versus duty to others." Fleischner, *Mastering Slavery*, 78.

55. Drew, *North-Side View of Slavery*, 114.

56. "It required all the moral courage that I was master of to suppress my feeling while taking leave of my little family," Bibb recalled. Bibb, *Narrative of the Life and Adventures of Henry Bibb*, 177–178, 46.

57. Drew, *North-Side View of Slavery*, 46, 47.

58. The interviewer noted that Atkinson's "eyes filled with tears" as he talked about his family. Drew, *North-Side View of Slavery*, 285, 82, 81, 71–72, 89; Jackson Whitney to William Riley, March 18, 1859, Blassingame, *Slave Testimony*, 115; Franklin and Schweninger, *Runaway Slaves*, 73–74; Gutman, *Black Family*, 265.

59. Drew, *North-Side View of Slavery*, 282, 161. William Williams insisted he would return to North Carolina "in three days if there was freedom there." Blassingame, *Slave Testimony*, 436; Williams, *Help Me to Find My People*, 132.

60. Henson, *Autobiography*, 52. Henry Williamson escaped with his family and a group of eighteen people. Drew, *North-Side View of Slavery*, 133.

61. Drew, *North-Side View of Slavery*, 181.

62. Josiah Henson is a good example of a man who moved through, and often combined, several masculine identities in his life. He only risked escape when it became clear he would be separated from family, taking his role as provider and protector into the realm of heroic resistance. From the vantage point of freedom, he later discussed and disavowed his time in a trustee position. Henson, *Autobiography*, 79, 80, 80–81, 95, 83–94; Blassingame, *Slave Testimony*, 526. David Doddington uses Henson's story of his wife's fears as an example of how fugitives "equated masculinity with resistance and femininity with passivity." Doddington, *Contesting Slave Masculinity*, 27, 69–70.

63. Before he ran away, and during their separation, he wrote, "My dear wife, I long to see you and the children." While this situation ended well, Jones lived with the anguish of having left his first family, from whom he had been forcibly separated, in slavery. Elsewhere, he wrote that only God "knows the bitter sorrow I now feel, when I think of my four dear children who are slaves. . . . I love those children with all a father's fondness." Jones, *Experience of Rev. Thomas H. Jones*, 43, 35; Jones, *Experience and Personal Narrative of Uncle Tom Jones*, 8.

64. Ward, *Autobiography of a Fugitive Negro*, 20, 15–20; Bragg, *Men of Maryland*, 54. Smart Edward Walker visited his children on another Kentucky plantation every night, and they planned a successful escape, made easier by the fact that two of the three were old enough to ride. Horses were ideal for a quick getaway, but like people, they required food, making them impractical for a long trip. Blassingame, *Slave Testimony*, 520–521.

65. Brown had a carpenter build a shipping box and ship him to Philadelphia. Ross escaped from Maryland. Brown, *Narrative of Henry Box Brown*, 56, 57, 58, 63; Blassingame, *Slave Testimony*, 405, 406; Ball, *Fifty Years in Chains*, 13; Schermerhorn, *Money over Mastery, Family over Freedom*, 161.

66. Drew, *North-Side View of Slavery*, 52–53, 87, 88, 89, 282; Jackson, *Story of Mattie J. Jackson*, 5–8, 17; Franklin and Schweninger, *Runaway Slaves*, 52, 66, 71; Gutman, *Black Family*, 264. A separation imminent, Harry Smith considered an escape attempt, but not wanting to part with his family, he arranged to be sold to a neighboring planter. Smith, *Fifty Years of Slavery*, 127. "Dey wuz gonna buy my 'pappy' an take him way off, but, my 'pappy' was smart. He had made baskets in the evenings and saved his earnings. Dat night he goes to de fireplace . . . pulls out a' bag a' money an' he runs away," George Bollinger stated. "I ain't never seed my 'pappy' since." *SNC*, Missouri, 10:42. As David Doddington notes, not all slaves saw heroic resistance as the only valid measure of a man. "Some enslaved people felt that to answer the rebel's call was to

abdicate masculine responsibilities as a provider and protector, and that to remain in chains to support dependents was not a mark of weakness," but rather "reflected a strength and selflessness." Doddington, *Contesting Slave Masculinity*, 103, 104, 74, 113.

67. After being emancipated at age thirty, Thomas Smallwood worked for the Underground Railroad. Men who successfully ran away appealed to Smallwood for help in freeing their families through escape or purchase. Smallwood, *Narrative of Thomas Smallwood*, 13, 18, 22, 36, 37. James Pennington tried to purchase his parents and when their master refused to sell, used the money to arrange for his father and two brothers to escape. His mother had been sold, "but she was eventually found" (63). Pennington, *Fugitive Blacksmith*, 75, 61–63.

68. Letters to kin show men's "loneliness and even guilt." Gutman, *Black Family*, 265; Still, *Underground Railroad*, 65, 42, 143–144, 164; Starobin, *Blacks in Bondage*, 154–155; Robert Brown, Dear Mille, Chatham, March 8, 1854, 29; Isaac H. Hunter to Brooklyn Star, Nov. 23, 1842, in Blassingame, *Slave Testimony*, 47.

69. Bibb, *Narrative of the Life and Adventures of Henry Bibb*, 79, 83, 100, 56, 59, 61, 66, 77–78, 80, 84, 87, 89, 110, 121, 122, 130, 134–146, 149; Clarke, *Narrative of the Sufferings of Lewis Clarke*, 39, 55; Brown, *Black Man*, 75–85. Included among the more than three hundred slaves rescued by Harriet Tubman were her brothers and parents. Her father aided in his sons' escape, with his cabin serving as a hiding place. When Tubman returned for her parents, "she found that her old father was to be tried the next Monday for helping off slaves," and Tubman responded, "I just removed my father's trial to a higher court, and brought him off to Canada." Bradford, *Harriet*, 82–83, 33, 64–65, 67, 108, 115, 116.

70. Bibb, *Narrative of the Life and Adventures of Henry Bibb*, 192; Williams, *Help Me to Find My People*, 135, 86, 133–136.

71. Fugitives "felt that they must flee to claim their manhood," but realized "doing so meant abdicating family responsibility." Doddington, *Contesting Slave Masculinity*, 74.

72. Ingram stated that after the war, "Pappy bought a place at De Berry, Texas, and I live with him til' after I wuz grown." Rawick, *AS*, supp., ser. 2, Texas, pt., 8, 9:3651, pt. 4, 5:1853, 1854, 1855; Franklin and Schweninger, *Runaway Slaves*, 52, 57; Gutman, *Black Family*, 264.

73. Family and community members fed truants, with husbands feeding absentee wives and wives feeding husbands. Rawick, *AS*, supp., ser. 2, Texas, pt. 3, 4:1366; Olmsted, *Cotton Kingdom*, 2:178; Franklin and Schweninger, *Runaway Slaves*, 57, 67; Gutman, *Black Family*, 80; Berry, *Swing the Sickle*, 102.

74. The paramount focus on family also became apparent in freedom, as thousands of formerly enslaved men, unable to marry locally, exercised their mobility. Pargas, *Quarters and the Fields*, 162; Rodrigue, *Reconstruction in the Cane Fields*, 30–31.

75. Ball, *Fifty Years in Chains*, 307, 387, 388, 389, 430, 308, 341, 382–383, 386, 391, 402, 425–426.

76. Enslaved people made different choices, "according to their own circumstances and calculations." Unlike many enslaved people presented with the chance, Ball chose not to run to the British during the War of 1812. Instead, he fought for the United States, a "lever he could use to protect his family." After being kidnapped and enslaved, Ball escaped and returned to his family in Maryland. He remarried and started a new family after Judah died in 1816. Only after losing his second family did he permanently go north. "Ball fled back to Maryland and possible reenslavement twice rather than forego bonds with wives, children, and — not inconsequently — his personhood as husband and father" (52, 54, 62). Schermerhorn, *Money over Mastery, Family over Freedom*, 51, 52, 43–60.

77. Green, *Narrative of the Events*, 15; Bradford, *Harriet*, 71.

Chapter Five

1. Loguen wrote in the third person. See Blassingame, *Slave Testimony*, xxxvii, xxxviii, for verification of his authorship. "It is almost impossible for slaves to give a correct account of their male parentage," said Henry Bibb, who also had a white father. Loguen, *Rev. J. W. Loguen*, 11; Douglass, *My Bondage*, 51; Bibb, *Narrative of the Life and Adventures of Henry Bibb*, 13.

2. "Resituating heritability was key in the practice of an enslavement that systematically alienated the enslaved from their kin and their lineage" (1). Morgan, "Partus Sequitur Ventrem: Law, Race, and Reproduction in Colonial Slavery," 12, 2, 3, 4, 14, 16; Kathleen Brown, *Good Wives, Nasty Wenches, and Anxious Patriarchs*.

3. "Thus, in essence, slaveowners and slaveowning legislators enacted the legal and material substitution of a thing for a child: no white man's *child* could be enslaved, while all black women's *issue* could" (5). Morgan, "Partus Sequitur Ventrem: Law, Race, and Reproduction in Colonial Slavery," 12, 11, 5, 17.

4. "Fatherhood, at best a supreme cultural courtesy, attenuates here on the one hand into a monstrous accumulation of power on the other," Spillers writes. "The denied genetic link becomes the chief strategy of an undenied ownership, as if the interrogation into the father's identity—the blank space where his proper name will fit—were answered by the fact, *de jure* of a material possession" (76). Spillers, "Mama's Baby, Papa's Maybe," 72, 74, 80.

5. Clinton, "Southern Dishonor," 54, 55, 56. Peggy Pascoe traces the role of law in stigmatizing interracial sex as illicit and defining interracial marriage as unnatural, and the links between this ideology and racial purity and white supremacy. Pascoe, *What Comes Naturally*, 3, 12, 27; Jones, *Fathers of Conscience*, 2, 6. Legal and social custom deterred illicit relationships between white women and black men. A white woman could not recover from a tarnished reputation and had to be careful to avoid blemishing the reputations of the men in her family, her protectors. Bertram Wyatt-Brown discusses men ruined by miscegenation, calling it "a weapon of social and familial suicide," as these men willingly subverted the unwritten rules that called for public silence and strict adherence to the social hierarchy. Wyatt-Brown, *Southern Honor*, 322, 294. "White women were paradoxically both powerless and powerful," Jeff Forret writes. "The ethic of honor inextricably bound the sexes together." Forret, *Slave against Slave*, 334.

6. Jack Maddox was enslaved in Georgia and Rosa in Mississippi. Rawick, *AS*, supp., ser. 2, Texas, pt. 6, 7:2531; Painter, "The Journal of Ella Gertrude Clanton Thomas," 65–66.

7. Miscegenation in New Orleans took on a formalized structure known as placage that led to a more distinct class hierarchy, particularly in the free black community. Though unable to legally marry their partners, mulatto women entered into brokered relationships with white men (sometimes negotiated by their mothers). The arrangements often produced long-term quasi-marriages that continued even after the man legally married, and men regularly educated and willed property to their illegitimate children. For less affluent men, such as merchants, this was not just about sex, but household labor. Unable to afford wives, who would require servants, they found it cost-effective to take a black mistress who then maintained the home. Olmsted, *Cotton Kingdom*, 1:302–306; Potter, *Hairdresser's Experience in High Life*, 113.

8. Rawick, *AS*, supp., ser. 1, Georgia, 4:373. Frederick Douglass believed Southern law catered to white men's "lusts," making "gratification of their wicked desires profitable as well as pleasurable; for by this cunning arrangement, the slaveholder, in cases not a few, sustains to his slaves the double relation of master and father." Bernie Jones argues, "without the law to force their obligations to the enslaved women who bore them children, only the men's consciences and fear of public scorn held sway over the men's behavior." "Rapes that created more property to be sold in the market were a double assertion of white manhood and a double denigration of black manhood," Edward Baptist writes. Douglass, *Narrative*, 4; Jones, *Fathers of Conscience*, 7; Baptist, "The Absent Subject," 142.

9. In private, Southerners admitted to the frequency of miscegenation and concubinage. Olmsted, *Cotton Kingdom*, 1:308; Painter, "The Journal of Ella Gertrude Clanton Thomas," 60. Masters were the greatest threat, followed by their sons. Thelma Jennings finds fewer instances of sexual abuse by overseers. Of the various forms of sexual exploitation, forced interracial sex was far more common than breeding. Based on the prevalence of abuse by masters, Emily West notes that sexual exploitation was not, as whites often argued, the province of lower-class men. Jennings, "Us Colored Women Had to Go though a Plenty," 61, 63; West, *Chains of Love*, 130.

10. Randolph, *From Slave Cabin to the Pulpit*, 206–207. See Amy Dru Stanley for a discussion of the abolitionist critique of slavery as a violation of the marriage contract. David Doddington

discusses abolitionists' denunciation of white sexual behavior within slavery. In juxtaposing honorable, monogamous enslaved men with debauched white men, they ignored the fact that some enslaved men also sexually coerced enslaved women. Stanley, *From Bondage to Contract*, 24–29; Doddington, *Contesting Slave Masculinity*, 136–140.

11. *SNC*, Georgia, pt. 4, 4:133; Hall and Elder, *Samuel Hall*, 38. John Payne's mother told him that his white father was the son of a neighboring planter. *SNC*, Arkansas, pt. 5, 2:304. Angela Davis discusses the "terroristic character" of slaveholder sexual violence. "Indirectly its target was also the slave community as a whole." Because men could not protect enslaved women, the situation led to his "entrapment in an untenable situation," fomenting "doubts about his ability to resist at all." Davis, "Reflections on the Black Woman's Role in the Community of Slaves," 13. While white women stressed their victimhood, and the sexual dynamics of slavery affected enslaved men, ultimately, the burden of suffering was most intense for enslaved women. Jennings, "Us Colored Women Had to Go though a Plenty," 60.

12. More recently, historians have had a tendency to focus on how rape impacts men. Hine, "Rape and the Inner Lives of Black Women in the Middle West," 917. Michael Gomez argues that the rape of African women, starting with the Middle Passage, created a sense of shared suffering that facilitated the transition from an identity based on ethnicity to one based on race. Gomez, *Exchanging Our Country Marks*, 166–167.

13. Fortman only learned of the family history later, and his mother never knew that her father also fathered her son. Fortman was raised by his mistress and treated kindly despite her awareness of her husband's transgressions. Contrary to expectations, he turned out normal. *SNC*, Indiana, 5:88, 86, 89; Rawick, *AS*, supp., ser. 2, Texas, pt. 1, 2:24; *SNC*, North Carolina, pt. 1, 11:219, 220. Ellen Sinclair's master had a daughter by a slave woman and then his son had a child with his half-sister. Rawick, *AS*, supp., ser. 2, Texas, pt. 8, 9:3593. Southerners worried about incest between white women and their mulatto half brothers, a good indication of the existence of incest on the part of white men. Wyatt-Brown, *Southern Honor*, 312–313.

14. Incest in the quarters was rare and swiftly censured by the slave community. "Slaves served as their own best police force," Jeff Forret writes, and incest violated their moral code. Forret, *Slave against Slave*, 18, 270–271, 335; *SNC*, Georgia, pt. 1, 4:142; Rawick, *AS*, supp., ser. 1, Georgia, 3:94. For a discussion of premarital sex, see Gutman, *Black Family*, 60–86.

15. Rawick, *AS*, supp., ser. 2, Texas, pt. 2, 3:537, pt. 2, 3:636, pt. 6, 7:2616. These anecdotes came from informants who grew up in Texas, Tennessee, and Louisiana.

16. Though a rarer occurrence and taboo subject, some former slaves had white mothers and black fathers. Hodes, *White Women, Black Men*; Foster, "Sexual Abuse of Black Men," 459–460. Matilda Perry, discussing her father's half-white child, a result of his being left in charge during the war, noted, "You had to do what the white man or the white woman said." The mother gave the child to Perry's father, who found a woman willing to rear it. Perdue et al., *Weevils*, 234–235.

17. "The brutal white race lacked important moral and spiritual qualities," Bay adds (110). Mallory, *Old Plantation Days*, 20–21; Anderson, *Life and Narrative of William J. Anderson*, 22; Bay, *The White Image in the Black Mind*, 214, 72; Webb, *History of William Webb*, 3; Jennings, "Us Colored Women Had to Go though a Plenty," 64. The mixed-race population contradicted the biblical justification for slavery and revealed Southern religious hypocrisy. "If the lineal descendants of Ham are alone to be scripturally enslaved, it is certain that slavery at the south must soon become unscriptural; for thousands are ushered into the world, annually, who, like myself, owe their existence to white fathers, and those fathers most frequently their own masters." Douglass, *Narrative*, 5, 118–119; Raboteau, *Slave Religion*, 294.

18. Sharony Green speculates that the man selling his concubine and child was probably Mississippi Judge Samuel S. Boyd. Virginia to Ballard, May 6, 1853, quoted in Green, *Remember Me*, 26. Olaudah Equiano had a similar reaction to white men in the Caribbean fathering children by bondwomen and holding them as slaves, considering it a perversion of paternal feeling and duty. Equiano, *Interesting Narrative*, 219.

19. Olmsted, *Cotton Kingdom*, 1:40; Redpath, *Roving Editor*, 234. In most areas of the South, and especially New Orleans, planters disproportionally manumitted women and children, usually

their concubines and children. Baltimore was an exception, a place where mixed-race individuals were not disproportionally freed. Gould, "Urban Slavery—Urban Freedom," 305–306. Whitman, *Price of Freedom*, 95; Rockman, *Scraping By*, 41.

20. Williamson traces the shift from partial "acceptance of free mulattos, especially in the lower South, to outright rejection." As a result, the mulatto elite came to identify with blacks and those with the resources fled the South. Williamson, *New People*, 63, 62, 26, 33, 56, 58, 65, 67, 71–87. In her study of the legal history of racial identity, Ariela Gross shows that although Southerners discussed the theory of the one-drop rule, in practice it "rarely decided actual cases." With no way to scientifically assess ancestry, disputed racial identity went before local juries, and rather than legal definitions of race as blood quantum, the cases often hinged on how the individuals in question performed whiteness. Gross, *What Blood Won't Tell*, 44.

21. Racial classification, more fluid in the earlier period, became increasingly rigid, legally and socially, in the nineteenth century. Rothman, *Notorious in the Neighborhood*, 204–238; Hodes, *White Women, Black Men*; Williamson, *New People*, 74–75.

22. White, *Ar'n't I a Woman?*, 38, 61, 44; Jones, *Fathers of Conscience*, 33–34; *Vail v. Bird*, 6 La. An. 223, March 1851, Catterall, *Judicial Cases*, 3:613.

23. Wyatt-Brown refers to this practice as "wenching." Wyatt-Brown, *Southern Honor*, 308, 309, 307–324; Rothman, *Notorious in the Neighborhood*, 133–134.

24. White men damaged their reputation if and when they failed to uphold proper social decorum and the racial order. Richard Mentor Johnson, a Kentucky war hero who fought with William Henry Harrison and reportedly killed Tecumseh at the Battle of the Thames, served one term as vice president under Martin Van Buren. Johnson had a long-term relationship with a mixed-race slave, Julia Chinn, and openly acknowledged, educated, and bequeathed his surname and property to their two daughters, Imogene and Adaline, who both married white men. Johnson treated Chinn as a wife, never denied the rumors that they had secretly married, and had no legitimate family to serve as a cover. Johnson's open relationship damaged his political career, in all likelihood causing him to lose his Senate seat in 1829. He was then elected to the House. In the 1836 national election, Van Buren secured the presidency, but Johnson had to be elected by the Senate when the Virginia delegation refused to honor the state's popular vote and chose to abstain rather than vote for him, leaving him shy of the needed electoral votes. The Democrats later dropped him from the ticket in 1840 when Van Buren ran for reelection. Although Chinn died in 1833, Johnson continued to alienate Southerners by publicly flaunting his illegitimate daughters. Meyer, *Life and Times of Colonel Richard M. Johnson of Kentucky*; Clinton, *Plantation Mistress*, 317–320.

25. Harper, *Memoir of Slavery*, 42, 57, 57–58; Hughes, "Treatise on Sociology," 243, 240. A Kentucky court saw a white man's "inclination to marry" a slave he freed as "evidence of insanity." *Patton v. Patton*, 5 J. J. Marsh. 389, April 1831, Catterall, *Judicial Cases*, 1:318.

26. Bleser argues that white descendants likely censored the records of Southern men, erasing any mention of sexual involvement with slaves. Catherine Hammond separated from her husband when he refused to end his relationship with Louisa. Two years later, Hammond sent Louisa away, but he reinstalled her in his home when Catherine declined to return. Bleser notes that Hammond also hinted at possible physical abuse of his wife. Bleser, ed., *Secret and Sacred*, 18, 17, xvi, 19, 23.

27. James Henry Hammond to Harry Hammond, Feb. 19, 1856, in Bleser, ed., *Secret and Sacred*, 19. Harry Hammond later also had an affair with and child by Louisa. Burton, *In My Father's House are Many Mansions*, 186.

28. Bleser, ed., *Secret and Sacred*, 20.

29. Macarty willed Patrice clothing and furniture from his "bed-chamber," and left the rest of the furniture and household goods to Celeste, who had permission to reside in his house for only six months following his death. The will also freed three unidentified enslaved children, possibly the children of Josephine Macarty, the concubine of the white executor, Francisco Tio. *Badillo et al. v. Francisco Tio*, 6 La. An. 129, February 1851, Catterall, *Judicial Cases*, 3:611–613; Clark, *The Strange History of the American Quadroon*.

30. In spite of widespread concubinage, Louisiana mirrored other Southern states in terms of manumission and inheritance patterns. Shafer, "Open and Notorious Concubinage," 169, 166–168, 171, 175, 182; Jones, *Fathers of Conscience*, 57–67.

31. Blassingame, *Slave Testimony*, 476, 478, 479, 486, 477; Gordon-Reed, *Thomas Jefferson and Sally Hemings*, 43–45; *Unwritten History of Slavery*, 18:207. Jefferson "never directly addressed the rumor," and never offered his illegitimate children the "respectability and legitimacy" that would indicate he considered them members of his family. Rothman, *Notorious in the Neighborhood*, 51, 46. See Gordon-Reed, *Hemingses of Monticello*, 647–649, for a discussion of Jefferson's lawyerly crafting of the will that freed his two younger sons. The two older children by Hemings had been emancipated earlier and in secret, but the two younger sons were freed publicly. "The way their father accomplished this suggests he knew that freeing these two young men might raise eyebrows," and Jefferson "never intended to make a public declaration—explicitly or implicitly—about his enslaved mistress and their children" (648). Jefferson freed Madison and Eston as apprentices to their uncle, John Hemings, an older, long-serving artisan slave. Madison Hemings was already beyond the age of an apprentice and Eston was given his time upon Jefferson's death and never served his uncle. Harriet Jacobs discussed slaveholders who fathered enslaved children and pretended otherwise: "I once saw a letter from a member of Congress to a slave, who was the mother of six of his children. He wrote to request that she would send her children away from the great house before his return, as he expected to be accompanied by friends. . . . The existence of the colored children did not trouble this gentleman, it was only the fear that friends might recognize in their features a resemblance to him." Jacobs, *Incidents*, 215.

32. Hughes's father had moved from Virginia to Kentucky. Blassingame, *Slave Testimony*, 211, 423.

33. Wyatt-Brown, *Southern Honor*, 311; Clinton, "Southern Dishonor," 62–63; West, *Family or Freedom*, 124–126, 129; Jones, *Fathers of Conscience*; Shafer, "Open and Notorious Concubinage," 170, 181. Challenging these wills enabled the white relatives to regain honor. Jones, *Fathers of Conscience*, 147.

34. In recounting the life of Amanda Dickson, Josephine Bradley and Kent Anderson Leslie note that her father and grandmother could not free her in Georgia except by legislative petition, and freeing her elsewhere meant she could not return to Georgia. She thus remained enslaved and vulnerable to the sudden death of her white father and grandmother. "They were not willing to send her away to freedom," the authors state. "They did not love her enough to part with her." Dickson remained a slave until 1864. Bradley and Leslie, "White Pain Pollen," 217.

35. For an example of a white man who moved to a free state and legally married a former slave, see Rawick, *AS*, supp., ser. 1, Indiana and Ohio, 5:133.

36. Townsend also freed the three living mothers. Townsend never married, and after seeing his brother Edmond's will voided and Edmond's two mixed-race children dispossessed, Townsend hired a lawyer to ensure that a similar fate would not befall his illegitimate kin. Townsend died in 1856, and although the Civil War intervened and there was a lengthy legal battle, his children were manumitted and sent to Ohio and eventually received financial support. Townsend's children had positive memories of their childhood, indicating an affectionate relationship with their father. Green, *Remember Me*, 93, 10, 86, 88, 90–92, 99, 115, 128.

37. "There is no hagiography here in describing these men as benevolent patriarchs," Bernie Jones writes. "Each act of heroism was infused with the villainy of slavery." Jones, *Fathers of Conscience*, 153.

38. Redpath, *Roving Editor*, 237–238.

39. These cases were decided by appellate judges and not by juries. White relatives challenged specific bequests and often challenged the entire will. If a will was ruled invalid, they stood to inherit under state probate law. Jones, *Fathers of Conscience*, 15, 19, 2, 11, 12, 14, 20, 55–56, 152. White relatives used the courts and also found other means of extracting wealth from an estate. A Louisiana concubine emancipated by her master charged that one of his relatives kept her children enslaved. The court ordered her children freed after finding that

this man forged papers to keep her and her children in bondage. The majority of white relatives could not be trusted to carry out the provisions of wills that deprived them of income or inheritance. *Marie Fanchonette v. Louis Grangé*, 5 Rob. La. 510, September 1843, 555; *Marie Fanchonette v. Grangé et al.*, 9 Rob. La. 86, September 1844, Catterall, *Judicial Cases*, 3:561–562.

40. *Mathews v. Springer*, 16 Fed. Cas. 1096 (2 Abb. U.S. 283), January 1871, 3:384–385; *Bedford v. Williams*, 5 Coldwell 202, December 1867, Catterall, *Judicial Cases*, 2:585–586.

41. Hutch. Code, 539 (1842), *Mississippi Reports: Vol. 46*, 439. According to the Code of 1857: "It shall not be lawful for any person either by will, deed, or other conveyance, directly or in trust, either express or secret, or otherwise, to make any disposition of any slave or slaves for the purpose, or with the intent to emancipate such slave or slaves in this state, or to provide that such slaves be removed to be emancipated elsewhere. . . . Nor shall it be lawful for any executor, trustee, or donee, legatee, or other person under any pretense whatever to remove any slave or slaves from this state with the intent to emancipate such slave or slaves. But all such wills, deeds, conveyances, dispositions, trusts or other arrangements . . . shall be denied and held entirely null and void, and the said slave or slaves thereby attempted or intended to be emancipated shall descend to, and be distributed among, their heirs at law of the testator, grantor or owner, or otherwise disposed of as though such testator, grantor or owner had died intestate." Code of 1857, *Mississippi Reports: Vol. 46*, 440. In addition, Mississippi did not allow free blacks to move to the state and had no recognition of free status conferred by other states (comity). Any free black person illegally residing or remaining in the state could be sold back into slavery. Currie, "From Slavery to Freedom in Mississippi's Legal System," 116, 117.

42. *Hinds v. Brazealle*, 2 How. Miss. 837, January 1838, Catterall, *Judicial Cases*, 3:286. Similarly, probable white father John Vick died without legitimate children and emancipated three slaves in his will. He wished for them to be sent to Ohio or Indiana. The court refused to recognize the will and the slaves became part of the estate. Vick's "emphatically expressed" desire that they be sent to the North indicates likely paternity. *Vick's Executor v. M'Daniel*, 3 How. Miss. 337, January 1839, Catterall, *Judicial Cases*, 3:287. Bernie Jones devotes his chapter on Mississippi mainly to the case of Mitchell v. Wells, in which Nancy Wells, then living as a free woman in Ohio, failed to collect the money and other items willed to her by her late white father, Edward Wells. A white cousin deemed Nancy part of the estate and challenged the will. The court ruled she had no rights in and could not inherit in Mississippi, although one judge dissented on the issue of comity. Wells likely would have been reenslaved had she remained in the South. Jones, *Fathers of Conscience*, 98–124.

43. *Winter and Scisson v. State*, 20 Ala. 39, January 1852, Catterall, *Judicial Cases*, 3:180–181.

44. *Shaw v. Brown*, 35 Miss. 246, April 1858, Catterall, *Judicial Cases*, 3:354–356. Ann Davis was an enslaved woman who lived with and had four children by a wealthy white man who traded in slaves. She ended up earning freedom as a result of the relationship. One son was named for the father, Hector Davis. "Was he aware of his father's business or that he was born his slave?" Calvin Schermerhorn asks. "Regardless, his naming choices suggest familial love and close bonds that endured the war and relocation." Schermerhorn, *Money over Mastery, Family over Freedom*, 118.

45. *Barksdale v. Elam*, 30 Miss. 694, April 1856, Catterall, *Judicial Cases*, 3:342–343; Jones, *Fathers of Conscience*, 55. On the other hand, Bernie Jones suggests that Edward Wells's failure to admit paternity of Nancy Wells gave the judges "room to treat the matter as an abstract one over the rights of a free woman of color to sue in Mississippi," rather than as an issue of familial responsibility (120).

46. Manumission by will was also risky because the law could change and a dead man had no power to make adjustments. A Louisiana man wanted his natural children and their mother to be freed in his will, "according to the laws of this State," or sent to a free state of their choice, and left them a third of his estate. Although the will was written and the man died before the Act of 1857 ended manumissions in the state, they were denied freedom based on that law, rendering the estate bequest void as well. *Turner, Curator v. Smith et al.*, La. An. 417, June 1857, Catterall, *Judicial Cases*, 3:655.

47. *Unwritten History of Slavery*, 18:34, 217, 106, 295.

48. *Unwritten History of Slavery*, 18:298, 251–252.

49. Hardy lived with her sister. *SNC*, Arkansas, pt. 3, 2:163; Albert, *House of Bondage*, 14. Some informants, like Betty Abernathy and Sarah Green, knew that the master was their father or grandfather, but provided little additional information. *SNC*, Missouri, 10:6, North Carolina, pt. 1, 11:341.

50. Benford grew up in Alabama. His mother was a seamstress, meaning there was a high likelihood his master was his father. *SNC*, Arkansas, pt. 1, 2:147; Drew, *North-Side View of Slavery*, 123; *SNC*, South Carolina, pt. 1, 14:240; Rawick, *AS*, supp., ser. 2, Texas, pt. 1, 2:181. Jeff Davis knew the name of his white father, but that was all. Davis's mother married his stepfather after freedom, so like all of the previous individuals cited, he had no father while he was enslaved. Victoria Perry knew only that her father was one of the white overseers. Preely Coleman knew that his father was one of a former master's sons, but he and his mother were sold as a result, so he never interacted with his biological father, though he did acquire a stepfather. *SNC*, Arkansas, pt. 2, 2:118, South Carolina, pt. 3, 14:261; Rawick, *AS*, supp., ser. 2, Texas, pt. 2, 3:856. Former slaves shared incomplete information about their white father's identity with white and African American fieldworkers. Perdue et al., *Weevils*, 90.

51. Finger grew up in Mississippi and Belle in Georgia. *SNC*, Arkansas, pt. 2, 2:287; Rawick, *AS*, supp., ser. 2, Texas, pt. 2, 3:573; *SNC*, Arkansas, pt. 1, 2:138. Nancy Boudry was identified as light skinned, and when asked about her family history responded, "I speck I is mos' white . . . but I ain't never knowed who my father was. My mother was a dark color." *SNC*, Georgia, pt. 1, 4:113.

52. Anderson grew up in Kentucky, and Williams and Mitchell in Tennessee. *SNC*, Arkansas, pt. 1, 2: 46, pt. 7, 2:149, pt. 5, 2:111; Douglass, *Narrative*, 3, 2.

53. Quinn's mother was unmarried. Fowler grew up in Georgia and had a stepfather on another plantation. Rawick, *AS*, supp., ser. 1, Mississippi, pt. 4, 9:1773, 1769; *SNC*, South Carolina, pt. 1, 14:35; Rawick, *AS*, supp., ser. 2, Texas, pt. 3, 4:1386. James Burleson said he had a white father but offered no specifics. "He doesn't know, or won't tell his name," the fieldworker noted. Rawick, *AS*, supp., ser. 2, Texas, pt. 2, 3:527.

54. Davis and Reese grew up in Georgia. *SNC*, Georgia, pt. 1, 4:253; Rawick, *AS*, supp., ser. 1, Georgia, 4:512; Perdue et al., *Weevils*, 108.

55. Perdue et al., *Weevils*, 205, 207. Mia Bay argues that former slaves believed white "meanness" stemmed from "power and privilege." Bay, *The White Image in the Black Mind*, 168.

56. Wallace was uneducated, a good sign that her father took no interest in her. Perdue et al., *Weevils*, 202, 255, 293, 295, xxxix.

57. Like Ray, William Singleton published his memoir in the 1920s and recalled growing up fatherless. As a young man, his aunt informed him that his master's brother was his father, but during his childhood, "I had nobody that I called father. I only knew my mother." Ray and Ray, *Twice Sold*, 54; Singleton, *Recollections of My Slavery Days*, 2, 5.

58. Rawick, *AS*, supp., ser. 1, Mississippi, pt. 5, 10:2045–2046; *SNC*, Arkansas, pt. 3, 2:203.

59. Washington, *Up from Slavery*, 2–3; Washington, *Autobiography*, 15; Rudd and Bond, *From Slavery to Wealth*, 141, 146.

60. Baptist argues that sexual abuse was worse on the frontier due to the skewed gender imbalance among whites and because forced migration removed enslaved women from social networks. Baptist, "The Absent Subject," 141.

61. "I was agent of a man who had eighteen of these headless families in one house." Drew, *North-Side View of Slavery*, 245. Ben Kinchlow and his mother were freed and sent to Mexico by a white father he never knew. *SNC*, Texas, pt. 2, 16:260. Free black hairdresser and Cincinnati resident Eliza Potter believed the large number of mixed-race people in the North were "gentleman's children from the South," sent there by their fathers. Potter, *Hairdresser's Experience in High Life*, 100.

62. Picquet and her husband exemplify the opposite potential outcomes for mulatto children. Though Picquet eventually achieved freedom, she had to endure sexual slavery to get there. Mattison, *Louisa Picquet*, 26. See Calvin Schermerhorn's discussion of Corrina Hinton and her

relationship with Richmond slave trader Silas Omohundro. Hinton lived as Omohundro's primary partner, bore him five children, assisted with his business affairs, and though enslaved benefited from the status imparted by this connection. Omohundro, an involved father, moved his family to Ohio before the war and freed them in his 1864 will. However, as was typical in these cases, their slave status up until his death caused legal problems. Mary F. Lumpkin had a similar relationship with Robert Lumpkin, a man who ran a slave jail in Richmond. Lumpkin sent the couple's children to school in the North and eventually moved them to Pennsylvania for fear they would be sold if he encountered financial difficulty. Schermerhorn, *Money over Mastery, Family over Freedom*, 112–117.

63. See her discussion of Avenia White and Susan Johnson, moved to the city and freed, along with four children, by a former slave trader turned planter, Rice C. Ballard. Ballard moved the group in 1838 before his legal marriage. White discussed Johnson's children in her letters in an attempt to gain Ballard's attention to their requests for financial support. As Green notes, white men "publically consolidated their power while privately addressing the entreaties of women and children of color" (56). Green, *Remember Me*, 3, 4, 12, 20–23, 33–37, 44–61.

64. While free blacks in Cincinnati tended to segregate by color within households, they did not do so by ward or neighborhood. Mixed-race individuals tended to marry other multi- or biracial individuals and leadership was dominated by, but not limited to, those with lighter skin. The black and mulatto communities were not isolated from one another. Horton and Flaherty, "Black Leadership in Antebellum Cincinnati," 81, 82, 84, 91; Taylor and Dula, "The Black Residential Experience and Community Formation in Antebellum Cincinnati," 104, 106, 108, 112, 115, 82, 84, 91.

65. Jones, *Fathers of Conscience*, 155, 153–155, 32; Green, *Remember Me*, 28, 47. Kenneth Aslakson argues that in the course of navigating a racially biased judicial system, free people of color in New Orleans unintentionally contributed to the creation of a firm legal "distinction between 'Negroes' and 'people of color.'" Aslakson, *Making Race in the Courtroom*, 2.

66. For examples of white men freeing and educating their children see Simmons, *Men of Mark*, 208, 510–511. John Mercer Langston and three brothers were born free after their father, Virginia slaveholder Ralph Quarles, manumitted Langston's mother and older sister. Quarles willed his property to his mulatto family. Only four when his father died, Langston had positive but limited memories of the man. Langston went on to study law, recruit for black regiments during the Civil War, and served as consul-general to Haiti and as the first black Congressional representative from Virginia. Langston Hughes was his grandnephew. Langston, *From the Virginia Plantation to the National Capitol*, 11–17, 22; Williamson, *New People*, 49–50. William Tiler Johnson was born a slave in 1809 and emancipated in 1820 by his master and probable father. Johnson's mother and sister had been freed earlier. A successful businessman and slaveholder, Johnson was murdered in 1851 by another free black man over a property disagreement. Johnson, *William Johnson's Natchez*.

67. Johnson was still living at home when freedom came. SNC, Arkansas, pt. 4, 2:73, 74; Simmons, *Men of Mark*, 538–539, 759, 760. Some former slaves, possibly because of the timing of emancipation, only discussed white fathers leaving property to their concubines and biracial children. SNC, North Carolina, pt. 2, 11:230, 227, pt. 2, 11:260, Tennessee, 15:50; Rawick, *AS*, supp., ser. 2, Nebraska, 1:339.

68. Rawick, *AS*, supp., ser. 1, Indiana and Ohio, 5:102, 103.

69. One informant noted that her Quaker father, a shopkeeper, wanted to buy her and send her to Philadelphia, but her owners would not sell. *Unwritten History of Slavery*, 18:227. Ella Johnson's white father lived on a nearby plantation and also unsuccessfully tried to buy her and take her North. While Johnson's master would not sell, "I was treated just like one of his own children." Rawick, *AS*, supp., ser. 1, Georgia, 4:343, 344.

70. Eliza Potter told a similar story with a happier ending. Another wealthy white man sold his Southern property, took his concubine north, married her, and provided for his wife and daughters. Potter, *Hairdresser's Experience in High Life*, 150–151, 153. Emily Clark points out that

"housekeeper" was often a euphemism for concubine. Clark, *Strange History of the American Quadroon*, 63.

71. One daughter purchased as a mistress committed suicide, while another brother and sister escaped. Craft, *Running a Thousand Miles*, 17, 18, 21, 25–26; Simmons, *Men of Mark*, 626. Even if a master had no intention of providing freedom, his death often led to a loss of status for concubines and his children. Smith, *Autobiography of James L. Smith*, 4, 5, 7; Rawick, *AS*, supp., ser. 2, Texas, pt. 3, 4:1360.

72. Northup later heard that Eliza had wasted away in her grief and died. Northup, *Twelve Years a Slave*, 52, 86–87, 53, 81, 85, 160. Calvin Schermerhorn discusses the risky nature of Eliza's strategy and relationship with Elisha Berry. Berry also miscalculated if he truly intended to free Eliza and Emily. Eliza also had an older son, Randall, who was not fathered by Berry. Schermerhorn, *Money over Mastery, Family over Freedom*, 107–108. One woman told her interviewer that her mother's master and father had manumitted his concubine and two daughters, but after his death, his white son burned their free papers and sold them to New Orleans. Cade, "Out of the Mouths of Ex-Slaves," 325. Peter Johnson's half-white brother hated him and immediately sold his father's concubine and her son when the Kentucky master died. Alexander Kenner's white father "told his mother she might go away" after he married. Though he had stated his intention to free her, he never manumitted his illegitimate family. Kenner's mother prospered in St. Louis and purchased three of her seven children, but the master's family kept one sibling and eventually claimed her assets. Kenner had to sue to reclaim his share of the money. Blassingame, *Slave Testimony*, 505, 392–393.

73. Drew, *North-Side View of Slavery*, 143–144.

74. Drew, 144, 145, 146; *SNC*, Arkansas, pt. 3, 2:267. Louisa Picquet's father and master thought "I had better hair than his daughter, and so he had it cut off." He also attempted to have sex with her. Mattison, *Louisa Picquet*, 17.

75. Curry was born in Tennessee and Pettus grew up in Georgia. Ross's interviewer commented, "It is not hard to realize the reason why Amanda was treated better than other children when you remember that she called her grandpa 'Master.'" *SNC*, Arkansas, pt. 2, 2:85, pt. 5, 2:339, pt. 6, 2:83, 85. Carrie Mason's husband was made overseer by his father and master, but given nothing after the war. Rawick, *AS*, supp., ser. 1, Georgia, 4:423–424.

76. "He allus tole Mammy dat she gwine habe a cabin an a patch ob ground' to raise her young'uns on, long as he got a spot ob land." However, the master was killed in the Civil War, "an' de family lost so much dey couldn't keep us atter Freedom." Van Hook was enslaved in Tennessee. Rawick, *AS*, supp., ser. 2, Texas, pt. 9, 10:3906; *SNC*, Arkansas, pt. 6, 2:222, pt. 6, 2:307, Oklahoma, 8:233.

77. Lawson came from Georgia and Hunter from North Carolina. *SNC*, Arkansas, pt. 4, 2:244, pt. 3, 2:365–366.

78. Cade, "Out of the Mouths of Ex-Slaves," 307–308. Bailey Cunningham and his half-white siblings in Virginia "were considered free until they were twenty years old and did not have to work." At the age of twenty-one, they were hired out. Cunningham worked in a hotel. Perdue et al., *Weevils*, 81. Green argues that the mixed-race children of Samuel Townsend "occupied an ambiguous space." Green, *Remember Me*, 85.

79. Although her father, William D. Waddell, acknowledged her, Daves suspected "some of the family would not like it if they knew I was telling this." Daves described her enslaved mother as nearly white. After she moved with her mother to Kansas, Daves lost touch with her father: "I don't know where my father is, living or dead, or what became of him." *SNC*, North Carolina, pt. 1, 11:234, 235, 233.

80. Rawick, *AS*, supp., ser. 1, Oklahoma, 12:72.

81. Grimes, *Life of William Grimes*, 5, 6. Cato Carter discussed what it meant to have white parentage, though he said almost nothing about his father. The son of his master's brother, Carter lived in the big house on an Alabama plantation while his mother and her other children lived in the quarters. "They were always good to me 'cause I was one of their blood. They never hit me a lick nor slapped me once and told me that they would never sell me away from them."

He nonetheless willingly discussed the sale of slaves, physical punishment, and patrols, acknowledging that while these negative aspects of slavery had little impact on him, they affected fellow slaves. Sim Younger's father and master willed his mother "a farm on which my brothers and sisters are still living." The will also included a provision for Younger's education. Because he was only five when his father died, Younger had little to say about the man, but he enlisted and fought for the Union army, an indication of his feelings about slavery. Nannie Eaves noted that her husband, the child of his Kentucky master, ran away from "his Massa en his Daddy en jine the U.S. Army." Rawick, *AS*, supp., ser. 2, Texas, pt. 2, 3:639, 643, 644, 646; *SNC*, Missouri, 10:380, 381, Kentucky, 7:61; *Unwritten History of Slavery*, 18:173.

82. Thompson was interviewed in Canada and owed his freedom to his father, who freed all of his slaves in his will. The will was rescinded and not everyone achieved freedom. While Thompson acknowledged that his father treated him fairly well, he disparaged the sexual dynamics of slavery, vilifying another master he knew who "had six children by a colored slave. Then there was a fuss between him and his wife, and he sold all the children but the oldest slave daughter. Afterward, he had a child by this daughter, and sold mother and child before the birth." Drew, *North-Side View of Slavery*, 136, 137.

83. Ensley's experience echoes that of Sally Hemings's children by Thomas Jefferson. James left South Carolina in 1865, attended Howard University, and included in his narrative a song celebrating freedom and William Tecumseh Sherman. Simmons, *Men of Mark*, 361; *SNC*, Maryland, 8:34, 35, 36. "I received no hard treatment and did little or no work. Yet, I wore the same clothing as did the rest of the slaves," Robert Grinstead recalled his upbringing as the only son of a master with no white wife or children. *SNC*, Oklahoma, 13:124.

84. Clarke, *Narrative of the Sufferings of Lewis Clarke*, 9, 10; Clarke and Clarke, *Narrative of the Sufferings of Lewis and Milton Clarke*, 69–70.

85. Clarke and Clarke, *Narrative of the Sufferings of Lewis and Milton Clarke*, 69–70; Clarke, *Narrative of the Sufferings of Lewis Clarke*, 20, 21. Ellen Craft's master was also her father. Because she was "almost white," her first mistress "became so annoyed, at finding her frequently mistaken for a child of the family, that she gave her when eleven years of age to a daughter, as a wedding present." Craft, *Running A Thousand Miles*, 2.

86. Picquet's mother "was fifteen years old when I was born." Douglass, *My Bondage*, 59; Mattison, *Louisa Picquet*, 6; Rawick, *AS*, supp., ser. 2, Texas, pt. 1, 2:336, supp., ser. 1, Minnesota, 2:101, 102; *SNC*, Arkansas, pt. 1, 2:162. Although prohibited to speak of it, the slave community whispered that Dr. Norcom had fathered eleven slaves. Harriet Jacobs noted that he sold the mothers and children to appease his wife. Jacobs, *Incidents*, 55, 85, 184.

87. "My daddy sold me to a preacher who raised me as though I were his own son," he added. Years later, during a political campaign, this biological father visited town and had Robinson "come to see him. . . . When I shook hands with him, he said, 'Gentlemen, he's a little shady but he's my son.'" *SNC*, Arkansas, pt. 6, 2:55, 56. Lettie Moonson told her African American interviewer about an enslaved woman whose mistress mistakenly believed that the master had fathered the woman's child. "By the time the baby was six months old the mistress had beaten it to death." The father actually lived on a neighboring plantation. Cade, "Out of the Mouths of Ex-Slaves," 308.

88. Roper was born in North Carolina. Alice Davis related a similar story of her birth in Mississippi: "When I was one month old they said I was so white Mandy Paine thought her brother was my father, so she got me and carried me to the meat block and was goin' to cut my head off." Her old mistress heard the commotion, ran in, and paid $40 for and raised the baby. Roper, *Narrative of the Adventures and Escape of Moses Roper*, 7, 8; *SNC*, Arkansas, pt. 2, 2:97. Some masters, who typically did not part with their slaves, sold only "social embarrassments," who were their own kin. Dunaway, *African-American Family*, 42.

89. "She is dead, thank God, and if I ever meet her again, I hope I shall know her," Grimes added. Wilson grew up in Louisiana and Grimes in Virginia. Douglass, *Narrative*, 4; *SNC*, Oklahoma, 13:347; Grimes, *Life of William Grimes*, 7–8; *SNC*, Georgia, pt. 3, 4:230; Jacobs, *Incidents*, 45, 46, 49, 51–54.

90. Perdue et al., *Weevils*, 91. One mistress, unable to convince her husband to sell his illegitimate children, refused to allow them to work in the house, which may have actually protected them. *Unwritten History of Slavery*, 18:261.

91. Jacobs, *Incidents*, 57. "Dey sell 'em jes' like de other slaves," Chris Franklin argued. "It seem like de white women didn't mind dat. Dey didn't object 'cause dat mean more slaves." Rawick, *AS*, supp., ser. 2, Texas, pt. 3, 4:1408. For a discussion of white women's reactions to the sexual exploitation of slave women, see White, *Ar'n't I a Woman?*, 40–43; Jones, *Labor of Love*, 25–26; Weiner, *Mistresses and Slaves*, 93, 96–97, 128; Clinton, *Plantation Mistress*, 188, 196; Fox-Genovese, *Within the Plantation Household*; Glymph, *Out of the House of Bondage*.

92. Jordon grew up in Lousisana. Albert, *House of Bondage*, 102, 103, 104; *SNC*, Arkansas, pt. 3, 2:205.

93. Burton, *Memories of Childhood's Slavery Days*, 7–8.

94. Young's family was from Tennessee. *SNC*, Indiana, 5:88, Oklahoma, 13:362, Florida, 3:186.

95. William managed to purchase his own freedom with the help of friends. *Ford v. Ford*, 7 Humphreys 92, September 1846, Catterall, *Judicial Cases*, 2:530; *SNC*, Maryland, 8:34; Douglass, *Life and Times*, 70, 73; *Unwritten History of Slavery*, 18:94.

96. Eliza was purchased and freed by a man from New York. *SNC*, Oklahoma, 13:77.

97. *SNC*, Arkansas, pt. 6, 2:187; Troy, *Hair-Breadth Escapes*, 2; Rawick, *AS*, supp., ser. 2, Texas, pt. 4:1218–1219; Drew, *North-Side View of Slavery*, 240, 239, 241.

98. Wyatt-Brown, *Southern Honor*, 312–313; Blassingame, *Slave Testimony*, 155; Rawick, *AS*, supp., ser. 1, Missouri, 2:217; Johnson, *Soul by Soul*, 151. Henry Bibb's light skin aided in his escapes, but also complicated his sale. Lewis Clarke also passed as white as he traveled, and John Hope Franklin and Loren Schweninger find that mulattos were a minority of fugitives, but overrepresented in proportion to their numbers in the population. William and Ellen Craft escaped from Georgia in 1848 using Ellen's whiteness, but only by disguising her as a man. "It occurred to me that, as my wife was nearly white, I might get her to disguise herself as an invalid gentleman, and assume to be my master, while I could attend as his slave," William wrote. Bibb, *Narrative of the Life and Adventures of Henry Bibb*, 49, 101–102, 108; Clarke, *Narrative of the Sufferings of Lewis Clarke*, 36; Franklin and Schweninger, *Runaway Slaves*, 214; Craft, *Running A Thousand Miles*, 29, 35–36, 30–78, 86, 88, 92, 93.

99. Drew, *North-Side View of Slavery*, 154–155; Brown, *Black Man*, 18–19; *SNC*, Arkansas, pt. 5, 2:328; Singleton, *Recollections of My Slavery Days*, 1, 3, 5. James Pennington disparaged an informer, "a confidential slave" who reported to the master. "This wretched fellow, who was nearly white, and of Irish descent, informed our master of the movements of each member of the family," he wrote. Pennington, *Fugitive Blacksmith*, 11.

100. Franks remembered secretly praying for freedom along with other house slaves. After emancipation, her brother snuck into the big house to tell her she was free and bring her to join her family. When she first went to work in the fields with her siblings, work she had never before performed, "I would faint away most every day." Williams grew up in Alabama. Rawick, *AS*, supp., ser. 1, Mississippi, pt. 2, 7:782, 786; *SNC*, North Carolina, pt. 2, 11:396, 397. Adora Rienshaw commented on being mulatto, but she did not say who treated her badly, blacks, whites, or both. Mixed-race individuals in North Carolina were generally referred to as Free Issue. Rienshaw called her family "Ole Issues," noting, "but I tell yo' it's bad ter be a' 'Ole Issue.'" *SNC*, North Carolina, pt. 2, 11:213, 215.

101. Perdue et al., *Weevils*, 108. Brenda Stevenson notes that the slave community assigned "an even deeper stigma to those children conceived as a result of the voluntary sexual relations between black women and white men," and their mothers often faced social ostracism. Stevenson, "Distress and Discord," 112.

102. In African American folklore, children were found in hollow logs or hatched from buzzard eggs. Katie Sutton related the following song lyrics: "'case you was hatched from a buzzard's egg, My little colored chile." It is unclear where Sutton was enslaved, but other references to hatching from a buzzard egg come from Virginia. Rawick, *AS*, supp., ser. 1, Indiana

and Ohio, 5:211; Schwartz, *Born in Bondage*, 103; Bay, *The White Image in the Black Mind*, 120. Michael Gomez discusses acceptance of mixed-race individuals based on whether or not they identified as black. Gomez, *Exchanging Our Country Marks*, 234–237.

103. When free to do so Galloway's mother left. Rawick, *AS*, supp., ser. 1, Mississippi, pt. 3, 8:803, 801–802, 805.

104. Billings's grandfather sent his stepchildren to school, but kept her working in the fields. Perdue et al., *Weevils*, 16, 15; *SNC*, Arkansas, pt. 1, 2:163. Donaville Broussard had a half-white mother and white father. After emancipation, he eventually left his mother and stepfather because "my steppapa didn't like me. I was light." *SNC*, Texas, pt. 1, 16:152, 151.

105. Pricilla Owens felt that her master and father "treated her fairly well." Of the Cade interviews conducted by African American fieldworkers, she was one of the only subjects who identified the present as worse than slavery. Cade, "Out of the Mouths of Ex-Slaves," 316, 325; Rawick, *AS*, supp., ser. 1, Indiana and Ohio, 5:88.

106. Fedric, *Slave Life in Virginia and Kentucky*, 45.

107. Neill came from Georgia. *Unwritten History of Slavery*, 18:3; Rawick, *AS*, supp., ser. 2, Texas, pt. 6, 7:2890; *SNC*, South Carolina, pt. 1, 14:128.

108. Rawick, *AS*, supp., ser. 2, Texas, pt. 5, 6:1943, pt. 5, 6:2298.

109. Watkins's father had a legal wife with whom he had no children. Watkins, *Narrative of the Life of James Watkins*, 7, 9; *SNC*, North Carolina, pt. 2, 11:271.

110. Miller, *"Dear Master,"* 145.

111. Roper, *Narrative of the Adventures and Escape of Moses Roper*, 56. A compromise strategy involved giving their children to white relatives rather than selling them outright. At age five, James Smith's father and master "gave me to his son, who was my half brother, and he raised me. This son then had children about my age. These children were sent to school, but I was not." The half brother later sold Smith to another owner. James Curry's mother had a white father who gave his two enslaved children to a white relative. Drew, *North-Side View of Slavery*, 351, 352; Curry, "Narrative of James Curry," 1.

112. Fedric, *Slave Life in Virginia and Kentucky*, 46; Rawick, *AS*, supp., ser. 2, Texas, pt. 2, 3:735; *SNC*, Missouri, 10:74, Kentucky, 7:23, South Carolina, pt. 1, 14:150; Perdue et al., *Weevils*, 86, 201.

113. Howell did not specify if her father was also her grandfather or if he forced his daughter to have a child with another slave. Rawick, *AS*, supp., ser. 2, Texas, pt. 7, 8:2989, 2990, 2991; Simpson, *Horrors of the Virginian Slave Trade*, 49, 58, 8, 12, 14, 15, 28, 29; *SNC*, Arkansas, pt. 3, 2:339, 340; Robinson, *From Log Cabin to the Pulpit*, 32. Jacob Aldrich knew his Louisiana master was his maternal grandfather and criticized his brutality, poor provisioning, and habit of sexually abusing enslaved women, a trait shared by his white sons. Rawick, *AS*, supp., ser. 2, Texas, pt. 1, 2:23, 24, 26.

114. The master forced Terrill's mother to "come be his mistress one night every week," but she also had an enslaved husband and two other children with whom Terrill was not allowed to interact. *SNC*, Texas, pt. 4, 16:80, 81.

115. "Do you wonder that when freedom came to me I preferred the maiden name of my sainted mother to the name of my father?" he asked (14). Johnson, *Slavery Days in Old Kentucky*, 8, 9, 13–14, 14, 32, 7, 11. Coleman Lee's white father "would not let me be called by his name. So mother gave me her name, which was Lee, and so I have kept it right along." Albert, *House of Bondage*, 158–159.

116. Brown, *Narrative of William W. Brown*, 98, 105, 106, 99. Adelaide Vaughn's father rejected the name of a white father who sold him and took the name of a kindly master. "He went in the Warren's name. He did that because he liked them. Phillips was his real father, but he sold him to the Warrens and he took their name and kept it." *SNC*, Arkansas, pt. 7, 2:10.

117. Douglass, *Narrative*, 3; Douglass, *Life and Times*, 39; Douglass, *My Bondage*, 424. A group freed by a will hoped to depart for Liberia, "the home of our Forefathers in Africa." John Scott to Rev and Dear Sir, Richmond, Sept. 19, 1853, in Starobin, *Blacks in Bondage*, 108. Later mis-

sionaries to Africa made similar comments, calling the continent "the land of my fathers." Johnson, *Twenty-Eight Years a Slave*, x.

118. *Unwritten History of Slavery*, 18:84, 81.

119. *SNC*, South Carolina, pt. 4, 14:161, 162, pt. 4, 14:45. As Bernie Jones notes, those manumitted by white fathers who successfully navigated the legal system to retain their freedom and financial inheritance became the "black elite, people of freedom and property," but their agency "was also tainted by slavery." Jones, *Fathers of Conscience*, 153–154.

120. Rawick, *AS*, supp., ser. 2, Texas, pt. 7, 8:3292–3294; *SNC*, North Carolina, pt. 2, 11:78.

121. *SNC*, South Carolina, pt. 4, 14:32, 33, 34; Gomez, *Exchanging Our Country Marks*, 235. Robert Kimbrough, who claimed to be three-quarters white, was also disdainful of his black stepfather. Rawick, *AS*, supp., ser. 1, Georgia, 4:366.

122. "Slaves did not necessarily constitute a class," Paul Lovejoy states of slavery more broadly. "Their dependence could result in the subordination of their identity to that of their master, on whom their position depended, or it could lead to the development of a sense of comradeship with other slaves, and hence a form of class consciousness. Both could take place in the same society." Stevenson, "Distress and Discord," 114, 112–115; Lovejoy, *Transformations in Slavery*, 5; Yarbrough, "Power, Perception, and Interracial Sex," 573–575; King, *Stolen Childhood*, 112–113.

123. "They did not despise them," Gomez adds of the black response to mixed-race individuals, "for they only knew too well the truth of their origins. But neither did they feel sorry for them, for many had already exchanged their lighter skin for privilege and distance from the black community" (235). Gomez, *Exchanging Our Country Marks*, 235, 237, 233. Annette Gordon-Reed discusses how Madison Hemings watched his three siblings pass as white while he identified with a black community. Gordon-Reed, *Thomas Jefferson and Sally Hemings*, 235.

124. The Chase sisters also discussed the "aristocratic pride of the F.F.V.s," former Virginia slaves who disparaged and refused to work with "North Carolina niggers." Swint, ed., *Dear Ones at Home*, 73, 60, 61. Dylan Penningroth discusses postwar migration, the lack of "a common identity or a unified black community," and how African Americans often "emphasized the *differences* among black people: between refugees and those who had grown up on a place, between free and the freed, between blacks from different regions, states, or even different islands." Penningroth, *The Claims of Kinfolk*, 175, 174, 171, 188.

125. Rawick, *AS*, supp., ser. 2, Texas, pt. 6, 7:2578.

126. Grinstead grew up in Mississippi. *SNC*, North Carolina, pt. 2, 11:391, 392, Oklahoma, 13:126; Rawick, *AS*, supp., ser. 2, Texas, pt. 2, 3:573.

127. Daugherty's family came from Kentucky. She was also sensitive about and revealed the story of her first husband's grandmother, a woman forced to serve as her master's concubine. "This was the first time Mrs. Daugherty said she had ever told anyone this. As the older Mrs. Grady always felt very badly about her origin." Patterson was born in Kentucky. Rawick, *AS*, supp., ser. 1, Indiana and Ohio, 5:62, 63; *SNC*, South Carolina, pt. 3, 14:41, Indiana, 5:152, 151, South Carolina, pt. 3, 14:195.

128. Childress was from Tennessee and Cheatham from Kentucky. *SNC*, South Carolina, pt. 2, 14:14, Indiana, 5:56; Drew, *North-Side View of Slavery*, 219; Rawick, *AS*, supp., ser. 1, Indiana and Ohio, 5:49; Blassingame, *Slave Testimony*, 649.

129. Jackson, *My Father's Name*, 126, 129, 137–139. When referring to mixed-race individuals, genealogical websites often list the first name of mother and "unk." (unknown) in place of the father. The omissions in genealogical records point to the number of white fathers who disappear from family histories. Heather Williams refers to contemporary African American attempts to trace genealogical information as the "larger work of naming people, of recognizing their existence, and of saying their existence is worthy of remembrance." White paternity complicates that effort. Williams, *Help Me to Find My People*, 197.

Chapter Six

1. In her study of white men who "invested emotionally and financially" in their enslaved concubines and children, Sharony Green emphasizes the "intimacy" that developed in these relationships, whether coerced or consensual. "Not all white men were as exploitative as generally presented, nor was their behavior consistent," Green writes. While affectionate relationships did develop, the power imbalance meant that these relationships began in exploitation. When one party is a slaveholder and the other a slave, exploitation inherently exists, even in the cases where women made strategic decisions and engaged in negotiations over the contours of the relationship. Green, *Remember Me*, 9, 8, 125, 132; Clinton, "Southern Dishonor," 66, 61–65; Clinton, *Plantation Mistress*, 213.

2. "Proximity to white men seemed to produce assertiveness, even callousness, in some African American women and girls," Green writes. "Such women were well aware of strategies of survival that could bring them benefits even as they enacted costs on others." Green, *Remember Me*, 84, 64; West, *Family or Freedom*, 130.

3. Gordon-Reed, *The Hemingses of Monticello*, 106; Clinton, "Southern Dishonor," 65; Jones, *Fathers of Conscience*, 6, 8, 9. Emily West refers to the fuzzy "line between rape and consent" in the case of Lucy Boomer, an enslaved woman involved with her master. West's study of free black petitioners for residency or re-enslavement addresses concubinage and consent. Male and female petitioners prioritized remaining with kin above all else, and those who petitioned for enslavement "often felt under the threat of expulsion and wanted to stay with beloved families in their homes and communities." West argues that re-enslavement petitions from free black women might indicate affection for white lovers, exploitation, and/or use of sex "to improve their quality of life." West, *Family or Freedom*, 129, 15, 130, 134, 139, 141, 152.

4. In this argument about consent, I differ slightly from other scholars. See for instance, L. Virginia Gould's discussion of Jacqueline Lemelle, a woman purchased in New Orleans in 1762 by Santiago Lemelle and eventually freed along with their three daughters. She argues that women knew sexual relationships could lead to freedom and used that to their advantage, leading to consensual unions, particularly in New Orleans. After being freed, Jacqueline stayed in Santiago's household, indicating the existence of a "mutual" relationship. Lemelle saved her money and purchased the freedom of another, earlier daughter, and also her granddaughter. After Santiago died, Jacqueline and her daughters inherited his property. While this was likely an affectionate relationship, it did begin with the purchase of a human being, which limited Jacqueline's options. That one of her free daughters chose to enter a union with a white man more fully conforms to the definition of consent. Gould, "Urban Slavery—Urban Freedom," 307, 303, 310; Shafer, "Open and Notorious Concubinage," 171. See also Pascoe's discussion of Leah Foster. In 1847, Alfred Foster took Leah and their five children to Cincinnati and freed them. She then returned to Texas with him, ostensibly as his servant. Her legal struggle to claim the inheritance he left to her and the children after his death in 1867, including her use of the term "widow," suggests a relationship of affection and a level of consent on her part. Leah Foster started as a slave, which means the relationship may have started in coercion, but she seems to have made her own choices later in her life. Pascoe, *What Comes Naturally*, 36, 17, 19, 32, 40.

5. "The notion of autonomy is undercut by their lack of legal standing," Jones writes, and these women were often pawns in the legal suits over such wills. Jones, *Fathers of Conscience*, 8, 9. A concubine had no concrete legal or economic power, but on occasion she could exert sway over a white man. Charles Ball told of a bachelor with a roughly forty-year-old mulatto housekeeper who "acquired a most unaccountable influence over" the much younger son of the master. The master sold the woman, but his son followed the trader, bought her back for a higher sum, and left his father to live with her. She fell in love with a slave man on another plantation, the young master forbade his visits, and the two murdered the master and were then executed. Ball, *Fifty Years in Chains*, 289, 290, 294.

6. "As with other forms of Victorian politeness, the rudeness lay with people who described things the way they saw them." Johnson, *Soul by Soul*, 114, 115.

7. Baptist defines slaves as "people converted into symbols and objects of economic power, social status, and psychosexual fulfillment" (1650). Baptist, "'Cuffy,' 'Fancy Maids,' and 'One-Eyed Men,'" 1623, 1621, 1647, 1648, 1620, 1627, 1631, 1640, 1643, 1649; Baptist, "The Absent Subject," 143. To buy a fancy maid was to purchase "fantasies about mastery and race," Walter Johnson writes. Calvin Schermerhorn argues that "networks exposed contradictions between the dominant familial ideology of nineteenth-century America and the idols of the marketplace." Johnson, *Soul by Soul*, 155; Schermerhorn, *Money over Mastery, Family over Freedom*, 207.

8. Unlike Fitzhugh, abolitionists discussed sexual exploitation in slavery, but they did adopt part of his thinking. They argued that "only a free market in labor, as in other commodities, ensured that the household would remain inviolate—a sphere insulated from commerce," Amy Dru Stanley writes. "Men's wages reconciled the worlds of market and the home." Fitzhugh, *Sociology for the South*, 106; Stanley, *From Bondage to Contract*, 142, 146.

9. Painter, "The Journal of Ella Gertrude Clanton Thomas," 62, 63, 39, 40–41, 42, 45, 50. Southern states passed or strengthened laws banning interracial marriage during the Civil War and in its immediate aftermath. Pascoe, *What Comes Naturally*, 29, 12. When Mary Chesnut commented on a hypothetical white man who "runs a hideous black harem with its consequences under the same roof with his lovely white wife, and his beautiful and accomplished daughters," she expressed concern over the impact of interracial sex on white women rather than the slave community. "You see," she continued, "Mrs. Stowe did not hit the sorest spot. She makes Legree a bachelor." While Harriet Beecher Stowe's character, Simon Legree, was cruel and violent, Chesnut described a cultured churchgoer and devoted husband and father. Such a man, she continued, was likely kind to his slaves, "and the unfortunate results of his bad ways were not sold. They had not to jump over ice blocks. They were kept in full view, and were provided for, handsomely, in his will." Biracial children were not people, but "consequences" and "unfortunate results." Chesnut admitted that white women were complicit in the culture of silence, and in doing so hinted at the toxicity of slaveholder family dynamics. "His wife and daughters, in their purity and innocence, are supposed never to dream of what is as plain before their eyes as the sunlight. And they play their parts of unsuspecting angels to the letter. They profess to adore their father as the model of all earthly goodness." Chesnut, *Diary from Dixie*, Aug. 26, 1861, 122.

10. The institution of slavery granted mistresses privilege and status, but "also gave them sexual nightmares. . . . Reluctant to put their class position against their gender interests, they avoided the facts and kept their secrets." White women's silence contributed to the sexual climate that caused them "jealousy, anger, and humiliation," and induced fears of "sexual competition." Painter, "The Journal of Ella Gertrude Clanton Thomas," 66, 59, 61.

11. Schermerhorn, *Money over Mastery, Family over Freedom*, 106, 116, 108, 112–119, 132, 201, 210, 211.

12. Bratton was born in Tennessee in 1881, so her mother was raped after freedom. *SNC*, Arkansas, pt. 1, 2:250, 249.

13. Enslaved women's sense of honor overlapped with that of white women and enslaved men, and Forret constructs "a portrait of enslaved femininity fundamentally at variance with contemporary whites' characterizations of unrestrained black female sexuality." Forret, *Slave against Slave*, 333, 20, 382.

14. Jane Peterson "never got to marry till after freedom. Then she had three more black children by her husband." *SNC*, Arkansas, pt. 1, 2:51, 52.

15. Peters was born in Missouri. *SNC*, Arkansas, pt. 5, 2:323, 328–329.

16. Smith's family came from Louisiana. *SNC*, Arkansas, pt. 6, 2:195; pt. 6, 2:257, 258. In his discussion of infanticide, Jeff Forret notes that enslaved women in Virginia "clearly indicated that white paternity was a source of shame." When enslaved women resorted to abortion or infanticide after being raped, such behavior enabled them to rid themselves of their shame and the reminder of being assaulted and also served as a form of retaliation against the perpetrator, especially if he was the master. Forret uses the story of Margaret Garner, who killed the likely child of her master in his presence. Infanticide was rare, but enslaved women's sense of honor

caused some to take the less drastic action of abandoning children born as a result of sexual violence. Forret, *Slave against Slave*, 377, 378, 372.

17. Lindsay was born in Louisiana, and Ray came from Georgia. *SNC*, Arkansas, pt. 6, 2:352, pt. 4, 2:255; Rawick, *AS*, supp., ser. 1, Indiana and Ohio, 5: 422, 423.

18. Keckley believed her father was her mother's master. Keckley, *Behind the Scenes*, 38, 39, 105, 49, 55, 63; King, *Stolen Childhood*, 111. Fleischner writes that Keckley "renounces her claim to the role of suffering slave mother," in her "suppression of her son in the narrative—he even remains unnamed." While Fleischner further argues that Keckley adopted a "tone of reproach and blame" in relation to her son, I believe she pinned the blame on slavery and his white father. Fleischner, *Mastering Slavery*, 96, 97. "Female slaves betrayed a remarkably acute understanding of gendered notions of sexual honor and nineteenth-century conventions of proper female sexual comportment," Jeff Forret writes in *Slave against Slave*, 380.

19. The master treated his "nearly white" sons by Phyllis no differently than other slaves, and when they grew older, they moved to the slave quarters. Rawick, *AS*, supp., ser. 2, Texas, pt. 5, 6:1973.

20. White grew up in Texas. Roper, *Narrative of the Adventures and Escape of Moses Roper*, 32; *SNC*, Oklahoma, 13:325; Brown, *Narrative of Henry Box Brown*, 23; *SNC*, Florida, 3:167, Indiana, 5:50. Cureton Milling's master "take 'vantage of de young gal slaves," by sending them to "shell corn in de crib" and then he "raise slaves to sell." South Carolina, pt. 3, 14:194; North Carolina, Part 2, 11:96. Mulattos were often sold as domestic slaves. Many Southerners believed that darker skin connoted better health and stamina for field labor. Owens, *This Species of Property*, 13; Johnson, *Soul by Soul*, 138–139; Olmsted, *Cotton Kingdom*, 2:211.

21. "Our sisters, if not by the law, are by common consent made the prey of vile men, who can bid the highest," Pennington stated. Brown, *Slave Life in Georgia*, 112; Craft, *Running a Thousand Miles*, 16; Pennington, *Fugitive Blacksmith*, v–vi, xi; Fedric, *Slave Life in Virginia and Kentucky*, 45; Jacobs, *Incidents*, 81, 160; Albert, *House of Bondage*, 119, 120. The "saddes'" event of Carol Randall's life occurred when her master sold her sister. "Marie was pretty, dat's why he took her to Richmond to sell her. You see, you could git a powerful lot of money in dose days for a pretty gal." Randall's narrative hints at possible white parentage. Perdue et al., *Weevils*, 236.

22. "Some of the half white and beautiful young women who were used by the marster and his men friends or who was the sweetheart of the marster only, were given special privileges. Some of 'em worked very little," Willie McCullough argued. "They had private quarters well fixed up and had a great influence over the marster. Some of these slave girls broke up families by getting the marster so enmeshed in their net that his wife, perhaps an older woman, was greatly neglected." From the perspective of these women, sex might have been defined as work. *SNC*, North Carolina, pt. 2, 11:78.

23. Brown, *Narrative of William W. Brown*, 46, 47, 48. While some concubines managed to achieve freedom, many were sold. Baptist, "'Cuffy,' 'Fancy Maids,' and 'One-Eyed Men,'" 1645; White, *Ar'n't I a Woman?*, 35–38; West, *Chains of Love*, 135.

24. Rawick, *AS*, supp., ser. 2, Texas, pt. 3, 4:1239, 1240, 1241, pt. 2, 3:719, 722.

25. Brown, *Slave Life in Georgia*, 132–133; *SNC*, Arkansas, pt. 3, 2:218; Florida, 3:89–90.

26. Angela Davis argues that rape of slave women was a function of oppression and mastery moreso than sexual gratification. Davis, *Women, Race & Class*, 23–24. Henry Brown believed sexual control motivated the maintenance of slavery. Brown, *Narrative of Henry Box Brown*, 23. Humans use rape as weapon of war. When exerting their dominance, humans do not typically force sex on other categories of property. Bestiality exists, but we view bestiality quite differently than rape. One is defined as a "crime against nature," whereas the other is recognized as having a human perpetrator and a human victim. "The trader's rapes are the most extreme example of the brutal recognition of their slaves' humanity," Walter Johnson writes. Johnson, *Soul by Soul*, 63.

27. Jacobs, *Incidents*, 79, 80, 119; Rawick, *AS*, supp., ser. 2, Texas, pt. 3, 4:1344, pt. 7, 8:3139; Perdue et al., *Weevils*, 92–93; Jennings, "Us Colored Women Had to Go though a Plenty," 61–63.

28. Mattison, *Louisa Picquet*, 15, 18, 10–13, 16–17.

29. Mattison, 19, 19–20, 23. According to the American Academy of Experts in Traumatic Stress, domestic abuse by intimate partners often includes "excessive possessiveness," and monitoring. De Benedictis et al., "Domestic Violence and Abuse: Types, Signs, Symptoms, Causes, and Effects."

30. Mattison, *Louisa Picquet*, 23, 24, 29, 30, 34–37, 46, 53. Williams purchased Picquet at age fourteen, meaning she was roughly twenty when he died. He may have cared about her and his children, but he was also possessive and he knew the appeal of a young mixed-race woman. Sending her north meant that he did not have to worry about another New Orleans slaveholder acquiring her. Picquet spent six years with Williams, and Green argues that they had a relationship based on "real intimacy," in which she "offered her body but also her companionship and labor until he died." This ignores the regular threats of violence. Green also suggests that Picquet could have escaped while Williams was on his deathbed. Because she could pass for white, "she presumably could have fled to freedom with her two equally 'white' children without waiting for his death. But she chose not to, perhaps out of fear of the unknown." This underestimates the dangers involved in escaping, especially as a woman with two small children. Williams did not free her until after his death, meaning that to flee and be caught would be to risk separation from her children, sale into a worse situation, and losing a potential avenue to freedom or property. Picquet instead bided her time, which was the strategic choice to make. Green, *Remember Me*, 66, 75, 66. Though prewar, Picquet is a good example of the noneconomic factors that motivated black women to migrate north following the Civil War. According to Darlene Clark Hine, black women fled the South out of "a desire to retain or claim some control and ownership of their own sexual beings and the children they bore." Hine, "Rape and the Inner Lives of Black Women in the Middle West," 914.

31. In her study of marriage in South Carolina, Emily West finds a low rate of manumission as a result of sex with white men: "Sexual contact with whites was much more likely to involve abuse than mutual affection. Love and respect was found in relationships slaves had with their spouses." West, *Chains of Love*, 135.

32. Galloway alluded to her mother's lack of consent. Rawick, *AS*, supp., ser. 1, Mississippi, pt. 3, 8:803; Farnham, "Sapphire?," 83.

33. Jones, *Fathers of Conscience*, 6, 7; *Walker v. Walker*, 25 Ga. 420, June 1858, 62–63; *Abercrombie's Executor v. Abercrombie's Heirs*, 27 Ala. 489, June 1855, 206; *Hooper v. Hooper*, 32 Ala. 669, June 1858, Catterall, *Judicial Cases*, 3:226–227.

34. Cade, "Out of the Mouths of Ex-Slaves," 308. One Fisk interviewee indicated that fathers gave their sons cooks, intended as concubines, as marriage gifts and that these women and their children lived in the big house with the legitimate wife and children and suffered abuse from the mistresses. "If they had nice long hair she would cut it off and wouldn't let them wear it long like the white children," she stated. *Unwritten History of Slavery*, 18:1.

35. Jacobs used pseudonyms, referring to Dr. James Norcom as Dr. Flint and Samuel Sawyer and Mr. Sands. Jacobs, *Incidents*, 82, 83, 84–85, 85; Yellin, *Harriet Jacobs*, 26–27. "At least some female slaves who gave birth either out of wedlock, to a mixed-race child, or at a young age believed that the delivery impugned the good character they possessed and strove to maintain," Jeff Forret writes. Forret, *Slave against Slave*, 380.

36. Jacobs technically belonged to Norcom's daughter, but he exerted control over the minor's property.

37. Jacobs referred to her children, Joseph and Louisa, by the pseudonyms Benny and Ellen. Jacobs, *Incidents*, 163, 189, 207, 209, 160; Yellin, *Harriet Jacobs*, 59.

38. Jacobs, *Incidents*, 282, 283.

39. *Unwritten History of Slavery*, 18:2; SNC, Missouri, 10:52; Rawick, *AS*, supp., ser. 2, Arkansas, 1:125. Albert Morgan discussed concubinage in Yazoo County, Mississippi, where a concubine's status reflected that of her lover. When their "supremacy" in the black community eroded after emancipation, with several expelled from churches for adultery, these women inquired about legal marriage and tried to use Reconstruction politics to their advantage. While it is clear that they valued and fought to maintain their status, and that after freedom they re-

mained at a distinct power disadvantage compared to their white sexual partners, how they felt about their relationships is unknown. Morgan hints that at least one woman he knew felt trapped, and that a concubine would, on occasion, commit suicide or kill her daughter to save the young woman from such a life, but these were rare responses. Morgan, *Yazoo*, 358, 361, 362, 432–435.

40. "Although not all white male–black female relationships were exploitative, most began that way, and most continued that way," Deborah Gray White writes. White, *Ar'n't I a Woman?*, 34; Jennings, "Us Colored Women Had to Go though a Plenty," 60; West, *Chains of Love*, 129; Baptist, "'Cuffy,' 'Fancy Maids,' and 'One-Eyed Men,'" 1644. Thomas Foster argues that the power differential makes it difficult to define relationships between white women and black men as fully consensual and that such relationships "ranged from affectionate to violent." Martha Hodes discusses the "coercion" of black men. Foster, "Sexual Abuse of Black Men," 459, 460; Hodes, *White Women, Black Men*, 133–139.

41. "By dissemblance I mean the behavior and attitudes of Black women that created the appearance of openness and disclosure but actually shielded the truth of their inner lives and selves from their oppressors." Hine, "Rape and the Inner Lives of Black Women in the Middle West," 912, 916; White, *Ar'n't I a Woman?*, 237–238.

42. SNC, North Carolina, pt. 1, 11:220; *Unwritten History of Slavery*, 18:208; Blassingame, *Slave Testimony*, 376.

43. The mistress had been raised in Cincinnati. *Bedford v. Williams*, 5 Coldwell 202, December 1867, Catterall, *Judicial Cases*, 2:585–586; Potter, *Hairdresser's Experience in High Life*, 93, 104, 113.

44. Rawick, *AS*, supp., ser. 2, Texas, pt. 3, 4:1360, supp., ser. 1, Indiana and Ohio, 5:286, supp., ser. 2, Washington, 1:397, 398.

45. Ary's commentary, as recounted by Lucy Chase, suggests that she had a good relationship with her white siblings, her white partner doted on their baby, and his sisters treated her well. Swint, ed., *Dear Ones at Home*, 61, 60, 55, 56, 73. The mixed-race daughters of white men were at high risk of being selected as concubines. A white man, Trudeau had a daughter, Robinette, with one of his slaves. Gardette, Trudeau's executor, bought Robinette from her father and had "three or four children by her." Robinette's mother secured freedom and purchased and emancipated her daughter, a move the court dismissed because Robinette was under the age of thirty as required by Louisiana law in any case of manumission. Gardette claimed Robinette as a slave and "confined" her. Robinette sued for and failed to obtain her freedom. *Trudeau's Executor v. Robinette*, 4 Mart. La. 577, January 1817; *Badillo et al. v. Francisco Tio*, 6 La. An. 129, February 1851, in Catterall, ed., *Judicial Cases*, 3:455, 611–613.

46. SNC, North Carolina, pt. 1, 11:234–235.

47. Murray, *Proud Shoes*, 42, 43, 46, 47, 39–52. None of the three white Smith children ever married, and Murray presents the complicated history of Harriet as the root of the family's downfall.

48. Julius was permanently crippled after getting caught in a snowstorm. Murray, *Proud Shoes*, 48, 49.

49. Sidney Smith promised to leave Cornelia his estate, but his unexpected death when she was sixteen left that promise unfulfilled. Murray, *Proud Shoes*, 49, 43, 51, 50. Mary Church Terrell's father, Robert Church, credited his father and master with teaching him to stand up for himself. Terrell had positive memories of her white grandfather and she avoided any direct allusion to the relationship that led to her father's birth. "I simply adored him," Terrell said of Captain Church. Her father "was so fair that no one would have supposed that he had a drop of African blood in his veins. As a matter of fact, he had very little," and yet she never mentioned his mother or how he came to be born. The fact that Captain Church raised Robert implies that the mother died early. Despite her hatred of slavery, Terrell credited some slaveholders with benevolence and believed "Captain Church was one of them, and this daughter of a slave father is glad thus publicly to express her gratitude to him." When exploring her mother's background, Terrell included a letter from a white man who had known her maternal grandmother,

which contained several hints of concubinage. When Terrell's great-grandmother, "a Malay princess," came to the United States on a slave ship, she was separated from the others and put in the cabin. In Virginia, she was sold "at what was then considered a fancy price." She became a "seamstress" to the mistresses and soon had a daughter. The letter failed to discuss or identify the father. The daughter, Emmeline, after being separated from her mother, ended up serving as a seamstress for another family and "was never treated as a slave and never had to do menial work." She "always passed as creole." In her condemnation of slavery, Terrell focused on her grandmother and great-grandmother's separation. She never openly discussed the probable sexual exploitation of one or both of them. Terrell had known white ancestry on one side of her family and her memoir suggests white ancestry on the other side, but she sidestepped the topic of illicit sex within slavery. Terrell, *Colored Woman in a White World*, 2, 5, 4.

50. Murray, *Proud Shoes*, 46, 43. Rachel Cruze, the child of the master's son and an enslaved cook, grew up in Tennessee. Until the age of twelve, Cruze thought her white grandmother was her mother. When another white son married a woman known to abuse slaves, Cruze was sent to live with her biological mother. Cruze had lived in the big house "as a member of the family all those years," sleeping in her grandparents' room. "Miss Nancy took especially good care of me," she recalled, "and one time when my stepfather gave me a lick I ran the two miles to tell Miss Nancy about it. I had never been whipped." Cruze had little to say about her white father, noting that he drank himself to death. She disliked living with her stepfather after emancipation because he put her to work, but she seems to have developed sense of identity based on both sides of her family. Rawick, *AS*, supp., ser. 1, Indiana and Ohio, 5:293, 294, 291, 318. Adaline Montgomery, who grew up in Alabama, "smiled in a cryptic manner" when asked about her father, a white man on a neighboring plantation who "allus give me close an' shoes." Montgomery lived with her white relatives after freedom and remembered her grandmother putting ribbons in her hair and taking her to church. Rawick, *AS*, supp., ser. 1, Mississippi, pt. 4, 9:1513, 1514, 1516.

51. Stevenson, "Distress and Discord," 112, 113.

52. Painter, *Soul Murder and Slavery*, 20. On structural violence, see Paul Farmer's exploration of how the history and political economy of the postcolonial world affect the emergence and spread of AIDS and tuberculosis in modern Haiti. Disease prevalence and patterns cannot be separated from the "large-scale social and economic structures in which affliction is embedded." Farmer, "An Anthropology of Structural Violence," 305, 306–325. Louisa, the daughter of James Hammond's concubine, Sally, who then herself became his prey at the age of twelve, remained on Hammond's property after emancipation. Her reasoning and feelings about him are unknown, but her extreme youth is diagnostic of the type of structural violence that may have left her socially isolated. Alice Marshall discussed a concubine on a neighboring Virginia plantation who lived with the planter "jes' same's dey's married." He provided for and treated her and their seven children well, but Marshall noted that he did not allow her to interact with black men. Perdue et al., *Weevils*, 202; McLaurin, *Celia*, 25.

53. Prior to his death, Dickson built a separate house on the plantation for Julia and Amanda and her children, ensured their legal ownership of that property, and had a brief, unsuccessful marriage to a much younger white woman (224, 225). Bradley and Leslie, "White Pain Pollen," 214, 215, 222, 217, 227, 230, 213–234. Julia is a good example of enslaved women's sense of sexual honor and shame in the wake of sexual assault. Forret, *Slave against Slave*, 380.

54. See Sharony Green's discussion of Samuel Townsend's will, which identified "first-class" and "second-class" slaves to be freed. The first-class slaves included his children, whereas their mothers were categorized as second-class slaves. Green, *Remember Me*, 91.

55. Those who succeeded in using the legal system to their own advantage often became part of the free black elite. An inheritance of freedom and/or property from a white father could influence feelings about one's paternity. Jones, *Fathers of Conscience*, 9, 153–154.

56. There is no record of what became of her two children by Newsom, though they likely remained enslaved to Newsom's white children. McLaurin, *Celia*, 18–20, 22, 25, 30, 31, 35, 38, 39, 46, 102, 103, 114, 115.

57. According to the American Academy of Experts in Traumatic Stress, domestic abuse includes controlling the victim through confinement and "isolation from friends and family." It can also involve "excessive possessiveness" and monitoring. Individuals abused by an intimate partner often develop symptoms that include disrupted sleep, anxiety, depression, compromised self-esteem as well as physical and mental health, difficulty trusting others, a sense of resentment or abandonment, and "poor relationships with their children and other loved ones." Children who grow up in a household where they witness or experience domestic violence are prone to low self-esteem, depression, drug use, and violence, and are more likely to exhibit criminal behavior, especially sexual assault. They are also more susceptible to suicide and to themselves becoming abusers. De Benedictis et al., "Domestic Violence and Abuse: Types, Signs, Symptoms, Causes, and Effects."

58. Green never saw his family again and their sale led to his ultimately successful attempts to escape. Green, *Narrative of the Life of J.D. Green*, 16, 22, 18, 19.

59. Jacobs, *Incidents*, 59, 23–24.

60. "Just as some male slaves stood as guardians of enslaved female honor, others attempted to violate it," Forret notes. While they had little defense against white men, as part of their assertion of their sense of honor, enslaved women "claimed the right to deny consent to predatory bondmen." Forret, *Slave against Slave*, 344, 333, 345–346, 348, 350–352; Doddington, *Contesting Slave Masculinity*, 83; West, *Chains of Love*, 68; Berry, *Swing the Sickle*, 80.

61. Some enslaved men used violence to compensate for their own subjugation within slavery. Forret, *Slave against Slave*, 286, 259–271, 259–271. "Intimate violence," David Doddington adds, "could be rationalized within a patriarchal framework that expected and normalized male dominance." Doddington, *Contesting Slave Masculinity*, 133, 131, 149, 151, 152; Stevenson, "Distress and Discord," 116, 121–122, 117. Christopher Morris, in his essay on domestic violence in the quarters, argues that enslaved men's lack of "patriarchal control . . . refutes the simple conclusion of some scholars that patriarchal families are the only settings for domestic violence." Morris, "Within the Slave Cabin: Violence in Mississippi Slave Families," 273.

62. Perdue et al., *Weevils*, 207.

63. Painter, *Soul Murder and Slavery*, 20.

64. Shackelford noted that the concubine he purchased had seven children and their father treated them well, "as if dey was by a white 'oman." Hayden's father, whose master had moved away from Kentucky and later returned, reunited with his former wife, the couple "finished their days together," and Hayden's mother "almost recovered her mind in her last days." Perdue et al., *Weevils*, 250; Blassingame, *Slave Testimony*, 695, 696.

65. Many white women and even men agreed, but white attitudes are not the focus of this chapter. Painter, "The Journal of Ella Gertrude Clanton Thomas," 34–66.

66. The illegitimate family remained, and while the mistress had no more children, the concubine's brood continued to grow. Brown, *Narrative of Henry Box Brown*, 28; Watson, *Narrative of Henry Watson*, 13; Rawick, *AS*, supp., ser. 2, Texas, pt. 7, 8:3294; Albert, *House of Bondage*, 30; Jacobs, *Incidents*, 51; Northup, *Twelve Years a Slave*, 189. Richard Macks told of another white wife who left her husband after he openly took a black concubine. When the child of the concubine drowned, his wife "left him; afterward she said it was an affliction put on her husband for his sins." *SNC*, Maryland, 8:54. See Clinton, *Plantation Mistress*, 110–122, for a discussion of "fallen" women.

67. *Richmond v. Richmond*, 10 Yerger 343, December 1837, 2:505; *Tewksbury v. Tewksbury*, 4 How. Miss. 109, December 1839, 3:287; *Farr v. Farr*, 34 Miss. 597, October 1857, 3:352; *Mosser v. Mosser*, 29 Ala. 313, June 1856, 3:212–213; *Mehle v. Lapeyrollerie*, 16 La. An. 4, January 1861, 3:687; *Edmonds v. her Husband*, 4 La. An. 489, September 1849, in Catterall, *Judicial Cases*, 3:600.

68. *Thomas v. Thomas*, 2 Coldwell 123, September 1865, 2:579–580; *Odom v. Odom*, 36 Ga. 286, June 1867, in Catterall, *Judicial Cases*, 3:95.

69. Jacobs noted that her master, Dr. Norcom, delayed sending her to the plantation, "owing to the fact that his son was there. He was jealous of his son; and jealousy of the overseer had

kept him from punishing me by sending me into the fields to work" (64–65). Stevens, *Anthony Burns*, 199; Jacobs, *Incidents*, 56–57, 81.

70. Sommerville argues that enslaved and free black men were exonerated about half of the time. They often had the support of masters who did not want to lose valuable property. Class concerns contributed to community support for black men, and poor white women's behavior was scrutinized. This changed in the early twentieth century as Southern elites granted poor white women the status of ladyhood in order to secure white supremacy. Sommerville, *Rape and Race in the Nineteenth-Century South*, 17. During Reconstruction, black politicians tried to target white men and punish them for sex with black women, focusing on interracial sex rather than interracial marriage. Pascoe, *What Comes Naturally*, 32.

71. "Incidents of sexual mutilation of black men rose" during Reconstruction. Sommerville, "Rape, Race and Castration," 83.

Chapter Seven

1. Douglass, *My Bondage*, 426; Green, *Narrative of the Events*, 22; James, *Life of Rev. Thomas James*, 23.

2. Anderson asked for nearly $12,000 in restitution and concluded, "P.S.—Say howdy to George Carter, and thank him for taking the pistol from you when you were shooting at me." Jourdan Anderson, Dayton, Ohio, "To My Old Master," Colonel P. H. Anderson, Big Spring, Tennessee, Aug. 7, 1865, in *New York Daily Tribune*, Aug. 22, 1865.

3. Chase had been hired out and wrote to his employer rather than his mistress. Anthony Chase to Jeremiah Hoffman, Aug. 8, 1827, in Starobin, *Blacks in Bondage*, 121; Rawick, *AS*, supp., ser. 1, Indiana and Ohio, 5:355.

4. Drew, *North-Side View of Slavery*, 86; Bibb, *Narrative of the Life and Adventures of Henry Bibb*, 17; Blassingame, *Slave Testimony*, 408. Fugitives argued that it was a masculine responsibility to "protect otherwise helpless female dependents." Doddington, *Contesting Slave Masculinity*, 28.

5. Hopper, *Narrative of the Life of Thomas Cooper*, 8, 9, 11–29; Parker, "The Freedman's Story," 288, 291–292; Ward, *Autobiography of a Fugitive Negro*, 3–4, 9, 26.

6. Craft, *Running a Thousand Miles*, 93. Those with the funds or contacts purchased their freedom and partial peace of mind. Though Harriet Jacobs "objected to having my freedom bought," the transaction "felt as if a heavy load had been lifted from my weary shoulders," and she thought of her father. "I hoped his spirit was rejoicing over me now." Jacobs, *Incidents*, 301; Fleischner, *Mastering Slavery*, 112–113; Douglass, *Life and Times*, 314, 315, 316.

7. Sterling, *Speak Out in Thunder Tones*, 85–102; Litwack, *North of Slavery*; Katzman, *Before the Ghetto*. Nancy Bertaux traces the confluence of structural economic change, immigration, racism, and discrimination in employment and educational opportunities that led to declining occupational status for free blacks in Cincinnati. Bertaux, "Structural Economic Change and Occupational Decline among Black Workers in Nineteenth-Century Cincinnati," 127–155; Prentiss, *Blind African Slave*, 172–186.

8. Drew, *North-Side View of Slavery*, 244, 248. The Ohio Black Laws of 1804 and 1807 were designed to discourage black migration to the state. The 1804 law required all blacks to register with the county and prove their freedom. The requirement to post a $500 bond was part of the 1807 law designed to add financial impediments. Love, "Registration of Free Blacks in Ohio," 38–47. Free blacks also faced increasing violence in the nineteenth century. Race riots in Cincinnati in 1829, 1836, and 1841 hurt the black community economically, with a decline in property ownership and many moving to Canada. Cheek and Cheek, "John Mercer Langston and the Cincinnati Riot of 1841," 46, 49; Sterling, *Speak Out in Thunder Tones*, 103–107.

9. One of Williamson's neighbors colluded with the kidnappers. Once he found them, Williamson needed the testimony of another white neighbor to prove his children's free status and he gave up his farm as payment. Drew, *North-Side View of Slavery*, 92; *The Liberator*, Dec. 10, 1841, in Sterling, ed., *Speak Out in Thunder Tones*, 145–147, 147–155, 257–262; Schermerhorn, *Money over Mastery, Family over Freedom*, 41, 42.

10. Joan Cashin argues that these impediments led to greater flexibility in gender roles among free blacks. "Parallel roles emerged for the sexes, revolving around family duty, political activism, and physical combat against slave catchers." Cashin, "Black Families in the Old Northwest," 463, 464, 476.

11. McCurry complicates the "standard account" of emancipation in which "slave men took the martial road to emancipation, and slave women, apparently, the marital one, which is to say that slave women got freedom at second hand, by way of marriage and in relation to their husband's rights" (122). She argues that the allegiance of enslaved women "simply never assumed the strategic significance of men's loyalty," which led to poor treatment by the government and that then limited women's opportunities in freedom. Union policy reflected "deep-seated assumptions about adult women's dependency and normative position as wives" (143). McCurry, "War, Gender, and Emancipation in the Civil War South," 142, 128, 123, 129–131, 135–136. Amy Dru Stanley examines the concurrent debate on the Thirteenth Amendment and the enlistment measure that awarded freedom to the wives and children of freedmen who served in the Union military, arguing that "the abolition of slavery fused with freedom endowed by marriage, thereby tethering a new birth of human rights to enduring domestic bonds." As a wife, a freedwoman "fell within her husband's dominion." Stanley, "Instead of Waiting for the Thirteenth Amendment," 733, 763, 735.

12. Berlin et al., eds., *Free at Last*, 99; Gutman, *Black Family*, 267–269. Robert Hickman described his father as a natural leader who was whipped for visiting his abroad family more often than allowed. During the war, he and several other men constructed a flat boat and then fled with their families to Union lines. George Johnson's father was trusted to regularly haul grit from Missouri to a mill across Iowa state lines. During the war, he and another slave concealed their families under a load and escaped. Rawick, *AS*, supp., ser. 1, Minnesota, 2: 109, 116. Martha Robinson, age six, escaped with her uncle, who carried her to the Union lines and to her parents, where it appears her father had enlisted. Perdue et al., *Weevils*, 239–240.

13. Rather than run to Union lines, Brown's father procured a cabin and employment on another farm. *SNC*, North Carolina, pt. 1, 11:79–80, 81; Rawick, *AS*, supp., ser. 1, Mississippi, pt. 1, 6:237. Nora Armstrong, frightened by reflections on the water as her family escaped a farm in Georgia, "lit into screamin'" and her parents, both carrying younger children, "tol' me to shut up or the Boss-man sho' come and git me." Rawick, *AS*, supp., ser. 2, Texas, pt. 1, 2:76.

14. Statement of Archy Vaughn, Berlin et al., eds., *Free at Last*, 113.

15. Rawick, *AS*, supp., ser. 2, Texas, pt. 7, 8:3316, 3313, pt. 3, 4:1092.

16. Serving as soldiers marked a "watershed for black manhood." Cullen, "I's a Man Now," 77.

17. Rawick, *AS*, supp., ser. 1, Minnesota, 2:135; *SNC*, Arkansas, pt. 6, 2:297; Johnson, *Slavery Days in Old Kentucky*, 37, 38; Bruner, *Slave's Adventures toward Freedom*, 43; Robinson, *From Log Cabin to the Pulpit*, 117. Eliza Million knit socks for her soldier father and received word of "how proud of them he was." Million's father enlisted in Kentucky, and the fact that the mistress facilitated this interaction indicates that he did so with a Unionist master's approval. Rawick, *AS*, supp., ser. 1, Indiana and Ohio, 5:131.

18. Hall and Elder, *Samuel Hall*, 23, 24, 25; Suggs, *Shadow and Sunshine*, 21, 22; *SNC*, Indiana, 5:146.

19. Dec. 27, 1864, 496; Jan. 26, 1865, in Berlin et al., eds., *Free at Last*, 505–506.

20. Military emancipation initially omitted women owned by slaveholders loyal to the Union, but on March 4, 1865, the Union emancipated the wives and children of Union soldiers regardless of the owners' allegiance and in areas not covered by the 1863 Emancipation Proclamation. In Kentucky, therefore, men gained liberty through military service and women through marriage. McCurry, "War, Gender, and Emancipation in the Civil War South," 132, 137, 138; Stanley, "Instead of Waiting for the Thirteenth Amendment," 733. See Herbert Gutman for a discussion of men from Kentucky who fought for the Union under coercion and voluntarily. Gutman, *Black Family*, 371–387. Dunaway, *African-American Family*, 190–192, 196–203, 199–211.

21. Edwin Stanton to Abraham Lincoln, March 3, 1865, in *The War of the Rebellion*, 1219. Escaped former slave John Boston enlisted in the Union army and wrote to his wife from New

York, asking her to kiss their son and expressing his hope for their eventual reunion. John Boston to "My Dear Wife," Jan. 12, 1862, in Berlin et al., eds., *Free at Last*, 30.

22. Glover wished her husband had stayed and informed him he should not ask any other married men to join the army. Ann to "My Dear Husband," Paris, Mo., Jan. 19, 1864, Martha Glover to My Dear Husband, Mexico, Mo., Dec. 30, 1863, 464, George Washington, Dec. 4, 1864, 495, William Deming, Benton Barracks, Mo., Feb. 1, 1864, 360, Patsey Leach affidavit, Camp Nelson, Ky., March 25, 1865, in Berlin et al., eds., *Free at Last*, 400. Stanley notes that letters from home and poor conditions "drew soldiers back to plantations." Stanley, "Instead of Waiting for the Thirteenth Amendment," 755.

23. S. R. Curtis, March 13, 1864, Berlin et al., eds., *Free at Last*, 113–115, 122; Eliot, *Story of Archer Alexander*, 79, 82. Louisa Alexander wrote to her husband to warn him that their bitter master was guarding them. She believed only military intervention would free the family. Louisa Alexander to Archer Alexander, Nov. 16, 1863, in Blassingame, *Slave Testimony*, 119.

24. Thomas objected to the fact that enslaved men could visit their wives "scarcely once a week." George Thomas, Battery L, 12th USCHA, Fort Smith, Bowling Green, Ky., July 18, 1865, 189–190, 6th USCI, Yorktown, Va., Feb. 8, 1864, in Redkey, ed., *Grand Army of Black Men*, 237.

25. Petition, Roanoke Island, N.C., March 9, 1865, 222, John Burnside, Camp Nelson, Ky., Dec. 1864, 395, Affidavit of Joseph Miller, Camp Nelson, Ky., 493–495, Richard Etheredge letter, in Berlin et al., eds., *Free at Last*, 228, 229, see also 529, 534–536, 538–539. In January of 1865, Miller, his wife, and three more children fell ill and died. Sears, *Camp Nelson Kentucky*, 220–221.

26. "If manhood was often conflated with the power to kill and destroy," Cullen writes, "at least some black men also saw it as a source of power to preserve and create." Cullen, "I's a Man Now," 90, 91, 82–85, 87, 89; Spotswood Rice, Benton Barracks Hospital, St. Louis, Mo., Sept. 3, 1864, in Berlin et al., eds., *Free at Last*, 481–482. The FWP narrative of Rice's daughter, Mary Bell, indicates that her father had a strong personality and the war gave him an opportunity to act on his beliefs. Her father once ran away after an undeserved whipping. "He scared my mother most to death because he had run away, and she done all in her power to persuade him to go back. He said he would die first," and he hid for three days before being caught. Rice asked to be sold, but his master refused because Rice was essential to the plantation. Rice told his master he would escape if whipped again. Bell stated that she was born in Missouri on May 1, 1852. She called her father Spot, "but that was his nickname in slavery. His full name was Spottwood Rice." Her spelling of the name differs from his. *SNC*, Missouri, 10:27, 30, 25, 29.

27. Rice's sons had escaped, were with their father in St. Louis, and sent their love. Spotswood Rice, Benton Barracks Hospital, St. Louis, Mo., Sept. 3, 1864, in Berlin et al., eds., *Free at Last*, 480–481.

28. Diggs owned all of Rice's children, and the letter he wrote possibly focused on Mary because she was hired out. *SNC*, Missouri, 10:25, 29, 30, 26, 27, 25, 25–31.

29. Hanks also testified that another man enlisted "for the avowed purpose of freeing the entire family." *SNC*, Missouri, 10:31; Testimony of the Superintendent of Negro Labor in the Department of the Gulf before the American Freedmen's Inquiry Commission, Deposition of Col. Geo. H. Hanks, Feb. 6, 1864, in Berlin, *The Wartime Genesis of Free Labor*, 519.

30. *SNC*, Arkansas, pt. 5, 2:359; Rawick, *AS*, supp., ser. 1, Oklahoma, 12:285; *SNC*, Arkansas, pt. 1, 2:153, South Carolina, pt. 2, 14:84, Indiana, 5:123; Simmons, *Men of Mark*, 439; Rawick, *AS*, supp., ser. 2, Texas, pt. 8, 9:3482, supp., ser. 1, Mississippi, pt. 3, 8:1250.

31. *SNC*, Arkansas, pt. 5, 2:252; Rawick, *AS*, supp., ser. 2, Texas, pt. 6, 7:2809, pt. 8, 9:3813, pt. 9, 10:4183–4184, supp., ser. 1, Mississippi, pt. 1, 6:153, pt. 3, 8:1284. William Hogue lost the man for whom he was named when his father died during his impressment into the Confederate army. Horace Overstreet's father went to war with his young master and though he returned alive, he "never got ober it." Rawick, *AS*, supp., ser. 1, Indiana and Ohio, 5:378, supp., ser. 2, Texas, pt. 7, 8:2996.

32. *SNC*, Arkansas, pt. 5, 2:308, South Carolina, pt. 4, 14:255, Arkansas, pt. 4, 2:44, pt. 2, 2:319, pt. 1, 2:160, Missouri, 10:318, 369, North Carolina, pt. 1, 11:391, South Carolina, pt. 1, 14:224, Alabama, 1:322; Rawick, *AS*, supp., ser. 2, Texas, pt. 5, 6:1995.

33. SNC, North Carolina, pt. 1, 11:221, Oklahoma, 13:108; Delaney, *From the Darkness*, 60, 61; SNC, Missouri, 10:264; *The Anglo-African*, Aug. 19, 1865; Wickham, *Lost Family Found*. Cora Horton visited her formerly enslaved maternal grandfather long after the war. "I had heard my mother speak of him being alive and he would write to her sometimes," she recalled. "I said if I ever got to be grown and my grandfather stayed alive, I was going to Georgia to see him. So the first opportunity I got I went." SNC, Arkansas, pt. 3, 2:321. Heather Williams details the postwar search for lost family, including former slaves appealing to the Freedmen's Bureau for assistance and transportation. Her most moving evidence consists of the numerous ads placed in newspapers in an attempt to locate kin, documents that speak to "hope and memory." Williams includes examples of fathers searching for their children and children searching for their fathers. Williams, *Help Me to Find My People*, 168, 159, 160, 166, 140–168, 191.

34. "I broke down and began to cry," he related. "Mother nor father did not know me, but mother suspicioned I was her child. Father had a few days previously remarked that he did not want to die without seeing his son once more. I could not find language to express my feelings." SNC, North Carolina, pt. 1, 11:339. An old man reunited with his escaped sons in the North, "took each one in his arms . . . exclaiming whilst hugging them closer and closer . . . in tears of joy and wonder." Still, *Underground Railroad*, 118; Northup, *Twelve Years a Slave*, 319, 320. When William Robinson found his mother and siblings, "the only thing which cast a shadow over the pleasure of our meeting was when mother asked, 'if we had heard anything from father?' The house of joy was turned into lamentation." Robinson, *From Log Cabin to the Pulpit*, 119–120; Williams, *Help Me to Find My People*, 172, 178–183.

35. SNC, Arkansas, pt. 1, 2:292; Missouri, 10:140. Frank Hughes saw his father only once. He arrived, found his wife with another man, and left permanently. Rawick, *AS*, supp., ser. 1, Mississippi, pt. 3, 8:1058. When Freedmen's Bureau officials helped slaves navigate postwar family arrangements, the existence and number of children could influence choices about which spouse to select for a legal marriage. Gutman, *Slave Family*, 420–425. Bureau officials expected African American men to "assume responsibility as protectors and providers for their dependents," and upheld the interests of freedwomen in custody battles, complaints of abuse, and requests for divorce when freedmen failed to meet Bureau standards as "responsible patriarchs," and if and when women presented themselves as "worthy" dependents rather than as "autonomous individuals." If a freedman met their standards, agents placed paternal authority above the wishes of mothers. Farmer-Kaiser, *Freedwomen and the Freedmen's Bureau*, 52, 139, 44, 98, 124, 128, 130–134, 138, 151, 154, 156; Jones, *Intimate Reconstructions*, 57.

36. Swint, ed., *Dear Ones at Home*, 242–243.

37. Rawick, *AS*, supp., ser. 2, Texas, pt. 1, 2:245; SNC, Texas, pt. 2, 16:125.

38. Rawick, *AS*, supp., ser. 2, Texas, pt. 1, 2:469, pt. 1, 2:448; SNC, South Carolina, pt. 2, 14:191, pt. 1, 14:301; Rawick, *AS*, supp., ser. 2, Texas, pt. 2, 3:899, pt. 9, 10:3974, supp., ser. 1, Mississippi, pt. 4, 9:1418. Several informants remembered being abandoned by their mothers. SNC, Arkansas, pt. 2, 2:331, pt. 1, 2:155; Rawick, *AS*, supp., ser. 1, Georgia, 3:245. Perhaps unable to support them, Alonzo Marshall's mother gave away all but two of her children. Emaline Watts and her siblings were abandoned by both of their parents. Rawick, *AS*, supp., ser. 1, Mississippi, pt. 4, 9:1436–1437, pt. 5, 10:2212.

39. "Papa was a little chunky man," Hadley stated of her childhood in Mississippi. "He'd steal flour and hogs. He could tote a hog on his back." SNC, Arkansas, pt. 3, 2:128; Rawick, *AS*, supp., ser. 1, Mississippi, pt. 4, 9:1454; Jones, *Intimate Reconstructions*, 55.

40. SNC, Arkansas, pt. 6, 2:234, Oklahoma, 13:244, Georgia, pt. 4, 4:166, South Carolina, pt. 3, 14:178, Texas, pt. 3, 16:131. Katherine Franke argues that the postwar requirement to form monogamous marriages pushed aside previous, more "fluid" slave family arrangements. Franke, *Wedlocked*, 15, 16, 17.

41. SNC, Arkansas, pt. 6, 2:122, pt. 3, 2:308, Oklahoma, 13:4, 5, North Carolina, pt. 1, 11:358.

42. After the war, Mattie Jackson and her half-brother went to live with her brother's biological father in Massachusetts. Her stepfather, whom she referred to as her father, was married to a physician who had lost her only son. They had a nice house and were better equipped to care

for children and send them to school than Jackson's recently emancipated mother. Jackson wrote her life story as a means of raising money to repay their generosity. Jackson, *Story of Mattie J. Jackson*, 27, 28, 29. Jane Montgomery lived with her father until her mother was settled. After freedom her mother "give me to my father 'cause she was married to another man. Her and my stepfather moved to Gilmore, Texas. They sent for me round 'bout Christmas." *SNC*, Oklahoma, 13:228.

43. Rawick, *AS*, supp., ser. 2, Texas, pt. 7, 8:3264, supp., ser. 1, Georgia, 3:242. His father sent him money to "come home" to Alabama, but Ben Chambers chose to stay in Texas. Rawick, *AS*, supp., ser. 2, Texas, pt. 2, 3:671, 673.

44. *SNC*, South Carolina, pt. 2, 14:179–180. Bureau officials, echoing wartime military emancipation policy, enshrined marriage and pushed the idea of patriarchal households and domesticity. In her study of freedwomen's appeals to and interactions with the Freedmen's Bureau, Mary Farmer-Kaiser shows that because agents "promoted female dependency, black manhood and independence," gender could work for and against petitioners. Agents were more likely to dispense aid and less likely to apply vagrancy laws to the "neediest and most worthy" women, giving them some advantages over freedmen. Farmer-Kaiser, *Freedwomen and the Freedmen's Bureau*, 11, 168, 169. While freedpeople used available legal channels in the postwar period, they did not abandon older, extralegal practices. "Rather than putting all their hopes into one institutional basket, ex-slaves tended to combine and move between legal and extralegal arenas," Dylan Penningroth writes. Penningroth, *The Claims of Kinfolk*, 130, 117.

45. Austin spoke to an African American fieldworker. *SNC*, Georgia, pt. 1, 4:21, South Carolina, pt. 2, 14:79, Missouri, 10:263, Texas, pt. 3, 16:184. For Mary Ellen Johnson, emancipation meant "that I am going to be raised free and that I don't b'long to nobuddy but God and my mammy and pappy." Rawick, *AS*, supp., ser. 2, Texas, pt. 5, 6:2032.

46. Rawick, *AS*, supp., ser. 2, Arkansas, 1:102, supp., ser. 1, Mississippi, pt. 5, 10:1995, supp., ser. 1, Indiana and Ohio, 5:435, Texas, pt. 4, 16:224.

47. Rawick, *AS*, supp., ser. 1, Mississippi, pt. 3, 8:976; *SNC*, Oklahoma, 13:51, Arkansas, pt. 3, 2:347. William Williams grew up in North Carolina and first met his father after the war. "After the war my mother joined my father on his little farm and it was then I first learned he was my father," he recalled. *SNC*, Ohio, 12:114.

48. Rawick, *AS*, supp., ser. 1, Mississippi, pt. 4, 9:1382, 1380; *SNC*, North Carolina, pt. 2, 11:378; Rawick, *AS*, supp., ser. 1, Minnesota, 2:133, supp., ser. 1, Mississippi, pt. 2, 7:384.

49. *SNC*, Arkansas, pt. 7, 2:111; Rawick, *AS*, supp., ser. 2, Texas, pt. 5, 6:2406; Perdue et al., *Weevils*, 211; Rawick, *AS*, supp., ser. 1, Mississippi, pt. 1, 6:183.

50. Rawick, *AS*, supp., ser. 2, Texas, pt. 6, 7:2876, pt. 9, 10:4010.

51. *SNC*, Arkansas, pt. 6, 2:128, 129, Alabama, 1:102, Arkansas, pt. 2, 2:122, pt. 5, 2:103, pt. 6, 2:35, North Carolina, pt. 2, 11:369, Indiana, 5:212.

52. *SNC*, Georgia, pt. 3, 4:117, Missouri, 10:209, 210; Jones, *Intimate Reconstructions*, 62. After her father was sold and her mother died, Armaci Adams was raised by the white family from the age of three, leading to severe neglect. After the war, Adams's owners never told her of freedom and disrupted her reunion with kin. "Dis de way I fin' out," she said of emancipation. "My pappy druv a team all de way f'om No'th Carlina up heah a-lookin' fur me once. He foun' me an' was goin' ter take me back." The mistress scared Adams by telling her that her stepmother had "fits." "I wouldn' go cause I believed her. When paw come ter git me, dey wouldn' let 'im see me so he went on 'way. Atter dat dey beat me worsen ever." Separation from fathers could destroy children's bonds with these men, but did not necessarily destroy a father's sense of duty to his children. Perdue et al., *Weevils*, 3, 4.

53. *Unwritten History of Slavery*, 18:62, 63, 64, 67. Children reared apart from biological family at times rejected parents who appealed to the Freedmen's Bureau for assistance. Such statements could be coerced by white employers or could reflect genuine allegiances. Farmer-Kaiser, *Freedwomen and the Freedmen's Bureau*, 136–137.

54. "Freedparents' struggles to achieve family autonomy remained constrained by white Southerners decidedly committed to reasserting control over black labor and restoring slavery

in all but name," Farmer-Kaiser writes. For Freedmen's Bureau agents, indenture functioned as "an indirect method of securing employment for mothers, for all involved understood that mothers were less likely to leave while their children were held to service." Farmer-Kaiser, *Freedwomen and the Freedmen's Bureau*, 99, 56.

55. "Apprenticeship emerged as the dominant mode of placing apparently orphaned children under household governance," Jones writes (115). Apprenticeships entailed fixed labor terms to age eighteen for girls and age twenty-one for boys. According to Herbert Gutman, Maryland antebellum apprenticeship laws that applied to free blacks granted judges broad discretion, which then enabled the courts to bypass parental consent in postwar indentures. Jones, *Intimate Reconstructions*, 189, 64–75, 105–132; Gutman, *Black Family*, 402–411; Mitchell, "'Free Ourselves but Deprived of Our Children,'" 163–170; King, *Stolen Childhood*, 144–154; Farmer-Kaiser, *Freedwomen and the Freedmen's Bureau*, 97–138. Forced indentures and apprenticeships that limited the mobility of black adults were not a new phenomenon in the postwar period. In the late 1790s, James Mars's family went into hiding when their Connecticut master attempted to move them to Virginia. Mars's father eventually negotiated a deal that assured the freedom of himself and his wife and daughter. His two sons fell under Connecticut's gradual emancipation law of 1784 and were sold as term labor and indentured locally. The family came out of hiding, and Mars went to his new employer. "I will not attempt to describe my feelings when he told me he had taken rooms in the same neighborhood," Mars said of his father, "and should be near me. That made the rough way smooth." Unable to exert complete control over his sons or keep his family under one roof, this father endeavored to maintain contact and influence. He had no choice but to remain in place in order to preserve a modicum of family integrity. Mars, *Life of James Mars*, 22, 17, 20, 21.

56. Rawick, *AS*, supp., ser. 1, Mississippi, pt. 5, 10:2169; *Comas (a Person of Color) v. Reddish*, 35 Ga. 236, December 1866, Catterall, *Judicial Cases*, 3:93–94; Statement of Daniel Chase, Washington, DC, Aug. 24, 1865, in Berlin et al., eds., *Free at Last*, 375–376. When the mistress declared her intention to keep two girls, Susan Rhodes's sister "stole us away," and eventually "she found our mother and daddy and they sent for us." *SNC*, Missouri, 10:286. While the Freedmen's Bureau more readily recognized the claims of biological parents, other relatives and surrogates fared poorly. Farmer-Kaiser, *Freedwomen and the Freedmen's Bureau*, 126.

57. *SNC*, Georgia, pt. 2, 4:330, 331. Men emancipated in early to mid-life worried not just about their children, but their parents and other kin. After the war, Harry Smith brought his family north, including his father, who died at Smith's Michigan home at the age of ninety. After mustering out of the Union army, Elijah Marrs set about providing for his parents and collecting his grandmother. Her former owners "were unwilling to part with her, but I insisted on caring for her in old age and took her home with me." Smith, *Fifty Years of Slavery*, 9, 167, 174; Marrs, *Life and History of the Rev. Elijah P. Marrs*, 77, 76.

58. Stanley, *From Bondage to Contract*, 46, 47–50; Penningroth, *The Claims of Kinfolk*, 177–179, 180, 182.

59. The Freedmen's Bureau "encouraged black men to control (and contract) the labor of all family members, including that of wives and children." Farmer-Kaiser, *Freedwomen and the Freedmen's Bureau*, 169.

60. Blassingame, *Slave Testimony*, 737, 738; *SNC*, Arkansas, pt. 1, 2:101, pt. 6, 2:87; Perdue et al., *Weevils*, 311; Rawick, *AS*, supp., ser. 2, Texas, pt. 4, 5:1801.

61. Rawick, *AS*, supp., ser. 1, Mississippi, pt. 5, 10:2317, 2316. Jacqueline Jones notes that the Department of Justice Peonage files show how white landowners used black family members as hostages to demand the return of a male head of household, even if that man had been intimidated and run off by his employer. Jones, "The Political Economy of Sharecropping Families," 209. Catherine Stewart argues that looking at subtext of FWP interviews offers another way of assessing freedpeople's decisions to stay on the plantations where they had been enslaved, as many may have done so "out of fear and not out of love and fealty." Stewart, *Long Past Slavery*, 226.

62. "Officials most readily came to the defense of former slave women who appealed either to principles of free labor or to their middle-class domestic ideals as dependent wives—that is, as

married women who, together with husbands, could support and care for their children" (138). Agents were most likely to back severe apprenticeships in the case of impoverished single mothers. Farmer-Kaiser, *Freedwomen and the Freedmen's Bureau*, 102, 103, 169.

63. Martin grew up in Louisiana. Rawick, *AS*, supp., ser. 2, Texas, pt. 6, 7:2581, 2586. In Wilma Dunaway's study, "Five years after emancipation, one-quarter of the black family units were still residing as laborers in white households, and the vast majority of them were women and their offspring." Jacqueline Jones discusses "disrupted households" with women in white homes and older sons and husbands hired out. Dunaway, *The African-American Family*, 262; Jones, "The Political Economy of Sharecropping Families," 212.

64. Overton grew up in Tennessee, Foltz in Virginia, and Brown in Mississippi. Rawick, *AS*, supp., ser. 2, Texas, pt. 7, 8:3005, supp., ser. 1, Mississippi, pt. 2, 7:753, supp., ser. 2, Texas, pt. 3, 4:1051, 1047; *SNC*, Arkansas, pt. 1, 2:313. James Brown had no knowledge of his father and lost his mother to sale. When his master informed the slaves they were free, he told them he would keep the children whose mothers had been sold, indenturing them to age twenty-one. Gabe Butler's father, the mistress's favorite slave, stole her finest horse and ran off during the war, abandoning his family. Before his mother died, she entrusted Butler to another slave woman. After the war, Butler was indentured for three years before this surrogate mother could secure his release. Rawick, *AS*, supp., ser. 2, Texas, pt. 2, 3:478, supp., ser. 1, Mississippi, pt. 1, 6:324, 326. Dylan Penningroth discusses the "powerlessness that came with not having a dense network of relatives." Penningroth, *The Claims of Kinfolk*, 175.

65. Gutman, *Black Family*, 204–205, 226. Care of orphans seems to be a feature of the black community across time and space. In her study of free black families in the Old Northwest, Joan Cashin finds that a quarter of the two-parent households in the 1850 census had children with a last name that differed from the male head of household, suggesting that many men opened their homes to orphans, as poor households lacked the resources to hire domestics. Virginia Young found similar arrangements in Georgia during the 1960s. Cashin, "Black Families in the Old Northwest," 464; Young, "Family and Childhood in a Southern Negro Community," 269–288.

66. Fairley's aunt had been sent from Mississippi to North Carolina to prevent her being freed. The two children were indentured to age twenty and denied an education. *SNC*, Ohio, 12:78, 77, 79; Rawick, *AS*, supp., ser. 2, Texas, pt. 3, 4:1060; *SNC*, Arkansas, pt. 2, 2:186, 187, pt. 2, 2:261. "Black mothers of 'orphan'—meaning, in reality, 'fatherless,' 'illegitimate,' or 'bastard'—children also endured the frequent wrath of labor-hungry white Southerners in the postwar South." Farmer-Kaiser, *Freedwomen and the Freedmen's Bureau*, 102.

67. Burton's mother collected her three children and brought with her two others. Burton, *Memories of Childhood's Slavery Days*, 11, 12. Single women trying to secure their children often had to appeal to Union authorities to release them from indentures. Rawick, *AS*, supp., ser. 1, Mississippi, pt. 1, 6:94–95; *SNC*, Texas, pt. 3, 16:136; Rawick, *AS*, supp., ser. 2, Texas, pt. 7, 8:3238, pt. 6, 7:2561. Annie Osborne knew she had a white father, and believed he was her master. She did not know about the parentage of her two brothers. After freedom, her master insisted on keeping the children. Osborne's mother obtained a paper from the provost marshal guaranteeing her children's liberty, but, too afraid to show it to her former master, she stole them away. Anna Clark, who had been a concubine from age fifteen and had six children with "no acknowledged father," went west. Most ex-slaves lacked the resources to make such a move. Rawick, *AS*, supp., ser. 2, Texas, pt. 7, 8:2992, supp., ser. 1, Colorado, 2:38.

68. Rudd and Bond, *From Slavery to Wealth*, 22, 37; Rawick, *AS*, supp., ser. 2, Texas, pt. 3, 4:1387, 1399. In a patriarchal society, free black men had an advantage over free black women, and courts tended to side with fathers when separated couples fought over children. In one case, a court noted that the father "privately and violently" removed his son from the mother without her permission. Although the court found both parents "unimpeached as to their industry and morality," according to the law the boy was "the legitimate child of Hector Jones." *Pascal v. Jones*, 41 Ga. 220, June 1870, Catterall, *Judicial Cases*, 3:101. On the other hand, during Reconstruction, Freedmen's Bureau agents supported claims of freedwomen over freedmen if

those men failed to uphold Northern standards of masculinity. Farmer-Kaiser, *Freedwomen and the Freedmen's Bureau*, 139, 154, 156.

69. Dunaway, *African-American Family*, 259, 265, 219–257. Dunaway disagrees with Gutman, who argued that the black household, even in postwar migration to the North, usually had two parents. He addressed "father-absent" postwar households, stating that many "had been conventional two-parent households in which the husband had died." Unmarried black women tended to live with their parents rather than head households. Gutman posited that black households changed more from 1905 to 1925 due to the Enclosure Movement and Poor Law. Gutman, *Black Family*, 433, 444, 445, 454, 468.

70. *SNC*, Arkansas, pt. 7, 2:140, South Carolina, pt. 3, 14:248; Rawick, *AS*, supp., ser. 2, Texas, pt. 5, 6:2370; *SNC*, Arkansas, pt. 1, 2:339. Joe Coney's father went into hiding to escape the "Bulldozers" and never returned. Rawick, *AS*, supp., ser. 1, Mississippi, pt. 2, 7:488, 489.

71. Rawick, *AS*, supp., ser. 1, North and South Carolina, 11:137, 138.

72. *SNC*, Missouri, 10:54; Rawick, *AS*, supp., ser. 2, Texas, pt. 3, 4:1327; *SNC*, South Carolina, pt. 4, 14:216, Kentucky, 7:93, South Carolina, pt. 1, 14:227, pt. 4, 14:16; Rawick, *AS*, supp., ser. 1, Indiana and Ohio, 5:143.

73. Naming shows that enslaved people did not practice unilineal descent. They also used first and last names to connect to grandparents and to an African heritage. Gutman, *Black Family*, 197, 188, 190, 95; Stevenson, "Gender Convention, Ideals, and Identity," 175.

74. Based on an analysis of South Carolina and Texas narratives, Herbert Gutman wrote, "Many ex-slaves remembered choosing surnames that revealed strong attachments to immediate slave families and to fathers and husbands. Among the nearly six hundred interviewed, two picked a mother's surname, and two others consciously rejected a father's surname." Gutman, *Black Family*, 246; Johnson, *Slavery Days in Old Kentucky*, 14.

75. *SNC*, Arkansas, pt. 1, 2:151, South Carolina, pt. 4, 14:251; Perdue et al., *Weevils*, 29; *SNC*, Arkansas, pt. 3, 2:267; *Unwritten History of Slavery*, 18:238; *SNC*, Texas, pt. 2, 16:55. Former slaves tended to choose the name of the first owner they recalled in a family history. Gutman, *Black Family*, 232–256.

76. *SNC*, Maryland, 8:66, 67, Texas, pt. 1, 16:257; Rawick, *AS*, supp., ser. 2, Texas, pt. 1, 2:405, pt. 8, 9:3646, supp., ser. 1, Mississippi, pt. 3, 8:1203. Tillman Bradshaw took the name of a father he "never really knew" because he saw the man, who died prior to emancipation, only once a year at Christmas. Rawick, *AS*, supp., ser. 1, Georgia, 3:92.

77. Robinson wrote, "After a diligent search of over fourteen years for the different members of our family, nine children met with mother and held what today would be known as a family reunion." They looked for their father, but never found him. Stroyer's father died six years before emancipation, but "mother is still enjoying liberty with her children." Robinson, *From Log Cabin to the Pulpit*, 158–159, 120; Stroyer, *My Life in the South*, 16, 37.

Chapter Eight

1. On the tax policies of Redeemer governments, see Foner, *Nothing but Freedom*, 70–71.

2. Rawick, *AS*, supp., ser. 2, Texas, pt. 3, 4:1069, 1070, 1072.

3. Hughes, *Thirty Years a Slave*, 191; Green, *Life of the Rev. Elisha W. Green*, 24, 21. Regardless of where they settled or how they achieved freedom, formerly enslaved men saw it as their responsibility to provide for kin. Peyton Skipworth wrote to his former master from Liberia mourning his wife's death and his own illness. "The idea of being in a new country with a large family of helpless children, who could depend only on me for support, & me being so indisposed as to be of no use to them nor myself . . . made me feel distressed and greatly so." He praised God for his improving health, and noted he had two children in school and "the others I instruct at home." Until his early death, Skipworth addressed his hopes and concerns for his children's education and self-improvement. Peyton Skipworth, Monrovia, Liberia, to J. H. Cocke, April 27, 1836, April 22, 1840, in Miller, *"Dear Master,"* 60–61, 74.

4. Holsey, *Autobiography*, 21; Blassingame, *Slave Testimony*, 503; Lane, *Autobiography of Bishop Isaac Lane*, 57.

5. *SNC*, Tennessee, 15:43–44; Rawick, *AS*, supp., ser. 2, Texas, pt. 3, 4:1105, pt. 1, 2:247; Foner, *Nothing but Freedom*, 65–67; Jones, "The Political Economy of Sharecropping Families," 203.

6. *SNC*, North Carolina, pt. 1, 11:377; Rawick, *AS*, supp., ser. 2, Texas, pt. 6, 7:2753.

7. *SNC*, Arkansas, pt. 5, 2:113; Rawick, *AS*, supp., ser. 1, Mississippi, pt. 3, 8:1143; Latta, *History of My Life and Work*, 11, 13, 14; Rawick, *AS*, supp., ser. 1, Mississippi, pt. 4, 9:1431. Margrett Nickerson also lost her father, though she never specified how, and described living for a time in a makeshift shelter built of saplings. "We didn' had no body to buil' a house fur us, cose pa was gone and ma jes had us gals." Enslaved women had ample experience with hard labor, but they rarely had trade skills. Nickerson mentioned having brothers, but they were not living with the family at this time. *SNC*, Florida, 3:255. The loss of adult men had a similar impact on manumitted Liberians in the 1830s. After her father and husband died, Matilda Skipworth lamented the difficulties of being "husbandless & fatherless," with three children. Not having a male provider exacerbated her hardship. Matilda Skipworth to John Hartwell Cocke, Oct. 18, 1851, in Miller, *"Dear Master,"* 106.

8. Love grew up in Tennessee. Love, *Life and Adventures of Nat Love*, 17, 18, 21, 24, 23. When both of Joseph Anderson's parents died in 1865, "my older sister took charge of me." *SNC*, North Carolina, pt. 1, 11:17.

9. Landrum grew up in Texas and Scott in Tennessee. Rawick, *AS*, supp., ser. 2, Texas, pt. 5, 6:2263, pt. 8, 9:3467, pt. 4, 5:1471, pt. 7, 8:2935, pt. 7, 8:3090, supp., ser. 1, Indiana and Ohio, 5:440; Perdue et al., *Weevils*, 319. Peter Gray and Kermyt Anderson argue that, across human societies, "earlier in life fatherhood may be a drain on a man's health, but that same relationship may have later, beneficial effects." Gray and Anderson, *Fatherhood, Evolution, and Human Paternal Behavior*, 239, 242.

10. Ray and Ray, *Twice Sold*, 24, 25, 26, 27.

11. Bouy knew his father came from South Carolina, but had no knowledge of his mother's background. Ray and Ray, *Twice Sold*, 31, 32; Rawick, *AS*, supp., ser. 1, Mississippi, pt. 1, 6:182. Booker T. Washington also lost his mother shortly after the war. "My sister Amanda, although she tried to do the best she could, was too young to know anything about keeping house. . . . Sometimes we had food cooked for us, and sometimes we did not. . . . More than once a can of tomatoes and some crackers constituted a meal. . . . It seems to me that this was the most dismal period of my life." Washington, *Up from Slavery*, 70–71.

12. Simms had been enslaved in Missouri. Bunton discussed her big wedding held at her father's cabin. *SNC*, Kansas, 6:13, 9; Rawick, *AS*, supp., ser. 2, Texas, pt. 2, 3:524, 525. Tolbert Bragg's wife died and "left him the care of several children," so he moved north from Tennessee, put them in school and eventually bought a home. Ann Mitchell's mother died in Mississippi when she was only a year old and her father left with Union soldiers, "but he come back to us . . . and we come to Arkansas." Mitchell never indicated if he remarried. Rawick, *AS*, supp., ser. 1, Indiana and Ohio, 5:20, supp., ser. 1, Arkansas, 2:13.

13. Franklin left his first family in Alabama. He had six children by his second wife and raised that family. Walker and his second wife had no children. *SNC*, Missouri, 10:367, 368; Rawick, *AS*, supp., ser. 2, Texas, pt. 3, 4:1415.

14. Holmes stayed with his grandfather until he married. At the time of his interview, Moye lived with a daughter. The town he moved into was Corsicana, Texas. *SNC*, South Carolina, pt. 2, 14:296; Rawick, *AS*, supp., ser. 2, Alabama, 1:1, supp., ser. 2, Texas, pt. 6, 7:2864, 2866, 2871. Nellie Smith's mother had died and she likely had a white father and was also raised by her grandparents. However, not all kinship connections worked out. Neal Upson's father made a pact with a cousin that if one died the other "would look atter de daid one's fambly and see dat none of de chillun was bound out to wuk for nobody." Upson's parents both died and Cousin Jim reneged on this vow, but Upson ran away from his employer. *SNC*, Georgia, pt. 3, 4:305, 309, 310, pt. 4, 4:66, 67.

15. See Shepard Krech for a discussion of family organization and the tendency toward multihousehold extended families. Krech, "Black Family Organization in the Nineteenth Century," 429–452; Jones, "The Political Economy of Sharecropping Families," 209. Nate Shaw's dictated memoir offers a good example of such multihousehold extended families. Rosengarten, ed., *All God's Dangers*. "The reestablishment and expansion of family networks after the Civil War and the growth of property controlled by families meant that family became more important to African Americans than ever," Penningroth argues. Penningroth, *The Claims of Kinfolk*, 186.

16. *SNC*, South Carolina, pt. 3, 14:188, 189.

17. Adams, *Narrative of the Life of John Quincy Adams*, 39, 11. Multihousehold extended families tended to coalesce around the leadership of an elderly individual, who could be male or female. Krech, "Black Family Organization in the Nineteenth Century," 433.

18. Rawick, *AS*, supp., ser. 1, Alabama, 2:419, supp., ser. 1, Indiana and Ohio, 5:421, supp., ser. 2, Texas, pt. 3, 4:1086; *SNC*, Arkansas, pt. 1, 2:297. "I have worked eighteen hours a day for fifty-five years, . . . raised fourteen kids, and taught Sunday School for sixty-five years," Bryl Anderson stated. Perdue et al., *Weevils*, 13.

19. *SNC*, North Carolina, pt. 2, 11:279, 279–280. Mia Bay argues that black intellectuals defined white men as "brutal, arrogant, and selfish," a critique echoed by these informants. Bay, *The White Image in the Black Mind*, 109.

20. Rawick, *AS*, supp., ser. 2, Texas, pt. 1, 2:34, 35, pt. 4, 5:1892. Louise Jones cried when her father took all of the money given to her by Union soldiers. Nelson Dorsey, who had served as a soldier and whose mother died, briefly returned home after the war before leaving his family, "because my father and older brothers didn't treat me right," and commandeered his wages. Perdue et al., *Weevils*, 187; Rawick, *AS*, supp., ser. 1, Minnesota, 2:106.

21. Rawick, *AS*, supp., ser. 1, Mississippi, pt. 2, 7:440. Ellen Sinclair said that her father "didn' have no sense," but she offered little context for this comment. Rawick, *AS*, supp., ser. 2, Texas, pt. 8, 9:3593. Wilma Dunaway finds "only one of every eight of the narrators spoke negatively of their fathers. In these instances, both parents were present in the households every day, but adult males engaged in negative behavior that disrupted family life." Dunaway, *African-American Family*, 80.

22. Rawick, *AS*, supp., ser. 1, Georgia, 4:512, 514; *SNC*, Arkansas, pt. 1, 2:89, South Carolina, pt. 4, 14:19–20; Jones, *Days of Bondage*, 1. After her family was freed by will and moved north, Mary McCray took on much of the workload because she "had no brothers to assist her father in the heavy work." In addition, her father, the free son of his master and a former distiller, "knew very little about farming," and liked to drink. McCray, *Life of Mary F. McCray*, 21, 22.

23. "Nothing so aroused Shaw as his recollections of his father," Rosengarten writes. "Shaw is still in conflict with a man who was a boy during President Lincoln's administration. While it is not unusual for a child to have unresolved feelings about a parent, it is disarming to see a struggle so open and honest" (xvi). Rosengarten, ed., *All God's Dangers*, 5, 6.

24. Rosengarten, ed., *All God's Dangers*, 9, 10, 18. Shaw's first whipping occurred because he was too physically immature to handle the labor his father expected of him (15).

25. Rosengarten, ed., *All God's Dangers*, 25, 7, 27, 33, 16, 26, 31; Painter, *Soul Murder and Slavery*, 14.

26. Nate and his wife raised Davey, "and I treated him just like he was our own child" (212). Rosengarten, ed., *All God's Dangers*, 26, 37, 55, 131, 57, 127, 206, 208, 210, 211, 212. In her field study of Georgiatown, Georgia, in 1962 and 1966, Virginia Young found that illegitimate and orphaned black children were "often cared for in the households of male kinsmen," including grandfathers and uncles. Young, "Family and Childhood in a Southern Negro Community," 272.

27. Rosengarten, ed., *All God's Dangers*, 48, 49, 50, 82, 83, 470, 273. Martin Jackson similarly expressed resentment of his father's accommodating attitude. Rawick, *AS*, supp., ser. 2, Texas, pt. 4, 5:1904–1905, 1908.

28. "My whole family come up respectable," he added. Rosengarten, ed., *All God's Dangers*, 274, 129, 24, 480.

29. Rosengarten, ed., *All God's Dangers*, 8, xx.

30. It may have been easier for Nate Shaw to make peace with his father because he could eventually defend himself. The same may not have been true of Hayes's wives. Rosengarten, ed., *All God's Dangers*, 352–353, 274, 276. Like Nate Shaw, Mary Church Terrell was never a slave. Unlike Shaw, she came from the black elite. Her assessment of her father, Robert Church, echoed Shaw's commentary. "He was a remarkable man in many respects," Terrell wrote. "I am not trying to paint him as a saint, for he was far from being one. He had the vices and defects common to men . . . reared as a slave, and environed as he was for so many years, from necessity rather than choice, after he was freed." Terrell remembered her father as a "courageous" man who "knew no fear," but he also had a dark side. "My father had the most violent temper of any human being with whom I have come in contact. In a fit of anger he seemed completely to lose control of himself." Terrell never mentioned if his temper led to domestic abuse, but her parents divorced and she did not explain why. Terrell, *Colored Woman in a White World*, 6.

31. "It weren't no use in climbin too fast; weren't no use in climbin slow, neither, if they was goin to take everything you worked for when you got too high," Nate Shaw continued (27). Rosengarten, ed., *All God's Dangers*, 27, 33, 30, 31. "The ending of slavery turned a smoldering negotiation over time into an open war over land and moveable property," Dylan Penningroth writes. Penningroth, *The Claims of Kinfolk*, 154.

32. In 1908, Jack Johnson became the first African American heavyweight world champion, provoking the animosity of white Americans. His marriages to white women and flamboyant behavior fueled the hostility. In 1913, based on flimsy evidence, an all-white jury convicted Johnson of violating the Mann Act and he fled the country. Blum, "A Subversive Savior," 152; Friend, "From Southern Manhood to Southern Masculinities," xx; Runstedtler, *Jack Johnson*.

33. "What little land they acquired often came under the control of families, not individuals," Penningroth writes of freedpeople. "Although many ex-slaves tried to make their property claims less dependent on social ties with white landlords, when it came to other blacks they often did just the opposite," an indication that former slaves' conceptions of property "did not conform to legal notions of private property." This likely helped to protect property. Penningroth, *The Claims of Kinfolk*, 160, 161, 158.

34. The Haywoods ranched in Texas and eventually had their own herd of cattle. Rawick, *AS*, supp., ser. 2, Texas, pt. 4, 5:1692; *SNC*, Arkansas, pt. 2, 2:39; Rawick, *AS*, supp., ser. 1, Mississippi, pt. 2, 7:730; *SNC*, South Carolina, pt. 3, 14:213; Rawick, *AS*, supp., ser. 2, Georgia, 1:269, supp., ser. 2, Texas, pt. 4, 5:1542–1543. Allen Wilson's father returned from his military service, collected his wife and children, moved to Petersburg, Virginia, and "worked and bought a home." Perdue et al., *Weevils*, 328.

35. Ford married and remained with her parents until they died, living in a separate house on the same property. Rawick, *AS*, supp., ser. 2, Texas, pt. 3, 4:1368, 1369; *SNC*, Georgia, pt. 4, 4:3, 5, Missouri, 10:109.

36. Jones, "The Political Economy of Sharecropping Families," 208–209, 196, 202, 203.

37. When KKK activity increased, the Powers family slept in the woods. Rawick, *AS*, supp., ser. 2, Texas, pt. 7, 8:3140, 3141, 3142; *SNC*, Arkansas, pt. 3, 2:263; *Unwritten History of Slavery*, 18:50. According to Dylan Penningroth, "It was kin who defined access to resources, and it was through the language of kinship, not race, that people rationalized and understood their claims on one another." Penningroth, *The Claims of Kinfolk*, 192.

38. Perdue et al., *Weevils*, 213; Rawick, *AS*, supp., ser. 1, Indiana and Ohio, 5:435.

39. Anderson also later hired his younger brother's time from his father and sent him to school. Moore claimed her parents lived to be 104 and 105 years old. Perdue et al., *Weevils*, 10, 12; *SNC*, Arkansas, pt. 1, 2:62, North Carolina, pt. 2, 11:137.

40. Beckwith came from Georgia, and Jackson from Alabama. *SNC*, Georgia, pt. 3, 4:260, Arkansas, pt. 1, 2:132, pt. 1, 2:179, pt. 4, 2:12.

41. *SNC*, Oklahoma, 13:7; Rawick, *AS*, supp., ser. 2, Georgia, 1:270; *SNC*, South Carolina, pt. 3, 14:246. Mary Childs fondly recalled the wedding dress her father purchased for her and wished she had kept it to show to her own children. Henry Lewis's artisan father "mek me a

good pair of shoes for me to git marry in." Rawick, *AS*, supp., ser. 1, Georgia, 3:202, supp., ser. 2, Texas, pt. 5, 6:2345.

42. Rawick, *AS*, supp., ser. 2, Texas, pt. 5, 6:2029; *SNC*, Virginia, 17:55. Nelson Cameron's father, a tanyard worker as a slave, earned a living "makin' boots and shoes" in the postwar period. *SNC*, South Carolina, pt. 1, 14:173; Rawick, *AS*, supp., ser. 1, Indiana and Ohio, 5:411, 414, supp., ser. 1, Mississippi, pt. 3, 8:1029, supp., ser. 2, Texas, pt. 2, 3:541.

43. Rawick, *AS*, supp., ser. 1, Alabama, 1:375, supp., ser. 1, Missouri, 2:248, 257. Most former slaves commented on their father's efforts to provide shelter and food, illustrating postwar hardships. A few had memories of more whimsical offerings. "Pa bought me a doll what would dance when you wound it up and I sho' did love dat little dancin' doll," Georgia Johnson remembered. *SNC*, Georgia, pt. 2, 4:333.

44. Nunn and his wife moved to live with his father after the death of his mother, and his father built them their own house on the property. *SNC*, Arkansas, pt. 1, 2:132, 133, 158; Rawick, *AS*, supp., ser. 2, Texas, pt. 7, 8:2955–2956; *SNC*, Florida, 3:260; Mississippi, 9:74. Sampson Willis's father saved money he earned from his cotton patch during slavery and purchased land after emancipation. "This place is part of the land I inherited from my father," he told his interviewer. Rawick, *AS*, supp., ser. 2, Texas, pt. 9, 10:4164. Dylan Penningroth argues that freedpeople lacked "any overarching rule on inheritance," though fathers more often made bequests, another example of the flexibility of enslaved and freedpeoples' sense of kinship. Penningroth, *The Claims of Kinfolk*, 90. After the war, fathers with connections secured apprenticeships and other opportunities for their children. Henry Flipper and London Ferebee had fathers who had been skilled slaves and who oversaw their son's career placements. Ferebee "contracted, by the consent of my father," with a judge, receiving lessons in law and Latin. Flipper was the first African American cadet at West Point, a placement his father countersigned. When a man offered him a large sum of money to forfeit his appointment, Flipper refused. "However, as I was a minor, I referred him to my father." Ferebee, *Brief History of the Slave Life of Rev. L. R. Ferebee*, 12; Flipper, *Colored Cadet at West Point*, 28, 7, 8, 26.

45. Meachum, *An Address*, 14, 20, 44–45, 19; Joseph Taper to former master, in Starobin, *Blacks in Bondage*, 152; Drew, *North-Side View of Slavery*, 87, 298; Jamison, *Autobiography and Work of Bishop M. F. Jamison*, 188. Josiah Henson established a vocational school and worked for racial uplift. Henson, *Autobiography*, 124.

46. Steward taught free black children with the help of another daughter. Jones, *Experience and Personal Narrative of Uncle Tom Jones*, 26; Steward, *Twenty-Two Years a Slave*, 306, 299; Douglass, *Life and Times*, 332. In a letter to Harriet Beecher Stowe, Frederick Douglass called for industrial education as a way to expand free black economic opportunities and reduce prejudice among the white working class. In addition, the poverty of the free black population made a university education unaffordable for many (354–357). J. W. Lindsay criticized prejudice in Canada that limited educational attainment. Blassingame, *Slave Testimony*, 397.

47. Ward, when speaking of a friend, illustrated his regard by comparing the man to his father. "Since the demise of my dear father, I have seen no man whom, in adversity and prosperity . . . I could so safely trust," he wrote (247). Lewis was raised in Louisiana. Ward, *Autobiography of a Fugitive Negro*, 27, 34; Lewis, *Out of the Ditch*, 18, 22; Suggs, *Shadow and Sunshine*, 22–24.

48. South Carolina, pt. 2, 14:3, pt. 3, 14:45; Jones, *Intimate Reconstructions*, 162–164.

49. Upson recalled his own graduation. "De grandest thing of all . . . was dat Daddy let me wear his watch." *SNC*, Arkansas, pt. 1, 2:278, Georgia, pt. 4, 4:63, Virginia, 17:56; Blassingame, *Slave Testimony*, 494.

50. *SNC*, Arkansas, pt. 7, 2:115; Blassingame, *Slave Testimony*, 745; Rawick, *AS*, supp., ser. 1, Mississippi, pt. 5, 10:2216: Albert, *House of Bondage*, 127. Eliza Suggs's father took a position at the Free Methodist Seminary in Orleans, Nebraska, because it offered educational opportunities for his daughters. Suggs, *Shadow and Sunshine*, 32. Other informants recalled getting their first instruction from their fathers. "My daddy learned me to spell . . . fore I went to school," Dinah Perry said. "My daddy was his old mistress' pet. He used to carry her to school all the time and guess that's where he got his learnin'." *SNC*, Arkansas, pt. 5, 2:319, Missouri, 10:239.

51. *SNC*, Georgia, pt. 1, 4:280, Oklahoma, 13:256; Robinson, *From Log Cabin to the Pulpit*, 150, 151; *Unwritten History of Slavery*, 18:125–126. Bill Reese ran a barbershop and also raised and sold chickens, pigs, and turkeys. He claimed his wife earned as much money teaching and sewing, and "both of us together raised and educated our children." Rawick, *AS*, supp., ser. 1, Georgia, 4:527; Rudd and Bond, *From Slavery to Wealth*, 178, 181.

52. McGee lived with a daughter and provided details of his children's careers. *SNC*, Missouri, 10:233, 234, Rawick, *AS*, supp., ser. 2, Arkansas, 1:215, 217, 215, 219; Perdue et al., *Weevils*, 170; Rawick, *AS*, supp., ser. 2, Texas, pt. 1, 2:374; *SNC*, South Carolina, pt. 4, 14:98.

53. *SNC*, Arkansas, pt. 1, 2:147; Ray and Ray, *Twice Sold*, 54.

54. Rawick, *AS*, supp., ser. 2, Texas, pt. 4, 5:1835; *SNC*, Arkansas, pt. 5, 2:40, pt. 1, 2:254, 265; Rawick, *AS*, supp., ser. 2, Texas, pt. 3, 4:1058; Henry, *Life of George Henry*, 5; Latta, *History of My Life and Work*, 11, 12, 14.

55. *SNC*, Arkansas, pt. 1, 2:284. The death or poor health of a parent made it difficult, though not impossible, for young people to attend school. Both of J. Vance Lewis's parents died not long after the war ended, "and I was left an orphan to fight life's battles." Another former slave boy "on the other hand was in school every day and had a loving mother to help and encourage him and a father to correct him and support him in whatever he undertook." Lewis and his friend both attended Leland University in New Orleans, but because he had to work, Lewis progressed slowly. After teaching for a time, Lewis attended law school and was eventually sworn in before the U.S. Supreme Court. Lewis, *Out of the Ditch*, 24, 24–25, 28, 31, 32. Sterling Brown had to leave school at age thirteen due to his father's "failing health" and the "sheer necessity" of providing food for a hungry family, but was later able to attend Fisk University with the support of his siblings and other relatives. Brown, *My Own Life Story*, 9, 11, 10.

56. *SNC*, Arkansas, pt. 2, 2:323; Rawick, *AS*, supp., ser. 2, Texas, pt. 8, 9:3461; *SNC*, Tennessee, 15:44, Maryland, 8:18, Tennessee, 15:29; Rawick, *AS*, supp., ser. 2, Texas, pt. 3, 4:1288, supp., ser. 1, Mississippi, pt. 5, 10:1913.

57. Rawick, *AS*, supp., ser. 2, Texas, pt. 7, 8:3304.

58. Washington's mother, who soon passed away, was more sympathetic. He found someone to give him lessons at night. Lowry, *Life on the Old Plantation*, 19, 20; Washington, *Up from Slavery*, 30, 31. Whereas Washington's stepfather was skeptical of the value of schooling, Anna Baker's mother and stepfather sent her to school. *SNC*, Mississippi, 9:15.

59. Blassingame, *Slave Testimony*, 743. Claiborne Bullen's father paid for his first two years of college and he worked to pay for the following two. Ben Robinson's abroad father taught his son the basics of literacy, so he had a head start when he entered school. Robinson eventually became a teacher and gave "full credit" to his father and teachers. Rawick, *AS*, supp., ser. 1, Mississippi, pt. 1, 6:303, pt. 4, 9:1846.

60. Smith, *Autobiography of James L. Smith*, 70; Brown, *My Own Life Story*, 36; *SNC*, Alabama, 1:392; Rawick, *AS*, supp., ser. 1, Georgia, 4:528–531; *SNC*, South Carolina, pt. 3, 14:25–26. In a departure from the typical narrative, Abner Griffin admitted that one son died in jail despite being "smart" and having been sent to school. Rawick, *AS*, supp., ser. 1, Georgia, 3:274.

61. *SNC*, South Carolina, pt. 4, 14:274, pt. 1, 14:102, Georgia, pt. 3, 4:311, 310; Rawick, *AS*, supp., ser. 2, Texas, pt. 7, 8:3112, pt. 5, 6:2024.

62. William Becker argues that the black church provided "models of manhood" that contributed to "the cause of black liberation." Becker identifies four aspects of black manhood in the church tradition: leadership, independence, black identity, and vocation. The black church protested slavery, later racism and lynching, and became heavily invested in mission work in Africa. Becker, "The Black Church: Manhood and Mission," 322, 323, 327. Edward Blum discusses the roots of black liberation theology in the South and the evolving image of the black Christ as "a subversive savior" linked to "a sacred black manhood to resist and someday overcome white supremacy." Blum, "A Subversive Savior," 168, 153, 150. Craig Friend argues that Southern African Americans "had greater options in formulating manhood" than were available within the Southern white church, which "had to account for the white men's imagined obligations to vigilantly oppress blacks and protect white womanhood. That demand did not

exist in the black church, thereby offering greater latitude to black Southern men in conceptu-
alizing masculinity." Friend, "From Southern Manhood to Southern Masculinities," xix.

63. Bruce, *The New Man*, 145. Martin Summers shows a "generational change" in conceptions
of manhood in the middle-class African American community, North and South, in the early
twentieth century and especially the late 1920s, that mirrored a similar transition in white society "from Victorian manliness to modern masculinity." Summers, *Manliness and Its Discontents*,
18, 19, 235.

64. Rawick, *AS*, supp., ser. 2, Texas, pt. 6, 7:2869; *SNC*, Arkansas, pt. 1, 2:282.

65. Rawick, *AS*, supp., ser. 2, Texas, pt. 9, 10:3932; *SNC*, Oklahoma, 13:104, 222; Rawick,
AS, supp., ser. 2, Texas, pt. 5, 6:1941.

66. *SNC*, North Carolina, pt. 1, 11:419; Rawick, *AS*, supp., ser. 2, Texas, pt. 1, 2:112, pt. 4,
5:1781, pt. 3, 4:1057, pt. 6, 7:2597. "Papa would tell us stories about the war," Betty Coleman
recalled. "I used to love to hear him on long winter evenings." Ella Maples would "beg" her
father to tell stories about "slavery days." *SNC*, Arkansas, pt. 2, 2:37; Rawick, *AS*, supp., ser. 2,
Texas, pt. 6, 7:2572. Thomas James, who escaped before the war, also taught his children to
celebrate emancipation: "With them I sing the old 'Liberty Minstrel' songs. . . . Blessed be
God that I have lived to see the liberation and the enfranchisement of the people of my color
and blood!" James, *Life of Rev. Thomas James*, 23.

67. *SNC*, North Carolina, pt. 2, 11:351, Oklahoma, 13:202. "As slaves we would be sold often
away from our children. In dat way we better off," Henry Gibbs added. Rawick, *AS*, supp., ser.
1, Mississippi, pt. 3, 8:835. As Catherine Stewart shows using the Georgia narratives, FWP interviews conducted by white Southerners tended to end with leading questions asking informants to compare slavery to the present. "Some informants equivocated by trying to
accommodate pro-Confederate views while still expressing their gratitude for emancipation,"
she writes. Stewart, *Long Past Slavery*, 213, 217. Stephanie Shaw notes that informants "refused
to answer without putting their response in the very specific context of the Great Depression."
Shaw, "Using the WPA Ex-Slave Narratives to Study the Impact of the Great Depression," 630.

68. *SNC*, Arkansas, pt. 1, 2:96, 174, 276; pt. 5, 2:154, Alabama, 1:175, Texas, pt. 1, 16:293,
Maryland, 8:43; Rawick, *AS*, supp., ser. 2, Texas, pt. 3, 4:1104, supp., ser. 1, Mississippi, pt. 2,
7:506; Clement, *Memoirs of Samuel Spottford Clement*, 25, 37; Ray, *Twice Sold*, 104, 188–189.

69. Rawick, *AS*, supp., ser. 2, Texas, pt. 9, 10:4280, pt. 1, 2:177; *SNC*, Ohio, 12:48. Simon
Durr also moved between the homes of his children. Mack Taylor lived on his own farm with
his grown son, and "my grandson, Mack, is a grown boy and de main staff I lean on as I climb
up to de hundred mile post of age." Bill Reese grew excited when the mailman arrived during
his interview and explained that his children took turns writing him a letter each day. Reese
missed his children, but he understood that "this town is too small for 'em now," and offered
little economic opportunity. Rawick, *AS*, supp., ser. 1, Mississippi, pt. 2, 7:657–658; *SNC*,
South Carolina, pt. 4, 14:159; Rawick, *AS*, supp., ser. 1, Georgia, 4:535.

70. *SNC*, South Carolina, pt. 1, 14:347; Rawick, *AS*, supp., ser. 2, Texas, pt. 5, 6:2192. During the Great Depression, elderly African Americans fared better when they had the support of
younger kin. The Great Migration left some without that crucial assistance. Shaw, "Using the
WPA Ex-Slave Narratives to Study the Impact of the Great Depression," 657, 645, 650.

71. Rawick, *AS*, supp., ser. 1, Indiana and Ohio, 5:86; *SNC*, Georgia, pt. 1, 4:280.

72. This information sometimes came from former masters as part of the announcement of
emancipation. "I's don' know 'zactly how ol' I's am, 'cause I's never gits de statement f'om my
Marster. My father keep de record in de Bible. Dat am somewhar 'roun', but I's don't know who
has it," Mandy Morrow stated. Rawick, *AS*, supp., ser. 2, Texas, pt. 6, 7:2774, pt. 5, 6:2021;
SNC, South Carolina, pt. 2, 14:107, Texas, pt. 3, 16:165–166, Arkansas, pt. 7, 2:244.

73. "Pappy is buried in the church yard on Four Mile branch," Thompson added. Rawick, *AS*,
supp., ser. 2, Texas, pt. 5, 6:2255, supp., ser. 1, Oklahoma, 12:309; *SNC*, Georgia, pt. 4, 4:178.

74. Bruner's daughter had originally written his story, and he ended the book with a poem
written by his granddaughter. Bruner, *Slave's Adventures toward Freedom*, 3, 7, 43, 53; Robinson,
From Log Cabin to the Pulpit; Washington, *Autobiography*, 13.

75. Rawick, *AS*, supp., ser. 2, Texas, pt. 4, 5:1906, 1903.

76. Early, *Life and Labors of Rev. Jordan W. Early*, 161; Edwards, *From Slavery to a Bishopric*, 137–138; Suggs, *Shadow and Sunshine*, 34. Josephine Brown added chapters to the narrative of her father, William Wells Brown, at the urging of peers in school eager to learn his history. Brown, *Biography of an American Bondman*, 4.

77. In railroad construction, the steel driver hammered a steel drill into rock to create holes for placing explosives. Lawrence Levine focused on Henry's appeal to black workers as a "natural man" who stood up to mechanization and represented the postwar "economic plight of black workers." African Americans who related the tale believed it was based on actual events. See Nelson, *Steel Drivin' Man*, for a recent account that traces the legend to the life of a real man. Levine, *Black Culture and Black Consciousness*, 424, 426, 427, 421, 422, 423.

Epilogue

1. Olwell, "'Loose, Idle, and Disorderly,'" 98.

2. George Bonanno discusses the heterogeneity of resilience and argues that there is "no single resilient type. Rather, there appear to be multiple and sometimes unexpected ways to be resilient," in the face of trauma, grief, and loss. Bonanno, "Resilience in the Face of Potential Trauma," 135.

3. "On the Management of Slaves," *Southern Agriculturist* 6 (June 1833): 281–287; "Management of Slaves, &c.," *Farmers' Register* 5 (May 1837): 32–33, in Breeden, *Advice among Masters*, 31, 35.

4. Hurricane, "The Negro and His Management," *Southern Cultivator* 18 (September 1860): 276–277, in Breeden, *Advice among Masters*, 332; Du Bois, *Black Reconstruction*, 647.

5. Rawick, *AS*, supp., ser. 2, Texas, pt. 6, 7:2806, pt. 8, 9:3453–3454.

6. Rawick, pt. 5, 6:2301–2302.

7. "Perhaps the most enduring legacy of slavery, then, was the persistence of a bifurcated society in which economic elites did not identify with or internalize the well-being of the majority of the population," Gavin Wright argues. Wright, *Slavery and American Economic Development*, 126. George Albright argued that poor whites initially felt "their interests lay with the Negroes," especially in terms of voting and education, but landlords and the Klan "got many of the poor whites on their side" and "split many of them away from their own best interests." Rawick, *AS*, supp., ser. 1, Mississippi, pt. 1, 6:19; Roediger, *Wages of Whiteness*.

8. On the criminalization of black men in American popular culture, see Linda Tucker, *Lockstep and Dance*. H. Bruce Franklin sees the criminalization of black men as rooted in the Constitution and Thirteenth Amendment. Franklin, *Prison Literature in America*.

9. Eberhardt et al., "Seeing Black: Race, Crime, and Visual Processing."

10. This study defines a mass shooting as one that claimed four or more victims, not including the perpetrator. The data set includes events that have been defined as workplace violence, gang violence, terrorism, and school shootings. Duxbury, Frizzell, and Lindsay, "Mental Illness, the Media, and the Moral Politics of Mass Violence: The Role of Race in Mass Shootings Coverage."

11. Coates, "Letter to My Son."

12. Greenbaum, *Blaming the Poor*.

13. Hamer, *What It Means to Be Daddy*, 31; Lempert, "Other Fathers," 189, 189–199. In the contemporary United States, out-of-wedlock births are a function of class, poverty, and economic inequality. Though long perceived as an African American problem, the number of children born outside marriage among poor whites has increased dramatically in recent decades. Kathryn Edin and Timothy Nelson conducted ethnographic fieldwork in inner-city Camden, New Jersey, and Philadelphia, interviewing 110 unwed fathers, half black and half white. Despite high expectations and a determination to be involved in their children's lives, these men regularly failed as fathers. They examine the disjuncture between ideals of fatherhood and the reality of life in poor communities, concluding that fatherlessness stems not

from men's desire to evade responsibility, but from the hardships of poverty. Edin and Nelson, *Doing the Best I Can*.

14. This term is also a reference to a genre of pornography. Dana Schwartz, "Why Angry White Men Love Calling People 'Cucks.'"

15. Coates, "We Should Have Seen Trump Coming." Michael Kimmel argues that "manhood is less about the drive for domination and more about the fear of others dominating us, having power or control over us." Kimmel, *Manhood in America*, 5.

Bibliography

Primary Sources

Aaron. *The Light and Truth of Slavery: Aaron's History*. Worcester, MA: Printed for the Author, 1845.

Adams, John Quincy. *Narrative of the Life of John Quincy Adams, When in Slavery, and Now as a Freeman*. Harrisburg, PA: Sieg, Printer, and Stationer, 1872.

Albert, Octavia V. Rogers. *The House of Bondage, or Charlotte Brooks and Other Slaves*. New York: Hunt and Eaton, 1890.

Aleckson, Sam. *Before the War, and After the Union: An Autobiography*. Windsor, VT: Gold Mind, 1929.

Alexander, Charles. *Battles and Victories of Allen Allensworth, A.M. Ph.D., Lieutenant-Colonel, Retired, U.S. Army*. Boston: Sherman, French, 1914.

Allen, Richard. *The Life, Experience, and Gospel Labours of the Rt. Rev. Richard Allen*. Philadelphia: Martin and Boden, 1833.

Anderson, Robert. *The Life of Rev. Robert Anderson*. Macon, GA: Printed for the Author, 1892.

Anderson, Thomas. *Interesting Account of Thomas Anderson, A Slave. Taken from His Own Lips*. Edited by J. P. Clarke, 1854.

Anderson, William J. *Life and Narrative of William J. Anderson, Twenty-Four Years a Slave*. Chicago: Daily Tribune, 1857.

Arter, Jared Maurice. *Echoes from a Pioneer Life*. Atlanta: A. B. Caldwell, 1922.

Ball, Charles. *Fifty Years in Chains; or, the Life of an American Slave*. New York: H. Dayton, 1859.

Bayley, Solomon. *A Narrative of Some Remarkable Incidents in the Life of Solomon Bayley*. London: Harvey and Darton, 1825.

Berlin, Ira. *The Wartime Genesis of Free Labor: The Lower South*. Cambridge: Cambridge University Press, 1990.

Berlin, Ira, Barbara J. Fields, Steven F. Miller, Joseph P. Reidy, and Leslie S. Rowland. *Free at Last: A Documentary History of Slavery, Freedom, and the Civil War*. New York: New Press, 1992.

Berlin, Ira, and Leslie S. Rowland. *Families and Freedom: A Documentary History of African-American Kinship in the Civil War Era*. New York: New Press, 1997.

Bibb, Henry. *Narrative of the Life and Adventures of Henry Bibb, An American Slave*. New York: Published by the Author, 1849.

Black, Leonard. *The Life and Sufferings of Leonard Black, A Fugitive from Slavery. Written by Himself*. New Bedford, MA: Press of Benjamin Linsey, 1847.

Blassingame, John, W. *Slave Testimony: Two Centuries of Letters, Speeches, Interviews, and Autobiographies*. Baton Rouge: Louisiana State University Press, 1977.

Bleser, Carol, ed. *Secret and Sacred: The Diaries of James Henry Hammond, a Southern Slaveholder*. New York: Oxford University Press, 1988.

Born in Slavery: Slave Narratives from the Federal Writers' Project, 1936–1938. Federal Writers' Project, Library of Congress, Manuscript Division, National Digital Library Program, Vols. 1–17. https://www.loc.gov/collections/slave-narratives-from-the-federal-writers-project -1936-to-1938/.

Bradford, Sarah H. *Harriet: The Moses of Her People*. New York: Geo. R. Lockwood and Son, 1886.

Bragg, George F. *Men of Maryland*. Baltimore: Church Advocate, 1914.

Breeden, James O. *Advice among Masters: The Ideal in Slave Management in the Old South*. Westport, CT: Greenwood, 1980.

Brown, Henry Box. *Narrative of Henry Box Brown, Who Escaped from Slavery Enclosed in a Box 3 Feet Long and 2 Wide*. Boston: Brown and Stearns, 1849.

———. *Narrative of the Life of Henry Box Brown, Written by Himself*. Manchester, UK: Lee and Glynn, 1851.

Brown, John. *Slave Life in Georgia: A Narrative of the Life, Sufferings, and Escape of John Brown, A Fugitive Slave, Now in England*. Edited by Louis Alexis Chamerovzow. London: W. M. Watts, 1855.

Brown, Josephine. *Biography of an American Bondman, by His Daughter*. Boston: R. F. Wallcut, 1856.

Brown, Sterling N. *My Own Life Story*. Washington, DC: Hamilton Printing, 1924.

Brown, William Wells. *Narrative of William W. Brown, An American Slave. Written by Himself*. London: Charles Gilpin, 1849.

Bruce, H. C. *The New Man. Twenty-Nine Years a Slave. Twenty-Nine Years a Free Man. Recollections of H. C. Bruce*. York, PA: P. Anstadt and Sons, 1895.

Bruner, Peter. *A Slave's Adventures toward Freedom. Not Fiction, but the True Story of a Struggle*. Oxford, OH: 1918.

Burton, Annie L. *Memories of Childhood's Slavery Days*. Boston: Ross, 1909.

Cade, John B. "Out of the Mouths of Ex-Slaves." *Journal of Negro History* 20, no. 3 (July 1935): 294–337.

Campbell, Israel. *An Autobiography. Bond and Free: Or, Yearnings for Freedom from My Green Brier House. Being the Story of My Life in Bondage and My Life in Freedom*. Philadelphia: Published by the Author, 1861.

Catterall, Helen Tunncliff, ed. *Judicial Cases Concerning American Slavery and the Negro. Vol. I: Cases from the Courts of England, Virginia, West Virginia, and Kentucky*. Washington, DC: Carnegie Institution, 1926.

———, ed. *Judicial Cases Concerning American Slavery and the Negro. Vol. II: Cases from the Courts of North Carolina, South Carolina, and Tennessee*. Washington, DC: Carnegie Institution, 1929.

———, ed. *Judicial Cases Concerning American Slavery and the Negro. Vol. III: Cases from the Courts of Georgia, Florida, Alabama, Mississippi, and Louisiana*. Washington, DC: Carnegie Institution, 1932.

"Caution." *National Anti-slavery Standard*. November 27, 1858.

Chesney, Pharaoh Jackson, and J. C. Webster. *Last of the Pioneers or Old Times in East Tenn., Being the Life and Reminiscences of Pharaoh Jackson Chesney*. Knoxville, TN: S. B. Newman, 1902.

Chesnut, Mary Boykin. *A Diary from Dixie*. Edited by Ben Ames Williams. Cambridge, MA: Harvard University Press, 1980.

Clarke, Lewis Garrard. *Narrative of the Sufferings of Lewis Clarke, during a Captivity of More Than Twenty-Five Years, among the Algerines of Kentucky, One of the So-Called Christian States of North America*. Dictated by Himself. Boston: David H. Ela, 1845.

Clarke, Lewis Garrard, and Milton Clarke. *Narratives of the Sufferings of Lewis and Milton Clarke, Sons of a Soldier of the Revolution, during a Captivity of More Than Twenty Years among the Slaveholders of Kentucky, One of the So-Called Christian States of North America*. Boston: Bela Marsh, 1846.

Clement, Samuel Spottford. *Memoirs of Samuel Spottford Clement Relating Interesting Experiences in Days of Slavery and Freedom*. Steubenville, OH: Herald Printing, 1908.

Cox, Mary L., and Susan H. Cox, ed. "Narrative of Dimmock Charlton, A British Subject, Taken from the Brig 'Peacock' by the U.S. Sloop 'Hornet,' Enslaved While a Prisoner of War, and Retained Forty-Five Years in Bondage." *Anti-slavery Reporter*. Philadelphia, 1859.

Craft, William. *Running a Thousand Miles for Freedom; or, the Escape of William and Ellen Craft from Slavery*. London: Richard Barrett, 1860.

Curry, James. "Narrative of James Curry, a Fugitive Slave." *The Liberator.* January 10, 1840.

Davis, Noah. *A Narrative of the Life of Rev. Noah Davis, a Colored Man. Written by Himself, at the Age of Fifty-Four.* Baltimore: John F. Weishampel Jr., 1859.

Delaney, Lucy A. *From the Darkness Cometh the Light or Struggles for Freedom.* St. Louis: J. T. Smith, n.d.

Douglass, Frederick. *Life and Times of Frederick Douglass, Written by Himself.* Boston: De Wolfe and Fiske, 1892.

———. *My Bondage and My Freedom. Part I. Life as a Slave. Part II. Life as a Freeman.* New York: Miller, Orton, and Mulligan, 1855.

———. *Narrative of the Life of Frederick Douglass, an American Slave. Written by Himself.* Boston: Anti-slavery Office, 1845.

Drew, Benjamin. *A North-Side View of Slavery. The Refugee: Or the Narratives of Fugitive Slaves in Canada. Related by Themselves, with an Account of the History and Condition of the Colored Population of Upper Canada.* Boston: John P. Jewett, 1856.

Early, Sarah J. W. *Life and Labors of Rev. Jordan W. Early, One of the Pioneers of African Methodism in the West and South.* Nashville: A. M. E. Church Sunday School Union, 1894.

Edwards, S. J. Celestine. *From Slavery to a Bishopric or the Life of Bishop Walter Hawkins of the British Methodist Episcopal Church Canada.* London: John Kensit, 1891.

Eliot, William G. *The Story of Archer Alexander from Slavery to Freedom, March 30, 1863.* Boston: Cupples, Upham, 1885.

Equiano, Olaudah. *The Interesting Narrative of the Life of Olaudah Equiano, or Gustavus Vassa, The African. Written by Himself.* Vol. 1. London: Printed for the Author, 1789.

Fedric, Francis. *Slave Life in Virginia and Kentucky; or, Fifty Years of Slavery in the Southern States of America.* London: Wertheim, Macintosh, and Hunt, 1863.

Ferebee, London R. *A Brief History of the Slave Life of Rev. L. R. Ferebee, and the Battles of Life, and Four Years of His Ministerial Life. Written from Memory. To 1882.* Raleigh, NC: Edwards, Broughton, 1882.

Fitzhugh, George. *Sociology for the South, or the Failure of Free Society.* Richmond, VA: A. Morris, 1854.

Flipper, Henry Ossian. *The Colored Cadet at West Point, Autobiography of Lieut. Henry Ossian Flipper, U.S.A., First Graduate of Color from the U. S. Military Academy.* New York: Homer Lee, 1878.

Gallaudet, Rev. Thomas H. *A Statement with Regard to the Moorish Prince, Abduhl Rahhahman.* New York: Daniel Fanshaw, 1828.

God Struck Me Dead: Religious Conversion Experiences and Autobiographies of Negro Ex-slaves. Fisk University, Department of Social Sciences, 1945. In *The American Slave.* Vol. 19. Westport, CT: Greenwood, 1972.

Grandy, Moses. *Narrative of the Life of Moses Grandy; Late a Slave in the United States of America.* London: C. Gilpin, 1843.

Green, Elisha W. *Life of the Rev. Elisha W. Green, One of the Founders of the Kentucky Normal and Theological Institute — Now the State University at Louisville; Eleven Years Moderator of the Mt. Zion Baptist Association; Five Years Moderator of the Consolidated Baptist Educational Association and over Thirty Years Pastor of the Colored Baptist Churches of Maysville and Paris. Written by Himself.* Maysville, KY: The Republican, 1888.

Green, J. D. *Narrative of the Life of J. D. Green, a Runaway Slave, from Kentucky Containing an Account of His Three Escapes in 1839, 1846, and 1848.* Huddersfield, UK: Henry Fielding, Pack Horse Yard, 1864.

Green, William. *Narrative of the Events in the Life of William Green, (Formerly a Slave) Written by Himself.* Springfield, MA: L. M. Guernsey, 1853.

Grimes, William. *Life of William Grimes, the Runaway Slave Brought Down to the Present Time. Written by Himself.* New Haven, CT: Published by the Author, 1855.

Hall, Samuel, and Orville Elder. *Samuel Hall, 47 Years a Slave: A Brief Story of His Life Before and After Freedom Came.* Washington, IA: Journal Print, 1912.

Harper, William. *Memoir of Slavery*. Read before the Society for the Advancement of Learning, of South Carolina, at its Annual Meeting at Columbia, 1837. Charleston, SC: J. S. Burges, 1838.

Hawkins, William G. *Lunsford Lane; or, Another Helper from North Carolina*. Boston: Crosby and Nichols, 1863.

Hazard, W. W. "On the General Management of a Plantation." *Southern Agriculturalist* IV, July 1831.

Heard, William H. *From Slavery to the Bishopric in the A. M. E. Church. An Autobiography*. Philadelphia: W. H. Heard, 1924.

Henry, George. *Life of George Henry. Together with a Brief History of the Colored People in America*. Providence, RI: H. I. Gould, 1894.

Henry, Thomas W. *Autobiography of Rev. Thomas W. Henry, of the A. M. E. Church*. Baltimore: Printed for the Author, 1872.

Henson, Josiah. *An Autobiography of the Rev. Josiah Henson ("Uncle Tom"). From 1789 to 1881. With a Preface by Mrs. Harriet Beecher Stowe and Introductory Notes by George Sturge, S. Morley, Esq., M. P., Wendell Phillips, and John G. Whittier*. Edited by John Lobb. London, Ontario: Schuyler, Smith, 1881.

Holsey, L. H. *Autobiography, Sermons, and Essays of Bishop L. H. Holsey, D. D*. Atlanta: Franklin, 1898.

Hopper, Isaac T. *Narrative of the Life of Thomas Cooper*. New York: Isaak T. Hopper, 1832.

Hughes, Henry. *Treatise on Sociology, Theoretical and Practical*. Philadelphia: Printed for the Author, 1854.

Hughes, Louis. *Thirty Years a Slave: From Bondage to Freedom, the Institution of Slavery as Seen on the Plantation and in the Home of the Planter. Autobiography of Louis Hughes*. Milwaukee: South Side Printing, 1897.

Jackson, Andrew. *Narrative and Writings of Andrew Jackson, of Kentucky; Containing an Account of His Birth, and Twenty-Six Years of His Life While a Slave; His Escape; Five Years of Freedom, Together with Anecdotes Relating to Slavery; Journal of One Year's Travels; Sketches, etc. Narrated by Himself; Written by a Friend*. Syracuse, NY: Daily and Weekly Star Office, 1847.

Jackson, John Andrew. *The Experience of a Slave in South Carolina*. London: Passmore and Alabaster, 1862.

Jackson, Mattie. *The Story of Mattie J. Jackson; Her Parentage — Experience of Eighteen Years in Slavery — Incidents during the War — Her Escape from Slavery. A True Story as Given by Mattie*. Edited by L. S. Thompson. Lawrence, MA: Sentinel Office, 1866.

Jacobs, Harriet A. *Incidents in the Life of a Slave Girl. Written by Herself*. Edited by Lydia Maria Child. Boston: Printed for the Author, 1861.

Jacobs, John S. "A True Tale of Slavery." Published serially in *The Leisure Hour: A Family Journal of Instruction and Recreation*, February 7, 14, 21, and 28, 1861. London: Stevens, 1861.

James, Thomas. *Life of Rev. Thomas James, by Himself*. Rochester, NY: Post Express, 1886.

Jamison, Monroe F. *Autobiography and Work of Bishop M. F. Jamison, D. D. ("Uncle Joe"), Editor, Publisher, and Church Extension Secretary, A Narration of His Whole Career from the Cradle to the Bishopric of the Colored M. E. Church in America*. Nashville: M. E. Church, South, 1912.

Jeter, Henry N. *Pastor Henry N. Jeter's Twenty-Five Years Experience with the Shiloh Baptist Church and Her History. Corner School and Mary Streets, Newport, R. I*. Providence, RI: Remington, 1901.

Johnson, Isaac. *Slavery Days in Old Kentucky. A True Story of a Father Who Sold His Wife and Four Children. By One of the Children*. Ogdensburg, NY: Republican and Journal Print, 1901.

Johnson, Thomas L. *Twenty-Eight Years a Slave, or the Story of My Life in Three Continents*. Bournemouth, UK: W. Mate and Sons, 1909.

Johnson, William Tiler. *William Johnson's Natchez: The Antebellum Diary of a Free Negro*. Edited by William Ransom Hogan and Edwin Adams Davis. New York: Kennikat, 1968.

Jones, Friday. *Days of Bondage. Autobiography of Friday Jones. Being a Brief Narrative of His Trials and Tribulations in Slavery*. Washington, DC: Commercial, 1883.

Jones, Thomas. *Experience and Personal Narrative of Uncle Tom Jones; Who Was for Forty Years a Slave. Also the Surprising Adventures of Wild Tom, of the Island Retreat. A Fugitive Negro from South Carolina*. Boston: H. B. Skinner, 1854.

Jones, Thomas H. *The Experience of Rev. Thomas H. Jones, Who Was a Slave for Forty-Three Years. Written by a Friend, as Related to Him by Brother Jones*. New Bedford, MA: E. Anthony and Sons, 1885.

Keckley, Elizabeth. *Behind the Scenes. By Elizabeth Keckley, Formerly a Slave, but More Recently Modiste, and Friend to Mrs. Abraham Lincoln. Or, Thirty Years a Slave, and Four Years in the White House*. New York: G. W. Carleton, 1868.

Kelley, Edmond. *A Family Redeemed from Bondage; Being Rev. Edmond Kelley, (the Author,) His Wife, and Four Children*. New Bedford, MA: Published by the Author, 1851.

Lane, Isaac. *Autobiography of Bishop Isaac Lane, LL. D.: With a Short History of the C. M. E. Church in America and of Methodism*. Nashville: Printed for the Author by M. E. Church, South, 1916.

Lane, Lunsford. *The Narrative of Lunsford Lane, Formerly of Raleigh, N. C. Embracing an Account of His Early Life, the Redemption by Purchase of Himself and Family from Slavery, and His Banishment from the Place of His Birth for the Crime of Wearing a Colored Skin. Published by Himself*. Boston: J. G. Torrey, 1842.

Langston, John Mercer. *From the Virginia Plantation to the National Capitol*. Hartford, CT: American, 1894.

Latta, Morgan London. *The History of My Life and Work. Autobiography by Rev. M. L. Latta, A.M., D.D.* Raleigh, NC: Printed for the Author, 1903.

Lewis, J. Vance. *Out of the Ditch; A True Story of an Ex-Slave*. Houston: Rein and Sons, 1910.

Loguen, Jermain W. *The Rev. J. W. Loguen, as a Slave and as a Freeman. A Narrative of Real Life*. Syracuse, NY: J. G. K. Truair, 1859.

Love, Nat. *The Life and Adventures of Nat Love Better Known in the Cattle Country as "Deadwood Dick" by Himself; a True History of Slavery Days, Life on the Great Cattle Ranges and on the Plains of the "Wild and Woolly" West, Based on Facts, and Personal Experiences of the Author*. Los Angeles: s.n., 1907.

Lowry, Irving E. *Life on the Old Plantation in Ante-bellum Days, or a Story Based on Facts. With Brief Sketches of the Author by the Late Rev. J. Wofford White of the South Carolina Conference, Methodist Episcopal Church*. Columbia, SC: The State, 1911.

Mallory, Col. William. *Old Plantation Days*. Hamilton, Ontario: s.n., 1902.

Marrs, Elijah P. *Life and History of the Rev. Elijah P. Marrs, First Pastor of Beargrass Baptist Church, and Author*. Louisville, KY: Bradley and Gilbert, 1885.

Mars, James. *Life of James Mars, A Slave Born and Sold in Connecticut. Written by Himself*. Hartford, CT: Case, Lockwood, 1868.

Mattison, Hiram. *Louisa Picquet, the Octoroon; or, Inside Views of Southern Domestic Life*. New York: Published by the Author, 1861.

McCray, S. J. *Life of Mary F. McCray: Born and Raised a Slave in the State of Kentucky*. Lima, OH: s.n., 1898.

Meachum, John B. *An Address to All the Colored Citizens of the United States*. Philadelphia: Printed for the Author by King and Baird, 1846.

Miller, Randall M., ed. *"Dear Master": Letters of a Slave Family*. London: Cornell University Press, 1978.

Mississippi Reports: Vol. 46. Being Cases Argued and Decided in the Supreme Court of Mississippi. Volume IV. By J. S. Morris, Reporter to the Supreme Court. Chicago: Callaghan, 1872.

Morgan, Albert Talmon. *Yazoo, or on the Picket Line of Freedom in the South*. Washington, DC: Published by the Author, 1884.

Murray, Pauli. *Proud Shoes: The Story of an American Family*. New York: Harper and Brothers, 1956.

"North American Slave Narratives." Documenting the American South, University of North Carolina. https://docsouth.unc.edu/neh/.

Northup, Solomon. *Twelve Years a Slave. Narrative of Solomon Northup, a Citizen of New York, Kidnapped in Washington City in 1841 and Rescued in 1853, from a Cotton Plantation Near the Red River in Louisiana*. London: Sampson Low, Son, 1853.

Olmsted, Frederick Law. *The Cotton Kingdom: A Traveller's Observations on Cotton and Slavery in the American Slave States*. Vol. 2. New York: Mason Brothers, 1861.

O'Neal, William O'Neal. *Life and History of William O'Neal: Or, the Man Who Sold His Wife*. St. Louis: A. R. Fleming, 1896.

Parker, Allen. *Recollections of Slavery Times*. Worcester, MA: Chas. W. Burbank, 1895.

Parker, William. "The Freedman's Story. In Two Parts." *The Atlantic Monthly* 17 (February 1866): 152–166, (March 1866): 276–295.

Pennington, James. *A Narrative of Events of the Life of J. H. Banks, an Escaped Slave, from the Cotton State, Alabama, in America*. Liverpool, UK: M. Rourke, 1861.

Pennington, James W. C. *The Fugitive Blacksmith; or, Events in the History of James W. C. Pennington, Pastor of a Presbyterian Church, New York, Formerly a Slave in the State of Maryland, United States*. London: Charles Gilpin, 1849.

Perdue, Charles L., Thomas E. Barden, and Robert K. Phillips. *Weevils in the Wheat: Interviews with Virginia Ex-Slaves*. Charlottesville: University Press of Virginia, 1975.

Pickard, Kate. *The Kidnapped and the Ransomed. Being the Personal Recollections of Peter Still and his Wife "Vina," After Forty Years of Slavery*. Syracuse, NY: William T. Hamilton, 1856.

Potter, Eliza, and Xiomara Santamarina. *A Hairdresser's Experience in High Life*. Chapel Hill: University of North Carolina Press, 2009.

Prentiss, Benjamin F. *The Blind African Slave, or Memoirs of Boyrereau Brinch, Nick-Named Jeffrey Brace*. St. Albans, VT: Harry Whitney, 1810.

Randolph, Peter. *From Slave Cabin to the Pulpit; the Autobiography of Rev. Peter Randolph: The Southern Question Illustrated and Sketches of Slave Life*. Boston: James H. Earle, 1893.

Rawick, George P., ed. *The American Slave: A Composite Autobiography: Supplement, Series 1*. Vols. 1–12. Westport, CT: Greenwood, 1977. https://publisher.abc-clio.com/~bookindex?indexLetter=All.

———, ed. *The American Slave: A Composite Autobiography: Supplement, Series 2*. Vols. 1–10. Westport, CT: Greenwood, 1979. https://publisher.abc-clio.com/~bookindex?indexLetter=All.

Ray, Emma J., and Lloyd. P. Ray. *Twice Sold, Twice Ransomed Autobiography of Mr. and Mrs. L. P. Ray*. Chicago: Free Methodist, 1926.

Redkey, Edwin S., ed. *A Grand Army of Black Men: Letters from African-American Soldiers in the Union Army, 1861–1865*. Cambridge: Cambridge University Press, 1992.

Redpath, James. *The Roving Editor or Talks with Slaves in Southern States*. New York: Burdick, 1859.

Robinson, William H. *From Log Cabin to the Pulpit, or, Fifteen Years in Slavery*. Eau Clair, WI: James H. Tifft, 1913.

Roper, Moses. *A Narrative of the Adventures and Escape of Moses Roper, from American Slavery*. Berwick-upon-Tweed, UK: Printed for the Author, 1848.

Rosengarten, Theodore, ed. *All God's Dangers: The Life of Nate Shaw*. Chicago: University of Chicago Press, 1974.

Rudd, Daniel A., and Theodore Bond. *From Slavery to Wealth: The Life of Scott Bond. The Rewards of Honesty, Industry, Economy and Perseverance*. Madison, AR: Journal Printing, 1917.

Scott, Robert N., H. M. Lazelle, George B. Davis, Leslie J. Perry, Joseph W. Kirkley, Fred C. Ainsworth, John S. Moodey, and Calvin D. Cowles. *The War of the Rebellion: A Compilation of the Official Records of the Union and Confederate Armies*. Washington, DC: Government Printing Office, 1880.

Simmons, William J. *Men of Mark: Eminent, Progressive and Rising*. Cleveland: Geo. M. Rewell, 1887.

Simpson, John Hawkins. *Horrors of the Virginian Slave Trade and of the Slave-Rearing Plantations. The True Story of Dinah, an Escaped Virginian Slave, Now in London, on Whose Body Are Eleven*

Scars Left by Tortures Which Were Inflicted by Her Master, Her Own Father. London: A. W. Bennett, 1863.

Singleton, William Henry. *Recollections of My Slavery Days*. Peekskill, NY: Highland Democrat, 1922.

A Sketch of Henry Franklin and Family. Philadelphia: Collins, 1887.

Smallwood, Thomas. *A Narrative of Thomas Smallwood (Coloured Man): Giving an Account of His Birth—The Period He Was Held in Slavery—His Release—and Removal to Canada, etc. Together with an Account of the Underground Railroad. Written by Himself*. Toronto: Printed for the Author by James Stephens, 1851.

Smith, Amanda. *An Autobiography: The Story of the Lord's Dealings with Mrs. Amanda Smith the Colored Evangelist: Containing an Account of Her Life Work of Faith, and Her Travels in America, England, Ireland, Scotland, India, and Africa, as an Independent Missionary*. Chicago: Meyer and Brother, 1893.

Smith, Harry. *Fifty Years of Slavery in the United States of America*. Grand Rapids, MI: West Michigan, 1891.

Smith, James L. *Autobiography of James L. Smith, Including, Also, Reminiscences of Slave Life, Recollections of the War, Education of Freedmen, Causes of the Exodus, etc.* Norwich, CT: Press of the Bulletin, 1881.

Starobin, Robert S. *Blacks in Bondage: Letters of American Slaves*. New York: New Viewpoints, 1974.

Sterling, Dorothy, ed. *Speak Out in Thunder Tones. Letters and Other Writings by Black Northerners, 1787-1865*. New York: Da Capo, 1998.

Stevens, Charles Emery. *Anthony Burns: A History*. Boston: John P. Jewett, 1856.

Steward, Austin. *Twenty-Two Years a Slave and Forty Years a Freeman; Embracing a Correspondence of Several Years, While President of Wilberforce Colony, London, Canada West*. Rochester, NY: William Alling, 1857.

Still, William. *The Underground Railroad*. New York: Arno, 1968.

Stroyer, Jacob. *My Life in the South. New and Enlarged Edition*. Salem, MA: Observer, 1885.

Suggs, Eliza. *Shadow and Sunshine*. Omaha, NE: s.n., 1906.

Swint, Henry Lee, Lucy Chase, and Sarah Chase. *Dear Ones at Home; Letters from Contraband Camps*. Nashville: Vanderbilt University Press, 1966.

Terrell, Mary Eliza Church. *A Colored Woman in a White World*. Washington, DC: Ransdell, 1940.

Thompson, Charles. *Biography of a Slave; Being the Experiences of Rev. Charles Thompson, a Preacher of the United Brethren Church, While a Slave in the South. Together with Startling Occurrences Incidental to Slave Life*. Dayton, OH: United Brethren, 1875.

Thompson, John. *The Life of John Thompson, a Fugitive Slave; Containing His History of 25 Years in Bondage, and His Providential Escape. Written by Himself*. Worcester, MA: John Thompson, 1856.

Towne, Laura. *Letters and Diaries of Laura M. Towne, Written from the Sea Islands of South Carolina, 1862-1884*. Edited by Rupert Sargent Holland. Cambridge, MA: Riverside, 1912.

Troy, William. *Hair-Breadth Escapes from Slavery to Freedom*. Manchester, UK: W. Bremner, 1861.

Twelvetrees, Harper, ed. *The Story of the Life of John Anderson, the Fugitive Slave*. London: William Tweedie, 1863.

Unwritten History of Slavery. Fisk University, Social Science Institute. In *The American Slave* Vol. 18. Westport, CT: Greenwood, 1972.

Ward, Samuel Ringgold. *Autobiography of a Fugitive Negro: His Anti-slavery Labours in the United States, Canada, & England*. London: John Snow, 1855.

Washington, Booker T. *An Autobiography: The Story of My Life and Work, Introduction by Dr. J. L. M. Curry*. Atlanta: J. L. Nichols, 1901.

———. *Up from Slavery: An Autobiography*. Garden City, NY: Doubleday, 1901.

Watkins, James. *Narrative of the Life of James Watkins, Formerly a "Chattel" in Maryland, U.S.; Containing an Account of His Escape from Slavery, Together with an Appeal on Behalf of Three Millions of Such "Pieces of Property," Still Held under the Standard of the Eagle*. Bolton, UK: Kenyon and Abbatt, 1852.

Watson, Henry. *Narrative of Henry Watson, a Fugitive Slave*. Boston: Bela Marsh, 1848.

Webb, William. *The History of William Webb, Composed by Himself*. Detroit: Egbert Hoekstra, 1873.

Wickham, Elizabeth Merwin. *A Lost Family Found; an Authentic Narrative of Cyrus Branch and His Family, Alias John White*. Manchester, VT: s.n., 1869.

Secondary Sources

Agresti, Barbara Finlay. "Household Composition, the Family Cycle, and Economic Hardship in a Postbellum Southern County: Walton County, Florida, 1870–1885." *International Journal of Sociology of the Family* 9, no. 2 (July–December 1979): 245–258.

Andrews, William L. "Reunion in the Postbellum Slave Narrative: Frederick Douglass and Elizabeth Keckley." *Black American Literature Forum* 23, no. 1 (Spring 1989): 5–16.

Arditti, Joyce A., Mathis Kennington, Joseph G. Grzywacz, Anna Jaramillo, Scott Isom, Sara A. Quandt, and Thomas A. Arcury. "Fathers in the Fields: Father Involvement among Latino Migrant Farmworkers." *Journal of Comparative Family Studies* 45, no. 4 (2014): 537–557. http://www.jstor.org/stable/24339640.

Aslakson, Kenneth R. *Making Race in the Courtroom: The Legal Construction of Three Races in Early New Orleans*. New York: New York University Press, 2014.

Bancroft, Frederic. *Slave Trading in the Old South*. New York: Ungar, 1959.

Baptist, Edward E. "The Absent Subject: African American Masculinity and Forced Migration to the Antebellum Plantation Frontier." In Friend and Glover, *Southern Manhood: Perspectives on Masculinity in the Old South*, 136–173.

———. "'Cuffy,' 'Fancy Maids,' and 'One-Eyed Men': Rape, Commodification, and the Domestic Slave Trade in the United States." *American Historical Review* 106, no. 5 (December 2001): 1619–1650.

Bay, Mia. *The White Image in the Black Mind: African-American Ideas About White People, 1830–1925*. New York: Oxford University Press, 2000.

Becker, William H. "The Black Church: Manhood and Mission." In Hine and Jenkins, *A Question of Manhood*, 322–339.

Berry, Daina Raimey. *"Swing the Sickle for the Harvest is Ripe": Gender and Slavery in Antebellum Georgia*. Urbana: University of Illinois Press, 2007.

Bertaux, Nancy. "Structural Economic Change and Occupational Decline among Black Workers in Nineteenth-Century Cincinnati." In Taylor, *Race and the City*, 127–155.

Black, Daniel P. *Dismantling Black Manhood: An Historical and Literary Analysis of the Legacy of Slavery*. New York: Garland, 1997.

Blassingame, John. *The Slave Community: Plantation Life in the Antebellum South*. New York: Oxford University Press, 1979.

———. "Status and Social Structure in the Slave Community: Evidence from New Sources." In *Perspectives and Irony in American Slavery: Essays*, edited by Carl N. Degler and Harry P. Owens, 137–151. Jackson: University Press of Mississippi, 1976.

———. "Using the Testimony of Ex-Slaves: Approaches and Problems." *Journal of Southern History* 41, no. 4 (1975): 473–492. http://www.jstor.org/stable/2205559.

Bleser, Carol K. Rothrock. *In Joy and in Sorrow: Women, Family, and Marriage in the Victorian South, 1830–1900*. New York: Oxford University Press, 1991.

Blum, Edward J. "A Subversive Savior: Manhood and African American Images of Christ in the Early Twentieth-Century South." In *Southern Masculinity: Perspectives on Manhood in the South Since Reconstruction*, edited by Craig Thompson Friend, 150–173. Athens: University of Georgia Press, 2009.

Bonanno, George A. "Resilience in the Face of Potential Trauma." *Current Directions in Psychological Science* 14, no. 3 (June 2005): 135–138.

Bradley, Josephine Boyd, and Kent Anderson Leslie. "White Pain Pollen: An Elite Biracial Daughter's Quandary." In *Sex, Love, Race: Crossing Boundaries in North American History*, edited by Martha Hodes, 213–234. New York: New York University Press, 1999.

Brown, Kathleen M. *Good Wives, Nasty Wenches, and Anxious Patriarchs: Gender, Race, and Power in Colonial Virginia*. Chapel Hill: University of North Carolina Press, 1996.

Burton, Orville Vernon. *In My Father's House Are Many Mansions: Family and Community in Edgefield, South Carolina*. Chapel Hill: University of North Carolina Press, 1985.

Camp, Stephanie M. H. *Closer to Freedom: Enslaved Women and Everyday Resistance in the Plantation South*. Chapel Hill: University of North Carolina Press, 2004.

Cashin, Joan E. "Black Families in the Old Northwest." *Journal of the Early Republic* 15, no. 3, Special Issue on Gender in the Early Republic (Autumn 1995): 449–475.

Cheek, William, and Aimee Lee Cheek. "John Mercer Langston and the Cincinnati Riot of 1841." In Taylor, *Race and the City*, 29–69.

Clark, Emily. *The Strange History of the American Quadroon: Free Women of Color in the Revolutionary Atlantic World*. Chapel Hill: University of North Carolina Press, 2013.

Clinton, Catherine. *The Plantation Mistress: Woman's World in the Old South*. New York: Pantheon Books, 1982.

———. "'Southern Dishonor': Flesh, Blood, Race, and Bondage." In Bleser, *In Joy and in Sorrow*, 52–68.

Coates, Ta-Nehisi. "Letter to My Son." *The Atlantic*, July 4, 2015. https://www.theatlantic.com/politics/archive/2015/07/tanehisi-coates-between-the-world-and-me/397619/.

———. "We Should Have Seen Trump Coming." *The Guardian*, September 29, 2017. https://www.theguardian.com/news/2017/sep/29/we-should-have-seen-trump-coming.

Cody, Cheryll Ann. "Cycles of Work and Childbearing: Seasonality in Women's Lives on Low Country Plantations." In Gaspar and Hine, *More Than Chattel*, 61–78.

Coltrane, Scott, Ross D. Parke, and Michele Adams. "Complexity of Father Involvement in Low-Income Mexican American Families." *Family Relations* 53, no. 2 (2004): 179–189. http://www.jstor.org/stable/3700261.

Cone, James H. *God of the Oppressed*. New York: Seabury, 1975.

Crawford, Stephen. "Quantified Memory: A Study of the WPA and Fisk University Slave Narrative Collections." PhD diss., University of Chicago, 1980.

Cullen, Jim. "'I's a Man Now': Gender and African American Men." In *Divided Houses: Gender and the Civil War*, edited by Catherine Clinton and Nina Silber, 76–91. Oxford: Oxford University Press, 1992.

Currie, James T. "From Slavery to Freedom in Mississippi's Legal System." *Journal of Negro History* 65, no. 2 (Spring 1980): 112–125.

Davis, Angela Y. "Reflections on the Black Woman's Role in the Community of Slaves." *The Black Scholar* (December 1971): 1–14.

———. *Women, Race & Class*. New York: Vintage Books, 1983.

De Benedictis, Tina, Jaelline Jaffe, and Jeanne Segal. "Domestic Violence and Abuse: Types, Signs, Symptoms, Causes, and Effects." American Academy of Experts in Traumatic Stress, 2006. http://www.aaets.org/article144.htm.

Dew, Charles B. "Disciplining Slave Ironworkers in the Antebellum South; Coercion, Conciliation and Accommodation." In Hine and Jenkins, *A Question of Manhood*, 205–226.

Deyle, Steven. *Carry Me Back: The Domestic Slave Trade in American Life*. New York: Oxford University Press, 2005. http://site.ebrary.com/id/10103588.

Doddington, David S. *Contesting Slave Masculinity in the American South*. Cambridge: Cambridge University Press, 2018.

Doherty, William J., Edward F. Kouneski, and Martha F. Erickson. "Responsible Fathering: An Overview and Conceptual Framework." *Journal of Marriage and Family* 60, no. 2 (1998): 277–292. doi:10.2307/353848.

Du Bois, W. E. B. *Black Reconstruction in America: An Essay toward a History of the Part Which Black Folk Played in the Attempt to Reconstruct Democracy in America, 1860-1880*. New York: Oxford University Press, 2007.

———, ed. *The Negro American Family*. The Atlanta University Publications, no. 13. Atlanta: Atlanta University Press, 1908.

Dunaway, Wilma. *The African-American Family in Slavery and Emancipation*. Cambridge: Cambridge University Press, 2003.

Durrill, Wayne K. "Slavery, Kinship, and Dominance: The Black Community at Somerset Place Plantation, 1786–1860." *Slavery & Abolition* 13, no. 2 (1992): 1–19.

Dusinberre, William. *Them Dark Days: Slavery in the American Rice Swamps*. Oxford: Oxford University Press, 1996.

Duxbury, S. W., L. C. Frizzell, and S. L. Lindsay. "Mental Illness, the Media, and the Moral Politics of Mass Violence: The Role of Race in Mass Shootings Coverage." *Journal of Research in Crime and Delinquency* 55, no. 6 (2018): 766–797. https://doi.org/10.1177/0022427818787225.

Eberhardt, Jennifer L., P. A. Goff, V. J. Purdie, and P. G. Davies. "Seeing Black: Race, Crime, and Visual Processing." *Journal of Personality and Social Psychology* 87, no. 6 (2004): 876–893. doi:10.1037/0022-3514.87.6.876.

Edin, Kathryn, and Timothy Jon Nelson. *Doing the Best I Can: Fatherhood in the Inner City*. Berkeley: University of California Press, 2013.

Elkins, Stanley. *Slavery: A Problem in American Institutional and Intellectual Life*. Chicago: University of Chicago Press, 1968.

Escott, Paul D. *Slavery Remembered: A Record of Twentieth-Century Slave Narratives*. Chapel Hill: The University of North Carolina Press, 1979.

Farmer, Paul. "An Anthropology of Structural Violence." *Current Anthropology* 45, no. 3 (June 2004): 305–325.

Farmer-Kaiser, Mary J. *Freedwomen and the Freedmen's Bureau: Race, Gender, and Public Policy in the Age of Emancipation*. New York: Fordham University Press, 2010.

Farnham, Christie. "Sapphire? The Issue of Dominance in the Slave Family, 1830–1865." In *"To Toil the Livelong Day": America's Women at Work, 1780–1980*, edited by Carol Groneman and Mary Beth Norton, 68–83. Ithaca, NY: Cornell University Press, 1987.

Fleischner, Jennifer. *Mastering Slavery: Memory, Family, and Identity in Women's Slave Narratives*. New York: New York University Press, 1996.

Fogel, Robert William. *Without Consent or Contract: The Rise and Fall of American Slavery*. New York: Norton, 1989.

Fogel, Robert William, and Stanley L. Engerman. *Time on the Cross*. Boston: Little, Brown, 1974.

Foner, Eric. *Nothing but Freedom: Emancipation and Its Legacy*. Baton Rouge: Louisiana State University Press, 1984.

Forret, Jeff. *Slave against Slave: Plantation Violence in the Old South*. Baton Rouge: Louisiana State University Press, 2015.

Forsyth, Craig J., and Robert Gramling. "Socio-Economic Factors Affecting the Rise of Commuter Marriage." *International Journal of Sociology of the Family* 28, no. 2 (1998): 93–106. http://www.jstor.org/stable/23070667.

Foster, Thomas. "Sexual Abuse of Black Men under American Slavery." *Journal of the History of Sexuality* 20, no. 3 (2011): 445–464.

Fox-Genovese, Elizabeth. *Within the Plantation Household: Black and White Women of the Old South*. Chapel Hill: University of North Carolina Press, 1988.

Franke, Katherine. *Wedlocked: The Perils of Marriage Equality: How African Americans and Gays Mistakenly Thought the Right to Marry Would Set Them Free*. New York: New York University Press, 2015.

Franklin, H. Bruce. *Prison Literature in America: The Victim as Criminal and Artist*. New York: Oxford University Press, 1989.

Franklin, John Hope, and Loren Schweninger. *Runaway Slaves: Rebels on the Plantation*. New York: Oxford University Press, 1999.

Fraser, Rebecca J. *Courtship and Love among the Enslaved in North Carolina*. Jackson: University Press of Mississippi, 2007.

———. "Negotiating Their Manhood: Masculinity amongst the Enslaved in the Upper South, 1830–1861." In *Black and White Masculinity in the American South, 1800–2000*, edited by Lydia Plath and Sergio Lussana, 76–94. Newcastle-upon-Tyne, UK: Cambridge Scholars, 2009.

Frazier, E. Franklin. *The Negro Family in the United States*. Chicago: University of Chicago Press, 1939.

———. "The Negro Slave Family." *Journal of Negro History* 15 (1930): 198–259.

Friend, Craig Thompson. "From Southern Manhood to Southern Masculinities: An Introduction." In *Southern Masculinity: Perspectives on Manhood in the South Since Reconstruction*. Athens: University of Georgia Press, 2009.

Friend, Craig Thompson, and Lorri Glover, eds. *Southern Manhood: Perspectives on Masculinity in the Old South*. Athens: University of Georgia Press, 2004.

Gaspar, David Barry, and Darlene Clark Hine, eds. *More Than Chattel: Black Women and Slavery in the Americas*. Bloomington: Indiana University Press, 1996.

Geary, Daniel. *Beyond Civil Rights: The Moynihan Report and Its Legacy*. Philadelphia: University of Pennsylvania Press, 2015.

Geggus, David P. "Slave and Free Colored Women in Saint Domingue." In Gaspar and Hine, *More Than Chattel*, 259–278.

Genovese, Eugene. *In Red & Black: Marxian Explorations in Southern and Afro-American History*. New York: Vintage Books, 1972.

———. *Roll Jordan Roll: The World the Slaves Made*. New York: Vintage Books, 1976.

Glymph, Thavolia. *Out of the House of Bondage: The Transformation of the Plantation Household*. Cambridge: Cambridge University Press, 2008.

Gomez, Michael A. *Exchanging Our Country Marks: The Transformation of African Identities in the Colonial and Antebellum South*. Chapel Hill: University of North Carolina Press, 1998.

Gordon-Reed, Annette. *The Hemingses of Monticello: An American Family*. London: W. W. Norton, 2008.

———. *Thomas Jefferson and Sally Hemings: An American Controversy*. Charlottesville, VA: University Press of Virginia, 1997.

Gould, L. Virginia. "Urban Slavery—Urban Freedom: The Manumission of Jacqueline Lemelle." In Gaspar and Hine, *More Than Chattel*, 298–314.

Gray, Peter B., and Kermyt G. Anderson. *Fatherhood: Evolution and Human Paternal Behavior*. Cambridge, MA: Harvard University Press, 2010.

Green, Sharony Andrews. *Remember Me to Miss Louisa: Hidden Black-White Intimacies in Antebellum America*. Dekalb: Northern Illinois University Press, 2015.

Greenbaum, Susan D. *Blaming the Poor: The Long Shadow of the Moynihan Report on Cruel Images About Poverty*. New Brunswick, NJ: Rutgers University Press, 2015.

Griffin, Rebecca. "Contest and Competition in the Folklore of Slaves." *Journal of Southern History* 71 (2005): 769–802.

Gross, Ariela Julie. *Double Character: Slavery and Mastery in the Antebellum Southern Courtroom*. Princeton, NJ: Princeton University Press, 2000.

———. *What Blood Won't Tell: A History of Race on Trial in America*. Cambridge, MA: Harvard University Press, 2008.

Gutman, Herbert. *The Black Family in Slavery and Freedom, 1750–1925*. New York: Pantheon Books, 1976.

Guyer, Jane I. "Household and Community in African Studies." *African Studies Review* 24, no. 2/3 (June–September 1981): 87–137.

Hadden, Sally E. *Slave Patrols: Law and Violence in Virginia and the Carolinas*. Cambridge, MA: Harvard University Press, 2001.

Hamer, Jennifer. *What It Means to Be Daddy: Fatherhood for Black Men Living Away from Their Children*. New York: Columbia University Press, 2001.

Hammel, E. A., and Kenneth W. Wachter. "Primonuptiality and Ultimonuptiality: Their Effects on Stem-Family-Household Frequencies." In *Population Patterns in the Past*, edited by Ronald Demos Lee, 113–134. New York: Academic Press, 1977.

Hilliard, Kathleen M. *Masters, Slaves, and Exchange: Power's Purchase in the Old South*. New York: Cambridge University Press, 2014.

Hine, Darlene Clark. "Lifting the Veil, Shattering the Silence: Black Women's History in Slavery and Freedom." In *The State of Afro-American History: Past, Present, and Future*. Baton Rouge: Louisiana State University Press, 1986.

———. "Rape and the Inner Lives of Black Women in the Middle West." *Signs* 14, no. 4 (Summer 1989): 912–920.

Hine, Darlene Clark, and Earnestine Jenkins. *A Question of Manhood: A Reader in U.S. Black Men's History and Masculinity*. Vol. 1. Bloomington: Indiana University Press, 2001.

Hodes, Martha. *White Women, Black Men: Illicit Sex in the Nineteenth-Century South*. New Haven, CT: Yale University Press, 1997.

hooks, bell. *Ain't I a Woman: Black Women and Feminism*. Boston: South End Press, 1981.

———. *Black Looks*. Boston: South End, 1992.

Horton, James Oliver, and Stacy Flaherty. "Black Leadership in Antebellum Cincinnati." In Taylor, *Race and the City*, 70–95.

Hrdy, Sarah Blaffer. *Mother Nature: A History of Mothers, Infants, and Natural Selection*. New York: Pantheon, 1999.

Hudson, Larry E., Jr. "'All That Cash': Work and Status in the Slave Quarters." In *Working toward Freedom: Slave Society and Domestic Economy in the American South*, 77–94. Rochester, NY: University of Rochester Press, 1994.

———. *To Have and to Hold: Slave Work and Family Life in Antebellum South Carolina*. London: University of Georgia Press, 1997.

Jackson, Lawrence Patrick. *My Father's Name: A Black Virginia Family After the Civil War*. Chicago: The University of Chicago Press, 2012.

Jennings, Thelma. "'Us Colored Women Had to Go though a Plenty': Sexual Exploitation of African-American Slave Women." *Journal of Women's History* 1, no. 3 (Winter 1990): 45–74.

Johnson, Michael, and James Roark. "Strategies of Survival: Free Negro Families and the Problem of Slavery." In Bleser, *In Joy and in Sorrow*, 88–102.

Johnson, Walter. "On Agency." *Journal of Social History* 37, no. 1 (2003): 113–124. http://www .jstor.org/stable/3790316.

———. *Soul by Soul: Life Inside the Antebellum Slave Market*. Cambridge, MA: Harvard University Press, 1999.

Jones, Bernie D. *Fathers of Conscience: Mixed-Race Inheritance in the Antebellum South*. Athens: University of Georgia Press, 2009. http://public.eblib.com/choice/publicfullrecord.aspx?p =3038991.

Jones, Catherine A. *Intimate Reconstructions: Children in Postemancipation Virginia*. Charlottesville: University of Virginia Press, 2015.

Jones, Jacqueline. *Labor of Love, Labor of Sorrow: Black Women, Work and the Family, from Slavery to the Present*. New York: Vintage, 1995, first pub. 1985.

———. "'My Mother Was Much of a Woman': Black Women, Work, and the Family under Slavery." *Feminist Studies* 8, no. 2 (Summer 1982): 235–269.

———. "The Political Economy of Sharecropping Families: Blacks and Poor Whites in the Rural South, 1865–1915." In Bleser, *In Joy and in Sorrow*, 196–214.

Jones, Jo, and William D. Mosher. "Fathers' Involvement with Their Children: United States, 2006–2010, National Vital Statistics Report." Centers for Disease Control, 2013.

Joyner, Charles. *Down by the Riverside: A South Carolina Slave Community*. Chicago: University of Illinois Press, 1984.

Katzman, David M. *Before the Ghetto: Black Detroit in the Nineteenth Century*. Urbana: University of Illinois Press, 1973.

Kaye, Anthony E. "Neighbourhoods and Solidarity in the Natchez District of Mississippi: Rethinking the Antebellum Slave Community." *Slavery & Abolition* 23 (April 2002): 1–24.

Kimmel, Michael S. *Manhood in America: A Cultural History*. New York: Oxford University Press, 2012.

King, Wilma. *Stolen Childhood: Slave Youth in Nineteenth-Century America*. Bloomington: Indiana University Press, 1997.

———. "'Suffer with Them Till Death': Slave Women and Their Children in Nineteenth-Century America." In Gaspar and Hine, *More Than Chattel*, 147–168.

Kiple, Kenneth F., and Virginia H. Kiple. "Slave Child Mortality: Some Nutritional Answers to a Perennial Puzzle." *Journal of Social History* 10 (Spring 1977): 284–309.

Koger, Larry. *Black Slaveowners: Free Black Slave Masters in South Carolina, 1790-1860*. London: McFarland, 1985.

Kolchin, Peter. *American Slavery, 1619-1877*. New York: Hill and Wang, 1993.

———. "Reevaluating the Antebellum Slave Community: A Comparative Perspective." *Journal of American History* 70, no. 3 (1983): 579–601. https://www.jstor.org/stable/1903484.

Krech, Shepard, III. "Black Family Organization in the Nineteenth Century: An Ethnographic Perspective." *Journal of Interdisciplinary History* 12 (Winter 1982): 429–452.

Lamb, Michael E. "The History of Research on Father Involvement: An Overview." *Marriage & Family Review* 29, no. 2–3 (2000): 23–42.

Lebsock, Suzanne. *The Free Women of Petersburg: Status and Culture in a Southern Town, 1784-1860*. New York: Norton, 1984.

Lempert, Lora Bex. "Other Fathers: An Alternative Perspective on African American Community Caring." In *The Black Family: Essays and Studies*, edited by Robert Staples, 189–199. New York: Wadsworth, 1999.

Levine, Lawrence W. *Black Culture and Black Consciousness: Afro-American Folk Thought from Slavery to Freedom*. Oxford: Oxford University Press, 1977.

Lichtenstein, Alex. "'That Disposition to Theft, with Which They Have Been Branded': Moral Economy, Slave Management, and the Law." *Journal of Social History* 21, no. 3 (Spring 1988): 413–440.

Litwack, Leon F. *North of Slavery: The Negro in the Free States, 1790-1860*. Chicago: University of Chicago Press, 1961.

Love, Edgar F. "Registration of Free Blacks in Ohio: The Slaves of George C. Mendenhall." *Journal of Negro History* 69, no. 1 (Winter 1984): 38–47.

Lovejoy, Paul E. *Transformations in Slavery: A History of Slavery in Africa*. Second Edition. Cambridge: Cambridge University Press, 2000, first pub. 1983.

Lussana, Sergio. *My Brother Slaves: Friendship, Masculinity, and Resistance in the Antebellum South*. 2016. http://public.eblib.com/choice/publicfullrecord.aspx?p=4458128.

Malone, Ann Patton. *Sweet Chariot: Slave Family and Household Structure in Nineteenth-Century Louisiana*. Chapel Hill: University of North Carolina Press, 1992.

Manfra, JoAnn, and Robert Dykstra. "Serial Marriage and the Origins of the Black Stepfamily: The Rowanty Evidence." *Journal of American History* 72, no. 1 (June 1985): 18–44.

Marks, Bayly. "Skilled Blacks in Antebellum St. Mary's County, Maryland." In Hine and Jenkins, *A Question of Manhood*, 227–251.

Marsiglio William, Kevin Roy, and Greer Litton Fox, eds. *Situated Fathering: A Focus on Physical and Social Spaces*. Lanham, MD: Rowman and Littlefield, 2005.

Martin, Jonathan D. *Divided Mastery: Slave Hiring in the American South*. Cambridge, MA: Harvard University Press, 2004.

Martin, Waldo E. *The Mind of Frederick Douglass*. Chapel Hill: University of North Carolina Press, 1984. http://site.ebrary.com/id/10202599.

Mattison, S. M., B. Scelza, and T. Blumenfield. "Paternal Investment and the Positive Effects of Fathers among the Matrilineal Mosuo of Southwest China." *American Anthropologist* 116, no. 3 (2014): 591–610.

McCurry, Stephanie. *Masters of Small Worlds: Yeoman Households, Gender Relations, and the Political Culture of the Antebellum South Carolina Low Country*. New York: Oxford University Press, 1995.

———. "War, Gender, and Emancipation in the Civil War South." In *Lincoln's Proclamation: Emancipation Reconsidered*, edited by William A. Blair and Karen Fisher, 120–150. Chapel Hill: University of North Carolina Press, 2009.

McDonnell, Lawrence T. "Money Knows No Master: Market Relations and the American Slave Community." In *Developing Dixie Modernization in a Traditional Society*, edited by Winfred B. Moore Jr., Joseph F. Tripp, and Lyon G. Tyler Jr., 31–44. New York: Greenwood, 1988.

McLaurin, Melton Alonza. *Celia, a Slave*. Athens: University of Georgia Press, 1991.

Merrit, Carol Elaine. "Slave Family and Household Arrangements in Piedmont Georgia." PhD diss., Emory University, 1986.

Meyer, Leland. *The Life and Times of Colonel Richard M. Johnson of Kentucky*. New York: Columbia University Press, 1932.

Mitchell, Mary Niall. "'Free Ourselves but Deprived of Our Children': Freedchildren and Their Labor after the Civil War." In *Children and Youth during the Civil War Era*, edited by James Alan Marten, 160–172. New York: New York University Press, 2012.

Morgan, Jennifer L. "Partus Sequitur Ventrem: Law, Race, and Reproduction in Colonial Slavery." *Small Axe* 22, no. 1 (2018): 1–17. muse.jhu.edu/article/689365.

Morris, Christopher. "Within the Slave Cabin: Violence in Mississippi Slave Families." In *Over the Threshold: Intimate Violence in Early America*, edited by Christine Daniels and Michael V. Kennedy, 268–285. New York: Routledge, 1999.

Moynihan, Daniel Patrick. *The Negro Family: The Case for National Action*. U.S. Government Printing Office, 1965.

Musher, Sharon. "Contesting 'The Way the Almighty Wants It': Crafting Memories of Ex-Slaves in the Slave Narrative Collection." *American Quarterly* 53, no. 1 (March 2001): 1–31.

Nelson, Dana D. *National Manhood: Capitalist Citizenship, Gender Relations, and the Imagined Fraternity of White Men*. Durham, NC: Duke University Press, 1998.

Nelson, Scott Reynolds. *Steel Drivin' Man: John Henry, the Untold Story of an American Legend*. Oxford: Oxford University Press, 2006.

Olwell, Robert. "'Loose, Idle and Disorderly': Slave Women and the Eighteenth-Century Charleston Marketplace." In Gaspar and Hine, *More Than Chattel*, 97–110.

Owens, Leslie. *This Species of Property: Slave Life and Culture in the Old South*. Oxford: Oxford University Press, 1976.

Painter, Nell Irvin. "The Journal of Ella Gertrude Clanton Thomas: An Educated White Woman in the Eras of Slavery, War, and Reconstruction." Introduction to *The Secret Eye: The Journal of Ella Gertrude Clanton Thomas, 1848–1889*, edited by Virginia Ingraham Burr. Chapel Hill: University of North Carolina Press, 1990.

———. *Soul Murder and Slavery*. The Fifteenth Charles Edmondson Historical Lectures. Waco, TX: Baylor University Press, 1995.

Pargas, Damian A. *The Quarters and the Fields: Slave Families in the Non-Cotton South*. Gainesville: University Press of Florida, 2010.

Pascoe, Peggy. *What Comes Naturally: Miscegenation Law and the Making of Race in America*. Oxford: Oxford University Press, 2009.

Penningroth, Dylan C. *The Claims of Kinfolk: African American Property and Community in the Nineteenth-Century South*. Chapel Hill: University of North Carolina Press, 2003.

Peres, Julio F. P., Alexander Moreira-Almeida, Antonia Gladys Nasello, and Harold G. Koenig. "Spirituality and Resilience in Trauma Victims." *Journal of Religion and Health* 46, no. 3 (September 2007): 343–350.

Proctor, Nicolas W. *Bathed in Blood: Hunting and Mastery in the Old South*. Charlottesville: University Press of Virginia, 2002.

Raboteau, Albert J. *Slave Religion: The "Invisible" Institution in the Antebellum South*, Updated Edition. Oxford: Oxford University Press, 2004, first pub. 1978.

Reuschke, Darja. "Living Apart Together over Long Distances—Time-Space Patterns and Consequences of a Late-Modern Living Arrangement. *Erdkunde* 64.3 (2010): 215–226. http://www.jstor.org/stable/29764827.

Richardson, Riché. *Black Masculinity and the U.S. South: From Uncle Tom to Gangsta*. Athens: University of Georgia Press, 2007.

Robertson, Claire. "'Africa into the Americas?' Slavery and Women, the Family, and the Gender Division of Labor." In Gaspar and Hine, *More Than Chattel*, 3–40.

Rockman, Seth. *Scraping By: Wage Labor, Slavery, and Survival in Early Baltimore*. Baltimore: Johns Hopkins University Press, 2009.

Rodrigue, John C. *Reconstruction in the Cane Fields: From Slavery to Free Labor in Louisiana's Sugar Parishes, 1862–1880*. Baton Rouge: Louisiana State University Press, 2001.

Roediger, David R. *The Wages of Whiteness: Race and the Making of the American Working Class*. London: Verso, 1991.

Rothman, Joshua D. *Notorious in the Neighborhood: Sex and Families across the Color Line in Virginia, 1787–1861*. Chapel Hill: University of North Carolina Press, 2003.

Runstedtler, Theresa. *Jack Johnson, Rebel Sojourner: Boxing in the Shadow of the Global Color Line*. Berkeley: University of California Press, 2012.

Sánchez-Eppler, Karen. "'Remember, Dear, When the Yankees Came through Here, I Was Only 10 Years Old': Valuing the Enslaved Child of the WPA Slave Narratives." In *Child Slavery Before and After Emancipation: An Argument for Child-Centered Slavery Studies*, edited by Anna Mae Duane, 27–49. Cambridge: Cambridge University Press, 2017.

Schermerhorn, Calvin. *Money over Mastery, Family over Freedom: Slavery in the Antebellum Upper South*. Baltimore: The Johns Hopkins University Press, 2011.

Schwartz, Dana. "Why Angry White Men Love Calling People 'Cucks': The Problematic History of the Alt-Right's Favorite New Insult." *GQ*, August 1, 2016. https://www.gq.com/story/why-angry-white-men-love-calling-people-cucks.

Schwartz, Marie Jenkins. *Born in Bondage: Growing Up Enslaved in the Antebellum South*. Cambridge, MA: Harvard University Press, 2000.

Sears, Richard D. *Camp Nelson Kentucky: A Civil War History*. Lexington: University of Kentucky Press, 2002.

Shafer, Judith K. "'Open and Notorious Concubinage': The Emancipation of Slave Mistresses by Will and the Supreme Court in Antebellum Louisiana." *Journal of the Louisiana Historical Association* 28, no. 2 (Spring 1987): 165–182.

Shaw, Stephanie. "Using the WPA Ex-Slave Narratives to Study the Impact of the Great Depression." *Journal of Southern History* 69, no. 3 (August 2003): 623–658.

Shengold, Leonard. *Soul Murder: The Effects of Child Abuse and Deprivation*. New Haven, CT: Yale University Press, 1989.

Sommerville, Diane. *Rape and Race in the Nineteenth-Century South*. Chapel Hill: University of North Carolina Press, 2004.

———. "Rape, Race, and Castration in Slave Law in the Colonial and Early South." In *The Devil's Lane: Sex and Race in the Early South*, edited by Catherine Clinton and Michele Gillespie, 74–89. Oxford: Oxford University Press, 1997.

Spillers, Hortense. "Mama's Baby, Papa's Maybe: An American Grammar Book." *Diacritics* (Summer 1987): 64–81.

Spindel, Donna J. "Assessing Memory: Twentieth-Century Slave Narratives Reconsidered." *Journal of Interdisciplinary History* 27, no. 2 (Autumn 1996): 247–261.

Stack, Carol B. *All Our Kin: Strategies for Survival in a Black Community*. New York: Harper and Row, 1974.

Stampp, Kenneth M. *The Peculiar Institution: Slavery in the Ante-Bellum South*. New York: Vintage, 1989, first pub. 1956.

Stanley, Amy Dru. *From Bondage to Contract: Wage Labor, Marriage, and the Market in the Age of Slave Emancipation*. Cambridge: Cambridge University Press, 1998.

———. "Instead of Waiting for the Thirteenth Amendment: The War Power, Slave Marriage, and Inviolate Human Rights." *American Historical Review* (June 2010): 732–765.

Steckel, Richard. "A Peculiar Population: The Nutrition, Health, and Mortality of American Slaves from Childhood to Maturity." *Journal of Economic History* 46, no. 3 (September 1986): 721–741.

————."Women, Work, and Health Under Plantation Slavery in the United States." In Gaspar and Hine, *More Than Chattel*, 43–60.

Stevenson, Brenda E. "Distress and Discord in Virginia Slave Families, 1830–1860." In Bleser, *In Joy and in Sorrow*, 103–124.

————. "Gender Convention, Ideals, and Identity among Antebellum Virginia Slave Women." In Gaspar and Hine, *More Than Chattel*, 169–190.

————. *Life in Black and White: Family and Community in the Slave South*. New York: Oxford University Press, 1996.

Stewart, Catherine A. *Long Past Slavery: Representing Race in the Federal Writers' Project*. Chapel Hill: University of North Carolina Press, 2016.

Summers, Martin. *Manliness and Its Discontents: The Black Middle Class and the Transformation of Masculinity, 1900–1930*. Chapel Hill: University of North Carolina Press, 2004.

Sutch, Richard. "The Breeding of Slaves for Sale and the Westward Expansion of Slavery, 1850–1860." In *Race and Slavery in the Western Hemisphere: Quantitative Studies*, edited by Stanley L. Engerman and Eugene Genovese, 173–210. Princeton, NJ: Princeton University Press, 1975.

Tadman, Michael. *Speculators and Slaves: Masters, Traders, and Slaves in the Old South*. Madison: University of Wisconsin Press, 1989.

Taylor, Henry Louis, ed. *Race and the City: Work, Community, and Protest in Cincinnati, 1820–1970*. Urbana: University of Illinois Press, 1993.

Taylor, Henry Louis, and Vicky Dula. "The Black Residential Experience and Community Formation in Antebellum Cincinnati." In Taylor, *Race and the City*, 96–125.

Townsend, Nicholas. "Men, Migration, and Households in Botswana: An Exploration of Connections over Time and Space." *Journal of Southern African Studies* 23, no. 3 (September 1997): 405–420.

Tucker, Linda G. *Lockstep and Dance: Images of Black Men in Popular Culture*. Jackson: University Press of Mississippi, 2007.

Wallace, Michele. *Black Macho and the Myth of the Super-Woman*. New York: Verso, 1990, first pub. 1978.

Weiner, Marli Frances. *Mistresses and Slaves: Plantation Women in South Carolina, 1830–1880*. Urbana: University of Illinois Press, 1997.

West, Emily. *Chains of Love: Slave Couples in Antebellum South Carolina*. Chicago: University of Illinois Press, 2004.

————. "The Debate on the Strength of Slave Families: South Carolina and the Importance of Cross-Plantation Marriages." *Journal of American Studies* 33, no. 2 (August 1999): 221–241.

————. *Family or Freedom: People of Color in the Antebellum South*. Lexington: University Press of Kentucky, 2012.

White, Deborah Gray. *Ar'n't I a Woman? Female Slaves in the Plantation South*. New York: W. W. Norton, 1985.

Whitman, T. Stephen. *The Price of Freedom: Slavery and Manumission in Baltimore and Early National Maryland*. Lexington: University Press of Kentucky, 1997. http://public.eblib.com /choice/publicfullrecord.aspx?p=1915670.

Williams, Heather Andrea. *Help Me to Find My People: The African American Search for Family Lost in Slavery*. Chapel Hill: University of North Carolina Press, 2012.

Williamson, Joel. *New People: Miscegenation and Mulattoes in the United States*. New York: The Free Press, 1980.

Wood, Betty. *Women's Work, Men's Work: The Informal Slave Economies of Lowcountry Georgia*. Athens: University of Georgia Press, 1995.

Wood, G., N. Hilti, C. Kramer, and M. Schier. "A Residential Perspective on Multi-Locality: Editorial." *Tijdschr Econ Soc Geogr* 106 (2015): 363–377. doi:10.1111/tesg.12158.

Woodson, Carter G. "Free Negro Owners of Slaves in the United States in 1830." *Journal of Negro History* 9 (January 1924).

Woodward, C. Vann. "History from Slave Sources." *American Historical Review* 79, no. 2 (April 1974): 470–481. https://doi.org/10.1086/ahr/79.2.470.

Wright, Gavin. *Slavery and American Economic Development*. Baton Rouge: Louisiana State University Press, 2006.

Wyatt-Brown, Bertram. "The Mask of Obedience: Male Slave Psychology in the Old South." *American Historical Review* 93, no. 5 (December 1988): 1228–1252.

———. *Southern Honor: Ethics and Behavior in the Old South*. New York: Oxford University Press, 2007, first pub. 1982.

Yarbrough, Fay A. "Power, Perception, and Interracial Sex: Former Slaves Recall a Multiracial South." *Journal of Southern History* 71, no. 3 (2005): 559–588.

Yellin, Jean Fagan. *Harriet Jacobs: A Life*. New York: Basic Civitas Books, 2004.

Yetman, Norman R. "The Background of the Slave Narrative Collection." *American Quarterly* 19 (1967): 534–553.

Young, Virginia Heyer. "Family and Childhood in a Southern Negro Community." *American Anthropologist* 72, no. 2 (April 1970): 269–288.

Zvonkovic, Anisa M., Catherine Richards Solomon, Aine M. Humble, and Margaret Manoogian. "Family Work and Relationships: Lessons from Families of Men Whose Jobs Require Travel." *Family Relations* 54, no. 3 (2005): 411–422.

Index

Campbell, Israel, 80–81, 89–90, 125–126, 139–140
Campbell, Letitia, 176, 177
Campbell, Maria, 125
Campbell, Samuel, 176
Camp Nelson (Ky.), 233–234
Canada, 125, 126, 136, 139, 141–142, 143, 144, 172, 182; fugitive life in, 228, 229
capitalism. See market economy
Carder, Sallie, 56
Carney, Cornelia, 68, 79
Carruthers, Richard, 72
Carter, Cato, 337–338n81
Carter, Harriet, 162–163
Carter, Jonathan, 162–163
Cates, Ralph, 170–171
Cates, Thomas (father), 171
Cauley, Zenie, 87
Celia (teenage slave), 218–219
Chambers, Lewis, 90
Chapman, Hannah, 41, 46
Charleston, Willie, 76
Charlton, Dimmock, 136
Chase, Anthony, 227
Chase, Lucy, 214
Chase, Sarah, 214
Cheatham, Robert, 194
Chesney, Pharaoh, 61
Chesnut, Mary, 343n9
children: as commodities, 149–150, 151; in cross-plantation households, 43, 44; emancipation and, 248; enforced neglect of, 49–50; forced sale of, 37–38; identity formation, 69; illegitimate, 180; labor and, 245–247; legal status of, 20, 149; limited contact with parents, 48–49; maternal-based slave status of, 2, 13, 40, 121, 122, 126, 149; response to freedom, 242; sale away from family, 58; slaveholder mistreatment of, 48–51, 58 (see also slave market); status of, 11–12. See also black fathers; black mothers; family; mixed-race children

Childress, James, 194
Chinn, Julia, 332n24
Choice, Jeptha, 34, 85
Christianity. See religion
Christmas, 43
Christopher, Anthony, 207
Church, Robert, 346n49
churches. See religion
Cincinnati (Ohio), 169, 170, 172–173, 191; free black communities, 336n64; as haven, 209; race riots, 349n9
citizenship, 230, 288
civil rights, 254
Civil War, 71, 75, 91, 92, 113, 116, 117, 204, 230–240; black military casualties, 237; Emancipation Proclamation (1863), 231, 232, 235; race relations following, 224; slave escapes during, 81, 86, 230–233, 237–240. See also Confederacy; postwar conditions; Union army
Claibourn, Ellen, 45
Clark, Anne, 77
Clarke, James, 175–176, 177
Clarke, Judith, 177
Clarke, Letitia, 177
Clarke, Lewis, 57, 138–139, 176, 177, 182, 339n98
Clarke, Milton, 176–177
class, 190–191, 194, 284, 286; black bourgeoisie, 170; miscegenation hierarchy, 190–191, 330n7; social networks, 93; stratification, 191–192
Clinton, Catherine, 150, 197
Coates, Ta-Nehisi, 286, 288
Coffee, Anna, 214
Coggin, John, 30, 31, 303n4
Coker, Abraham, 73
Cole, Thomas, 86, 111
Coleman, Betty, 72, 75, 76
Coley, Annie, 262
college students, 259, 275
Colonization Society, 229
community, 5, 19
commuter marriages (modern), 295n35

Fitzhugh, George, *Sociology for the South, or the Failure of Free Society*, 199–200
Fitzpatrick, Sarah, 47
Fleischner, Jennifer, 11, 77, 115, 344n18
Fleming, George, 251
Fluker, Ida, 97, 276
folklore, 281; John Henry, 314n42, 363n77; trickster tales, 113, 313n30, 319–320n46; turkey buzzard, 183–184, 339n102; Uncle Remus, 208
Foltz, Sally, 248
football kneeling controversy, 4, 287–288
forced breeding, 31, 34, 35–36, 48, 75, 304–305n18
Ford, Aaron, 242
Ford, Loyd, 180
Ford, Sarah, 96–97, 146, 214, 269
Ford, Wash, 71
Forman, George, 153
Forret, Jeff, 17, 19, 32, 47, 93, 202, 343–344n16
Fortman, George, 153, 180
Foster, Thomas, 33, 345n40
Fountain, Della, 278
Fowler, Louis, 166
Franklin, Ann, 118
Franklin, Jared, 117–118
Franklin, Jim, 260
Franklin, John Hope, 138, 339n98
Franks, Dora, 183
Fraser, Rebecca, 17, 57, 79, 297n52
Frazier, E. Franklin, 292n9
free blacks, 23–24, 57, 121, 323n6, 323n7; antebellum obstacles, 126–128, 160–161, 169–170, 181, 228–229; focus on reuniting family, 233; as slaveholders, 133–134; Union army enlistments, 231
Freedmen's Bureau, 242, 245, 248, 250
freedom, 90–91, 116, 120–147, 191, 226–253; empowerment from, 227; hardships of, 284; masculinity model of, 227, 247; surname choices, 251–253; valuation of, 115, 279.

See also emancipation; fugitive slaves; manumission; self-purchase
Freeman, Alice, 214
Freeman, Frank, 78
Freeman, Mittie, 71
Friend, Craig, 13, 16–17, 268, 361–362n62
Fugitive Slave Act (1850), 228
fugitive slaves, 11, 37, 40, 50, 55, 59, 92, 100–102, 116, 117, 125–126, 137–148, 152, 184, 205, 227–228, 328n65; abolitionists and, 57, 103, 104; Civil War and, 81, 86, 230–233, 237–240; economic challenges, 228; education discrimination, 273–274; factors hindering, 138–141; family considerations, 57, 96–97, 99, 120, 129, 136–143, 145, 148; fatherhood and, 23, 67, 115, 120; federal legislation and, 228; Jacobs as, 211; kidnapping fears, 228; light-skin advantage, 182, 339n98; narratives, 27–28, 115–116; new names, 187–188; profile of, 138; risks faced by, 122, 128, 129, 228; view of former masters, 89
FWP narratives, 24–28, 30–32, 35, 37, 51, 54, 59, 146, 163, 283, 302n95, 318–319n30; black vs. white field-workers, 27; on commendable traits, 91; focus of, 70–73, 280; on slaveholders, 88–89; style of informants, 76–77; on white fathers, 154

Galloway, Lucy, 183–184, 209
gang rape, 203
Gardner, Nancy, 238
Garner, Cornelius, 59, 79
Garner, Margaret, 343–344n16
Garner, Remulus, 79
Garnet, Henry, 144
Gassaway, Menellis, 276
Gause, Louisa, 74
Geary, Daniel, 292n9
gender roles, 99, 116, 138, 309n90; slave fluidity of, 22, 68

Macarty, Augustin, 158
Macarty, Josephine (daughter), 158
Macarty, Patrice, 158
Madden, Perry, 275
Maddox, Jack, 151
Maddox, Rosa, 151
Madison, Reuben, 62
Mallory, William, 153–154
Manning, Allen, 278–279
manumission, 133, 228, 323n9, 326n42;
  of mixed-race children, 170, 172;
  self-purchase as, 121; state restric-
  tions on, 160–163; by will, 158,
  333–334n39, 334n46
market economy, 121, 195, 282. *See also*
  slave market
marriage, 9, 39–50, 240, 305n33, 345n31;
  assigned spouses, 41–42; church
  weddings, 305n33; emancipation
  policy, 230; interracial ban, 156,
  343n9; slave conventions, 40;
  slaveholder control of, 32, 40, 100.
  See also abroad marriages
Marshall, Adline, 38
Marshall, Alice, 167, 347n52
Marshall, Sam, 233
Martin, Charlotte, 205
Martin, Eva, 248
Maryland, 144, 147, 148, 159, 188,
  323n9. *See also* Baltimore
masculinity, 16–24, 39–50, 81, 134,
  209–210; American essential traits of,
  1, 17, 20–21, 91; antebellum hallmarks of, 13, 39, 146; black contemporary negative stereotypes of,
  285–287; black definition of, 53, 225,
  267; black expressions of, 4, 19–20,
  79, 281, 282; black forced denial of, 1,
  3–4, 13, 14, 42, 50–66, 234, 285;
  caretaker model of, 124–125, 221;
  color hierarchy and, 246; definitions
  of, 277; distorted images of, 4, 21,
  285–287; dominant social concept of,
  19, 57, 83–84, 96; freedmen's models
  of, 227, 247; hegemonic model of,

267; hierarchy of, 182, 246, 284, 286;
  Jim Crow impact on, 12, 267; partial
  whiteness and, 182, 284; paternalist
  component of, 88 (*see also* paternalism); sexual prowess linked with,
  34–35; skills and, 82–83; slave system
  and, 12, 13, 17, 57, 72, 91, 98–99, 100,
  282, 283; traits linked with, 20–21, 23,
  52, 69, 78, 80, 98, 194, 278; white
  Southern concept of, 2, 13, 195, 267,
  268, 282–284, 288–289
Massie, Ishrael, 110, 167, 221, 243
Mathews, Louise, 44
matrifocality, 43, 45, 93, 201, 218, 250,
  253; distorted image of, 3, 5, 7–8, 16,
  285, 286, 287, 292n13; slave
  households and, 8, 209–210; white
  father and, 15, 191
Matthews, Ann, 255, 276
Matthews, John, 240
Matthews, Sue, 244
McCastle, Duncan, 243
McCurry, Stephanie, 230
McDonnell, Lawrence, 93
McGee, Perry, 275
McLaurin, Melton, 218–219
McLean, James, 88
McMullin, Charles, 128
McNeil, Bill, 46
Meachum, John, 132, 273, 325n33
Meadow, Charlie, 241
men. *See* black fathers; masculinity;
  white fathers
Michener, Patsey, 31
Miller, Jason, 260–261
Miller, Joseph, 234
Millner, Archie, 270
miscegenation, 14–15, 30, 154–163, 288,
  298n62, 330n7, 330n8, 330n9; laws
  against, 150, 170, 215. *See also*
  mixed-race children; mixed-race
  identity
Mississippi, 161
Missouri, 235
Mitchell, Hettie, 165

Tucker, Reeves, 62
turkey buzzard, 183–184, 339n102
Turner, Charlie, 261
Turner, Nat, 79; revolt (1831), 110, 323n9

Uncle Remus tales, 108
Union army, 75, 86, 113, 116, 230, 236–237; black recruits, 230–236, 242–243; families of black recruits, 230–232, 234–236
Unwritten History of Slavery (Fisk University), 24
Upson, Neal, 82, 274

Van Buren, Martin, 332n24
Van Hook, Winger, 173
Vaughn, Adelaide, 59–60, 340n116
violence, 361–362n62; black male targets of, 254; Ku Klux Klan, 76, 147, 250–251, 278, 284; lynching, 224, 361n62; Southern climate of, 3, 4, 18, 19, 284, 286. *See also* domestic abuse; rape
Virginia, 63, 154, 245–246
Virginia Act of 1662, 149
Virginia Writers' Project, 26

Walker, Irella, 278
Walker, James, 129–132
Walker, Minksie, 260
Wallace, Annie, 168
Waller, Richard, 195
Walton, Henry, 246
Ward, Samuel, 143–144, 273–274
Ward, William, 152
Washington, Booker T., 169, 195, 276, 357n11
Washington, Ella, 49
Washington, George (former slave), 233
Watkins, James, 185
Watson, A. P., 24, 64
Watson, Charley, 46
Watson, Henry, 222
Weatherall, Eugenia, 83
Weathersby, George, 87

Weathersby, Steve, 87
Webb, Ishe, 78
Webb, William, 139–140
Weeks, Emma, 244
Weevils in the Wheat (slave narratives), 68
West, David, 89, 141, 144, 296n44
West, Emily, 5, 9, 296n44, 307n52, 330n9, 342n3, 345n31
West Africa. *See* African culture
White, Avenia, 336n63
White, Deborah Gray, 11, 14, 155, 296n44, 297n53, 346n40
White, George, 95, 247, 314n42
White, John, 36, 74, 205
White, Julia, 243, 274
White, Mingo, 74
white fathers, 2, 14–15, 149–196; black community's view of, 183–184; complicated family dynamics of, 180; evaluation of, 163–196; former slaves' evasiveness on, 164–166; justifications of, 155–156; loathing of, 204; manumission by, 159–160; moral deficits of, 151; paternalistic ideology of, 160; surname choice and, 253. *See also* mixed-race children
white masculinity. *See under* masculinity
white supremacists, 225, 250, 284, 287–289. *See also* Ku Klux Klan
white women, 179, 200, 206, 219
Whitman, Stephen, 121–122, 133, 134, 323n4
Whitmore, Sarah, 250
Whitney, Jackson, 141–142
Wiggins, James, 252
Wilcox, Tom, 243
Wilks, William, 181
Williams, Bell, 165
Williams, Charles, 76–77, 275
Williams, Frank, 248
Williams, Heather, 59, 145, 305n29, 341n129, 352n33
Williams, John, 38, 193
Williams, Lizzie, 183
Williams, Nancy, 84–85